What's New to This Edition

This edition, the second edition, marks drastic changes for *What Every Paradox for Windows Programmer Should Know*. I was very proud of the first edition, but also thought there was plenty of room for enhancement. The following are just some of the changes since the first edition:

- Revised for version 5.0 (OLE2, SQL, new methods, new procedures, new properties).
- Many new and advanced techniques added.
- Many completely new chapters—for example, Chapter 20, "Properties," Chapter 30, "The Event Model Revisited," Chapter 35, "Using Paradox with SQL", and Chapter 36, "Delivering Your Application," just to name a few.
- I have eliminated the goal section of each tutorial and combined it with the text right below the tutorial heading.

WHAT EVERY PARADOX® 5 FOR WINDOWS™ PROGRAMMER SHOULD KNOW

SECOND EDITION

WHAT EVERY PARADOX® 5 FOR WINDOWS™ PROGRAMMER SHOULD KNOW

SECOND EDITION

MIKE PRESTWOOD

A Division of Macmillan Computer Publishing
201 West 103rd, Indianapolis, Indiana 46032 USA

To my wife, Lisa, for raising our daughter, Felicia; the most important job in the world.

OVERVIEW

CONTENTS

ACKNOWLEDGMENTS

A book of this nature demands input from as many different people as possible. I'm lucky enough to work with many talented engineers. Their contributions and their openness to my inquiries are greatly appreciated. I would particularly like to acknowledge those who contributed applications to the disk set that comes with this book: James Arias-LaRheir, Mark Duquette, Marco Romanini, Ronald Tanikawa, Charles Gallant, Eldridge "E.J." Johns, Dave Orriss, Jr., and Randy Sell.

The following software engineers deserve mention for either giving me ideas on style and content, contributing clip-objects, or just giving me support: Keith Bigelow, Robert Ramirez, Mark Nelson, Michael Johnson, and Dave Murphy.

I also would like to thank Joe Nuxoll for updating Rich Jones' LOADER.EXE (new name is LAUNCH.EXE). I am sure many Paradox developers will greatly appreciate his hard work.

A special thanks goes to Randy Spitz for technically editing the book. Randy Spitz works in Borland's Quality Assurance, helping to ensure that ObjectPAL works as designed. I have complete faith that he has ensured that the content of this book is correct as designed.

While I'm on the subject of quality assurance: The following engineers assured the quality of the disk set: Randy Spitz, Ben Matterson, Sharon Curry, and Gene Matts.

I probably could go on for another page or two, but let me finish with a big thank you to Sams Publishing for giving me this opportunity and guidance. In particular, thanks goes to Stacy Hiquet, Dean Miller, and Susan Christophersen for their support. Finally, a warm thank you goes to Paul Perry for recommending me to Sams.

ABOUT THE AUTHOR

Mike Prestwood works for Borland International, Inc. in technical support. Mike has reached the highest technical position possible in Technical Support: Consulting Engineer. His duties at Borland include serving as Advanced Training Coordinator, member of the SQL team, and a sysop on Compuserve.

As the Advanced Training Coordinator for the Paradox team, Mike is responsible for putting together training courses for SQL, advanced ObjectPAL, and more. Mike teaches a 40-hour, week-long ObjectPAL course (now based on this book), and helped put together 21 advanced ObjectPAL training courses for Paradox technical support (more than 100 engineers).

Mike has supported Paradox for Windows since before it shipped. He answers questions on the Paradox Help desk and SQL lines, and he reviews technical bulletins about Paradox. In the past, Mike has also answered questions from Borland's international subsidiaries through Borland's international BBS. Before joining the Paradox technical support team, Mike was part of the ObjectVision technical support team for one and one-half years.

In preparation for the release of version 5.0 of Paradox, Borland hired Mike as an outside consultant. Mike helped with over 100 of the new 5.0 ObjectPAL commands for the online help and ObjectPAL *Reference Guide*.

Mike also contributed to the Sams book, *Paradox 5 for Windows Developer's Guide, Second Edition*, by James Arias-LaRheir. Mike helped update it to Paradox for Windows version 5.0 by contributing Chapter 9, "Using Crosstabs and Graphs," Appendix C, "Prestwood's Coding Convention," and one application, "Paradox Desktop 2.0" (also included in this book).

INTRODUCTION

This book is for anyone who wants to learn or get better at ObjectPAL and is ready to tackle ObjectPAL with a hands-on approach. This includes beginner, intermediate, and advanced ObjectPAL programmers, and everyone who wants to write a database application with Paradox. Through instruction and example, you will learn the intricacies of ObjectPAL and how to write a complete database application.

If you already know the basics of ObjectPAL, this book is a good source for ideas, tricks, tips, short code routines, undocumented features, and advanced concepts. This book doesn't document every feature of Paradox. That's the job of the manuals. Nor does it show you how to use interactive features, except for occasional interactive solutions to programming problems. That is the job of beginner-level Paradox books. If you need a beginning book, then I recommend another Sams book, *Paradox 5 for Windows Developer's Guide*, by James Arias-LaRheir.

The goal of this book is to add to the manuals with as little duplication as possible to present a complete study of ObjectPAL. It teaches you how to use ObjectPAL and how to bring all the elements of Paradox together to develop a complete application. This book concentrates on ideas, solutions, and learning ObjectPAL. If you own several ObjectPAL books, I'm confident you will find this book to be most useful with many more advanced examples and discussions presented in clear English—you don't need a PH.D. to understand this book.

WHAT YOU SHOULD KNOW BEFORE READING THIS BOOK

This book assumes that you understand interactive Paradox. If you can create a table, form, report, and query, you fall into this category. Although you don't need to know how to use every interactive feature of Paradox, you must be familiar with the majority of its interactive—non-ObjectPAL—features. Specifically, you should

- Know the basics of the Windows environment
- Be familiar with the Paradox desktop environment
- Know how to create a table
- Know how to create a single-table form and a multitable form
- Be familiar with the basic features of queries and reports

Part I: Getting Ready for ObjectPAL

Part I, "Getting ready for ObjectPAL," addresses some of the elements of interactive Paradox that the ObjectPAL programmer needs to keep in mind when developing an application. For example, Chapter 1, "The Paradox System," starts you off with an overview of the Paradox development system. Part I also introduces you to ObjectPAL and the ObjectPAL Editor.

This part of the book is intended to help the beginning ObjectPAL programmer get ready for ObjectPAL. It is also intended as a review for intermediate and advanced ObjectPAL programmers. If you are a beginner to ObjectPAL and you wish to learn ObjectPAL very well, I recommend that you read straight through this book.

Part II: ObjectPAL Basics

Part II, "ObjectPAL Basics," is a formal study of the concepts and ideas behind ObjectPAL. It presents all the concepts and ideas used in ObjectPAL in a logical, step-by-step approach.

This part of the book is intended to help bring the beginning ObjectPAL programmer to an intermediate level. The beginning ObjectPAL programmer should consider reading Part II twice—perhaps after reading the book all the way through. Intermediate and advanced users will enjoy a concise review of the ObjectPAL basics, perhaps filling in some holes in their knowledge.

PART III: EXPLORING OBJECTPAL

Part III, "Exploring ObjectPAL," is the "meat and potatoes" of this book. This part explores almost every area of developing in ObjectPAL.

This part of the book is for every level of ObjectPAL programmer. To help become an advanced ObjectPAL programmer, beginning and intermediate ObjectPAL programmers should go straight through Part III, whereas advanced ObjectPAL programmers may wish to use this part mainly for reference.

PART IV: SPECIAL TOPICS

Part IV, "Special Topics," concludes the discussion of ObjectPAL by exploring advanced topics. In addition to revisiting the event model, it covers topics such as debugging, networking, SQL, and delivering your application.

All ObjectPAL programmers should read Part IV, perhaps skipping Chapter 35, "Using Paradox with SQL," until you need to implement them in your application.

EACH CHAPTER'S FORMAT

Each chapter contains two types of information: text and tutorials. Scattered throughout the text are short examples of code. Unless the text specifically tells you to type the code, don't type it; it's simply meant to drive home the text. This partial code focuses on the subject being discussed, and the tutorials are clearly marked and give you the full code needed.

Tutorials are broken into sections: On Disk, Quick Steps, Step By Step, and Analysis. The On Disk section tells you where you can find the tutorial's code on the disk that comes with this book. This is valuable if you have mistyped a tutorial, just check your work against the answer in the ANSWERS directory. The Quick Steps summarize how you can accomplish the goal. Quick Steps also are useful when you're reviewing the concept illustrated. The Step By Step section guides you through every step. If you're well-versed in the subject of the tutorial, you can skip this section. Most tutorials end with an Analysis section that puts everything in perspective.

Also scattered throughout the text are sidebars. These boxes contain extra information, reminders, concepts, tips, and tricks. The On Disk sidebar, which has a picture of a disk next to it, tells you about a program included on the disk that comes with this book.

Conventions Used in This Book

Built-in
Bold text is used to highlight built-in methods—locations to put code. For example: **pushButton**, **newValue**, and **canDepart**. This is important to distinguish built-in methods from methods and procedures of the same name. For example, "Put code in the built-in **open** method."

`code`
Whenever code elements are referred to in text, the element is in monospace. This includes methods, procedures, keywords, and Object variables. In addition, if the command is a method or procedure, it is followed with (). Now, in this edition, you can easily tell the difference between a built-in method such as **open** and the ObjectPAL runtime library method with the same name: `open()`. For example, "You can use the `open()` method in the built-in **open** method to open another form."

structures
In the first edition, I used the term *block* to refer to a structure of code. In this edition, I use the term *structure*. For example, in the first edition, I wrote, "Place code in a `method...endMethod` block." In this edition, however, I write, "Place code in a `method` structure." There are exceptions—for example, I write "`if` statement" because the manual does. In addition, in the first edition I might have written, "In a `while...endWhile` block, you can loop 10 times," whereas now I write, "In a `while` loop, you can loop 10 times."

variables
Whenever variables, table field names, object names, or text values are referred to in text, they are in *italics*.

TABLE.DB
Whenever filenames are referred to in text, they are in all capital letters. When tables are referred to in text, they are in initial capital letters. For example: "Along with the ORDERS.DB file on diskette, there is a primary key file with the name ORDERS.PX. You can use a TCursor and open the Orders table from disk."

The Mulitconcept icon highlights an advanced tutorial.

 The Great Idea icon highlights a great idea.

 The New 5 Feature icon highlights new features to version 5.

 Any new terms that are defined in the surrounding text are in bold and Italic. The glossary term icon is used if the term is of particular importance.

A NOTE ON BUGS

The goal of this book is to address how Paradox should work as discussed with my coworkers from technical support, quality assurance, and research and development. This is important because the product does change frequently and Borland will likely fix any anomalies in the product that exist at the time of writing. As a developer, however, you need to know about problem areas in the product so that you can avoid them. Therefore, on the diskette that accompanies this book is a help file called SECRETS2.HLP. Among other things, this help file documents any known problems about the product at the time of shipping the book. Because I can update this file very close to shipment of the book and long after the book goes to press, the disk is the place for such information.

P A R T

I

GETTING READY
FOR OBJECTPAL

THE PARADOX SYSTEM

This first chapter's goal is to talk about Paradox from an overall development perspective. It begins with a discussion of why you should use Paradox. It then leads into a little history of Paradox and discusses the new features of version 5. Then it moves into a discussion of types of applications and which types Paradox is suitable for. This chapter then follows up with this idea and introduces the disk set and the types of applications on it. Finally, it discusses design methodology—overall design concept.

WHY SHOULD YOU USE PARADOX?

paradox—Something that appears to contradict itself or be contrary to common sense but might be true.

A **database** is an organized collection of information. For Paradox users, this meaning is stretched to mean a set of related tables (usually in the same directory). Paradox is much more than a simple database program. It's really several programs in

GLOSSARY TERM

one: a Database Manager System (DBMS) capable of using either local tables (Paradox or dBASE) and remote tables (Oracle, Sybase, Interbase, Informix, and more).

This means that as a Paradox or dBASE developer, you can read and write Paradox and dBASE tables and indexes without importing them. This is important. Many developers call Borland, asking how to convert a dBASE table to a Paradox table or vice versa. The answer is, you don't. If you have a need to copy the data from dBASE to Paradox format, or vice versa, then simply copy it with Tools | Utilities | Copy.

In addition to local table structures such as Paradox and dBASE, you can use any of the SQL servers supported by the IDAPI engine. As of this writing, this includes Borland's Interbase, Oracle, Sybase, Microsoft SQL, and Informix. In addition, the IDAPI engine is ODBC compliant. This means you can use most any ODBC driver to connect to almost anything including text files, BTrieve, and Excel spreadsheets.

Every version of Paradox has made complex databases accessible to the average user. In my opinion, Paradox has three levels of usability: easy database access, complex database access, and database application development. A ***database application*** is a cohesive set of files. Your database, with all its tables, forms, queries, reports, and anything else you include within the scope of the files, including utilities and accessories, makes up your database application.

Easy database access enables you to create simple database tables and to enter and browse through data quickly with the traditional table window or a more flexible form. In addition, you can print in table and form view by selecting File | Print. Or, you can create more complex printing with a report.

Complex database access enables you to ask complex questions about your data. In Paradox, you can set a filter in a form or ask a question of your data with a query. After you find the answer, you can use crosstabs, graphs, and advanced reports to communicate the answer to your users.

Database application development includes bringing all the elements that display data—table views, forms, and reports—into a cohesive presentation. The application development side of Paradox brings a friendly user interface to the end user, and a powerful language called ObjectPAL to the programmer. Both of these elements together enable you to better control the application environment. Developing an application in Paradox is a process of taking small steps.

dBase for Windows versus Paradox for Windows

Now that Borland has moved both dBASE and Paradox to the Windows environment, which should you use? The Windows versions of both dBASE and Paradox support each other's table formats and act as a front-end to SQL servers. (This is accomplished by the IDAPI engine, which both use.) Which table structure is better is no longer the developing issue. The decision now centers around which development environment you prefer.

If you have the time and money, I urge you to get and try both. Both database managers have their strong and weak points. If you make a living at developing databases, then this suggestion is reasonable. If you don't, then hopefully this section will reassure you that you made the right choice. The two products differ primarily in feel. dBASE is a language-based product and Paradox is an object-based product. If you code in dBASE, then it makes good sense to use the Windows version of dBASE. If you use ObjectPAL, then use Paradox for Windows. If you are new to both, then it really is a difficult choice. If you have not used either and are a heavy programmer, then you may wish to try dBASE (a programmer-oriented development environment). If you have never programmed before, then you may prefer Paradox (a user-oriented development environment). Even though I love to code, I prefer the user-oriented Paradox development environment because it saves me lots of time. Here are some of the strong points of dBASE for Windows.

- Truly OOP
- It's the dBASE standard
- VBX controls
- dBASE DOS applications port right over
- It has two-way controls
- You can see all code (nothing hidden)
- It is a programmer-oriented development environment

dBASE does not have OBEX, a datamodeler (although queries do the job), or OLE 2 support. In general, developing in dBASE takes longer.

Paradox for Windows' strong points are as follows:

- It now has OLE 2.0 support with version 5.0
- It is a mature product
- It has OBEX support

- It is ODBC compliant
- It has better SQL support (user tools, show SQL, local SQL, and so on)
- Most award-winning Windows database since its introduction
- It is the market share leader in Windows databases
- It has a much richer object-based programming language
- It is a user-oriented development environment

As you can see, both are full-featured products capable of accomplishing any database task.

Tables, dBASE, and Paradox

Paradox handles Paradox tables best and dBASE handles dBASE tables best. For example, with dBASE for Windows, you can store a graphic in a binary field and dBASE for Windows knows it's a graphic and displays it. Paradox for Windows 5 does not. It simply displays <BLOB Binary>. Another example is the Paradox table supports an OLE field type. Because Paradox supports OLE 2 and dBASE does not, Paradox handles this Paradox table field better. Each DBMS—Paradox and dBASE—handles its own native table structures best. Because the Paradox table structure is superior to the dBASE table structure and because Paradox handles Paradox tables best, my choice of development environment is Paradox for Windows. For more on dBASE and Paradox table structures, see the section, "dBASE Tables versus Paradox Tables" in Chapter 2, "Tables and Developing."

DESIGN METHODOLOGY

It's important to understand the elements of ObjectPAL. If you don't keep the big picture in mind, however, the end product suffers. With this book, you will learn the skills to develop in ObjectPAL. This first chapter deals with broad design issues and the following chapters deal with issues that an ObjectPAL programmer must keep in mind.

Before you jump into ObjectPAL, let's review a few concepts. The first few chapters deal with issues such as planning, table design, and interactive form design. These chapters also discuss the interactive issues that an ObjectPAL programmer needs to keep in mind. The rest of this chapter talks about the design process and gives you ideas about how a database application should look. The whole point of this section can be summed up in two words: *be consistent*.

When you develop a database application, you follow a series of steps. First, you design and create your tables. Next, you design your forms. Then you add cross tabs, graphs, queries, and reports. Finally, you add bits of ObjectPAL code to alter or add to the built-in behavior. This final step of adding ObjectPAL code often brings the various elements of interactive Paradox together. This book's primary concern is the final step—adding ObjectPAL. The next section gives you a quick overview of this process, along with some specific issues and considerations.

Top-Down Planning

Any programmer with any experience will tell you that planning an application is just as important as getting started on it. In other words, the first step in designing a database application is to sit down, take some time, and think through the process.

> When you're finishing an application for a client, nothing is more frustrating than the client telling you that the application is all wrong. Do yourself a favor: During or shortly after the planning stage, be sure to echo to the client what you heard him say. Also consider putting your general plan in writing and have both you and your client sign it. This makes you a more professional consultant.

Dealing with Business Rules

Creating a database isn't just about creating tables and linking them. It is also about implementing business rules on the data. For example, in an invoicing system, you need to multiply quantity times price to get each line total on an invoice. Then you sum up the line total and multiply it by the local tax rate and perhaps add shipping costs. These are all business rules. Another less obvious business rule might be to start charging interest on invoices that still have a balance due after 30 days. If you're a database consultant, remember to ask your client about all his or her business rules and incorporate as many as appropriate into your database application.

Creating Your Tables

In a separate session with your client, sit down and gather all the data components and categorize them into tables. After you gather the business rules and data components, you need to decide on table structures. Whether you're developing a complete invoicing system or an application that just keeps track of phone numbers, planning your table structures correctly can save you hours of work later. Although Paradox makes it easy to restructure your tables later, you can never recover the time and frustration wasted because of poorly designed table structures.

As you develop your tables, think about the data model. The **data model** is a diagram of the table relationships for a form. Each form has only one data model. With the Data Model dialog box, you can bind tables to documents and specify how they are linked to one another. In particular, think about all the possible relationships between tables that you need for this project. What fields will make this table unique? What fields must be in common? Develop your tables with your primary keys in mind. (Chapter 2 discusses this further.) It's easy to increase or decrease the length of your fields in Paradox, so keep in mind the minimum size needed as you develop your field lengths. A little careful planning can save you hours of backtracking later. Remember to plan and create your tables with the data model in mind before you start working on your forms.

Forms Are Your Application

In Paradox for DOS, the script is the center of your application, and the form is used to present data. A form in Paradox for Windows is used to present data, but it also doubles as the center of your application. A form has many Objects that you can use to develop an application. It's important that you have a good grasp of what these Objects can do. A table frame is an Object used to display multiple records on a form. A field is a multipurpose Object that enables you to display a single value from a table. It also enables you to show users extra bits of information, calculated values, and other values not stored directly in the

table. An **object** such as a button, field, or box is an item that the user interacts with to create events. The more you know about Paradox's objects, the better your application will be. Chapter 3, "Forms and Developing," shows you a good technique for developing forms.

A form stores the code for an application. A form can have up to 64K of compiled code—that is, about 32 full pages of compiled code. If an application needs more than 64K of code, break it into multiple forms or use libraries to store extra code. (Storing and centralizing code is discussed later in Chapter 23.) When you deliver your form, Paradox compiles it into what is actually a Windows DLL with a .FDL extension.

Screen Resolution

The main window in Paradox is the **Desktop**. The Desktop is the highest level of interaction with all Paradox objects. The desktop varies its size depending on your screen resolution. The Desktop is also known as your application workspace. In ObjectPAL, there is an application variable type for manipulating it. The application variable is discussed in Chapter 13, "The Display Managers."

Forms designed for one screen resolution don't necessarily look good under a different resolution. If you will be porting applications from one machine to another, you should use the same resolution on both systems. (Also, be sure to use the same fonts on both systems.) If it's impossible to use the same resolution, develop the form for the lowest common resolution—for example, VGA rather than SVGA. Later, in part three, you will revisit this topic and see several ObjectPAL solutions.

Forms versus Pages

A form can consist of multiple pages, and an application can consist of multiple forms. It's often difficult to decide when to add a page or start a new form. In general, think about adding a new page to the existing form first. If a new page won't work, add a new form. Because every page of a form has to be the same size, usually size dictates whether to use a new page or form.

When all the forms and pages are the same size, then I let the data model dictate whether to add a new page or a new form. The general rule is one data model per form. When the data model gets in the way, then start a new form. For example, in a typical invoicing system, you might link Orders to Customers. I would use one form with this data model and simply add pages until another data model is indicated. For example, suppose that you need to have a page or form for the user to browse through the Customer table. The preceding data model does not work because the Customer table is the second table in a one-to-one relationship; it is restricted by the Orders table. Common sense tells me to create a new form with a new data model; that is, a data model with just the

Customer table in it. (Table relationships are discussed more in the next chapter.)

The Main Form

A typical application consists of tables, indexes, forms, reports, queries, and possibly scripts or libraries. This presents a problem to the user: how to start up the application. The common practice for developers is to give the main form the same name as the directory that contains it; for example, C:\SECRETS2\SECRETS2.FDL. If you stick with this practice, the users of your Paradox applications will soon learn how to start them up. (For more coding conventions such as this, see "Prestwood's Coding Convention" in Chapter 9, "Syntax.")

TYPES OF APPLICATIONS

This section discusses types, or categories, of applications, introduces the files on the disk set, and discusses how those files fall into these categories. It's just as important to study the files on the disk as it is to study the code, techniques, and concepts presented in this book. In fact, the programs on the disk provide you with a wealth of code.

What's On the Disk Set

Before we jump into our formal discussion, let's see what Paradox is capable of. Sometimes it is nice to see what a product can do. As they say, "Seeing is believing." Knowing what a product can do is half the battle. This section demonstrates the capabilities of Paradox by showing you what comes in the two diskettes that accompany this book. If you haven't done so yet, take a few minutes now to install the disk set.

Whenever I refer to a directory in this book that is part of the disk set, I refer to the subdirectory under the SECRETS2 directory. For example, when you see \APPS\INVOICE\INVOICE.FSL, the actual path is C:\SECRETS2\APPS\INVOICE\INVOICE.FSL. (This example assumes that you installed the SECRETS2 directory at the root level of C:\).

The disk set that comes with this book includes several types of files: support files for the tutorials, answers to the tutorials, clip-objects, utilities, and sample applications. You can access all the support files through one main form, SECRETS2.FSL, which loads MAINMENU.FSL (see Figure 1.1). All the forms are nondelivered (FSL) forms (except for the Paradox Desktop). All the code in the sample applications is commented and uses a consistent naming convention for naming objects and variables.

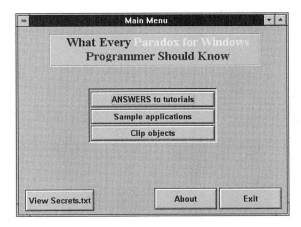

Figure 1.1. MAINMENU.FSL.

While on the Main Menu, press the Configuration button to move to the configuration screen. While on the Configuration screen you can install some of the more useful utilities to your Tools menu or click on the SECRETS2.TXT button to view the text file for the latest information (see Figure 1.2). Also, press F1 while on the Main Menu to view the SECRETS2.HLP Windows help file (see Figure 1.3).

The tutorial support files are in the TUTORIAL directory. Before going through any tutorial, set your working directory to the TUTORIAL directory. The answers to all tutorials are in the ANSWERS directory. If you have any problems with a tutorial, then run the answer from the ANSWERS directory. In addition, the ANSWERS directory is a fun directory to browse. Use the form \ANSWERS\ANSWERS.FSL to browse the files (see Figure 1.4).

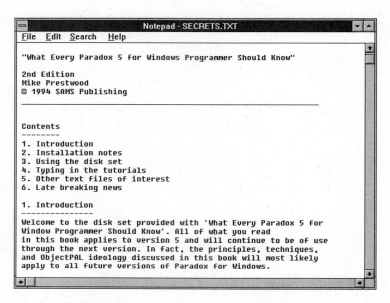

Figure 1.2. SECRETS2.TXT: Late-breaking information on the book.

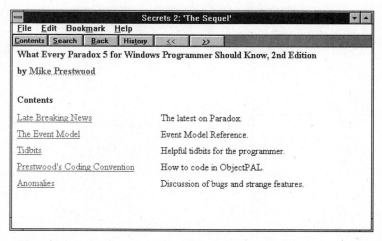

Figure 1.3. SECRETS2.HLP: Late-breaking information on Paradox.

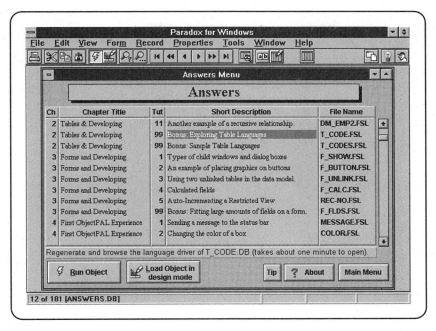

Figure 1.4. \ANSWERS\ANSWERS.FSL.

The clip-objects are in the DEV-SRC directory, short for development source. Use the form \APPS\APPS.FSL to browse the files. Each of the sample applications are in a subdirectory below the \APP directory. Use the form \APPS\APPS.FSL to browse the files.

Suitable Applications

Studying the different types of applications could be a whole book by itself. In fact, discussing how to develop the various parts of just one type of application could take up a whole book. For example, a book could be devoted to developing all the nuances of an invoicing application. This section addresses some of the issues involved in developing the types of applications for which Paradox is best suited.

There are many types of applications. Because Paradox is a database management system (DBMS), it's best suited for developing databases. This doesn't mean that databases are the only type of application you can develop. In fact, you can develop many types of applications with Paradox. Table 1.1 discusses how suited Paradox is for developing each type of application.

TABLE 1.1. TYPES OF APPLICATIONS AND PARADOX.

Category	Suitability	Comments
Manager system	Sometimes yes	Suitable when one of the applications is written in Paradox
Database	Yes	Paradox's strong point
Informational	Yes	Paradox's strong point
Kiosk	Yes	Paradox's strong point
Educational	Usually yes	Educational software often uses tables
Desk accessory	Sometimes yes	Suitable only when a Paradox application is used
Games	No	A few interesting games can be created, however
Prototype	Yes	Prototyping applications in Paradox is very fast

Usually, choosing a tool is easy. When you are asked to do a certain project or when you get an inspiration to develop an application, you usually know what tool you should use. Clearly, Paradox isn't the best tool for every category of software. For example, you probably would not wish to write a file utility with it. If a project involves extensive amounts of data, Paradox will likely be well suited for the job. ObjectPAL is the powerful backbone of Paradox and therefore can be the backbone of a large DBMS. Paradox is also useful for *prototyping* an application you plan to write in C or Pascal. Prototyping is the process of application development, in which small parts or the general structure of an application are designed and tested. These models are used as the basis for building the finished system. If you are going to develop applications, it is important to know what tool—or developing environment—to use.

Manager Systems

A manager system is an application that manages other applications. For example, the MAINMENU.FSL form in the main \SECRETS2 directory manages all the sample applications and forms that come with this book (see Figure 1.1). The MAINMENU.FSL form is your gateway to all of the files and subdirectories in the \SECRETS2 directory. MAINMENU.FSL uses a splash screen (SECRETS2.FSL), a main menu, and a help screen. These three elements give this manager system a professional touch. The code in the splash screen—SPLASH.FSL—contains timers that offer interesting effects.

In general, Paradox isn't the best tool for developing a manager system. When one or more of the managed applications is written in Paradox, however, you might consider using it.

> Take the time now to open and browse through each application on the disk set. Perhaps spend at least five minutes per application. It is important to become familar with what Paradox can do. Don't worry about the code at this point, just learn what is on the disk set. More particularly, learn what features are demonstrated in each application.

Database Applications

A database is any clearly identified collection of data. One example is a telephone book. In Paradox terms, a database is a set of related tables. It is a cohesive set of files—specifically, all the tables, forms, queries, reports, and anything else that you include within the scope of the files. This includes utilities, accessories, and so on.

A superset of a database application is a Database Manager System (DBMS). Typically, a DBMS differs from a database application only in its completeness. A DBMS is a collection of hardware and software that organizes and provides access to a database. Paradox is a perfect tool for both a database application and a DBMS. Several of the applications on the disk set demonstrate this category of an application. These applications are as follows:

Personal Budget Planner
Author: Marco Romanini
Version: 1.0
Set Working Directory to \APPS\BUDGET
File to open: BUDGET.FSL
The Personal Budget Planner is an application for keeping track of your personal financial information (see Figure 1.5). It keeps track of all aspects of your financial info, from paying bills, to budgeting your money. It will also help you balance your bank accounts, and retrieve expense summaries at a glance.

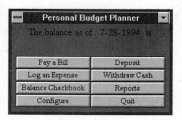

Figure 1.5. BUDGET.FSL.

Mail Merge
Version: 2.0
Set Working Directory to \APPS\DDE-WORD
File to open: DDE-WORD.FSL
The Mail Merge demonstrates an interesting technique for doing mail merge. It uses a DDE link to Word for Windows (see Figure 1.6).

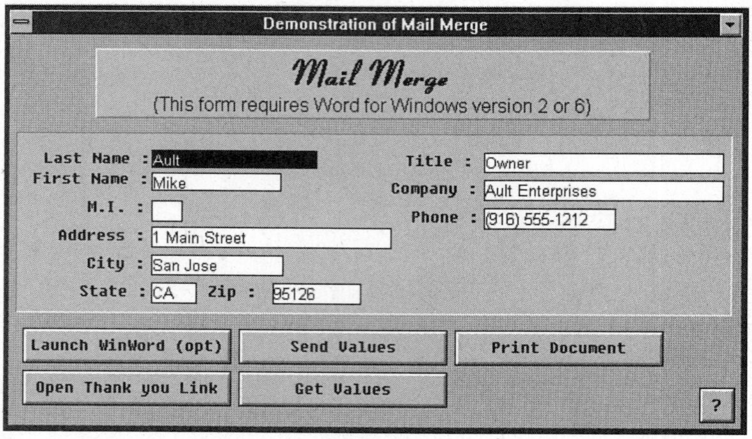

Figure 1.6. DDE-WORD.FSL.

Dialer
Version: 2.0
Set Working Directory to \APPS\DIALER
File to open: DIALER.FSL
DIALER.FSL uses a single field for a person's name and demonstrates how to dial and hang up the telephone (see Figure 1.7). The list page centralizes code. Figure 1.8 shows a listing with an alphabetical search.

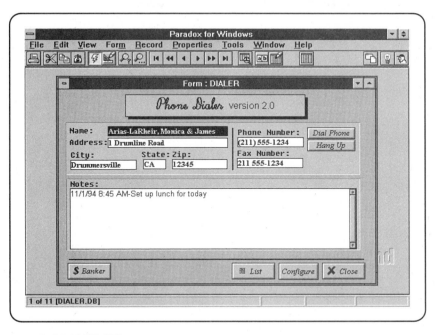

Figure 1.7. DIALER.FSL.

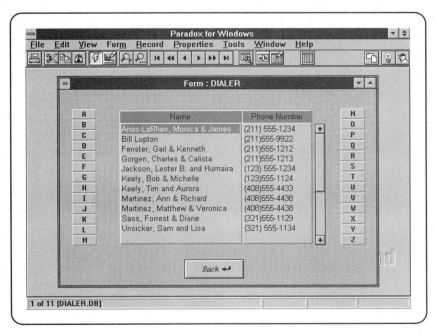

Figure 1.8. DIALER.FSL and a listing with an alphabetical search.

PMail

Authors: Mark Duquette and James Arias-LaRheir
Version: 1.0
Set Working Directory to \APPS\PMAIL
File to open: MAIL.FSL
This full-featured mail application is faster than most commercial mail applications. To run it, run the PMAIL.FSL form. The MAILCFG.FSL form is the configuration form (see Figure 1.9).

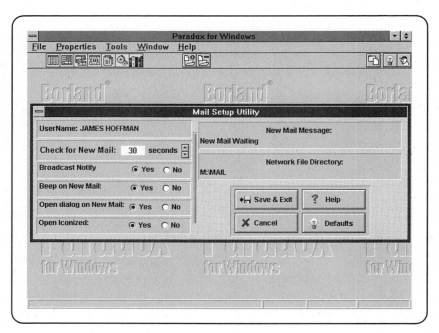

Figure 1.9. MAILCFG.FSL.

The People Keeper

Version: 1.0
Set Working Directory to \APPS\PEOPLE
File to open: PEOPLE.FSL (see Figure 1.10).
The People Keeper tracks various information on people. This application has an interesting data model that demonstrates linking several types of table relationship (these relationships will be discussed in Chapter 2).

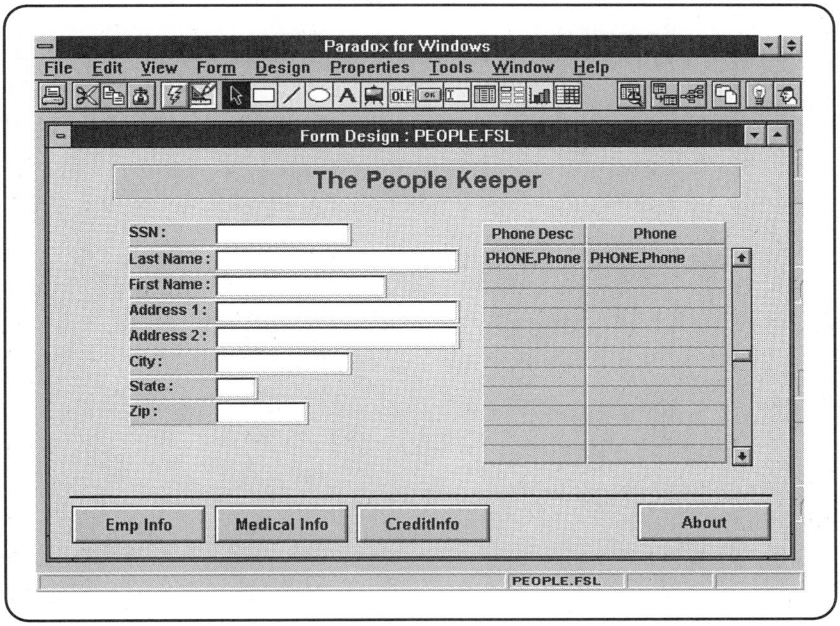

Figure 1.10. PEOPLE.FSL.

The Invoice System
Version: 2.0
Set Working Directory to \APPS\INVOICE
File to open: INVOICE.FSL
The Invoice System is a multiform application that resides in the
APPS\INVOICE directory. It contains a simple invoicing application
that gets you started (see Figure 1.11). The Invoice System is not
intended to be a complete invoicing application. You can use the
Invoice System application as a template for your own invoicing
system. I recommend that you use it for at least one hour. Study its
code thoroughly before you alter it to your liking.

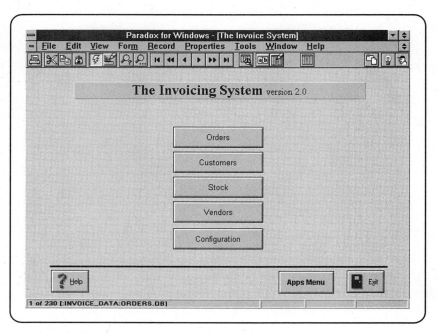

Figure 1.11. The main menu form of the Invoice System application.

Kiosk Applications

You've probably seen kiosk applications in airports, malls, and museums. They are stands with a monitor and some type of keyboard. You might use them to find your way, locate a store, or learn about a particular dinosaur. Generally, kiosk applications are user friendly. They're similar to informational applications. A kiosk application is geared toward people who aren't computer users, however. It has a simple user interface, and the user can't exit the application.

When you create a kiosk application, you often want to make Paradox the Windows shell and to boot directly into Windows. To do this, put WIN.EXE in the AUTOEXEC.BAT file and set up your application as the Windows shell. Make sure that PDOXWIN.EXE is in your path, and put the following statement in the WIN.INI file:

```
SHELL = C:\KIOSK\KIOSK.FDL
```

Graphics and Multimedia

Paradox is suitable for some types of databases that traditional database managers don't handle well. You can use the Fomatted Memo, Graphic, and OLE field types to store formatted text, bitmaps, sound, and movies. For example, you can use the Graphic field type to store graphics in your application easily. The MMEDIA.FSL sample application demonstrates this.

Multimedia Demo
Version: 1.0
Set Working Directory to \APPS\MMEDIA
File to open: MMEDIA.FSL
You can use this multimedia application as a template for your own multimedia application. Simply collect text, pictures, animations, and sounds on a particular subject and paste them into the appropriate fields (see Figure 1.12).

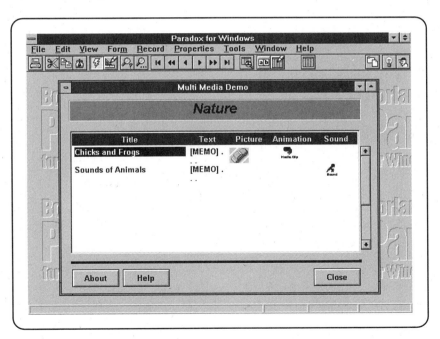

Figure 1.12. MMEDIA.FSL.

Informational Applications

Database applications display, alter, and add data. Informational applications are a subcategory of database applications. They provide information, but they don't enable the user to alter the data presented to them.

Paradox 5 Reference Material
Version: 1.0
Set Working Directory to \APPS\REF
File to open: REF.FSL
The APPS\REF directory contains reference material generated by ObjectPAL methods and procedures. You use the REF.FSL form to access various reference tables in the same directory. You can use these tables to look up various commands, properties, error messages and more. Figure 1.13 shows REF.FSL and Figure 1.14 shows one of the reports included with Paradox 5 Reference Material.

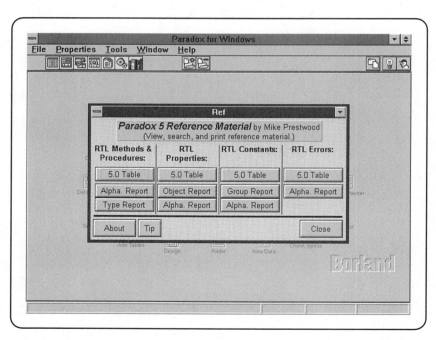

Figure 1.13. REF.FSL.

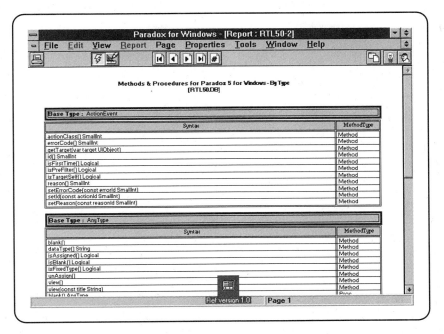

Figure 1.14. REF.FSL.

Utility Applications

Another category of applications that Paradox is well equipped to handle is utilities. A *utility* is an application that helps the developer run, create, or analyze other applications. For a small utility, the best tools to use are C or Pascal because a utility written in C or Pascal compiles into a single executable—that is, .EXE—file. You can develop two types of utilities with ObjectPAL. One type is a utility that helps developers create, modify, or analyze an application; the other type is a utility that helps end users run or use applications.

Because of the vast array of database commands and support for local tables (Paradox and dBASE) and remote tables (SQL), Paradox is a great candidate for database utilities.

Paradox Desktop
Version: 2.0
Set Working Directory to \APPS\DESKTOP

File to open: DESKTOP.FSL

Paradox Desktop version 2.0 by Mike Prestwood is a utility to help the Paradox for Windows 5 developer. This small form (small in visual size only), aids the developer in four tasks: managing multiple instances of PDoxWin, replacing File | Open, inspecting objects for code, properties, and so on, and easy access to information. It offers browsing features to browse files and launch or open your aliases, forms, reports, tables, and so on. It helps you use multiple instances by managing your private and working directories. It also offers the PDoxWin Task List to switch among multiple instances. In addition, it provides an "Inspector" that allows you to view table structures, link information, source code, properties, and object names. Finally, it provides easy access to the most often used utilities and information. Keep an eye on the status bar for tips and information to guide you while using Paradox Desktop (see Figure 1.15). Refer to the DESKTOP.WRI file for a full description of Paradox Desktop's features.

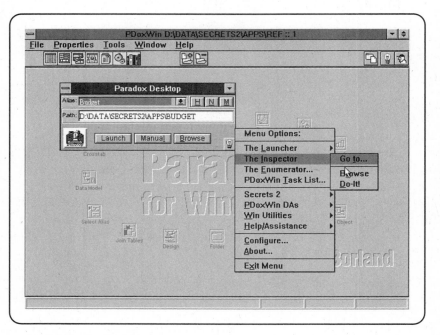

Figure 1.15. Paradox Desktop.

The Property Setting Utility
Author: Randy Sell
Version: 2.0
Set Working Directory to \APPS\PROPERTY
File to open: PROPERTY.FSL
This wonderful utility aids you in making an application dazzle. It goes through and sets the properties of all of your objects on a form. This helps you develop consistent applicatons (see Figure 1.16).

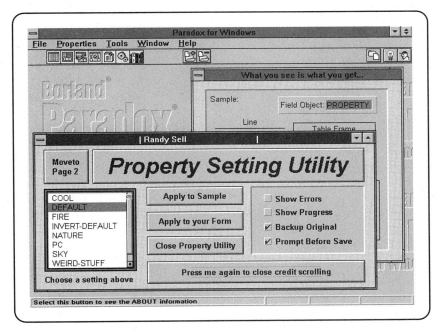

Figure 1.16. PROPERTY.FSL.

Field Conversion Utility
Author: E.J. Johns
Version: 1.0
Set Working Directory to \APPS\STRING
File to open: STRING.FSL
The Field Conversion Utility aids you in manipulating data. With it you can make all the data in a field of a table proper, strip leading zeros and more (see Figure 1.17).

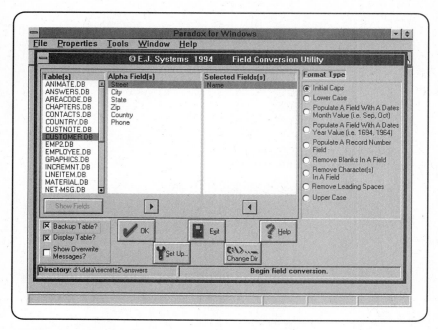

Figure 1.17. STRING.FSL.

Educational Applications

Another category of software for which Paradox is perfectly suited is educational software. Most educational software uses some type of database to store the information. Paradox, of course, has the database power. With its capability to manipulate objects during runtime, Paradox is perfect for developing educational software.

Desk Accessories

A term originally used in the Macintosh world, *desk accessory* refers to a small application that adds functionality to an application. Adding this type of application to your Paradox application is a good idea. It's not a good idea, however, to develop a desk accessory in Paradox for use outside of Paradox because Paradox takes such a long time to load—usually 17 to 25 seconds. Sometimes it's a matter of using the right tool for the job.

Games

Paradox isn't suited for every game. You wouldn't develop a "shoot 'em up" game in Paradox because the game would run too slowly. Paradox is a suitable tool for educational games or games with a lot of data, however. The disk set that comes with this book contains another game that demonstrates an appropriate match of tool and game—Felicia.

Felicia

Version: 2.0
Set Working Directory to \APPS\FELICIA
File to open: FELICIA.FSL
The FELICIA.FSL form, shown in Figure 1.18, is a child's keyboard game. All the keys are disabled except for the letters and the numbers. When the user presses a letter key, a random sound is generated and both the uppercase and lowercase forms of that letter are displayed. If a number key is pressed, the number is displayed and a random three-note melody is played. To keep the youngster's attention, a picture of a horse scrolls across the top.

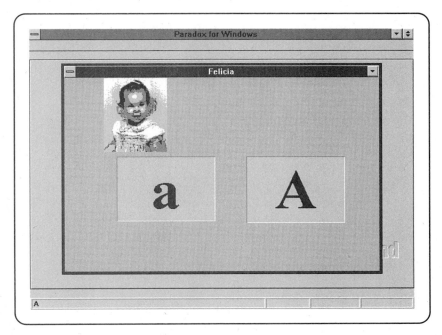

Figure 1.18. The Felicia game.

The next two chapters deal with the development theory behind tables and forms. For example, they do not show you how to set up a one-to-many table relationship but do tell you why. You will learn what a many-to-many table relationship is, when to use cascade delete, the six steps to developing a great form, and more.

MusicKey
Author: Ronald Tanikawa
Version: 1.0
Set Working Directory to \APPS\MUSICKEY
File to open: MUSICKEY.FSL
At the heart of the form is a custom method—plays at the Form level. plays takes in a note number, and plays the corresponding note as well as highlighting the key on the keyboard that has been selected. The note number ranges from 1 to 49. There are twelve half-steps (notes) in a scale, and the range of the keyboard is 4 octaves (1 scale). The frequency is determined by the following formula:

```
1:  Freq = 110 * 2 ^ (1 / 12) ^ n
```

where n is the note number. The frequency of a note doubles for each octave, hence the 2 with the exponent. We have the ration 1/12 because there are 12 half-steps (includes sharps and flats—the black keys) in an octave. Finally, we multiply by 110 to put the frequency in a practical and clearly audible range (see Figure 1.19).

Skunk
Author: Ronald Tanikawa
Version: 1.0
Set Working Directory to \APPS\SKUNK
File to open: SKUNK.FSL
Because this is a game of luck, it does not take much time or skill to beat the computer. It might take some time to become familiar with the game, but once you do, you might try changing the "Winning Value" goal to a higher number than the default 100 (see Figure 1.20).

Figure 1.19. MUSICKEY.FSL.

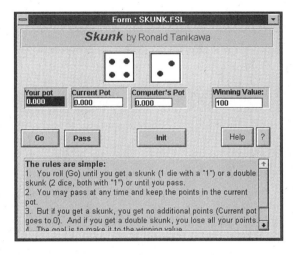

Figure 1.20. SKUNK.FSL.

After opening and browsing through all these applications, you are getting a good sense of what types of applications you can develop in Paradox for Windows. By now, you should be getting a sense of the look and feel of Paradox applications; that is, the look and feel of real Windows applications. After you become familar with ObjectPAL, you may wish to print all the source code for these applications and store them in a three-ring binder. In addition to this book, the code on the disk set is a wonderful source for code routines.

TABLES AND DEVELOPING

The table is a tool that you the developer use to store data. In our continuing quest to gear up for ObjectPAL, this chapter talks about constructing a database; that is, creating tables with relationships in mind. It discusses all three types of database relationships and their variations—the one-to-one (1:1) relationship, the one-to-many (1:M) relationship, and the many-to-many (M:M) relationship. This chapter also helps you decide which table structure to use—namely, Paradox or dBASE. Finally, the chapter covers a few of the interesting characters of both dBASE and Paradox tables. First, though, let's consider the importance of aliases to the developer.

Aliases

An *alias* is the name you assign to a directory path and implement to solve a big problem. In the past, when you developed an application and moved the data, you had to redefine all your *links* (a link establishes a relationship between tables by connecting corresponding fields). Paradox uses aliases to refer to a location of files; such as a directory or SQL server. In Paradox terms, the location that is pointed to by the alias often is called a database. Although aliases might be new to you, they are a great time saver. They make using hundreds of tables, queries, and forms in many different directories manageable. There's tremendous value in having the capability to select File | Open | Table and browse through the aliases that you set up.

Using an alias offers several benefits:

- Long path names are shortened to a single word.
- Your applications are instantly portable. ObjectPAL code can refer to objects by means of an alias. When the path of your tables changes, you simply change the path of the alias.
- You can use multiple sets of data with the same application. Once an application is set up with an alias, you can change the path of the alias; instantly, you are working with a different set of data. This makes it possible to develop an application on your local drive and then switch the tables it uses to network tables.

You can browse through and easily set the aliases of a system with the Aliases page in the IDAPI Configuration Utility (see Figure 2.1). To get to this dialog box, open the IDAPI Configuration Utility and select the Aliases page.

When you're ready to start structuring your tables, you need to decide where you want to place them. You have two choices: the current directory or some other directory. If you're developing a single-user application, it makes good sense to put all the files in the same directory. If you are developing what might become a multiuser application, consider separating the tables from the rest of the application. Because Paradox doesn't search for a table, you must develop your application with tables in the same directory or use an alias. Hard-coding table paths usually is a mistake.

If I may be so bold as to suggest a technique, put your tables in a directory different from the one that contains the forms, reports, and libraries. Refer to the tables by using an alias. This makes your application instantly a network-compatible application, and portable. When you install the application on site, you simply have to ask where to put the data and where to put the application. The application can be local or on the network. Put the data files where they need to be, and change the alias path.

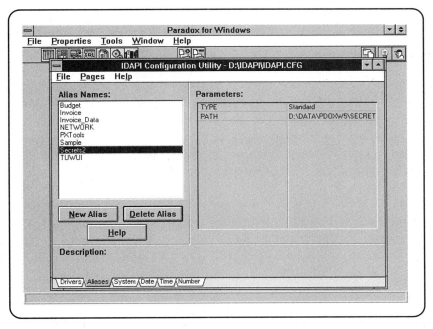

Figure 2.1. The Aliases page from the IDAPI Configuration Utility.

The Invoicing System uses the aforementioned technique of using aliases. The forms are in the \APPS\INVOICE directory and the data is in the \ANSWERS directory. It uses two aliases to manage the files: the Invoice alias points to the forms and reports, and the Invoice_Data alias points to the data files. See Prestwood's Coding Convention in Chapter 9, "Syntax," for more suggestions on the application development process.

PUBLIC AND PROJECT ALIASES

Version 5 adds a new feature to aliases. Now you can create either a public or project alias. A public alias is the same as a regular alias in versions 1 and 4.5. Project aliases are stored in a new PDOXWORK.CFG file, which is loaded whenever you change working directories. You can think of project aliases as aliases that belong to a certain project stored in a specific working directory.

PARADOX AND dBASE FIELD TYPES

Why talk about Paradox and dBASE field types in a book on ObjectPAL? Partially because ObjectPAL is the backbone language to a DBMS, and understanding the field types into which you can store data is important. But the main reason to discuss these field types is so that you can become familiar with what types of data can go into what type of field. Later, table field types and ObjectPAL data types will be discussed. For now, browse and study the following field types. Pay attention to the field types that are new to you. In particular, study what data can go in what field, and study each field type's maximum and minimum value limits. Understanding what type of data can go into fields will help you understand the ObjectPAL data types better.

Alpha (A)—A general-purpose field type that can contain up to 255 letters and numbers. The Paradox 3.5, 4, and 5 table structures can use this field type. This field type was called Alphanumeric in previous versions. It is similar to the Character field type in dBASE.

Autoincrement (+)—This is a special field type that contains unique non-editable numbers. Paradox begins with the number 1 and adds one number for each record in the table. Deleting a record does not change the field values of other records. This field type can be very useful when designing tables, and is useful especially for adding an artificial unique primary key to a table. (See "Using Primary Keys" later in this chapter.) This field type is valid for Paradox 5 tables only.

BCD (#)—Let's first consider what a BCD field is supposed to do. Paradox BCD fields contain numeric data in a BCD (Binary Coded Decimal) format. Use BCD fields when you want to perform calculations with a higher level of precision than that available with the use of other numeric fields. Calculations on BCD fields are not performed as quickly as those on other numeric fields. In the initial release of Paradox for Windows version 5, the BCD field type is provided only for compatibility with other applications that use BCD data. Paradox correctly interprets BCD data from other applications that use the BCD type. When Paradox performs calculations on BCD data, however, it converts the data to the numeric float type, then converts the result back to BCD. This field type is valid with Paradox 5 tables only.

Binary (B)—This is a field used by programmers to store custom data that Paradox cannot interpret. A binary field typically is used for sound and animation. This field is valid with Paradox for Windows 1 and 5 and dBASE5 tables.

Bytes (Y)— Only advanced users who need to work with data that Paradox cannot interpret should use the Bytes field type because Paradox does not know how to interpret bytes fields. You can access a Bytes field with ObjectPAL for example, to store bar codes or magnetic strips. Unlike binary fields, bytes fields are stored in the Paradox table (rather than in the separate .MB file), allowing for faster access. These fields are valid for Paradox 5.

Character (C)—A dBASE character field can contain up to 254 characters (including blank spaces). This field is valid for dBASE III+, IV, and V. This field is similar to the Paradox Alpha field type.

Date (D)—Paradox Date fields can contain any valid date from January 1, 100, to December 31, 9999. This field type is valid for dBASE III+, IV, V, and Paradox 3.5, 4, and 5.

Float (F)—dBASE provides two ways to store numeric data. The float number type contains numeric data in a binary floating-point format. Use the float number type on fields that will not require precise calculations to be performed on them; some degree of precision is rounded or truncated during calculation. Float number fields are best used to contain whole numbers, or numbers of up to two decimal places. The size of a dBASE float number field can be from 1 to 20. This field type is valid for dBASE IV and V.

Formatted Memo (F)—Paradox formatted memo fields are like memo fields except that you can format the text. You can alter and store the text attributes typeface, style, color, and size. This field type is valid for Paradox for Windows 4 and 5.

Graphic (G)—Paradox graphic fields contain pictures in .BMP, .PCX, .TIF, .GIF, and .EPS file formats. Not all graphic variations are available. For example, currently you cannot store a 24-bit .TIF graphic. When you paste a graphic into a graphic field, Paradox converts the graphic into the .BMP format. This field type is valid for Paradox for Windows 1 and 5.

Logical (L)—Paradox logical fields contain values representing True or False (yes or no). By default, valid entries include T and F (case is not important). This field type is valid for Paradox 5 and dBASE III+, IV, V.

Long Integer (I)—Paradox long integer fields are 32-bit signed integers that contain whole numbers in the range 2,147,483,647 to –2,147,483,647. Long integer fields require more space to store than Short fields. This field type is valid for Paradox 5.

Memo (M)—This is a special type of BLOB field used for storing text. BLOB is an acronym for *binary large object*. A BLOB is not a field type, but rather a data type. Field types that can contain BLOBs include binary, memo (both Paradox and dBASE), formatted memo, graphic, and OLE.

The file is divided into blocks of 512 characters. Each block is referenced by a sequential number, beginning at zero. Block 0 begins with a four-byte number in hexadecimal format, in which the least significant byte comes first. This number specifies the number of the next available block. It is, in effect, a pointer to the end of the memo file. The remainder of Block 0 isn't used. This data type is valid for Paradox 4 and 5. dBASE III+, IV, and V.

Money ($)—Paradox money fields, like number fields, can contain only numbers. They can hold positive or negative values. By default, however, money fields are formatted to display decimal places and a money symbol. Regardless of the number of decimal places displayed, Paradox recognizes up to six decimal places when performing internal calculations on money fields. Valid for Paradox 3.5, 4, and 5, this field type was called Currency in previous versions of Paradox.

Number (N)—This is a field that can contain only numbers from –10307 to +10308 with 15 significant digits. A number field can contain some valid nonnumerical characters, such as a decimal point or a minus sign. This field type is available in Paradox 3.5, 4, and 5, and dBASE III+, IV, and V table structures.

dBASE number fields contain numeric data in a Binary Coded Decimal (BCD) format. Use number fields when you need to perform precise calculations on the field data. Calculations on number fields are performed more slowly but with greater precision than are calculations on float number fields. The size of a dBASE number field can be from 1 to 20. Remember, however, that BCD is in Paradox for Windows version 5 only for compatibility and is mapped directly to the Number field type. In a future version, you'll benefit from the advantages of the BCD field type.

OLE (O)—Use the OLE field to store different kinds of data, such as images, sound, documents, and so on. The OLE field provides you with a way to view and manipulate this data without leaving Paradox. Paradox 5 now supports OLE 1 and OLE 2. This field is valid for Paradox for Windows 1 and 5 and dBASE 5.

Short (S)—This is a Paradox field type that can contain integers from −32,767 through 32,768—no decimal. A short number field type uses less disk space than the number field type. It's perfect for storing ages, years of employment, invoice numbers, item numbers, and so on. It is valid for Paradox 3.5, 4, and 5.

Time (T)—Paradox time fields contain times of day, stored in milliseconds since midnight and limited to 24 hours. This field type is valid for Paradox 5.

TimeStamp (@)—Paradox time stamp fields contain a value comprised of both date and time values. To enter today's date and the current time, press Spacebar repeatedly until Paradox enters the data. Rules for this field type are the same as those for date fields and time fields. This field type is valid for Paradox 5.

ATTENTION, STACKER USERS: SPEED UP WINDOWS TODAY!

If you compress your drive with Stacker or any other compression utility, consider not compressing all of your drive. That way, you can put your Windows swap file, TEMP directory, and perhaps even your PRIVATE directory on the noncompressed part. This speeds up Windows and, of course, Paradox. See Appendix A, "Installation and Setup," for more tips on speeding up Windows.

PRIMARY KEYS

Paradox enables you to manage many types of data in its fields. A *field* in Paradox terms is a single value in a record—for example, City—a column of a table. In addition to standard types of data, such as text, number, date, and currency, you can store a variety of new data types, such as graphic, OLE, and binary. With version 5, Borland added even more data types to the Paradox table structure. For example, time, TimeStamp, BCD, and Autoincrement.

The *structure* of a table is the arrangement of fields in a table: their data types, indexes, validity checks, and so on. Now, more than ever, deciding on table structure and relationships is a crucial element of developing an application. Develop tables in two steps: decide on data components and then decide on the table relationships. The first step in deciding table relationships is to decide what fields need to be a part of the primary key.

A *record* is the horizontal row in a Paradox table that represents a set of data for that item—for example, a person's address information. A primary key sorts your table and makes each record unique. A primary key isn't required but it is highly recommended. In fact, I suggest that every table you create should contain a primary key. A key on a Paradox table orders records and ensures unique records and allows *referential integrity*—a way of ensuring that the ties between similar data in separate tables can't be broken. Referential integrity is defined at the table level in Paradox. Establishing a key has several effects. It prevents duplicate records, sorts records, enables use of the table in a detail link, and speeds general access to the table.

A Paradox primary key can consist of more than one field. These fields are treated as one—a composite. A *composite key* or *index* is a key or index composed of two or more fields of a table. A composite primary key must be made up of the first fields of the table. Use composite key fields when a table contains no single field in which every value is unique. Together, the combination of the fields in the key sorts the table. Define the primary key from the first field through however many fields will make each record unique.

When a table has a composite key field, duplicate values are permitted in an individual key field as long as the values are not duplicated across all the key fields. In other words, the key fields, taken as a group, must uniquely identify a record. Should you go crazy and key most or all of the fields in a table? No. Your goal is always to find the least number of fields that will make each record unique. To sort tables that have composite key fields, Paradox starts with the first field and then sorts the following fields. Paradox's primary key also promotes normalized table structures (more on this later).

Primary Keys and Secondary Indexes

An *index* is a file that determines the order in which a table displays records. It also enables objects such as UIObjects, TCursors, and Table variables to point to any record. A *secondary index* is an extra index primarily used for linking, querying, and sorting tables. Paradox tables can have a primary key and secondary indexes, whereas a dBASE table can have only indexes—that is, files with .MDX or .NDX extensions. You can refer to any file that sorts a table as an index.

> Tables need indexes to speed them up. In Paradox, get used to the idea of creating maintained and case-sensitive secondary indexes. Accepting and doing this simple step will greatly improve the overall speed of your application—especially queries.

Using a Primary Key

Let's develop a typical address table to demonstrate the proper use of primary keys and secondary indexes. In the following development cycle, you will see how a table may change over time as you realize what truly makes each record unique. This natural process is normal. You can learn from this example that you do not have to finalize your table structures too early in the development cycle.

In a typical table consisting of addresses, you might index on the combination of first and last name. This combination of first name and last name makes every record in the table unique. Here is a typical address table with * representing the composite primary key.

```
1:  First Name*
2:  Last Name*
3:  Address
4:  City
5:  State
6:  Zip
7:  Phone
```

This table, however, first sorts by first name and then by last name. Abe Smith will come before Bobby Brown. For a more standard sort, you might sort by last name and then first name. If you need to search by first name, create a secondary index that consists of first names so that you can search and sort by a person's last name, first name, or last and first names. The following is a typical address table with a more standard sort order. It has a secondary index represented by **.

```
1:  Last Name*
2:  First Name*     **
3:  Address
4:  City
5:  State
6:  Zip
7:  Phone
```

After entering records for a few days, you may discover that you have two identical names; for example, *John Smith*. Because the combination of last name and then first name no longer makes each record unique, you come to the conclusion that it is a good idea to include the person's middle initial. With really large amounts of data, you might even include the street address. This takes into account people with the same name and also people's home and work addresses. Here is an example of a fully unique address table with a secondary index:

```
1:  Last Name*
2:  First Name*          **
3:  Middle Initial*
4:  Address*
5:  City
6:  State
7:  Zip
8:  Phone
```

Keying from the first field through however many fields needed to make each record unique works in most cases. This technique is awkward at times, however. A different approach involves using a single, unique field entry, such as a Social Security number, or an autoincrementing field to make each record unique and using secondary indexes for alternate sorting and searching. Here is an example of a fully unique address table with two composite secondary indexes:

```
1:  SSN*
2:  Last Name      1 **    2 ***
3:  First Name     2 **    1 ***
4:  Middle Initial 3 **
5:  Address
6:  City
```

```
7:   State
8:   Zip
9:   Phone
```

Now if this table is developed for the government, then you might discover that the government actually reuses Social Security numbers. Therefore, if you need to keep a history, you may need to find another unique identifier. For example, Birth Date:

```
 1:   Social Security Number*
 2:   Birth Date*
 3:   Last Name          1 **      2 ***
 4:   First Name         2 **      1 ***
 5:   Middle Initial     3 **
 6:   Address
 7:   City
 8:   State
 9:   Zip
10:   Phone
```

If, for example, it is illegal to ask for a customer's Social Security number in your state, then the above table structure will not work. Because of a business rule, you might have to find another keying solution. The following presents a final solution, an autoincrementing key or artificial key:

```
 1:   ID*
 2:   Last Name          1 **      2 ***
 3:   First Name         2 **      1 ***
 4:   Middle Initial     3 **
 5:   Address
 6:   City
 7:   State
 8:   Zip
 9:   Phone
10:   Social Security Number
11:   Birth Date
```

In this final solution, a random unique identifier is used to make each record unique. The new Autoincrement field is perfect for this situation. The new Autoincrement field type is a special field type that contains unique non-editable numbers. Paradox begins with the number 1 and adds one number for each record in the table. This field type can be very useful when designing tables. In particular, it is useful for adding an artificial, unique, primary key to a table.

In general, try to avoid this final solution and use it only as a last resort. Using an artificial, unique, primary key is generally considered a bad idea. Have you ever gone into a store and been asked whether you know your customer number? Sometimes it's your phone number or your social security number, but sometimes it's a random number that you were expected to remember (and you probably didn't). If you use this last solution, make sure that you build an easy-to-use and effective way to quickly look up a customer's ID number.

As you can see, deciding what fields to include in a table is only half the battle. The other half of the battle is deciding what makes each record unique.

:PRIV:STRUCT.DB NO LONGER CREATED

In versions 1.0 and 4.5, whenever you restructured a table or viewed its structure with the Info Structure option, a table named STRUCT.DB was created in your private directory. Many users have grown used to printing that table to print a table's structure. In version 5, no :PRIV:STRUCT.DB table is created.

Tutorial: Printing a Table's Structure

Now that you have created your table structure, suppose that you wish to print the structure of it to study and to keep in a safe place. Paradox doesn't have a direct command for printing the structure of a table. Most long-term Paradox users were hoping for a direct and easy solution in version 5, but it did not come. The following is a brief tutorial on how to print the structure of a table in Paradox.

Quick Steps

1. View the structure with the Info Structure option.
2. Choose the Save As button. Name the table (perhaps use :PRIV:STRUCT.DB).
3. Open and print the table.

Step By Step

1. Select Tools | Utilities | Info Structure from the main pull-down menu.
2. Select a table. This brings up the Info Structure dialog box.
3. Choose the Save As button.
4. Name the table (perhaps use :PRIV:STRUCT.DB). This creates a table with the name you entered.

5. Select File | Open | Table, and open the table you created in steps 3 and 4.

6. Select File | Print. To format the data, you could select Quick Report instead.

PRINT FANCIER STRUCTURES

Follow the preceding instructions. Then design a few reports based on :PRIV:STRUCT.DB, and add your own style to your structure printouts. Perhaps save your favorite report as STRUCT.RSL. If you stick with saving structures as :PRIV:STRUCT.DB, then you can simply open your favorite STRUCT.RSL report to view the table's structure; otherwise, you have to use the Change Table option of the Open Document dialog box.

RELATING TABLES

The following material reviews the concepts and theories behind setting up table relationships. If you need help linking tables with the data model, refer to the *Paradox User's Guide*.

When you hear developers talk about table relationships, you hear things such as "the two tables are linked in a one-to-many." What they are really describing is the theoretical number of records possible in each table. The term *one-to-many* translates into the following: For every unique record in the first table, the second table can have many records. Let's examine a few cases to clearly understand relating tables, the terminology, and the theory behind relating tables.

THE ONE-TO-ONE RELATIONSHIP (1:1)

Suppose that you're working with two tables that are both keyed on the Social Security number (the field name is SSN). One table contains personal information; the other contains medical information. You want to pull data from both of them and display that information as though it came from one database. You need to relate the two tables based on a common field or common fields—in this case, SSN. Once you relate these two tables in a 1:1 relationship, the medical database will display the correct record whenever you display a record from the personal database. Whenever you want to relate two tables, they must have one or more fields in common.

Okay, now for the theory. Although you may not see a good reason that you can't dump all the information from both tables into a single table, there is one. In general database theory, it's a good idea to group data into smaller databases based on logical splits of the data—for example, address, employee, and medical information. If you dump all the data into one huge database, managing the data can get out of control and the tables can grow unnecessarily. Imagine a table with address, employee, and medical information in it. It is a single table with perhaps 50 fields in it. Every time you create a new entry and store just address information or work information, the database reserves room on your hard drive for all 50 fields—even though the majority of the fields are empty! Now, imagine that this table is broken into three tables: ADDRESS.DB, EMPLYEE.DB, and MEDICAL.DB. If you enter a record into the Address table, no room is necessarily reserved in the Employee and Medical tables. Breaking large tables into several tables saves disk space and makes working with your data faster and easier to analyze.

An Example of a 1:1 Relationship

A 1:1 relationship is really just a large table split into multiple tables and linked on a common field or fields. In the following table relationship, for every record in Customer, there can be only one record in Custnote. The form \ANSWERS\DM_1-1.FSL and data model file \ANSWERS\DM_1-1.DM demonstrate this table relationship (see Figure 2.2 that follows).

```
      Customer.db           Custnote.db
1:    Customer No* ===>     Customer No*
2:    Name                  Notes
3:    Street                Picture
4:    City
5:    State
6:    Zip
7:    Country
8:    Phone
```

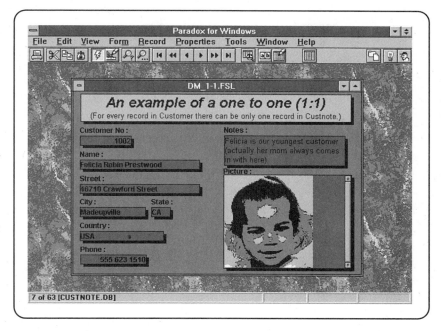

Figure 2.2. This form DM_1-1.FSL demonstrates a 1:1 relationship.

THE ONE-TO-MANY RELATIONSHIP (1:M)

A *master table* in a multitable relationship is the primary table of your data model. If there is only one table in your data model, it is the master table. A *detail table* in a multitable relationship is the table whose records are subordinate to those of the master table. A detail table is also called a *slave table*, a *child table*, or a *many table*. A clearer way to state this is as follows: For every record in the master table, there can be many records in the detail table.

An Example of a 1:M Relationship

When you look at an invoice from a store, you typically are seeing the end product of tables set up in a series of 1:1 and 1:M relationships. This next example shows two tables from a typical invoicing system. For every order in the Orders table, there can be many line items in the Lineitem table. Note that the two tables are linked on Order No and that the Lineitem table uses a composite primary key. The form \ANSWERS\DM_1-M.FSL and data model file \ANSWERS\DM_1-M.DM demonstrate this table relationship (see Figure 2.3 that follows).

```
        Orders.db                    Lineitem.db
1:   Order No* ------------>> Order No*
2:   Customer No              Stock No*
3:   Sale Date                    Selling Price
4:   Ship Date               Qty
5:   Total Invoice
6:   Amount Paid
7:   Balance Due
8:   Payment Method
```

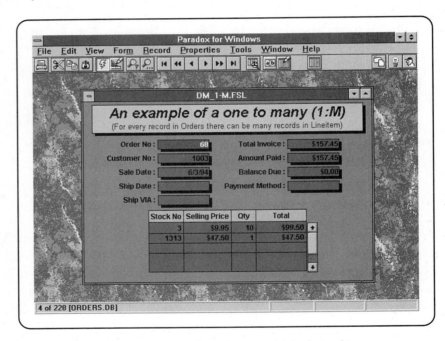

Figure 2.3. This form DM_1-M.FSL demonstrates a 1:M relationship.

THE MANY-TO-ONE RELATIONSHIP (M:1)

Usually, when discussing table relationships, you're talking about the primary key. More specifically, however, you should be talking about the fields on which the tables are linked. The next example does not use an index on the first table; it demonstrates a M:1 relationship. At first glance this may seem like a

1:1 relationship, but on closer inspection it is actually a M:1. You can have many records in Orders with the same Customer No for any one Customer No in the Customer table. The Customer No field in the Orders table in this case is called a foreign key. The form \ANSWERS\DM_M-1.FSL and data model file \ANSWERS\DM_M-1.DM demonstrate this table relationship (see Figure 2.4 that follows).

```
        Orders.db              Customer.db
1:   Order No*
2:   Customer No <<--------   Customer No*
3:   Sale Date                Name
4:   Ship Date                Street
5:   Total Invoice            City
6:   Amount Paid              State
7:   Balance Due              Zip
8:   Payment Method           Country
9:                            Phone
```

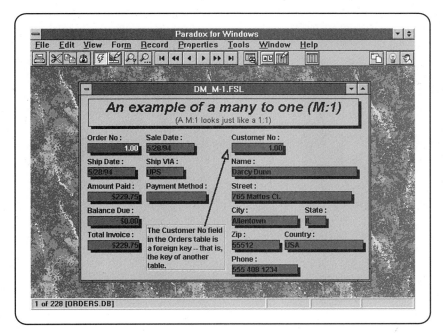

Figure 2.4. This form DM_M-1.FSL demonstrates a M:1 relationship.

THE MANY-TO-MANY RELATIONSHIP (M:M)

A many-to-many (M:M) relationship is when two tables share a common field or fields. Both can have multiple values based on the field(s) in common. Here is an example of a M:M database; Figure 2.5 shows the form equivalent.

```
        Phone.db             Credit.db
1:  SSN* <<---->>        SSN*
2:  Phone Desc*          Credit Card*
3:  Phone                Number
4:                       Expiration
5:                       Credit Limit
```

The form \ANSWERS\DM_M-M.FSL and data model file \ANSWERS\DM_M-M.DM demonstrate this table relationship (see Figure 2.5).

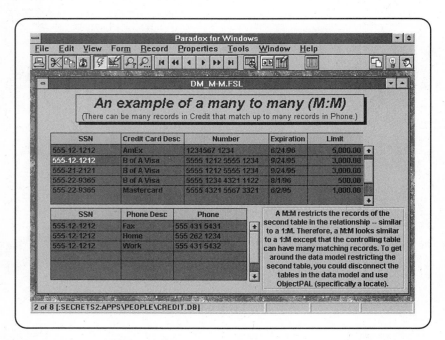

Figure 2.5. The form DM_M-M.FSL is an example of a many-to-many relationship.

The preceding M:M relationship becomes clearer when you add an intermediate table and make the relationship a M:1:M (see M:1:M section later).

RELATING THREE TABLES

Now that you understand the basic three table relationships, let's add a third table to the scenario and study some case examples.

An Example of a 1:1:1 Relationship

Earlier in this chapter, I mentioned breaking a large table full of address, employee, and medical information into three tables: ADDRESS.DB, EMPLOYEE.DB and MEDICAL.DB. The following is that table relationship. The form \ANSWERS\DM_1-1-1.FSL and data model file \ANSWERS\DM_1-1-1.DM demonstrate this table relationship (see Figure 2.6 that follows).

```
1:  Address.db          Employee.db          Medical.db
2:  SSN* ---------->     SSN* ------------->  SSN*
3:  Last Name           Department           Male or Female
4:  First Name          Desk Phone           Color of Hair
5:  Address 1           Manager SSN          Color of Eyes
6:  Address 2           Start Date           Weight (lbs)
7:  City                Salary (per year)    Height
8:  State               Shift Start Time     Blood type
9:  Zip                 Shift End Time
```

The tables in the preceding 1:1:1 example actually have more fields in the table than listed. The fields in the preceding list reflect the fields displayed on the DM_1-1-1.FSL form.

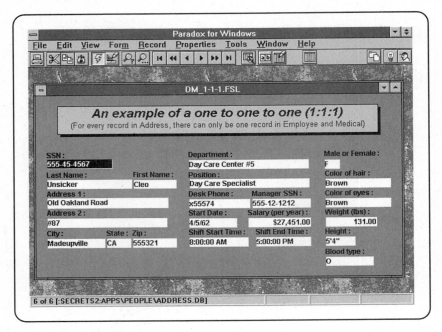

Figure 2.6. This form DM_1-1-1.FSL demonstrates a 1:1:1 relationship.

An Example of a M:1:M Relationship

The next example is a follow up to the M:M relationship presented earlier. This three-way table relationship is really just two 1:M relationships. For every record in the Address table, there can be many records in the Phone table and in the Credit table. The form \ANSWERS\DM_M-1-M.FSL and data model file \ANSWERS\DM_M—1-M.DM demonstrate this table relationship (see Figure 2.7 that follows).

```
      Phone.db        Address              Credit.db
1:  SSN* <<-----    SSN*        ----->>   SSN*
2:  Phone Desc*     Last Name             Credit Card*
3:  Phone           First Name            Number
4:                  Address 1             Expiration
5:                  Address 2             Credit Limit
6:                  City
7:                  State
8:                  Zip
```

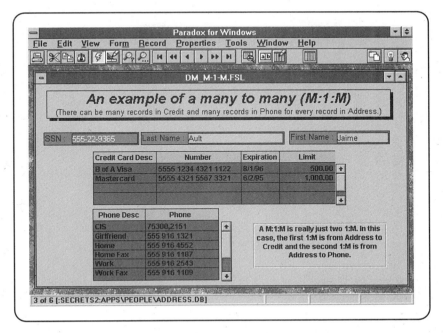

Figure 2.7. An example of the M:1:M form.

A Deceiving Example of a M:1:M Relationship

As stated earlier, a typical invoicing system is simply a series of 1:1 and 1:M table relationships. The next example is of a M:1:M relationship. More precisely, it is a M:1 between Orders and Customer and a 1:M between Orders and Lineitem. There can be many records in the Orders table for every one record in the Customer table. For every record in the Orders table, there can be many records in the Lineitem table. The Customer No field in the Orders table is a *foreign key*; that is, the key of another table. The form \ANSWERS\DM_M-1-M2.FSL and data model file \ANSWERS\DM_M-1-M2.DM demonstrate this table relationship.

GLOSSARY TERM

```
 1:  Orders.db              Customer.db        Lineitem.db
 2:  Order No* ----------------------------->>  Order No*
 3:  Customer No <<--------  Customer No*       Stock No*
 4:  Sale Date              Name               Selling Price
 5:  Ship Date              Street             Qty
 6:  Total Invoice          City
 7:  Amount Paid            State
 8:  Balance Due            Zip
 9:  Payment Method         Country
10:                         Phone
```

AN EXAMPLE OF A 1:M:M RELATIONSHIP

The next example is a 1:M:M (or more precisely, a 1:M with a 1:M). This example uses the same tables as the preceding example, but it views the data differently. A secondary index is used on the Orders table. The form \ANSWERS\DM_1-M-M.FSL and data model file \ANSWERS\DM_1-M-M.DM demonstrate this table relationship (see Figure 2.8 that follows).

```
 1:  Customer.db        Orders.db          Lineitems.db
 2:                     Order No* ------>> Order No*
 3:  Customer No* --->> Customer No**      Stock No*
 4:  Name               Sale Date          Selling Price
 5:  Street             Ship Date          Qty
 6:  City               Ship Via           Total
 7:  State              Total Invoice
 8:  Zip                Amount Paid
 9:  Country            Balance Due
10:  Phone              Payment Method
```

A good technique to use when you present this much data is to show the user only one or two identifying fields from each table and to use another page or form to show the details.

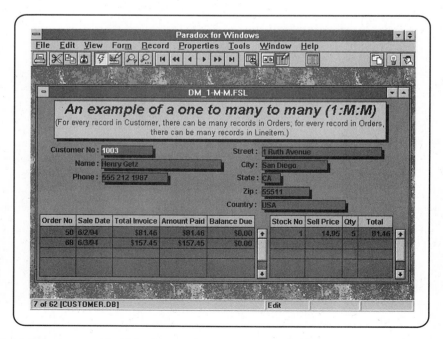

Figure 2.8. An example of the one-to-many-to-many relationship.

AN EXAMPLE OF A 1:M:1 RELATIONSHIP

Let's take a look at a table relationship that often throws developers off. In this scenario, you are developing the table structure for a clothing manufacturer. You have two tables: types of material and outfit patterns (MATERIAL.DB and PATTERNS.DB). You need to connect any one record in the Material table to any one record in the Patterns table. Initially, this sounds like a M:M, but it is not. After you start developing this table relationship, you will discover that you need a third intermediate table, as in the following:

```
1:  Material.db       Outfits.db        Patterns.db
2:  Cloth ID* --->>    Cloth ID*
3:  Cloth Desc        Pattern ID* <<----  Pattern ID*
4:  Cost              Total cost        Pattern Desc
5:                                      Cost
```

This three-table relationship is a 1:M:1. For every record in the Material table, you can have many records in the Outfits table; and for every record in the Patterns table, you can have many records in the Outfits table. The file ANSWERS\DM_1-M-1.FSL demonstrates this table relationship.

THE RECURSIVE RELATIONSHIP

The last table relationship to be demonstrated is a recursive relationship. A *recursive* relationship is when a single table is used as though it were two tables. In certain table structures, a single table contains all the fields needed to link to itself in a 1:M relationship. For example, take a look at the following table:

```
        Employee.db
1:  SSN*
2:  Department
3:  Desk Phone
4:  Manager SSN      **
5:  Start Date
6:  Salary (per year)
7:  Shift Start Time
8:  Shift End Time
```

Any one Manager SSN field can link to many records defined by the SSN field. To do this relationship, you need a primary key and a secondary index.

Putting a table multiple times in a data model allows you to do a recursive relationship. With version 5, Borland introduced the concept of a **table alias** to the data model. In a data model, a table alias is an alternate name for a table. A table alias allows you to rename a table in a data model. This allows you to refer to the table in the data model by the table alias rather than the table name.

This is important in ObjectPAL when you need to refer to a table in a data model. Instead of referring to the table name, you can refer to the table alias. This way, if you change the underlying table, you do not have to change your code if it refers to a table alias. Table aliases also help when using a recursive relationship in a data model. You can give the same table that appears multiple times in your data model different table alias. This doesn't have any real advantages except to help clarify your data model.

The form \ANSWERS\DM_EMP1.FSL and data model file \ANSWERS\DM_EMP1.DM demonstrate this table relationship (see Figure 2.9 that follows).

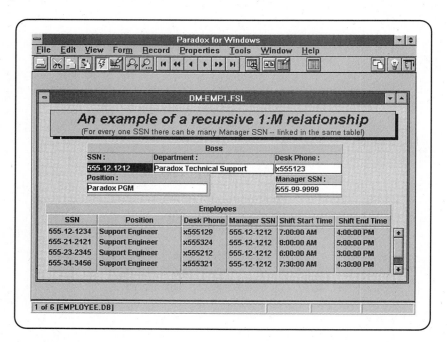

Figure 2.9. The form DM_EMP1.FSL demonstrates a recursive one-to-many relationship.

The recursive relationship is easier to understand if you look at a variation of it, as follows:

```
    Emp2.db
1:  Manager SSN*
2:  Employee SSN*              **
3:  Department
4:  Desk Phone
```

```
5:   Start Date
6:   Salary (per year)
7:   Shift Start Time
8:   Shift End Time
```

Now you can easily see that the combination of Manager SSN and Employee SSN makes each record unique. In addition, there is a secondary index on Employee SSN, so you can still use the table in the same manner as the previous example. The form \ANSWERS\DM_EMP2.FSL and data model file \ANSWERS\DM_EMP2.DM demonstrate this table relationship.

> One technique for doing a recursive relationship in Paradox is to use a live query in the data model.

Normalizing a Data Structure

A *normalized data structure* arranges data to minimize disk space. Each record includes the smallest number of fields necessary to establish a category. Instead of dumping all possible fields into a large table, normalized tables distribute information over many tables. This saves disk space each time a user doesn't need to use a particular table. In addition, normalized tables provide more flexibility in terms of analysis. Normalized data should be your goal at all times. It enables you to optimize disk space, analyze data better, and make data easier to manipulate.

In this method of organizing information, you group fields into categories in which each record contains the least number of fields necessary to establish a unique group. A normalized data model is not required in Paradox, but it is highly recommended. The normalization process discussed next is broken into three steps: remove identical records, remove repeating groups, and move fields that do not relate to the key.

Step One: Remove Identical Records

In the first step, you remove all identical records. Keying a table in Paradox removes all duplicate records. (See the section, "Using a Primary Key," earlier in this chapter for a complete discussion.)

Step Two: Remove Repeating Groups

In the second step, you remove repeating groups—a process that is more difficult to explain. You can learn about the second step with an example. In a traditional name and address table, you store a person's telephone number as part of the main table. In today's fast-paced, high-technology world, someone can have many telephone, fax, and communication numbers. A person can have several home and work numbers, as well as fax and modem numbers—perhaps even MCI and Compuserve account numbers. You could guess the maximum number of potential fields in the table. (Typically, developers will put Home, Work, and Fax fields in their tables.) Some users would have no numbers, however, and some would have all three. Because of the way database products allocate disk space, this is a terrible waste of disk space.

In addition, this scheme does not work when you need to have four or more numbers. Data with the potential for so many telephone numbers should be normalized. Again, the second rule to normalizing your data is to remove repeating groups. A traditional table with a Home field, a Work field, and a Fax field repeat a single field phone number three times. A good solution to this problem is to break apart the two bodies of information and link them in a 1:M relationship with a data model. In other words, for every *one* record in the parent table, there can be many records in the child table. Here is an example of using a second table for telephone numbers:

```
       Rolodex.db                   Rolodx-p.db
 1:    Last Name*     ----->>       Last Name*
 2:    First Name*    ----->>       First Name*
 3:    Middle Name*   ----->>       Middle Name*
 4:    Address 1                    Phone # Name*
 5:    Address 2                    Phone Number
 6:    City                         Phone Ext
 7:    State
 8:    Zip
 9:    Zip Ext
10:    Notes
```

SECRETS\APPS\ROLODEX\ROLODEX.FSL uses the preceding table structures. It demonstrates how to use a separate table for telephone numbers.

Step Three: Move Nonrelating Fields

The third—and final—step to normalizing your data involves tables that have more than one key field. If a nonkey field relies on only part of the total key, it should be moved to a separate table. This means that every field in the table must be directly related to all the key fields—not just some of them. For example, in a typical invoicing system, the child or detail table consists of at least the following:

```
    Lineitem.db
1:  Order No*
2:  Stock No*
3:  Description
4:  Selling Price
5:  Qty
```

Note that Description is related only to the Stock No field of the two-field composite index. Because Description does not directly pertain to Order No, it should be moved to another table and the two tables linked by the common field Stock No. The following structure accomplishes this:

```
    Lineitem.db       Stock.db
1:  Order No*
2:  Stock No* --->    Stock No*
3:  Selling Price     Vendor No
4:  Qty               Description
5:                    Qty on Hand
6:                    Cost Price
7:                    Selling Price
```

> INVOICE.FSL uses the preceding table structures. It demonstrates how to use a separate table for the item description.

If you study and learn the three rules of normalizing data presented above, you will be able to create larger databases that are optimized for disk space. In addition, the data will be better organized and, therefore, easier to analyze. I suggest that you reread this section—or this whole chapter—in a month or two in order to drive the point home.

dBASE TABLES VERSUS PARADOX TABLES

Once you decide to use Paradox as your DBMS, you still need to decide whether to use a local table structure like dBASE and Paradox or move to SQL table structures and the client server model. For a complete discussion of the client server model, see Chapter 35, "Using Paradox with SQL." Once you decide on a local table structure, you still need to decide between Paradox or dBASE table structures. You can store both Paradox and dBASE tables on either your hard drive or on a networked drive. Both have their advantages and disadvantages. What follows is intended to help you decide, but I must tell you up front that my strong preference is Paradox.

The primary key in Paradox promotes normalized table structures. On the other hand, dBASE allows for the flexibility of non-normalized tables because it does not use the concept of a primary key. Both dBASE 5 and Paradox 5 offer improved table structures. (Paradox 5 has many more new field types, however.) In addition, the Paradox table structure allows you to have spaces, lowercase characters, and special characters in the field's name. This one feature alone would decide the issue for me. The Paradox table structure allows you to humanize field names.

The new table structures of Paradox support so many advanced features that the choice seems clear. For example, the Paradox 5 table structure has referential integrity and supports such advanced field types as Formatted Memo, Graphic, Time, and Autoincrement. dBASE, however, has the benefit of being supported on almost every platform, including DOS, Windows, OS/2, Macintosh, Amiga, and UNIX. If Borland doesn't have the dBASE database product on that platform, remember that other companies do. dBASE index expressions also permit tremendous flexibility. Refer to the "Using dBASE Expressions" section later in this chapter.

Whether you use dBASE or Paradox tables is up to you. Each one has its advantages and disadvantages. dBASE gives you more flexible indexes and compatibility across platforms. Paradox is faster, promotes normalized data structures, has referential integrity, and has more flexible field types. If after reading this short section you are still not sure which table structure to use, I suggest you read the rest of this chapter carefully and use both structures a little until you decide.

NOTES ON THE dBASE TABLE STRUCTURE

The following section contains notes on various important features of the dBASE table structure. The intent is to let you know about some of the key differences between the Paradox and dBASE table structures and to highlight features of each.

dBASE Tables Mark Records for Deletion

In dBASE, records are marked for deletion by the active index. They are deleted only after you pack the table. If you never pack the table, it will keep growing forever. This is an advantage; it is also, however, a disadvantage, but one that is easily overcome. You can put routines in your application to retrieve and purge deleted records. Just remember that dBASE tables must be packed.

dBASE Allows Duplicates in the Main Index

Another difference is that with dBASE you have the option of having duplicate key values in all the indexes except unique indexes. Even with a unique index, however, duplicate values are allowed in the table; duplicate values are prevented only in the index.

dBASE Record Numbers Are Not Dynamic

In Paradox, the record numbers are dynamic; in dBASE, they are not. With Paradox tables, the record numbers change whenever you delete a record. To accomplish this, Paradox uses the concept of a heap stack. When you delete a record in dBASE, the record still exists in the table until you pack the table.

However, when you select Table | Filter for paradox or dBASE tables, the record numbers are the same, no matter what index you use. The status bar shows you only what record you are on, not what *record number* of *how many* (see Figure 2.10 that follows). Also, the original record numbers shift accordingly whenever you select different indexes (see Figure 2.11 that follows).

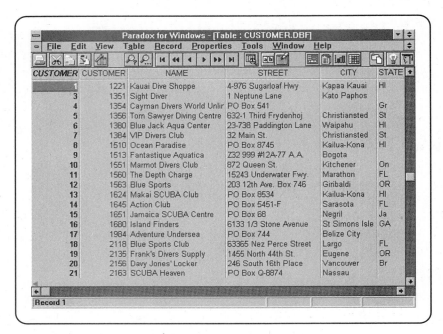

Figure 2.10. Screen shot of Customer table sorted by Customer.

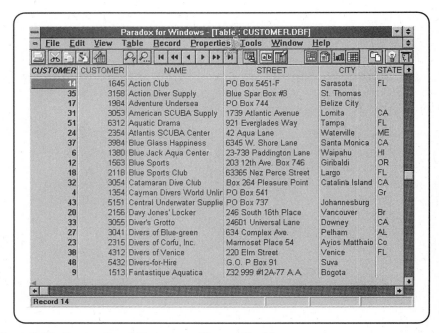

Figure 2.11. Screen shot of Customer table sorted by Name.

USING DBASE EXPRESSIONS

One advantage that dBASE tables have over Paradox tables is that dBASE indexes are very flexible. You can write elaborate expressions using dBASE keywords in the Define Index dialog box (see Figure 2.12). The following are all the dBASE functions supported by the expression engine:

ABS	DTOR	LOG10	SIGN
ACOS	DTOS	LOWER	SIN
ASC	DTOS	LTRIM	SPACE
ASIN	EXP	MAX	SQRT
AT	FIXED	MIN	STR
ATAN	FLOAT	MOD	STUFF
ATN2	FLOOR	MONTH	SUBSTR
CEILING	FV	PAYMENT	TAN
CHR	IIF	PI	TRANSFORM
COS	INT	PV	TRIM
CTOD	ISALPHA	RAND	UPPER
DAY	ISLOWER	REPLICATE	VAL
DIFFERENCE	ISUPPER	RIGHT	YEAR
DIV	LEFT	ROUND	
DOW	LEN	RTOD	
DTOC	LOG	RTRIM	

Here are some examples of index expressions:

DEPT+UPPER(LNAME) lists records by DEPT and LNAME fields. In this case, the index ignores case in the LNAME field.

UPPER(Field1)+UPPER(Field2)+UPPER(Field3) lists records by the Field1, Field2, and Field3 fields. In this index, case is ignored completely.

SUBSTR(DEPT,1,3)+SUBSTR(UPPER(LNAME),1,3)

DEPT+DTOS(DATE_HIRED)

DEPT+STR(DATE()-DATE_HIRED,4,0)

DEPT + STR(YEAR(DATE_HIRED),4,0) + STR(MONTH(DATE_HIRED),2,0) + STR(DAY(DATE_HIRED),2,0)

IIF(DEPT="SALES",SUBSTR(LNAME,1,3),SUBSTR(CITY,1,3))

IIF(STATE="AZ".OR.STATE="CA",STATE+"A",STATE)

DEPT+STR(YEAR(DATE_HIRED),4,0)+STR(SALARY,7,0)

```
DEPT+STR(MONTH(DATE_HIRED),2,0)+STATE
DEPT+STATE+STR(100000-SALARY,8,0)
```

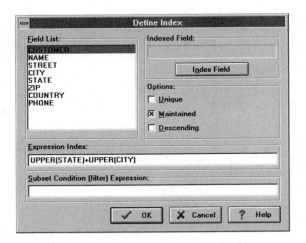

Figure 2.12. Entering dBASE expressions.

The preceding examples of index expressions show you how flexible dBASE indexes are. You are limited to expressions that have a length of no more than 220 characters and that result in no more than 100 characters. The CUSTOMER.DBF in the ANSWERS directory has a few indexes defined.

DBASE IS NOT ALWAYS DBASE

Not All dBASE Structures Are the Same!

Because dBASE is a database format and the most popular database in the world, slight variations with the .DBF table and drastic variations in the index exist. In general, all .DBF database files are similar enough in format not to cause any problems. Indexes are another story, however. Paradox is compatible with only .NDX and .MDX indexes. For example, you can't use Clipper .NTX indexes or FoxPRO's proprietary (.COX) indexes.

NOTES ON THE PARADOX TABLE STRUCTURE

As an ObjectPAL programmer, you must keep in mind the things that are better accomplished in interactive mode—for example, at the table level. Figure 2.13 shows the Restructure dialog box with the Table Properties drop list displayed. This section talks about the various Paradox table properties. It concentrates on using pictures to aid data development and to control data. This section also discusses how various concepts of referential integrity apply to Paradox tables.

Paradox Table Properties

The Paradox table properties are important. They consist of Validity Checks, Table Lookup, Secondary Indexes, Referential Integrity, Password Security, Table Language, and Dependent Tables.

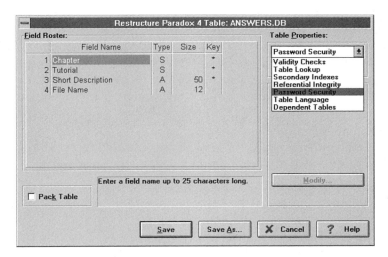

Figure 2.13. The Restructure dialog box.

The following is a quick review of table properties:

Validity Checks—These control the values that a user can enter in a field. They enable you to set up default values, data input checks, required values, and more.

Table Lookup—This is a data entry tool that ensures that data from one table is entered correctly in another table.

Secondary Indexes—These are very useful in interactive mode. In ObjectPAL, secondary indexes are useful for speeding up operations and viewing data in different ways.

Referential Integrity—This enables you to ensure data across table relationships. With referential integrity, you can make sure that ties between data won't be broken. For example, if a record in the master table has child records, you can't delete the master.

Password Security—Full-password encryption at the table and field levels guarantees the security of your data.

Table Language—The language driver for a table determines the table's sort order and the available character sets. The default table language is set by the IDAPI Configuration Utility. When you create or restructure a table, you can override the default table language with the Table Language option in the Table Properties panel in the Restructure dialog box. Paradox 5 offers many new language drivers, including several new ANSI language drivers, which allow you to store Windows ANSI high characters.

Dependent Tables—This is a table property that shows all the tables that are recognized as children in a referential integrity link.

PICTURE STRINGS

A *picture* is a pattern of characters that defines what a user can type into a field during editing or data entry. A picture aids data entry and promotes—but does not ensure—consistent data. Picture strings are an input aid and a means of validating data. They are implemented at the table level. Every ObjectPAL programmer needs to keep this in mind. If you must limit what someone can enter into a field, implement the limiting factor at the table level with a validity check if possible. You should use ObjectPAL only when you have determined that a picture won't work. Remember, ObjectPAL is on the form only. Unless you password-protect your table, nothing can prevent the user from selecting File | Open | Table and entering data directly into the table—in other words, bypassing your ObjectPAL code.

Use the Picture Assistance dialog box to enter new pictures (see Figure 2.14). When you add to the list of sample pictures, the pictures actually are written to the [Pictures] section of PDOXWIN.INI.

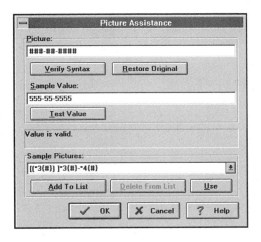

Figure 2.14. The Picture Assistance dialog box.

Table 2.1 lists the picture string characters you can use to validate data.

TABLE 2.1. PICTURE STRING CHARACTERS.	
Character	Description
#	A numeric digit
?	Any letter (uppercase or lowercase)
&	Any letter (converts to uppercase)
@	Any character

continues

Character	Description
Table 2.1. continued	
!	Any character (converts to uppercase)
;	Interprets the next character as a literal character—not as a special picture-string character
*	The character that follows can be repeated any number of times
[xyz]	The characters between square brackets are optional
{x,y,z}	Optional characters separated by commas
{}	Grouping operator
,	Alternative choices of values

If you use any other characters in a picture string, Paradox treats each character as a constant. Paradox automatically types the constant when the user comes to a point in the picture string where that constant is specified—except for the first character. The user must tell Paradox that he or she wants to enter data by entering the first character or by pressing the spacebar for autofill.

> Remember, autofill is a great feature that you should promote to your users. For example, to automatically fill in a date field with today's date, just press the spacebar a couple of times.

A Note on Using Multiple PDOXWIN.INI Files

Using the Picture Assistance dialog box makes good sense when you develop. You can enter and maintain a long list of frequently used pictures. This information is stored in your PDOXWIN.INI file. With the -i startup parameter, you can use multiple PDOXWIN.INI files. If you maintain multiple PDOXWIN.INI files, however, using the Picture Assistance dialog box to maintain multiple PDOXWIN.INI files might take a lot of time. If you do use multiple PDOXWIN.INI files using the startup parameter -i, then consider keeping a master list of pictures.

For example, you can maintain a master PDOXWIN.INI file in your Windows directory with all your pictures in it, and keep a separate PDOXWIN.INI file in each working directory you use. This technique enables you to customize each working directory with a different title, background, and other features. If you use this technique, do yourself a favor: Maintain a list of your favorite pictures—perhaps in the Windows PDOXWIN.INI file.

This technique is not recommended, however. If you always use the same PDOXWIN.INI, your settings remain the same for whatever working directory you use. Using one PDOXWIN.INI file is especially important when maintaining your customized pictures and other information stored in the PDOXWIN.INI file (such as number formats).

> The PICTURES.TXT file is on the disk that comes with this book in the \DEV-SRC directory. You can use the Notepad or any editor to open your PDOXWIN.INI file and copy the picture strings to it.

Useful pictures include the following:

```
Phone with auto fill = ###-####
Phone with auto fill (area opt) = [(###)]###-####
Phone w/1-800 optional = [{1-800-,(###)}]###-####
Flexible Phone Number = [1 (*3{#}) ]*3{#}-*4#
US 5 or 9 Zip Code = #####[-####]
US 5, US 9, or Canada zip code = *5{#}[*4#],@#@ #@#
SSN with auto fill = ###-##-####
SSN no auto fill = ###{-}##{-}####
Letters only (no spaces) = *?
Letters only (capitalize first) = &*?
Capital Letters = *&
Capital First letter = !*@
Capitalize every word 1 = *[![*?][* ]]
Capitalize every word 2 = !*[ * !,@]
Capitalize every word 3 = *{ ,.}!*{{ ,.}*{ ,.}!,@}
Capitalize every word 4 = *[[*#[ ]]![*?][@][ ]]
Capital After = !*[{ ,.,(,;,}*{ ,.,(,;,}!,@]
Time (HH:MM:SS:) = {0#,1#,2{0,1,2,3}}:{0,1,2,3,4,5}#:{0,1,2,3,4,5}#
Time with SS optional = {0#,1#,2{0,1,2,3}}:{0,1,2,3,4,5}#[:
  {0,1,2,3,4,5}#]
Time (HH:MM AM) or (HH:MM PM) = {1{:,{0,1,2}:},{2,3,4,5,6,7,8,9}:}
  {0,1,2,3,4,5}# {AM,PM}
Date with auto fill = {##/##/##,#/##/##}
Date 2 = {##/01/##,#/01/##}
```

```
Allow Miss, Ms., Mr., or Mrs. = M{iss,s.,r{.,s.}}
Allow Dr., Doctor, Father, Miss, Mrs., Mr., Mr. & Mrs., Ms., Msgr.,
  Pastor, and Reverend: = {D{r.,octor},Father,M{iss,r{s.,.[ ;& Mrs.]},
  s{.,gr.}},Pastor,Reverend}
```

Using a Table Lookup Effectively

When the user presses Ctrl+spacebar to bring up a lookup table, the lookup table respects the table properties set for the table. You can use this feature to jazz up the way the table lookup dialog box looks. For example, you can change the colors of a table in a table window and the changes will carry over to the table lookup dialog box. The table properties you alter are stored in the tableview file with the same name as the table and a .TV extension. When you use that table in the lookup, it will appear with the new property values.

Educate Your Users on the Interactive Features

When the user presses Ctrl+Spacebar to bring up a lookup table, remember to let him or her know that they can use Ctrl+Z (zoom) to locate a value. This one interactive feature can greatly enhance the user's perception of your application.

Table Lookup Does Not Use Aliases

The reason Paradox for Windows 1.0 table structures do not support aliases when setting up lookup tables is for compatibility with Paradox for DOS 4.5. The concept of aliases does not exist in Paradox for DOS. If Paradox for Windows allowed the use of aliases in lookup tables, then Paradox for DOS would not know how to interpret the alias. Therefore, even if you specify an alias, the path (not the alias name) is stored along with the table name.

What about Paradox for Windows 5 tables? Paradox for Windows 5 tables behave the same as Paradox for Windows 1 tables do with respect to lookup tables. Because Paradox for DOS cannot open a Paradox for Windows 5 table, I do not know why this occurs. Perhaps Borland is planning a Paradox for DOS version 5 that still will not support aliases.

THE TABLE LANGUAGE AND SORTING

How do you get support for special character sets in Paradox? For languages whose characters are written with an alphabet—not languages such as Chinese and Japanese—a language driver that supports the character set needs to exist, or Borland must create and release one.

In addition, the sort order of a table depends on the **language driver**. The three main language drivers with which we are concerned here in the United States are Paradox "ascii," Paradox "intl," and the new Paradox ANSI INTL. The Paradox "intl" (international) and Paradox ANSI INTL drivers sort alphabetically, mixing uppercase and lowercase; for example, aAbBBccC. The Paradox "ascii" (ASCII) driver sorts by the ASCII table, putting all the lowercase characters first; for example, aabbbcdAAABCCCD. How Paradox sorts a table depends on the language driver.

SECONDARY INDEXES

Earlier in this chapter, the importance of primary keys was addressed. Before Paradox 4.0, most users didn't even know what a secondary index was. With Paradox 4.0, secondary indexes became one of the options on the Main pull-down menu. In Paradox for Windows, secondary indexes are an integral part of the table structure. If you need help with secondary indexes, refer to this chapter for theory, and the *User's Guide* for interactive instructions.

REFERENTIAL INTEGRITY

Referential integrity (RI) is extremely important. Point-and-click referential integrity enables you to set up rules between tables so that your data is always valid. **Data integrity** is a guarantee that the values in a table are protected from corruption. Data integrity for autoincrementing means that no two records have the same key values. For referential integrity, data integrity means that the records in one table will always match the records in another table.

There are various types of referential integrity. Paradox supports Prohibit, Cascade, and Strict Update rules. Figure 2.15 shows a referential integrity link being set up between LINEITEM.DB and STOCK.DB. Note the two options selected in the Update Rule panel.

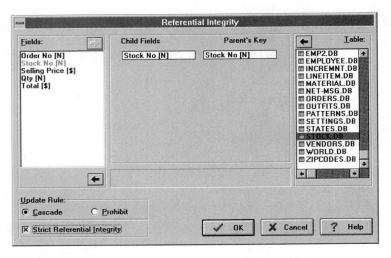

Figure 2.15. The Referential Integrity dialog box, which shows a link between
LINEITEM.DB and STOCK.DB.

Setting up Referential Integrity

You must be in the child table to create a referential integrity link. In addition,
you must make sure that the child table contains all key fields of the parent.
Besides controlling data entry, the referential integrity link provides an update
feature: either Cascade or Prohibit.

Cascade enables you to update child tables when a value changes in
the parent table. With Cascade referential integrity, any changes that
are made to the parent table's primary key are automatically made to
the child table. Therefore, if you make a change to the parent table's
primary key, the child table's foreign key is also updated. Referential
integrity links don't have to be made on key fields in the child table.
Whenever a change is made to the parent key, the change is cascaded
to all the child records that match that key. For example, if you
change the spelling of a customer's name from *Smith* to *Smythe,* the
data in the reference field of all the child table records that consist of
this key will also change.

> **WHERE IS CASCADE DELETE?**
>
> If you delete a record in the parent table, the related records in the child tables are not deleted. Although Paradox supports cascade updates with a convenient table level feature, it does not support cascade deletes with a table level feature. See "Implementing Cascade Delete Using ObjectPAL" in Chapter 16, "Using Table and TCursor Variables."

Prohibit referential integrity prevents a change in the parent's key if any records match the value in the child table. You can use Prohibit in an invoicing system to prevent the invoice numbers in existing line-item entries from being changed or deleted.

Strict Referential Integrity Check Box

Strict Referential Integrity should have been called "Prohibit Paradox 4.0" because it prevents Paradox 4.0 and its earlier versions from writing to the table because they don't support referential integrity. When the Strict Referential Integrity option in the Update Rule panel is checked (see Figure 2.15 shown previously), Paradox 4.0 for DOS can't alter data. This feature is designed entirely for interoperatability with Paradox for DOS. When strict integrity is selected, Paradox 4.0 sees the table as being write protected. Therefore, the data can be viewed in Paradox for DOS but can't be changed. If you are going to use referential integrity, and absolute data security is important, then you should also turn Strict Referential Integrity on.

The Parent Must Use a Primary Key

The parent table in a referential integrity link must use all the fields of the parent table's primary key. A parent table holds the master values for the link. It has the power to change these values, delete them, and add new values. A child table depends on the values in the parent table for its matching fields. Only the ones that exist in the parent table are available to a user to alter or view in a form.

Automatic Secondary Index

A referential integrity link can be defined between the primary key in a parent table and any index in a child table. The fields must match in number, type, and size. In other words, a parent table with two fields in its primary key must link to an index—primary or secondary—with two fields of the same type in the child table. You can use composite secondary indexes on the child table in a referential integrity link.

If Paradox needs to, it will automatically create any secondary indexes needed to establish a referential link. If Paradox needs a single field secondary index, it creates it Case Sensitive and Maintained and names it the same name as the field. If more than one field is needed, it names it the same name as the name you gave the referential integrity link.

Blank Field Caution

In referential integrity, blank fields are permitted to exist in the child even when no matching blank field exists in the parent. Blank fields are considered to be outside the referential integrity link. This feature comes in handy when you want to enter a child record without matching it immediately to a parent record; you can add the link value later.

You should *not* blank out a primary key value in the parent table, however. If you do, the corresponding fields in the child records are made blank as the change cascades from the parent. When you change the blank primary key to a nonblank value, the child records that were linked to it will remain blank. This is known as **orphaning records**. Remember, blanks in the master are considered to be outside the link.

To prevent orphaning of child records, restructure the table and use the Required Field validity check for all the key fields. In fact, it is generally considered good database design to make all the fields in a Paradox primary key Required Fields.

KILL VALIDITY CHECKS TODAY

Deleting .VAL Files Is OK!

Referential integrity and other settings stored in .VAL files sometime interfere with a project. If this happens to you and you don't mind losing the validity checks for a table or for a set of tables, go ahead and delete or, better yet, rename them. Be careful, though. All the validity checks will be deleted. For example, the ORDERS.DB, CUSTOMER.DB,

> LINEITEM.DB, STOCK.DB, and VENDORS.DB tables in the SAMPLE directory that comes with Paradox are a wonderful starting point for an invoicing system. The .VAL files—or more precisely, the table validity checks and referential integrity—might interfere, however, with you using the tables.

The form is a wonderful tool, but it isn't the place where data is stored. The table is. Therefore, the table is a much better place to implement data integrity. You can use pictures, table lookups, and referential integrity to implement data integrity. Only after you've determined that a data restriction can't be implemented at the table level should you move to the form level and use ObjectPAL to manipulate a user's input.

QUESTIONS AND ANSWERS

Q: When I open a .DBF table and select an index, why does the vertical scroll bar seem to freeze?

A: When you open a dBASE table, the vertical scroll bar button is enabled. If you select an index with Table | Order Range, the vertical scroll bar button is disabled. The records still move when you click on the Up and Down arrows, but the button remains stationary. This is as designed because dBASE tables carry record numbers as a permanent part of each record. This is different than Paradox, which uses a Heap Table concept. Therefore, records don't carry a permanent record number with Paradox tables.

Q: Does Paradox support Alpha Four?

A: Alpha Four version 3.0 is a relational database management system available on DOS platforms. Alpha Four 3.0 saves files directly in dBASE III+ and dBASE IV formats (.DBF), which can be used directly by Paradox.

Q: When I attempt to open a Paradox 4 or Paradox for Windows 5 table in Paradox 3.5 (or similar product), and I am prompted for a password, what is really happening?

A: Paradox 3.5, and any Paradox Engine 2.0 application like ObjectVision 2.0, do not support the versions of the Paradox table format past version 3.5 (this includes Paradox for Windows 5 tables).

Q: What is the purpose of the .FAM file that is sometimes created when I use my tables?

A: It is a file that contains a pointer to the location of a "family" file for the table—specifically, the .TV (tableview) file and the default report and form. The .FAM file is created when a .TV file is created. This file can occasionally cause problems when sorting tables in Paradox. The file can safely be deleted because the file will be recreated if needed.

Q: When I attempt to store high ASCII characters (extended ASCII) I get the error message "Character(s) not supported by Table Language." What is going on?

A: When storing data in tables, Paradox for Windows supports only the characters supported by the table language driver that the table is using. For most drivers, this is DOS Code Page 437. This is done to stay compatible with Paradox for DOS. You can change the code page to other languages using the IDAPI Configuration Utility, but, by default, Paradox uses Code Page 437. You also can turn off the Strict Translation property for the table in the data model of a form.

Q: What are the differences between an index created by Paradox for DOS and Paradox for Windows? It seems that the index created by Paradox for Windows is larger than the one created by Paradox for DOS. What can explain this difference?

A: Paradox for DOS creates indexes fully packed, whereas Paradox for Windows creates them with some space in them. Fully packed is faster for searches, but the extra space that Paradox for Windows leaves allows quicker record updates when adding records to the table.

Q: How easy is it to import data from Access?

A: Access and Paradox for Windows both can use Paradox 3.5 file format and dBASE file format. Therefore, all you need to do is export your Access files into one of these formats. Select File | Export from Access menus, then change the option to Paradox 3.x. Currently, ODBC, the Access engine, does not support Paradox 4 or Paradox for Windows 5 table structures.

Be aware that Access writes Paradox tables improperly. If a field in Access has no value, Access writes it to Paradox with a value of 1 space (" "), so a query searching for a blank field will make no matches.

No matter which table structure you choose, use aliases and make sure that your data model is correct. Aliases are your ticket to portability. No matter what type of relationship you set up, your data model is simply a series of 1:1, 1:M, M:1, and M:M relationships. When you study a complex data model, examine the relationship between any two tables. Set up data validity checks at the table level if possible.

3

CHAPTER

FORMS AND DEVELOPING

With Paradox, you can create forms and reports visually. You can create dazzling single- or multitable forms for viewing, editing, and adding data. This chapter shows you how to begin integrating design elements into a complete application. It deals with issues, problems, and solutions with design documents from a developing point of view. A **design document** is a form or a report that a developer uses to display data. This chapter also dives into special, summary, and calculated fields.

GLOSSARY TERM

Learning from others

Developing forms

Spicing up forms

Getting the most from style sheets

Notes on forms and the data model

Special fields

Summary fields

Calculated fields

STUDY APPLICATIONS FOR A BETTER USER INTERFACE

The user interface is the first element of your application that a user sees. Because first impressions are important, the user interface carries more weight than any other part of your application. It deserves much planning and effort.

Often when you start a new form, you already have an idea of what you want it to look like. When you're inspired, go with it. When you're struggling to find the right look and feel for a form or application, however, why reinvent the wheel?

Software companies spend millions of dollars studying the look and feel of software. You can benefit from all this effort by looking through the software right on your machine. Take some time—perhaps now—to open up and browse through your favorite software. In general, what does the application look like? Look for consistent features. Are all the buttons the same size? What color scheme did they develop? What things do you like, and what do you dislike? What would you change? Be really picky. Closely examine the details of these professionally developed applications.

Your applications don't have to look as professional as commercial applications. The closer you get, however, the better. You should at least pick a design concept and stick to it. Pick your colors, form size, button size, frame style, and fonts. Don't stray from the standard that you set for a particular project. If you don't know what the look and feel should be, design with the simple Paradox defaults—white background, transparent box colors, black letters, and no borders. After your forms have all their elements, you can decide on a look and feel.

> APPS\PROPERTY\PROPERTY.FSL is a utility you can use to universally change a form or a set of forms.

STUDY OBJECTS BEFORE YOU START DESIGNING

Paradox comes with a plethora of objects and options. Browse through them and look at their many characteristics. Many people get caught up in a particular project and never explore the many visual features of Paradox.

Spend some time studying the visual properties of objects. The objects from the speedbar tools that you can place in forms and reports are **design objects**. The better you know the design objects of Paradox, the better your applications will look. Make sure that you know what all the properties do. For example, a field has several Run Time properties. What are the differences among Read Only, Tab Stop, and No Echo? Know the properties of design objects before you start programming in ObjectPAL.

GETTING THE MOST OUT OF STYLE SHEETS

The prototyping of objects is a feature of Paradox that allows you to create great-looking and consistent forms and reports. This option enables you to save default settings such as color, font information, ObjectPAL code, and so on. Use this feature to expedite the creation of consistent objects complete with all the properties and ObjectPAL code. The following section discusses style sheets in general. If you need help changing the contents of the style sheet, consult the *Paradox User's Guide*.

Style sheets are a powerful tool for design development. You can maintain several different looks and switch among them before you create a design document—either a form or a report. You can set up several .FT form and .FP report Style Sheet files—with different fonts, colors, frame styles, and so on—and save them to your working directory.

You can even use custom color schemes, which are saved as part of the Style Sheet file. You also can create your own color schemes that are independent of the Windows color palette. The possibilities are limitless.

Keep in mind, however, that many users are still bound to only 16 colors. If you have a better video card, remember that the custom colors you define probably will be dithered on lesser video cards. Therefore, be sure to test your work on a standard 16-color VGA card. It's also a good idea to test your application with at least three different Windows color schemes. Check out the Windows Control Panel for possible color schemes. The following color schemes work best with Paradox:

> Arizona
> Black Leather Jacket
> Bordeaux
> Cinnamon
> Emerald City

Fluorescent
Hot Dog Stand
LCD Reversed = Light
Monochrome
Ocean
Patchwork
Rugby
Valentine

If you get into the habit of choosing a style sheet before you create the first form for a project, you guarantee a consistent look and feel for your entire application—with little or no effort.

On the disk set are several .FT files to get you started:

FANCY.FT: A fancier custom look

CLOWN.FT: A simple colorful look

SECRETS1.FT: My preferred style sheet (no ObjectPAL code)

SECRETS2.FT: My preferred style sheet (with lots of ObjectPAL code)

SECRETS2.FP: My preferred printer style sheet

Also on disk are two scripts for creating your own style sheets based on an existing form or report.

The Six Steps to Create a Form

Everybody has his or her own technique for developing a form. This section explores one technique. Study this technique and use it to improve your own technique for developing forms. Here are the six steps of developing a form that I use:

1. **Create the data model.** This includes gathering data components and business rules, and planning and structuring the tables. See Chapter 2, "Tables and Developing," for an in-depth discussion of tables.

2. **Prototype several forms.** Design several versions of forms with the data models you created and the business rules you gathered in step 1. Let someone else decide which prototype form has the best look and feel.

3. **Test the built-in behavior.** Run the form and see whether the basic data model and fields are what you need. Make sure that you use the application the way that the user will. For example, search for values, insert a new record, change, and delete records.

4. **Add objects and design elements.** Once you have decided on the prototyped forms and tested the built-in behavior, the next step is to add text objects, graphics, buttons, and so on to get the overall visual effect you want.

5. **Add ObjectPAL.** Decide what more you want an object to do and add the appropriate code (more on this starting with the next chapter).

6. **Do a beta test.** Large companies thoroughly test their software, and so should you.

Step 1: Create the Data Model

You can use what Borland calls the data model designer, to create relational table links visually. New to version 5, you can even save and load data model files (.DB). Whether you're working on forms, reports, or queries, all you do is draw lines between tables. The linking expert automatically does all the relational work for you by showing you how the tables can be linked. No matter how complex the relationship is, Paradox graphically displays the linked tables.

The first step in creating a form is to decide on a data model. The better you understand how the data model works and the theory behind relating tables, the easier it is for you to create forms and applications. See Chapter 2 for more information on the theory behind linking tables. For information on how to link tables in the data model, an interactive feature, consult the *Paradox User's Guide*.

Step 2: Prototype Several Forms

Creating forms in Paradox is easy and fun. Within a couple of hours you could create nearly a dozen variations of a form. Design several versions of forms for your application and let someone else, such as the client, decide which prototype form he or she likes the look and feel of best.

When you prototype a form, set the form's properties, decide on a Style Sheet, create the form using either the data model or an Expert, decide whether you want the form to be a Window or a Dialog box, set the title of the form, and so on.

Set the form's properties (see Figure 3.1). Get into the habit of setting the properties of a form whenever you create one. Give it a name, take the scroll bars off, and so on. Now is a good time to choose a look and feel for your application. (Refer to the section titled "Getting the Most Out of Style Sheets" earlier in this chapter.) Figure 3.1 shows the Form Window Properties that I prefer.

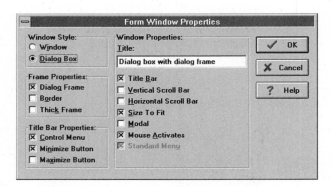

Figure 3.1. The Form Window Properties dialog box.

Step 3: Test the Built-In Behavior

Because Paradox has a tremendous amount of built-in functionality, exploring the built-in behavior of the form is important. Users often waste time because they don't know the built-in behavior. Sometimes, the built-in behavior is different from what they assume it is. After programming for many hours, they finally give up and either call Borland or post a message on Compuserve, only to be told that the default behavior already does what they were trying to do. In other words, if you don't know the default behavior, you might waste time duplicating it. Even worse, your added code may cause problems that you may then try to write more code to fix. This is a programming loop you must try to avoid.

Testing your form before you begin to add to it also gives you an overall sense of what you're trying to accomplish. Developers often get caught up in one detail of an application and lose sight of the big picture. Use your forms the way your users will. Your applications will have a much better look and feel.

Step 4: Add Objects and Design Elements

The next step is to add objects—calculated fields, lines, graphics, boxes used to contain fields (a wonderful way to set the tab order for a group of objects), and so on. You add more objects only after you thoroughly test the built-in behavior of your newly created form.

When first developing a form, consider using the snap to grid options to help you quickly place many objects on a form in orderly positions. The **grid** consists of horizontal and vertical lines that help you place objects. You can show or hide the grid; you also can resize it. Use Snap To Grid when you first design a form. Doing so cuts down the time needed to design the form.

Step 5: Add ObjectPAL

After you thoroughly test how your objects and design elements operate with the built-in behavior of Paradox, the next step is to decide what more you want the form to do. Do you want the form to automatically put values in fields? Do you want it to open another form? Do you want to add pull-down menus and keyboard shortcuts?

Whatever ObjectPAL you decide to add, develop in small steps and test as you go. If you add code and the code doesn't work, take it out! I can't tell you how many times I have talked to programmers who swear that the problem they have is a bug in Paradox and it turns out to be their overcoding. Often, when faced with a task, you will experiment with code to see what happens. If you just keep adding code to your form in hopes of solving the problem, you will end up with a mess.

Remember to remove code experiments. Also, remember to step back and remind yourself what you are trying to do, and try to think of different ways of accomplishing the same task.

> ### Note for Programmers Who Have Already Started ObjectPAL
>
> If you are already familiar with ObjectPAL, here is a tip. If, in experimentation, you use `sleep()`, `doDefault`, or `DisableDefault` to overcome some odd or misunderstood behavior, do not leave the commands in your code. If using the command didn't seem to make a difference, then take it out. Use commands only when they are called for.

One great way to really learn the event model and the power of these—and other—commands is to experiment with adding them. Remember to take them out, however, if they did not do what you wanted.

If you really think you have found a bug in Paradox, then don't waste any time on your complicated form. Instead, try to duplicate the problem on a brand new form with no extra code on it. Only after you have duplicated the problem on a new form should you even consider notifying Borland. I believe that you will find, more times than not, that the problem is not a bug in Paradox, however.

Step 6: Do a Beta Test

The final step in developing a form is to test your form as a whole. You'll see whether you are done or need to go back to steps 4 and 5. You should test your ObjectPAL code as you go. In this step, you test the whole application, not its individual elements. Does the form behave the way you thought it would? Does it behave the way your users will expect it to? Does it integrate with the rest of the application? Chapter 36, "Delivering Your Application," discusses techniques you can use to beta test your own custom written software.

NOTES ON CREATING FORMS

The following section discusses various design issues of creating forms.

Child Windows versus Dialog Boxes

Put some thought into whether you want a form to be a child window or a dialog box. Forms that are child windows obey Microsoft's Multiple Document Interface (MDI). The MDI, for example, dictates that when you maximize one child window, all child windows are maximized.

A box that requests or provides information is a **dialog box**. Many dialog boxes present options from which you must choose before you can perform an action. Other dialog boxes display warnings or error messages. Some are even utilities—such as the Paradox Desktop that comes on the disk set that comes with this book.

A **model dialog box** is a dialog box that the user can't leave to interact with Paradox until he or she responds to it. Use the form ANSWERS\F_SHOW.FSL to experiment with the various form types (see Figure 3.2). Each form type has different characteristics. Open F_SHOW.FSL and experiment with the various types of dialog boxes. Figures 3.3 through 3.5 show several of the various types of dialog boxes that you can design.

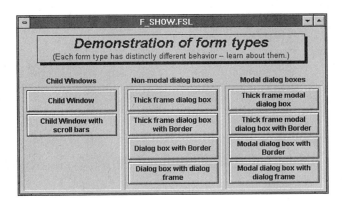

Figure 3.2. ANSWERS\F_SHOW.FSL demonstrates the various form types.

Figure 3.3. ANSWERS\F_DIA2.FSL demonstrates a nonmodal thick frame dialog box.

Figure 3.4. ANSWERS\F_DIA4.FSL demonstrates a nonmodal dialog frame dialog box.

Figure 3.5. ANSWERS\F_MOD3.FSL demonstrates a modal dialog box with a border.

If you leave the form as a child window to Paradox and hide the Paradox desktop, the child window hides with it. If you want to hide the Paradox desktop so that the form is the only visual object on your screen, you must define the form as a dialog box. Remember that a form is a dialog box only when it is opened in View Data mode. If you're in Design mode, running the form isn't the same as reopening it. You must reopen it. Using forms as dialog boxes is discussed more in Chapter 15, "Handling Reports."

Spicing Up Your Forms

Windows is a wonderful color graphics environment. With the early versions of Windows, most applications had white backgrounds with black letters. Microsoft added three-dimensional buttons to version 3.0 to improve the look. Borland's dynamic link library gives Borland and many other applications a chiseled, three-dimensional look. Windows applications are just starting to come to life visually. Keep this in mind, because your users will demand a high degree of visual appeal from your database applications. Just remember not to overdo it and keep your applications looking professional.

Spicing Up Your Applications

UIObjects are objects that you can draw by using the speedbar, such as circles, lines, fields, and buttons. You can add pictures to spice up UIObjects. Use bitmaps whenever possible. Small bitmaps on buttons are particularly attractive; they give your application a professional look. The form ANSWERS\F_BUTTON.FSL demonstrates adding graphics to buttons (see Figure 3.6).

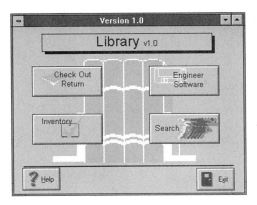

Figure 3.6. *To spice up an application, add pictures to buttons.*

I once added five little bitmaps to five buttons on a form. Each bitmap was about 1/2 inch by 1/2 inch. When I saved and reloaded the form, it ran incredibly slowly. I studied the situation and discovered that my form took up 960K of space. I had accidentally used five full-screen bitmaps and had Paradox shrink the graphics by selecting Magnification | Best Fit. I opened the bitmaps in Photo Styler, changed them to their actual sizes (about 1/2 inch by 1/2 inch). The size of the form shrank from 960K to 48K, and the form ran as it should.

A **crosstab** is an object that enables you to summarize data in one field by expressing it in terms of two other fields. These spreadsheet-like structures are easy for the user to understand. Unfortunately, crosstabs aren't used enough by developers. Therefore, keep in mind that another way to improve the look and feel of an application is to use crosstabs to show summaries of information. In today's technological world, people are bombarded with information. Users expect to be presented with neat little packages of information. Crosstabs are your gateway to creative summaries and graphs.

Graphs add visual excitement and flair to your forms and reports. Using a graph to represent data visually is appealing to the eye and brain. You can use many kinds of graphs, including line, bar, and three-dimensional pie. You can even combine line and marker graphs. Graphs change as data is changed. They are a wonderful visual aid. Most database users agree that graphs are not used enough—especially for analyzing data.

Do Not Overcrowd a Form

Many users use Paradox to duplicate printed forms: applications, records, and so on. Your natural inclination might be to put all the fields on a single page—just like the real form. Try to resist this temptation, because it causes problems with the user interface. Typically, a form that mimics a form is larger than the screen, and the user must scroll around it to fill in all the data. A better user interface approach is to break the fields into categories on forms—or a multipage form—that are the same size as or smaller than the screen. When you are ready to print, use a report or a large form. Although this means some duplication of effort, your users will appreciate your extra effort in the user interface.

Consistency is the Key to Creating Good-Looking Forms

Choose consistent colors when you create and place objects. If you choose a white background for your forms, stick to it. If you choose another color or a special color scheme, such as Borland's chiseled steel look, stick to it. As stated previously, when you design forms, a good approach is to set your colors to the Windows default by using the Control Panel.

To achieve a good user interface, you need to be consistent. Choose a color scheme and stick to it. Make similar objects the same size. Buttons are especially noticeable; try to use only one or two sizes for them. Use a consistent line width and frame style.

At the same time, don't use too many visual elements in your application. A good-looking application doesn't have an abundance of colors or objects. Instead, good-looking applications use subtle design elements. Use patterns sparingly—only one or two styles for each application. When you pick colors, feel free to choose as many as you need for the foreground, background, text, title, and user input—just be consistent. Realize, however, that just because your users have at least 16 colors, you don't have to use every color on a single form or in a single application.

Just as Borland has found a look and feel it likes—the chiseled steel look—you should strive to find your own style. You can create several looks and switch among them with each project, or you can develop a single look; your users may soon recognize your applications. Keep in mind, however, that the data is more important then the flashy objects around it.

Increase Your Productivity

Run Multiple Instances of Paradox!

One benefit of running multiple instances of Paradox is that you can easily copy and paste objects from one form to another. For example, I frequently develop with another instance of Paradox running with its working directory set to DEV-SRC (the developer source directory with clip objects in it that ships with the disk set from this book).

You can use the Paradox Desktop utility in APPS\DESKTOP\ DESKTYOP.FDL or set up icons in your Paradox group to run more than one copy of Paradox. First, create more private directories in your Paradox directory. Call them PRIV2, PRIV3, and PRIV4. Next, set up three more icons with the following command lines:

```
PDOXWIN -e -y -pC:\PDOXWIN\PRIV2
PDOXWIN -e -y -pC:\PDOXWIN\PRIV3
PDOXWIN -e -y -pC:\PDOXWIN\PRIV4
```

Now you can run up to four copies of Paradox: your original copy and the three new ones. One machine can have up to eight instances of Paradox running at the same time. Remember that whenever you're sharing data on the same machine, it is recommended that you load SHARE.EXE and turn on Local Share in the IDAPI configuration utility. If you are running a non-IDAPI application along with Paradox, then SHARE.EXE and turning on local share is required. Refer to Appendix A, "Installation and Setup," for more information on setting up icons.

Data Model and Table Lookup Notes

This section does not tell you how to use the data model; data model theory was discussed in the last chapter and it is assumed that you already know the basics of linking tables with the data model. Instead, this section points out some common pitfalls of the data model and table lookups with respect to forms.

Link the Correct Way

When using referential integrity, make sure that you link from the master to the detail. If you accidentally link from the detail to the master, the data model will attempt to update the child table before updating the master table; this causes the error message "Master Record missing."

If you wish to test this, then create two tables with a single field primary key. Save the first table as REF1.DB and the second as REF2.DB. Restructure REF2.DB (the child table) and set up a Cascade Delete referential integrity link to REF1.DB (the parent table). Next, create a form and link the tables in a one-to-one relationship. The goal in this case was to update the REF2.DB child table whenever a new record is inserted or updated in REF1.DB. But because we linked the wrong way—from the child to the parent—the data model first tries to update REF2.DB, then REF1.DB. The message on the status bar is "Master Record missing." To fix the form, go into design mode, open the data model, unlink the two tables, and relink them; this time link from REF1.DB (the parent table) to REF2.DB (the child table).

Do Not Hard Code Table Lookups

For compatibility with the DOS product, aliases are not allowed on table lookups. This, unfortunately, limits the usefulness of table lookups. If your data needs to be portable, then put the table lookups in the same directory as the main data or a subdirectory below it. This second technique is called *relative directory addressing (RDA)*. This allows you to move your entire data directory (along with its subdirectories) to a different location.

The Second Table in a 1:1 Relationship Is Read-Only

When you link two tables in the data model of a form, the second table is set to read-only by default. If you do this and attempt to modify the second table, you will get the error message, "Cannot modify this table."

To change this setting, view the forms data model and right click the detail table. The pop-up menu should show read-only with a check mark next to it. Select the read-only property to toggle it off. You will now be able to edit the detail table.

The 1-by-1 MRO Is No Longer Needed for Unlinked Tables

The last trick dealing with the data model I wish to show you is the very important 1-by-1 multirecord object, which is sometimes referred to incorrectly as a single record object.

With earlier versions it was important for two reasons: for use with the data model and ObjectPAL. Suppose that you need to have two unlinked tables in your data model. If you have ever tried this in earlier versions, you know that it isn't as straightforward as it seems. You can define the first table to fields as easily as if there were only one table in the data model. When you try to add fields for the second table, however, the data model allows you to use only summary fields. The solution for versions 1 and 4.5 is to put both of the sets of fields in two 1-by-1 MROs.

With version 5 of Paradox, Borland increased the functionality of the data model so that it can now handle unlinked tables in the data model; a 1-by-1 MRO is no longer needed interactively to scroll through either table (see Figure 3.7).

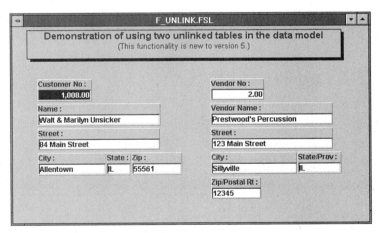

Figure 3.7. Screen shot of ANSWERS\F_UNLINK.FSL.

The 1-by-1 MRO is still very important to the ObjectPAL programmer; it adds a record object to fields on a form. We'll return to this later in Chapter 18, "Fields, Table Frames, and MROs" in the section titled, "Using a 1-by-1 MRO."

SPECIAL, SUMMARY, AND CALCULATED FIELDS

Many users have trouble understanding calculated fields. For this reason, and so that you don't try to duplicate this functionality by using ObjectPAL, this next section explores how to use special, summary, and calculated fields.

Using Special or Calculated Fields

To use a special or calculated field, select the field that you want the value to go into, inspect its properties, choose Define Field, and select the ellipsis points (...).You can use the tools in the Define Field Object dialog box to set up a special or calculated field.

When you **define** a field object, you attach it to data from a table. For example, you define a field object in a form as a field in a table. You cannot define calculated fields to a field in a table. Do not confuse defining with binding. You **bind** or associate an object such as a table frame or multirecord object (MRO) with a table, whereas you **define** a field.

A **special field** is a field, placed in a design document, that contains information about a table or design. These fields are predefined by Paradox, such as Now and Table Name.

Special Fields and Summary Fields

Table 3.1 describes special fields, Table 3.2 describes special table fields, and Table 3.3 describes the summary fields.

TABLE 3.1. SPECIAL FIELDS.	
Field	*Description*
Now	Displays the current running time in the field. This is an excellent and easy way to add a clock to your application. Because you can't define a field to a table and also use it as a special Now field, use the `time()` method via ObjectPAL to time-stamp a record or use the new TimeStamp field type.
Today	Displays the current date in the field.

Field	Description
TimeStamp	Displays the current time and date in the field. (This feature is new to version 5.)
Page Number	Displays the current page number of the form.
Number of Pages	Displays the total number of pages in the current form.

TABLE 3.2. SPECIAL TABLE FIELDS.	
Field	**Description**
Table Name	Displays the name of the table in the field. Table Name is particularly useful in reports.
Record Number	Displays the current record number in the field. Using a table's record number is particularly useful for auto-numbering records in forms and reports when you don't need to store the number with the table. Record Number obeys restricted views. That is, if the number of records is restricted by the data model, Record Number reflects this and starts numbering at 1. This makes it useful for auto-numbering items in a typical invoicing system.
Number of Records	Displays the total number of restricted records.
Number of Fields	Displays the number of fields in the table.

TABLE 3.3. SUMMARY FIELDS.	
Field	**Description**
Sum	Adds all the values.
Count	Displays a count of all the records.
Min	Displays the smallest value for this field in the table.
Max	Displays the largest value for this field in the table.

continues

TABLE 3.3. CONTINUED	
Field	Description
Avg	Displays the average value for this field in the table.
Std	Displays the standard deviation of the values in the set.
Var	Displays the statistical variance of the values in the set.

Figure 3.8 shows the Define Field Object dialog box, which displays the special and summary fields.

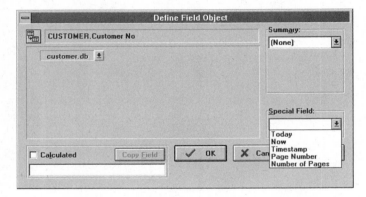

Figure 3.8. The Define Field Object dialog box showing the special and summary fields.

Tutorial: Auto-Incrementing a Restricted View

Suppose that you wish to number the detail records in a typical invoicing system. To do this, you do not need ObjectPAL. The special table field Record Number can handle the task.

On Disk: ANSWERS\REC-NO.FSL

Quick Steps

1. Create a form that uses ORDERS.DB and LINEITEM.DB in its data model set up in a 1:M.
2. Add a column to the detail table.
3. Define the new column field as a Record Number field.

Step By Step

1. Launch Paradox, and make the TUTORIAL directory your working directory.
2. Select File | New | Form and link ORDERS.DB to LINEITEM.DB in a 1:M relationship. Select OK.
3. At the Design Layout screen, select By Rows under the Object Layout: section, and select OK.
4. Add a column to the detail table frame. Your form should now look similar to Figure 3.9.

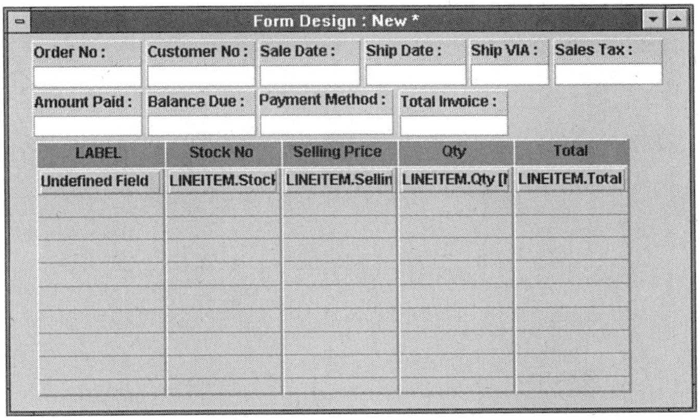

Figure 3.9. Adding a column to a table frame.

5. To bring up the Define Field Object dialog box, select the undefined field of the column you added in step 4. Right click (or press F6) to inspect the field. Select Define Field and the ellipsis points (. . .).
6. Select the drop-down arrow of the LINEITEM.DB table and then select the Record Number special table field. Select OK.
7. Label the column Item Number if you want, and run the form. It should look similar to Figure 3.10.
8. Save the form as REC-NO.FSL.

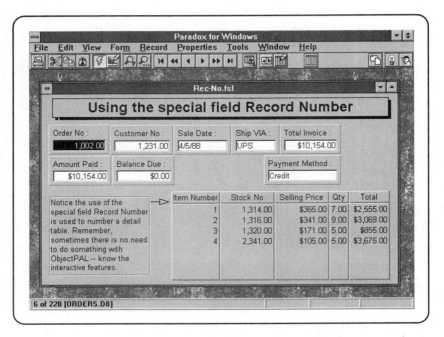

Figure 3.10. The completed form from REC-NO.FSL showing the use of a table field for the line item in the first column.

NOTE

If you had any problems with this tutorial (or any tutorial in this book), then open up the completed form in the \SECRETS2\ANSWERS directory.

Analysis

The first column is numbered 1 through however many records there are in the restricted view. The restricted view is determined by the table relationships set up in the data model. This operation is built into Paradox. You could do this same operation in ObjectPAL, but with difficulty.

TIP

Before you code in ObjectPAL, ask yourself two questions: Does Paradox already do this? Is there a better and easier way?

You also can use the Record Number table field with reports; for example, when you want the records of a report to be numbered. Special and summary fields have many uses, so make sure that you know what all these field types do. The Now special field is particularly useful. To put a clock on the main menu of your form, simply place an undefined field on the form and define it as the Now special field type. Voilá! In an instant, you have created a running clock on your form.

CALCULATED FIELDS

Calculated fields use the Calculated edit region of the Define Field Object dialog box to set up a user-defined formula. When you combine two or more alphanumeric values, you **concatenate** them. An **operator** is a symbol that represents an operation to be performed on a value or values. For example, the + operator represents addition, and the * operator represents multiplication. The **arithmetic operators** in ObjectPAL are +, -, *, /, and ( ). Use these operators to construct mathematical expressions in queries and calculated fields. For example, to concatenate two or more alphanumeric values in a calculated field (or ObjectPAL), use the + operator. For example, the formula

```
1:  City + ", " + State
```

concatenates three strings to form a value such as

```
1:  Milpitas, CA
```

In addition to arithmetic operators, you can use in a calculated field any expression that returns a single value. This includes any ObjectPAL statement that returns a single value. Although we have not formally started our study of ObjectPAL, here are some fairly self-explanatory, single-command expressions you can use in a calculated field:

```
startUpDir()
privDir()
workingDir()
windowsDir()
windowsSystemDir()
isLeapYear(today())
isSpeedBarShowing()
getMouseScreenPosition()
version()
isDir("C:\\DOS")
fieldName1 + fieldName2
number(fieldName1) + number(fieldName2)
```

Here are some combination-method expressions you can use in a calculated field:

```
size(startUpDir())
dow(today())
doy(today())
```

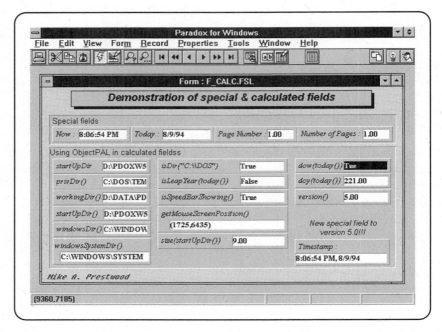

Figure 3.11. The form ANSWERS\F_CALC.FSL demonstrates calculated and special fields.

Using *iif()*

You can use the `iif` (immediate if) statement in both calculated fields and ObjectPAL to make decisions. With an `iif` statement, you can in essence say, "If the following expression is true, this field's value is A. Otherwise, this field's value is B."

Syntax

```
iif(Condition, ValueIfTrue, ValueIfFalse)
```

Examples

```
iif(field1=blank(), today, field1)
iif(taxable = "Yes", ([LINEITEM.Selling Price] * [LINEITEM.Qty]) * .06, blank())
```

> ## YOU CAN FORCE A CALCULATED FIELD TO REFRESH
>
> If you ever have a calculated field on a form not updated with one of the values in the calculation change, then you can use the ObjectPAL method `forceRefresh()` to make the calculated field display the correct values. This can occur, for example, when you update a field involved with a calculated field using a Tcursor. More on `forceRefresh()` later in Chapter 18, "Fields, Table Frames, and MROs."

Special fields, special table fields, summary fields, and calculated fields are important to the ObjectPAL programmer. Many times, tasks are easier to accomplish with these fields than through ObjectPAL.

In addition to designing and creating tables, designing good forms makes your application great. Forms are the backbone of your application. In fact, in Paradox, forms *are* your application. The better you are at designing forms, the better your applications turn out.

So far, this book has covered some of the more important nonprogramming aspects of ObjectPAL and interactive Paradox. The rest of this book concentrates on pure ObjectPAL. Remember: The more you know about interactive Paradox, the easier it is to develop your applications. Also note that 80 percent or more of your application is completed even before you start to code in ObjectPAL. Understanding interactive Paradox is crucial. Whenever you have a question about or an interest in a particular interactive feature, press F1 for help or consult the *User's Guide*.

YOUR FIRST OBJECTPAL EXPERIENCE

Although Paradox is powerful, it still can't do some things interactively. You have to accomplish some tasks using its programming language. The Paradox Application Language is **ObjectPAL**. Why would you need to use ObjectPAL? You use ObjectPAL to automate or customize objects on a form. An example of a task that requires ObjectPAL is creating a custom menu system for a form. If you plan to develop a complete custom Paradox application, you probably will need to use ObjectPAL.

*The elements of
ObjectPAL*

Where to put code

*The six beginner-level
built-in methods*

Types of commands

Altering properties

First database routines

This first chapter exclusively on ObjectPAL is geared toward the beginning ObjectPAL programmer. If you have never programmed in ObjectPAL before, then this chapter is for you. If you have programmed in ObjectPAL a little—or a lot—then I recommend that you read it as review material. Especially important are the sections on the event model and types of commands.

ObjectPAL: An Overview

ObjectPAL is for both programmers and nonprogrammers. If you have experience with another language, especially an object-oriented programming language such as C++ or Pascal with objects, you will find ObjectPAL especially interesting. If you have never programmed, ObjectPAL is a good language to learn first, because it allows you to paint objects with built-in behavior on a form and then attach bits of code to the object.

You use the user interface to design forms with objects on them—such as fields, tables, and buttons. When you're happy with the way the form works interactively, you attach ObjectPAL code to the objects that require it. This system of programming falls into the category of an event-driven language. The fact that you draw objects on a form and attach code to the objects allows even the nonprogrammer to create applications easily.

Features of ObjectPAL

ObjectPAL's features include an event handler, data types, strong program control, the runtime library, user-defined commands, and support for dynamic link libraries.

The event handler built into ObjectPAL cuts down the amount of time you spend programming. It also makes the language accessible to nonprogrammers. ObjectPAL has many data types, including `String`, `Number`, `SmallInt`, `Date`, `Time`, `Array`, and `DynArray`. The language supports programming control—branching—such as `if`, `for`, `while`, and `scan`. ObjectPAL also has a long list of commands called methods and procedures that a programmer can use. Methods and procedures either stand alone or work on an object, and they include such commands as `open()`, `attach()`, `moveTo()`, `setTitle()`, `getPosition()`, and `setPosition()`. ObjectPAL also lets you read or set all the properties with which you are already familiar such as Color, Tab Stop, and Next Tab Stop.

As with C and Pascal, you can create your own commands with ObjectPAL. These user-created commands are called custom methods and custom procedures. Custom methods and procedures consist of methods and procedures from the runtime library and other user-defined routines. You also can make calls to dynamic link libraries (DLLs). DLLs are functions and procedures usually written in C, C++, or Pascal. After you register the user created-function in ObjectPAL, you can use it as though Borland included it. This offers you almost unlimited expandability.

A Powerful High-Level Programming Language

ObjectPAL is a complete programming language. Like Basic, Pascal, and C, ObjectPAL supports variables, control structures, loops, and more. The power of ObjectPAL pleases traditional programmers. You will appreciate ObjectPAL's power to manipulate databases. The ObjectPAL language contains a rich array of functionality for managing data. You can find and manipulate values in a table. You can add records from one table to another. You can even scan a table, find every field that has a certain word, and change that word. No language can do it all, but ObjectPAL certainly comes close.

Sometimes, you might spend a few minutes in ObjectPAL adding a few lines of code to an object on a form, and then you are done. Other times, you might spend hours coding many different objects that interact with one other. If you program in small steps and test as you go, programming in ObjectPAL can be fun and easy.

Do I Have to Learn a Programming Language?

Most of the time, ObjectPAL is easy to program. It can be hard, however. Every programming language can be tough. At the same time, every programming language is easy if you take it in small increments. It is just a matter of how much you want to learn in a given period of time. If you want to learn all of ObjectPAL by next week, ObjectPAL is as hard as hard can get. If you're willing to spend a little time, however, it's one of the easiest languages to learn. The goal of this chapter is for you to learn how to add small bits of ObjectPAL code to objects to accomplish specific tasks.

WHAT DO I NEED TO KNOW TO USE OBJECTPAL?

An ObjectPAL master programmer must be multitalented. To become an ObjectPAL master, you must have a firm grasp of database technology and know Windows, DOS, and object-oriented programming (OOP). You must know how to use DDE, OLE, and DLLs effectively. You must be a graphic artist and a program designer. You also need to be a mind reader so that you can know what your client actually wants. In short, an ObjectPAL master must know everything there is to know about Windows programming.

But what is a mere mortal to do? In one way or another, you can incorporate almost all you've learned about computers into your application. If your strength is in application design, concentrate on that. If your strength is in graphics, concentrate on that. If you don't have a strength, do what Borland originally intended for you to do: concentrate on developing good database applications. Later, you can go back and explore all the fun, nondatabase features. The point is that whatever your previous experience with databases, Paradox for DOS PAL programming, other programming languages, or graphics is, all you know about computers will come in handy with Paradox.

WHAT IS ELEGANT PROGRAMMING?

Elegant programming is the best way to accomplish a particular task. It can mean many things, but most often elegant programming means a routine that takes the *least amount of code* to complete a task. Try to resist overcoding a task. Remember what I said in the last chapter: If you add some code that doesn't work, take it out!

The term *elegant code* has many meanings. For example, fast code is elegant. Code that uses a TCursor (a pointer to a table) can be more elegant than code that uses a UIObject (a user interface object). A TCursor is faster because it doesn't have the overhead of screen refreshes. (In many cases, however, you can accomplish the same objective by using a UIObject—especially if it's already there.)

Code that is free of bugs and takes into account all possibilities is elegant. The least amount of code is not always the most elegant. If code does not take care of all possibilities, then it is not adequate. This is the reason you need to beta test your software. For example, test the effect of putting blanks into date fields. Try putting negative numbers where you normally expect a positive number. If users can do it, they will!

Portable code is elegant. The capability to copy an object with code from one form to another with little modification is elegant. ObjectPAL is an Object-Based Programming (OBP) language that allows you to create objects you can copy from one form to another. In most cases, this is not automatic, but with a little creative programming, you can create objects that you can paste into other forms.

Even where you put code determines how elegant it is. The places—methods— to which you attach ObjectPAL code is part of the event handler. The event model that the event handler uses determines when your code will fire off. In ObjectPAL, where you code is as important as what you code. This book devotes three chapters to this subject: Chapter 7, "Event Model Basics," Chapter 8, "Where to Put Code," and Chapter 30, "The Event Model Revisited."

Although no book can claim to have the correct answer for everything, this book does attempt to demonstrate elegant programming. This book won't always have the perfect solution for every problem; indeed, no book can make that claim. After typing in a routine, you might think of a more elegant way to code it. This is good: the challenging and fun part of programming is coming up with a better solution. The most elegant way isn't always obvious. As a programmer with limited time, you must balance your time between elegant and adequate programming.

As you will see in later chapters, a problem often has several solutions that range from simple to complicated and elegant. You learn the most by studying simple solutions first, and then more complicated solutions (rather than the other way around). You see the quickest and best way to complete a task. By seeing various levels of solutions to a problem, you learn more about what elegant programming is.

For example, even though the Paradox table structure offers an Autoincrement field type with version 5. Chapter 16, "Using Table and TCursor Variables," shows you several techniques for autoincrementing a field with ObjectPAL. First, you add a record to a form. Second, you set up a simple autoincrement field. Third, you autoincrement a nonkey field. Fourth, you autoincrement the master table on a form with a 1:M. For the most elegant solution, you add locking to the routine. By studying simple and elegant solutions, you learn how to implement different routines under different situations. This gives you the ability to balance your time between elegant and adequate programming.

SETTING YOUR OBJECTPAL LEVEL

Enough hype. Let's jump right in and do some ObjectPAL. First, make sure that your ObjectPAL level is set to Beginner. To do this, start Paradox. Select Properties | ObjectPAL to bring up the ObjectPAL Preferences dialog box, shown in Figure 4.1. This is where you set the ObjectPAL Preferences. From the Level panel, select Beginner. Later, in the next chapter, you will switch to the Advanced level.

> Whether your ObjectPAL level is set to Beginner or Advanced, you can use all the ObjectPAL methods, procedures, properties, constants, keywords, and so on. The Level panel is a help filter used just for learning purposes.

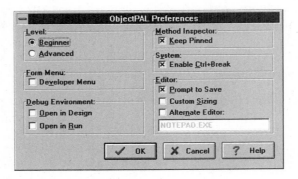

Figure 4.1. The ObjectPAL Preferences dialog box.

Starting ObjectPAL

A built-in *method* is the location in a form, script, or library where you place ObjectPAL code. This code is attached to the object, and defines the object's response to that event. An *event* is an action sent by the event handler that triggers an ObjectPAL method. For example, pushing a button triggers **pushButton**, clicking on a box triggers **mouseDown**, and opening a form triggers **open**.

Code in ObjectPAL is attached to objects in these built-in methods. When you right-click on an object, the Object Inspector displays options you can select. Select Methods from the Object Inspector (see Figure 4.2) to gain access to the Method Inspector (see Figure 4.3). Use the Method Inspector to gain access to the ObjectPAL Editor. You type code into the ObjectPAL Editor. The Editor is closely tied to the compiler; you type commands—that is, text—into the editor that the compiler uses to compile code.

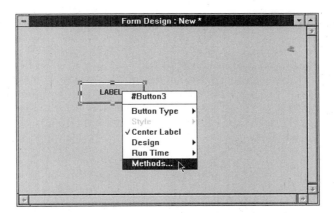

Figure 4.2. The Methods option takes you to the Method Inspector.

After you've selected the Methods option, you can edit any of the built-in methods. For example, you can add code to the **pushButton** method of a button. These built-in methods are the events that trigger your code. Figure 4.3 shows the Method Inspector.

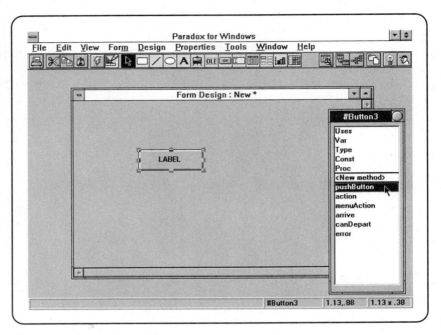

Figure 4.3. The Method Inspector.

In the ObjectPAL Editor, you enter code much as you would in other Windows editors, such as Notepad. The Editor has the normal features of any Windows editor: cut, copy, paste, and so on. In addition, the editor has some features specific to ObjectPAL that check your syntax, help you build a line of code, and debug your code (see Figure 4.4).

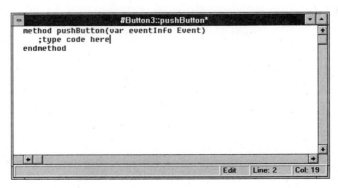

Figure 4.4. The ObjectPAL Editor.

PROGRAMMING A BUTTON TO SEND A MESSAGE TO THE STATUS BAR

A wonderful way to jump into ObjectPAL is to see what it can do. One type of command in ObjectPAL is called a procedure. Procedures are generally the easiest ObjectPAL commands to use because they usually are straight forward. For example, to send a message to the status line, you use the `message()` procedure. Here is the syntax for `message()`.

message (const **message** String [, const **message** String]*)

To use this procedure, you type in the keyword `message` followed by an open parenthesis, and then the string you wish to show up on the status line. For example:

```
1:  message("type string here")
```

> In general, do not type the code that appears as part of the body of text. It is included to illustrate what the text is talking about. Generally, every discussion is followed by a tutorial, which is where you can get your feet wet. Any exceptions to this are noted.

You can also send a message composed of many different strings (I tested a message composed of 30 strings). For example, the following lines of code display the same message on the status line.

```
1:  message("Hello World")        ;Displays "Hello World".
2:  message("Hello ", "World")    ;Displays "Hello World".
3:  message("H", "e", "l", "l", "o", " ", "W", "o", "r", "l", "d")
```

The following first few tutorials in ObjectPAL lead you step-by-step through the exercise. In most of the later tutorials, you are given only a setup description and the code for all the objects. It's important in these first few tutorials to understand how to get to the ObjectPAL Editor, and how to enter code in the built-in methods.

Tutorial: Sending a Message to the Status Line

Suppose that you wish to send a message to the status bar when a user clicks a button. This tutorial acquaints you with the **pushButton** method of a button and the `message()` procedure. When you click on the button, a message is displayed on the status bar.

On Disk: \ANSWERS\MESSAGE.FSL

Quick Steps

1. Add a button to a form.
2. Use the `message()` procedure in the button's **pushButton** method to display a message on the status bar.

Step By Step

1. Change your working directory to the TUTORIAL directory and create a new form by selecting File | New | Form.
2. Place a button on the form with the Toolbar button. Change the label of the button to Display Message. Your form should now look like Figure 4.5.

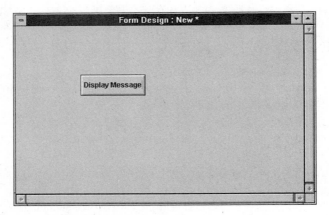

Figure 4.5. Change label to Display Message.

3. Right-click the button to display the Object Inspector and select Methods (see Figure 4.6).

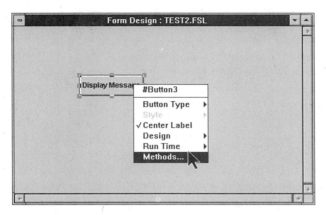

Figure 4.6. The Object Inspector.

4. Select **pushButton** from the Method Inspector and press the Enter key (see Figure 4.7). Between method and endMethod, there is a blank line with a blinking cursor ready for you to type code.

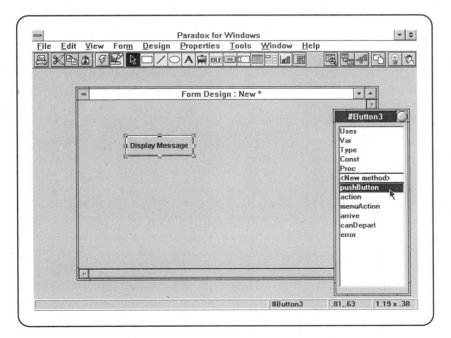

Figure 4.7. The Method Inspector.

5. In the **pushButton** method, type line 3 that follows.

```
1:    ;button :: pushButton
2:    method pushButton(var eventInfo Event)
3:        message("We put some words on the status bar.")
4:    endmethod
```

6. Check your syntax by selecting Program | Check Syntax. If you have any syntax errors, correct them. (Watch out for opening and closing parentheses and quotation marks.)

7. Close the ObjectPAL Editor window.

8. Then save the form by selecting File | Save As. Save the form as MESSAGE.FSL.

9. Run the form by selecting View | View Data.

10. Click the Display Message button. The message appears in the status bar. Figure 4.8 shows MESSAGE.FSL. Your completed form should look similar.

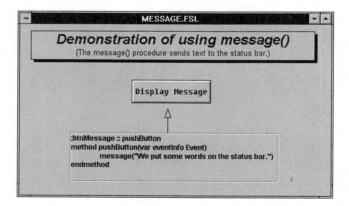

Figure 4.8. MESSAGE.FSL.

Analysis

Paradox enters two of the three lines required to display a message in the status line. In step 6, line 1 identifies what object and method the following code applies to. You never need to type this code in. It is in this book to help guide you through the tutorials. Lines 2 and 4 signify the beginning and the end of the built-in method. Line 3 does the actual work you want it to do. It uses the `message()` procedure to display a message in the status line.

All modifiable methods—built-in and custom—start with `method` and end with `endMethod`. Take a closer look at line 2. After `method` in line 2 is its name, **pushButton**. This identifies what built-in method (event) you are attaching code to; in this case, **pushButton**. Following **pushButton** is the parameter that **pushButton** takes, var *eventInfo* Event. var signifies that the method expects a variable. *eventInfo* Event signifies that the *eventInfo* variable is of type Event. For now, realize that ObjectPAL is an event-driven type of language that sends events from object to object and line 2 identifies what type of event the event handler is sending.

THE ELEMENTS OF OBJECTPAL

Now that you have gotten your feet wet, take a closer look at ObjectPAL. ObjectPAL consists of many different elements. When you study a broad subject such as a programming language, it's often helpful to categorize what you are about to learn. The following paragraphs describe the elements of ObjectPAL.

The ***built-in methods*** are the triggers that start your code, such as **pushButton**, **open**, and **changeValue**. Built-in methods are part of the event handler. An ***event handler*** is a type of programming language that has preset triggers to which the programmer can attach code. The idea of attaching code to triggers on objects puts Paradox in this category. Do not confuse the category of *event handler* with the term *event model*. An event model is the map that an event handler uses to process events.

The actual words or building blocks of ObjectPAL are called ***keywords***, such as `doDefault`, `DisableDefault`, `method`, `endMethod`, `var`, `endVar`, `if`, `endIf`, `switch`, and `endSwitch`. For example, an `if` statement is comprised of the following keywords: `if`, `then`, the optional `else`, and `endIf`.

The ***methods***—commands—act on objects, such as `open()`, `setPosition()`, and `moveTo()`. Examples of methods include `formVar.open("form")`, `theBox.setPosition(100,100)`, and `fieldName.moveTo()`. Methods differ from ***procedures***, which are commands that don't have a specified object on which they work, such as `close()`, `setTitle()`, and `setAliasPath()`. Examples of procedures include `close()`, `setTitle("My Application")`, and `setAliasPath("MyAlias", "C:\\WORK\\DATA")`.

In ObjectPAL, you can manipulate the **properties**—the characteristics—of objects, such as `value`, `color`, and `tabStop`. Examples of properties include `fieldName.value = 12`, `theBox.frame.color = Blue`, and `buttonName.tabStop = True`. Most of the properties that you set interactively by inspecting an object can be set using ObjectPAL.

Object variables are built into the language, such as `self`, `container`, and `active`. Examples of using Object variables include `self.color = Red`, `container.color = Blue`, and `message(active.Name)`.

A **constant** is a word that represents an unchanging value you can use in ObjectPAL. `Red`, `DataInsertRecord`, and `True` are all constants. With constants, the number the constant represents does not matter (and can change in a future version). This humanizes ObjectPAL; that is, it makes it easier to relate to. You use a meaningful word rather than a number in your code. Examples of using constants include `box1.color = Red`, `action(DataInsertRecord)`, and `fld3.tabStop = True`.

INTRODUCING THE EVENT HANDLER

In the first tutorial earlier in this chapter, you used the **pushButton** method of a button, but how do you know which built-in method to add code to? One thing that makes ObjectPAL easy to learn is that it is an event-driven language. You can refer to the event-driven part of ObjectPAL as the event handler. In a traditional procedural language, you have to write everything, including the interface—one of the least favorite tasks for a developer. In Paradox, you design the interface interactively with little trouble. In fact, it's fun to design forms with Paradox. With the interface out of the way, you simply attach code to enhance or restrict the interface and its built-in behavior. In most cases, you want to put the code on the object on which you want it to act. If you want a button to do something, put code on the **pushButton** method of the button. If you want to prevent a user from leaving a field, put code on the **canDepart** method of that field. Whenever you search for a place to put code, ask yourself, "What object am I working with or on?" Think of programming in ObjectPAL as attaching small bits of code to events or triggers.

Table 4.1 lists some common built-in on which methods to place code. This table can be valuable for beginning ObjectPAL programmers.

	TABLE 4.1. COMMON PLACES TO PUT CODE.	
Object	*Location*	*How to Use*
Form	**open**	To initialize variables
Form	**arrive**	To maximize a form and set values in the form
Form	**menuAction**	To process menu events
Form	**action**	To trap for key violations on a single table form
Form	**mouseExit**	To clear the status bar if you use **mouseEnter**
Page	**arrive**	To set up a custom pull-down menu
Button	**pushButton**	To execute code when the user selects a button
Button	**mouseEnter**	To add help by sending a message to the status bar
Field	**changeValue**	To check a new value against an old value in a table

Every object has a default behavior that you can modify with built-in methods. Most objects share the same built-in methods: **action**, **menuAction**, **arrive**, **canDepart**, **mouseClick**, and **error**. Some objects have unique built-in methods, such as **pushButton** for a button.

THE SIX BEGINNER-LEVEL BUILT-IN METHODS

Whenever you're looking for a place to put code, consider ObjectPAL's six beginner-level built-in methods first. These core built-in methods are the built-in methods that Borland believes new users to ObjectPAL will use most. Table 4.2 provides a short description of each.

Table 4.2. The six built-in methods.

Method	Description
action	Used when a user calls, or triggers, a built-in method. Typically, action is used for trapping events and processing them. For example, action is useful for trapping database actions such as inserting a record, and moving in and out of edit mode.
menuAction	Called whenever a user selects a menu option. Put code in the menuAction method to trap for when the user selects an option from the menu, Toolbar, or form control box.
arrive	**arrive** occurs whenever focus moves to a field. At first, **arrive** seems identical to **setFocus**, which occurs whenever focus moves to an object (and with fields this appearance is somewhat accurate). With some objects, however, it is not. Let's examine a form opening to illustrate. First, the **open** method occurs, then the **arrive**, and finally **setFocus**. **arrive** occurs only after **open**, whereas **setFocus** occurs whenever the form becomes active; for example, with a multiple form application. You can use **arrive** to instruct the user what to enter. An **arrive** only occurs after **canArrive**.
canDepart	Think of canDepart as the opposite of arrive. Typically, canDepart is used for data integrity. For example, if the value is less than 100, canDepart can prevent the user from leaving the field until the correct value is entered.
mouseClick	This is triggered whenever the logical left mouse button is pressed and released when the mouse is on an object.
error	This event is triggered whenever an error occurs. The error built-in method is used to add to the built-in **action** (response).

Types of Commands

ObjectPAL has several types of commands you can use in a built-in method. This section is going to address procedures, methods, keywords, and properties that are some of the commands you can use in a built-in method.

Procedures

You have already used a procedure in your first tutorial. A procedure is a powerful type of command that always does the same thing. It can stand alone. In other words, a procedure would be complete on a line by itself. For example, each of the following is a procedure.

```
1:     message("Press OK to continue")
2:     msgInfo("Warning", "You are about to delete a record")
3:     isFile("C:\\DOS\\COMMAND.COM")
```

Methods

A method is a weak type of command. It requires an object to hold it up. For example:

```
1:     TaxableField.isBlank()                 ;Returns True if blank.
2:     f.open("FORM1")                        ;Opens a form named "FORM1".
```

Another way to look at methods versus procedures is to say that a procedure always knows the object it works on or with, but a method does not. Some commands can serve as both procedures and methods. For example:

```
1:     close()       ;Closes the current form.
2:     f.close()     ;Close the form associated with f
3:                   ;(f is a form variable).
```

Line 1 uses the `close()` command as a procedure—it knows to close the current form. If, however, you use `close()` as a method, you need to specify an object. In line 2, *f* is a form variable you have opened previously.

> Do not confuse a command that can be both a method and procedure with the alternate syntax. Whenever you code `object.method()`, the alternate syntax allows you to code `method(object)`. For example:
>
> ```
> Phone_Number.moveTo()`      ;Regular syntax.
>
> moveTo(Phone_Number)        ;Alternate syntax.
> ```

> When a single command supports the alternate syntax, which syntax
> should you use? Although it doesn't really matter, the regular syntax
> `object.doIt()` as seen in the preceding first line is preferred. It's more
> consistent with the rest of the language. Don't worry too much about
> these variations in syntax at this point. I revisit syntax and present a
> coding convention later in Chapter 9, "Syntax."

Keywords

Keywords are words reserved for use with certain commands in ObjectPAL.
They are special language construct commands that are neither procedures nor
methods. Keywords include `Proc`, `endProc`, `method`, `endMethod`, `doDefault`, `iif`,
and `Database`. A complete list of keywords appears in Chapter 9, "Syntax." At
this point, just be aware that you shouldn't use keywords in ObjectPAL for the
names of objects or variables.

Here's an example of keywords that are used properly:

```
1:    method pushButton(var eventInfo Event)   ;method is a keyword.
2:       if taxable.value = "Yes" then         ;if & then are keywords.
3:          tax.value = subtotal * .06
4:       else                                  ;else is a keyword.
5:          tax.value = 0
6:       endIf                                 ;endIf is a keyword.
7:    endmethod                                ;endMethod is a keyword.
```

`method`, `if`, `then`, `else`, `endIf`, and `endMethod` are all keywords. You can't give
objects or variables names that are the same as these keywords. In fact, it's a
good idea not to give an object or a variable the same name as any element of
the ObjectPAL language. This optional rule is a good idea. It makes your code
more readable and avoids possible problems. Chapter 9, "Syntax," presents
many more coding conventions.

ALTERING PROPERTIES AND DOT NOTATION

Objects that you place on a form have properties. You have already set many
of the properties of objects; for example, when you change the color of a box
on a form. With ObjectPAL, you can alter an object's property with *dot
notation*. Dot notation is the basic syntax structure used in ObjectPAL. It uses

dots to separate elements in a complex statement. Here is the basic syntax structure:

```
ObjectName.property = Constant
```

The capability to alter properties while the form is running is powerful and sets Paradox above many other DBMS systems. Following are some examples of altering the properties of objects.

```
1:   box1.color = Blue              ;Change box1 to blue.
2:   box1.visible = False           ;Make box1 disappear.
3:   Last_Name.color = Yellow       ;Change field color.
4:   City.tabStop = False           ;Do not allow focus to City.
```

Dot notation can also represent a complete path to an object. The following examples set the properties of objects in other objects.

```
1:   pge1.box1.Last_Name.color = DarkGray
2:   f.pge3.visible = False
3:   box1.Last_Name.Frame.Style = Windows3DGroup
```

The example in line 3 of the preceding code represents a compound property. The path of the object is `box1.Last_Name`. The compound property is `Frame.Style`. This is confusing—especially when learning ObjectPAL. For now, understand that both the object path and the property can be composed of multiple values. The following are three instances for which dot notation is used in ObjectPAL:

- To separate an object and property. For example:

  ```
  Last_Name.value = "Hall"
  ```

- To separate or indicate an object's path. For example:

  ```
  pge2.boxSection3.Last_Name.value = "Hall"
  ```

- To separate an object and a method. For example:

  ```
  Last_Name.moveTo()
  ```

For now, think of the containership path of an object as analogous to a directory path. When you open a file, you specify its path; for example, `C:\PDOXWIN\DATA\MYFORM.FSL`. When referring to objects, you need to specify the path of the object with dots rather than a slash. For example, `pge2.boxSection3.Last_Name`.

Properties are another type of code you can use in ObjectPAL to get or alter the property of an object. Think of objects as having a set of data attached to them. Some of the properties of a field object are value, color, font.color, TabStop, Name, FieldName, and TableName. The next tutorial demonstrates that you can alter the properties of objects with ObjectPAL.

Tutorial: Changing the Color of a Box

Suppose that you wish to change the color of a box when the user clicks the box. This tutorial uses the mouseClick method of a box to alter the property color. The object variable self is used to refer to the object to which the code is attached. This tutorial also demonstrates using dot notation.

On Disk: \ANSWERS\COLOR.FSL

Quick Steps

1. Add a box to a form.
2. Through dot notation, change the color of the box on its mouseClick method.

Step By Step

1. Change your working directory to the TUTORIAL directory and create a new form and add a box to the form with the Toolbar box icon (see Figure 4.9).

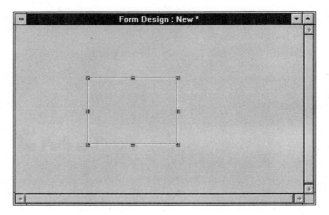

Figure 4.9. Set up form for tutorial.

2. Right-click the box to display its Object Inspector.

3. Select Methods.

4. Open the built-in **mouseClick** method.

5. In the **mouseClick** method, type in lines 3 and 4:

```
1:    ;theBox :: mouseClick
2:    method mouseClick(var eventInfo MouseEvent)
3:       ;The following changes the color of self
4:       self.color = Red
5:    endmethod
```

6. Check your syntax and save the form as COLOR.FSL.

7. Close the Edit box by clicking the close icon—that is, the arrow icon.

8. Go into View Data mode—that is, run the form—by clicking on the Toolbar lightning bolt icon. Click the box and watch the color change. Figure 4.10 shows COLOR.FSL. Your completed form should look similar (minus the button).

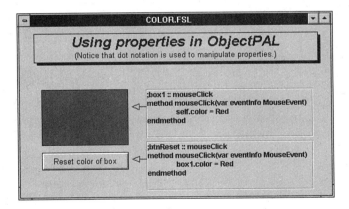

Figure 4.10. The completed COLOR.FSL form.

Analysis

In step 5, lines 2 and 5 begin and end the method. These lines of code are always provided for you by ObjectPAL. In line 2, note that the *eventInfo* variable type is MouseEvent. This is important to note and is discussed more later. For now, understand that ObjectPAL is an event-driven language and, in this case, an event of type MouseEvent was sent to **mouseClick**. Line 3, in step 5, starts with a semicolon, followed by a comment. Lines that start with a semicolon are stripped out when the form is compiled or run. Do yourself a favor and comment all your code heavily. You'll appreciate your efforts when you go back to the code a month later. The semicolon is also a good way to disable a line of code; it's useful when you debug code. For the tutorials in this book, you do not need to type the comments.

Look at line 4, which uses a special built-in object variable, `self`, to refer to the object to which the code is attached. If you named the box `box1`, you could have used `box1.color = Red` rather than `self.color = Red`. `color` is a property of the object type `Box`. The rest of the line sets that property to a certain value or constant. A *constant* is a specific, unchanging value; in this case, the color `Red`. Contrast this with a *variable*, which is a place in memory used to store data temporarily.

One type of code that you write in ObjectPAL gets or alters the property of an object. Think of objects as having a set of data attached to them. Some of the properties of a field object are `value`, `color`, `font.color`, `tabStop`, `name`, `fieldName`, and `tableName`. As demonstrated in the previous tutorial, you can alter the properties of objects with ObjectPAL.

OBJECTPAL IS DESCRIPTIVE

In addition to altering an application's look by manipulating properties, there are many ObjectPAL commands that can have an effect on an application. For example, you can change the look of the desktop with the procedures `hideToolbar()` and `showToolbar()`. They hide and show the Toolbar. For example:

```
1:    hideToolbar()   ;Hide Toolbar.
2:    sleep(1000)     ;Wait for 1 second.
3:    showToolbar()   ;Show toolbar.
```

Notice how descriptive ObjectPAL is. It uses real words that describe what you're doing. Sounds easy so far, right? Well, that's because it *is* easy. The reason ObjectPAL has such a steep learning curve is that it's so rich in commands. Every procedure and method is as easy to understand as the previous examples, however. Because there are so many procedures, methods, and properties, it takes a while just to get a handle on ObjectPAL.

LANGUAGE ELEMENTS

Now that you have looked at ObjectPAL from the big picture, this next section introduces basic programming elements common to most programming languages and relates these common elements to ObjectPAL. If you have programmed in another language before, then read quickly through this section.

A *variable* is a place in memory used to store data temporarily. You first declare a variable and then you use it. For example, a *string* is an alphanumeric value or an expression consisting of alphanumeric characters. You can convert a number to a string with `string(x)` or you can declare a string variable and use it as the following code demonstrates. For example, line 2 that follows declares *s* as a string.

```
1:    var                         ;Begin variable block.
2:       s      String            ;Declare s as a string.
3:    endVar                      ;End variable block.
4:
5:    s = "Press OK to continue." ;Set s to string value.
6:    message(s)                  ;Display s.
```

> If you wish to type and run the examples in this section, then use the **pushButton** method of a button and type the code, run the form, and select the button. (There is no need to type the comments.)

An *operator* is a symbol that represents an operation to be performed on a value or values. For example, the + operator represents addition, and the * operator represents multiplication. Line 8 in the code that follows multiplies x and y and then displays the result on the status line.

```
1:    var                         ;Start variable block.
2:       x      Number            ;Declare x as a number.
3:       y      Number            ;Declare y as a number.
4:    endVar                      ;End variable block.
5:
6:    x = 10                      ;Set x to 10.
7:    y = 5                       ;Set y to 5.
8:    message(x * y)              ;Displays 50 on the status line.
```

When you ***concatenate*** two values, you combine two or more alphanumeric values with the + operator. For example, line 9 that follows concatenates two strings and then assigns the value to *s2*.

```
1:    var                              ;Begin variable block.
2:       s1    String                  ;Declare s1 as a string.
3:       s2    String                  ;Declare s2 as a string.
4:    endVar                           ;End variable block.
5:
6:    s1 = "Enter name here"           ;Set s1 to string.
7:    s1.view("What is your name?")    ;View s1 in a view box.
8:
9:    s2 = "Hello " + s1               ;Set s2 to string plus s1.
10:   message(s2)                      ;Display s2 on status line.
```

Comparison operators are symbols used to compare two values in a query, in a calculated field, or in an ObjectPAL expression. The comparison operators are <, >, <=, >=, and =. For example, lines 11–13 below compare x and y. Depending on which value is greater, a different message is displayed.

```
1:    var                              ;Begin variable block.
2:       x    Number                   ;Declare x as a number.
3:       y    Number                   ;Declare y as a number.
4:    endVar                           ;End variable block.
5:    x = 0                            ;Set x to 0.
6:    x.view("Enter value for x")      ;View x in a view box.
7:    y = 0                            ;Set y to 0.
8:    y.view("Enter value for y")      ;View y in a view box.
9:
10:   switch                           ;Begin switch block.
11:      case x > y : message("x is bigger")     ;Is x > y?
12:      case y > x : message("y is bigger")     ;Is y > x?
13:      case x = y : message("They are equal")  ;Is x = Y?
14:   endSwitch                        ;End switch block.
```

A ***constant*** is a specific, unchanging value. ObjectPAL uses two types of constants; those used in calculations and defined in the Const window of an object and constants predefined by ObjectPAL. For example, line 2 that follows uses a user set constant that sets the value of pi to 8 decimal points.

```
1:    const                    ;Begin constant block.
2:       pi = 3.14159265       ;Set the permanent value of pi.
3:    endConst                 ;End constant block.
4:
5:    ;Display the square root of pi.
6:    message("The square root of pi is ", sqrt(pi))
```

We already have used predefined constants; all property values are actually predefined constants. For example, in the previous tutorial, you used self.color = Red. Red is a constant that represents a number ObjectPAL associates with the color red. You use constants with methods and procedures, such as

`DataNextRecord`, `DarkBlue`, and `FieldForward`. Examples of constants include `fieldName.action(DataNextRecord)`, `fieldName.font.color = DarkBlue`, and `active.action(FieldForward)`.

A ***branch*** transfers program control to an instruction other than the next sequential instruction. When you used the `switch` block in the example for comparison operators, you branched to one line of code or another depending on a comparison. Normally, a programming language executes line after line in sequential order. This is true whether the language is a line-oriented language, such as BASIC, or a statement-oriented language, such as C.

In programming languages, a ***control structure*** is a set of keywords used to branch or loop. With control structures, you can alter the sequence of execution and add logic to your code. A ***loop*** is a set of instructions that is repeated a predetermined number of times or until a specified condition is met. For example, lines 6 and 7 in the code that follows are repeated 10 times as indicated in line 5.

```
1:    var                      ;Begin variable block.
2:       x     Number          ;Declare x as a number.
3:    endVar                   ;End variable block.
4:
5:    for x from 1 to 10       ;Begin loop.
6:        message(x)           ;Display x.
7:        sleep(500)           ;Wait 1/2 second.
8:    endFor                   ;End Loop.
```

A ***logical value*** is a True or False value that is assigned to an expression when it is evaluated. ***Logical operators*** are operators used in queries, in calculated fields, and in ObjectPAL methods. The three logical operators are `and`, `or`, and `not`. For example, line 2 in the code that follows declares `l` as a logical variable, and line 6 uses the `not` logical operator to display the opposite of `l` in a view box.

```
1:    var                   ;Begin variable block.
2:       l     Logical      ;Declare l as a logical.
3:    endVar                ;End variable block.
4:
5:    l = True              ;Set l to True.
6:    view(not l)           ;Display False in view box.
```

A ***subroutine*** is a sequence of instructions that performs a specific task, usually more than once in a program. The sequence may be invoked many times by the current program or by multiple applications. Although ObjectPAL doesn't have *actual* subroutines, you can think of custom methods and custom procedures as subroutines. There is more on this subject in Chapter 23, "Storing and Centralizing Code."

HIDING THE DESKTOP

At one point or another, most users want to create a form that hides the Paradox desktop. To do this, define an Application variable and use that variable with the `hide()` and `show()` methods. For example:

```
1:    var
2:        app  Application    ;App is now an application variable.
3:    endVar
```

Then, use the `hide()` method to hide it. Unless you have defined your form as a dialog box and have reopened it, your form will disappear with the desktop. At first, hide the desktop only for a period of time—for example, three seconds:

```
1:    app.hide()
2:    sleep(3000)
3:    app.show()
```

After a variable is defined as an application, you can use any of the application-type methods on it. In addition to `hide()` and `show()`, you can use and manipulate an application variable with the following methods: `bringToTop()`, `getPosition()`, `getTitle()`, `isMaximized()`, `isMinimized()`, `isVisible()`, `maximize()`, `minimize()`, `setPosition()`, `setTitle()`, `windowClienthandle()`, and `windowHandle()`. Don't bother experimenting with these at this early stage. Just realize that you can set the title of an application, check whether it's maximized, maximize it, and get and set its position. The next tutorial shows you how to put the `hide()` and `show()` methods to work.

Tutorial: Hiding the Desktop

Suppose that you wish to hide the desktop for five seconds using the **pushButton** method of a button. This tutorial uses the following methods and procedures: `hide()`, `show()` and `sleep()`. In addition, it acquaints you with how to declare and use a variable in ObjectPAL. Finally, it demonstrates that a form is a child window of the desktop that hides when the desktop is hidden.

On Disk: \ANSWERS\APP.FSL

Quick Steps

1. Add a button to the form.
2. Use the `hide()`, `sleep()`, and `show()` methods to hide the desktop for five seconds.

Step By Step

1. Change your working directory to the TUTORIAL directory and create a new form. Add a button to the form and change its label to Hide Desktop (see Figure 4.11).

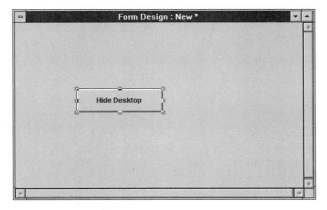

Figure 4.11. Your form should look like this.

2. Open the **pushButton** method by selecting the button and pressing Ctrl+Spacebar. Open the ObjectPAL Editor for the **pushButton** method.

3. Add lines 3–8 to the **pushButton** method. There is no need to type the comments after the semicolons.

```
1:   ;btnHide :: pushButton
2:   method pushButton(var eventInfo Event)
3:      var
4:         app  Application    ;App is a application variable.
5:      endVar
6:      app.hide()            ;Hide the desktop.
7:      sleep(5000)           ;Wait 5 seconds.
8:      app.show()            ;Show the desktop.
9:   endmethod
```

4. While you're still in the ObjectPAL Editor, right-click to bring up the Editor's Object Inspector. Select Check Syntax to check your syntax.

5. Save the form as APP.FSL, close it, and then reopen it. Press the Hide Desktop button. After five seconds, Paradox should come back.

Analysis

In step 3, lines 2 and 9 mark the beginning and the end of the method. Lines 3–5 mark the variable section. In line 4, you declare app as a variable of type Application. In lines 6 and 8, you use that variable with the hide() and show() methods. Note that even though hide() and show() don't have a parameter passed to them, you still use parentheses. Parentheses are part of the basic syntax for all methods and procedures. Contrast this with properties, which never use parentheses. In line 7, you use the sleep() procedure to sleep for 5000 milliseconds (5 seconds). You can tell that sleep() is a procedure and not a method because it has no object on which to work. A method requires an object on which to work; a procedure does not.

Line 1 of the code in step 3 is a comment that isn't part of the ObjectPAL code. (The semicolon signifies that this is a remark.) All code in the tutorials will have this remark line above it for reference. The first word of this special identifying remark is either the name of the object or the type of the object. Following the name or type is the window in which you will place the code. This window can be any of the built-in methods—for example, Var for variable window, Const for the constants window, the name of a custom method, and so on. This technique of referring to objects comes straight from the Editor window. This naming convention is consistent with what it displays on the title bar, which indicates where you are (see Figure 4.12) that follows.

FIRST DATABASE ROUTINES

All this programming theory and manipulating properties and the desktop is necessary and useful, but it probably isn't the reason you purchased Paradox. This section discusses some of the basic commands used to edit data. ObjectVision users will appreciate this section, because it simulates some of the most important database functions from ObjectVision.

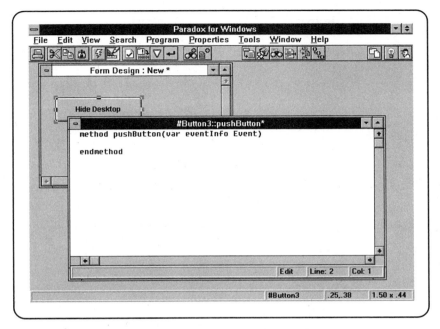

Figure 4.12. The title bar of the ObjectPAL editor indicates where you are.

home(), end(), priorRecord(), and nextRecord()

In ObjectPAL, you often have several ways to do something. For example, to go to the beginning of a table, you could use either a method or an action constant. The following two lines of code are equivalent:

```
1:    nextRecord()
2:    action(DataNextRecord)
```

These two methods represent two techniques for maneuvering through a table. Both of these methods move the pointer from the current record to the next record. The first line requires less typing and is my preferred usage. The second line represents more clearly what ObjectPAL is doing, however. The `action()` method sends an event to the built-in method `action`. When the constant `DataNextRecord` reaches the `action` method, `action` knows to insert a record. In addition to `nextRecord()`, there is a whole set of table-related methods, including `home()`, `end()`, and `priorRecord()`.

In addition to using self—which refers to the object the code is attached to—you can use `active`, which represents the object with focus. You can combine these with the two distinctly different techniques for positioning the pointer. For example:

```
1:      self.nextRecord()             ;Move to the next record.
2:      active.nextRecord()           ;Move to the next record.
3:      self.action(DataNextRecord)   ;Move to the next record.
4:      active.action(DataNextRecord) ;Move to the next record.
```

These two groups of code use two built-in object variables: `self` and `active`. `self` refers to the object that executes the code.

edit() and endEdit()

When you go into edit mode—with a command such as `edit()`—it is important to note that you put the whole form into edit mode. In other words, you can go to any field and enter or edit values. When you issue an `endEdit()` command, the whole form is taken out of Edit mode. The `edit()` method is intelligent enough to act on the table that is connected to `self`. `active` refers to the object that currently has the focus. In a multitable form, you could use `active` to move the record pointer to the table that is attached to the selected object.

insertRecord() and deleteRecord()

The final two database methods used in the next tutorial are `insertRecord()` and `deleteRecord()`. Until now, you've seen how to use database-type methods on a form with a single table in the data model. But what if you want to delete a record from only one table in a 1:M relationship? You can use the name of an object to refer to the underlying table. For example:

```
1:    Last_Name.insertRecord() ;Insert a new blank record.
2:    LineItem.DeleteRecord()  ;Delete current record.
```

Using the name of an object enables you to specify what table you want to work with, which is crucial when you work with multiple tables. This tutorial puts the commands together.

Tutorial: Basic Database Buttons

Suppose that you wish to put eight buttons on a form that simulate the ObjectVision menu actions: Top, Bottom, Previous, Next, Edit, Store, New, and Delete (see Figure 4.13). This tutorial introduces you to the following ObjectPAL methods: `home()`, `end()`, `priorRecord()`, `nextRecord()`, `edit()`, `postRecord()`, `endEdit()`, `insertRecord()`, and `deleteRecord()`. It also introduces the `if` structure.

On Disk \ANSWERS\OV-LIKE.FSL

Quick Steps

1. Place eight buttons on a form that uses a table in its data model.
2. Use `home()`, `end()`, `priorRecord()`, `nextRecord()`, `edit()`, `postRecord()`, `endEdit()`, `insertRecord()`, and `deleteRecord()` on the buttons.

Step By Step

1. Make your working directory the TUTORIAL directory and create a new form with the CUSTOMER.DB table in its data model.
2. Place eight buttons on the form. Change their labels to Top, Bottom, Previous, Next, Edit, Store, New, and Delete (see Figure 4.13).
3. Add line 3 to the button labeled Top.

```
1:    ;btnTop :: pushButton
2:    method pushButton(var eventInfo Event)
3:       active.home()              ;Move to the first record.
4:    endmethod
```

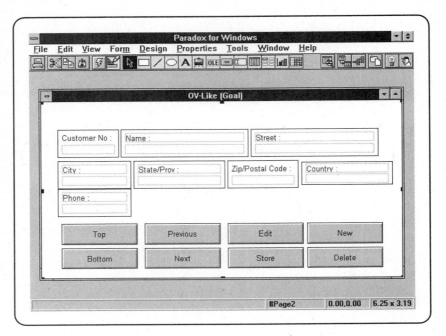

Figure 4.13. The set up of the form for the tutorial Basic Database Buttons.

4. Add line 3 to the button labeled Bottom:

```
1:    ;btnBottom :: pushButton
2:    method pushButton(var eventInfo Event)
3:       active.end()       ;Move to the last record.
4:    endmethod
```

5. Add line 3 to the button labeled Previous:

```
1:    ;btnPrevious :: pushButton
2:    method pushButton(var eventInfo Event)
3:       active.priorRecord()     ;Move to the previous record.
4:    endmethod
```

6. Add line 3 to the button labeled Next:

```
1:    ;btnNext :: pushButton
2:    method pushButton(var eventInfo Event)
3:       active.nextRecord() ;Move to the next record.
4:    endmethod
```

7. Add lines 3 and 4 to the button labeled Store:

```
1:    ;btnStore :: pushButton
2:    method pushButton(var eventInfo Event)
3:       active.postRecord() ;Write the record to the table.
4:       endEdit()           ;End edit mode.
5:    endmethod
```

8. Add line 3 to the button labeled Edit:

```
1:    ;btnEdit :: pushButton
2:    method pushButton(var eventInfo Event)
3:       edit()              ;Put form into edit mode.
4:    endmethod
```

9. Add lines 3–5 to the button labeled New:

```
1:    ;btnNew :: pushButton
2:    method pushButton(var eventInfo Event)
3:       action(MoveTopLeft) ;Move to first field on form.
4:       edit()              ;Put form into edit mode.
5:       active.insertRecord();Insert a new blank record.
6:    endmethod
```

10. Add lines 3–7 to the button labeled Delete:

```
1:    ;btnDelete :: pushButton
2:    method pushButton(var eventInfo Event)
3:       if deleteRecord() then
4:          message("Record deleted")
5:       else
6:          message("Could not delete record")
7:       endIf
8:    endmethod
```

11. Check the syntax, save the form as OV-LIKE.FSL, and run it. Try out all the various buttons. Your form should look similar to the \ANSWERS\OV-LIKE.FSL form (see Figure 4.14).

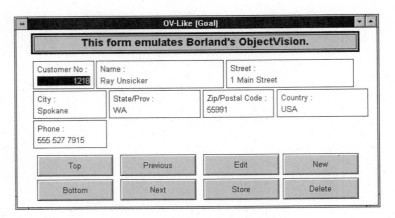

Figure 4.14. OV-LIKE.FSL.

Analysis

In step 5, line 3 issues the `home()` command, which takes you to the beginning of the active table. If you have multiple tables on this form, how does `home()` know which table to work with? When you use a method by itself, `active` is implied, as in `active.home()`.

You also could use the active variable, as in `active.home()`. In fact, this third variation in syntax is the clearest and the most elegant. In all these methods, the name of the object worked on is left out. This is exactly how the built-in functionality works.

In step 6, line 3 issues the `end()` command, which takes you to the last record in the table. In step 7, line 3 uses `priorRecord()` to move the pointer back one record. In step 8, line 3 uses `nextRecord()` to move the pointer forward one record.

In step 9, lines 3 and 4 commit the user's changes to the record and end the edit session. Both `postRecord()` and `endEdit()` were used in this example to explicitly post the change to the table and end the edit mode. Note, however, that this was done just to introduce the method `postRecord()`. In a real application, ending edit mode with `endEdit()` automatically sends `DataPostRecord` to the built-in **action** method (changes, if any, to a record are committed when you end an edit session).

In step 10, line 3 puts the form in edit mode with `edit()`.

In step 11, with the New button, you want to get the form ready for the user edit. Move the focus to the upper-left field using the `MoveTopLeft` action constant with `action(MoveTopLeft)`. Go into Edit mode and insert a record with `edit()` and `insertRecord()`.

The syntax of the Delete button in step 12 deserves special attention. There are times when `deleteRecord()` is not a valid command. Therefore, you need to do some error checking. `deleteRecord()` returns a logical True or False in an `if` structure. If `deleteRecord()` is successful, the message in line 4 is sent to the status bar. `deleteRecord()` sometimes fails—for example, when the user isn't in Edit mode or when `deleteRecord()` interferes with referential integrity. Whenever `deleteRecord()` fails, a different message is sent to the message box in line 6.

The user can't use the pull-down menus and the Toolbar whenever you use a custom menu, hide the Toolbar, or use a modal dialog box. These eight buttons are very useful in such situations. Now that you have created these buttons, simply copy and paste them to other forms as needed.

REFERRING TO OBJECTS

The techniques shown in the previous tutorial used the object variable `active` and a method. They are useful for single-table forms. Most often, however, you'll create multitable forms. Therefore, you must be more precise. In the next tutorial, you learn how to use a method on a single table in a multitable form.

Tutorial: Using a UIObject Name to Refer to the Underlying Table

Suppose that you wish to set up a button on a 1:M form that deletes only the currently selected detail record. This tutorial shows you how to use dot notation in combination with a method. It also introduces the procedure `msgQuestion()`, which displays a message question dialog box.

On Disk: \ANSWERS\DELETE.FSL

Quick Steps
1. Create a form with a 1:M relationship.
2. Add a button called Delete Item.
3. On a button, use the name of a `UIObject` in the detail table with `deleteRecord()`.

Step By Step

1. Create a new form with a 1:M relationship between ORDERS.DB and LINEITEM.DB, and place a button on the form. Change the button's label to Delete Line Item.

2. Alter the button's **pushButton** method to look like the following:

```
1:    ;deleteLineButton :: pushButton
2:    method pushButton(var eventInfo Event)
3:        if msgQuestion("Warning", "Are you sure you wish to
              delete the current item?") = "Yes" then
4:            edit()
5:            Stock_No.deleteRecord()
6:        endIf
7:    endmethod
```

3. Test your syntax, correct any errors if necessary, save the form as DELETE.FSL, and run the form.

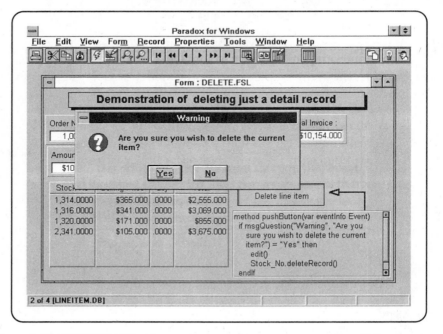

Figure 4.15. DELETE.FSL. Use `msgQuestion()` *in an* `if` *statement to ask the user a question and act on the answer.*

Analysis

In step 3, line 3, the `msgQuestion()` procedure is used to ask the user whether he or she really wants to delete the record (see Figure 4.15). If the answer is yes, lines 4 and 5 delete the record. Otherwise, the `if` statement ends at line 6. To delete the record, you put the form into edit mode in line 4. In line 5, you use the name of an object to signify exactly which table to delete a record from. Just as easily, you could have used any other object that is connected to the table, or even the name of the table frame. Remember that when you use the name of an object with a method that uses a table, the method will use the table that the object is connected to.

FURTHER STUDY

If you haven't done so already, install and browse through the disk set that came with this book. After you install it, you'll have a directory called SECRETS2. Inside the SECRETS2 directory is a main menu form called SECRETS2.FSL. Load and run this form. It's the gateway to all the secrets contained on the disk. At this stage, you'll be interested in the button called Answers to tutorials. Take a half-hour to browse through these sample forms. Pay special attention to the code that makes sense to you. If you come across something you don't understand, don't worry about it—just move on.

THE OBJECTPAL EDITOR

This chapter explores the ObjectPAL Editor, which is part of the Paradox integrated development environment (IDE). The IDE of Paradox consists of the ObjectPAL Editor and Debugger. This chapter is primarily concerned with the ObjectPAL Editor; the Debugger is discussed in Chapter 29, "Dealing with Errors."

Exploring the ObjectPAL Editor

Exploring ObjectPAL

USING THE OBJECTPAL EDITOR

The ObjectPAL Editor is a typical Windows editor that has special features for use with ObjectPAL. The Editor is where you enter, edit, and check your code. Because of these features, the Editor has tremendous functionality. In fact, although you can change editors, very few people actually switch to a different editor. The better you know the Editor, the easier it will be for you to enter, edit, and debug your application.

Features of the ObjectPAL Editor include:

- Writing code: The ObjectPAL Editor is the main viewing area. It's where you write code.

- Checking syntax: You can easily check your syntax for typos and other basic mistakes before you execute your code.
- Debugging: With the built-in Debugger, you can inspect variables, trace execution, and step through code.
- Reference: The Tools menu in the ObjectPAL Editor contains useful reference options—specifically, Keywords, Types, Properties, and Constants.

Entering the Editor

You move into the Editor whenever you select a method from the Method Inspector. You get to the Method Inspector by selecting Methods from the Object Inspector. (You already should be familiar with this two-step process from the last chapter.) My favorite way to get to the Editor is by selecting the object I wish to put code on and then pressing Ctrl+Spacebar. This bypasses the Object Inspector and takes you straight to the Method Inspector. I then press the first letter of the method I wish to edit.

Whether you add code to a form, a library, or a script, the Editor works the same. First, you enter the Method Inspector. Then, you select a method to which you want to add code. The one exception is a script. When you create a new script or open an existing script in design mode, Paradox assumes that you want to edit the run method, and it automatically opens the ObjectPAL Editor for you.

The Method Inspector

To open the Method Inspector, you first need to select the object with which you want to work. Then you have several options:

- Select an object and either click the right mouse button or press F6 to bring up the Object Inspector. Select Methods to go to the Method Inspector.
- Select an object and press Ctrl+Spacebar to go directly to the Method Inspector.

Every object has a set of built-in methods attached to it. Figure 5.1 shows the Method Inspector, which contains a list of all the available built-in methods and custom methods. It also lists an option for <New method> where you can enter a new custom method. The Var, Type, Const, Proc, and Uses options allow you to declare variables, types, constants, procedures, and external library routines to use in a method or procedure. Either select the option and press Enter, or double-click an option. You can use Ctrl+Left-Click and Shift+Left-Click to select multiple built-in methods. You can right-click an option to bring up a pop-up menu with more options (see Figure 5.1).

Figure 5.1. The Method Inspector.

The list of built-in methods that the Method Inspector shows could have been called Triggers. Technically, these methods are triggers. Don't confuse the built-in methods with the methods in the runtime library. Just remember that built-in methods are triggers that dictate when—or whether—your code gets executed.

Custom methods are routines you create. They make a set of frequently used commands easier to use. For now, think of custom methods as being analogous to batch files in DOS. With batch files, you can use any DOS command, execute an external program, or even call another batch file. It's similar with custom methods. You can use any runtime library method or procedure, execute or call functions in DLLs, or even call other custom methods.

You create custom procedures in the Procs window. Custom procedures and custom methods are similar. They both store code you can call, and they can receive and return values. Because of the how they're stored, however, custom procedures are faster than custom methods. And unlike custom methods, custom procedures are private to an object. Therefore, you can't call them with dot notation from another containership hierarchy. Think of custom procedures as subroutines private to the current object and to the other objects in its containership hierarchy. Custom methods and custom procedures are discussed further in Chapter 23, "Storing and Centralizing Code."

The Uses window enables you to add functionality to ObjectPAL. You can make custom methods available from libraries and functions available from DLLs. With the Uses window, ObjectPAL can be expanded virtually forever.

You use the Var window to declare a variable global to an object. You may wish to do this to increase the scope of a variable. A variable declared in an object's Var window can be used by all the built-in methods, custom procedures, and so on of that object and by all the objects that are contained by it.

You use the Const window to declare constants global to an object. A constant declared in an object's Const window can be used by all the built-in methods, custom procedures, and so on of that object and by all the objects that are contained by it.

You define custom data types in the Type window. Just as variables and constants can be global to an object, so can custom data types. Within a custom method, you can declare the private versions of custom procedures, custom types, variables, constants, and uses. The difference between global to an object and private to a method is important. It's discussed further in Chapter 8, "Where to Put Code."

Keyboard Shortcuts

The Editor is your tool for entering code. The better you know the Editor, the faster you can enter code. One thing you can do to expedite entering code is to memorize the keyboard shortcuts. For example, pressing Home moves you to the beginning of a line, and pressing End moves you to the end of a line. Table 5.1 describes what the function keys do in the ObjectPAL Editor. F8, Shift+F8, and F9 are particularly useful.

Table 5.2 describes the keyboard shortcuts that you can use with the ObjectPAL Editor. Ctrl+Left Arrow and Ctrl+Right Arrow are particularly useful.

Key	Description
TABLE 5.1. THE FUNCTION KEYS IN THE OBJECTPAL EDITOR.	

Key	Description
F1	Help
F2	Accepts
Shift+F2	Accepts and closes
F3	Inspects variable
Shift+F3	Stacks backtrace
Ctrl+F3	Sets breakpoint
F5	Goes to line
Ctrl+F5	Next warning
F6	Object inspector
F7	Steps over
Shift+F7	Steps into
F8	Runs
Shift+F8	Saves to disk and runs
F9	Checks syntax
Ctrl+F9	Saves and then delivers form
F10	Menu

TABLE 5.2. KEYBOARD SHORTCUTS WITH THE OBJECTPAL EDITOR.

Key	Description
Ctrl+Left Arrow	Moves the cursor one word to the left
Ctrl+Right Arrow	Moves the cursor one word to the right
Home	Moves the cursor to the beginning of a line
End	Moves the cursor to the end of a line
Ctrl+Home	Moves the cursor to the beginning of the text
Ctrl+End	Moves the cursor to the end of the text

continues

TABLE 5.2. CONTINUED	
Page Up	Moves one window-full backward
Page Down	Moves one window-full forward
Backspace	Deletes the character to the left of the cursor
Delete	Deletes the character to the right of the cursor
Insert	Has no effect
Ctrl+Insert	Copies selected text to the clipboard
Shift+Insert	Pastes text from the clipboard into a method
Shift+Delete	Cut text to the clipboard
Tab	Inserts a tab character and pushes text to the right

> The Insert key has no effect because the Editor is always in Insert mode. As you type, characters are pushed to the right.

You also can use shortcuts to select text in the ObjectPAL Editor. To select a word, double-click it. To select an entire line of text, click to the left of the line. You know that the mouse is in the correct position when the I-beam cursor changes to an arrow. There are two ways to select a block of text. You can click and drag the mouse, or you can click to indicate the starting position, and then press Shift and one of the arrow keys.

The Editor Toolbar

The Toolbar gives you quick access to many of the most-used features in the ObjectPAL Editor. Figure 5.2 shows the Editor Toolbar.

Figure 5.2. The ObjectPAL Editor Toolbar.

The first six and last three icons on the Tool Toolbar with which you are already familiar. The first six are the Print, Cut to Clipboard, Copy to Clipboard, Paste from Clipboard, View Data, and Design. The Print icon sends a copy of your code to the default printer. Use it to print copies of your code. It's equivalent to File | Print. This is a great way to archive your code—perhaps keep a binder of most frequently used code bits. The Cut tool cuts text to the Windows clipboard. It works like any other Windows cut tool. It's equivalent to Edit | Cut. The Copy tool copies text to the Windows clipboard. It works like any other Windows copy tool. It's equivalent to Edit | Copy. The Paste tool pastes text from the Windows clipboard. It works like any other Windows paste tool. It's equivalent to Edit | Paste. The lightning bolt is the View Data icon. This icon puts your form in View Data mode. It's equivalent to Form | View Data or F8.

From the right, the three icons are Coaches, Expert, and Open Project Viewer. The Coaches icon takes you through a series of tutorials. The Experts allow you to create forms, reports, and mailing labels with your own data. The Open Project Viewer opens the Project Viewer.

The remaining icons are used primarily for debugging your code. Chapter 29, "Dealing with Errors," discusses debugging your code. For now, the following introduces the icons.

The checkmark is the Check Syntax icon. Use it to check the syntax of your code. It's equivalent to Tools | Check Syntax, F9, or Ctrl+Y. When you use this icon, the current editor window syntax is checked. To check all your code, use the Compile icon next to the Check Syntax icon.

> Use F9 and F8 in sequence to check your syntax and to go into Run mode quickly.

If you get an error while checking your syntax, you can use the Go to next warning icon to see whether it is the only error.

The icon with an arrow is the Close icon, which saves and exits. When you have Prompt on Save unchecked, it's the same as the Close button in the upper-right corner of the edit window.

The next two icons allow you to add watches and breakpoints. You can watch a variable by using the watch window. A breakpoint is a place in the code where the Debugger automatically stops execution. Set a breakpoint when you debug your code. It's a good idea to set a breakpoint when you're getting an error or when part of the code doesn't seem to execute. You can place breakpoints at various spots to evaluate whether your code is executing up to that point.

The next six icons toggle various windows open and close. The icons are Methods, Debugger, Watches, Breakpoints, Tracer, and Stack windows. The Methods icon brings up the Methods window (also known as the Method Inspector). Use this icon to quickly bring up other editor windows for the object with which you are currently working. You will most often use this to bring up the Var window for the current object.

The File, Tools, and Window Menus

You're familiar with these menus in the Editor. They're the same whether you are in Design or View Data mode.

The Window menu lists the open windows and has four options: Tile, Cascade, Arrange Icons, and Close All. These menu options are the same as the ones in Design and Run modes. You're already familiar with them from standard Windows applications.

The Edit Menu

You use the ObjectPAL Edit menu to manipulate code. It has a few more options than the Edit menu in Design mode. Paste From, Copy To, and Undo All Edits are particularly useful. Figure 5.3 shows the ObjectPAL Edit menu.

Figure 5.3. The Edit menu from the ObjectPAL Editor.

The Undo All Edits option restores your code to what it was before you started editing. The Cut, Copy, and Paste options do what they do in any other Windows application. The Delete option deletes the code without placing it on the Windows clipboard.

The Paste From and Copy To options are of particular interest to anyone interested in saving time. To save code to a text file, first highlight the code, then select Edit | Copy To. The Select All option selects all the text in the current window.

ARCHIVE YOUR CODE

Save Time By Reusing Your Code!

Create a directory just for pieces of code, and use Copy To and Paste From to store and retrieve code. You could even use this technique extensively and categorize code into directories. (Another way to archive code is to use a dummy set of forms with the code on the appropriate object—my personal favorite.)

The Search Menu

The Search menu allows you to search and replace code with its Find, Find Next, Replace, and Replace Next options. These options are similar to the search and replace options available in word processors. You'll seldom use the Goto Line option. Rarely will you write code long enough to require jumping to a particular spot.

Compiling an Object

After you complete a form, script, library, or report, you can compile it with Program | Deliver. This option creates another version of the file, but with a different extension. This compiled version can't be edited by anyone. Because of the way the code is stored, it's actually a little faster. Table 5.3 lists the extensions used for undelivered and delivered objects.

TABLE 5.3. EXTENSIONS OF UNDELIVERED AND DELIVERED OBJECTS.

Type	Undelivered	Delivered
Form	FSL	FDL
Library	LSL	LDL
Script	SSL	SDL
Report	RSL	RDL

Browse Sources

Of particular interest from the Tools menu is the Browse Sources option. Normally, you edit your code in small pieces. You see only small sections of your application at a time. Sometimes it's useful to view all your code at once. You can do this with Tools | Browse Sources. This option creates a table called PAL$SRC.DB in your private directory, then generates a quick report based on it. This option is particularly useful with large applications. If you create a large application, you can print all the forms, libraries, and scripts. You also can view the entire application. This also is a good way to document the application for archiving purposes.

> The DEV-SRC\SOURCE.RSL report on the disk that comes with this book uses :PRIV:PAL$SRC.DB. You can use this report to print nicer print outs of your code.

The Editor's Object Inspector

The Object Inspector shown in Figure 5.4 is one of the most important menus in the Editor. You can bring up the Editor's Object Inspector menu by right-clicking inside the Editor window. This menu aids you as you develop code.

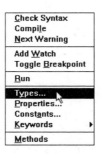

Figure 5.4. The ObjectPAL Editor's Object Inspector.

You can check your syntax with the Check Syntax, Compile, and Next Warning options. After you've entered your code, select Check Syntax to see whether it contains any errors. If you find an error, you can select Next Warning to bring out all the errors in your code. Next Warning is a great time saver.

The Methods option brings up the Methods dialog box so that you can move quickly from one editor to another. You don't have to leave one edit window to bring up another.

The Keywords, Types, Properties, and Constants options are important. They help you to piece together code. The Keywords option brings up a list of some—but not all—keywords. The keywords in this list are used for program control. You can use this menu to insert a keyword into a method without typing the keyword.

The next option is the Types option, which brings up the Types and Methods dialog box (see Figure 5.5). This dialog box contains the types you can use to declare variables and the methods that can act on each type of variable. When you select a type and one of its available methods, the syntax is displayed. Use this dialog box when you're working with an object and you want to know what methods are available for that object—in other words, what you can do with that object.

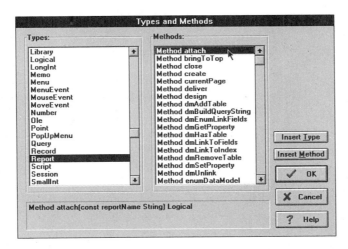

Figure 5.5. The Types and Methods dialog box.

The Properties option on the Tools menu brings up the Display Objects and Properties dialog box (see Figure 5.6). This dialog box displays all the objects you can use. A list of the properties of each object is on the right. Below it are all the possible values for each property.

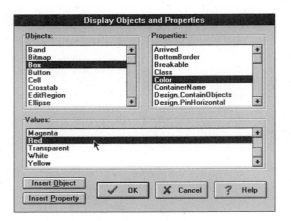

Figure 5.6. The Display Objects and Properties dialog box.

Only display or UIObjects can have properties. They describe attributes an object has.

The Constants option brings up the Constants dialog box. These constants are grouped by type. If you select a type of constant on the left, its available constants appear on the right. You use these constants in many different methods. Typically, you use constants to specify colors, mouse shape, menu attributes, window styles, and printer orientation. Everything a user does interactively generates a constant. You trap for and execute many of the constants. In particular, you can trap for any of the constants in any of the action classes in the built-in **action** method, or execute any of the action constants with the `action()` method. For example, you can trap for when the user tries to delete a record by trapping for the constant `DataDeleteRecord` in the **action** method. Also of particular mention is the MenuCommands class of constants; you can execute most of them with the `menuAction()` method (see Figure 5.7).

Rather than have to remember numbers to specify something that might change from version to version, you can use descriptive constants that Paradox evaluates for you.

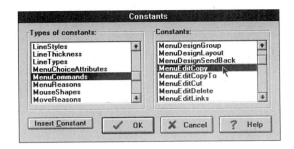

Figure 5.7. The Constants dialog box.

Building an Expression

The next tutorial shows you how to use the Editor's Object Inspector to build an expression. Choosing a keyword from the Keywords menu option pastes the frame for that keyword into your code. The Types, Properties, and Constants dialog boxes all have buttons on them. Use them to paste pieces into your code. Entering code in this way isn't too practical, because it's much slower than just typing the code. It's useful when you're treading in an uncharted programming language, however.

Tutorial: Using the Tools Menu to Construct an Expression

Suppose that you wish to create a button that beeps ten times. You can do this by constructing it piece by piece using the Tools menu.

Quick Steps

1. Use the Types, Constants, Properties dialog boxes and the keyboard to piece together a `for` loop.

Step By Step

1. Change your working directory to the TUTORIAL directory and create a new form. Place a button on it.

2. Enter the button's **pushButton** method by using the keyboard. Select the button and press Ctrl+Spacebar to bring up the Method Inspector, and press Enter to open the editor window for the **pushButton** method.

3. Select Tools | Keywords | var. The Editor places the `var` block for you.

4. Enter x Number where the cursor is; that is, immediately after var. Your code should look like this:

```
1:    method pushButton(var eventInfo Event)
2:    var x Number
3:    endvar
4:
5:    endmethod
```

5. Move the cursor to the blank before endmethod and select Tools | Keywords | for. The Editor places the for loop block for you.

6. Enter x From 1 To 10 Step 1 where the cursor is; that is, immediately after for. Your code should look like this:

```
1:    method pushButton(var eventInfo Event)
2:    var x Number
3:    endvar
4:    for x From 1 To 10 Step 1
5:    endfor
6:
7:    endmethod
```

7. Add a blank line just before endFor and place the cursor on it. Select Tools | Types. Choose System from the Types section and Proc beep from the Methods section. Click the Insert method button and OK.

8. The syntax for beep() requires parentheses after it. The Insert method button pastes only the name of the method. It's up to you to type the syntax. Therefore, be sure to type the left and right parentheses after beep(). Your final code should look like this:

```
1:    method pushButton(var eventInfo Event)
2:    var x Number
3:    endvar
4:    for x From 1 To 10 Step 1
5:    beep()
6:    endfor
7:    endmethod
```

9. Check the syntax by selecting Program | Check Syntax. If you have syntax errors, correct them. If you don't, run the form by selecting Program | Run.

Analysis

Although building applications with the Tools menu is impractical, it's a good aid when you're writing code. The Properties and Constants options are especially useful. If you want to alter the property of an object (or when you're curious about which properties you can alter), select Tools | Properties, and browse. Whenever you're searching for constants to use with methods and procedures, select Tools | Constants, and then select the type of constant you need.

The Properties Menu

With the ObjectPAL in the Properties menu, you can:

- Set whether the Method Inspector stays pinned
- Save the size of the Editor window
- Specify an alternate Editor
- Set Object user level to Beginner or Advanced
- Specify whether to save code automatically or be prompted
- Specify the Debug Environment

The ObjectPAL Preferences Dialog Box

While in the ObjectPAL Editor, you can select Properties | ObjectPAL to display the ObjectPAL Preferences dialog box. Use this dialog box to configure the ObjectPAL Editor (see Figure 5.8). You have already used the Level panel to make sure your ObjectPAL level was set to Beginner. Setting it to advanced shows the entire ObjectPAL language.

Check Developer Menu in the Form Menu panel to add many of the ObjectPAL Editor menu options to the form designer menus. In the beginning, leave this box unchecked; until you are used to all the options, it only confuses you and makes the product harder to use. After you have programmed in ObjectPAL awhile, you probably will wish to leave it checked all the time.

The Debug Environment panel allows you to specify if and when the ObjectPAL Debugger is displayed. Choose both Open in Design and Open in Run to display the Debugger always. Choose just Open in Run to display the Debugger only when the form is running.

Check the Keep Pinned box in the Method Inspector panel to keep the Method Inspector pinned—opened—while in the ObjectPAL Editor. This is a nice feature, especially for SVGA users.

When the Enable Ctrl+Break option in the System panel is checked, you can press Ctrl+Break while the form is running to go straight into the Debugger. More on this feature and the Debugger later in Chapter 29, "Dealing with Errors."

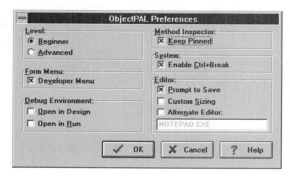

Figure 5.8. The ObjectPAL Preferences dialog box.

Always Use Compiler Warnings and Compile with Debug

The Compiler Warnings option is particularly interesting. It toggles the display of warning messages from the compiler. When this item is checked, messages in the status line warn you about undeclared variables and other conditions that might cause runtime errors. In addition, the Compile with Debug option allows for better error messages. You should always toggle these two options on. If you don't, you aren't taking advantage of extra help from the compiler.

The Help Menu

The Help menu has eight options with which you are already familiar. The Help menu is your online desk reference. You can select any menu option and press F1 for immediate information on what it does and how to use it.

Context-level help at the ObjectPAL level is new to the version 5. Now you can press F1 to get help on the closest ObjectPAL keyword.

Two Hidden Features

There's More to About Than Meets the Eye!

Borland uses internal version numbers to track the many different builds any product goes through before it ships. The internal number of the initial shipping version of Paradox 5 for Windows is 6.135B, Lego: 7/30/94. To check the internal version number, select Help | About and press I.

In addition, when the About Paradox dialog box is open, you can view a secret credits slide show (see Figure 5.9). To view it follow the following steps:

1. Make sure Num Lock and Scroll Lock are set.

2. Press Alt+Shift+Z.

3. While holding down the Ctrl key, left mouse click the icon.

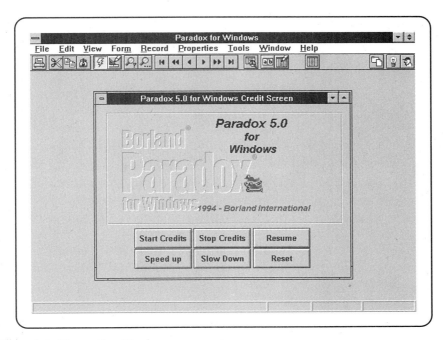

Figure 5.9. The credits slide show.

Exploring the Beginning-Level Runtime Library

One of the most difficult things about ObjectPAL is getting a grasp on all it can do, especially all the thousands of combinations of types of objects, methods, method parameters, and constants. This next section is intended to ease you into ObjectPAL. The next two tutorials explore the Tools menu.

The next tutorials are a quick overview of the beginning-level methods, procedures, properties, and constants. Your goal is to become familiar with the beginning-level types of objects and their methods, procedures, properties, and constants.

Tutorial: Exploring the Tools Menu

In this tutorial, you look at types of objects and the methods and procedures that can act on them. You'll group the 21 different beginner-level types into random pseudo-groups. For example, you'll start by lumping Date, DateTime, and Time into a category.

Part 1: Types of Objects and Methods and Procedures

1. Open the ObjectPAL Editor for any object. The type of object doesn't matter. Select Tools | Types.

2. From the Types section of the Types and Methods dialog box, browse through the Date, DateTime, and Time data types by clicking them. Note the methods available for each one. Date and Time have no methods in common. DateTime, however, has methods in common with both Date and Time (see Figure 5.10).

   Although you can't tell exactly how all beginner-level methods and procedures act on their data types, the descriptive names for the methods give you a good idea. daysInMonth() returns the number of days in a month. isLeapYear() returns True if the Date or DateTime data is in a current leap year, and False if the data is not. hour() returns the hour portion of the Time() or DateTime() data format. If a method looks useful to you, select it and view its syntax.

   If you need more explanation, refer to the ObjectPAL reference book or use the context-sensitive help new to version 5 by pressing Ctrl+F1.

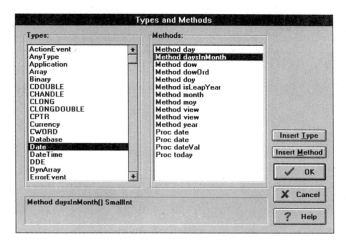

Figure 5.10. The Types and Methods dialog box.

3. Browse through Number, SmallInt, and LongInt methods and procedures. View their methods and procedures. Even though these three data types are all types of numbers, Number has many more available methods and procedures. This isn't because of Beginner mode. When you switch to Advanced mode, the methods and procedures for Number are completely different from the methods and procedures for SmallInt and LongInt. If you have a variable defined as a SmallInt and you want to use one of the Number methods, you have to cast the SmallInt as a Number with either the Number() or NumVal() procedures.

4. Browse through the AnyType, Logical, and String types. Although AnyType and Logical have few methods and procedures, String has 17. (It has 29 in Advanced mode.)

5. Browse through Form and Report. These two display managers have no methods in common in Beginner mode. When you switch to Advanced mode, they have several methods and procedures in common, although they do slightly different things. Select a few of the methods and procedures whose names catch your attention, and view their syntax.

6. Browse through Table, TCursor, and UIObject. These three types have many methods in common. Their methods deal with accessing a table.

7. Browse through ActionEvent, ErrorEvent, Event, MenuEvent, MoveEvent, and ValueEvent. These types are all events, or packets of information sent from one object to another. The methods that apply to these event packets retrieve, set, or trigger them.

8. Browse through the System procedures. Select System and view the 14 beginning-level System procedures. You'll recognize what many of these System procedures do just by looking at their names.

Part 2 Step By Step: Display Objects and Properties

Now, explore the Display Objects and Properties dialog box (see Figure 5.11). In Beginner mode, 17 objects each have up to 36 properties, and each property has up to 17 constants. Advanced mode raises these numbers by a factor of three or four. Many of these numbers are duplicates, however. For example, most objects have one or more color properties. The constants for every color property are the same 17. This duplication holds true for most properties and their constants.

From the Objects section of the Display Objects and Properties dialog box, select Box. From the Properties section, select `frame.style` (see Figure 5.11). Note the available values that are constants.

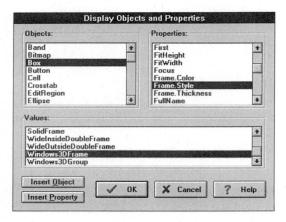

Figure 5.11. The Display Objects and Properties dialog box.

Part 3 Step By Step: Constants

1. Bring up the ObjectPAL Editor from any object. Select Tools | Constants.

2. Select `ActionDataCommands`. These 14 constants are the beginning-level action constants. You can use these constants with the `action` method. For example:

```
1:    Last_Name.action(DataLockRecord)    ;Lock a record.
2:    Last_Name.action(DataEnd)           ;Move to last record.
3:    Last_Name.action(DataBeginEdit)     ;Start edit mode.
4:    Last_Name.action(DataUnlockRecord)  ;Unlock a record.
```

3. Select `PatternStyles`. These 24 constants are the pattern styles that are available in Paradox. You can use them in ObjectPAL with dot notation to change patterns on-the-fly. For example:

```
1:    theBox.Pattern.color = Yellow
2:    theBox.Pattern.Style = FuzzyStripesDownPattern
```

There are thousands of combinations of types of objects and their methods, procedures, properties, and constants. Many of them are related, however, and you can categorize them and cross-reference them mentally.

ADVANCED-LEVEL TYPES

Now, kick ObjectPAL into high gear and look at the rest of the methods and properties. Select Properties | Desktop and toggle the ObjectPAL level from Beginner to Advanced.

Tutorial: The Runtime Library in Advanced Mode

Your goal is to become familiar with the advanced-level types of objects and their methods, procedures, properties, and constants.

Step By Step: Types of Objects

1. Bring up the ObjectPAL Editor from any object and select Tools | Types. In Advanced mode, the Types section of the Types and Methods dialog box (see Figure 5.12) lists the 50-plus types of methods and procedures.

If you check the Developer Menu option in the ObjectPAL preferences dialog box, then the Types, Constants, and Properties options appear on the Tools menu if the current window is a form, script, or library and it is in design mode.

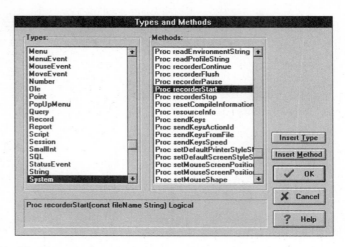

Figure 5.12. The Types and Methods dialog box when set to Advanced.

2. Select the System type. The number of methods and procedures has grown from 14 in Beginner mode to more than 100 in Advanced mode—and this is just one of the 50-plus types! No wonder ObjectPAL has a steep learning curve! Borland could have stripped ObjectPAL down, but then the language wouldn't have been so robust.

3. Look at Database, FileSystem, and Session. See how they belong in a pseudo-category with System.

4. Browse through the design objects: Application, Form, Library, Query, Report, UIObject, and Script. Note the methods and procedures that are available to these object types.

5. Browse through the Table, TableView, TCursor, and UIObject object types. These object types are one of the reasons you bought Paradox. They are the centerpiece objects with the majority of database power. Note which object types have an attach method, and note their syntax. For example, UIObject has six attach methods, whereas TableView has none.

Return to the Tools menu as often as you can while you learn ObjectPAL. After you learn the basic concepts of ObjectPAL, the Tools menu is an indispensable reference tool.

OBJECTPAL
BASICS

ObjectPAL Concepts

OBJECT-BASED PROGRAMMING

ObjectPAL isn't a true object-oriented programming language. It is, however, object-based programming (OBP). Take a look at what objects are, the three elements of Object-Oriented Programming (OOP), and see how both relate to ObjectPAL. First up is a discussion of objects.

ObjectPAL theory explored

Objects

ObjectPAL is event driven

Object-oriented programming

Containers

Containership hierarchy

Scope

What Are Objects?

Many people have trouble understanding how objects relate to programming. Normally, an object is something perceived by the senses —something material. An object also is something perceived by the mind. From buttons you can place on a form to TCursors you use to get data, everything in Paradox is an object. All the elements of an ObjectPAL application are objects. Some are obvious objects, such as fields, buttons, boxes, and pages. Others are less obvious objects, such as TCursors, tables, and strings.

The biggest advantage of using object-based programming rather than procedural programming is that you can cut these independent objects from one place or container and paste them to another place or container without affecting any other objects (at least in most cases). This makes your code highly portable. For example, if you create a button that launches the Windows Calculator, you can copy it from one form to another form without affecting other objects or code. With ObjectPAL, you can reuse code more easily than you can with a procedural language such as PAL, Basic, C, or Pascal. With ObjectPAL, you can develop many self-contained routines only once.

Another advantage of object-based programming is that it is easier to maintain than a procedural programming language. Your code is contained in objects. Therefore, if something goes wrong, it generally affects only one module or part of your application. If you develop with a group of programmers, you will appreciate that each programmer's code is protected from the others' code. For example, code in one form generally will not affect code in another form.

The Six Categories of Methods and Procedures

When you study a subject as broad as the more than 1,200 ObjectPAL methods and procedures and their variations, it helps to break them into categories. The ObjectPAL methods and procedures act on objects. The objects on which the methods and procedures act fall into six categories:

- Data types
- Display managers
- Data model objects

- Design objects
- System data objects
- Event objects

Following is an overview of each of the object categories. They are discussed in detail throughout this book.

Data Types

You use the 18 data types to store data (see Table 6.1). After you store data in a particular type of variable, you can manipulate the data by using the methods associated with that type of variable.

TABLE 6.1. THE 18 TYPES OF DATA.		
AnyType	*DynArray*	*OLE*
Array	Graphic	Point
Binary	Logical	Record
Currency	LongInt	SmallInt
Date	Memo	String
DateTime	Number	Time

Chapter 11, "Data Types," discusses the 18 data type methods and procedures in detail.

Display Managers

Display managers manage how objects are displayed. ObjectPAL has five display managers:

NEW
5

- Application
- Form
- TableView
- Report
- Script

The Application display manager is the Paradox desktop. It manages the display of the other display managers—Form, TableView, Report, and Script. A Form display manager manages all the Objects that you put on it. The form is the center of every ObjectPAL application. A TableView display manager manages and displays tables. A Report display manager manages the formatted display and how table information is printed. A Script is a special display manager that has no UIObjects on it but can display information on the status bar and in message boxes. In general, you deal with display managers in ObjectPAL as a complete unit. For example, you might maximize, minimize, or hide any of the display managers except for a Script.

Data Model Objects

You use data model objects to manipulate data in tables and databases. ObjectPAL has five kinds of data model objects:

- Database
- Query
- Table
- TCursor
- SQL

You use the Database methods and procedures on a database—a set of tables in a directory. For example, with Database methods and procedures, you can open a database or delete a table. You use the Query methods and procedures to execute and manipulate queries. The Table methods and procedures represent the table itself.

The Table object is distinct from a TCursor, which is a pointer to the data. It also is distinct from a table frame and a TableView, which are objects that display the data. Use the Table methods and procedures to add, copy, create, and index tables, to do column calculations, and to get information about a table's structure. Don't use Table methods to edit records, however. Use a TCursor or a table frame—a UIObject—instead.

Design Objects

Design object methods and procedures are commands used to manipulate menus, pop-up menus, and UIObjects. The three kinds of design objects are as follows:

- Menu
- PopUpMenu
- UIObject

You use Menu and PopUpMenu methods and procedures to build and manipulate menus. Similarly, you use UIObject—short for *user interface object*—methods and procedures to manipulate UIObjects. For example, when you change the color of a box to red or when you set the value of a field, you manipulate UIObject properties. UIObject methods and procedures add to this functionality. For instance, they enable you to set the position of an object.

Scripts, libraries, forms, and UIObjects are the only objects that have built-in methods. The form, for example, is a display manager that behaves like a UIObject. A form has built-in methods to which you can attach code, and it responds to events. There also are methods and procedures that you can use to manipulate a form.

Many of the UIObject methods are duplicated among the TCursor methods. For example, `insertRecord()` works on both a UIObject and a TCursor. The UIObject methods that work with tables work on the underlying table by means of a visible object. Actions directed to the UIObject that affect a table are immediately visible in the object to which the table is bound.

On the other hand, TCursor methods work with a table behind the scenes as if another user were making the changes. When you work with a TCursor that affects a table to which a UIObject is bound, the result isn't visible in any UIObject until you use the `resync()` method.

System Data Objects

The six kinds of system data objects are as follows:

- DDE
- Library
- TextStream
- FileSystem
- Session
- System

You use the DDE (dynamic data exchange) types of methods and procedures with DDE. DDE allows you to send and receive data between Windows applications (see Chapter 29 for more information on DDE). The Library methods and procedures work with libraries. A library is a place to store code (see Chapter 23 for more information on libraries). TextStream methods and procedures manipulate streams of text.

The other three categories—FileSystem, Session, and System—are used for objects outside Paradox, such as DOS-level or Windows-level procedures. FileSystem methods and procedures enable you to manipulate a FileSystem variable to provide access to and information about disk files, drives, and directories. A FileSystem variable provides a handle; that is, a variable you use in an ObjectPAL statement in order to work with a directory or a file. Session methods and procedures give you a channel to the database engine. For example, you can add and delete aliases by using Session methods. You use System procedures to display messages, find out about the user's system, get a filename with the file browser, and work with the help system.

Event Objects

Events are packets of information sent from one object to another. Built-in methods are the events in action. You use the Event methods and procedures to manipulate that packet. Ten kinds of methods and procedures manipulate the various *eventInfo* variables:

```
Event          MouseEvent
ActionEvent    MoveEvent
ErrorEvent     StatusEvent
KeyEvent       TimerEvent
MenuEvent      ValueEvent
```

As an example, the following paragraphs discuss the Event, ActionEvent, ErrorEvent, and KeyEvent categories. The Event category is the base type from which the other event types are derived. Many of the methods listed in this section are used by the other event types.

You generate an ActionEvent primarily by editing and navigating in a table. ActionEvent methods and procedures enable you to get and set information in the **action** method.

An ErrorEvent is sent to the built-in **error** method. Use **error** to add to the built-in error behavior.

You use KeyEvent methods and procedures to manipulate and retrieve information about keystroke events in **keyPhysical** and **keyChar**.

MenuEvent methods and procedures enable you to retrieve and to set data in the MenuEvent event packet that is related to menu selections in the application menu bar—in other words, menu constants. For example, when the user chooses an item from the Toolbar, it triggers the **menuAction** method by sending it the appropriate menu constant. You use the methods in the MenuEvent class to manipulate the MenuEvent *eventInfo* packet.

Free Reference Sheet

Print Your Own Reference Sheet!

Create and run the following one-line script:

```
enum RTLMethods("RTLMETH.DB")
```

This script creates a table that lists all the runtime library methods and procedures and their variations. That's more than 1,200 commands. By using the RTLMETH.DB, you can create and print elaborate reports and use them as reference sheets. You also can query the table to view the methods in various ways.

IS OBJECTPAL OOP?

Now that you have a firm grasp of the various objects used in ObjectPAL, look at the three elements of Object Oriented Programming (OOP), and see how they relate to ObjectPAL. The three elements are encapsulation, polymorphism, and inheritance.

Encapsulation

In OOP, *encapsulation* is the bundling of methods and variables within an object so that access to the variables is permitted only through the object's own methods. ObjectPAL supports encapsulation. The code you write is stored with the object that triggers it. The code is completely independent of other objects and other code. In other words, if the object is moved inside another object or to another form, the code goes with it. This is encapsulation.

The key benefit of encapsulation is that your code is self-contained and protected from other objects. If another object needs to access variables inside your object, you can grant access through a custom method. If a group of people develop an ObjectPAL application, each programmer needs to be concerned only with his or her particular section. A section in ObjectPAL means a group of objects. If an external object needs access to something in the current object, the current object must have a method to allow it to be accessed.

For example, a team of programmers could designate one programmer to be in charge of the library for an application. (The library is where generic code is put.) When another programmer wants a routine to be included in the library, that person gives the programmer in charge of the library the specifications for the custom method—that is, what the custom method should be passed and what it should do and return. When another programmer wants to add to or alter that custom method, the programmer in charge of the library decides whether the modification is possible, given what the method already does.

Encapsulation makes it possible to bring foreign code together. With a traditional procedural language, a team of programmers must be sure not to use the same function and variable names. Because ObjectPAL supports encapsulation, you don't have to worry about the names of methods, procedures, objects, or variables. Each programmer can use his or her own variable-naming convention and not worry about the other programmers. When it comes time to bring all the sections of an application together, you simply have to worry about how the objects communicate. If you are an individual programmer, this means that you can reuse more of your code.

The capability to have duplicate names for variables and custom methods is a great relief to a programmer. For example, you can have a variable called `Counter` in two different places or two custom methods called `cmRoutine()`.

Dot Notation and Encapsulation

The dot notation syntax of ObjectPAL supports encapsulation and enables you to grab values from other objects. For example, from `field1` of `form1`, you can open `form2` and grab the value in its `field1` with the following code:

```
1:    var
2:       f2 form
3:    endVar
4:
5:    f2.open("form2")
6:    field1.value = f2.field1.value
```

The rules about when you can use duplicate names and about which code can see other code refer to scope. (Scope is discussed in more detail later in this chapter.)

Tutorial: Encapsulation

The goal of this tutorial is to demonstrate one element of encapsulation in ObjectPAL. Encapsulation allows you to use the same variable name in two different containers. Encapsulation is closely related to scope. In this tutorial, you refer to two variables that have the same name but are in separate containers above a button. The name of both variables is s. It is encapsulation that enables you to use duplicate named variables. This tutorial also introduces you to assigning a value to a variable and using the msgInfo() procedure.

On Disk: \ANSWERS\ENCAP.FSL

Quick Steps
1. Declare a variable in the Var window of the form.
2. Define the value of the variable in the **open** method of the form.
3. Declare the same variable in the Var window of a box on the page.
4. Define the variable in the **open** method of the box.
5. Create a button on the page—outside the box—that uses the variable. Click the button.
6. Move the button inside the box and click it.

Step By Step
1. Change your working directory to the TUTORIAL directory and create a new form with a box and a button on it.
2. Declare s as a string in the form's Var window. Do this by adding line 3 to the form's Var window.

```
1:    ;Form :: Var
2:    Var
3:         s      String
4:    endVar
```

3. When the **open** method of the form is called, set the value of the form's version of s. Do this by adding line 8 to the form's **open** method.

```
1:    ;Form :: open
2:    method open(var eventInfo Event)
3:    if eventInfo.isPreFilter()
4:    then
5:    ;This code executes for each object on the form
6:    else
```

```
7:      ;This code executes only for the form
8:      s = "Text from form open"
9:        endif
10:     endmethod
```

4. Declare the box's version of s in the box's Var window. Do this by adding line 3 to the box's Var window.

```
1:      ;Page.Box :: Var
2:      Var
3:        s      String
4:      endVar
```

5. When the **open** method of the box is used, set the value of the box's version of s. Do this by adding line 3 to the **open** method of the box.

```
1:      ;Page.Box :: open
2:      method open(var eventInfo Event)
3:        s = "Text from box"
4:      endmethod
```

6. When the button is clicked, use the variable. Do this by adding line 3 to the **pushButton** method of the button.

```
1:      ;Page.#Button4 :: pushButton
2:      method pushButton(var eventInfo Event)
3:       msgInfo("Value of s from button", s)
4:      endmethod
```

7. Check the syntax and save the form as ENCAP.FSL. See "Analysis" that follows for more instructions.

Analysis

With the button outside the box, run the form and press the button. Note that the button searches for a variable named s. The **pushButton** method searches for a Var block within the method block, then above the method block, then in the button's Var window; and then it searches the container's Var window, and so on. The button finally finds the variable s declared at the form level. The string variable that is declared in step 2, line 3 and set in step 3, line 8 is used by the button in step 6, line 3.

Go into Design mode, move the button inside the box, and run the form again. This time, the button uses the variable declared in the box's Var window (step 4, line 3) and set in step 5, line 3. The button now has context. The s variable's value depends on the container in which the button is contained. Containership, hierarchy, encapsulation, and scope are tightly intertwined. (Containers are discussed in more detail later in this chapter.)

Polymorphism

In OOP, the capability of the same command to be interpreted differently when used with or received by different objects is called polymorphism. In ObjectPAL, *polymorphism* is the capability of an object to act differently depending on the context in which it is being used. For example, methods require an object with which to work. Depending on the object's type, the method does different things. The following expression opens the object named *Orders*, depending on how *varName* is defined:

```
1:        varName.open("Orders")      ;varName is an object.
```

Orders can be a table, a form, a script, or many other objects. What ObjectPAL tries to open depends on what variable type you declare *varName* as. You can define *varName* to be a database, a DDE link, a form, a library, a report, a session, a TableView, a TCursor, a TextStream, or something else. As the programmer using this object-based language, you don't need to concern yourself with the details of opening these various objects. You write code that is based on this simple formula:

```
var
     object ObjectType            ;First declare a variable.
endVar
object.open( parameterList )      ;Then use the variable.
```

ObjectPAL takes over and handles the details. For example, to open another form, you could use:

```
1:    var
2:       tempVar    Form     ;tempVar is a form variable.
3:    endVar
4:
5:    tempVar.open("Orders")  ;Open form.
```

TCursors and Polymorphism

A *TCursor* is a tool used to manipulate a table behind the scenes. A TCursor (table cursor) is a pointer to a record in a table. You will get a closer look at TCursors later, in Chapter 16, "Using Table and TCursor Variables," so this will be a brief introduction here.

If you change the variable type of `tempVar`, the same `open()` method can open something else, such as a TCursor:

```
1:    var
2:       tempVar      TCursor       ;tempVar is a TCursor.
3:    endVar
4:
5:    tempVar.open("ORDERS.DB")    ;Open a TCursor to Orders.db.
```

In the future, when Borland adds another type of object that can be opened, you won't need to learn the new syntax; you'll need to learn only the new characteristics of the object. This certainly beats learning syntax for 10 to 15 different open routines. In fact, polymorphism goes deeper than this. Throughout ObjectPAL, methods use the following syntax model:

```
object.doIt()
```

where `object` is the name of the variable or the name given to the object, and `doIt()` is what you want done. This syntax model is called dot notation and is highly flexible. It enables you to manipulate objects in other objects. Here are some examples of syntax that supports polymorphism:

```
1:    Container.xyz.value = 27        ;xyz can be any field.
2:    container.container.xyz.doIt()  ;doIt is a custom method.
3:    Form2Var.PageName.xyz.color = red  ;xyz can be a line or box.
```

Tutorial: Polymorphism

This tutorial demonstrates the existence of polymorphism in ObjectPAL. The same method, `setPosition()`, is used on the application, the page, and two UIObjects. This tutorial also introduces you to the `maximize()` method.

On Disk: \ANSWERS\POLY.FSL

Quick Steps

1. Use application `setPosition()` on the **open** method of the application to set the size of the application.
2. Use the UIObject `setPostion()` in the **open** method of the page, a box, and a button to set their size and position.

Step By Step

1. Change your working directory to the TUTORIAL directory and create a new form with a box and a button on it.
2. Declare *app* as an application variable by adding line 3 to the form's Var window.

```
1:    ;Form :: Var
2:    Var
```

```
3:        app      Application
4:     endVar
```

3. When the **open** method of the form is triggered, maximize and set the position of Paradox. Do this by adding lines 9 and 10 to the form's **open** method.

```
1:     ;Form :: open
2:     method open(var eventInfo Event)
3:
4:         if eventInfo.isPreFilter() then
5:             ;// This code executes for each object on the
               form:
6:
7:         else
8:             ;// This code executes only for the form:
9:             app.maximize()
10:            app.setPosition(100, 100, 9000, 6000)
11:        endif
12:    endmethod
```

4. When the **open** method of the page occurs, set the page's color and position it. Do this by adding lines 3 and 4 to the **open** method of the page.

```
1:     ;Page :: open
2:     method open(var eventInfo Event)
3:         self.color = Gray
4:         self.setPosition(0, 0, 7000, 3000)
5:     endmethod
```

5. When the **open** method of the button occurs, set its position. Do this by adding line 3 to the **open** method of the button.

```
1:     ;Page.#Button4 :: open
2:     method open(var eventInfo Event)
3:         self.setPosition(2000, 1000, 2000, 1000)
4:     endmethod
```

6. When the **open** method of the box occurs, set its position. Do this by adding line 3 to the **open** method of the box.

```
1:     ;Page.#Box3 :: open
2:     method open(var eventInfo Event)
3:         self.setPosition(100, 100, 1000, 1000)
4:     endmethod
```

7. Check the syntax, save the form as POLY.FSL, and run it. When you run this form, note the size and position of the application, the form, the page, the box, and the button change.

Analysis

In steps 3, 4, 5, and 6 the same `setPosition()` method is used. In fact, in steps 4, 5, and 6, the command is almost identical. `setPosition()` works on three different types of objects with the same command. `setPosition()`, in this sense, has context; that is, it behaves differently depending on where the code is attached.

In step 3, line 9 maximizes the application and line 10 sets its position and size. This was done to show that a maximized Paradox application doesn't have to be full screen, which is useful when you're developing for several screen resolutions. You could develop for VGA and set the position and size depending on the screen resolution.

In step 4, line 3 sets the color of the page to gray. This illustrates the difference between the page and the form. There is white space around the page. This white space is the form; the only object you can put directly on the form is a page. Every form must have at least one page, and all the objects are contained within the page.

To learn more about the commands in ObjectPAL that have polymorphism, consult the *Quick Reference* book. It shows clearly which commands work on more than one type of object.

INHERITANCE—WELL, ACTUALLY, DELEGATION

In OOP, a mechanism for automatically sharing methods and data types among objects is called *inheritance*. In ObjectPAL, an object inherits all the variables, types, and custom procedures of the objects by which it is contained.

Also, the fact that methods and procedures from one object type are derived— inherited—from other types shows the existence of inheritance in ObjectPAL. Figure 6.1 depicts the on-line help showing the methods and procedures for the report type that are derived from the form type. The benefit of derived methods is that, once you learn how to use a particular method for one type, you know how to use it on all the other objects that have inherited it.

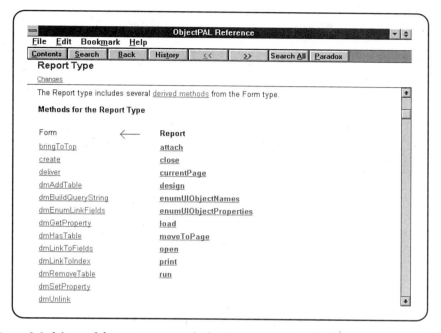

Figure 6.1. Many of the report type methods are inherited from the Form type.

Paradox UIObjects—objects you place on a form—don't have true inheritance. UIObjects, however, do have a form of inheritance that Borland calls *delegation*. You also can refer to it as cloning. How would UIObjects behave if they had true inheritance? Suppose that you put a button on a form, change its label, attach a method to it, and copy it. If you change the original—that is, the parent—the child also changes. This doesn't happen in Paradox. Instead, Paradox clones the original. If you change the original, nothing happens to the copy. In Paradox, the link between the parent and the child is broken after the copy is made.

Every object in Paradox supports delegation. When you copy an object, the copy is delegated the properties and methods of the parent. Be careful when you use Design | Copy To Toolbar. If the object that you copy to the Toolbar has ObjectPAL code on it, the code is copied, too.

Containers

Earlier in this chapter, a variable called `container` was used in a few examples. In ObjectPAL, this built-in `container` variable refers to the object that contains the current object. A container object completely surrounds and controls the behavior of all the objects within it. The rules of a container dictate that when you move a container, its contained objects also move. Likewise, when you delete a container, its contained objects are also deleted.

When you have objects that can contain other objects, the containership, or path, has to stop somewhere. In ObjectPAL, the form is the highest level of container. A form contains at least one page, and the page contains design objects such as fields, buttons, table frames, and bitmaps (see Figure 6.2). Note that the page contains the larger box, and that the larger box contains the circle, the smaller box, and the button. The field is contained by the small box. Remember that the form contains all these objects and that it is the highest level of container in Paradox.

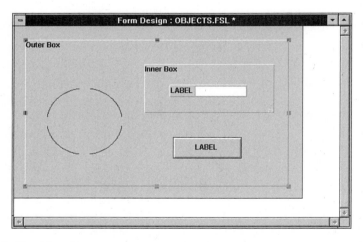

Figure 6.2. Containership.

The keywords and object variables that you use with containers are as follows:

`disableDefault`	;Stop the built-in behavior
`doDefault`	;Execute the built-in behavior now
`enableDefault`	;Allow the built-in behavior
`passEvent`	;Pass event up to container

`self`	;Refers to the object the code is on
`active`	;Refers to the object with focus
`container`	;Refers to the container
`lastMouseClicked`	;Last object to receive a left mouse click
`lastMouseRightClicked`	;Last object to receive a right mouse click
`subject`	;Refers to another object

You can refer to a container with the container variable. For example, `message(self.container.name)` displays the name of the object that contains `self`. More on the built-in object variables later in Chapter 9, "Syntax."

Containership Hierarchy: What Contains What

Paradox employs what is called containership, which enables you to put a smaller object inside a larger object. You could say that the smaller object is contained by the larger object. The Object Tree visually shows you the containership hierarchy of a form. It is one of the most important tools for developing forms and writing ObjectPAL code (see Figure 6.3). The Object Tree shows you what objects contain what other objects.

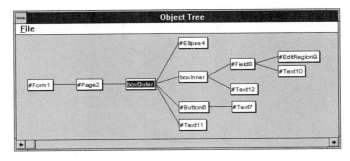

Figure 6.3. The Object Tree inspector.

Use the Object Tree to rename objects quickly. Also use it to see what contains what and to see which objects have code on them. Objects that have code are underlined.

You can attach code to the objects that show up in the Object Tree. You can attach code to as many objects as you want, in any order that you want. Attaching code directly to the object with which you want to work makes ObjectPAL a great programming language to learn first. For example, you can place a box and a circle on a form and place code in the **mouseClick** methods of both objects. Because the form is an event handler that follows an event model, when you run the form, Paradox takes care of trapping a mouse click when the user clicks on either the box or the circle.

Containership Rules

The following are several rules dealing with containership.

- Deleting a container deletes all embedded objects.
- Containership determines dot notation.
- Containership allows you to have duplicate named objects in the same form.
- Noise names are not part of the containership path. A noise name is the default name Paradox gives new objects. Noise names always start with #.
- An object is embedded only if it is completely within the boundaries of the container.
- Objects inside a container can see the variables, custom methods, and custom procedures of its container.
- A container cannot see the variables, custom methods, and custom procedures of its embedded objects.

Scope: What Can See What

The scope of an object is the range of objects that have access to it. For example, if you declare a variable in the form's Var window, that variable may be used by any object in the form, but not by objects outside the form. Scope has a definite path determined by the containership hierarchy. An object can see all the variables or constants above it and within it, but not below it. In other words, an object can't see the variables, constants, and procedures of the objects it contains. Also, an object can't see variables, constants, or procedures that are on another branch of the Object Tree. Objects that are contained can see their containers' variables, constants, and procedures. That is, they "inherit" them (and can overwrite them with their own, an OOP feature).

For example, in Figure 6.4, a box labeled Inner Box is contained by a box labeled Outer Box. Inner Box can see all its own variables and all the variables of Outer Box. Outer Box, on the other hand, can see only its own variables. It can't see the variables of Inner Box.

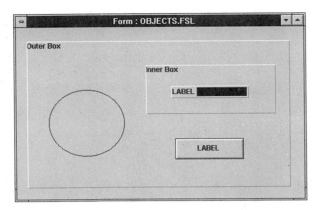

Figure 6.4. Scope is determined by containership hierarchy.

Scope can be summed up by the phrase *what can see what*. Noise names don't interfere with scope, but real names do. Understanding this difference is absolutely crucial to understanding scope. When you view the containership hierarchy, you can find out which objects see which objects. You need to know where and when you can use duplicate names of objects on forms. The next tutorial explores duplicate object names and duplicate variables.

Tutorial: Scope

The goal of this tutorial is to demonstrate the difference between scope and containership. To do this, you will try to rename two fields the same name. You will fail at first because the scope of the objects interferes. After this fails, you will rename one of the field's containers and try again.

Quick Steps

1. Put two boxes on a form. Put a field into each box so that each box contains a field.
2. Name both fields `Field1`. (You won't be able to name them the same way until you name one of the boxes.)

Step By Step

1. Change your working directory to the TUTORIAL directory and create a new form. Put two boxes on a form, then put a field in each box (see Figure 6.5).

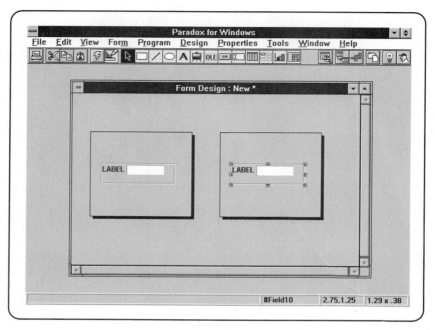

Figure 6.5. Set up form for tutorial.

2. Name one of the fields *Field1*.

3. Try to give the other field the same name, *Field1*.

   You can't. Why? Aren't they in different containers? Yes and no. The two fields are in different containers, but they still can see each other because there is nothing between them except noise names. This is the difference between scope and containership. Browse the Object Tree for a visual representation of this. In Figure 6.6, note that all the names start with a pound symbol (except for the one that was renamed). This signifies that the object name is a noise name.

4. Rename either box—*#Box4* in Figure 6.6—to *Box2*.

5. Rename the field inside *Box2* to *Field1*. Now you can use a duplicate name, as Figure 6.7 shows.

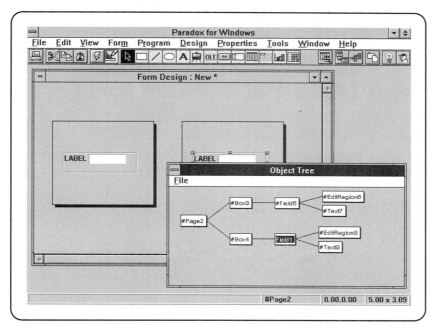

Figure 6.6. The Object Tree inspector shows scope.

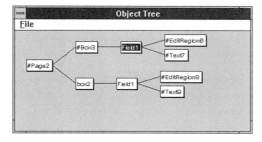

Figure 6.7. Now a duplicate name can be used.

ObjectPAL Is Event Driven

How does Paradox execute all these independent routines? ObjectPAL is an event-driven language much like ObjectVision, Visual Basic, Hypercard, and Toolbook. You paint objects on the screen and attach code directly to them. The event handler monitors what events or triggers occur, and automatically executes your code when it should, based on its event model. This mechanism of triggering events is known as an event handler. The plan or guideline that the event handler uses to trigger events is known as the event model.

To understand ObjectPAL, you first must understand the event model. Nothing else will make sense until you understand it. (The next chapter explores the event model in detail.) For now, keep the following points in mind:

- Every event has a target. When you click a field, it becomes the target of the event.

- Every event goes to the form first. With the form prefilter, you can intercept an event before the target gets it. If you don't place code in the form's prefilter, the event is not affected by the prefilter.

- The form sends the event to the target. The form serves as a kind of dispatcher. An event goes to the form, and then the form sends the event packet to the target object.

- Internal events stop after the target. Internal events such as **open**, **close**, and **arrive** go to the form and then to the target, and then they terminate.

- External events bubble. If an external event such as mouseDown, keyPhysical, and error are not trapped for at the form level or the target level—in other words, no built-in code responds to the event—the object passes the event to its container. If the container has no built-in code that traps for that external event, it is passed to its container and so on, until it reaches the form for the second time, where it stops.

- The form can see external events twice. If an external event has no built-in code that traps for it, the form sees it twice. The prefilter equals False when the form is the target of the event. The prefilter also equals False when another object is the target of the event and the form is seeing it for the second time.

Bubbling: The Path of Events

An event has one of two definite paths: either form and then target, or form, target, and bubble back up to the form. An external event such as mouseDown goes to the form, then to the target, and then it bubbles up the containership hierarchy until it reaches the form a second time, where it stops. The event might go through the entire path. If any of the objects in the path have built-in code that uses the event, the event might get cut short. (Your code does not stop bubbling; only built-in code does.) For example, mouseDown normally bubbles up to the form. If you left-click a field, however, the field knows what to do with **mouseDown** and the **mouseDown** event is not bubbled.

Most of the time, your code executes on the target. The target object executes an event such as **mouseDown**. The event goes first to the form. If the form doesn't have the appropriate code on the correct method, the event is returned to the target for execution. If the target doesn't have the appropriate code, the code is bubbled up through the containership path to the form, where it stops. The form sees the code twice—at the start and at the end—unless another object, such as the target's container, intercepts the event with built-in code, such as the preceding field example.

Now, follow what happens to a button's **pushButton** method when a user clicks it. The target object—the button—sends the **pushButton** method to the form. Because the form doesn't use a **pushButton** method, the event is returned to the target for execution. If the target—the button—doesn't have the appropriate built-in code, the event is bubbled up through the containership path to the form, where it stops. The form can see an event twice—at the start and at the end of its life cycle. You can place code anywhere on the containership path to trap for the event. In fact, you can place it several times on the path and all the code will execute.

Suppose that you want to trap for an event whenever the user arrives on a record. At the form's prefilter, you can trap for `DataArriveRecord`, as in the following:

```
 1:    method action(var eventInfo ActionEvent)
 2:       if eventInfo.isPreFilter()
 3:          then
 4:          ;This code executes for each object on the form
 5:          if eventInfo.id() = DataArriveRecord then
 6:             beep()  ;Do your stuff here
 7:          endIf
 8:       else
 9:          ;This code executes only for the form
10:       endif
11:    endmethod
```

If you are using a table frame, which has a record object, you can't move lines 5, 6, and 7 to the `else` part of the `if` structure because the record object of the table frame will use up the event and not allow it to bubble up to the `else` clause of the form. The action `DataArriveRecord` is never bubbled up to the form.

The event you're interested in applies to a table frame—one of the many other objects that are caught by the prefilter test. The comment after the `then` part of the `if` structure reads, "This code executes for each object on the form." This refers to all the objects on the form except the form itself, which is tested in the `else` clause.

If you create a single record form—that is, a form with just fields on it—you can use the preceding `else` clause to trap for `DataArriveRecord` because it bubbles back up to the form.

Containership, Scope, and Bubbling Are Intertwined

The containership hierarchy is the branching tree represented in the Object Tree. The Object Tree enables you to see the containership hierarchy, or path, of objects. Containership hierarchy is closely related to bubbling and scope. Events go to the form and then to the target. Then, the event bubbles up the containership hierarchy. The event packet path is determined by the containership hierarchy. Scope is what can see what. Use the ObjectTree to determine the scope of objects. If an object on the containership path has been renamed, then it has defined part of the scope path. If the object has not been renamed, then it is not part of the scope path.

Whew! You have just survived, learned, and absorbed what most programmers consider the toughest aspect of ObjectPAL. This chapter definitely is the toughest in this book—at least as far as concepts go. If you understood most of this chapter, great! The following checklist lists the important topics in this chapter:

- Objects
- Encapsulation
- Polymorphism
- Inheritance
- Cloning objects
- Containers
- Containership hierarchy
- Scope

If you still don't understand a certain topic, read the section that discusses it again. Is it absolutely crucial that you understand these topics? Yes and no. Not understanding this chapter won't hold you back. The better you understand the concepts in this chapter, however, the better you will understand the big picture—and the better your applications can be.

This chapter covered many aspects of ObjectPAL, including objects, containers, containership hierarchy, and bubbling. The next chapter discusses the basics of the event model in detail.

CHAPTER 7

EVENT MODEL BASICS

The event model is such an important topic, it deserves two chapters. In your first look at the event model, you'll take a look at its basics. In Chapter 30, "The Event Model Revisited," you will revisit the event model and take an in-depth view of it.

Why two chapters on the event model? Quite simply because it is the heart of Paradox. Once you understand it, you will be able to program in ObjectPAL with ease.

Internal built-in methods

External built-in methods

Special built-in methods

The eventInfo packet

Default behavior

Bubbling

The Event Model Makes Sense

The event model is an important aspect of ObjectPAL. This section explores a simplified view of a form and the built-in **open** method. The event model is not linear, but can be used in a linear fashion. Much like a procedural language, you can attach code to the **open** method of the form, page, box, field, and button. The code executes in order. First the code on the form executes, then the code on the page, box, and field executes. Finally, the code on the button executes.

The goal of this next tutorial is to show you that any single built-in method can be linear. Specifically, it demonstrates that **open** occurs from the outer form object inward, object after object, in a linear fashion.

Tutorial: The Event Model Can Be Linear

The following tutorial demonstrates that a single, built-in method can trigger in a linear fashion.

On Disk: \ANSWERS\OPEN.FSL

Quick Steps

1. Put `msgInfo()` in the **open** method of the form, page, and all objects in the page.
2. Run the form. Note that the order of the message boxes is from outer container inward in a linear fashion.

Step By Step

1. Change your working directory to the TUTORIAL directory and create a new form with a box, a button, and a field on it (see Figure 7.1).

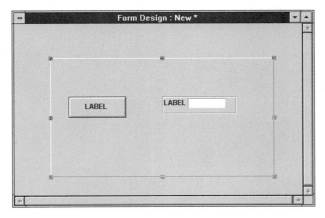

Figure 7.1. Set up form for tutorial.

2. To display a message when the form is opened, add line 8 to the form's **open** method.

```
1:    ;Form :: open
2:    method open(var eventInfo Event)
3:       if eventInfo.isPreFilter()
4:          then
5:             ;This code executes for each object on the form
6:          else
7:             ;This code executes only for the form
8:             msgInfo("Form :: Open", "Triggered by Form ::
                 Open")
9:       endif
10:   endmethod
```

3. To display a message when the page is opened, add line 3 to the page's **open** method.

```
1:    ;Page :: open
2:    method open(var eventInfo Event)
3:       msgInfo("Page :: Open", "Triggered by Page :: Open")
4:    endmethod
```

4. To display a message when the box is opened, add line 3 to the box's open method.

```
1:     ;Page.Box :: open
2:     method open(var eventInfo Event)
3:         msgInfo("Box :: Open", "Triggered by Box :: Open")
4:     endmethod
```

5. To display a message when the field is opened, add line 3 to the field's open method.

```
1:     ;Page.Box.Field :: open
2:     method open(var eventInfo Event)
3:         msgInfo("Field :: Open", "Triggered by Field :: Open")
4:     endmethod
```

6. To display a message when the button is opened, add line 3 to the button's open method.

```
1:     ;Page.Box.Button :: open
2:     method open(var eventInfo Event)
3:         msgInfo("Button :: Open", "Triggered by Button ::
            Open")
4:     endmethod
```

7. Check the syntax, save the form as OPEN.FSL, and run it. Note the order of the message information boxes. Your form should look similar to \ANSWERS\OPEN.FSL (see Figure 7.2).

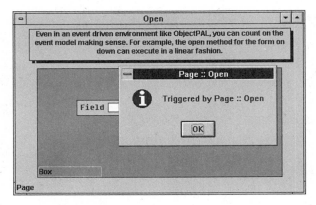

Figure 7.2. \ANSWERS\OPEN.FSL.

Analysis

The form is the highest container in ObjectPAL. It always contains at least one page. You place objects such as fields, table frames, and buttons inside a page. All UIObjects, including both forms and pages, have an **open** built-in method. Code in the **open** method is triggered whenever the object is opened. When you launch a form, first the form is opened, and then the page is opened. The code on the form's **open** built-in method is triggered before the code on the page's **open** built-in method. When you run this tutorial, you'll see that msgInfo() is executed from the top container downward: the form, the page, then UIObjects inside the page.

The five message information boxes you just saw are executed in a linear fashion. When the box and the button are on the same level, however, they both can't execute at the same time. What dictates the order of execution? The containership hierarchy determines which code is executed first. Generally, the order in which objects are placed on the page dictates which object is opened first. For an experiment, place a larger box around both of these objects, and alternate moving them onto the page level. What do you expect to happen? Try it and find out.

> You can alter the path of objects by moving objects around in the containership hierarchy. Move objects on the same level by selecting Design | Bring to Front and Design | Send to Back.

Although ObjectPAL and Paradox can execute in a linear fashion—that is, one built-in method executes after another—you don't program ObjectPAL in a linear fashion. When you program in Paradox, think, "What object do I want to alter?" For example, if you want to check a value in a field after the user enters it, go to that field and put code on the built-in **canDepart** method. You can use **canDepart** to check the field's contents before it permits the cursor to leave the field.

Default Behavior Occurs Last

The default behavior of the built-in **open** method is to open the objects within it. When exactly does an object open? All default behavior occurs just before endMethod.

Take a closer look at the built-in methods **open** and **arrive** and when the default behavior occurs. An object is always opened before it is arrived on. Therefore, code in the **open** method always executes before code in the **arrive** method. Any code that you want to execute as a form opens or before a form opens goes in the **open** method. Any code that you want to execute after a form opens goes in the **arrive** method. The **arrive** method is a good place for code that requires user interface objects, because UIObjects aren't opened until the end of the **open** method (just before `endMethod`).

Tutorial: Default Behavior Occurs Last

The goal of this tutorial is to demonstrate the difference between **open** and **arrive**, and to demonstrate that the default behavior occurs just before the keyword `endMethod`.

On Disk: \ANSWERS\LAST.FSL

Quick Steps

1. Put `msgInfo()` in both the **open** and **arrive** methods of the form.
2. Run the form. Note the order of the message boxes.
3. Put an undefined field on the form.
4. In the **open** method of the form, assign a value to the field.
5. Run the form. The value doesn't get put in the field.
6. Put `doDefault` before the `assign` statement and run the form again.
7. When you run the form again, note the value changes.

Step By Step

1. Change your working directory to the TUTORIAL directory and create a new form with a field on it. Name the field *fldTest* (see Figure 7.3).

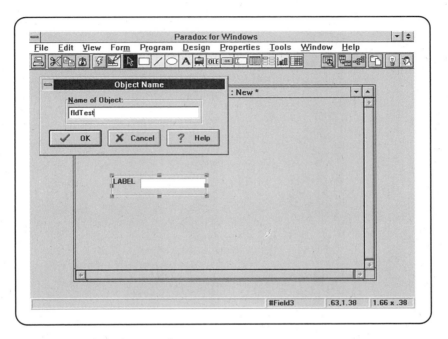

Figure 7.3. Set up form for tutorial.

2. To display a message and try to assign a value to the field *fldTest* when the form is opened, add lines 8 and 9 to the form's **open** method.

```
 1:    ;#Form1 :: open
 2:    method open(var eventInfo Event)
 3:        if eventInfo.isPreFilter()
 4:            then
 5:            ;This code executes for each object on the form
 6:        else
 7:            ;This code executes only for the form
 8:            fldTest.value = "text from open method"
 9:            msgInfo("Form", "open method")
10:        endif
11:    endmethod
```

3. To display a message when you **arrive** on the form, add line 8 to the form's **arrive** method.

```
1:    ;#Form1 :: arrive
2:    method arrive(var eventInfo MoveEvent)
3:       if eventInfo.isPreFilter()
4:          then
5:             ;This code executes for each object on the form
6:          else
7:             ;This code executes only for the form
8:             msgInfo("Form", "arrive method")
9:          endif
10:   endmethod
```

4. Check the syntax, save the form as LAST.FSL, and run it. Note that the message information box for the **open** method shows before the one for the **arrive** method. In addition, note that the value from step 2, line 8 never makes it to the field.

5. Add a doDefault just before the assignment in the **open** method (see line 8 that follows).

```
1:    ;#Form1 :: open
2:    method open(var eventInfo Event)
3:       if eventInfo.isPreFilter()
4:          then
5:             ;This code executes for each object on the form
6:          else
7:             ;This code executes only for the form
8:             DoDefault
9:             fldTest.value = "text from open method"
10:            msgInfo("Form", "open method")
11:         endif
12:   endmethod
```

6. Check the syntax, save the form, and run it. Note that with the doDefault the value does make it to the field *fldTest*. Your form should look similar to \ANSWERS\LAST.FSL (see Figure 7.4).

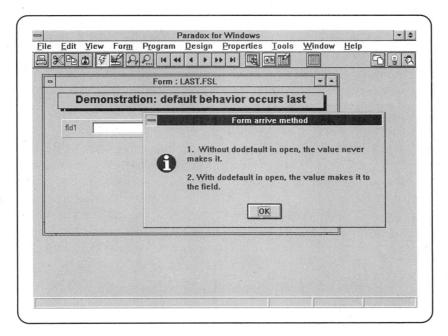

Figure 7.4. \ANSWERS\LAST.FSL.

Analysis

The default built-in behavior always occurs just before endMethod. Using keywords such as doDefault and disableDefault, you as the programmer have full control over if and when the default behavior occurs.

BUILT-IN METHODS ARE THE EVENT MODEL

Objects in ObjectPAL come with built-in methods, or triggers, for each event to which an object can respond. As stated before, the part of ObjectPAL that sets up triggers that are trapped for when the user interacts with the application is called an *event handler*.

Built-in methods specify an object's default behavior in response to a certain event. Sometimes an event is used by an object, and sometimes it's passed to another built-in method. This using and passing of events is known as the *event model*—a map of the order in which events are triggered in an event handler. You cannot see this hidden code, but it is there and you can effect it—for example, with `doDefault`, `disableDefault`, and `enableDefault`.

Events can be generated by a user action—such as moving the mouse or pressing a key—or by ObjectPAL. An event generated by ObjectPAL usually is generated or called from a user's actions. So, in a sense, all events are started in one way or another by the user. Thinking of the event model in this simplified way is a good way to program. An **open** event occurs because the user chooses File | Open | Form. It's easier to think of a user opening a form, which causes the **open** method to trigger, than it is to think of the built-in **open** method as a method that receives an internal event generated by ObjectPAL.

Likewise, when a user clicks a button, the button's **pushButton** method is triggered, right? Wrong. **pushButton** is an internal method that is called by the external method **mouseUp** only when the cursor is inside the boundaries of the button. It's much easier, however, to think that when the user clicks a button, several built-in methods are triggered in order—**mouseDown**, **mouseUp**, **mouseClick**, and **pushButton**. There are times when it's important to understand that **mouseUp** calls **pushButton** only when the cursor is within the boundaries of the button. Even so, most of the time you can think in terms of simple user actions.

Understanding the event model is key to understanding ObjectPAL. The better you know when code executes, the better and cleaner your applications will be. Although you usually use **pushButton** when you program a button, occasionally you will want to use **mouseDown**, **mouseUp**, or **mouseClick**. Understanding what the differences are is important.

The form \ANSWERS\BUTTON.FSL demonstrates the order of execution of a button's **mouseDown**, **mouseUp**, **mouseClick**, and **pushButton** methods. In addition, it demonstrates **mouseEnter** and **mouseExit**.

SOME EVENT MODEL RULES

There are many rules that govern the event model. The following are some introductory rules to keep in mind:

- All events generate a packet of information. This event packet contains information on what generated the event, the target of the next event, and more. Events are generated either by ObjectPAL or by a user interacting with a form. A few examples of methods for which ObjectPAL generates events are open, arrive, and depart. A few examples of methods for which a user generates events are **mouseClick**, **keyChar**, and **menuAction**.

- All events go to the form first. If the target is an object other than the form, the event goes through the form's prefilter and the event is sent to the target. This is important because the prefilter of the form is a great location to code certain types of generic code.

- Internal events are passed from the form's prefilter to the target object. Internal events, discussed in detail in the next section, are events triggered from within Paradox.

- External events, like internal events, are passed from the form's prefilter to the target object. Unlike internal events, however, external events can bubble back up to the form.

INTERNAL, EXTERNAL, AND SPECIAL BUILT-IN METHODS

Built-in methods are triggered by internal, external, and special events. These three categories of built-in methods follow very specific rules. Table 7.1 lists the built-in methods.

TABLE 7.1. BUILT-IN METHODS.

Internal	External	Special
open	**mouseClick**	**pushButton**
close	**mouseDown**	**changeValue**

continues

	TABLE 7.1. CONTINUED	
Internal	*External*	*Special*
canArrive	mouseUp	newValue
arrive	mouseDouble	
setFocus	mouseRightDown	
canDepart	mouseRightUp	
removeFocus	mouseRightDouble	
depart	mouseMove	
mouseEnter	keyPhysical	
mouseExit	keyChar	
timer	error	
	status	
	action	
	menuAction	

Internal Built-In Methods

Internal built-in methods are triggered by events generated by Paradox. A good case study example of an internal event is **open**. **open** occurs from outer container inward. The form is opened, then the page, then the objects in the page. **canArrive**, **arrive**, and **setFocus** also trigger from outer container in.

Their counterparts **close**, **canDepart**, and **depart** trigger from inner container out. To study this, suppose that you have a field inside a box on the first page of a form and you try to **close** the form. In what order do the various object's **canDepart** methods trigger? First, the **canDepart** for the field is triggered, or called. Then its container, the box's **canDepart**, is triggered, then finally the box's container, the page **canDepart**, is triggered. **close**, **canDepart**, and **depart** are called—triggered—from inner container outward.

Like external events, internal events go first to the form and then to the target object. Unlike external and special events, internal events stop at the target. In other words, the complete path for an internal event is sent to the form and back to the object. Table 7.2 describes the internal built-in methods. The concept of bubbling back up to the form does not exist for internal events.

	TABLE 7.2. INTERNAL BUILT-IN METHODS.	

Method	Short Description
open	Triggered once for every object when the form is opened
close	Triggered once for every object when the form is closed
canArrive	Triggered before moving to an object
canDepart	Triggered before moving off an object
arrive	Triggered after moving to an object
depart	Triggered after moving off an object
setFocus	Occurs whenever an object gets the focus
removeFocus	Occurs whenever an object loses the focus
mouseEnter	Generated whenever the mouse pointer enters an object
mouseExit	Generated whenever the mouse pointer exits an object
timer	Triggered at a time interval specified by the programmer

Default Behavior of Internal Events

Take a closer look at the default behavior of each internal built-in method. Internal methods are always called either from other internal methods or from an external built-in event. There is much built-in default behavior in Paradox. The following paragraphs describe the internal built-in methods and their default behavior.

Every object has to be opened. The **open** event is called only once for every object, starting with the form, then the page, then the objects contained by the page, and finally the objects contained within that container. After the first page is completely open, the process starts over with the next page in the form. Remember that the prefilter of the form sees the **open** event before the target object sees it. The default code for **open** calls the **open** method for each of the objects it contains. Then, the **open** method for each one of those objects calls the **open** method for the objects it contains, and so on. The default behavior for the **close** method acts in the same way but in reverse. If a table is bound to the object, the object also opens the table. Any errors will abort the **open** process.

The form \ANSWERS\OPEN2.FSL demonstrates the **open** method and the prefilter section of the form's **open** method.

The **canArrive** method is interesting. It occurs before movement to an object is permitted. Think of **canArrive** as asking permission to move to the object. Contrary to what is implied in the manuals, **canArrive** is not used just for restricting entrance to a field. You can use this method to execute almost any kind of code just before arriving on an object. The **canArrive** method blocks arrival for records beyond the end of a table—except, of course, when you are in Edit mode and the Auto-Append option is checked in the data model. Any object whose tab stop property is unchecked also is blocked.

The **arrive** method is executed after movement has arrived on an object. An **arrive** method can be called only after a **canArrive** method. Pages, table frames, and multirecord objects move to the first tab stop object they contain. When you **arrive** on a field or a record, the object is made current; if you're in Edit mode, an edit window is created for the edit region of a field. If the object is a drop-down edit list, the focus moves to the list. If the object is a radio button, the focus moves to the first button.

The **setFocus** method occurs every time an object gets the focus. If the object getting the focus is contained in another object, **setFocus** is called for each container—from the outer-most container inward. For example, if a page contains a box, which contains a field, **setFocus** is triggered first for the page, next for the box, and then for the field. In an edit field, the default code highlights the currently selected edit region and causes the insertion point to blink. The focus property is set to True, and the status message reports the number of the current record and the total number of records. For buttons, if the tab stop property is set, a dotted rectangle is displayed around the label.

The **canDepart** method is triggered before a move off an object. Field objects try to post their contents and trip **changeValue**. If the record is a changed record, the object tries to commit the current record. If the record is locked, the form tries to unlock it.

The **removeFocus** method occurs when an object loses the focus. On field objects, the flashing insertion point and highlight are removed. On a button, the dotted rectangle is removed. The object's focus property is set to False. This is called for the active object and its containers.

After **canDepart** and **removeFocus** have executed successfully, the **depart** method is called. Field objects close their edit windows, then repaint and clean up the screen.

The **mouseEnter** method is generated whenever the mouse pointer enters an object. Form, page, and button objects set the pointer to an arrow. Field objects set the pointer to an I-beam. If a button is still down, its value toggles between True and False.

The **mouseExit** method is generated whenever the mouse pointer exits an object. Field objects set the pointer back to the arrow.

External Built-In Methods

External built-in methods are events generated by the user interacting with a form and by ObjectPAL. Both internal and external events go first to the form and then to the target object. External events, however, unlike internal events, bubble back up to the form. The default behavior for an external method is to pass the event to its container, which is how it bubbles up to the form. External built-in methods are generated when a user interacts with the user interface. Table 7.3 describes the external built-in methods.

TABLE 7.3. EXTERNAL BUILT-IN METHODS.

Method	Short Description
mouseMove	Occurs whenever the mouse moves
mouseDown	Occurs when the left mouse button is pressed
mouseUp	Occurs when the left mouse button is released
mouseClick	Occurs when the pointer is inside an object and the left mouse button is pressed and released

continues

	TABLE 7.3. CONTINUED	
Method	*Short Description*	
mouseDouble	Occurs when the left mouse button is double-clicked	
mouseRightDown	Occurs when the right mouse button is pressed	
mouseRightUp	Occurs when the right mouse button is released	
mouseRightDouble	Occurs when the right mouse button is double-clicked	
keyPhysical	Occurs whenever any key is pressed	
keyChar	Occurs whenever a character key is pressed	
action	Executes when a keystroke or menu option maps to an action	
menuAction	Occurs when a menu option or a Toolbar icon is selected	
error	Occurs whenever an error is encountered	
status	Occurs whenever a message is displayed in the status bar	

Default Behavior of External Events

Now take a closer look at the default behavior of each external built-in method. The following paragraphs explain the default behavior of the external built-in methods that do something in addition to bubbling their events.

The **mouseDown** method occurs when the left mouse button is pressed. The event packet for **mouseDown** contains the mouse coordinates in twips (1/1440 of an inch) relative to the last object that executed a **mouseEnter** method. If the object is a field that is active, the field is put into Field View. If the object is a button, its value is toggled between True and False.

The **mouseRightDown** method occurs when the right mouse button is pressed. It is the same as the **mouseDown** method, except that it uses the right mouse button instead. If the object is a formatted memo, a graphic, OLE, or an undefined field, a pop-up menu is displayed.

The **mouseUp** method occurs when the left mouse button is released. **mouseUp** is called for the last object that received a **mouseDown** method. Therefore, an object always sees the **mouseDown** and **mouseUp** methods in a pair. If you select text, **mouseUp** ends the selection. If the object is a button and the pointer is still inside the button, **mouseUp** calls the **pushButton** method. The **mouseRightUp** method is the same as the **mouseUp** method, except that it uses the right mouse button instead.

The **mouseDouble** method occurs when the left mouse button is double-clicked. A field object enters Field View. The **mouseRightDouble** method is the same as the **mouseDouble** method, except that it uses the right mouse button.

The movement of the mouse is tracked with the **mouseMove** method. Whenever the pointer is moved within an object, the **mouseMove** method is triggered.

The **keyPhysical** method occurs whenever any key is pressed and each time a key is autorepeated. **keyPhysical** includes all the physical keys on the keyboard, including the character keys, the function keys, and the Alt, Ctrl, and Esc keys. The **keyChar** method, on the other hand, triggers only when a character key is pressed. A keystroke goes first to Windows and then to Paradox, which gives it to the form's prefilter. The form sends it to the active object for processing. The object's **keyPhysical** determines whether the keystroke represents an action or a display character. Actions are passed to the **action** method, and display characters are passed to **keyChar**.

The **keyChar** method occurs whenever a character key is pressed. Actually, the **keyPhysical** method for the active object sends action events such as `DataNextRecord` to the action method, and it sends characters such as `a` to **keyChar**. If the active object is a field in Edit mode, a lock is put on the table before the first character is inserted. If the active object is a button and the character is a spacebar, the button's **pushButton** method is called. Remember a button can be active only if its Tab Stop option is set to True.

The **action** method is called frequently. It executes when it is sent an action keystroke from **keyPhysical**, when **menuAction** maps to a menu option, or when a method such as `DataPostRecord` calls for an action. The default behavior for **action** is extensive because all actions go through it. For example, Page Down moves to the next record, F9 toggles Edit mode, and Insert inserts a record only if the form is in Edit mode.

The **menuAction** method occurs when a menu option, a Toolbar icon, or an option from the Control box is selected. The option is sent first to the form's **action** method for processing and then to the active object.

The **error** method occurs right after an error is encountered. You shouldn't test for errors with the built-in error method. Use action instead. An error is passed to its container until it gets to the form. The form might or might not display a message, depending on the severity of the error. You can trap for errors and alter the default behavior in the **action** method before the error gets to the **error** method. You can use the **error** method to add to the built-in default error behavior.

The **status** method occurs whenever a message is displayed on the status bar. The default behavior of **status** is too extensive to be described here. In short, any time you see a message in one of the four status areas, an event has gone through the built-in **status** method.

Special Built-In Methods

Special built-in methods are specific to a few objects, such as **newValue** of a field. Table 7.4 describes the special built-in methods.

Method	Description
TABLE 7.4. SPECIAL BUILT-IN METHODS.	
pushButton	Occurs whenever you click a button
newValue	Triggered whenever the value in a field changes
changeValue	Triggered whenever the value in a table changes

Default Behavior of the Special Built-In Methods

The following paragraphs explain the default behavior of the special built-in methods.

The only UIObjects that have a **pushButton** method are buttons and fields displayed as a list box. The form has a **pushButton** method because it dispatches it with its prefilter clause. **pushButton** occurs when the pointer is inside an object for both the **mouseDown** and **mouseUp** methods. In fact, **mouseUp** calls **pushButton**. Button objects visually depress and pop out. Check boxes check or uncheck. Radio buttons push in or pop out. If the Tab Stop property is set to True, the focus moves to it.

The **newValue** method is triggered after the value in a field changes. **newValue** is triggered even if the value is changed only on screen.

The **changeValue** method on a defined field, on the other hand, is triggered by a change in a table. The **changeValue** method on an undefined field is triggered when the value in the field changes.

The **changeValue** method is triggered before a value in a table is changed. If you have code on both **changeValue** and **newValue**, the code on **changeValue** occurs first—that is, before the value changes. **newValue** is triggered after the value changes. Therefore, if you want to do validity checks on a field, **changeValue** is a good place to put them.

TRACING THE EVENT MODEL

Although the Debugger is not introduced until Chapter 29, "Dealing with Errors," the Tracer—one feature of the debugger—is introduced now to help demonstrate the event model.

Tutorial: Tracing the Event Model

In this tutorial, you study the built-in action method. Your goal is to use the Tracer to demonstrate the event model and default behavior.

Quick Steps
1. Open the Tracer by selecting View | Tracer.
2. Choose Properties | Trace Built-Ins.
3. In the Select Built-In Methods for Tracing dialog box, choose a built-in method to trace.

Step By Step
1. Create a new form by selecting File | New | Form.
2. Open the Editor window for the action method of the form.
3. Open the Tracer by selecting View | Tracer.

4. From the Tracer window, choose Properties | Built-Ins.

5. This dialog box lists all the built-in methods you can trace. In the Select Built-In Methods for Tracing dialog box, choose select All and click on OK (see Figure 7.5).

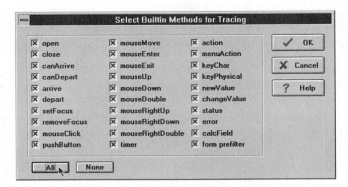

Figure 7.5. The Select Built-in Methods for Tracing dialog box.

6. Make sure that Properties | Trace On is checked (see Figure 7.6).

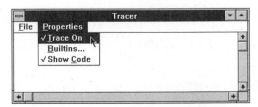

Figure 7.6. The Tracer window.

7. Run the form (there is no need to save the form). Note how many events occur even on an empty form (see Figure 7.7).

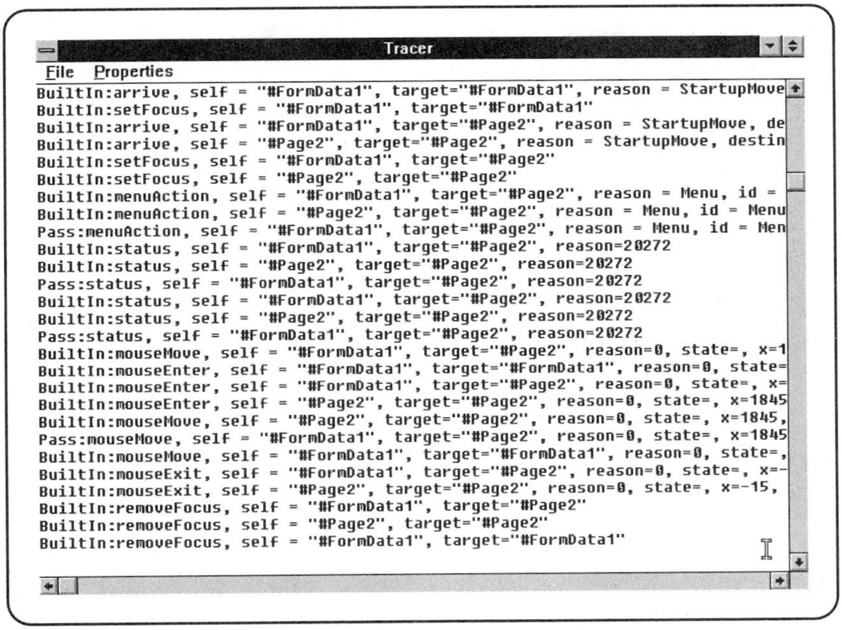

```
┌──────────────────────────────────────────────────────────────┐
│ ─                          Tracer                      ▼ │ ♦ │
├──────────────────────────────────────────────────────────────┤
│  File   Properties                                             │
│ BuiltIn:arrive, self = "#FormData1", target="#FormData1", reason = StartupMove ▲
│ BuiltIn:setFocus, self = "#FormData1", target="#FormData1"     │
│ BuiltIn:arrive, self = "#FormData1", target="#Page2", reason = StartupMove, de
│ BuiltIn:arrive, self = "#Page2", target="#Page2", reason = StartupMove, destin
│ BuiltIn:setFocus, self = "#FormData1", target="#Page2"         │
│ BuiltIn:setFocus, self = "#Page2", target="#Page2"             │
│ BuiltIn:menuAction, self = "#FormData1", target="#Page2", reason = Menu, id =
│ BuiltIn:menuAction, self = "#Page2", target="#Page2", reason = Menu, id = Menu
│ Pass:menuAction, self = "#FormData1", target="#Page2", reason = Menu, id = Men
│ BuiltIn:status, self = "#FormData1", target="#Page2", reason=20272
│ BuiltIn:status, self = "#Page2", target="#Page2", reason=20272
│ Pass:status, self = "#FormData1", target="#Page2", reason=20272
│ BuiltIn:status, self = "#FormData1", target="#Page2", reason=20272
│ BuiltIn:status, self = "#Page2", target="#Page2", reason=20272
│ Pass:status, self = "#FormData1", target="#Page2", reason=20272
│ BuiltIn:mouseMove, self = "#FormData1", target="#Page2", reason=0, state=, x=1
│ BuiltIn:mouseEnter, self = "#FormData1", target="#FormData1", reason=0, state=
│ BuiltIn:mouseEnter, self = "#FormData1", target="#Page2", reason=0, state=, x=
│ BuiltIn:mouseEnter, self = "#Page2", target="#Page2", reason=0, state=, x=1845
│ BuiltIn:mouseMove, self = "#Page2", target="#Page2", reason=0, state=, x=1845,
│ Pass:mouseMove, self = "#FormData1", target="#Page2", reason=0, state=, x=1845
│ BuiltIn:mouseMove, self = "#FormData1", target="#FormData1", reason=0, state=,
│ BuiltIn:mouseExit, self = "#FormData1", target="#Page2", reason=0, state=, x=-
│ BuiltIn:mouseExit, self = "#Page2", target="#Page2", reason=0, state=, x=-15,
│ BuiltIn:removeFocus, self = "#FormData1", target="#Page2"      │
│ BuiltIn:removeFocus, self = "#Page2", target="#Page2"          │
│ BuiltIn:removeFocus, self = "#FormData1", target="#FormData1"   I ▼
├──────────────────────────────────────────────────────────────┤
│ ←│                                                          │→ │
└──────────────────────────────────────────────────────────────┘
```

Figure 7.7. The Tracer tracing code.

Analysis

Tracing one or two built-in methods at a time is a great way to get acquainted with the event model. Take some time right now—perhaps 30 minutes—to try tracing various combinations of built-in methods.

Tutorial: Tracing Your Own Code

This tutorial demonstrates how to use the tracer to trace just your code. Suppose that while you are developing an application, an error occurs and you have no idea what code is causing the error.

Quick Steps

1. Open a form that has code in it.
2. In the Tracer, turn on Properties | Show Code.
3. Run the form.

Step By Step

1. Change your working directory to the TUTORIAL directory and open
   the OV-LIKE.FSL form that you created in Chapter 4. If you skipped
   that tutorial (shame on you), change your working directory to the
   ANSWER directory and open up the OV-LIKE.FSL form (see Figure 7.8).

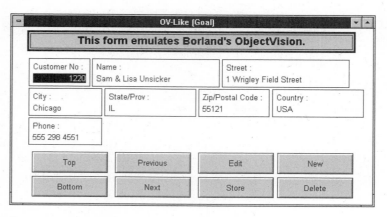

Figure 7.8. \ANSWERS\OV-LIKE.FSL

2. Open the Editor window for any built-in method.

3. Select View | Tracer to open the Tracer.

4. Select Properties | Builtins and make sure that no built-in methods
   are selected for tracing.

5. Make sure that Properites | Trace On and Properties | Show Code
   are checked.

6. Run the form, select the various buttons, and see what happens (see
   Figure 7.9).

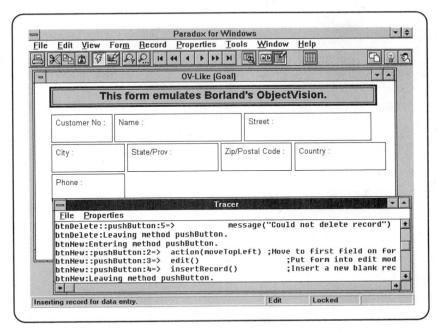

Figure 7.9. Using the Tracer to trace your own code.

Analysis

You can use the Tracer for two purposes: to analyze the built-in methods and/ or to analyze your code. When analyzing or debugging your code, the Tracer is great for finding the location of bugs.

SPEED UP TRACE EXECUTION

Problem: Tracing execution on a large form is very time consuming.

Reason: The tracer updates the screen every time it executes a line of code. As usual in a GUI, screen updates dramatically slow you down.

Solution: Shrink the trace execution window as small as possible. When you wish to see the trace execution, then open the window. Here are the steps:

1. Run it.

2. Press Ctrl+Break.

3. Minimize it.

This solution works so well, you can now just leave the trace execution windows minimized on your screen.

THE EVENT PACKET

When you open a form interactively, many events are generated by ObjectPAL. The form opens and then the prefilter tells the page to open by sending an event to it. Understanding the sending and receiving of events is understanding the event model.

Whenever a method is called, an information packet is generated. This information packet often is passed from one method to the next. This information is called the event packet. You can read any value in the event packet with the **eventInfo** variable. Table 7.5 describes the different types of events.

TABLE 7.5. TYPES OF EVENTS.

Type of Event	Information about	Built-in methods
ActionEvent	Editing and navigating a table	**action**
ErrorEvent	Errors	**error**
Event	Base event type from which all others are derived—inherited	**open, close, setFocus, removeFocus, newValue, and pushButton**
KeyEvent	Keystroke events	**keyChar and keyPhysical**

Type of Event	Information about	Built-in methods
MenuEvent	Menu selections	menuAction
MouseEvent	The mouse and pointer	mouseClick, mouseDown, mouseUp, mouseDouble, mouseRightUp, mouseRightDown, mouseRightDouble, mouseMove, mouseEnter, and mouseExit
MoveEvent	Navigating from field to field	arrive, canArrive, canDepart, and depart
StatusEvent	Messages in the status line	status
TimerEvent	Events at specified intervals	timer
ValueEvent	Changes to a field's value	changeValue

The type of *eventInfo* a method generates is declared in its prototype syntax. Every time you open the ObjectPAL Editor for a built-in method, Paradox automatically prototypes the built-in method for you: the first line of every built-in method. For built-in methods, simply go into the method, and it will tell you on the first line what type of event the *eventInfo* variable is. Take a look at a button's built-in pushButton method:

```
1:   ;Button :: pushButton
2:   method pushButton(var eventInfo Event)
3:
4:   endmethod
```

Notice var eventInfo Event in parentheses. In this prototype, *eventInfo* is a variable that is declared as an Event. This is important because it tells you what types of methods can be used to extract and set information in the *eventInfo* variable. With **pushButton**, all the event methods can be used.

Next, look at the **keyPhysical** method of a field.

```
1:    ;Field :: keyPhysical
2:    method keyPhysical(var eventInfo KeyEvent)
3:
4:    endmethod
```

eventInfo is defined as a `KeyEvent`. This indicates that you can use any of the `KeyEvent` methods to extract and deal with the event information. To see a list of all the methods that work with `KeyEvent`, select Tools | Types to bring up the Types and Methods dialog box, and then `KeyEvent` from the Types panel (see Figure 7.10).

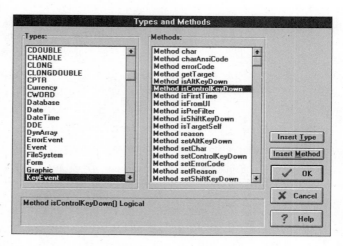

Figure 7.10. The Types and Methods dialog box.

You can use any of the **KeyEvent** methods in the **keyPhysical** or **keyChar** methods to deal with and alter an event created by the keyboard. For example, to prevent all Ctrl keystroke combinations on a certain field, alter the field's **keyPhysical** as follows:

```
1:    ;Field :: keyPhysical
2:    method keyPhysical(var eventInfo KeyEvent)
3:       if eventInfo.isControlKeyDown() then
4:          disableDefault
5:          msgInfo("", "Control key combinations are invalid here")
6:       endIf
7:    endmethod
```

In this routine, the Ctrl key is trapped for, and `disableDefault` prevents the default behavior.

THE PATH OF *eventInfo* FROM FIELD TO FIELD

One important part of the event model is the sequence of execution from field to field. Figure 7.11 shows the sequence of execution of the built-in methods when moving from field to field.

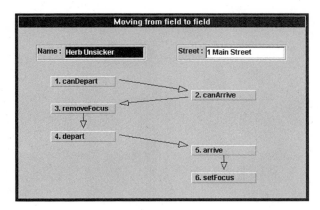

Figure 7.11. The sequence of events from field to field.

MANIPULATING DEFAULT BEHAVIOR

The default behavior for built-in methods was described earlier in this chapter. The preceding section introduced you to the *eventInfo* packet. To use and manipulate the default behavior, you must understand the default behavior and the *eventInfo* packet. You can use the following keywords and variables to control the default behavior: `disableDefault`, `doDefault`, `enableDefault`, and `passEvent`.

`disableDefault` prevents the built-in behavior from executing. Normally, the default behavior is executed just before `endMethod`. `doDefault` explicitly executes the default behavior ahead of time. If you have disabled the default behavior—at the beginning of the method, for example—you can re-enable it with `enableDefault`. `passEvent` passes an event to the object's container.

This chapter formally introduced you to the event model. The event model is the core piece to understanding how and where to program in ObjectPAL. You will revisit the event model many times. For example, in Chapter 19, "Manipulating Strings and Handling the Keyboard," you will take a close look at the path of a key press and later, in Part IV, you'll revisit the event model for an advanced discussion. The next chapter discusses where you should put code.

WHERE TO PUT CODE

One of the hardest aspects of using ObjectPAL is deciding where to place code. Novice ObjectPAL programmers tend to place code everywhere. Rather than work with the default behavior, the event model, and the data model, beginners often tend to put code in the wrong place. Later, they add more code to try to fix an inelegant approach.

Programmers who use DOS PAL and traditional procedural languages are used to writing a lot of code. In the Windows version of Paradox, they tend to overcode to get the results they want. Understanding the system can make the difference between inelegant and elegant code.

Taking the time to understand the default behavior of objects, the event model, and the data model can save you much time. If you don't fully understand how an object works, you could end up working harder and accomplishing less. Much of this book deals with this issue. This chapter concentrates on it and offers guidelines, tips, and techniques on where and when to code.

Code placement

Levels of code

Global versus private code

Using built-in methods in combination

Don't Overcode

When new users to Paradox begin writing code in ObjectPAL, they often write tremendous amounts of code. The amount of code can become overwhelming if you don't understand the fundamentals of the product.

Usually you follow certain steps whenever you develop an application. Before writing a single line of ObjectPAL code, you always should build the data model and arrange the form until it's similar to what you want. Then, run the form and work with it to see what it does and doesn't do. When you find something that you want to work differently, ask yourself, "What do I want to happen?" and "When do I want it to happen?" Try to do this for only one task or object at a time. In other words, develop in small steps.

Go back and forth between Design mode and Run mode and test your work incrementally. When you're done coding and testing a single object, move to the next. By refining your application in steps, you end up with functioning code in bite-sized chunks. If you try to tackle in one step all the work that an application requires, you can easily end up frustrated, with messy code. Remember, program and test one task at a time.

Watch Out for Spaghetti Code

BASIC, early Pascal, and early C promoted spaghetti code—intertwined code with many repeated parts. These procedural languages required you to write line after line of code. Although modern languages don't lend themselves to spaghetti code, it's still possible to write it. During the development process, you might copy a routine from one spot to another and later find a bug in it. You would have two pieces of code to correct. This is fine if you are perfect and can remember to change both pieces of code. But this method of programming is hard on upkeep, and it makes reusing code nearly impossible. You would have to start every new project from scratch.

Use an Object-Oriented Methodology

Object-oriented programming involves compartmentalizing and reusing code. Your goal should be to avoid duplicating code by developing self-contained, reusable units. After a while, you will spend the majority of your developing time copying, pasting, and putting together previously developed units. When a bug in a certain unit turns up, you can debug that one unit, and every application from that point on that uses that unit is cleaned up or enhanced. In addition, when you enhance some code that many applications share, those applications are enhanced instantly.

Keep in mind that you can still write spaghetti code in ObjectPAL. If you duplicate parts, you inevitably introduce bugs into your application. ObjectPAL, however, promotes good programming. If you follow the rules of object-oriented methodology, develop in compartments, and avoid duplicating code, your programs will be clean.

LOCALIZE CODE

Because you're programming in ObjectPAL (an object-based programming language), the code should be as local to the object as possible. For example, if you're trying to decide to put code on a button or the form, then choose the button. If the situation warrants moving up to the form level, it will become obvious. There are many benefits for coding as low as possible, including the ability to copy objects with code on them from one form to another and still have it work.

Whenever you have a choice, try adding ObjectPAL code directly to the object to get the desired results. Do you ever want to not code locally? Yes—when you want to work with more than one of the same object. You can use a container above all the objects and put code on the object's container.

CODE AS LOW AS POSSIBLE

Put code on the lowest possible container. If you later need to use the same code elsewhere, move the code up the container path to the lowest container that both objects can see. If you follow this rule, your code will be compartmental-ized and portable. By developing in compartments, you keep code segments apart. A bug introduced in one compartment is less likely to affect other parts of your application.

If you are programming a button, put all the code, including variables, on the button. This makes the button a self-contained unit that is easily copied and pasted to other forms. If you later need that same code on another button, convert it to a custom method and move it up the container path to the button's container object. A container object is an object that completely surrounds and controls the behavior of all the objects within it.

If you then decide you need to use the code with several pages within the form, then move the custom method to the form. If you need the same routine in several forms, consider putting it in a library. A library is an object that stores custom ObjectPAL code. Libraries are useful for storing and maintaining frequently used routines, and for sharing custom methods and variables among forms.

Using this general rule of coding as low to the object as possible gives you maximum access to your code and saves you time. In addition, if you later find a problem with the routine, you need to correct it in only one spot; instantly, all code that uses the routine benefits from the improvement.

Although you can write spaghetti code with an object-based language, ObjectPAL supports and promotes good object-oriented practices. By using contained objects and custom methods properly, you can keep your code clean. Develop in self-contained units whose code is protected from other objects.

LEVELS OF CODE

As I have hinted, in an ObjectPAL application, you put code on various levels. You can put code on objects, on the object's container, on the page, on the form, or even in a library. When you place code in your application, imagine that you are placing your code at various levels. The levels of coding are as follows:

- Script
- Library
- Form
- Page
- Container in a page—for example, a box object
- Object on a page or in a container—for example, a field object
- Elements of an object—for example, the record object of a table frame
- The table level—for example, picture strings and other validity checks

Script Level

A script is an object consisting of ObjectPAL code that a user can run independently of a form or that can be called from ObjectPAL. Unlike forms and reports, scripts have no objects. Unlike libraries, scripts can be run without ObjectPAL. You will hardly ever use the script level in a project. It's useful, though, for enabling the user to execute code without opening a form. You occasionally might use the script level to start off an application—perhaps for setting up data for a form, such as adding or deleting records. Another use for scripts is to enable the user to run part of the code without launching the whole application. You will seldom use either of these techniques.

Library Level

A library is a good place to put code that you need to call from multiple forms. Many ObjectPAL programmers think of the library as a way to code above the highest container—the form. Libraries are discussed in Chapter 23, "Storing and Centralizing Code." For now, just remember that a library is a place to put code that is shared among forms.

The Form Level

The form actually has two levels: a prefilter and a form level. All events go through the form's prefilter, and external events can go to the form twice. First, the event is prefiltered, and then it is sent to the target and can bubble back up to the form. If you want to intercept another object's built-in method, use the form's prefilter. Think of the prefilter as a special level and the `else` part of the form's `if` statement as the form level. For example, if you want to do something after the form is opened, use the `else` portion of the form's built-in **arrive** method. If you want to trap for an error so that you can do something in addition to the built-in behavior, use the form's `else` portion of the **error** method. If you wish to trap for an error before it happens, then most likely the built-in **action** method is where you will want to code. If you wish to write generic code that does something every time you arrive on any one of a set of fields, then use the prefilter of the form's **arrive** method.

The arrive Method of a Form

Immediately after an object opens, the **arrive** method occurs. The form's **arrive** is a good place to put code that you want executed when the form is first opened and whenever it is selected. For example, you could maximize the form and display a message upon arriving with the following code:

```
1:   ;Form :: arrive
2:   method arrive(var eventInfo MoveEvent)
3:       if eventInfo.isPreFilter()
4:           then
5:               ;This code executes for each object on the form
6:
7:           else
8:               ;This code executes only for the form
9:               maximize()
10:              msgInfo("Our database", "Welcome")
11:          endif
12:  endmethod
```

With this code, the form maximizes and displays the message every time the form is opened and selected. Compare the preceding routine to the following routine. They both accomplish the same thing: they maximize the application desktop and display a message when the form is opened. The following **open** version requires a doDefault, however.

```
1:   ;Form :: open
2:   method open(var eventInfo Event)
3:       if eventInfo.isPreFilter()
4:           then
5:               ;This code executes for each object on the form
6:
7:           else
8:               ;This code executes only for the form
9:               maximize()
10:              doDefault
11:              msgInfo("Our database", "Welcome")
12:          endif
13:  endmethod
```

Note in line 10 that doDefault is added after the maximize line. Without the doDefault, the message would interrupt the opening of the form, and the form would look peculiar. For this reason, the **arrive** is considered the better, more elegant location.

The Form's Prefilter

People often have trouble using events prefiltered at the form level. If you have 50 fields on a form and want to set the colors on the **arrive** of each one, it doesn't make sense to add the code to every field's **arrive** method. Even if the code that sets colors is in a custom method, you don't need to call the custom method in each **arrive**. The form's prefilter enables the programmer to write code that intercepts the **arrive** for each object and performs the work for each object.

Rather than modify 50 fields, the programmer has to deal with only one generic method at the form level. If you want to set the color of every object in the Box class when the form opens, you could do the following:

```
 1:    ;Form :: open
 2:    method open(var eventInfo Event)
 3:       var UIObj UIObject endVar
 4:       if eventInfo.isPreFilter()
 5:       then
 6:          ;This code executes for each object on the form
 7:          eventInfo.getTarget(UIObj)
 8:          if UIObj.class = "Box" then
 9:             UIObj.color = Red
10:          endIf
11:           else
12:              ;This code executes only for the form
13:
14:       endif
15:    endmethod
```

Using the form's prefilter to work on a group of objects is an important technique. With it, you can cut down on the amount of code you need to write.

\ANSWERS\GETTARG.FSL also demonstrates how to use the form's prefilter.

Tutorial: Using the Form's Prefilter

Suppose that you or your users are having a hard time seeing which field is currently active. One solution is to make the field highlight yellow while it is active. This tutorial demonstrates how to alter the appearance of a field whenever it has focus using the form's prefilter.

On Disk: \ANSWERS\PREFILT.FSL

Quick Steps

1. Create a quick form based on CUSTOMER.DB.
2. Declare a UIObject variable.
3. In the prefilter of the form's **arrive**, use eventInfo.getTarget(UI) to find the target object. Then use the property class to find out whether the target is a field, and change its color if it is.
4. In the prefilter of the form's **canDepart**, use eventInfo.getTarget(UI) to find the target object. Then use the property class to find out whether the target is a field, and change its color back to transparent.

Step By Step

1. Change your working directory to the TUTORIAL directory and create a quick form based on the CUSTOMER.DB table. Figure 10.1 shows what the quick form should look like after you create it.

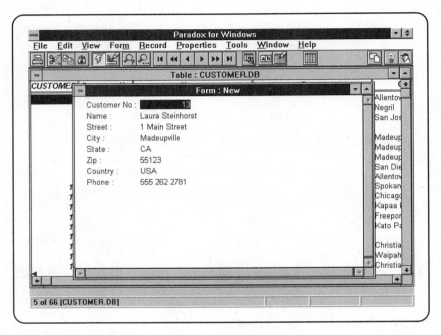

Figure 8.1. The quick form should look like this after you create it.

2. Add lines 3–5 and 8–11 to the form's **arrive** method.

```
1:   ;Form :: arrive
2:   method arrive(var eventInfo MoveEvent)
3:       var
4:       ui      UIObject              ;Declare ui as a UIObject.
5:       endVar
6:       if eventInfo.isPreFilter() then
7:          ;// This code executes for each object on the
            form:
8:          eventInfo.getTarget(ui)    ;Set ui to target.
9:          if ui.class = "Field" then ;Is ui a field, then
10:         ui.color = Yellow          ;change it to yellow.
```

```
11:        endIf
12:        else
13:            ;// This code executes only for the form:
14:
15:        endif
16:    endmethod
```

3. Add lines 3–5 and 8–11 to the form's **canDepart** method.

```
 1:    ;Form :: canDepart
 2:    method canDepart(var eventInfo MoveEvent)
 3:        var
 4:            ui      UIObject      ;Declare ui as a UIObject.
 5:        endVar
 6:        if eventInfo.isPreFilter() then
 7:            ;// This code executes for each object on the
                form:
 8:            eventInfo.getTarget(ui)      ;Set ui to target.
 9:            if ui.class = "Field" then  ;Is ui a field, then
10:            ui.color = Transparent      ;make it transparent.
11:        endIf
12:        else
13:            ;// This code executes only for the form:
14:
15:        endif
16:
17:    endmethod
```

4. Check the syntax, save the form as PREFILT.FSL, and run it. Move from field to field using the Tab key or mouse and note that the `active` field changes color. Figure 8.2 shows what they should look like.

Analysis

In step 2, line 4, a UIObject variable *ui* is declared. In line 8, a handle to the target object is put in the UIObject variable *ui*. Line 9 uses the handle to test whether it is a field by comparing the property class to the string Field. If they are the same, then a UIObject variable is used to change the field's color to yellow.

Step 4 is the same as step 3 except for location—the code is in the form's **canDepart**—and it changes the color back to transparent.

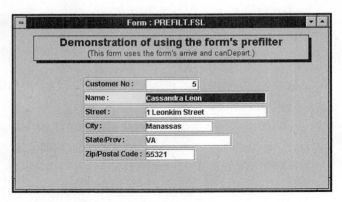

Figure 8.2. The PREFILT.FSL form demonstrates using the form's prefilter.

You can use the form's prefilter whenever you want to work with a group of objects. A group of objects can be categorized by class, color, font, and so on. You can check for all objects in a certain class or for objects with a certain name. You also can check for multiple criteria. For example:

```
1:    ;Form :: isPreFilter
2:    if UI.class = "Field" then
3:         if UI.name <> "Last_Name" then
4:              UI.color = Red
5:         endIf
6:    endIf
```

The prefilter of the form's **arrive** method is a good place for setting colors or other settings that need to be initialized at the beginning of a session, such as user configuration settings. You could write settings to a table or to an .INI file, read them in when the form is opened, and set all the object properties with this technique. More often, however, you will use the other built-in methods, such as **action** and **menuAction**, to manipulate a group of objects. Remember that all the form-level, built-in methods have a prefilter you can use.

GLOBAL CODE TIP

Put message("") *on the Prefilter of the Form's* mouseExit *Method*

Have you ever noticed that the status bar continues to display the last message even when it's no longer needed? For most applications, this is what you want. Occasionally, though, you might want a cleaner look. You

---

can put `message("")` in the form-level **mouseExit** method to turn off messages when a user leaves an object. In addition to cleaning up the status bar whenever you leave an object, this technique enables you to put a message on the **mouseEnter** methods of objects you want to inform the user of. For example:

```
;Button :: mouseEnter
message("This button exits the application")
```

Page Level

Normally, your first choice for high-level code should be either a library or the page level. Why not the form level? Because the form level forces the prefilter to fire for every object. In general, avoid the form level `else` portion for faster applications. When you have a multipage form and you need to distinguish between pages, use the page level. A classic example of this is when building menus. Generally, an application will need a different menu for every page. In this case, the page's **arrive** method is the perfect location to build a menu.

In addition, use the **menuAction** trigger of the page when you build a custom menu and need to trap for the user's selection. This enables you to have different menus for different pages of a form. If you need the same menu choices on all the pages of a form, use the form-level **menuAction** method. To learn more about menus, see Chapter 25, "Using Menus, Toolbars, and the Filesystem."

Container Level

Sometimes it's advantageous to put a container such as a box object in a page. Put objects inside the container, and put code at the container level that deals with the objects it contains.

Grouping Objects to Centralize Code

In addition to putting a box around objects, you could group them. This puts an invisible box type object around the objects. If you want to test something about a group of objects, you can group them and test them with the **arrive** and **canDepart** methods, for example. In a typical 1:M invoicing system, you might want to verify that a telephone number has been entered, but only when the user attempts to leave the header information. You can group the header field objects and test the telephone field on the **canDepart** method of the grouped objects. For example:

```
1:    ;Group :: canDepart
2:    if Phone.isBlank() then
3:        beep()
4:        message("Enter a phone number.")
5:        eventInfo.setErrorCode(CanNotDepart)
6:    endIf
```

Tutorial: Grouping Objects to Centralize Code

The goal of this tutorial is to return the values 0 through 9, depending on which object the user clicks. This tutorial uses the technique of grouping objects to centralize code on the grouped object.

On Disk: \ANSWERS\GROUP.FSL

Quick Steps

1. Create the 10 objects.
2. Group them.
3. On the **mouseDown** method of the object, get either the name of the object or its value, depending on which one has the value you want.

Step By Step

1. Change your working directory to the TUTORIAL directory, create a new form, and place 10 text objects with the values 0 through 9. Then, group them by selecting all of them and choosing Design | Group (see Figure 8.3).

2. Add lines 3–11 to the **mouseDown** of the grouped object.

```
1:    ;Group :: mouseDown
2:    method mouseDown (var eventInfp MouseEvent)
3:        var
4:            obj   UIObject
5:        endVar
6:
7:        eventInfo.getObjectHit (obj)
8:        obj.color = Yellow
9:        message ("You pressed the number , obj.value)
```

```
10:      sleep (100)
11:      obj.color = Gray
12:    endmethod
```

3. Check the syntax, save the form as GROUP.FSL, and run it. When you click on one of the nine text objects, it changes color and displays the correct value in the status bar.

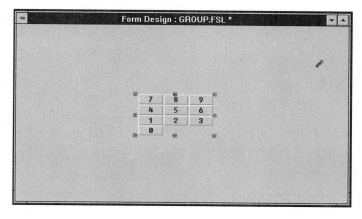

Figure 8.3. GROUP.FSL.

Analysis

Line 4 declares a UIObject variable that is used in line 7 to get the intended object of a mouse action—in this case, the objects in the grouped object. Line 8 changes the object that is clicked to the color yellow, and line 9 notifies the user which object is hit (see Figure 8.4). Line 10 sleeps for one-tenth of a second so that the user can see the object highlighted. Line 11 sets the color back to gray.

Rather than use the `message()` procedure in line 9 to notify the user of which object was clicked, you might want to use the data for something more practical. For example, you could turn this routine into a calculator. Figure 8.5 shows how this technique is used in the Dialer application to capture the letter of the alphabet that the user types. Chapter 23, "Storing and Centralizing Code," gives you more tips and techniques for writing more elegant code.

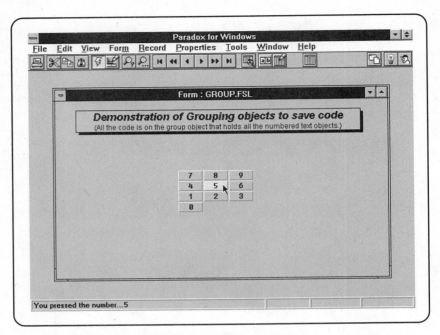

Figure 8.4. GROUP.FSL after an object has been clicked.

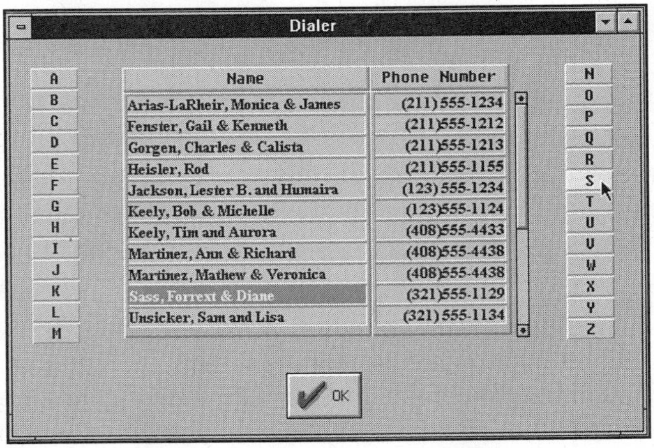

Figure 8.5. DIALER.FSL.

Object Level

The optimal place to put code—and also the first place you should think about putting code—is directly on the object itself. Most of the time, you put objects such as fields, buttons, and table frames within a page or in a container and attach code directly to them. See the tutorial, "Using **mouseEnter** and **mouseExit**," later in this chapter.

Elements of Objects

The lowest level for code is on the elements of an object. Many objects are actually composed of several objects. A field object is composed of a text label object and an edit region object (see Figure 8.6). When you put code on a field, you have a choice of 27 built-in methods at the field level, 10 at the edit region level, and 25 at the text label level. In the case of a field, you rarely use the edit region and text levels.

A button has two levels where you can attach code: the button object and the text object it contains. You usually use the **pushButton** built-in method with buttons.

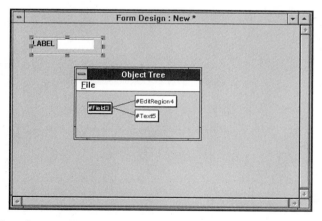

Figure 8.6. The Object Tree of a field.

Figure 8.7 shows the Object Tree of a table frame. Note that a two-column table frame is composed of seven objects. Normally, you wouldn't place code on the header or on the column labels. That leaves three levels where you can place code on a table frame: the field level, the record level, and the table-frame level.

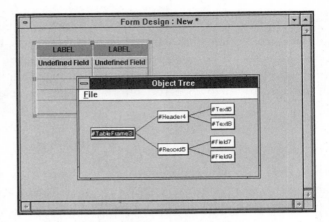

Figure 8.7. The Object Tree of a table frame.

Figure 8.8 shows the Object Tree of a crosstab. A crosstab is composed of seven objects. Therefore, it has seven places where you can attach code.

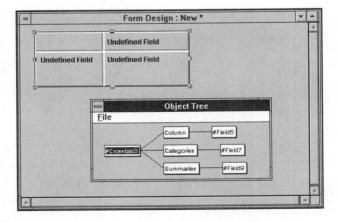

Figure 8.8. The Object Tree of a crosstab.

Thinking of attaching code to various levels of an application or object is easier than randomly guessing where to put code. It gives you an idea of what can see what. Whenever a routine isn't behaving properly, ask yourself, "Is there a better level or location for this routine?" Sometimes—especially when you're dealing with multiple objects—the answer is yes.

DECLARING VARIABLES

The concepts of various levels, containership, and what can see what are important in ObjectPAL. One of the most important elements of ObjectPAL code placement is where to declare a variable. The discussion of scope and instance in this section also applies to the other object windows: Const, Type, Uses, and Proc.

The place where you declare a variable determines the scope and instance of a variable. The term *scope* means *accessiblity*. The scope of the variable means what other objects, if any, can see it. The scope of a variable—that is, the range of objects that have access to it—is defined by the objects in which it is declared, and by the containership hierarchy. Objects can access only their own variables and the variables defined in the objects that contain them. The scope of a variable depends on where it is declared.

The *instance* of the variable means how long the variable exists. For example, if you declare a TCursor variable within a button and you want to use the same TCursor variable in another button, you could declare the TCursor in both buttons—a waste of resources. Or you could move the declaration to higher ground—that is, to a place where both buttons can see and reuse one variable. In the case of two buttons on a page, the page level is a good choice. All the objects on the page, including the two buttons, have access to page-level variables.

Declare Private Variables within a Method

After you choose which object to declare a variable on, you must decide whether you want the variable to be private to a method or global to the object. Variables declared within a method are visible only to that method and are dynamic; that is, they are accessible only while that method executes. They are initialized—reset—each time the method executes. A private variable can be seen only by the built-in method in which it is declared. Its scope is limited. Therefore, if you want to use the variable in only a single method, use a variable that is private to the method.

If you declare a variable within a method (either within or above `method...endMethod`), then the variable is private to the method; that is, no other methods or objects can see or use the variable. In essence, the variable is private to the method.

Most often, the first place you choose to put a variable is inside
method...endMethod. When you do this, the variable's scope is limited to the
method and its existence is only for the duration of the method. Use this
technique when no other objects need to use the variable and the variable can
be initialized each time. For example, you can put both the variable declaration
and the code in the same method window, as in the following:

```
1:   ;Btn1 :: pushButton
2:   method pushButton(var eventInfo Event)
3:       var                         ;Private variables are declared
4:          s     String             ;inside method/endMethod.
5:       endVar
6:
7:       s = "Hello World"
8:       msgInfo("", s)
9:   endMethod
```

The first technique is easier to read; all code is located in the same place. In
addition, the variable is a private, or local. More specifically, the variable is
local to only this method; no other built-in methods of this object or of another
object can see the variable.

Declare Global Variables in the Var Window

The Var window of an object creates a variable that is global to the object.
Variables declared in an object's Var window are visible to all methods attached
to that object, and to any objects that object contains. A variable declared in
an object's Var window is attached to the object and is static, accessible as long
as the object exists.

A variable with broader scope in ObjectPAL is said to be global to the object.
Any object can access it from that point down in the containership hierarchy.
Do not confuse the concept of a variable being global to an object with a global
variable in other languages. A variable that is global to an object in ObjectPAL
is global only to that object and not to any other objects.

After you choose the object, you have three places in which you can declare a
variable: in the Var window of the object, inside the method...endMethod
structure of a method, or above the method...endMethod structure.

As an alternative to putting the variable declaration with the code, you can put
the variable in the Var window and the code in the method, as in the following:

```
1:   ;Btn2 :: Var
2:   var                      ;Global to an object variables
3:          s     String      ;are declared in the Var window
4:   endVar                   ;of the object.
```

```
1:    ;Btn2 :: pushButton
2:    method pushButton(var eventInfo Event)
3:        s = "Hello World"
4:        msgInfo("", s)
5:    endMethod
```

This second technique uses a variable that is global to the object. It is more elegant if you need to use the variable elsewhere. The variable is global to the object; all the other methods of the object and of the objects it contains can see the variable. In other words, the scope you need for a particular variable is the determining factor. If no other object needs the variable, declare it privately.

Are there any exceptions to this rule? Yes. In the preceding example, either inside method...endMethod or in the Var window is equally elegant because the button's **pushButton** method occurs only once for each click of the button, which doesn't tax the system. In fact, you can declare a variable in any custom or built-in method that executes once. Methods such as **pushButton**, **open**, and **arrive** are prime candidates for declaring variables privately inside method...endMethod.

In the case of a built-in method such as **newValue**, which is triggered many times by many different events, the second technique of separating the variable in the Var window from the code in the built-in method is more elegant. Typically, **newValue** is triggered so many times during a session that redeclaring a variable each time doesn't make sense. A variable could be redeclared thousands of times in a **newValue** method.

Var window variables are declared for the instance of the object. Therefore, they are more elegant in most cases. It's better programming practice to declare your variables only once so that the system won't be taxed. The declaring of variables in the Var window occurs only once, and it occurs even before the **open** method of the object. If you want to see this for yourself, put the following code on a button and run the form. The message box will display the correct variable declaration.

```
1:    ;Button :: open
2:    method open(var eventInfo Event)
3:        msgInfo("", data Type(o))
4:    endmethod

1:    ;Button :: Var
2:    var
3:        o      OLE
4:    endVar
```

When you declare variables, you usually use one of the two techniques just discussed. The scope and instance of the variable is the determining factor. In general, it's a good rule of thumb to use the Var window as your first choice. Move the declaration from the Var window (which is global to the object) to within `method...endMethod` (which is private to the method) only when needed.

Another reason to use the Var window of an object is because the symbol table can get full. You are limited to a 64K symbol table. Various information is stored in the symbol table including variables, constants, and names of objects. (Refer to Appendix B for more ObjectPAL limitations.) By putting variables in the Var window of an object, more built-in methods have access to it.

Declaring Variables Outside a Method

What if you want the scope of a variable to be private to a method, but have its instance be for the duration of the object? Is this possible? Yes. Variables declared before the word method in a `method...endMethod` block are visible only to that method and are static. This technique has the benefit of declaring the variable only once—that is, when the object is created—yet the variable remains private to the method. In addition, it's existence is for the duration of the object.

```
1:    ;Button :: pushButton
2:    var
3:        O    OLE          ;Private variable declared only once.
4:
5:    endVar
6:    method pushButton(var eventInfo Event)
7:        msgInfo("", DataType(O))
8:    endmethod
```

This third technique is not used often enough. It is an elegant way to declare a variable private to a method, because the variable is declared only once. Declare permanent variables in either the Var window (scope that is global to the object with an instance of the duration of the object) or above the `method...endMethod` (scope that is private to the method with an instance of the duration of the object).

Variable Level

After you decide that you need a variable that is global to an object—in other words, you have decided to use the Var window of an object—you must decide the level on which you want to declare the variable—the form, the page, the object's container, or the object. The answer depends on what you want the scope of the variable to be. In a way, it depends on how global you need the variable to be. In general, I declare the variable either at the form level or at the lowest possible container. If you declare a variable at the form level, you don't have to worry about the scope of the variable because the variable is global to the form. That is, all objects in the form can see it.

The better of these two approaches is to declare variables in the Var window of the lowest possible container. You can move them up the containership path when a broader scope is needed. For example, if you're going to use a variable on a button, declare it on the button. Declare the variable in the built-in method itself—for example, within **pushButton**. If you use it in another of the button's built-in methods—for example, **mouseEnter**—move it to the button's Var window. If you later need that variable for another object on that page or on another page in the form, move the variable back to the Var window of the page or form. In general, declare the variable on as low a level as possible, and use the Var window whenever you need the same variable with two different built-in methods or two different objects.

BUILT-IN METHOD COMBINATIONS

An excellent technique for placing code on an object is to place code in "before and after" combinations. Many built-in methods have counterparts—for example, **open** and **close**, **arrive** and **depart**, **canArrive** and **canDepart**, and **mouseEnter** and **mouseExit**. If you need to code in a "before and after" maneuver, think and code in one of these method combinations. For example, occasionally you might need to create a table when a form is opened and delete it when the form is exited. The **open** and **close** combination is a good place to do this. **open** and **canDepart** might be even better, but that's up to you as the programmer.

mouseEnter and mouseExit

Whenever you want something to occur when the pointer is within the boundaries of an object, use the **mouseEnter** and **mouseExit** combination.

Tutorial: Using mouseEnter and mouseExit

Suppose that you wish to display a message on the status bar whenever the mouse pointer is over a button.

On Disk: \ANSWERS\M-ENTER.FSL

Quick Steps

1. Set up a button with some code on it.

2. Add the `message("This button...")` command to `mouseEnter`.

3. Add `message("")` to `mouseExit`.

Step By Step

1. Change your working directory to the TUTORIAL directory and create a new form with a button on it. Change the label of the button to Close (see Figure 8.9).

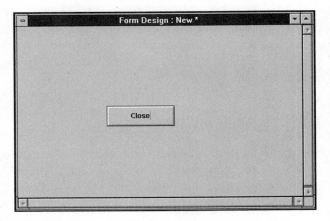

Figure 8.9. Set up form for tutorial.

2. Add commands to the button. In this case, let's close the form by adding line 3 to the **pushButton** method.

```
1:    ;Button :: pushButton
2:    method pushButton(var eventInfo Event)
3:        close()
4:    endmethod
```

3. Place the message on the status bar by adding line 3 to the **mouseEnter** of the button.

```
1:    ;Button :: mouseEnter
2:    method mouseEnter(var eventInfo MouseEvent)
3:        message("This button closes the form")
4:    endmethod
```

4. Remove the message from the status bar by adding line 3 to the
mouseExit of the button.

```
1:     ;Button :: mouseExit
2:     method mouseExit(var eventInfo MouseEvent)
3:        message("")
4:     endmethod
```

5. Check the syntax, save the form as M-ENTER.FSL, and run it. Move
your cursor over the button and keep an eye on the status bar.

Analysis

In step 2, line 3 closes the current form. Note that `close()` is used as a
procedure in this case—it knows what object to work with.

In step 3, line 3, the **mouseEnter** method sends a message to the status bar
whenever the mouse pointer enters the boundaries of the button.

In step 4, line 8 posts a new message, the null character.

Rather than use the **mouseExit** method of every object, you can put code in the
prefilter of the form's **mouseExit** method. Remember that external commands
always bubble up. Therefore, putting `message("")` at the form level clears the
status bar whenever the mouse leaves an object.

COMPARISONS OF BUILT-IN METHODS

Many of the built-in methods are so similar that it's confusing to use them. The
following comparisons should clear the muddy waters.

open **versus** arrive

An object is always opened first, then arrived on. Therefore, **open** occurs before
arrive. Remember that the default behavior happens last. When you **open** an
object, the code on the form's built-in **open** method executes, and the form is
opened. If you put code that deals with a UIObject in the **open** method, the
code might not execute correctly because the objects don't exist yet. You could
put `doDefault` before your code to execute the default behavior, or you could
move your code to the **arrive** method.

open is a good place to initialize a variable, create a table, and deal with the
form—for example, to maximize or resize it. **arrive** is a good place to set the
properties of the objects on the form—for example, the values of the field
objects.

newValue versus changeValue

newValue occurs whenever the value for an edit region changes value on-screen. This occurs whether or not the field is defined. changeValue occurs with both defined and undefined fields but behaves quite differently for each. changeValue on an undefined field occurs whenever the value in it changes. With defined fields, however, it occurs only after a field is read from a table and changed by the user.

changeValue is a good place to do something based on a change in the table value. For example, you could perform some operation when payment type changes from cash to credit. If you want something to happen whenever a user changes a value in a field—undefined or defined—use changeValue.

keyChar versus keyPhysical

The keyChar and keyPhysical built-in methods trap for the user pressing keys on the keyboard. keyChar traps for only the character keyboard keys—that is, the keys that print characters to the screen. keyPhysical traps for all the keyboard keys—both character keys and physical keys. keyPhysical filters the keyboard first and passes printable characters to the screen.

Use keyChar to trap for character keys, such as A, B, 1, 2, (, and ;. Use keyPhysical to trap for keys such as Esc, F1, F8, and Tab. If you need to trap for both physical and character keys in a routine, use only keyPhysical because it can trap for both.

action, menuAction, and error

Use action to trap for table actions such as DataInsertRecord and DataPostRecord. Whenever a user does something related to the table—inserting a record, deleting a record—an action constant is sent to the action method. Use menuAction to catch user selection of menus, the Toolbar, and the contol box. Whenever a user selects a menu option or clicks a button on the Toolbar, a menu constant is sent to the menuAction built-in method of the form. You could use the error method to trap for errors, but because the built-in error method is always called after errors occur, use action instead. A good use for error is to add to the built-in error behavior; for example, to log all errors to a table.

EXAMPLES OF WHERE TO PUT CODE

Good examples are valuable. The following examples of where to put code might not be the most elegant, but they're good.

- Field validation: Validate fields at the object level with **canDepart** or **changeValue**.

- Record validation: Validate records at the record level with action or **canDepart**.

A REMINDER THAT WILL SAVE YOU TIME

Know the Built-In Behavior

Before you construct a certain behavior, be sure that the built-in behavior doesn't already do what you need with a great deal more sophistication. Knowing what Paradox does is important to the programmer. ObjectPAL is a rich and powerful language. If you duplicate functionality, you're wasting time. Always ask yourself, "What already happens in this event?"

Where code is placed in the event model is important. Ultimately, you must find the perfect place to put your code. Only through trial and error—and some experimentation—will you learn the good and bad places to put code. The guidelines presented in this chapter will get you started.

SYNTAX

This chapter addresses syntax, the object variables, and coding conventions. These topics may not seem related, but they all have to do with knowing how to type code in and making what you code readable and reuseable.

DOT NOTATION AND *object.doIt*

The `object.doIt()` syntax style of ObjectPAL is important. The section "Object-Oriented Programming" in Chapter 6, "ObjectPAL Concepts," mentioned that this style of syntax is easier to remember than a dozen different syntax variations for a single command. This next section builds on the idea that ObjectPAL is easy to remember, and compares ObjectPAL with everyday language.

In the real world, you can rudely say to people:

Hey. Do it. Now.
You. Do it. Pick up trash.
Lisa. Do it. Swim.
Glenn. Do it. Golf.

Dot notation

Syntax variations

Variables

Constants

Using properties

Using built-in object variables

Developing readable code

Coding convention

To turn these statements into ObjectPAL code, you would write them as follows:

```
1:    var
2:        Hey, You, Lisa, Glenn      People
3:    endVar
4:
5:    Hey.doIt("Now")
6:    You.doIt("Pick up trash")
7:    Lisa.doIt("Swim")
8:    Glenn.doIt("Golf")
```

In this example, in effect you program a human type or class of object. If Borland ever adds a human type or class of object to ObjectPAL, you could program a button as follows:

```
1:    method pushButton(var eventInfo Event)
2:       var
3:          p             Person
4:          pm1, pm2  Person Movement
5:          house, store   Building
6:       endVar
7:
8:       p = "Lisa"
9:       p1 = "Swim"
10:      p2 = "Run"
11:      house.p.doIt(p1)
12:      store.p.doIt(p2)
13:    endmethod
```

With dot notation, you can tell two different people called Lisa in two different locations what to do.

THE ALTERNATE SYNTAX

Because ObjectPAL's core syntax is taken directly from PAL, PAL programmers will be familiar with many of the commands. PAL is a procedural language; ObjectPAL is an object-based, event-driven language. Therefore, the syntax of Paradox has migrated from the DOS version to the Windows version to more closely resemble Pascal and C.

Although ObjectPAL's `object.doIt()` syntax is its syntax template, ObjectPAL does have an alternate syntax. Here is the template for the standard syntax.

```
object.methodName(argument [, argument])
```

Now, here is the template for the alternate syntax.

```
methodName(object, argument [, argument])
```

For example, the following three statements all close the current form:

```
1:    close()          ;This uses close as a procedure.
2:    self.close()     ;This is the standard syntax.
3:    close(self)      ;This is the alternate syntax.
```

Here is another example that demonstrates manipulating strings. These two lines of code are equivalent:

```
1:    s = test.subStr(2,3)     ;Regular syntax.
2:    s = subStr(test,2,3)     ;Alternate syntax.
```

If you want to try these syntax variations, put the following code on a button:

```
1:    ;Button :: pushButton
2:    method pushButton(var eventInfo Event)
3:        var
4:                s,s1,s2    String
5:        endVar
6:
7:        s = "Mike Ault"
8:        s1 = s.subStr(1,4)
9:        s2 = subStr(s,6,4)
10:       msgInfo("Syntax 1", s1)
11:       msgInfo("Syntax 2", s2)
12:   endmethod
```

The Alternate Syntax Uses Dot Notation

Just like the regular syntax, the alternate syntax can use dot notation. For example, the following two lines of code are equivalent:

```
1:    pge1.tfCustomer.Last_Name.moveTo()
2:    moveto(pge1.tfCustomer.Last_Name)
```

Although ObjectPAL gives you this freedom when you write code, be consistent. Whenever you have a choice, use the regular object.methodName() style of syntax. If you do this, your code will be more consistent. It also will be easier for others to read and easier for you to understand two months after you've coded it.

Using the Alternate Syntax in a Calculated Field

Q: How can I use round() in a Calculated Field?

A: Most of the Number type methods will work in a calculated field. The syntax is as follows:

```
methodname(fieldname)
```

For example, to use round() and truncate(), you need a slightly different syntax. The syntax for round() and truncate() is as follows:

> **truncate(*fieldname.value, places*)**   ;Truncate the value in fieldname.
> **round(*fieldname.value, places*)**   ;Round the value in fieldname.

where *places* is the number of decimal places you want to round or truncate to.

For example, if the field being rounded is *Total_Invoice*, and it needs to be rounded to 2 decimal places, an example of a calculated field that rounds the total is as follows:

```
1:     Round(Total_Invoice.value,2)
```

This also can be incorporated in more complex calculated fields. For example:

```
1:     Round(SUM(Total_Invoice),2)
```

The preceding rounds the grand total of the field *Total_Invoice*.

CASE SENSITIVITY

When is Paradox case sensitive? Paradox is case sensitive with string comparisons and locates. For example, Yes is not the same as YES. When you locate a record, Lupton is not the same as lupton or LUPTON. Case sensitivity applies even when you check against parts of the ObjectPAL language if the part is in a string. For example, box isn't the same as Box. You can check which class an object belongs to with the following:

```
1:     var ui UIObject endVar
2:     eventInfo.getTarget(ui)
3:     if ui.class = "Box" then
4:        ;Put your code here. For example:
5:        message(ui.name)
6:     endIf
```

If you accidentally typed box or BOX, the routine would fail. Therefore, you need to watch your string constants. You can use ignoreCaseInStringCompares() and ignoreCaseInLocate() procedures, however, to force case insensitivity. For example:

```
1:     var ui UIObject endVar
2:     eventInfo.getTarget(ui)
3:     ignoreCaseInStringCompares(Yes)
4:     if ui.class = "box" then
5:        ;Put your code here. For example:
6:        message(ui.name)
7:     endIf
```

Other than string compares and locates, ObjectPAL syntax is not case sensitive.

VARIABLES

Declaring variables already has been introduced by implication because variables have been used in many examples before now. In addition, the last chapter went into detail about where to declare variables. What follows in this section is a formal introduction/review of declaring variables in ObjectPAL. You declare variables in a var block. For example:

```
1:    var          ;Start of variable block.
2:                 ;Declare variables here.
3:    endVar       ;End of variable block.
```

When you declare variables of the same type, you can either put them on the same line or separate lines. The choice is yours; it does not matter to the compiler. For example, the following declares four variables: two numbers and two strings.

```
1:    var
2:         s1      String    ;You can declare like variables on
3:         s2      String    ;separate lines, or
4:         n1,n2   Number    ;on the same line separated by commas.
5:    endVar
```

Here are some examples of how variables are declared:

```
1:    si    SmallInt      ;Declare si as a small integer. This
2:                        ;is useful for smaller numbers.
3:    s     String        ;Declare s as a string.
4:    f     Form          ;Declare f as form.
5:    app   Application    ;Declare an application variable
6:                        ;when you want to deal with the
7:                        ;desktop. For example,
8:                        ;to maximize or hide the
9:                        ;application.
10:   t     Time          ;Declare t as type
11:                       ;time to deal with time.
```

Here are some examples of using variables in expressions:

```
1:    x = x + 1
2:    s = "Nicole Kimberly Prestwood"
3:    s = "The new value is " + string(x)
4:    s = "The time is " + string(t)
5:    message(a.name())
```

Constants

As already stated, an ObjectPAL constant is a value that represents a number. A constant is a specific, unchanging value used in calculations and defined in a const block very similar to a variable block. Just as variables have scope and instance in ObjectPAL, so do constants. The following declares a constant with private scope; the instance of the constant is for the duration of the object.

```
1:    ;Button :: pushButton
2:    const
3:        youngest = "Veronica Renee Martinez"
4:    endConst
5:    method pushButton(var eventInfo Event)
6:        view(youngest, "New family member")
7:    endmethod
```

The value of constants, of course, doesn't change. You use these constants in ObjectPAL statements to do a variety of tasks. Two advantages of using constants is that they humanize your code and help make managing your code easier. They humanize your code by making your code easier to read. A constant named tax is easier to remember and understand than 8.125. Constants help you maintain your code by centralizing values. If the tax rate in your area changes from 8.125 to 8.5, you change the constant in one location. Imagine having to change it throughout a form.

Using Properties

One reason ObjectPAL is powerful is that you can change the properties of an object. You are already familiar with various properties of objects; you have set them in previous examples. This section explores the syntax used to manipulate them. You can set most of an object's properties while the form is running—another feature that sets Paradox apart from other database systems. You can set not only the value of a field and the color of a box, but also the size and position of objects, the alignment, tab stop, and so on.

Using the Apostrophe

There is a problem when you use properties. What if you wish to change the color of a box named *color*? This is an ambiguous use of ObjectPAL. Furthermore, what if there is an object inside the box named *color* too (see Figure 9.1).

This really is an ambiguous use of ObjectPAL. The following is what ObjectPAL does with various commands when you run the form.

```
color.color = Red              ;Error (invalid property).
color.color.color = Red        ;Change inner box to red.
```

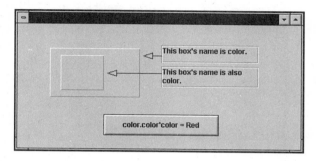

Figure 9.1. Do not name objects the same name as a property.

How do you write code that changes the outer box? Do this using the apostrophe. For example:

```
1:    color'color = Red          ;Change outer box to red.
2:    color.color'color = Red    ;Change inner box to red.
```

Using the apostrophe makes your code incredibly easy to read. The real solution in this case, of course, is to not use any part of ObjectPAL to name objects. Should you start doing this in your code? This is completely up to you. I have not adopted using the apostrophe in my own coding convention yet because it has not been widely used or accepted by the developing community. If you name your objects carefully, then there is no need to use it. But one more time: it does make your code incredibly easy to read and I truly hope it eventually catches on, especially with compound properties.

COMPOUND PROPERTIES

Just as there are compound objects in ObjectPAL, there are also compound properties. A compound property is a property that has several parts to it separated by dots. For example, Table 9.1 lists some sample compound properties.

TABLE 9.1. SAMPLE COMPOUND PROPERTIES.	
Compound Property	Sample Usage
`design.SizeToFit`	box1.design.SizeToFit = True
`font.style`	fld1.font.style = FontAttribBold
`Background.Pattern.Style`	grph1.Background.Pattern.Style = CrosshatchPattern
`List.Value`	fld1.lst1.list.value = "Bill Lupton"

BUILT-IN OBJECT VARIABLES

ObjectPAL offers built-in variables in addition to its built-in methods. These variables are predefined by Paradox for you to use in your ObjectPAL routines. The object built-in variables are an integral part of ObjectPAL. Like so much of ObjectPAL, they are self-explanatory. In fact, you've already used several of them. The built-in object variables are `self`, `subject`, `container`, `active`, `lastMouseClicked`, and `lastMouseRightClicked`. Use the built-in object variables as much as possible. They make your code very readable and more portable.

self

With one exception, `self` always refers to the object to which the code is attached. The exception is when `self` is used in a library. When `self` is used in a library, it always refers to the object that calls the custom method. The technique of using `self` in a library is discussed in Chapter 23, "Storing and Centralizing Code." For now, concentrate on using `self` within code on an object like a field.

Use `self` whenever possible; it makes your routines more generic. Use `self` whenever code refers to itself. If you have a choice between the following two lines of code, always choose the one that uses `self`:

```
1:    Last_Name.value = "Hoffman"
2:    self.value = "Hoffman"
```

If you later change the name of the *Last_Name* field, you don't have to change the name used in the code. In addition, when you copy an object with code attached to it, the code is more likely to work if you use `self`.

subject

When self is used in a library, it refers to the calling object. Wouldn't it be nice if you could do the same with custom routines in a form? You can with subject. With dot notation and subject you can have a routine work on another object. Custom methods and subject are discussed later in Chapter 23, "Storing and Centralizing Code."

container

When you use container in your code, it refers to the object that contains the object to which the code is attached. If you have a small box inside a large box and you execute the following code attached to the small box, the large box turns red:

```
1:    ;SmallBox :: mouseClick
2:    container.color = red
```

active

active refers to the object that is currently active—in other words, the last object to receive a moveTo() command. Usually, it's the object that currently has the focus—that is, the object ready to be edited. In the following example, active is used to indicate the object that has the focus:

```
1:    active.nextRecord()
```

In a multitable form—a form with several tables bound to it—this line of code acts differently, depending on which object has the focus.

```
1:    lastMouseClicked and lastMouseRightClicked
```

LastMouseClicked refers to the last object to receive a mouseDown/mouseUp combination. A mouseDown/mouseUp combination occurs whenever the user presses the left mouse button while the pointer is over an object. This variable enables you to deal with the user's most recent mouse clicks without writing special code. lastMouseRightClicked is the same as lastMouseClicked, except that the right mouse button is pressed.

Tutorial: Using Object Variables

In this tutorial you use the object variables: self, active, lastMouseClicked, and lastMouseRightClicked. The goal of this tutorial is to build a somewhat crazy form that uses the ObjectPAL built-in variables.

On Disk: \ANSWERS\OPALVAR.FSL

Step By Step

1. Change your working directory to the TUTORIAL directory and create a new form with the Customer table in the data model. Add three boxes and a button, as indicated in Figure 9.2.

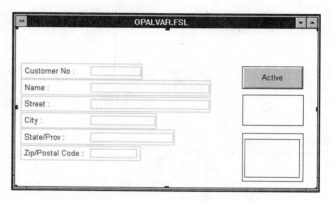

Figure 9.2. After you've set up your form, it should look like this.

2. Toggle the color of `self` and `container` when the user clicks the small box. Do this by adding lines 3–9 to the **mouseClick** method of the small box.

```
1:   ;SmallBox :: mouseClick
2:   method mouseClick(var eventInfo MouseEvent)
3:       if self.color = Red then
4:           self.color = Green
5:           container.color = White
6:       else
7:           self.color = Red
8:           container.color = Gray
9:       endIf
10:  endmethod
```

3. To display the name of the object when the mouse is clicked, add line 3 to the page's **mouseDown**.

```
1:   ;Page :: mouseDown
2:   method mouseDown(var eventInfo MouseEvent)
3:       message(lastMouseClicked.name)
4:   endmethod
```

4. To display the name of the object when the mouse is right-clicked, add line 3 to the page's **mouseRightDown**.

```
1:    ;Page :: mouseRightDown
2:    method mouseRightDown(var eventInfo MouseEvent)
3:        message(lastMouseRightClicked.name)
4:    endmethod
```

5. To display the active field's name and value in the status bar when the user presses a button, add line 3 to the **pushButton** method of the button.

```
1:    ;Button :: pushButton
2:    method pushButton(var eventInfo Event)
3:        message(active.name + ": " + active.value)
4:    endmethod
```

6. Check the syntax, save the form as OPALVAR.FSL, and Run it. Click the single box to the right (see Figure 9.3). Click the small box inside the larger box. The mouse click toggles the colors of the two boxes. If you click any of the three boxes on the right, the name of the box is displayed in the status bar. Press the button. Note the name and the value of the current object in the status bar.

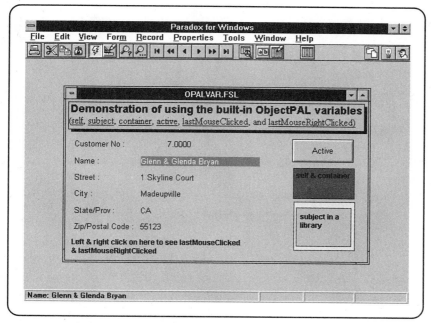

Figure 9.3. After you've completed this tutorial, your form should look similar to this.

Analysis

In step 2, lines 3–9 toggle the color of `self` (the small box) and `container` (the large box) when the small box is clicked. Line 3 checks the current color of the small box. Then, based on that current color, lines 4, 5, 7, and 8 change the colors.

Step 3, line 3 and step 4, line 3 use the fact that external methods bubble up to the form. Line 3 in step 3 displays the name of the last object that was left-clicked. Line 3 in step 4 displays the name of the last object that was right-clicked.

Step 5, line 3 uses `active` to display in the status bar the name and value of the current field whenever the user clicks the button.

The built-in object variables—`self`, `subject`, `container`, `active`, `lastMouseClicked`, and `lastMouseRightClicked`—are used in developing generic routines. Generic routines are important. The more generic routines you use, the less coding you have to do.

> You can use any property that applies to the type of object with which you are working. Properties that don't apply won't work. For example, because buttons don't have frames or color properties, `self.color = Red` doesn't work on a button.

CODING CONVENTION

A coding convention consists of the rules you use to type your code, names objects, and so on. Every programming language is flexible in how you use it. For example, the idea to use the built-in object variables `self`, `subject`, and `container` as much as possible can be part of a coding convention. How you personally use these flexible areas of the language is your own personal coding convention—for example, what names you choose to name variables, UIObjects, forms, and so on. Developing a consistent coding convention is very important. With a good, consistent coding convention, your code is much easier to read and, in the long run, saves you time. It needs to be simple and easy to remember. The rest of this chapter is comprised of my own personal coding convention. Please feel free to use, study, and copy it.

Use Descriptive Names to Make Code More Readable

Many times you will forget how a custom method or procedure works and perhaps even what it does. Even if you're the one who wrote it, you might have to study it as if someone else wrote it. You can avoid this problem if you take a little extra time while developing to format and comment your code.

It is not code that obfuscates readability; it is the programmer. ObjectPAL has the potential to be very comprehensible. The use of consistent programming standards can make code quite easy to read. If you format your code consistently and use common sense when naming variables, others will be able to understand your code and so will you.

Paradox Is Self-Documenting

If you use real names for variables and object names, your code will be self-documenting. The capability to use real names in ObjectPAL shouldn't be taken lightly. Easy-to-read code is very helpful when several people are developing an application or when an application becomes very large. Resist using archaic computer initials. For example, decide which of the following you consider clearer:

```
1:    x = x + 1
2:    Counter = Counter + 1
```

Obviously, the Counter version, line 2, is a much clearer use of a variable name. You might remember that in algebra, x is used to substitute for numbers. That familiarity might lead you to overuse x as a variable name. For the sake of clarity, resist the temptation to use arcane variables. Use descriptive variable names and descriptive object names.

Don't Use Reserved Words for Names

The names of commands, keywords, functions, system variables, and operators are all reserved words. These words should not be used as object variable names. Even though you can use reserved words in certain circumstances and not get an error—for example, you are permitted to name an object array—don't. Sometimes your code can pass the syntax checker but still cause a runtime error. Also, it's confusing to read code in which you can't distinguish the names of objects and variables from the names of commands. For example, although you could use to as the name of an object, you couldn't use it in ObjectPAL. If you used *to* as the name of an object and typed the following command, you would get the message, "Error: Identifier expected error":

```
1:      to.moveTo()     ;to is incorrectly named. You can't use keywords
2:                      ;for names of objects.
```

You also might get a runtime error in addition to immediate syntax errors. At the very least, your code will be hard to read. Table 9.2 lists the keywords in ObjectPAL.

TABLE 9.2. THE KEYWORDS.

active	endSwitchMenu	proc
and	endTry	query
array	endUses	quitLoop
as	endVar	record
case	endWhile	refIntStruct
caseInsensitive	for	retry
const	forEach	return
create	from	scan
database	if	secStruct
descending	iif	self
disableDefault	in	sort
doDefault	index	step
DynArray	indexStruct	struct
else	is	subject
enableDefault	key	switch
endConst	like	switchMenu
endCreate	loop	tag
endFor	maintained	then
endForEach	method	to
endIf	not	try
endIndex	ObjectPAL	type
endMethod	of	unique
endProc	on	uses
endQuery	onFail	var
endRecord	or	where
endScan	otherwise	while
endSort	passEvent	with
endSwitch	primary	without

In addition to not using keywords to name objects, it's good programming practice to make sure that you don't name objects the same name as a method or procedure (or any language element). Avoid using the names of methods and procedures for object names (even though it's permitted). For example, in

```
1:    moveTo.moveTo()
```

the first `moveTo` is the name of an object. This is permitted, but the code is confusing.

White Space

In ObjectPAL, white space does not matter. For example, you can place more then one command per line, as in the following:

```
1:    var s String endVar s = "Monica Arias" s.view()
```

However, the preferred way to write the preceding line is as follows:

```
1:    var
2:        s String
3:    endVar
4:
5:    s = "Monica Arias"
6:    s.view()
```

Use white space to make your code easier to read.

Should I Use 'Camel Caps' for Method Names?

Although method and procedure names are not case sensitive, be consistent. For methods, procedures, and variables, stick with the capitalization that the manuals use. Except for the first word of the name, the first letter of every word is capitalized, as in `setMouseShape()`, `setMouseScreenPosition()`, `play()`, and `msgYesNoCancel()`. Take advantage of descriptive variable names—for example, `tblOrders`, `arNames`, and `nCounter`. You might use all capital letters for filenames—for example, ORDERS.DB and `ADDRESS."Last Name"`. Being consistent with your code increases its readability.

Here is an example of code that is hard to read because its syntax style is inconsistent:

```
1:    method pushButton(var eventInfo Event)
2:    VAR s      String  Endvar
3:    s="Enter your name" s.VIEW()
4:    if  s.isBlank() or s="Enter your name" Then
5:    MSGStop("Operation Stopped","You must type in your name.")
```

```
6:      return else msgInfo("","Hello "+s)  EndIf
7:      Message("Goodbye " + s)
8:      endmethod
```

s is used for a string variable. In this case, that's not so bad because *s* is the only variable. When you have three or more variables, however, nondescriptive variable names make the code difficult to read.

The formatting in this example is poor. The capitalization and formatting are inconsistent. Whether you choose to capitalize some characters and not others is not important. Whether you choose to tab sections of code or insert several spaces to set off sections of code also is not important. What is important is that you remain consistent.

Here is the same piece of code formatted in a consistent style:

```
1:      method pushButton(var eventInfo Event)
2:          var
3:              str      String
4:          endVar
5:
6:          str = "Enter your name"
7:          str.view()
8:
9:          if str.isBlank() or str = "Enter your name" then
10:            msgStop("Operation Stopped","You must type in your name.")
11:            return
12:          else
13:            msgInfo("","Hello " + str)
14:          endIf
15:          message("Goodbye " + str)
16:      endmethod
```

How much faster can you figure out what this second piece of code does? It's much easier to read and understand. The variable has a new name. Tabs are used in sections of code, and the capitalization is consistent. White space is also used.

Now, add comments and the Prestwood Coding Convention (PCC) to the code to help others read it—or to refresh your memory later:

```
1:      method pushButton(var eventInfo Event)
2:          ;This code demonstrates using view() for input
3:          var
4:              sName      String              ;Declares sNameStr as a string.
5:          endVar
6:
7:          sName = "Enter your name"          ;Setup variable to prompt user.
8:          sName.view()                       ;Shows user the current value. Also
9:                                             ;prompts user.
10:
11:         ;Test user input.
```

```
12:        if sName.isBlank() or sName = "Enter your name" then
13:           msgStop("Operation Stopped","You must type in your name.")
14:           return                  ;If bad data, displays above
15:                                   ;message and aborts.
16:        else
17:           msgInfo("","Hello " + sName) ;Displays message.
18:        endIf
19:        message("Goodbye " + sName)    ;Says goodbye.
20:     endmethod
```

Obviously, this version of the code is the clearest. Sometimes, though, you don't have time to remark a piece of code. You should, however, always have time to format it because you can do this as you go. If you're working under a deadline, you might set aside these good programming techniques in order to get the job done. Usually, however, you can afford to spend a little time now to document your code in order to save yourself and others a lot of time later. Here's a good rule of thumb: If you are writing code that others will see or that you might reuse, take the time to format and comment it.

Naming Convention

By looking at your code, you should be able to easily distinguish between objects and variables. Furthermore, you should be able to distinguish between UIObjects you have named and the UIObjects Paradox has named. Use any naming convention you wish. Just be consistent.

The following are some naming rules and warnings:

- Generally, rename an object only if you reference it in your ObjectPAL code.

- Do not reference noise names. Noise names are the default names that Paradox gives objects; they always start with #.

- Names of objects and variables are limited to 64 characters. Shorter is better, however.

- The first character must be a letter A–Z, a–z or an underscore.

- After the initial character, you can use letters, digits, extended ANSI, and any of the following three characters: $, !, _. Although you can use $, !, and _, avoid them.

- No spaces or tabs are allowed.

- Object and variable names are case insensitive.

- Generally, it is considered good programming not to duplicate language elements. Do not use date, time, method, var, and so on to name objects or variables.

Modified Hungarian Notation for Naming Variables

Hungarian notation is a variable naming scheme. All variables of a given type should start with a lowercase prefix. The system I use is a variation on the Hungarian notation style of naming objects.

1. Start with a lowercase descriptor (a character or characters that represent the variable or object type)—for example, *s* for string, *si* for small integer, *tc* for TCursor, *mnu* for a menu variable, *sec* for secondary indexes, and so on. This descriptor should be one to three characters and as consistent with Borland's *ObjectPAL Reference Guide* as possible (although it is not always consistent).

2. Follow the variable descriptor with a short description of the variable in camel caps—for example, *sFirstName*, *siCounter*, *tcCustomer*, *fOrders*, *secState*, and so on.

3. If you need two or more variables with similar names, increment the descriptor—not the short description (*tc1Customer*, *tc2Customer*).

4. Use common sense when naming objects. After the initial 1- to 3-character beginning, use a common sense, camel-caps description. For example, use the table name for Table and TCursor variables (*tcOrders*, *tcCustomer*, *tc1Lineitem*, *tc2Lineitem*). Use the name of the table or field to name objects that are defined to a table or a field (*fldLast_Name*, *tfOrders*).

5. Use full English words for the short camel-cap description, but also keep it short—for example, *tblOrders* and *fldLastName*. In addition, avoid useless extra characters such as *siCounterVariable* (instead use *siCounter*). As one final example, if you have a field UIObject with a label of *Working Directory*, do not use *fldWorkingDirectory* (instead use *fldWorking*, or, better yet, *fldWork*). Remember, a coding convention should save you time in the long run; shorter names are preferred.

6. The preferred naming convention for temporary variables is to just use the descriptor. If you declare a variable within a method, it is acceptable to just use the descriptor. This may seem as if it is making your code more ambiguous, but in the long run, it helps the programmer code fast. For example:

```
1:    method pushButton(var eventInfo Event)
2:        var
3:            s1, s2   String   ;Strings start with s.
```

```
 4:          si        Smallint ;Small integers start with si.
 5:          tc        TCursor  ;TCursors start with tc.
 6:      endVar
 7:
 8:      s1 = "CUSTOMER.DB"
 9:      tc.open( s1 )
10:
11:      si = 3
12:      s2 = tc.(si)          ;Note in this line you can easily
13:      s2.view()             ;tell what each variable type is.
14:  endmethod
```

Note several conventions in the preceding text that I use to make my code easier to read. In the preceding example, all code is indented a single tab inside a code block. All code inside the method block is indented an additional tab. In addition, the variable declarations are indented one more tab than the var block. Also note that when two string variables were needed, I used *s1* and *s2*. Finally, note that when I used a DOS file in my code, I made it all uppercase because DOS is case insensitive.

7. When using a TCursor to refer to fields in a table, always use quotation marks, or dereference with parentheses. Although I haven't talked much about the various ways to refer to fields using a TCursor, in brief, there are three: *tc.Last_Name*, *tc."Last_Name"*, and *tc.(2)*. The preferred usage is to use quotation marks. For example, in *tc."Name"* it is clear that *Name* is a field.

8. When referring to the value of an object, it is always preferred to use the value property. This one is not mandatory, but it does make your code more readable, as you can tell at a glance that you are looking at a UIObject. Table 9.4. shows a few examples.

Rules for Naming Objects

Naming UIObjects requires a little different naming convention than naming variables. The following are the rules I use when naming an object. Rules 2, 3, and 4 are very important basic ObjectPAL rules necessary because of the 64K symbol table limit (see Appendix B, "Specifications of Paradox for Windows," for more information).

1. If you rename an object, start it with a lowercase descriptor and use

camel caps after the descriptor—just as with variables. For example, `fldName`, `boxHeaderFrame`, `tfOrders`, and `recOrders`.

2. Do not rename objects that Paradox names for you. Renaming objects unnecessarily is a waste of time and energy. For example, when you define a field object to a field in a table, Paradox names the field object the same name as the field.

3. Only rename objects if you use them in your ObjectPAL code. Renaming objects from noise names unnecessarily is a waste of time and energy. In addition, you are limited to a 64K symbol table. The symbol table holds variables and object names.

4. Never refer to noise names in your ObjectPAL code. Object noise names can be reshuffled when you deliver your form. This includes record objects of TableFrames and MROs. If you need to distinguish among the various duplicated record objects during View Data mode, then use the `rowNo` property of the record object.

Tables 9.3 through 9.7 show you many examples of naming variables and objects in ObjectPAL.

TABLE 9.3. PRESTWOOD'S CODING CONVENTION FOR DATA VARIABLES.

Object	Example	Description
AnyType	anyUserInput	Start with *any*
Array	arNames	Start with *ar*
Binary	bCorelDrawing	Start with *b*
Currency	cTotal	Start with *c*
Date	dBeginDate	Start with *d*
DateTime	dtFileStamp	Start with *dt*
DynArray	dynSysInfo	Start with *dyn*
Graphic	gEmployee	Start with *g*
Logical	lFlag	Start with *l*
LongInt	liCounter	Start with *li*
Memo	mNotes	Start with *m*
Number	nCounter	Start with *n*
OLE	oWinword	Start with *o*
Point	pBoxPosition	Start with *p*
Record	recCustomerInfo	Start with *rec*
SmallInt	siCounter	Start with *si*

Object	Example	Description
String	sLastName	Start with *s*
Time	tBeginTime	Start with *t*

TABLE 9.4. USING THE VALUE PROPERTY IS PREFERRED.

Preferred	Acceptable
fldName.value = "Greg Unsicker"	fldName = "Greg Unsicker"
Cust_No.value = 12	Cust_No = 12
btnToggleDates.value = True	btnToggleDates = True
txtReportTitle.value = "Sales Report"	txtReportTitle = "Sales Report"

TABLE 9.5. PRESTWOOD'S CODING CONVENTION FOR OBJECT VARIABLES.

Object	Example	Description
Application	app	Just use *app* (you never need more than one)
Database	dbOracle	Start with *db* and follow with type of database
DDE	ddeWinword	Start with *dde* and follow with server name
FileBrowserInfo	fbi	Start with *fbi*
FileSystem	fs	Start with *fs*
Form	fOrders	Start with *f* and follow with form file name
FormOpenInfo	fiOrders	Start with *fi* and follow with form file name
Library	libSecrets	Start with *lib* and follow with file name

continues

TABLE 9.5. CONTINUED

Object	Example	Description
Menu	mnuMain	Start with *mnu*
PopUpMenu	popEdit	Start with *pop* and follow with menu name
Query	qOrders	Start with *q* and follow with first table name
Report	rOrders	Start with *r* and follow with report file name
ReportOpenInfo	riOrders	Start with *ri* and follow with report file name
Session	ses	Start with *ses*
SQL	sqlCommit	Start with *sql* and follow with SQL file name
Table	tblCustomer	Start with *tbl* and follow with table name
TableView	tvOrders	Start with *tv* and follow with table name
TCursor	tcCustomer	Start with *tc* and follow with table name
TextStream	tsAutoexecBat	Start with *ts* and follow with file name
UIObject	uiTargetStart	UIObject variables with ui

TABLE 9.6. PRESTWOOD'S CODING CONVENTION FOR MISCELLANEOUS OBJECTS.

Object	Example	Description
Custom methods	cmCalculateTotal	Start custom methods with *cm*
Custom procedures	cpCalculateTotal	Start custom procedures with *cp*

Object	Example	Description
Custom actions	caCalculateTotal	Start with *ca* (see postAction)
Secondary Indexes	secLast_Name	Start Paradox secondary indexes with *sec*
Indexes	iLASTNAME	Start dBASE indexes with *i*
Constants	kPi	Start user defined constants with a *k*
Types	ct	Start user defined types with *ct*

TABLE 9.7. PRESTWOOD'S CODING CONVENTION FOR UIOBJECTS.		
Object	**Example**	**Description**
Field	fldLastName	Start field objects with *fld*
Button	btn	Start button objects with *btn*
TableFrame	tf	Start table frame objects with *tf*
MultiRecord Object	mro	Start multirecord objects with *mro*
Record	rec	Start record objects with *rec*
Crosstab	ct	Start crosstab objects with *ct*
Text	txt	Start text objects with *txt*
Box	box	Start box objects with *box*
Ellipse	cir	Start ellipse objects with *cir*
Graph	gph	Start graph objects with *gph*
Grouped Objects	grp	Start grouped objects with *grp*
Line	lin	Start line objects with *lin*

One of the problems with many naming conventions is that they are cumbersome and overwhelming. Some naming conventions actually slow the programmer down. The nice thing about the naming convention I have adopted is that you can still use simple 1- to 3-letter variable names if you wish and still stay within all the rules. For example, you can still use *tc* for a TCursor and *s* for a string. Yet, when you need to be more descriptive, you can add the short description. For example, you can use *tcOrders* and *tcCustomer* for descriptive variables. My naming convention even has the power to have many similarly named objects. For example, if you need several TCursor variables all pointing to the Customer table, you would use *tc1Customer*, *tc2Customer*, *tc3Customer*, and so on. In addition, you can easily tell the difference between UIObject names and variables. When reading your code weeks later, you instantly know whether you are looking at a string, TCursor, form, report variables, or a specific type of UIObject such as a field or a table frame.

UNNAMING OBJECTS

In order not to fill up the symbol table, you may occasionally need to revert an object's name back to its original noise name. To revert back to an object's noise name, delete the name you gave it.

1. Inspect the object with the Object Inspector.
2. Select its name option.
3. Delete the name in the Object Name view box.
4. Click OK or press the Enter key.

Other Conventions

While we're on the subject of conventions, here are a few of the other rules I use while developing applications.

- Unless you can think of a good reason not to, every form should have errorTrapOnWarnings(Yes) in the form **open** method. This raises warning errors to critical errors and makes developing in ObjectPAL much easier.

- Every form should have Properties | Compiler Warnings and Properties | Compile with Debug checked. These two options allow for better warning messages making developing and debugging in ObjectPAL much easier and therefore more enjoyable.

- Use a descriptive name for the main directory of your application. Use names such as SECRETS, DESKTOP, and INVOICE. Do not use names such as DATA, WORK, WORKING, or FORMS.

- Name the main form in the directory the same name as the directory. For example, INVOICE.FSL is the main form in the INVOICE directory.

- If at all possible, use a single alias. As they say, less is more in many cases. If, however, your data is in another directory, using an alias for the data is in order. For example, the Invoicing System is in a directory called INVOICE, the main form is INVOICE.FSL, the `Invoice` alias is used to open all objects in the INVOICE directory, and the `Invoice_Data` alias is used to access the data for the Invoicing System.

- Comment your code liberally. Use a complete sentence starting with a capital and ending with a period. Seeing normal English in code really sets your remarks apart from your code.

- In general, avoid putting code at the form level. When you put code at the form level, ObjectPAL executes the method for every object even when you don't use the prefilter level. In general, consider putting code that does not require the prefilter at the page level. The code still executes when the event bubbles. Do not confuse the form level with the prefilter level. The prefilter level is still a great location for writing generic routines.

- In general, use `setErrorCode(1)` rather than `disableDefault` to disable the built-in behavior whenever possible.

- When building menus, the preferred way to trap for user selection is to use menu IDs (not strings).

- Use the built-in object variables as much as possible.

- A `switch` block is always preferred over nested `if` statements even if the nested `if` statements are only two deep.

- When you have an option and there is no clear reason to do otherwise, use specific coding. For example, although `tc.open("CUSTOMER")` will open a Paradox table, the preferred syntax is `tc.open("CUSTOMER.DB")`. One other example: when executing `action()` and `menuAction()`, be specific. Do not use `action(Constant)`; instead, use `active.action(Constant)`.

- The tab stop property for buttons should be set to True. Because the default for Windows applications is to allow the user to move from button to button with the tab key, so should Paradox applications. However, keep in mind that if you have a record of a detail table locked and move focus to a button, the record does post. Therefore, if you have an undo type button for a detail table, do not set the Tab Stop property.

- Use the wide scroll bar only—the thin default scroll bar just isn't standard.

- Use only one style sheet for forms and one style sheet for reports per application. This alone will go a long way to giving your appellation a consistent look and feel. For example, I use SECRETS2.FT form style sheet and SECRETS2.FP report style sheet for all my large projects. For the sample forms, I used a style sheet with the name GRAY.FT.

Application Checklist

Whenever you start a new project, you should develop an application checklist. Usually, you do this before you start to code. A checklist guides you through an application. It enables you to step back and look at the features that you want to include in your application. A checklist helps you develop clearer, more professional applications. Here is a checklist that you can follow:

1. Use a splash screen.
2. Use a Main menu form.
3. Use an alias.
4. Either the splash screen or the Main menu form should check for the aliases and add them if possible.
5. If possible, set the correct working directory in open. If your application depends on objects in the current working directory, then you should either change the working directory for the user (if necessary) or at least check and automatically close with an error.
6. Use a consistent color and object scheme.
7. Use a Help button or option on the main form or menu.
8. If you include a text file or a Microsoft Write file, include a button—or some other easy way—to launch the file with Notepad or Write. For example:

```
1: if isFile("TEXTFILE.WRI") then   ;Check for TEXTFILE.WRI.
2:    execute("WRITE TEXTFILE.WRI") ;If it is there, open it.
3: else
```

```
4:   beep()                        ;If it is not, let the user
5:   message("File not found")     ;know.
6: endIf
```

9. Include a button or menu option to exit the application. Having the
   user double-click on the Close box in the upper-left corner of the form
   isn't sufficient for full applications.

Gradually, you will develop your own application checklist and even a
few template forms to speed your developing time. The \DEV-SRC
\TEMPLATE.FSL form on the disk that comes with this book is one
example of a template. Your goal is to create a master checklist that you can use
to develop applications that have your own style stamped on them.

A programming language's syntax is something you learn as you go along. The
syntax is the structure of the language. With the guidelines presented in this
chapter, you now have a foundation of knowledge about ObjectPAL syntax on
which to build. Whenever you type a routine, you are practicing and learning
syntax.

The next chapter continues your voyage into ObjectPAL syntax. It deals with
all the control structures available to the ObjectPAL programmer.

CONTROL STRUCTURES

In programming languages, control structures are keywords used to alter the sequence of execution and add logic to your code. All programming languages contain control structures. They are a fundamental element of any programming language. Normally, a programming language executes line after line in sequential order. This is true whether the language is a line-oriented language, such as BASIC, or a statement-oriented language, such as C. A branch transfers program control to an instruction other than the next sequential instruction. A set of instructions that is repeated a predetermined number of times or until a specified condition is met is called a *loop*. Control structures enable you to branch and loop based on whether a certain condition is True. They also enable you to add logic to your code. The techniques you learn in this chapter will help you when you learn other programming and macro languages. Although the syntax might vary, the control structures in ObjectPAL apply to other macro, procedural, and event-driven languages.

Branching with iif

Branching with if, switch, *and* try *structures*

Using the loop *and* quitLoop *keywords*

Looping with while, for, *and* scan *loops*

Programming languages and control structures

Branching

Branching involves testing a condition and doing something based on the result of that test. It enables you to code a Logical decision into your application. ObjectPAL has four types of branching: iif, if, switch, and try.

Using *iif*

iif()—short for *immediate if*—returns one of two values, depending on the result of a Logical expression. iif() enables you to branch within a single statement. You can use iif() wherever you use any other expression. iif() is especially useful where an if statement is illegal, such as in calculated fields and reports. The syntax for an iif() is as follows:

```
iif (Condition, TrueValue, FalseValue)
```

For example,

```
1:      ans = iif(Total > 100, Yes, No)
```

The true and false sections of iif() simply return a value. They don't execute commands.

The *if* Statement

You're familiar with the if statement. if executes one set of commands or another, depending on the result of a Logical expression. When ObjectPAL comes to an if statement, it evaluates whether the expression is true. If the expression is true, ObjectPAL executes the statements in the *TrueStatements* sequence. If the expression isn't true, ObjectPAL skips the *TrueStatements* sequence. Then, if the optional else keyword is present, ObjectPAL executes the *FalseStatements* sequence. In both cases, execution continues after the endIf keyword. For example:

```
if Condition then            ;If condition, then
     TrueStatements          ;execute these statements.
[else                        ;Otherwise,
     FalseStatements]        ;execute these statements.
endIf
```

The following is an example of an if statement using the else clause:

```
1:      if self.value < 0 then              ;If negative, then set
2:          self.font.color = Red           .;the font color to red, &
```

```
3:         message("Value is negative")      ;display a message.
4:      else
5:         self.font.color = Black           ;Otherwise, color is black
6:         message("")                       ;and clear message.
7:      endIf
```

The `if` statement is highly flexible; you can nest `if` statements. Nesting an `if` statement means that any statement in TrueStatements or FalseStatements sequences also can be an `if` statement. For example:

if *Condition1* then	;If condition1, then
TrueStatements1	;execute these statements.
else	;Otherwise,
if *Condition2* then	;if Condition2, then
TrueStatements2	;execute these statements.
endIf	;End inside if block.
endIf	;End outside if block.

The following is an example of a nested `if` statement.

```
1:      if skillLevel = "Beginner" then
2:         if skillBox.color = "Red" then
3:            skillBox.color = "Green"
4:         endIf
5:      endIf
```

The next two examples demonstrate how to use compound conditions with `and` and `or`.

if *Cond1* and *Cond2* then	;If both are true, then
TrueStatements	;execute these statements.
else	;Otherwise,
FalseStatements	;execute these statements.
endIf	;End of if block.

For example:

```
1:      if self.value > 0 and self.value < 10 then
2:         self.font.color = Yellow
3:         message("Balance is low")
4:      endIf
```

if *Cond1* or *Cond2* then	;If either are True, then
TrueStatements	;execute these statements.
else	;Otherwise,
FalseStatements	;execute these statements.
endIf	;End of if block.

For example:

```
1:      if x = 1 or x = 2 then
2:          message("True")
3:      else
4:          message("False")
5:      endIf
```

One of the tutorials, "Basic Database Buttons," in Chapter 4 used this keyword sequence:

```
1:      if    deleteRecord() then
2:                  message("Record deleted")
3:            else
4:                  message("Could not delete record")
5:            endIf
```

Line 1 tries to delete a record. If the delete is successful, the code after the `then` keyword and before the `else` keyword is executed. If the delete fails, the code after the `else` keyword and before the `endIf` keyword is executed.

If you wanted to check the data of a field before the user leaves it, you could use an `if` statement in the **canDepart** built-in method of the field that you want to check. Essentially, **canDepart** asks for permission to leave the field. In other words, the **canDepart** built-in method is triggered just before the cursor leaves the field:

```
1:      if self.value > 100 then
2:          eventInfo.setErrorCode(canNotDepart)
3:          msgStop("!!! Warning !!!","Value too large.")
4:      endIf
```

This example has more than one line of code between the `if` and `endIf` keywords. Take a close look at line 2. *eventInfo* is a variable. In essence, this *eventInfo* variable represents a packet that ObjectPAL sends from object to object. `setErrorCode()` is a method that works on this packet. In this case, `setErrorCode()` uses the `CanNotDepart` error constant to set the error code in the packet to the error code `CanNotDepart`. You can inspect this error code with the `errorCode()` method. Setting the error code in the packet in this way prevents the cursor from leaving the field.

The *switch* Block

You can use nested `if` statements to execute one set of commands out of many sets. ObjectPAL offers a better way, however, to make compound decisions: the `switch` block. `switch` executes a set of alternative statement sequences, depending on which of several conditions is met.

switch uses the values of the condition statements in each case to determine which sequence of statements to execute. Each case works like a single if statement, and the switch structure works like multiple, compound, or nested if statements.

As soon as the first case evaluates to True, the corresponding sequence of statements is executed and the remaining cases are skipped. If no case evaluates to True and the optional otherWise clause is present, the statements in otherWise are executed. If no case evaluates to True and no otherWise clause is present, switch has no effect. Here is the syntax.

switch
        case *Condition1*   : *Statements1*
        [**case** *Condition2*   : *Statements2*] ;Repeat as
                                              needed.
        [**otherWise**   : *Statements3*]
    endSwitch

For example:

```
1:    switch
2:        case AmountField < 0      : message("We're in the red")
3:        case AmountField < 10     : message("Balance is very low")
4:        case AmountField < 100    : message("Balance is low")
5:        case AmountField > 1000   : message("Go spend some money")
6:        otherWise                 : message("Balance is looking good")
7:    endSwitch
```

This first example is formatted well because each resulting sequence of commands was short enough to fit nicely on a single line of code, but how do you keep your code readable when you need to use multiple lines of code in the resulting sequence? This next example shows how you can use compound expressions and execute multiple statements, and still keep the code very readable.

```
 1:    switch
 2:        case Field1 < 0 and Field2 = True
 3:            :  ans = 1
 4:               message("One")
 5:               Page1.moveTo()
 6:        case Field1 < 0 and Field2 = False
 7:            :  ans = 2
 8:               message("Two")
 9:               Page2.moveTo()
10:        case Field1 >= 0 and Field2 = True
11:            :  ans = 3
12:               message("Three")
13:               Page3.moveTo()
14:        case Field1 >= 0 and Field2 = False
```

```
15:              :  ans = 4
16:                 message("Four")
17:                 Page4.moveTo()
18:        endSwitch
```

The *try* Block

Use try as your basic ObjectPAL error recovery tool. With try, you can attempt
to execute a block of code. If all the commands succeed, execution skips to just
after the endTry keyword. If any one command generates a critical error, the
recovery block executes starting just after the onFail keyword. Here is the
syntax:

> **try**
>
> > [*Statements*]   ;The transaction block.
> > [**fail()**]   ;Optional.
>
> **onFail**
>
> > [*Statements*]   ;The recovery block.
> > [**reTry**]   ;Optional.
>
> **endTry**

You can call the keyword reTry to execute the transaction block again. For
example:

```
 1:     var
 2:        nCounter     Number
 3:     endVar
 4:
 5:     nCounter = 1
 6:
 7:     try
 8:        Last_Name.postRecord()
 9:     onFail
10:       sleep(250)
11:       if nCounter >= 5 then
12:          msgStop("Warning", "Could not post record")
13:       else
14:          nCounter = nCounter + 1
15:          reTry
16:       endIf
17:     endTry
```

A method or procedure that generates a warning error or returns a False does
not cause the onFail block to execute. You can raise warning errors to critical
errors by using errorTrapOnWarnings(). For example:

```
 1:     errorTrapOnWarnings(Yes)     ;Raise warning errors to critical
 2:                                  ;so try will catch it.
```

In addition, you can use the keyword `fail()` to force a branch to the `onFail` portion. Use this technique to force a block of code to fail, such as when a method or procedure returns a False. For example, type the following line of code in the **pushButton** method of a button.

```
1:      ;Button :: pushButton
2:          method (var eventInfo Event)
3:      try
4:          if not isfile("C:\\NOFILE.TXT") then fail() endIf
5:          message("File exists.")
6:      onFail
7:          message("File does not exist.")
8:      endTry
9:          endMethod
```

You can nest `fail()` inside several procedure calls—far from where the block begins. If you decide in a recovery block that the error code is not what you expected, or if the error code is too serious to be handled in the current `onFail` block, call `fail()` again to pass it up to the next `try` block's `onFail` clause.

If no higher-level `try` block exists, the whole application fails. It cancels existing actions, closes resources, and causes a critical error. This is done by the implicit `try` block that ObjectPAL wraps around every method (see Figure 10.1).

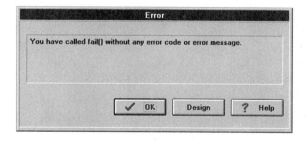

Figure 10.1. The error message you get when you call `fail()` *and* `fail()` *has no place to fail to.*

Tutorial: Using *try* to Test a Date in an Undefined Field

Suppose that you wish to test whether the value in an undefined field is a valid date. How can you tell whether the user has typed a valid date into an undefined field? ObjectPAL doesn't have an `isDate` type method, so how do you test? One way to test whether the user typed in a valid date is to try to cast the value as a date. If the test fails, you know that the date isn't valid. Although blanks are normally a legal date, in this tutorial, blanks are not allowed.

On Disk: \ANSWERS\TRY.FSL

Quick Steps

1. Put an undefined field and a button on a form.

2. In a `try` structure on the button, try to cast the value in the field as a date.

3. Inside the `try` structure, test for a blank in an `if` statement. If the `isBlank()` returns False, then force a fail.

Step By Step

1. Change your working directory to the TUTORIAL directory and create a new form. Put an undefined field and a button on a new form. Label the button Test Date and name the field *fldDate*, and change its label to Enter date (see Figure 10.2).

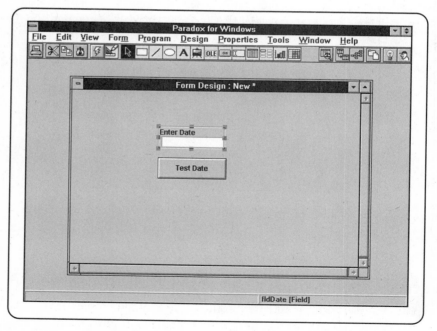

Figure 10.2. Set up form for tutorial.

2. Add lines 3–9 to the **pushButton** method of the button.

```
1:      ;Button :: pushButton
2:      method pushButton(var eventInfo Event)
3:          try
4:              if fldDate.isBlank() then fail() endIf
5:              date(fldDate)
6:              msgInfo("","Valid date")
7:          onFail
8:              msgInfo("Warning", "Invalid date")
9:          endTry
10:     endmethod
```

3. Check the syntax, save the form as TRY.FSL, and run it. Enter various dates into the field. Test each date after you've entered it by clicking on the button (see Figure 10.3). For example, try 1/8/65, 10/33/93, 001/1/1991, and a blank. This form uses isBlank() and a try structure to test whether the data typed into an undefined field is valid.

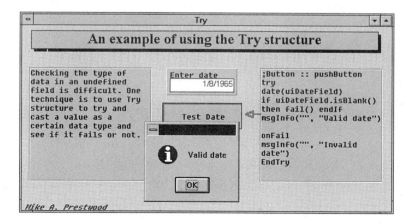

Figure 10.3. ANSWERS\TRY.FSL.

Analysis

In step 2, lines 3–9 make up the try block. Line 3 begins the structure with the keyword try. Line 4 uses an if statement along with the isBlank() method to test whether something was entered. If nothing was entered, the fail() procedure forces a fail, and the execution skips to onFail in line 7. If something was entered, the execution drops through to line 5. Line 5 attempts to cast the value in the *fldDate* field as a date. If the value is cast as a date, execution continues to line 6, which displays a message information box. After line 6 displays the message, the execution skips to endTry in line 9. If the casting of the *fldDate* field with the Date() procedure in line 5 fails, the execution skips to onFail in line 7.

Remember that, in a try structure, if any command in the try portion generates a critical error, the execution skips to onFail. If you don't care about blank entries, you can leave out the if statement. For example:

```
1:    ;Button :: pushButton
2:    try                              ;Begin try block.
3:       date(fldDate)                 ;Cast fldDate as a date.
4:       msgInfo("","Valid date")      ;Display a message box.
5:    onFail                           ;Begin onFail block.
6:       msgInfo("","Invalid date")    ;Display a message box.
7:    endTry                           ;End try block.
```

You can use a try block to add function to ObjectPAL. For example, this tutorial showed you how to add an isDate() type of method. A try block is also a great way to put error checking into your application. You could surround a piece of code with a try structure and display a generic message if any command fails.

Looping

When you program, you often need to repeat a number of commands. One of the most important aspects of a programming language is its ability to loop—that is, to go through a series of commands a certain number of times. ObjectPAL has four ways to loop: scan, for, forEach, and while.

Using the *loop* and *quitLoop* Keywords

All four loops have two keywords in common: loop and quitLoop. Therefore, let's address these before we get into the four loops. loop passes program control to the top of the nearest loop. When loop is executed within a for, forEach, scan, or while structure, it skips the statements between it and endFor, endForEach, endScan, or endWhile and returns to the beginning of the structure.

quitLoop terminates a loop. quitLoop immediately exits to the nearest for, forEach, endScan, or endWhile keyword. Execution continues with the statement that follows the nearest endFor, endForEach, endScan, or endWhile. quitLoop causes an error if it's executed outside a for, forEach, scan, or while structure.

The *while* Loop

A while loop enables you to execute a set of commands while a condition is true. Specifically, while repeats a sequence of statements as long as a specified condition evaluates to True. At the end of the set of commands, the condition is tested again. In a typical while loop, you must make the condition False somewhere in the set of commands.

```
while Condition     ;Test condition, if true
   [Statements]     ;execute these statements.
                    ;Don't forget to make
                    ;the condition false some          place.
endWhile            ;Go back to while.
```

while starts by evaluating the Logical expression *Condition*. If *Condition* is false, the execution continues after endWhile. If *Condition* is true, *Statements* are executed. When the program comes to endWhile, it returns to the first line of the loop, which re-evaluates *Condition*. *Statements* are repeated until *Condition* evaluates to False.

Tutorial: Using a *while* Loop

The goal of this tutorial is to demonstrate a simple while loop that counts to 10.

On Disk: \ANSWERS\LOOPS.FSL

Quick Steps

1. Declare a *Counter* variable as SmallInt.

2. Initialize the *Counter* variable.

3. Use a while loop to count to 10 and to display the *Counter* variable in the status bar. Make sure that you increment the *Counter* within the loop.

Step By Step

1. Change your working directory to the TUTORIAL directory and create a new form with a button labeled While loop.

2. Add lines 3–14 to the **pushButton** method of the While loop button.

```
1:    ;Button :: pushButton
2:    method pushButton(var eventInfo Event)
3:       var
4:          Counter    SmallInt       ;Counter is a SmallInt.
```

```
 5:        endVar

 6:

 7:        Counter = 0           ;Variables must be
 8:                                  ;initialized.
 9:        While Counter < 10    ;Start of while loop.
10:           message(Counter)         ;Display Counter.
11:           sleep(250)          ;Sleep for 1/4 second.
12:           Counter = Counter + 1    ;Increments counter.
13:        endWhile                 ;End of while loop.
14:        message("Final value for Counter is " +
           StrVal(Counter))
15:      endmethod
```

3. Check the syntax, save the form as LOOPS.FSL, and run the form. Click the While Loop button. Watch the status bar count from 0 to 9 in the loop and display the number 10 after the loop is finished (see Figure 10.4).

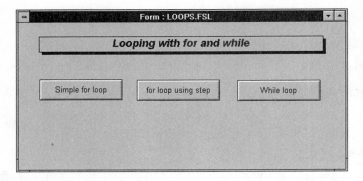

Figure 10.4. Using for *and* while *loops.*

Analysis

In step 3, line 4 declares *Counter* as a SmallInt variable. In line 7, *Counter* is initialized to 0. (All variables must be initialized before you use them.) Lines 9–13 form the while loop. When *Counter* is less than 10, lines 10–12 are executed. In line 12, the *Counter* variable is incremented. If you leave this line out, the counter will loop forever. (You'll have to use Ctrl+Break to exit the loop.) With while loops, you have to make the condition False at some point. This example uses a simple *Counter* variable that eventually makes the condition in line 9 False, which in turn ends the loop. Execution continues after endWhile.

This example uses a while loop as a counter. Normally, you would use a for loop for a loop that has a counter. while loops are useful for executing a set of commands as long as a condition is True. For example, you might execute a set of commands while the left character of a string is equal to *Sm* or while a box's color is red. The important thing to remember about a while loop is that it's your responsibility to make the condition false and exit the loop.

The *for* Loop

Use a for loop to execute a sequence of statements a specific number of times. You don't have to increment the counter in a for loop, as you must in a while loop.

> **for** *Counter* [from *startVal*] [to *endVal*] [step *stepVal*]
>   *Statements*
> **endFor**

The three values *startVal*, *endVal*, and *stepVal* are values or expressions that represent the beginning, ending, and increment values. for executes a sequence of statements as many times as the counter specifies. The specific number of times is stored in *Counter*, and it is controlled by the optional from, to, and step keywords. You can use any combination of these keywords to specify the number of times that the statements in the loop should be executed. You don't have to declare *Counter* explicitly, but a for loop runs faster if you do. If you previously didn't assign a value to *Counter*, from creates the variable and assigns the value of *startVal* to it.

You can use for without the from, to, and step keywords. If *startVal* is omitted, the counter starts at the current value of Counter. If *endVal* is omitted, the for loop executes indefinitely—not too practical! Finally, if *stepVal* is omitted, the counter increments by 1 each time through the loop. For example:

```
1:    ;Button :: pushButton
2:    for Counter from 1 to 3      ;Count from 1 to 3.
3:        Counter.view()           ;Execute these statements.
4:    endFor                       ;End for block.
```

Tutorial: Using a *for* Loop

The goal of this tutorial is to demonstrate two for loops: with and without step.

On Disk: \ANSWERS\LOOPS.FSL

Step By Step

1. Change your working directory to the TUTORIAL directory and open the LOOPS.FSL form you created in the previous tutorial (or create it now). Place two buttons named Simple for loop and For loop using step on it (see Figure 10.4 shown previously).

2. Add lines 3–9 to the **pushButton** method of the Simple for loop button.

```
1:    ;Button1 :: pushButton
2:    method pushButton(var eventInfo Event)
3:       var
4:          Counter    SmallInt          ;Declare Counter.
5:       endVar
6:       for Counter from 1 to 5          ;Start of for loop.
7:          msgInfo("Counter", Counter) ;Commands to loop.
8:       endFor                           ;End of for loop.
9:       message("Note the final value for Counter is " +
              string(Counter))
10:   endmethod
```

3. Add lines 3–15 to the **pushButton** method of the For loop using step button.

```
1:    ;Button2 :: pushButton
2:    method pushButton(var eventInfo Event)
3:       var
4:          Counter, CountTo    Number
5:       endVar
6:
7:       CountTo = 20
8:       CountTo.view("Enter a number")
9:
10:      for Counter from 0 to CountTo Step .5
11:         message(Counter)
12:         sleep(250)
13:      endFor
14:
```

```
15:        message("Note the final value for Counter after loop
           is " + string(Counter))
16:        endmethod
```

4. Check the syntax, save the form, and run it. Press the Simple for loop and For loop using step buttons. Watch the status bar as they loop.

Analysis

In step 2, line 4 declares *Counter* as a SmallInt variable. You also could use `Number`, `LongInt`, or `AnyType`. In fact, you could choose not to declare *Counter* at all, but that would be poor programming. Lines 6–8 make up the `for` loop. Line 6 sets up the *Counter* variable to count from 1 to 5 at the default increment step of 1. Between `for` and `endFor`, you put all the commands that you want to loop through five times. In this case, a message information dialog box is displayed. Line 8 ends the `for` loop. Remember that, in a `for` loop, all the commands between `for` and `endFor` are executed once every time the loop is executed. Line 9 displays the final value for *Counter*, which is always one increment beyond the *CountTo* value.

In step 3, line 4 declares *Counter* and *CountTo* variables of type `Number`. Because of containership and encapsulation, you can use the same name—*Counter*—in both buttons. Line 7 initializes *CountTo* to 20, and line 8 displays it so that the user can either accept it or change it. Line 10 sets up the *Counter* variable to count from 0 to the value stored in *CountTo* at the increment step of .5.

Lines 10–13 make up the `for` loop. Line 11 displays the counter in the status bar, and line 12 sleeps for a quarter second. Line 15 reminds you that the counter value is always one increment beyond the value used in the last loop.

The *forEach* Loop

A `forEach` loop works similarly to a `for` loop. You use a `forEach` loop to move through the elements in a `DynArray`. Chapter 11, "Data Types," discusses the `DynArray` data type and `forEach` loops.

The *scan* Loop

The `scan` loop is an extremely powerful tool that you can use to manipulate a whole table or, with the `for` keyword, a subset of a table. The `scan` loop scans a TCursor and executes ObjectPAL instructions. The syntax for a `scan` loop is as follows:

```
scan tcVar [for booleanExpression]:
    Statements
endScan
```

The colon at the end of the first line is required. It separates the first line from the following statements. scan starts with the first record in a TCursor and moves from record to record, executing Statements for every record. scan automatically moves from record to record through the table, so you don't need to call action(DataNextRecord) within your statements. When an indexed field is changed by a scan loop, the changed record moves to its sorted position in the table. Therefore, it's possible to encounter the same record more than once. As with all the loops discussed in this chapter, be sure to put statements that occur only once before the loop.

The for expression is used to filter the records. Only the records that match the expression are acted on. All other records are skipped. When you use the for keyword with scan, it must be followed by a colon to differentiate it from a for loop.

If you use ObjectVision, you're familiar with the @PROPER command, which takes a text field and converts the first letter of every word to a capital letter. Although ObjectPAL doesn't have a proper command, you can use the format() command to achieve the same result, as the next tutorial demonstrates.

Tutorial: Using a scan Loop to Make a Field Proper

Suppose that you wish to use a scan loop to change a field to a proper format. This tutorial uses a scan loop and the format() command to change a field named Name in the CUSTOMER.DB table to a proper format. Before you make drastic changes to a table, you should always make a backup copy. This tutorial acquaints you with the script, the scan loop, and format().

On Disk: \ANSWERS\PROPER.SSL

Quick Steps
1. Open a TCursor and put it in Edit mode.
2. Use a scan loop to loop through the table record by record.
3. As you loop through the table, use the format() method to format any field that you want.
4. Tidy up by exiting Edit mode and closing the TCursor.

Step By Step

1. Make TUTORIAL your working directory. Open the CUSTOMER.DB file. Change some of the last names to all uppercase or all lowercase.

2. Choose File | New | Script and type in lines 3–16.

```
 1:    ;Script :: Run
 2:    method run(var eventInfo Event)
 3:       Var
 4:          tc    TCursor
 5:       endVar
 6:
 7:       if msgQuestion("Question?",
             "Make Name field proper?") = "Yes" then
 8:          tc.open("CUSTOMER.DB")
 9:          tc.edit()
10:       scan tc:
11:          tc."Name" = format("cl,cc", tc."Name")
12:       endScan
13:       tc.endedit()
14:       tc.close()
15:       msgInfo("","All done converting Name field")
16:       endIf
17:    endmethod
```

3. Check the syntax, save the form as PROPER.SSL, and run the script. After the script has finished executing, reopen CUSTOMER.DB. Now the Name field is in a proper format.

Analysis

In step 2, line 4 declares tc as a TCursor variable. Line 7 asks for permission to continue using a message question box. If the answer is yes, then line 8 opens the TCursor and puts it in Edit mode in line 9. In this code, the scan loop uses only three lines—lines 10–12. Line 13 ends the Edit session, and line 14 closes the TCursor. Line 15 tells the user that the program is done.

You bought Paradox so that you could view, enter, and manipulate data. For the ObjectPAL programmer, the scan loop is very easy to use, and it's a powerful tool for manipulating the data in a table. In many ways, using a scan loop is similar to using a query in Interactive mode. In fact, there are occasions when using a scan loop is faster then doing a complicated query.

> Don't use a scan loop whenever the record number for a record might
> change. As mentioned earlier, it's possible for records to be encountered
> more than once or to be missed entirely if the record number for any
> record is changed. Therefore, you should never use a scan loop when you
> delete records or when you change the value of the primary key. Instead,
> use a for loop with nRecords(). An example of this technique is presented
> in Chapter 16, "Using Table and TCursor Variables."

This chapter introduced you to branching and looping in ObjectPAL. The
main reason you purchased Paradox was to manipulate data. Manipulating data
depends on data types. Chapter 11 discusses the ObjectPAL data types.

11

CHAPTER

DATA TYPES

What are data types? Data typing is the classifying of data into categories such as string, number, and date. This classification is necessary so that the compiler knows how to treat and store the data. For example, a number takes up more room in memory than a small integer. I talked about the various types or classes of methods and procedures back in Chapter 5, "The ObjectPAL Editor," and I've mentioned them sporadically since then. In ObjectPAL, you can declare a variable to be any of 50 or more variable types. How do you know what types are available? You already know the answer to that question. Remember near the end of Chapter 5 when you browsed through all the variable types and their methods by selecting Tools | Types from the ObjectPAL Editor? Those are the variable types you can declare a variable as (see Table 11.1). The methods and procedures that correspond to them are the methods and procedures you use to manipulate them.

Using AnyType variables

Using the Logical data type

Dealing with number data

Dealing with character data

Using custom data types

TABLE 11.1. THE 50-PLUS VARIABLE TYPES AVAILABLE IN ObjectPAL.			
ActionEvent	Date	Memo	SmallInt
AnyType	DateTime	Menu	StatusEvent
Application	DDE	MenuEvent	String
Array	DynArray	MouseEvent	System
Binary	ErrorEvent	MoveEvent	Table
CDOUBLE	Event	Number	TableView
CHANDLE	FileSystem	OLE	TCursor
CLONG	Form	Point	TextStream
CLONGDOUBLE	Graphic	PopUpMenu	Time
CPTR	KeyEvent	Query	TimerEvent
Currency	Library	Record	UIObject
CWORD	Logical	Report	ValueEvent
Database	LongInt	Session	SQL

CREATE AN UP-TO-DATE TABLE OF CLASS NAMES

Create and run the following one-line script:

```
enumRTLClassNames("RTLCLASS.DB")
```

This one line of code creates a table with all the current class names. Why should you do this if the preceding table has all the classes? When Borland releases a new version of Paradox, you can run this same script and check to see whether Borland added any new classes of objects.

As soon as you find a variable type with which you want to work, you declare a variable as that type in a var block. As soon as the variable is declared, you can use any of the methods in its class to manipulate it. For example, as soon as a TCursor is defined, you then can use any of the TCursor type or class of methods to manipulate it:

```
1:    var                            ;This is the start of a var structure.
2:        tc   TCursor               ;Set variable types in between.
3:    endVar                         ;This marks the end of a var structure.
4:    tc.open("ZIPCODES")
```

The *tc* variable is a handle to a TCursor object. A TCursor is a type of object. How do data types relate to object types? Data types are simply a very important subset of all the variable types. Remember that in ObjectPAL there are more than 50 object types. All these object types are variables that you can manipulate with the appropriate method or procedure. For example, you use the 18 data types to store data in memory. As soon as data is stored in a particular type of variable in memory, you can use the methods associated with the type or class of variable to manipulate it. Table 11.2 describes the 18 data types and the kind of data each stores.

TABLE 11.2. THE 18 DATA TYPES.

Type	Description
AnyType	A catch-all data type
Array	An indexed collection of data
Binary	A handle to a binary object (machine-readable data)
Currency	Money (for example, $1.00, $.05, $12.50)
Date	Calendar data (for example, 12/25/93)
DateTime	Calendar and clock data combined (for example, 10:00:00 am 12/25/65)
DynArray	A dynamic array
Graphic	A bitmap image
Logical	True or false
LongInt	Represents relatively large integer values
Memo	Holds lots of text
Number	Floating-point values
OLE	A link to another application
Point	Information about a location on-screen
Record	A user-defined structure
SmallInt	Used to represent integer values from –32,768 to 32,767
String	Letters (for example, A–Z, 0–9, %, and $)
Time	Clock data (for example, 11:04:00 PM)

Just as you define fields in tables to store various types of data, you declare variables in ObjectPAL to store data in memory. As you can see from Table 11.3, field types in a table are related to data types in memory.

TABLE 11.3. OBJECTPAL DATA TYPES, PARADOX FIELD TYPES, AND DBASE FIELD TYPES.		
Data Type	Paradox Field Type	dBASE Field Type
AnyType		
Array		
Binary	Binary-B	Binary-B
Currency	Money-$	
Date	Date-D	Date-D
DateTime	TimeStamp - @	
DynArray		
Graphic	Graphic-G	
Logical	Logical - L	Logical-L
LongInt	Long Integer-I	Float Number-F
Memo	Memo-M	Memo-M
Number	Numeric-N	Number-N
OLE	OLE-O	OLE-O
Point		
Record		
SmallInt	Short-S	Number-N
String	Alpha-A	Character-C
Time	Time-T	

Although Paradox 5 table structures support many more data types then previous versions of Paradox, as you can see, ObjectPAL picks up where Paradox and dBASE tables leave off. There are more ObjectPAL data types than either Paradox or dBASE field types. If you wanted to store time in a dBASE table, what field type would you choose? dBASE, unlike the Paradox table structure, does not offer a time format. One technique is to use a character field of size 12 to store the characters and then use ObjectPAL to manipulate them. The important thing to note at this point is that the 18 data types in

ObjectPAL enable you to deal with more types of data than the set Paradox and dBASE field types allow. You declare or cast a variable as a particular type of variable. This is known as type casting.

USING ANYTYPE

AnyType is the catch-all variable type for the times when you can't predict what type of variable you'll need. Table 11.4 lists all the data types AnyType accepts.

TABLE 11.4. ANYTYPE VARIABLE TYPES.		
Array	Graphic	Point
Binary	Logical	Record
Currency	LongInt	SmallInt
Date	Memo	String
DateTime	Number	Time
DynArray	OLE	

After you declare a variable as an AnyType variable, you can use the seven AnyType methods and procedures to manipulate it. These methods are very important because most of them are the core methods for the rest of the datatypes. Following is a description of each.

blank()	Returns a blank value
dataType()	Returns a string representing the data type of a variable
isAssigned()	Reports whether a variable has been assigned a value
isBlank()	Reports whether an expression has a blank value
isFixedType()	Reports whether a variable's data type has been explicitly declared
unAssign()	Sets a variable's state to unAssigned
view()	Displays in a dialog box the value of a variable

Implicit Casting with AnyType

Whenever the compiler comes across a variable or value in your code, it stores it in memory. If the value was not type cast, then the compiler casts it at that time. This can create problems. For example, if you type and run the following code, you'll get an error.

```
 1:     ;Button :: pushButton
 2:     method pushButton(var eventInfo Event)
 3:        var
 4:           n      Number              ;Declare n as a number.
 5:        endVar
 6:
 7:         ;Set n to 40000.
 8:         n = 2 * 20000              ;This gives an error.
 9:         n.view()
10:     endmethod
```

Why? Isn't 40,000 within the range of a Number? Yes, but when ObjectPAL came across the equation 2 * 20000, it had to store the numbers in memory and, because the first number is an integer, the numbers were stored in temporary small integer variables. Small integers cannot store the value 40,000. To fix this, change the preceding line 8 to the following.

```
 8:         n = 2.0 * 20000.0
```

More on implicit casting of numbers later when SmallInt, LongInt, and Number are discussed. For now, here are some examples of implicit casting that you can type into a button if you like.

```
 1:     x = 1                      ;x is cast as a SmallInt.
 2:     view(Datatype(x))          ;Displays SmallInt.
 3:
 4:     x = 1.1                    ;x is cast as a Number.
 5:     view(Datatype(x))          ;Displays Number.
 6:
 7:     x = 40000                  ;x is cast as a LongInt.
 8:     view(Datatype(x))          ;Displays LongInt.
 9:
10:     x = "Darcy"                ;x is cast as a String.
11:     view(Datatype(x))          ;Displays String.
12:
13:     y = 1.1                    ;This is a Number.
14:     z = "Mike"                 ;This is a string.
15:     x.view()
```

In the next tutorial, you use the same variable as a number and then as a string without declaring it again. It demonstrates using an AnyType variable. Several of the tutorials in this chapter are demonstrated in the form \ANSWERS\DATATYPE.FSL (see Figure 11.1).

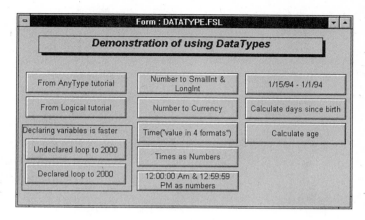

Figure 11.1. The \ANSWERS\DATATYPE.FSL form demonstrates using datatypes.

Tutorial: Using AnyType

Suppose that you need to use *x* as both a number and a string. In this tutorial, *x* is used first as a number, then as a string.

On Disk: \ANSWERS\DATATYPE.FSL

Quick Steps

1. Define a variable as AnyType.
2. Assign a value to the variable (string, number, time, and so on).
3. Use the variable in code.

Step By Step

1. Change your working directory to the TUTORIAL directory, create a new form, and place a button on it.

2. Open the **pushButton** method of the button and add lines 3 through 13 to it.

```
1:    ;Button :: pushButton
2:    method pushButton(var eventInfo Event)
3:       var
4:          x      AnyType      ;Declare x as AnyType.
5:       endVar
6:
7:          x = 12.3           ;First use x as a Number.
```

```
8:              x.view()          ;View x.
9:              msgInfo("DataType", dataType(x))
10:
11:             x = "12.3"         ;Then use x as a String.
12:             x.view()          ;View x.
13:             msgInfo("DataType", dataType(x))
14:     endmethod
```

3. Check your syntax, save the form as DATATYPE.FSL, and run it. Click the button. First, you see the number 12.3 in a number-style viewer. After you click OK, you see a message box confirming that the current data type for x is indeed Number. After you click OK to the message box, you see the characters 12.3, but this time they are in a string box. After you click OK to the viewer, a message box confirms that x indeed is now a string.

Analysis

Line 4 declares x as an AnyType variable, which means that you can store many types of data in it without declaring it again. Line 7 sets x to the number 12.3. It is viewed with the number class viewer in line 8. In line 9, `msgInfo()` uses `dataType()` to confirm that the type of x has been declared by ObjectPAL as type Number.

Lines 11–13 are just like lines 7–9, except that in line 11, x is set to the string "12.3." In line 12, the string viewer is used when the user is shown the value. In line 13, `msgInfo()` confirms that, internally, ObjectPAL has changed the data type to a string type.

YOU DON'T HAVE TO DECLARE VARIABLES, BUT YOU SHOULD

Although x was specifically declared as an AnyType variable in the preceding tutorial, declaring an AnyType variable isn't required. Whenever the ObjectPAL compiler comes across a variable that hasn't been declared, it declares it as AnyType. In general, it's good programming practice to always declare variables. Get in the habit of declaring variables so that the compiler can catch typing mistakes. If you declare a *siCounter* variable at the form and accidently type *liCounter*, the compiler will catch it when Properties | Compiler Warnings is turned on. Declaring variables also makes your code easier to read.

Is it a good idea to declare all variables as AnyType so that you don't have to worry about variable type? No. Avoid using AnyType variables because they slow your code down. Declaring a variable as an AnyType variable is the same as not declaring the variable at all. If you explicitly declare all your variables, your code will run faster. AnyType variables are useful when you don't know what the datatype will be.

Tutorial: Declared Variables Run Faster

The goal of this tutorial is to demonstrate that declaring variables makes your code faster.

On Disk: \ANSWERS\DATATYPE.FSL

Quick Steps

1. In a `for` loop, count to 2000. Don't declare the counter variable.
2. In a second `for` loop, count to 2000. This time, declare the counter variable as a SmallInt.

Step By Step

1. Change your working directory to the TUTORIAL directory and create a new form with two buttons on it. Label them Undeclared and Declared.

2. Add lines 3–5 to the **pushButton** method of the Undeclared button.

```
1:    ;Undeclared Button :: pushButton
2:    method pushButton(var eventInfo Event)
3:        beep()
4:        for Counter from 1 to 2000 endFor
5:        beep()
6:    endmethod
```

3. Add lines 3–9 to the **pushButton** method of the Declared button.

```
1:    ;Declared Button :: pushButton
2:    method pushButton(var eventInfo Event)
3:        var
4:            Counter SmallInt
5:        endVar
```

```
6:
7:        beep()
8:        for Counter from 1 to 2000 endFor
9:        beep()
10:    endmethod
```

4. Check the syntax, save the form as DATATYPE.FSL, and run the form. Click both buttons. Note how much closer together the beeps are for the button labeled Declared.

Analysis

Let's take a closer look at the preceding tutorial for two reasons: to explain compile time binding and to review scope.

When the compiler compiles your source code, it casts all the variable types of the variables you have used. This process is called *binding*. When the compiler comes across a variable, it needs to find out whether the variable is declared. It first searches the `method...endMethod` structure in which the variable is used. Then, the compiler searches for a `var...endVar` structure above the current `method...endMethod` structure. After this, it searches the Var window of the object to which the code is attached, and then the Var window of the Object's container, and so on until it reaches the form. When the compiler comes across the first occurrence of the variable declaration, it stops searching. If the compiler goes all the way up to the Var window of the form and the variable is not declared anywhere, then the variable is declared as AnyType.

The Logical Data Type

A variable declared as Logical can contain only two values: True or False. It can, however, be at any one of four states/values: unassigned, blank, True, or False. For example, type the following code on the **pushButton** method of a button.

```
1:    ;Button :: pushButton
2:    method pushButton(var eventInfo Event)
3:       var
4:          l      Logical           ;Declare l as a logical variable.
5:          endVar
6:
7:          l.view("Unassigned")     ;View l.
8:
9:          l = blank()              ;Set l to blank.
10:         l.view("Blank")          ;View l.
11:
12:         l = True                 ;Set l to True.
13:         l.view("True")           ;View l.
```

```
14:
15:        l = False              ;Set l to False.
16:        l.view("False")        ;View l.
17:    endmethod
```

A field that is either blank or zero is considered null. Whenever you store an empty field, Paradox and dBASE actually store a null. This condition for a field is called *blank* in Paradox. The ObjectPAL Logical data type is equivalent to the dBASE and Paradox Logical field types. You can use the Logical methods and procedures. The Logical type includes several derived or inherited methods from the AnyType type and are marked with an asterisk in Table 11.5.

TABLE 11.5. LOGICAL METHODS AND PROCEDURES.

blank*

dataType*

isAssigned*

isBlank*

isFixedType*

Logical

view*

*Inherited from the AnyType type

In your ObjectPAL code, you can use Yes/No or On/Off in place of True/False, but the value that is displayed to the user is still dependent on the display format, usually True or False. If you type the following code on the **pushButton** method of a button, you'll notice that, although l is specifically set to Yes in line 7, True is displayed when line 8 displays a Logical view box.

```
1:    ;Button :: pushButton
2:    method pushButton(var eventInfo Event)
3:        var
4:            l    Logical
5:        endVar
6:
7:            l = Yes
8:            l.view()
9:    endmethod
```

Why use a Logical data type when you could just as easily use a `String`? One reason is that a Logical variable occupies only 1 byte of storage, and in computer languages, smaller is faster.

MANY METHODS RETURN A LOGICAL

Nearly all methods and procedures return something. In many cases, they return a simple Logical True or False. You can use this return value to determine whether a method or procedure succeeded. For example, the following line of code displays True in the status bar if it can take the form out of Edit mode, and False if it can't:

```
1:      message(endEdit())
```

This simple example shows you that almost every method and procedure returns something. In most cases, you can use this fact to add error checking to your routines. For example, the following line of code displays the error box, complete with an error message when the locate() method returns False:

```
1:      if not Last_Name.locate("Last Name", "Unsicker") then
2:          errorShow()
3:      endIf
```

This and other error-checking techniques are addressed further in Chapter 29, "Dealing with Errors." The following tutorial shows that most methods and procedures return a value. You can return a value to a Logical variable and then display the value of the variable.

Tutorial: Showing a Returned Logical with *isFile*

Suppose that you wish to use the fact that isFile() returns a Logical to find out whether a file exists.

On Disk: \ANSWERS\DATATYPE.FSL

Quick Steps

1. Use isFile() to check whether a file exists.
2. Show the result with view() box.

Step By Step

1. Change your working directory to the TUTORIAL directory, create a form, and add a button to it. Label the button Using a logical.

2. Add lines 3–8 to the **pushButton** method of the Using a logical button.

```
1:      ;Button :: pushButton
2:      method pushButton(var eventInfo Event)
```

```
3:        var
4:          l          Logical
5:        endVar
6:
7:        l = isFile("C:\\AUTOEXEC.BAT")
8:        l.view("Does file exist?")
9:      endmethod
```

3. Check the syntax, save the form as ISFILE.FSL, and run it. Click the button. The logical viewer will display True or False, depending on whether the file exists.

Analysis

In step 2, line 4 declares *l* as a Logical variable. `isFile()` returns True if the file exists and False if it doesn't. In line 7, *l* is given this return value from `isFile()`. Line 8 displays the result. Note that you passed `view()` a title to display.

DEALING WITH NUMBERS

Often, you need to calculate and convert numbers—time, date, currency, and others. You either manipulate them or convert them so that you can manipulate them. For example, a Number is different from a String. When you have number characters stored in a String variable or Alpha field, you need to convert the string to a Number before you can use it in a calculation. ObjectPAL offers many methods and procedures for accomplishing this task. When declaring a variable as a number, you actually have three choices: Number, LongInt, and SmallInt.

Number

A Number variable is the most flexible of the three number data types and takes up the most room in memory. A Number variable can contain up to 18 significant digits, and the power of 10 can range from $\pm 3.4 * 10^{-4930}$ to $\pm 1.1 * 10^{4930}$. In addition to the Number methods and procedures, you also can use methods and procedures from the AnyType class to manipulate Number data. The Number type includes several derived or inherited methods from the AnyType type marked with an asterisk (see Table 11.6).

TABLE 11.6. NUMBER METHODS AND PROCEDURES.		
abs	fv	pow10
acos	isAssigned*	pv
asin	isBlank*	rand
atan	isFixedType*	round
atan2	ln	sin
blank*	log	sinh
ceil	max	sqrt
cos	min	tan
cosh	mod	tanh
dataType*	number	truncate
exp	numVal	view*
floor	pmt	
fraction	pow	

*Inherited from the AnyType type

LongInt

A LongInt (long integer) variable can range from –2,147,483,648 to +2,147,483,647. Why use a data type that is limited by design when you have more powerful data types? Very simply, LongInt variables occupy only four bytes of storage, and in computer terms, smaller means faster. In addition to the LongInt methods and procedures, you also can use methods and procedures from the AnyType class and the Number class to manipulate LongInt data (see Table 11.7). The LongInt type includes several derived methods from the Number and AnyType types. The AnyType methods are marked by a single asterisk and the Number methods are marked with two asterisks.

TABLE 11.7. LONGINT METHODS.		
abs**	exp**	numVal**
acos**	floor**	pmt**
asin**	fraction**	pow**

atan**	fv**	pow10**
atan2**	isAssigned*	pv**
bitAND	isBlank*	rand**
bitIsSet	isFixedType*	round**
bitOR	ln**	sin**
bitXOR	log**	sinh**
blank*	LongInt	sqrt**
ceil**	max**	tan**
cos**	min**	tanh**
cosh**	mod**	truncate**
dataType*	number**	view*

*Inherited from the AnyType type   **Inherited from the Number type

SmallInt

A SmallInt (small integer) variable can range from –32,768 to +32,767. Again, the reason you may wish to use a data type that is limited by design when you have more powerful LongInt and Number data types is because a SmallInt variable occupies only two bytes of storage, which is half of what LongInt variables take up. A SmallInt uses up the least amount of bytes to store small numbers. In computer terms, smallest is best. You can manipulate the SmallInt datatype with methods listed in Table 11.8. The SmallInt methods have inherited a number of methods from the AnyType and Number types. The AnyType methods are marked by a single asterisk and the Number methods are marked with two asterisks.

TABLE 11.8. SMALLINT METHODS AND PROCEDURES.

abs**	floor**	pmt**
acos**	fraction**	pow**
asin**	fv**	pow10**
atan**	int	pv**

continues

TABLE 11.8. CONTINUED		
atan2**	isAssigned*	rand**
bitAND	isBlank*	round**
bitIsSet	isFixedType*	sin**
bitOR	ln**	sinh**
bitXOR	log**	SmallInt
blank*	max**	sqrt**
ceil**	min**	tan**
cos**	mod**	tanh**
cosh**	number**	truncate**
dataType*	numVal**	view*
exp**		

*Inherited from the AnyType type **Inherited from the Number type

As introduced earlier, whenever ObjectPAL comes across a number, it casts the number internally as the most appropriate type of number. If the number is an integer, ObjectPAL casts the number as either a small integer, a large integer, or a number, depending on its size, as the following code indicates. If the number contains a decimal point, it is cast as a Number. If you wish, type the following in the **pushButton** method of a button:

```
1:    msgStop("Datatype of 320", dataType(320))
```

This first example returns SmallInt, which takes up the smallest possible room in memory—only two bytes.

```
1:    msgStop("Datatype of 33000", dataType(33000))
```

This second example returns LongInt because the data is too large to be a SmallInt.

```
1:    msgStop("Datatype of 2200000000", dataType(2200000000))
```

This third example returns Number because the data is too large to be a LongInt.

```
1:    msgStop("Datatype of 320.0", dataType(320.0))
```

This final example is rather interesting. Although the value clearly can fit into a SmallInt, the compiler puts it into a Number because of the decimal point.

Why is this so important? Doesn't ObjectPAL take care of this for you? Well, yes and no. In most cases, you don't have to worry about it. The following code passes a syntax check but fails during runtime, however. You could pull your hair out for hours trying to figure out why.

```
1:    ;Button :: pushButton
2:    method pushButton(var eventInfo Event)
3:       si = 60 * 24 * 24
4:       si.view()
5:    endmethod
```

When ObjectPAL comes to line 2, it casts all the numbers in the expression as small integers. When the code is executed and the three numbers are multiplied, they result in a number larger than a small integer can handle, and a runtime overflow error occurs (see Figure 11.2). This problem has many solutions, all of which rely on the fact that ObjectPAL looks at an expression as a whole and sets the data types to the lowest common data type. You simply have to make any one of the elements involved with the calculation a larger number type (for example, LongInt or Number). Line 2 can be replaced with any of the following:

Solution 1

```
1:    si = Number(60) * 24 * 24
```

The first solution casts the first number in the calculation as a Number. ObjectPAL internally casts the other two numbers, and the result is the same type.

Solution 2

```
1:    si = 60.0 * 24 * 24
```

The second solution simply uses a floating-point number (indicated by .0).

Solution 3

```
1:    si = 60. * 24 * 24
```

The third solution is a variation of the second solution. ObjectPAL checks only for the existence of a decimal point in a number. It doesn't check whether the number is a floating-point number. The third solution uses this fact and simply adds a decimal point to the first of the three values.

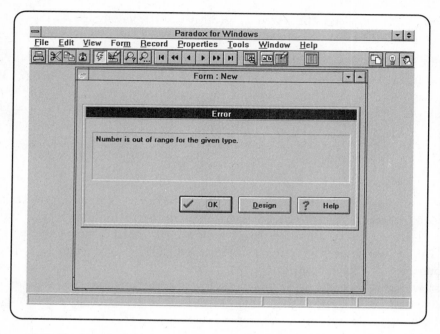

Figure 11.2. If you multiply two numbers that result in a number out of a small integer's range, you get this error.

Tutorial: Converting Number to SmallInt and LongInt

Suppose that you wish to convert a Number variable first to a SmallInt, then to a LongInt. This tutorial demonstrates how to do that.

On Disk: \ANSWERS\DATATYPE.FSL

Quick Steps

1. Use SmallInt to convert a number to a small integer.
2. Use LongInt to convert a number to a long integer.

Step By Step

1. Change your working directory to the TUTORIAL directory. Open the DATATYPE.FSL form and put a button on it. Label the button Number to SmallInt & LongInt.

2. Add lines 3–18 to the **pushButton** method of the Number to SmallInt & LongInt button.

```
1:     ;Button :: pushButton
2:     method pushButton(var eventInfo Event)
3:        var
4:           n      Number        ;Declare n as a number.
5:           si     SmallInt      ;Declare si as a SmallInt.
6:           li     LongInt       ;Declare li as a LongInt.
7:        endVar
8:
9:        n = 3.8                 ;Set number to 3.8.
10:       n.view()                ;Displays 3.80.
11:
12:       si = SmallInt(n)        ;Set si to SmallInt of n.
13:       si.view()               ;Displays 3.
14:
15:       li = LongInt(n)         ;Set li to LongInt of n.
16:       li.view()               ;Displays 3.
17:
18:       n.view()                ;Displays 3.80.
19:    endmethod
```

3. Check the syntax, run the form, and click the button.

Analysis

The first viewer displays 3.80 in the number viewer. Note that the number is formatted according to the Windows number format (the Windows default is two decimal points). When you click OK, the number is converted internally to a SmallInt variable and is displayed in a SmallInt viewer. Note that the number was chopped down to just 3 and not rounded up to 4. Click OK again. The number is again converted, this time to a LongInt. It's displayed one last time to show you that the original n Number variable is unchanged.

Whenever you need a number of a different type than is declared, cast it. In this tutorial, you cast a number as both a long integer and a small integer, but you can go either way. Note, however, that converting a noninteger causes the decimal points to be stripped. For example, values of 1.1, 12.85, and .001 would be converted to 1, 12, and 0.

THE CURRENCY DATA TYPE

A Currency variable can range from $3.4 * \pm 10^{-4930}$ to $1.1 * \pm 10^{4930}$, precise to six decimal places. The number of decimal places displayed depends on the user's Control Panel settings. The value stored in a table does not, however. A table stores the full six decimal places. As well as using the Currency methods and procedures, listed in Table 11.9, you can use methods and procedures from the AnyType class marked with a single asterisk and the Number class marked with two asterisks.

TABLE 11.9. CURRENCY METHODS.		
abs**	fraction**	pow**
acos**	fv**	pow10**
asin**	isAssigned*	pv**
atan**	isBlank*	rand**
atan2**	isFixedType*	round**
blank*	ln**	sin**
ceil**	log**	sinh**
cos**	max**	sqrt**
cosh**	min**	tan**
currency	mod**	tanh**
dataType*	number**	truncate**
exp**	numVal**	view*
floor**	pmt**	

*Inherited from the AnyType type **Inherited from the Number type

Currency variables are rounded, not truncated. Although internally ObjectPAL keeps track of Currency variables to six decimal places, the values are rounded when they're displayed to the user. The number of decimal places depends on the user's Control Panel settings. Most users use the default of two decimal points.

If you type in the following code, ObjectPAL shows you a dialog box with the correctly rounded figure of 19.96 in a currency view box.

```
1:     ;Button :: pushButton
2:     method pushButton(var eventInfo Event)
3:        var
4:           n Number          ;Declare n as a number.
5:        endVar
6:
7:        n = 19.9599           ;Set n to a number.
8:        view(Currency(n))     ;Displays 19.96.
9:     endmethod
```

> The preceding code can be found on the disk under \ANSWERS\DATATYPE.FSL.

ON THE
DISK

Although the number of decimal places depends on your Control Panel settings, the number will be rounded correctly. Also, note the alternative syntax used for view().

THE DATE, TIME, AND DATETIME DATA TYPES

Although time and date data types aren't related, each shares data and methods with the DateTime data type. When deciding between these three data types, ask yourself whether you need time in the same field as the date information. Whenever possible, separate date and time.

Date

There are differences between dates stored in a table and Date variables. The Date data type can be any valid date, whereas a Paradox table can store only dates from 01/01/100 to 12/31/9999. Use the methods and procedures to bridge the gap and manipulate date data. As well as using the Date methods and procedures, you also can use methods and procedures inherited from the AnyType class and the DateTime class (see Table 11.10).

TABLE 11.10. DATE METHODS AND PROCEDURES.
blank*
dataType*
date
dateVal
day**
daysInMonth**
dow**
dowOrd**
doy**
isAssigned*
isBlank*
isFixedType*
isLeapYear**
month**
moy**
today
view*
year**

*Inherited from the AnyType type **Inherited from the DateTime type

You can store any valid date with the ObjectPAL Date data type. For example, type the following code into the **pushButton** method of a button.

```
1:    ;Button :: pushButton
2:    method pushButton(var eventInfo Event)
3:       msgInfo("Beginning Date", Date(0))
4:    endMethod
```

This displays the string 00/00/0000 in a dialog box. You can type in negative numbers that represent B.C. dates, too.

Subtracting Two Dates

If you subtract two dates, you get another date. For example, type the following code into the **pushButton** method of a button.

```
1:     ;Button :: pushButton
2:     method pushButton(var eventInfo Event)
3:         message(date("01/15/94")-date("01/01/94"))
4:     endMethod
```

This displays 01/14/0001 in the status bar. This information isn't very useful. Usually you want the number of days or years between the two dates. The trick to getting the number of days between two dates is to cast the result as a number. For example, type the following code into the **pushButton** method of a button.

```
1:     ;Button :: pushButton
2:     method pushButton(var eventInfo Event)
3:         var
4:             dBorn Date
5:         endVar
6:
7:         dBorn = Date("01/20/1967")
8:         dBorn.view("Enter your birthdate")
9:         msgInfo("Days since your birthdate", Number(Today() - dBorn))
10:    endmethod
```

Calculating Years

To calculate years, simply cast the value as a year. For example, type the following code into the **pushButton** method of a button.

```
1:     ;Button :: pushButton
2:     method pushButton(var eventInfo Event)
3:         var
4:             dBorn Date
5:         endVar
6:
7:         dBorn = Date("01/20/1967")
8:         dBorn.view("Enter your birthdate")
9:         msgInfo("Your age", Year(Today() - dBorn))
10:    endmethod
```

Time

A Time variable is stored in the format HH:MM:SS AM/PM. You could use any of the following as separators: blank, tab, space, comma, hyphen, slash, period, colon, or semicolon. If you wish, type the following code into the **pushButton** method of a button. (All the following strings are legal time strings in ObjectPAL.)

```
1:     ;Button :: pushButton
2:     method pushButton(var eventInfo Event)
3:         var t Time endVar
4:             t = time("10:05:32 AM")
5:             t.view()
6:
```

```
 7:               t = time("10;05;32 AM")
 8:               t.view()
 9:
10:               t = time("10 05 32 AM")
11:               t.view()
12:
13:               t = time("10,05,32 AM")
14:               t.view()
15:
16:               t = time("10/05/32 AM")
17:               t.view()
18:    endMethod
```

Note, however, that although the value in each case is given in ObjectPAL in a certain format, it's still displayed to the user in the format specified in Control Panel. The values the user inputs must be in accordance with his Control Panel settings. Internally, ObjectPAL stores the time all the way down to the millisecond. In addition to using the Time methods and procedures, you also can use methods and procedures inherited from the AnyType class and the DateTime class to manipulate time values (see Table 11.11).

TABLE 11.11. TIME METHODS AND PROCEDURES.

blank*

dataType*

hour**

isAssigned*

isBlank*

isFixedType*

milliSec**

minute**

second**

time

view*

*Inherited from the AnyType type **Inherited from the DateTime type

Using Time

Call `Time()` with no parameters to return the current time. For example, type the following code into the **pushButton** method of a button.

```
1:    ;Button :: pushButton
2:    method pushButton(var eventInfo Event)
3:        msgInfo("Current time", time())
4:    endMethod
```

Converting a String to Time

Use the `Time()` procedure to cast a string value as a time variable:

```
1:    time(fldTime.value)
```

If you wish to subtract two times, then cast the values as times and put the remainder into a number variable. For example:

```
1:    DiffTime = Time(Ending_Time) - Time(Beginning_Time)
```

Converting Regular Time to Military Time

The user's Control Panel settings determine whether the 12-hour time format (HH:MM:SS AM/PM) or the 24-hour (military) time format is used. Sometimes you want to convert 12-hour time to 24-hour time, however. The following routine casts a string as Time and then displays it in 24-hour format. You can type the code into the **pushButton** method of a button.

```
1:    ;Button :: pushButton
2:    method pushButton(var eventInfo Event)
3:        var
4:            s string
5:            t time
6:        endVar
7:
8:            formatSetTimeDefault("hh:mm:ss am")
9:            s="2:20:00 PM"
10:           t = time(s)
11:           formatAdd("24","to(%h:%m:%s)na()np()")
12:           formatSetTimeDefault("24")
13:           t.view()
14:    endmethod
```

Subtracting Time

Suppose that you need to get the number of seconds between two times. Type the following into the **pushButton** method of a button.

```
 1:    ;Button :: pushButton
 2:    method pushButton(var eventInfo Event)
 3:       var
 4:          t1, t2 Time
 5:       endVar
 6:
 7:       t1=time("1:35:30 PM")
 8:       t2=time("2:10:15 PM")
 9:       view(Number(t2-t1)/1000)            ;For seconds.
10:       view(Number(t2-t1)/1000/60)         ;For minutes.
11:       view(Number(t2-t1)/1000/60/60);For hours.
12:    endmethod
```

DateTime

DateTime is a special data type that stores both date and time values in the same variable. Normally, you shouldn't use this data type, because you lose the advantages of the date field type. When date- and time-stamping a record in a single field is important, however, DateTime makes it easier.

DateTime stores data in the form of hour-minute-second-millisecond year-month-day. If you don't care about milliseconds, you can use an alphanumeric 23- to 30-field type to store the values. When you do care about milliseconds, you probably are going to use the data in a calculation. A numeric field type is best in that case. As well as using the DateTime methods and procedures, you also can use methods and procedures from the AnyType class (see Table 11.12).

TABLE 11.12. DATETIME METHODS AND PROCEDURES.

blank*	doy	minute
dataType*	hour	month
dateTime	isAssigned*	moy
day	isBlank*	second
daysInMonth	isFixedType*	view*
dow	isLeapYear	year
dowOrd	milliSec	

*Inherited from the AnyType type

The `DateTime()` method returns the current date and time. For example, to return the current date and time in a message information box, type line 3 into the **pushButton** method of a button.

```
1:    ;Button :: pushButton
2:    method pushButton(var eventInfo Event)
3:        msgInfo("Current Date & time", DateTime())
4:    endMethod
```

As an interesting experiment, you can cast values with the procedure `DateTime()` and display the results. This experimenation helps you to understand the numbers behind the DateTime datatype. For example, type line 3 into the **pushButton** method of a button.

```
1:    ;Button :: pushButton
2:    method pushButton(var eventInfo Event)
3:        msgInfo("Beginning Date/Time", DateTime(0))
4:    endmethod
```

Line 3 displays 12:00:00 AM, 00/00/0000 in a dialog box. This shows you that going back all the way to year 0 is legal in ObjectPAL. In fact, you can even use negative numbers!

If you store data in an alphanumeric field type and later need to do a calculation on the value, you must cast the string in the field as a number. To cast a string as a number, use Number and `DateTime()` together. For example, type line 3 into the **pushButton** method of a button.

```
1:    ;Button :: pushButton
2:    method pushButton(var eventInfo Event)
3:        msgInfo("Lisa's Birthday", Number(DateTime("07:30:00 PM, January 20,
          ➥1967")))
4:    endMethod
```

The preceding line 3 displays the number 62042700600000 in a dialog box. This isn't very useful, but you can use this code in a calculation with values (including another DateTime converted to a Number).

DEALING WITH CHARACTERS

When you're dealing with characters, use the `string` data type. The `string` data type allows strings as long as 32,767 characters. A quoted string typed into a method can't be more than 255 characters long, however. As well as using the `string` methods and procedures, you also can use methods and procedures from the AnyType class (see Table 11.13).

TABLE 11.13. STRING METHODS AND PROCEDURES.	
advMatch	keyNameToVKCode
ansiCode	lower
blank*	lTrim
breakApart	match
chr	oemCode
chrOEM	rTrim
chrToKeyName	search
dataType*	size
fill	space
format	string
ignoreCaseInStringCompares	strVal
isAssigned*	substr
isBlank*	toANSI
isFixedType*	toOEM
isIgnoreCaseInStringCompares	upper
isSpace	view*
keyNameToChar	vkCodeToKeyName

*Inherited from the AnyType type

Use "" to represent an empty string. This is equivalent to the null character. Alternatively, you can use the `blank()` method to empty a string. For example, type lines 3–10 into the **pushButton** method of a button.

```
1:    ;Button :: pushButton
2:    method pushButton(var eventInfo Event)
3:       var
4:          s      String
5:       endVar
6:
7:       s = "Bradley Scott Unsicker"
8:       s.view()                  ;Displays Bradley Scott Unsicker.
9:       s.blank()                 ;Set s to null.
```

```
10:      s.view()               ;Displays null.
11:   endMethod
```

Line 9 empties, or blanks out, the string. This is only one technique to empty a string. You also could replace line 6 with either of the following:

```
1:   s = ""
2:   s = blank()
```

Embedding Codes in Strings

Sometimes you might want to code some special characters or backslash codes to add to a string when it's displayed to the user. Special characters are ANSI characters not found on the keyboard. Backslash codes are the way to include some special characters in ObjectPAL. For example, \t represents a tab.

You use the string procedure chr() to display an ANSI code. Suppose that you're going to display a message to the user and you want to embed a few returns (ANSI character 13) into the text. You could use the following code (see Figure 11.3):

```
1:   ;Button :: pushButton
2:   method pushButton(var eventInfo Event)
3:      msgInfo("Message from programmer","Warning!" + chr(13) + chr(13) +
          "You have violated the license agreement. Send me money.")
4:   endMethod
```

This technique can add a little extra flair to your applications that other programmers might not think to include. Refer to Appendix H, "ASCII and ANSI Character Sets," for a complete listing of ANSI characters that you can use with chr().

A keycode is a code that represents a keyboard character in ObjectPAL scripts. A keycode can be an ASCII number, an IBM extended keycode number, or a string that represents a keyname known to Paradox.

It would be easier to use the Windows and C++ standard escapes:
chr(13) = \r = \n = <enter>
\t = <tab>
\b = <backspace>

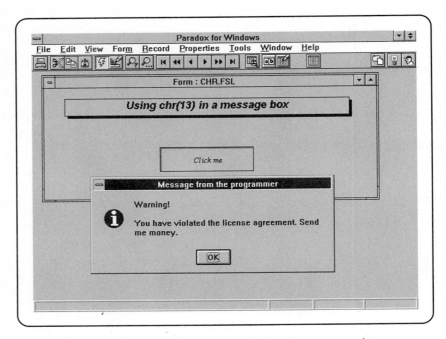

Figure 11.3. An example of using the chr() procedure to format text within a message information dialog box.

The Memo Data Type

When you need to work with a string longer then 32,767 characters, use a Memo variable. As soon as you set up a Memo variable, you can use writeToFile() and readFromFile() to set and retrieve data from a Memo file. Memo fields can be as large as 512MB! As well as using the Memo methods and procedures, you also can use methods and procedures from the AnyType class (see Table 11.14).

TABLE 11.14. MEMO METHODS AND PROCEDURES.

```
blank*

dataType*

isAssigned*

isBlank*

isFixedType*
```

```
memo

readFromFile

writeToFile
```

*Inherited from the AnyType type

Three of the Memo type methods are of particular interest for manipulating a Memo variable: `memo()`, `readFromFile()`, and `writeFromFile()`. Following are descriptions of the three.

`memo()`	Casts a value as a Memo
`readFromFile()`	Reads a memo from a file
`writeToFile()`	Writes a memo to a file

THE ARRAY DATA TYPE

An *array* is a group or series of related items identified by a single name and referenced by an index. An array is a special type of variable. It enables you to store a group of elements identified by a single name. Arrays are stored in consecutive locations in memory. Think of each one of these locations as being a cell reserved for your data. If, for example, you declare an array with five elements, you can put a value directly in cell three and later pull it out. Following this analogy, an array is very similar to a one-field table. Arrays are limited to 65,535 elements.

In addition to using the array methods and procedures, listed in Table 11.15, you also can use methods and procedures inherited from the AnyType class (indicated with an asterisk) to manipulate an array.

TABLE 11.15. ARRAY METHODS AND PROCEDURES.

addLast	grow	isResizeable
append	indexOf	remove
blank*	insert	removeAllItems
contains	insertAfter	removeItem
countOf	insertBefore	replaceItem
dataType*	insertFirst	setSize
empty	isAssigned*	size

continues

TABLE 11.15. CONTINUED		
exchange	isBlank*	view
fill	isFixedType*	

*Inherited from the AnyType type

Using a Static Array

There are two types of arrays: static and resizeable. A static array has a fixed number of elements. A resizeable array can be resized. The size of a static array is set when you declare the array, and a resizeable array is set in code after you declare it. The following is the syntax model to declare a static array:

```
arrayName Array[size] dataType
```

For example, the following declares a three-element array ready to store three small integers:

```
1:   var
2:          arNumbers    Array[3] SmallInt
3:   endVar
```

As soon as the array is declared, you can reference any of the elements of the array directly:

```
arrayName[element] = value
```

For example, the following sets the second and third elements in arNumbers to 10 and 20:

```
1:      arNumbers[2] = 10
2:      arNumbers[3] = 20
```

As soon as the elements of the array have values, you can retrieve the values much like you retrieve values from regular variables and fields. For example, the following displays the second element in the array in the status bar:

```
1:      message(arNumbers[2])
```

If you think that using an array is just like using multiple variables, you're right. One benefit of using arrays is that they group multiple variables into a single group of variables called an array. This gives you a way to address a set of values. For example, type the following piece of code into the **pushButton** method of a button. It uses a three-element array to store a user's first, middle, and last name. Then it displays all three variables with a single line of code.

```
 1:     ;Button :: pushButton
 2:     method pushButton(var eventInfo Event)
 3:        var
 4:           name array[3] String      ;Declare a 3 element fixed array.
 5:        endVar
 6:
 7:        name[1] = "Lester"           ;Set first element of array.
 8:        name[2] = "Earl"             ;Set second element of array.
 9:        name[3] = "Prestwood"        ;Set third element of array.
10:
11:        name.view()                  ;View array.
12:     endmethod
```

Using a Resizeable Array

If you don't know the size of the array needed at declaration, use a resizeable array. The following is the syntax model to declare an array variable:

```
arrayName Array[] dataType
```

After you declare a resizeable array, use the `setSize()` method to set its size. As soon as the array is declared and its size is set, you can reference any of the elements of the array the same way you reference the elements of a static array. For example, type the following code into the **pushButton** method of a button. It declares a resizeable array, sets its size to 10, and fills it with numbers:

```
 1:     ;Button :: pushButton
 2:     method pushButton(var eventInfo Event)
 3:        var
 4:           myArray    Array[] SmallInt
 5:           Counter    SmallInt
 6:        endVar
 7:
 8:        myArray.setSize(10)
 9:
10:        for Counter from 1 to 10
11:           myArray[Counter] = Counter
12:        endFor
13:
14:        myArray.addLast(100)
15:
16:        myArray.view()
17:     endmethod
```

Note that line 14 uses the `addLast()` method to add one additional element to the array before displaying it.

The following tutorial shows you how to loop through an array using a `for` loop with the `size()` method. This technique is important because an array can't use a `forEach` loop. (A `forEach` loop applies only to dynamic arrays.) Both forms ARRAY.FSL (see Figure 11.4) and ARRAYS.FSL (see Figure 11.5) in the ANSWERS directory demonstrate using arrays, dynamic arrays, and records.

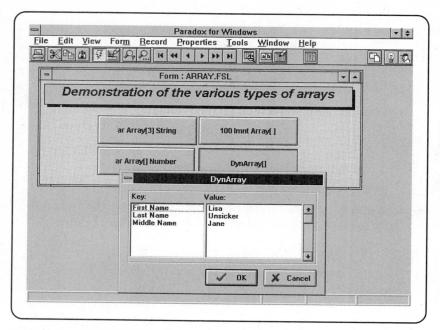

Figure 11.4. \ANSWERS\ARRAY.FSL. Using sets of information.

Tutorial: Using an Array and *enumFormNames* to Check for an Open Form

Suppose that you wish to use an array with the enumFormNames() procedure to check for an open form. If the form is not open, display all the open forms in an array view box.

On Disk: \ANSWERS\ARRAYS.FSL

Quick Steps

1. Enumerate form names into an array with enumFormNames().
2. Use a for loop to move through the array, checking for a form name.
3. If the form name is found, display a dialog box indicating this, and exit with return.
4. If the form is never found, display a dialog box indicating this, and display all open forms with view().

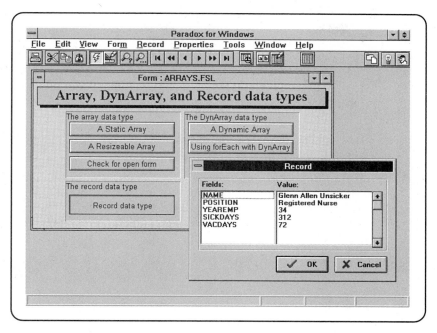

Figure 11.5. ANSWERS\ARRAYS.FSL. Using the array, DynArray, and record data types to store sets of information.

Step By Step

1. Change your working directory to the TUTORIAL directory and create a new form. Place a button labeled Check for open form on it.

2. In the **pushButton** method of the button, type lines 3–18:

```
1:    ;Button :: pushButton
2:    method pushButton(var eventInfo Event)
3:       var
4:          arForms          Array[] String
5:          siCounter     SmallInt
6:       endVar
7:
8:       enumFormNames(arForms)
9:
```

```
10:        for Counter from 1 to arForms.size()
11:           if arForms[Counter] = "Arrays" then
12:              msgInfo("Found","Form 'Arrays' is open")
13:              return
14:           endIf
15:        endFor
16:
17:        msgInfo("Not Found","Form 'Arrays' is not open")
18:        arForms.view("Current forms open")
19:     endmethod
```

3. Check the syntax, save the form as ARRAY.FSL, and run it. Click the button. A dialog box indicates whether the form is open. After you click OK, the routine either stops or displays all the open forms. If a form with the name Arrays is open, the routine stops. Otherwise, an array view box displays all the open forms.

Analysis

In step 2, line 4 declares a resizeable array, *arForms*, that is populated in line 8 with enumFormNames(). Note that you don't have to set the size of the resizeable array ahead of time. Line 5 declares a string variable named *siCounter*. Line 10 uses *siCounter* to scan through the array from the first element to however many elements are in the array. This is determined by arForms.size(). Line 11 checks to see whether the current array element is *Arrays*. If it is, a message information box is displayed in line 12, and execution stops in line 13 with the keyword return. If the element is not *Arrays*, the loop continues. This cycle continues until either *Arrays* is found or the end of the array is reached. If the routine is never exited, line 17 tells the user that the form isn't open. Line 18 shows the user all the currently open forms.

THE DYNARRAY DATA TYPE

A DynArray (dynamic array) is very similar to a regular array, except that it uses address names rather than index numbers. Just as static and resizeable arrays are for using sets of data, so is the DynArray. The number of elements—indexes—you can have in a DynArray is limited only by memory. An index can be up to 255 characters. As well as using the DynArray methods and procedures, listed in Table 11.16, you can use methods and procedures inherited from the AnyType type indicated with an asterisk.

TABLE 11.16. DYNARRAY METHODS AND PROCEDURES.
blank*
contains
dataType*
empty
getKeys
isAssigned*
isBlank*
isFixedType*
removeItem
size
view

*Inherited from the AnyType type

Of the many DynArray methods, the following are some of the most useful:

contains()	Searches a DynArray for a pattern of characters
empty()	Removes all items from a DynArray
getKeys()	Loads a resizeable array with the indexes of an existing DynArray
removeItem()	Deletes a specified item from a DynArray
size()	Returns the number of elements in a DynArray

The following is the syntax model to declare a DynArray:

DynArrayName DynArray[] dataType

The following declares *dyn1* as a DynArray:

```
1:    var
2:        dyn1      DynArray[] SmallInt
3:    endVar
```

As soon as the array is declared, you can reference any of the elements of the DynArray directly:

DynArrayName[ElementName] = value

The following creates two elements in dyn1 and sets their values:

```
1:    myDynArray["Last_Name"] = "Megan"
2:    myDynArray["First_Name"] = "Miles"
```

As soon as the elements of a DynArray have values, you can retrieve the values
much like you retrieve values from a regular array. Instead of using a numbered
index, however, you use named indexes. For example, the following displays
the First_Name element in the array in the status bar:

```
1:     message(myDynArray["First_Name"])
```

Now let's look at a completed example. Type lines 3–10 in the **pushButton**
method of button.

```
 1:    ;Button :: pushButton
 2:    method pushButton(var eventInfo Event)
 3:        var
 4:            myDynArray      DynArray[] String
 5:        endVar
 6:
 7:            myDynArray["Last_Name"] = "Megan"
 8:            myDynArray["First_Name"] = "Miles"
 9:
10:            myDynArray.view()
11:    endmethod
```

When you run the preceding code, note that the indexes are in alphabetical
order.

Using *forEach*

The forEach structure enables you to loop through a DynArray much like scan
enables you to loop through a table. The syntax for forEach is as follows:

> forEach *VarName* in *DynArrayName*
>
>   *Statements*
>
> **endForEach**

For example:

```
1:    forEach sElement in Dyn1
2:            message(DynArrayVar[sElement])
3:            sleep(500)
4:    endForEach
```

The next tutorial shows you how to move through a DynArray using a forEach
loop.

Tutorial: Using *forEach* with *sysInfo()*

Suppose that you wish to use a forEach loop to move through a DynArray of
your system information, showing the user each element until you get to the

`IconHeight` element. In addition to the `forEach` loop, this tutorial acquaints you with `sysInfo()`.

On Disk: \ANSWERS\ARRAYS.FSL

Quick Steps

1. Use `sysInfo()` to fill a DynArray.
2. Use `forEach` to move through each element.
3. Use `msgInfo()` to show the element's name and value.
4. After the `forEach` loop, use `view()` to show all the elements at once.

Step By Step

1. Create a new form and add a button to it. Label the button Using forEach with DynArray.

2. Add lines 3–15 to the **pushButton** method of the Using forEach with a DynArray button.

```
1:    ;Button :: pushButton
2:    method pushButton(var eventInfo Event)
3:       var
4:          dynSys      DynArray[] Anytype
5:          s                  String
6:       endVar
7:
8:       sysInfo(dynSys)
9:
10:      forEach s in dynSys
11:         if s = "IconHeight" then quitLoop endIf
12:         msgInfo(s, dynSys[s])
13:      endForEach
14:
15:      dynSys.view()
16:    endmethod
```

3. Check the syntax, run the form, and click the button. A message information dialog box appears for each element of the DynArray. Rather then cycle through all 30 bits of information, the program stops after the most important information is displayed. At the end of this parade of system information, a DynArray view box shows you all the elements at once.

Analysis

In step 2, line 4 declares the DynArray *dynSys*. Note that no size is indicated in line 3 or in the body of the code. Line 5 declares s as a string variable. In line 8, the sysInfo() procedure is used to put information about your system into the DynArray. *s* is used in line 10 to store the index name, which is used in lines 11 and 12. Lines 10–13 comprise the forEach block, which moves through each element in the DynArray, checking to see whether the element name is equal to *IconHeight*. If it is equal, the loop is exited with the keyword quitLoop. If the loop hasn't reached *IconHeight* yet, the element name and value are displayed. Finally, line 15 shows the complete DynArray all at once. In this case, a view is a better way to see all the elements of the array than looping through and showing one element at a time.

This simple example merely shows you how to loop through a DynArray and acquaints you with sysInfo(). Normally, you will do much more than this example does, using or manipulating each element as you go.

CUSTOM DATA TYPES

A custom data type is a way for you to create your own data type. You do this in a Type structure in either the Type window or in the built-in method, much like you declare variables and constants. That is, the scope and instance of a custom type follows the same rules as a var block. The following is the syntax model:

> **type**
>
> > *UserType = ExistingType*
>
> **endType**

Borland renamed the old Currency type of Paradox tables to Money, but left ObjectPAL to the same old Currency data type. If you don't like this inconsistency, then you could declare a new variable type called Money and use it in place of Currency.

```
1:    Type                        ;Begin type block.
2:         Money = Currency       ;Set custom types.
3:    endType                     ;End type block.
```

After you do this, you could use either Currency or Money whenever you deal with money. You could use either line 2 or line 6 in the following code (lines 1–3 and 5–7 declare total as a Currency data type).

```
1:    var
2:       Total      Currency
3:    endVar
```

```
1:    var
2:       Total      Money
3:    endVar
```

You will put custom types to use when you pass an Array or DynArray variable to a custom method or procedure later in Chapter 23, "Storing and Centralizing Code." For now, let's take a closer look at the type block. Another use of the type block is to define a data type as a set or record of existing types. For example, type lines 3–23 into the **pushButton** method of a button.

```
1:    ;Button :: pushButton
2:    method pushButton(var eventInfo Event)
3:       type                              ;Start type block.
4:          employee = Record              ;Start record block.
5:             Name        String          ;Set elements of record.
6:             Position    String          ;type employee.
7:             YearEmp     SmallInt
8:             SickDays    SmallInt
9:             VacDays     SmallInt
10:            endRecord                    ;End record block.
11:       endType                           ;End type block.
12:
13:       var                               ;Begin var block.
14:          emp employee                   ;Set emp to employee.
15:       endVar                            ;End var block.
16:
17:       emp.Name = "Glenn Allen Unsicker"
18:       emp.Position = "Registered Nurse"
19:       emp.YearEmp = 34
20:       emp.SickDays = 312
21:       emp.VacDays = 72
22:
23:       emp.view()                        ;View emp record.
24:    endmethod
```

As soon as a custom type is defined as a record, you can deal with a set of variables all at once.

The capability to manipulate data types is the core of every programming language. You should understand now that ObjectPAL is not weak in the area of data types. With SmallInt, LongInt, and Number data types, you can deal with almost any number. Date, Time, and DateTime data types give you the capability to deal with the passage of time. String and Memo types enable you to manipulate characters. With Array, DynArray, and Record data types, you can manipulate sets of data. The study of data types in ObjectPAL concludes this book's discussion of the individual elements of ObjectPAL. Now that I've talked about all the elements of ObjectPAL, Chapter 12 brings the methods and procedures of ObjectPAL into focus.

CATEGORIES OF COMMANDS IN OBJECTPAL

You've learned about many elements of ObjectPAL and used many of the commands. This chapter's goal is to bring together the knowledge you have gained so far by giving you a formal review of the types of commands available in ObjectPAL: methods, procedures, constants, and properties. You can type most of the examples (the ones you can type are indicated).

Methods and procedures

Action Constants

MenuAction Constants

Properties

Using Methods and Procedures

The most often used types of commands are methods and procedures in the runtime library. The runtime library (RTL) is the predefined set of methods and procedures used for operating on objects (see Figure 12.1). Methods and procedures differ from built-in methods in that they actually do something tangible. The primary use of a built-in method is to trigger events—for example **open**, **newValue**, **mouseDown**, and **action**. A built-in method triggers a series of methods and procedures that you put between `method` and `endMethod`.

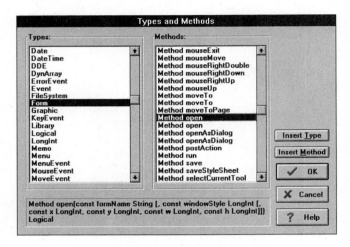

Figure 12.1. The Types and Methods dialog box is the runtime library.

Here are two quick definitions from the glossary to remind you about the difference between a method and a procedure.

method—A function or command in ObjectPAL that acts on an object. A method uses dot notation to work on an object set by the programmer, as in `object.method()`.

procedure—A function or command in ObjectPAL that has no object to work on. The programmer doesn't specify an object.

Here's an example of using the `open()` method. You can type lines 3–7 into the **pushButton** of a button (make sure that your working directory is set to TUTORIAL).

```
1:    ;Button :: pushButton
2:    method pushButton(var eventInfo Event)
```

```
3:        var
4:            f        Form
5:        endVar
6:
7:        f.open("OV-LIKE.FSL")
8:    endMethod
```

open() is the method and the *f* form variable is the object. A procedure, on the other hand, has no object to work on.

Here's an example of using the isDir() procedure. You can type line 3 into the **pushButton** method of a button.

```
1:    ;Button :: pushButton
2:    method pushButton(var eventInfo Event)
3:        view(isDir("C:\\DOS"))
4:    endMethod
```

isDir() is the procedure. It checks whether a directory exists.

It's not always necessary to keep in mind the difference between a method and a procedure. This book takes a formal look at the ObjectPAL language. It's enough to know that methods and procedures are two types of commands.

Using the action() Method

One method in the runtime library opens up a whole world of commands—the **action** method. As an ObjectPAL programmer, you're interested in five action constant classes: ActionDataCommands, ActionEditCommands, ActionFieldCommands, ActionMoveCommands, and ActionSelectCommands. Use these commands with the action() method. The syntax for action constants is as follows:

ObjectName.action(ActionConstant)

ObjectName is the name of the object on which you want the action to occur—for example, theBox or Last_Name. The actionConstant can be any constant category whose name starts with action. If you want, you can precede this expression with an object path, as in the following:

```
1:    f.pge3.tf.action(DataNextRecord)
```

f is a handle to another form (see Chapter 13, "The Display Managers"). pge3 and tf are the names of two objects contained in the form (the third page and its table frame). The constant DataNextRecord moves the cursor forward one record (if possible).

Using Action Constants

The constants in the `ActionDataCommands` category deal with data in a table as a whole (see Figure 12.2). They are used for navigating the pointer in a table, locking a record, posting a record, toggling Edit mode, and positioning the record pointer. Here are three examples:

```
1:    action(DataPrint)              ;Prints a form or table view.
2:    action(DataTableView)          ;Open the master table in a window.
3:    action(DataSaveCrosstab)       ;Writes the crosstab data
4:                                   ;to :PRIV:CROSSTAB.DB.
```

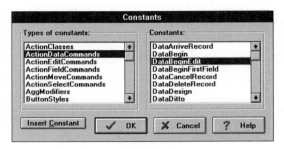

Figure 12.2. `ActionDataCommands` *deal with data as a whole.*

ActionEditCommands

In general, the constants in the `ActionEditCommands` category are used for altering data within a field (see Figure 12.3). With these constants, you can copy text to the clipboard, enter persistent field view, bring up the help system, and search your text. Here are three examples:

```
1:    action(EditDropDownList)    ;Drops down pick list.
2:    action(EditEnterMemoView)   ;Enters memo view.
3:    action(EditPasteFromFile)   ;Pastes from file into current field.
```

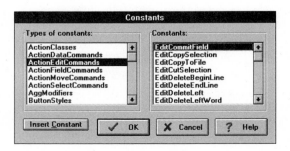

Figure 12.3. `ActionEditCommands` *alter data within a field.*

ActionFieldCommands

The constants in the `ActionFieldCommands` category are used for moving between field objects (see Figure 12.4). With these constants, you can invoke and control tab order. You can move the focus forward or backward in the tab order. You can ignore the tab order and move up, down, left, or right. You can even move from one table frame to another. Here are three examples:

```
1:      action(FieldRotate)      ;Rotates columns in a table frame
2:      action(FieldNextPage)    ;Moves to the next page in a form
3:      action(FieldForward)     ;Moves one field forward
```

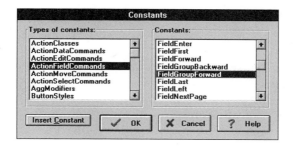

Figure 12.4. `ActionFieldCommands` are used for moving from field to field.

ActionMoveCommands

The constants in the `ActionMoveCommands` category are used for positioning within a field object (see Figure 12.5). With these constants, you can move to the beginning or end of a field, move left one word, or scroll a field up or down. In general, these commands behave differently in a memo field than they do in a set of fields. Here are three examples:

```
1:      action(MoveEnd)              ;Moves to the end of the document or
2:                                   ;to last field.
3:      action(MoveLeftWord)         ;Moves cursor to word on the left.
4:      action(MoveScrollPageDown)   ;Scrolls the page image down.
```

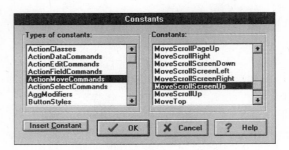

Figure 12.5. ActionMoveCommands are used for positioning within a field.

ActionSelectCommands

The ActionSelectCommands constants are similar to the ActionMoveCommands constants, but they are for selecting data within a field object (see Figure 12.6). With these constants, you can select from the current position to the beginning of the document. Here are three examples:

```
1:     action(SelectEnd)         ;Select to the end.
2:     action(SelectLeft)        ;Selects one character to the left.
3:     action(SelectSelectAll)   ;Selects the entire document.
```

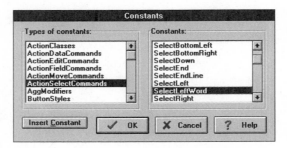

Figure 12.6. ActionSelectCommands are used for selecting data within a field.

ANSWERS\CONSTANT.FSL demonstrates how to use move and select constants.

Browse through the online constants section by selecting Tools | Constants. Select the categories whose names start with action. If you find a constant that is not self-explanatory, press Ctrl+F1 and look it up for a complete description. These constants are your gateway to more powerful data manipulation and, therefore, to more powerful applications.

Trapping Action Constants

In addition to executing action constants, you can trap for them. The basic idea is to use the action method and inspect the *eventInfo* variable. For example, to trap for when the form enters edit mode, type lines 3–6 in the page's **action** method.

```
1:    ;page :: action
2:    method action(var eventInfo ActionEvent)
3:       if eventInfo.id() = DataBeginEdit then
4:          beep()
5:          message("You are now in edit mode.")
6:       endIf
7:    endmethod
```

Using MenuAction Constants

Another method in ObjectPAL that opens up a whole world of power is menuAction(). The menuAction() method allows you to execute any of the MenuCommand constants (see Figure 12.7). Anytime you wish to execute or trap a menu-equivalent task, consider using the menuAction() method or **menuAction** built-in method.

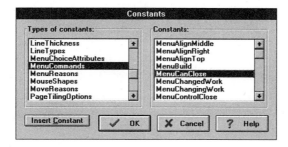

Figure 12.7. The Constants dialog box showing the MenuCommands.

For example, to have a button do the same thing as selecting Edit | Copy, add line 3 to the **pushButton** method of a button.

```
1:    ;Button :: pushButton
2:    method pushButton(var eventInfo Event)
3:        active.menuAction(MenuEditCopy)
4:    endmethod
```

Trapping MenuAction Constants

Just as you can trap for action constants, you can trap for MenuCommand constants.
For example, to trap for the user pressing the form maximize button, add lines
3–5 to the **menuAction** method of a page.

```
1:    ;Page :: menuAction
2:    method menuAction(var eventInfo MenuEvent)
3:        if eventInfo.id() = MenuControlMaximize then
4:            disableDefault
5:        endIf
6:    endmethod
```

USING PROPERTIES

The final type of command you can use in ObjectPAL is the properties of
objects (see Figure 12.8). All properties of an object are either read-only or
read-write.

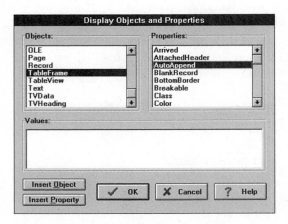

Figure 12.8. The Display Objects and Properties dialog box.

Read-Only Properties

Some properties are read-only. That is, you cannot set their value. You can only read it. For example, to display the record number of the active field in a message information box whenever a button is pressed, add line 3 to the **pushButton** method of a button.

```
1:    ;Button :: pushButton
2:    method pushButton(var eventInfo Event)
3:        msgInfo("Record number", active.recNo)        ;recNo is a property.
4:    endmethod
```

Read-Write Properties

Another type of property is a read-write property. For example, to toggle the AutoAppend property of a table frame when a button is pressed, add line 3 to the **pushButton** method of a button.

```
1:    ;Button :: pushButton
2:    method pushButton(var eventInfo Event)
3:        tf.autoAppend = not tf.autoAppend        ;tf is a table frame.
4:    endmethod
```

You don't need to memorize all the methods, procedures, constants, keywords, control structures, and properties of ObjectPAL. What you should learn is how all the various elements of ObjectPAL are categorized. Therefore, when you need to find a command, you'll know where to check to see whether it exists and how to use it. By now, you should feel comfortable with the categories of ObjectPAL commands.

Part II of this book, "ObjectPAL Basics," has taught you the concepts you need in order to master ObjectPAL. Part II is the heart of this book. To get the most out of ObjectPAL, you must understand the information in Part II. Each piece of information about ObjectPAL relies on something else. If you've read other books on ObjectPAL or the ObjectPAL manuals, maybe everything in Part II made sense. If this is your first experience with ObjectPAL, however, I recommend that you reread this part of the book in a few weeks.

PART

III

EXPLORING OBJECTPAL

THE DISPLAY MANAGERS

A **display manager** is a group of ObjectPAL data types that includes the application, the form, the report, TableView, and new to version 5, the script. Except for the script, these object types are used to display data. This chapter tells you how to turn database ideas and concepts into real applications. This chapter covers handling the desktop, moving from one page in a form to another page, moving from form to form, integrating reports, and using a table window. You also learn about techniques that you can use to develop a complete Windows application.

Controlling the application environment

Manipulating an Application variable

Manipulating a Form variable

Using a table window in ObjectPAL

Display managers are what Paradox uses to display data. Display managers are objects that contain design objects. There are five kinds of display managers:

- Application
- Form
- TableView
- Report
- Script

This chapter deals with the Application, Form, and TableView display managers. The Report display manager is dealt with in Chapter 15, "Handling Reports." Scripts are discussed in detail in Chapter 23, "Storing and Centralizing Code."

THE APPLICATION DISPLAY MANAGER

In Paradox, the application can refer to a group of files in a directory. In this chapter, *application* refers to the Paradox desktop. Specifically, an Application variable in ObjectPAL is an ObjectPAL data type that provides a handle to the Paradox desktop. The Application variable is one of the display manager objects.

You can manipulate the display managers. For example, you can open, close, minimize, maximize, and move them. The first step in manipulating a display manager is to define a variable as a display manager. For example:

```
1:    Var
2:        app    Application
3:        f      Form
4:        r      Report
5:        tv     TableView
6:        sc     Script
7:    endVar
```

As soon as you've defined a variable, you can manipulate it with any of the object methods that belong to that object. For example, to set the title of the application, use

```
1:    var
2:        app  application
3:    endVar
4:
5:    app.setTitle("My Custom Application")
```

After you've defined the application variable *app*, you can manipulate the *app* variable with any of the application methods. To browse through the various application methods from the Types and Methods dialog box, select Language | Types from within the ObjectPAL Editor. Figure 13.1 shows the Types and Methods dialog box showing the application type.

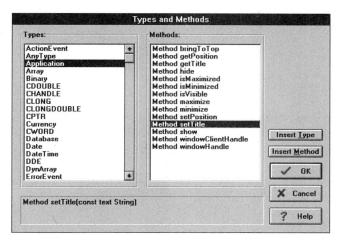

Figure 13.1. The Types and Methods dialog box.

USING hide(), SHOW(), MINIMIZE(), AND MAXIMIZE()

If you want to hide the desktop, you must define the form as a dialog box. To do this, select Properties | Form | Window Style and check the Dialog Box check box in the Window Style panel. Figure 13.2 shows the Form Window Properties dialog box.

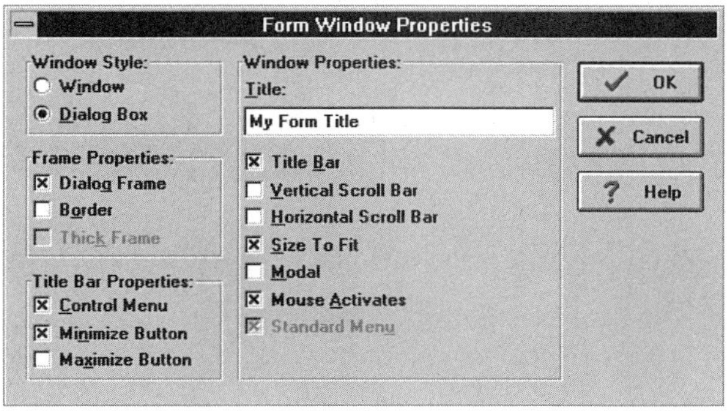

Figure 13.2. The Form Window Properties dialog box.

If the form isn't a dialog box, it will disappear when you hide the desktop. After you've defined the form as a dialog box, the next step is to define a variable of type Application:

```
1:      var
2:          app    Application
3:      endVar
```

Now, you can hide or show the application in View Data mode:

```
1:      app.hide()
2:      sleep(5000)
3:      app.show(5000)
```

The form is a dialog box only when you open it in View Data mode. If you're in Design mode, running the form is not equivalent because the form is still a child window of Paradox. You must close the form and open it in View Data mode to view it as a dialog box.

Table 13.1 lists the Application methods.

TABLE 13.1. APPLICATION METHODS AND PROCEDURES.			
bringToTop*	isMaximized*	minimize*	show*
enumWorkItems	isMinimized*	windowClientHandle*	
getTitle*	isVisible*	setPosition*	windowHandle*
hide*	maximize*	setTitle*	

*Inherited from the Form type

The following tutorial demonstrates how to use the `hide()`, `show()`, `minimize()`, and `maximize()` methods from the form type. These methods are important because they enable you to control your form and the Paradox desktop to achieve different looks.

Tutorial: Using *hide()*, *show()*, *minimize()*, and *maximize()*

Suppose that you wish to create a new form with buttons that hide, show, minimize, and maximize the application and the form. Once you create this form, you can use it to test different looks.

On Disk: \ANSWERS\HIDE.FSL

Quick Steps

1. Create a form that is defined as a dialog box with eight buttons on it and label the buttons as they are shown in Figure 13.2.
2. Use `hide()`, `show()`, `maximize()`, and `minimize()` with both the Application variable and the form.

Step By Step

1. Change your working directory to the TUTORIAL directory and create a new form with eight buttons on it. Label the buttons Hide Application, Show Application, Maximize Application, Minimize Application, Hide Form (3 seconds), Show Form, Maximize Form, and Minimize Form. Select Properties | Form | Window Style, and choose Dialog Box from the Window Style panel (see Figure 13.3).

2. In the Var window of the form, add line 3.

```
1:    ;Page2 :: Var
2:    Var
3:        App Application
4:    endVar
```

3. Add line 3 to the **pushButton** method of the Hide Application button.

```
1:    ;Button :: pushButton
2:    method pushButton(var eventInfo Event)
3:        App.hide()
4:    endmethod
```

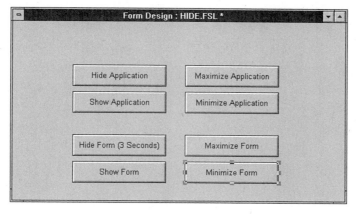

Figure 13.3. Set up form.

4. Add line 3 to the **pushButton** method of the Show Application button.

```
1:    ;Button :: pushButton
2:    method pushButton(var eventInfo Event)
3:        App.show()
4:    endmethod
```

5. Add line 3 to the **pushButton** method of the Maximize Application button.

```
1:    ;Button :: pushButton
2:    method pushButton(var eventInfo Event)
3:        App.maximize()
4:    endmethod
```

6. Add line 3 to the **pushButton** method of the Minimize Application button.

```
1:    ;Button :: pushButton
2:    method pushButton(var eventInfo Event)
3:        App.minimize()
4:    endmethod
```

7. Add lines 3–5 to the **pushButton** method of the Hide Form (3 Seconds) button.

```
1:    ;Button :: pushButton
2:    method pushButton(var eventInfo Event)
3:        hide()
4:        sleep(3000)
5:        show()
6:    endmethod
```

8. Add line 3 to the **pushButton** method of the Show Form button.

```
1:      ;Button :: pushButton
2:      method pushButton(var eventInfo Event)
3:          show()
4:      endmethod
```

9. Add line 3 to the **pushButton** method of the Maximize Form button.

```
1:      ;Button :: pushButton
2:      method pushButton(var eventInfo Event)
3:          maximize()
4:      endmethod
```

10. Add line 3 to the **pushButton** method of the Minimize Form button.

```
1:      ;Button :: pushButton
2:      method pushButton(var eventInfo Event)
3:          minimize()
4:      endmethod
```

11. Check the syntax and save the form as HIDE.FSL. Close the form, then open it. Click all eight buttons in any order to see how they work. Then, select buttons in various combinations. Different combinations produce different effects.

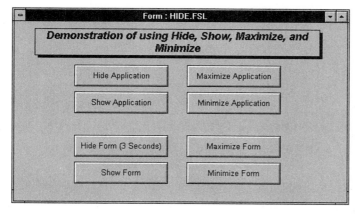

Figure 13.4. HIDE.FSL.

Analysis

In step 2, line 3 declares the application variable app. Because there is only one application—namely, the current application—you don't need to attach or open the application variable; simply use it. This app variable is used in steps 3–6 to hide, show, maximize, and minimize the application—in other words, the Paradox desktop.

Steps 7–10 call these same procedures for the form. The only difference in syntax is that the form versions don't use the optional variable in the preceding example. You could use the name of the form or the built-in object variable self to refer to the form, but a variable is not needed with these methods. In addition, you could use attach() to attach a Form variable to the current form. To demonstrate this important technique, type the following into the **pushButton** method of a button.

```
1:     ;Button :: pushButton
2:     method pushButton(var eventInfo Event)
3:        var
4:           f      Form         ;Declare f as a Form variable.
5:        endVar
6:
7:        f.attach()             ;Attach f to the current form.
8:        view(f.getTitle())     ;Show title in a view box.
9:     endmethod
```

The capability of controlling the application and the form during runtime is an important part of Paradox. Use this form whenever you want to experiment with various combinations—such as minimizing and maximizing the form and the application. For example, you can hide the application and minimize the form.

THE FORM DISPLAY MANAGER

Chapter 3, "Forms and Developing," discussed interactive and design issues about forms. This section discusses how to manipulate forms and pages in ObjectPAL.

Table 13.2 lists the form methods and procedures. Note that hideSpeedBar() from previous versions is now hideToolBar().

TABLE 13.2. FORM METHODS AND PROCEDURES.

action	dmSetProperty	isMaximized	mouseRightUp
attach	dmUnlink	isMinimized	mouseUp
bringToTop	enumDataModel	isToolbarShowing	moveToPage
close	enumSource	isVisible	open
create	enumSourceToFile	keyChar	openAsDialog
delayScreenUpdates	enumTableLinks	keyPhysical	postAction
deliver	enumUIObjectNames	load	run
design	enumUIObject Properties	maximize	save
disableBreak Message	formCaller	menuAction	saveStyleSheet
dmAddTable	formReturn	methodDelete	selectCurrentTool
dmAttach	getFileName	methodGet	setPosition
dmBuildQueryString	getPosition	methodSet	setProtoProperty
dmEnumLinkFields	getProtoProperty	minimize	setSelectedObjects
dmGet	getSelected Objects	mouseDouble	setStyleSheet
dmGetProperty	getStyleSheet	mouseDown	setTitle
dmHasTable	getTitle	mouseEnter	show
dmLinkToFields	hide	mouseExit	showToolbar
dmLinkToIndex	hideToolbar	mouseMove	wait
dmPut	isDesign	mouseRightDouble	windowClientHandle
dmRemoveTable	isAssigned	mouseRightDown	windowHandle
dmResync			

Maximizing with sysInfo()

When designing a form, you need to consider screen size. You must decide on whethor your application is going to be full screen or smaller. If you choose full screen, you must decide which resolution you're going to develop for— 640×480, 800×600, 1024×768, or something else. One solution is to check the user's screen size and to make a decision based on the answer. Use the `sysInfo()` procedure to get the current user's system information. The `sysInfo()` procedure supplies much information about your system. For example, type the following into the **pushButton** method of a button.

```
1:      ;Form :: Var
2:      Var
3:          dynSys    DynArray[]      AnyType  ;Variable for sysInfo()
4:      endVar
5:
6:      sysInfo(dynSys)
7:      dynSys.view()
```

Once you get this information, you can extract the width of the monitor resolution and use it to decide what to do. The `FullWidth` index contains the horizontal working area in pixels in a maximized window. You can use this information to determine whether your form will fit on the screen. For example, if you develop a form for 800×600, you can use the following to let the user know.

```
1:      ;Form :: open
2:      if dynSys["FullWidth"] < 800 then
3:          msgStop("Startup Error!", "This form requires at least 800 x 600
            resolution")
4:          close()
5:      endIf
```

This, unfortunately, eliminates standard VGA (640×480) users from using your form. A good solution to this problem is to develop all your forms with a 640×480 maximized resolution. In today's computer industry, most users have at least VGA. You can check whether the user is using VGA; maximize if he is. If the user's resolution is higher than that, the default Size to Fit setting centers the form on his screen (remember to check the Size to Fit property of the form). This enables users of higher-resolution monitors to get the benefit of their larger screens and still use all the screen real-estate of a VGA setup.

Tutorial: Maximizing If the Resolution is VGA

Suppose that you wish to develop a form for use on a VGA or higher-resolution monitor. If the form is open on a VGA system, then maximize the form. If the form is open on a higher-resolution system, let the default behavior take over centering the form on the desktop. This next tutorial uses sysInfo() from the System class of methods and procedures and maximize() from the form type of methods and procedures.

On Disk: \ANSWERS\VGA.FSL

Quick Steps

1. Declare a DynArray for use with sysInfo() and use the DynArray to get the current setup information.
2. Check the FullWidth index of the DynArray. If it is equal to 640, maximize the form.

Step By Step

1. Create a form for which the size of the page is VGA—6.67 inches by 4.11 inches. Make sure that the Size to Fit option is checked for the form.

2. In the Var window of the form, add line 3.

```
1:   ;Form :: Var
2:   Var
3:       dynSys   DynArray[] AnyType ;Variable for sysInfo()
4:   endVar
```

3. In the open method of the form, add lines 8–11.

```
1:   ;Form :: Open
2:   method open(var eventInfo Event)
3:      if eventInfo.isPreFilter() then
4:         ;This code executes for each object on the form
5:
6:      else
7:         ;This code executes only for the form
8:         sysInfo(dynSys)
9:         if dynSys["FullWidth"] = 640 then
10:            maximize()
11:         endIf
12:      endif
13:   endmethod
```

4. Check the syntax, save the form as VGA.FSL, and run it. If you're using a VGA monitor, the form will maximize (see Figure 13.5). If you have another resolution, the form won't maximize (see Figure 13.6).

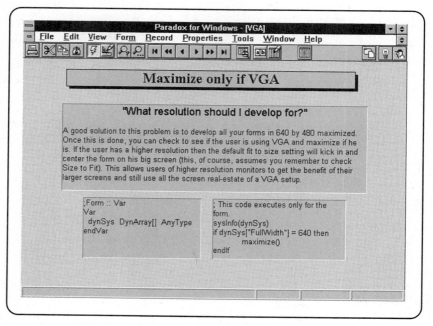

Figure 13.5. VGA.FSL on a VGA system uses the full screen.

Analysis

In step 2, line 3 declares `dynSys` as a DynArray variable that is ready to accept any type of data. In this case, you could declare *dynSys* private to the **open** method; but the data retrieved with `sysInfo()` is so useful, I like to make it global to the form for use throughout the form.

In step 3, line 8 uses `sysInfo()` to grab system information and put it into the DynArray `dynSys`. Line 9 checks whether the *FullWidth* index in *dynSys* equals 640. If it does, line 10 maximizes the form.

Another technique that is not too popular is to design a form for each resolution and to use a script to decide which version to load. You also can create a dynamic form that resizes itself depending on the resolution. This final technique is my preferred way of handling screen resolution. See the section, "Dynamic Forms," later in this chapter.

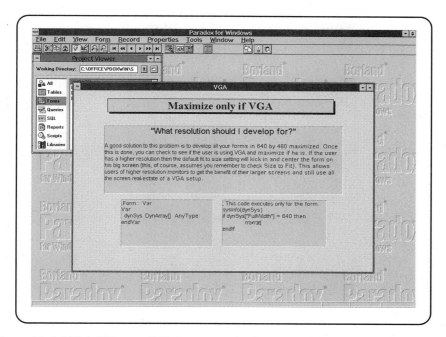

Figure 13.6. VGA.FSL on a SVGA system. The form is nicely fitted and centered.

PAGES AND FORMS

Your data model dictates whether you should use a new page or a new form. If the page that you want to add uses a table in the current data model, first consider adding a page. If a new page won't work because of size or some other reason, add a new form.

If you add another form to your application, you need to know how to move from form to form and how to pass information between forms. These two issues are discussed later in this chapter. There are two techniques to move from page to page. The first technique uses `moveTo()` and the second technique uses `moveToPage()`. To use `moveTo()`, first rename the page. Then, use `pageName.moveTo()`.

Tutorial: Moving from Page to Page

Suppose that you wish to move back and forth from the first page in a form to the second by using buttons. This tutorial acquaints you with `moveTo()`.

On Disk: \ANSWERS\PAGES.FSL

Quick Steps

1. Rename each page.
2. Use the `PageName.moveTo()` syntax. You could also use the alternative syntax `moveTo(PageName)` or `moveToPage()`.

Step By Step

1. Create a form with two pages on it. Name the first page *pge1* and the second page *pge2*. On *pge1*, create a button labeled Page Two. On *pge2* create a button labeled Page One. Make sure that the pages are stacked and not tiled horizontally or vertically.

2. Add line 3 to the **pushButton** method of the Page Two button on pge1.

   ```
   1:    ;Button :: pushButton
   2:    method pushButton(var eventInfo Event)
   3:        pge2.moveTo()
   4:    endmethod
   ```

3. Add line 3 to the **pushButton** method of the Page One button on pge2.

   ```
   1:    ;Button :: pushButton
   2:    method pushButton(var eventInfo Event)
   3:        pge1.moveTo()
   4:    endmethod
   ```

4. Check the syntax, save the form as PAGES.FSL, and run it. Click the Page Two button to move to the second page. When you're on the second page, click on the Page One button to return to the first page.

Analysis

In step 2, line 3 moves to the page named pge2, and line 3 of step 3 moves to the page named pge1. An alternative technique is to use the order of the pages instead of page's UIObject name. For example,

```
1:    moveToPage(2)
```

Added to version 5 the page now has a `positionalOrder` property you can use to know what page a user is on. Use this property, if you need to know what page the user is currently on.

MOVING FROM FORM TO FORM

To open a new form you need to do two things: define a variable as a form, and use the `open()` method:

```
1:      var
2:         f     form
3:      endVar
4:
5:      f.open(":ALIAS:FILENAME")
```

If you specify an alias, Paradox looks in only the alias directory for the file. If you don't specify an alias, Paradox looks in the working directory. Paradox doesn't search for a form that you want to open. For example, if you specify

```
1:      f.open("ORDERS.FDL")
```

Paradox looks in only the working directory for a delivered form. If you specify

```
1:      f.open("C:\DATA\ORDERS.FDL")
```

Paradox looks in only the DATA directory on drive C (it does not look in the working directory). If you specify

```
1:      f.open(":DATA:ORDERS.FDL")
```

Paradox looks in only the directory specified in the DATA alias.

Paradox looks first for the nondelivered version of a form—for example, FILENAME.FSL—and then for its delivered version—for example, FILENAME.FDL. The following searches first for ORDERS.FSL and then for ORDERS.FDL in the current working directory only.

```
1:      f.open("ORDERS")
```

If you want to search only for a specific name, use an extension:

```
1:      f.open("ORDERS.FDL")
```

If you want to reverse the search order, use

```
1:      if not f.open("ORDERS.FDL") then
2:            f.open("ORDERS.FSL")
3:      endIf
```

To move to a form that is already open, you must do three things:

1. Define a variable as a Form variable (if you haven't done so already).
2. Use the `attach()` method to attach to the form.
3. Use the `moveTo()` or `bringToTop()` method to go to the form.

Here's an example:

```
1:      var
2:          f     form
3:      endVar
4:
5:      f.attach("Form : ORDERS.FSL")
6:      f.moveTo()
```

First, check whether the form is open. If it is, attach and move to it. If the form isn't open, you can combine the preceding methods with an `if` method:

```
1:      var
2:          f     form
3:      endVar
4:
5:      if f.attach("Form : ORDER.FSL") then
6:          f.moveTo()
7:      else
8:          f.open("ORDER")
9:      endIf
```

The only other problem is the title of the form. You had to specify `Form :` `ORDER.FSL`. When you're ready to deliver your forms, you must rewrite all your code to reflect the new name. In other words, you must specify `Form :` `ORDER.FDL`—an unsuitable situation.

You can rename the form with the `setTitle()` method and use this name when you attach. For example, on the built-in `open()` method of the form, use

```
1:      ;Form2 :: open
2:      setTitle("Order Entry")
```

You can open either the delivered (.FDL) or nondelivered (.FSL) forms without modifying your code at delivery time if you use

```
1:      ;Form1.Button :: pushButton
2:      if f.attach("Order Entry") then
3:          f.moveTo()
4:      else
5:          f.open("ORDER")
6:      endIf
```

To save yourself a line of code and some time, get into the habit of explicitly naming a form every time you create a new one. If you don't need to change the title of a form during runtime, name the form, as discussed in Chapter 3, "Forms and Developing." Doing so makes it easier to attach, and the form has a more professional appearance. Instead of `Form :` `MYFORM.FSL`, you can place a more meaningful title.

For example, you might use Order Entry System. With this title, the program tries to attach to a form called Order Entry System and moves to it if `attach()`

is successful. If `attach()` fails, the program attempts to open ORDER.FSL or ORDER.FDL. This is important; it's the best way to open another form. (The last tutorial in this section adds a twist to this; it uses the `if` method to check whether the final `open()` method worked.)

Tutorial: Opening Another Form

Suppose that you wish to open a second form or to move to that second form, depending on whether the second form is already open. The following tutorial demonstrates what I believe is the best way to open another form.

On Disk: \ANSWERS\FORM1.FSL

Quick Steps

1. Explicitly set the title of both forms.
2. Try to attach to the second form. If you're successful, move to it.
3. If `attach()` fails, open the form.

Step By Step

1. Create two forms. In the Form Window Properties dialog box (see Figure 13.7), set the form title of one form to Form One, and save it as FORM1.FSL. Name the other form Form Two, save it as FORM2.FSL, and close it. On Form One, put a button labeled Other form on it.

Figure 13.7. The Form Window Properties dialog box.

2. In the **pushButton** method of the Other form button on Form One add lines 3–13.

```
1:    ;Button :: pushButton
2:    method pushButton(var eventInfo Event)
```

```
 3:        var
 4:            f       Form
 5:        endVar
 6:
 7:        if f.attach("Form Two") then
 8:            f.moveTo()
 9:          else
10:            if not f.open("FORM2") then
11:               errorShow("Form open error")
12:            endIf
13:          endIf
14:      endmethod
```

3. Check the syntax, save the form, and run it. Click the button labeled Other form. When the other form opens, leave it open and select the first form by selecting Window | 1 Form One. Click the button a second time. The second form isn't opened again. Instead, it's brought to the front very quicly.

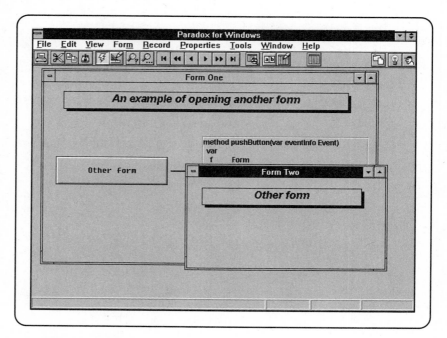

Figure 13.8. Opening another form.

Analysis

In step 2, line 4 declares *f* as a Form variable. Line 7 tries to attach `f` to Form Two. If `attach()` is successful, line 8 moves control to the newly attached form. If `attach()` fails, the execution moves to line 10, where another `if` structure executes. Line 10 of the new `if` structure opens the FORM2 file on disk. If line 10 fails to open the form, line 11 displays the error stack with `errorShow()`. Line 10 uses only the name of the form; no extension is used. This enables ObjectPAL to try to open FORM2.FSL first. If FORM2.FSL doesn't exist, ObjectPAL automatically tries to open FORM2.FDL. No extra code is required.

Using an `if` statement is a great way to test whether a method has been successful. Use `if` with `errorShow()` whenever you can. It helps safeguard your applications, and it makes them more professional. Using `if` with an `errorShow()` is another way of developing good programming skills.

NONDELIVERED OBJECTS TAKE PRECEDENCE

Whenever you use `var.open("FILENAME")` for which `var` is defined as a form, report, library, or script, Paradox always looks first for the nondelivered .?SL file and then for the delivered .?DL file.

USING WINSTYLEDEFAULT

If you use WinStyleHidden, or any of the constants in the WindowStyles category, make sure that you also use WinStyleDefault. For example, do not do the following:

```
1:      var
2:        f       Form
3:      endVar
4:
5:      f.open("MYFORM", WinStyleHidden)      ;This is wrong.
6:      sleep(1000)
7:      f.show()
```

Instead, do the following:

```
1:      var
2:        f       Form
3:      endVar
4:
```

```
5:      f.open("MYFORM", WinStyleDefault + WinStyleHidden)      ;Correct.
6:      sleep(1000)
7:      f.show()
```

To see why, try the above with a dialog box style form or with a form with scroll bars. This rule also applies to reports.

USING OPENASDIALOG()

Here is an example of using openAsDialog() with the WindowStyles. Create a form and in the Window Style panel, choose the Dialog Box. In the Title Bar Properties panel, turn off the Contol Menu. Open the dialog form from another form with the following:

```
1:      ;Button :: pushButton
2:      method pushButton(var eventInfo Event)
3:         var
4:             f       Form
5:         endVar
6:
7:         f.openAsDialog("MYFORM", WinStyleDefault + WinStyleModal +
               WinStyleControl)
8:      endMethod
```

DYNAMIC FORMS

A dynamic form is a form that automatically resizes itself and all the objects it contains so that it fits when a user resizes the form. When a user changes the size of a form, the constant MenuControlSize goes through the form's **menuAction** method. You can trap for this constant and, after the user is finished, set the form's sizeToFit property to True.

Tutorial: Dynamic Forms

Suppose that you need to create a form that dynamically resizes itself when the user resizes it.

On Disk: \ANSWERS\DYNAFORM.FSL

Quick Steps

1. Set the form's zoom property to best fit.
2. In the form's **menuAction**, trap for MenuControlSize. When it is detected, do a doDefault and set the form's sizeToFit property to True.

Step By Step

1. Change your working directory to the TUTORIAL directory and create a new form.

2. In the **setFocus** method of the form, type lines 9 and 10:

```
1:      ;Form :: setFocus
2:      method setFocus(var eventInfo Event)
3:
4:          if eventInfo.isPreFilter() then
5:              ;// This code executes for each object on the
                form:
6:
7:          else
8:              ;// This code executes only for the form:
9:              doDefault
10:             menuAction(MenuPropertiesZoomBestFit) ;Set zoom
                                                       ;to best
                                                       ;fit.
11:         endif
12:     endmethod
```

3. In the **menuAction** method of the form, type lines 9–12:

4. In the close method of the form, type lines 9–11:

```
1:      ;Form :: close
2:      method close(var eventInfo Event)
3:
4:          if eventInfo.isPreFilter() then
5:              ;// This code executes for each object on the
➥form:
6:
7:          else
8:              ;// This code executes only for the form:
9:          if not isMaximized() then show() endIf    ;If
➥maximized, show.
10:         menuAction(MenuPropertiesZoom100)  ;Set zoom to
➥100%.
11:         self.sizeToFit = True                       ;Size
➥the form to the page.
12:         endif
13:     endmethod
```

5. Check the syntax, put a few objects on the form, save the form as DYNAFORM.FSL, and run it. Resize the form and notice how the page resizes itself to fit the form. The ANSWER.FSL form also uses this technique (see Figure 13.9).

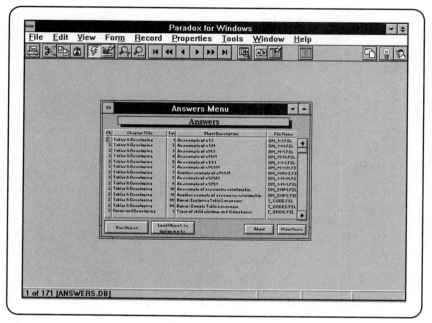

Figure 13.9. ANSWER.FSL form uses this technique to dynamically resize itself.

Analysis

In step 2, line 9 executes a `doDefault`, which finishes bringing focus to the form. In line 10, the form is set to best fit. This is equivalent to the user selecting View | Zoom | Best Fit.

```
1: if eventInfo.id() = MenuControlSize then ;When the user resizes the form
2:     doDefault                              ;then make the form size too.
3:   self.sizeToFit = True
4: endIf
```

In step 3, the **menuAction** of the form is used to trap for a menu event. In this case, you are trapping for `MenuControlSize` in line 9. This means that the user is resizing the form. Line 10 executes a `doDefault` so that the form will finish resizing and size the page because best fit is set. Finally, the form property `sizeToFit` is set to True in line 11 so that the form will match the aspect ratio of the newly resized page.

MAINMENU.FSL uses these two techniques together. All the code is located in the **open** method.

USING SETWORKINGDIR() AND SETPRIVDIR()

With version 5 of Paradox, Borland added two much needed procedures: setWorkingDir() and setPrivDir(). setPrivDir() emulates a user selecting File | Private Directory, typing a new private directory and pressing OK. setWorkingDir() does the same for your working directory. These two procedures are fairly straightforward except that the default behavior, when changing either your working or private directory, is to close all its windows. To stop this, you can trap for either MenuChangingWork or MenuChangingPriv in the **menuAction** method. For example, the following code traps for ObjectPAL changing the working directory, and stops it from closing the form to which this code is attached.

```
1:      if eventInfo.id() = MenuChangingWork then
2:          eventInfo.setErrorCode(1)
3:      endIf
```

The next two tutorials show you a good technique for using both setPrivDir() and setWorkingDir().

Tutorial: Setting Your Private Directory

Suppose that you wish to set your private directory when you open a form. Perhaps because you have a preferred private directory where you keep some favorite forms and tables.

On Disk: \ANSWERS\PRIV1.FSL

Quick Steps

1. Use setPrivDir() to change the current private directory to the one you want.
2. In order to keep the form open, trap for the constant MenuChangingPriv and set the error code to any nonzero value (perhaps 1).

Step By Step

1. Change your working directory to the TUTORIAL directory and create a new form.

2. In the **open** method of the form, type lines 3–5 and 14–17:

```
1:            ;Form :: open
2:            method open(var eventInfo Event)
3:                 var
4:                      s        String
5:                 endVar
6:
7:                 if eventInfo.isPreFilter() then
8:                      ;// This code executes for each object on
   ➡the form:
9:
10:                else
11:                     ;// This code executes only for the form:
12:
13:                     ;Set private directory to my preferred
   ➡directory.
14:                     s = "D:\\OFFICE\\PRIVATE"      ;My
   ➡preffered priv dir.
15:                     if privDir() <> s and isDir(s) then
16:                          setPrivDir(s)
17:                     endIf
18:
19:                endif
20:
21:           endmethod
```

3. In the **menuAction** method of the form, type lines 9–11:

```
1:            ;Form :: menuAction
2:            method menuAction(var eventInfo
   ➡MenuEvent)
3:
4:                 if eventInfo.isPreFilter() then
5:                      ;// This code executes for each object on
   ➡the form:
6:
7:                 else
8:                      ;// This code executes only for the form:
9:                      if eventInfo.id() = MenuChangingPriv then
10:                          eventInfo.setErrorCode(1)
11:                     endIf
```

```
12:
13:                 endif
14:
15:            endmethod
```

4. Check the syntax, save the form as PRIV1.FSL, and close it. Change your private directory to a different directory (perhaps C:\) and open the form. After the form opens, check the current private directory by selecting File | Private Directory.

Analysis

In step 2, line 4 declares s as a string variable. Step 14 sets s to a string that points to my preferred private directory. The if statement in lines 15–17 starts off in line 15 by checking two conditions. First, it compares the current private directory with s. Then, it makes sure that the directory path s represents exists. If both of these conditions are true, line 16 changes the private directory to s.

In step 3, line 9 checks for the constant MenuChangingPriv. If it is detected, line 10 sets an error code to a nonzero value.

Tutorial: Setting Your Working Directory

Suppose that you have code that relies on objects that are in the same directory as the form, and you wish to automatically change your working directory to that directory when the form is opened.

On Disk: \ANSWERS\WORK1.FSL

Quick Steps

1. Use setWorkingDir() to change the current working directory to the same directory the form is in.

2. In order to keep the form open, trap for the constant MenuChangingWork and set the error code to any nonzero value (perhaps 1).

Step By Step

1. Change your working directory to the TUTORIAL directory and create a new form.

2. In the **open** method of the form, type lines 3–6 and 15–21:

```
1:          ;Form :: open
2:          method open(var eventInfo Event)
3:               var
4:                    f              Form
```

```
5:                    dyn1      DynArray[] String
6:              endVar
7:
8:              if eventInfo.isPreFilter() then
9:                     ;// This code executes for each object on
   ➥the form:
10:
11:                else
12:                     ;// This code executes only for the form:
13:
14:                     ;Set working directory to this directory.
15:                     f.attach()
16:                     if not isFile(":WORK:ANSWERS.FSL") then
17:                          splitFullFileName(f.getFileName(),
   ➥dyn1)
18:                             if not setWorkingDir(dyn1["Drive"] +
   ➥dyn1["Path"]) then
19:                                errorShow()
20:                          endIf
21:                     endIf
22:
23:                endif
24:
25:          endmethod
```

3. In the **menuAction** method of the form, type lines 9–11:

```
1:          ;Form :: menuAction
2:          method menuAction(var eventInfo
   ➥MenuEvent)
3:
4:              if eventInfo.isPreFilter() then
5:                     ;// This code executes for each object on
   ➥the form:
6:
7:              else
8:                     ;// This code executes only for the form:
9:                     if eventInfo.id() = MenuChangingWork then
10:                        eventInfo.setErrorCode(1)
11:                     endIf
12:
```

```
13:              endif
14:
15:          endmethod
```

4. Check the syntax and save the form as WORK1.FSL. Change your working directory to a different directory (perhaps C:\) and open the form. After the form opens, check the current working directory by selecting File | Working Directory.

Analysis

In step 2, line 4 declares *f* as a form variable and *dyn1* as a DynArray ready to accept string values. Line 15 is rather interesting. It uses `attach()` to attach `f` to the current form. When you attach to the current form, you do not have to include its title. Line 16 checks to see whether the current working directory is the same directory the form is in. If it is not, then line 17 uses `getFilename()` and `splitFullFileName()` to extract the form's path. Line 18 sets the working directory.

Similar to the previous tutorial, in step 3, line 9 checks for the constant `MenuChangingWork`. If it is detected, line 10 sets an error code to a nonzero value.

GETTING USER INPUT

With ObjectPAL you have several ways to get input from a user. You could simply place an undefined field on the form for the user to type in to. This passive way of getting user input works for many situations. Another, more decisive technique is to use a view dialog box. We have used `view()` several times already; here is one more example for you to type into the **pushButton** method of a button.

```
1:      method pushButton(var eventInfo Event)
2:          var
3:              s       String
4:          endVar
5:
6:          s = "Enter your name"
7:          s.view("Full name")
8:          if s = "Enter your name" then
9:              ;Either user did not change text or clicked Cancel.
10:             return
11:          endIf
12:          message("Your name is " + s)
13:      endMethod
```

You could also use some of the simple built-in dialog boxes with `msgQuestion()`, `msgYesNoCancel()`, and so on. For example:

```
1:    if msgQuestion("Question", "Do you wish to proceed?") = "No" then
2:        return
3:    endIf
```

USING FORMRETURN()

To get more complex data input from a user, you must use another form for input. Once the user types a value in to an undefined field on the other form, you need to return the value from the second form to the first. You can use formReturn() to return a value from one form to another.

To use formReturn() actually requires several steps. Suppose that you wish to return a value from a form form2 to form1. First, you open form2 and wait for it from form1. For example:

```
1:    var
2:        f      Form
3:        s      String
4:    endVar
5:
6:    f.open("FORM2")
7:    s = string(f.wait())
```

Note that the variable s is set up to wait for a value from form2. On form2, use formReturn() to return a value to s. For example:

```
1:    formReturn("Hello first form")
```

After the form2 returns a value to form1, close form2 with close(). For example:

```
1:    f.close()
```

Here is the code for both forms.

```
1:    ;btnCallForm :: pushButton
2:    method pushButton(var eventInfo Event)
3:        var
4:            f      Form
5:            s      String
6:        endVar
7:
8:        f.open("FORM2")
9:        s = f.wait()
10:       f.close()
11:       s.view()
12:    endmethod
13:
14:    ;btnCalledForm :: pushButton
15:    method pushButton(var eventInfo Event)
16:        formReturn("Hello first form")
17:    endMethod
```

Note that the form is closed immediately after using `wait()`. Here are a couple of rules to keep in mind when using `formReturn()`.

1. If `formReturn()` has a `wait()` waiting on it, `formReturn()` returns a value but does not close the current form.

2. If `formReturn()` does not have a `wait()` waiting, `formReturn()` closes the form.

As long as you keep the preceding rules in mind, `formReturn()` is easy to use.

Tutorial: Using *formReturn()* with Dot Notation

Suppose that you need to return more than one value from a called form. This tutorial demonstrates how to use `formReturn()` in conjunction with dot notation to return three values from the called form to the calling form. In addition, it demonstrates that text objects have a value property that you can read (and set) from another form. In this case, the calling form reads two text boxes on the called form. Finally, it demonstrates that you do not have to close the called form immediately after using `wait()`.

On Disk: \ANSWERS\FORMRET1.FSL & FORMRET2.FSL

Quick Steps

1. Use `formReturn()` with `wait()` as described in the preceding text.

2. Between the `wait()` and `close()`, use dot notation to grab values from any of the objects on the second form.

Step By Step

1. Change your working directory to TUTORIAL. Create two forms. On the first form place a button labeled Call Other Form (see Figure 13.10) and save it as FORMRET1.FSL. Place two button objects on the second form, and two text objects. Label the two buttons as OK and Cancel. Name the two text boxes txt1 and txt2. Set the value of txt1 to Hello and set the value of txt2 to World (see Figure 13.11). Save this second form as FORMRET2.FSL.

   Optional: Make FORMRET2.FSL a modal dialog box. This forces the user to press one of the two buttons.

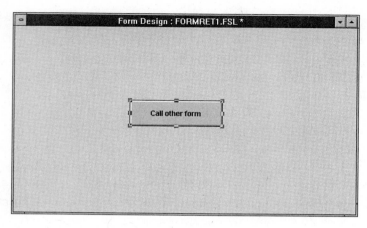

Figure 13.10. Set up form for FORMRET1.FSL.

2. On the first form (FORMRET1.FSL), add lines 3–15 to the
   pushButton method of the button labeled Call Other Form.

```
1:              ;BtnCall :: pushbutton
2:              method pushButton(var eventInfo Event)
3:                  var
4:                      f       Form
5:                          s1, s2, s3      String
6:                  endVar
7:
8:              f.open("FORMRET2")    ;Open 2nd form.
9:              s1 = string(f.wait())         ;Wait on 2nd form.
10:             s2 = f.txt1.value             ;Grab value from
        ➥txt1 object.
11:             s3 = f.txt2.value             ;Grab value from
        ➥txt2 object.
12:                 f.close()                        ;Close 2nd
        ➥form.
```

```
13:                s1.view()                      ;View returned
   ➥value.
14:                s2.view()                      ;View txt1
   ➥value.
15:                s3.view()                      ;View txt2
   ➥value.
16:            endmethod
```

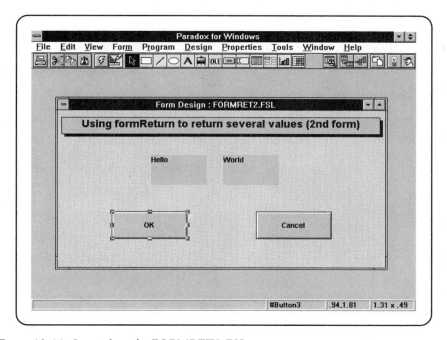

Figure 13.11. Set up form for FORMRET2.FSL.

3. On the second form (FORMRET2.FSL), add line 3 to the **pushButton** method of the button labeled OK.

```
1:            ;BtnOK :: pushbutton
2:            method pushButton(var eventInfo Event)
3:                  formReturn("OK")
4:            endmethod
```

4. On the second form (FORMRET2.FSL), add line 3to the **pushButton** method of the button labeled Cancel.

```
1:        ;BtnOK :: pushbutton
2:        method pushButton(var eventInfo Event)
3:           formReturn("Cancel")
4:        endmethod
```

5. Check the syntax, save both forms, and close the second form (FORMRET2.FSL). Run FORMRET1.FSL and click the button. On the second form, click either the OK or Cancel button (see Figure 13.12).

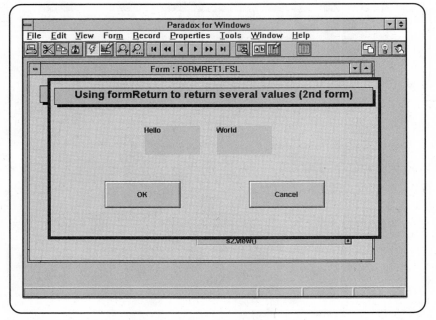

Figure 13.12. FORMRET1.FSL and FORMRET2.FSL.

Analysis

In step 2, lines 4 and 5 declare f as a form variable and s1, s2, and s3 as string variables. Line 8 uses the f variable with open() to open the second form. Line 9 waits for the second form to return a value; pay special attention to the syntax used in this line.

Now skip over to steps 3 and 4. Line 3 in both uses formReturn() to return a value and control back to the calling form. It is interesting to note that, at this point, you could use formCaller() to find out what form is the calling form. formCaller() assigns the calling form to a form variable.

After `formReturn()` returns a value and control back to the calling form, the `wait()` in step 2, line 9 returns a value to the string variable `s1`. Lines 10 and 11 grab two values from two text objects on the second form. Finally, line 12 closes the second form only after you have grabbed two values from two of its text objects. Lines 13, 14, and 15 view the three values in view boxes.

PASSING VALUES WITH CLOSE()

If you do not need to keep the second form open, then do not use `formReturn()`. Instead, just use `close()` in its place. To see this in action, follow these steps:

1. In step 2, delete lines 10, 11, 12, 14, and 15.
2. In step 3 and 4, change `formReturn()` to `close()`. For example, change `formReturn("OK")` to `close("OK")`.

If you do not need to keep the second form open, this technique of using `close()` is the preferred technique. `formReturn()` is used too much.

PASSING VALUES BETWEEN FORMS

Often, you need to pass values from one form to another. As with many things in ObjectPAL, you have several ways of approaching this task. You can't pass a variable directly from one form to another; you must use a custom method or procedure that changes or sets a variable. You can, however, change the value of a field directly.

PASSING VALUES DIRECTLY TO A UIOBJECT

With ObjectPAL, you can pass values directly from one object to another. Because a form is an object, you also can pass values directly from one form to another. You can use statements such as

```
1:    field1Name.value = field2Name.value
```

Likewise, you can declare a Form variable, attach it to another form, and use dot notation to transfer values. For example, to put the value in `field1` on `form1` into `field2` on `form2`, use

```
1:    var
2:        f    form
3:    endVar
```

```
4:
5:        f.attach("Form : Form2.fsl")  ;Watch those form titles
6:        field1.value = f.field2.value
```

This technique works well if both forms currently are open and the names of the form titles don't change. You use this technique to manipulate the `value` property of objects. After you've attached `form2` to a variable, you can expand this technique to manipulate, call, and use any of the properties of the other form's objects:

```
1:        f.box3.color = red
2:        f.line4.visible = false
3:        f.maximize()
4:        f.hide()
5:        f.button3.pushButton()
6:        f.ID_No.locate("ID No", ID_No)
```

Here's an example of opening a form and setting a field's value:

```
1:        ;Button :: pushButton
2:        var
3:              f       form
4:        endVar
5:
6:        f.open("MYFORM2")
7:        f.Last_Name = "Prestwood"
```

This example illustrates that a form is just another object, which can be manipulated like UIObjects. As soon as you have a handle to the other form, you can manipulate it.

PASSING VARIABLES WITH A TABLE

You can write values to a table from the first form and read in the values from the other form. You use a TCursor to write to and read from a table in either the working or the private directory. You even can include a mechanism for cleaning up, or deleting, the tables when you exit the application—perhaps on the `canDepart` method of the form.

This technique works well for passing large amounts of data, nontextual data, or data you want to hang around for the next time you enter your application. For example, if you need to pass a sound file or a picture from one form to another, use this method.

PASSING VARIABLES THROUGH A LIBRARY

You can use a library to store and pass values. Because external objects have access only to the custom methods of a library, you must use at least two custom methods. One custom method puts the value into the library's variables; the other custom method gets the value. This technique works well if you already are using a library with your application.

This technique is valuable if you're going to close and open forms. You could write one custom method that sets a variable in the library and another that checks it. As soon as you have the two custom methods in the library, you can call them from various forms. Chapter 23, "Storing and Centralizing Code," contains a tutorial that demonstrates this technique.

KEEPING TWO FORMS IN SYNC

With a relational database manager system such as Paradox, you often gather data into compartments. Usually, you display the data on a form in a 1:1 relationship. Occasionally, though, you need to display the data on separate forms. Having independent forms is a convenient way of displaying parts of a complete database a little at a time.

For example, in an address book application, you might separate personal information from business information. One table is connected to a form that shows personal information—home address, home telephone number, and so on. The other table is connected to a form that shows business information—title, work address, work telephone number, and so on. You might make the business form the main, or master, form and include on it a button that brings up the person's home information.

When both forms are displayed, you need to keep them in sync. A form is a display manager, and display managers in Paradox are objects—just as a field is an object. Therefore, you can manipulate objects on another form. In this address book example, you can use a button to open a second form and position it on the same record or on the corresponding record. You can use two techniques to accomplish this.

You use the first technique if both forms use the same table or if they use different tables that are related. The following code represents an elegant and clean way to keep two forms in sync.

```
1:      ;button :: pushButton
2:      var
3:          f2    form
4:      endVar
5:
6:      f2.open("homeinfo", WinStyleDefault + WinStyleHidden)
7:      f2.Last_Name.locate("Last Name", Last_Name1, "First Name", First_Name1)
8:      f2.bringToTop()
```

Last_Name1 and First_Name1 are two fields on the master business form.

The second technique assumes that you're using the same table in both forms.
Its code is as follows:

```
1:      var
2:          tc      TCursor
3:          f       Form
4:      endVar
5:
6:    • tc.attach( fldInCurrentForm )
7:      f.open("form2", WinStyleDefault + WinStyleHidden)
8:      f.fldInform2.reSync(tc)
9:      f.bringToTop()
```

Tutorial: Keeping Two Forms in Sync

Suppose that you have two forms that are connected to the same table—or two
similar tables—and need to keep them in sync.

On Disk: \ANSWERS\SYNC1.FSL

Quick Steps

1. Attach or open the second form.

2. Use dot notation to locate the same record, then move to the other
   form.

Step By Step

1. Change your working directory to the TUTORIAL directory and
   create a new form with the Customer table in the data model. Add a
   button to the form and label it View Notes (see Figure 13.13). Save
   the form as SYNC1.FSL.

2. Create a second form with the Custnote table in the data model. Add
   a button to the form and label it Close (see Figure 13.14). Change the
   title bar name to SYNC2 and save the form as SYNC2.FSL.

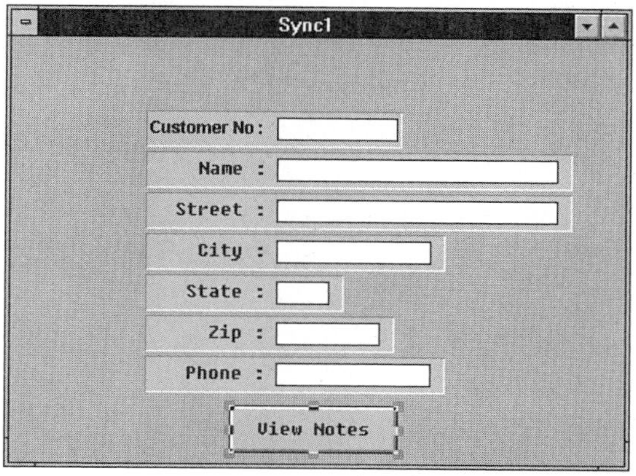

Figure 13.13. SYNC1.FSL set up form.

Figure 13.14. SYNC2.FSL set up form.

3. In the **pushButton** method of the View Notes button on SYNC1.FSL, type lines 3–17:

```
1:          ;Button :: pushButton
2:          method pushButton(var eventInfo Event)
3:              var
4:                   f      Form
5:              endVar
6:
7:              if not f.attach("Sync2") then
8:                   f.open("SYNC2", WinStyleDefault +
```

```
             ➥WinStyleHidden)
 9:                    endIf
10:
11:                    if not f.Customer_No.locate("Customer No",
      ➥Customer_No) then
12:                        f.Customer_No.edit()
13:                        f.Customer_No.insertRecord()
14:                        f.Customer_No = Customer_No.value
15:                    endIf
16:
17:                    f.bringToTop()
18:              endmethod
```

4. In the **pushButton** method of the Close button on SYNC2.FSL, type
   line 3:

```
1:          ;Button :: pushButton
2:          method pushButton(var eventInfo Event)
3:              close()
4:          endmethod
```

5. Check the syntax, save the forms, and run it. Move to any record and
   then press the View Notes button (see Figure 13.15). Type in some
   notes and press the Close button.

Analysis

In step 3, line 4 declares f as a form variable for use in lines 7 or 8 to either attach
to or open SYNC2.FSL. Once a handle is opened, lines 11, 12 ,13, and 14 use
it to manipulate what record the other form is on, and then line 17 shows the
form.

In step 4, line 3 closes the form and returns control back to the calling form.
Also note that edit mode is automatically ended and any unposted changes to
the table are posted.

The highest container level in an ObjectPAL application is the form. Often,
you need to pass data from form to form. You can use any of the techniques
outlined in this section to exchange data between forms or to sync forms.

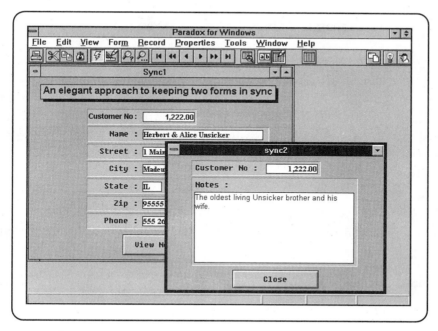

Figure 13.15. SYNC1.FSL calling SYNC2.FSL.

PRINTING A FORM

One of the first things that you'll want to do is print a form. Unlike the report type of methods, the form type does not have a print() command. You can print a form from ObjectPAL, however. Just as a user can select File | Print, you can send a form to the printer with ObjectPAL. To print the current form, use either of these lines of code:

```
1:    menuAction(MenuFilePrint)   ;Emulates the menu.
2:    action(DataPrint)           ;Preferred technique.
```

You can use either of these techniques to print a form. The technique of using the menuAction() procedure in the preceding line 1 uses the technique to invoking a menu constant. In versions 1 and 4.5, Borland officially warns against using menu constants with this technique, for they might not work in the future. With version 5, however, all the constants seem to work—at least all the constants I tested.

PREVENTING A USER FROM EXITING

Two techniques work well for preventing the user from exiting your application. The first technique traps for the `MenuControlClose` constant with `eventInfo.id() = MenuControlClose` or `eventInfo.id() = MenuCanClose` in the **menuAction** method, and sets the `CanNotDepart` error code. The second technique uses `canDepart` of the form. Both of them use a flag. A *flag* is a variable used in a routine to indicate whether a condition has occurred. The next tutorial demonstrates how to use **menuAction** to prevent exiting. The second technique of using `canDepart` is demonstrated next.

Tutorial: Using *menuAction* to Prevent Exiting

Suppose that you wish to prevent a user from exiting a form unless you let him or her. In this tutorial, however, the user can go into design mode. The next tutorial demonstrates trapping for `MenuCanClose` and `MenuControlClose` in the **menuAction** method.

On Disk: \ANSWERS\NOCLOSE1.FSL

Quick Steps

1. Trap for `MenuCanClose` and `MenuControlClose` in the **menuAction** method of the form.
2. Check the value of a flag. If the flag is true, set the error code to `CanNotDepart`.

Step By Step

1. Create a new form. On the form, place a radio button field named *fldFlag*. Add two choices to the radio button: Allow close and Do not allow close. Figure 13.16 shows how the form should look.
2. Add lines 7–12 to the **menuAction** method of the form.

```
1:       ;Form :: menuAction
2:       method menuAction(var eventInfo MenuEvent)
3:       if eventInfo.isPreFilter() then
4:            ;This code executes for each object on the form
5:       else
6:            ;This code executes only for the form
7:            if eventInfo.id() = MenuCanClose or
8:                 eventInfo.id() = MenuControlClose then
9:                 if fldFlag = "Do not allow close" then
```

```
10:                         eventInfo.setErrorCode(CanNotDepart)
11:              endIf
12:         endIf
13:    endif
14:    endmethod
```

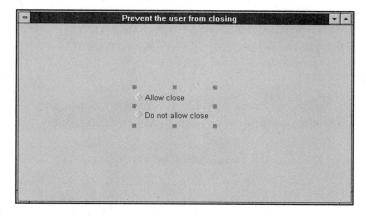

*Figure 13.16. NOCLOSE1.FSL. Using **menuAction** to prevent the user from exiting the application.*

3. Check the syntax, save the form as NOCLOSE1.FSL, and run it. Set the field fldFlag to Do not allow close, and try all the various ways of exiting. Then, set the flag field to Allow close, and exit or move into design mode.

Analysis

In step 2, lines 7 and 8 check for MenuCanClose and MenuControlClose. MenuControlClose is called when the user attempts to close the form, and MenuCanClose is called when the application tries to close or when the user selects Window | Close All. The menu command constants are listed online under Language | Constants. You can use this technique to trap for any of the menu command constants. Line 9 enables you to exit. (You need a way to exit at some point in your code.) Line 10 does the real work. It sets the CanNotDepart error code.

The next tutorial demonstrates how to use **canDepart** to prevent exiting. You use the **canDepart** method of a form to prevent a form from closing—thereby preventing the application from closing. It also provides a way to toggle this effect on and off—perhaps with a flag field.

Tutorial: Using *canDepart* to Prevent Exiting

Suppose that you wish to prevent a user from exiting a form unless you let him or her (including going into design mode).

On Disk: \ANSWERS\NOCLOSE2.FSL

Quick Steps

1. On the **canDepart** of the form, check a flag.
2. If the flag is true, set the error code to CanNotDepart.

Step By Step

1. Create a new form. On the form, place a radio button field named *fldFlag*. The radio button field has two choices, which are Allow close and Do not allow close. The form should look like it did in the last tutorial (refer back to Figure 13.16).

2. Add lines 9–11 to the **canDepart** method of the form.

```
1:          ;Form :: canDepart
2:          method canDepart(var eventInfo MoveEvent)
3:          if eventInfo.isPreFilter()
4:          then
5:               ;This code executes for each object on the form
6:
7:          else
8:               ;This code executes only for the form
9:               if FlagField = "Do not allow close" then
10:                    eventInfo.setErrorCode(CanNotDepart)
11:                endIf
12:          endif
13:          endmethod
```

3. Check the syntax, save the form as NOCLOSE2.FSL, and run it. Set the flag field to Do not allow close and try all the various ways of exiting. You cannot go into Design mode, as you could in the previous tutorial. Set the flag field to Allow close, and exit.

Analysis

In step 2, line 9 checks the value of the *fldFlag* field. If the value is Do not allow close, line 10 sets the error code to CanNotDepart.

Both the techniques presented in this section are important. Trapping for a constant in **menuAction**—or **action**—at the form level enables you to centralize your code. Using the **canDepart** method and setting the error code to `CanNotDepart` also is useful. Both these techniques have broad uses.

THE TABLEVIEW DISPLAY MANAGER

In Paradox, a table window is an object that displays data in its own window. A table window is what opens when you select File | Open | Table and choose a table. A TableView variable is a handle to that window. Sometimes, you want to bring up a table and work with it in a TableView. Although a TableView is limited in functionality, you can open and manipulate it similarly to how you open and manipulate a form. Table 13.3 lists the TableView methods and procedures.

TABLE 13.3. TABLEVIEW METHODS AND PROCEDURES.

```
action

bringToTop*

close

getPosition*

getTitle*

hide*

isAssigned

isMaximized*

isMinimized*

isVisible*

maximize*

minimize*

moveToRecord

open

setPosition*
```

continues

```
setTitle*

show*

wait

windowHandle*
```

*Inherited from the Form type

TABLEVIEW VARIABLES

Just as there are Application and Form variables, there is a variable for use with a table window—it is the TableView variable. As soon as you declare a variable as a TableView and open the TableView, you establish a handle to a table window. With that handle, you can open, wait, and close table windows similar to manipulating a form with a Form variable.

You also can use ObjectPAL to manipulate TableView properties. For example, you can manipulate the TableView object as a whole—for example, background color, grid style, and the value of the current record. You can also manipulate the field-level data in the table (TVData)—for example, font characteristics and display format. Finally, you can manipulate the TableView heading (TVHeading)—for example, font, color, and alignment.

The following code declares a TableView variable named tv:

```
1:    Var
2:         tv    TableView
3:    endVar
```

Because this variable now exists, you can use it to open a table window:

```
1:    tv.open("ZIPCODES.DB")
2:    tv.wait()
3:    tv.close()
```

The TableView action() method is powerful. It gives you access to many of the form methods and procedures. You can do many operations on a table, including hide and show:

```
1:      tv.hide()
2:      message("Table is hidden for 3 seconds")
3:      sleep(3000)
4:      tv.show()
```

To tell the user how to start and end Edit mode, you can use the TableView
setTitle() method, as in

```
1:      TableViewVar.setTitle("F9 for edit mode :: Close to return")
```

This next tutorial demonstrates opening a table window from a button.

Tutorial: Bringing up a TableView from a Button

Suppose that you wish to have a button on a form bring up a table window.

On Disk: \ANSWERS\TVIEW1.FSL

Quick Steps

1. Define a TableView variable.
2. Use the open() method to open a table window.

Step By Step

1. Set your working directory to TUTORIAL. Create a new form and put
   a button on it labeled ZIPCODES.DB.

2. Add lines 4–8 to the **pushButton** method, which open
   ZIPCODES.DB in a table window.

```
1:          ;Button :: pushButton
2:          method pushButton(var eventInfo Event)
3:              ;This routine brings up a TableView
4:              var
5:                  tv      TableView
6:              endVar
7:
8:              tv.open("ZIPCODES.DB")
9:          endmethod
```

3. Check the syntax, save the form as TVIEW1.FSL, and run it. Click
   the button. Figure 13.17 shows how the form looks when you click the
   button.

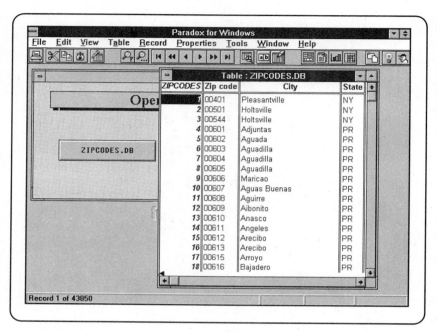

Figure 13.17. TVIEW1.FSL. How to open a table in TableView mode.

Analysis

In step 2, line 5 declares *tv* as a TableView variable, which line 8 uses to open the ZIPCODES.DB table.

GETTING A TABLEVIEW READY FOR INPUT

The next step in dealing with a table window is to get it ready for data entry. You can use the action() method with constants to manipulate a table window. I like the technique presented in the next tutorial because of its simplicity. It demonstrates how to get a table window ready for input.

Tutorial: Getting a TableView Ready for Input

Suppose that you wish to have a button on a form that opens a table window ready for input when the user clicks it.

On Disk: \ANSWERS\TVIEW2.FSL

Quick Steps

1. Define a TableView variable.
2. Use the open() method to open a TableView.
3. Use action constants to move to the end of the table, to switch into Edit mode, and to move to the next record.

Step By Step

1. Set your working directory to TUTORIAL. Create a new form and place a button on it labeled Add a Customer.
2. Add lines 4–11 to the **pushButton** method of the button to open Customer table window that is ready for input.

```
1:              ;Button :: pushButton
2:              method pushButton(var eventInfo Event)
3:                    ;this routine brings up a table view ready for
input
4:                  var
5:                      tv        TableView
6:                  endVar
7:
8:                      tv.open("CUSTOMER.DB")
9:                      tv.action(MoveEnd)
10:                     tv.action(DataBeginEdit)
11:                     tv.action(DataNextRecord)
12:              endmethod
```

3. Check the syntax, save the form as TVIEW2.FSL, run it, and click the button. The TableView does exactly what you told it to do, and it's ready for input. Your form should look similar to Figure 13.18. The CUSTOMER.DB table is ready for input.

Analysis

In step 2, line 5 declares *tv* as a TableView variable. It's used in lines 8–11. Line 8 opens the CUSTOMER.DB table with the *tv* variable in a table window. Lines 9–11 use action constants to move to the end of the table, to switch into Edit mode, and to move to the next record. Now, the table window is ready for input.

Chapter 14 discusses a topic related to display managers—queries. Chapter 15 discusses the fourth display manager, the report.

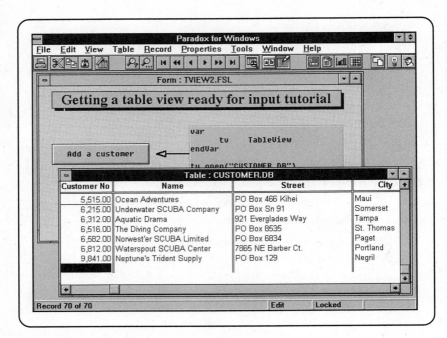

Figure 13.18. TVIEW2.FSL.

USING QUERIES

QUERIES AND DEVELOPING

The technique of asking questions about data by providing an example of the answer you expect is called *query by example* (QBE). You can use this tool to ask questions about your data and analyze it. A query is a means of extracting sets of information from a database or table. You can base forms and reports off a subset of your data by using a query as the first table in your data model. You can even use a live query as this first table—a dynaset. You can even create queries on the fly in ObjectPAL.

The Query variable is a handle to a QBE query. Table 14.1 lists the methods and procedures available in the Query Type. Version 4.5 users should note that the `readFromFile()` replaced the Database procedure `executeQBEFile()`, and `readFromString()` replaced `executeQBEString()`.

TABLE 14.1. QUERY METHODS AND PROCEDURES.
executeQBE
getQueryRestartOptions
isAssigned
isExecuteQBELocal
query
readFromFile
readFromString
setQueryRestartOptions
wantInMemoryTCursor
writeQBE

QUERIES

Queries are a very important part of any database. Having a large amount of data isn't useful unless you can analyze it. Queries are what you use to analyze your data. Sometimes they are the only way to get certain information about a product. Paradox delivers a graphical query by example (QBE) that makes it easier than ever to create queries and get fast answers. You can access up to 24 tables in a single query. Join, outer join, inclusion, and set operations are available for full relational queries.

QBE has two functions—namely, as an end user tool and as a way to use a subset of all the data. You can use QBE to develop specialized forms and reports.

Important Query methods and procedures are as follows:

executeQBE()	Executes a QBE query
QUERY	Begins a QBE statement or string
readFromFile()	Reads a QBE file into a query variable
readFromString()	Reads a string into a query variable
writeQBE()	Writes a Query statement to a specified file

BRINGING UP THE QUERY WINDOW

Suppose that you wish to bring up the query window with a particular query.
To do this, you can use sendKeys() from the system type. For example, change
your working directory to the TUTORIAL directory and type line 3 into the
pushButton method of a button.

```
1:  ;Button :: pushButton
2:  method pushButton(var eventInfo Event)
3:      sendKeys("%foqworld{ENTER}")  ;Emulates pressing keys.
4:  endmethod
```

sendKeys() emulates the user pressing keys. The first part of the preceding code
emulates the user pressing ALT+O+Q, which is the same as selecting
File | Open | Query. The second half, WORLD{ENTER}, specifies the name of the
query to open and presses the Return key. Figure 14.1 shows the final result. The
form ANSWERS\QUERY_O.FSL demonstrates this technique.

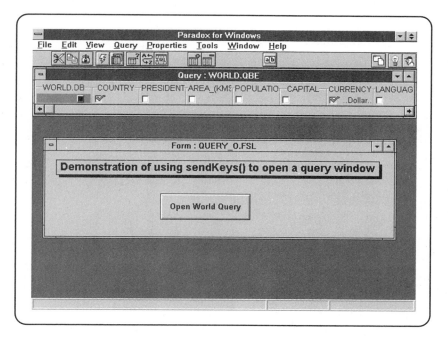

Figure 14.1. WORLD.QBE.

This important procedure `sendKeys()` is addressed further in Chapter 19, "Manipulating Strings and Handling the Keyboard."

Executing a Saved Query

The term *query* in ObjectPAL refers to the Query variable. The Query variable is your handle to a query. Just as you can declare a `Form` variable and open it, you can declare a Query variable, read a file into it, and execute it. For example, change your working directory to the TUTORIAL directory and type lines 2–7 into the **pushButton** method of a button.

```
1:   method pushButton(var eventInfo Event)
2:       var
3:           q       Query                   ;Declare a Query variable.
4:       endVar
5:
6:       q.readFromFile("WORLD.QBE")    ;Read in QBE.
7:       q.executeQBE()                 ;Execute QBE.
8:       ;Open up the ANWSER table in your private directory.
9:   endMethod
```

Note for 1.0 and 4.5 Users

executeQBEFile( ) Is Now readFromFile( )

In versions 1.0 and 4.5, you used `executeQBEFile()` to execute a saved query. For backward compatibility reasons, you can still use this undocumented feature. For example:

```
executeQBEFile("WORLD.QBE", ":PRIV:__ANS.DB")
```

The preceding line of code executes WORLD.QBE and generates the answer table to `:PRIV:.ANS.DB`. The new technique in version 5 is to use `readFromFile()` and `executeQBE()` from the Query type, as discussed previously.

The following tutorial demonstrates how to run an existing query.

Tutorial: Running a Query from a Button

Suppose that you have an existing query, WORLD.QBE, that you wish to run, show the results in a TableView, and enable Paradox to delete the answer table automatically when it exits.

On Disk: \ANSWERS\QUERY.FSL

Quick Steps

1. Define a Query and TableView variable.
2. Use the `readFromFile()` to read the query file into the Query variable. Then use `executeQBE()` to run the query and to create a file named `:PRIV:__ANS.DB` in your private directory.
3. Open the table by using the TableView variable.

Step By Step

1. Change your working directory to TUTORIAL. Create a new form and place a button labeled Run query file on it.
2. Add lines 3–10 to the **pushButton** method of the Run query file button to execute the query.

```
1:      ;Button :: pushButton
2:      method pushButton(var eventInfo Event)
3:          var
4:              q    Query              ;Declare query variable.
5:              tv   TableView
6:          endVar
7:
8:          q.readFromFile("WORLD.QBE") ;Read in QBE.
9:          q.executeQBE(":priv:__ans") ;Optional: specify answer table.
10:         tv.open(":priv:__ans")
11:     endmethod
```

3. Check the syntax, save the form as QUERY.FSL, run the form, and click the button. The query runs and creates a table named __ANS.DB in your private directory. Then the table is opened (see Figure 14.2). When you exit Paradox, the table is deleted.

Analysis

In step 2, line 4 declares a Query variable and line 5 declares a TableView variable. Line 8 uses `readFromFile()` to read the QBE file WORLD.QBE into the q Query variable. Then `executeQBE()` is used in line 9 to run the query and create a table named __ANS.DB in your private directory.

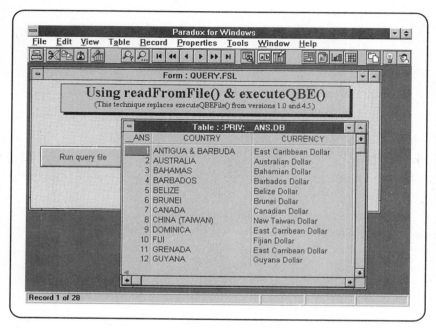

Figure 14.2. QUERY.FSL.

This last step of using two underscores at the beginning of a file in your private
directory is important. It is also interesting, because it takes advantage of an
undocumented feature of Paradox. Any file in the private directory that starts
with two underscores is deleted when the program is exited. This is a normal
part of the clean-up process of Paradox. In addition, the files are not listed in
the browser or Project Viewer.

USING A QUERY STATEMENT WITH *executeQBE()*

In addition to executing a query file—for example, WORLD.QBE—you can
code a query inside your code with ObjectPAL. First, you declare a Query
variable:

```
1:   var
2:      q     Query
3:   endVar
```

Next, you use the defined Query variable to start the query section in your code.
Then comes the actual Query string. For example:

```
1:  q = Query
2:       WORLD.DB ¦ COUNTRY ¦ CURRENCY        ¦
3:                         ¦ Check   ¦ Check ..Dollar.. ¦
4:  EndQuery
```

Typing all these field names, checks, and values would be a hassle, to say the least. In essence, you have to learn a whole new programming language, the QBE language. Luckily, ObjectPAL provides an easier way. A saved QBE file is simply a text file. Therefore, you can use the Edit | Paste From option to paste the text file and alter it as needed. Then, use `executeQBE()` the way you did in the previous tutorial. For example:

```
1:  q.executeQBE(":PRIV:ANSWER.DB")
```

This next tutorial demonstrates how to use `executeQBE()`.

Tutorial: Using *executeQBE*

Suppose that you wish to execute a query by using the ObjectPAL Query variable.

On Disk: \ANSWERS\QUERY1.FSL

Quick Steps

1. Create a query interactively.

2. Paste the QBE text file into the Editor.

3. Alter it as you like.

4. Use `executeQBE()` to execute the Query variable.

Step By Step

1. Create a new query based on WORLD.DB that queries all the records with Dollar in the CURRENCY field, as in Figure 14.3. Save the query as WORLD.QBE (this file already exists in the ANSWERS subdirectory).

2. Create a new form and add a button labeled Query WORLD.DB to it.

3. The easiest way to a build a query in ObjectPAL is to build it interactively and paste it into the Editor. A QBE file is simply a text file (see Figure 14.4). It can be pasted directly into the Editor. The easiest way to do this is to use the Edit | Paste From option of the Editor. Figure 14.5 shows how the code looks after you insert the QBE file.

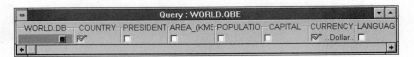

Figure 14.3. WORLD.QBE.

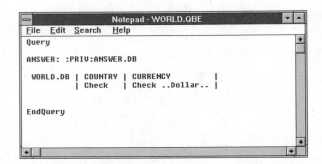

Figure 14.4. The text file WORLD.QBE in Notepad.

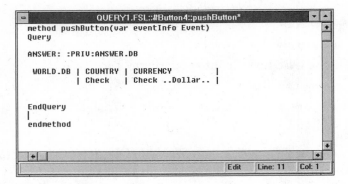

Figure 14.5. After inserting the QBE file.

4. Alter the **pushButton** method of the Query WORLD.DB button as follows.

```
1:    ;Button :: pushButton
2:    method pushButton(var eventInfo Event)
3:       var
4:          q  Query
5:          tv TableView
6:       endVar
```

```
 7:
 8:        q = Query
 9:        ANSWER: :PRIV:ANSWER.DB
10:
11:        WORLD.DB ¦ COUNTRY ¦ CURRENCY        ¦
12:                ¦ Check   ¦ Check ..Dollar.. ¦
13:
14:        EndQuery
15:
16:        executeQBE(q)
17:        tv.open(":PRIV:ANSWER.DB")
18:    endmethod
```

5. Check the syntax, save the form as QUERY1.FSL, and run it. Click the button. The query is run, and the table is shown in a table window (see Figure 14.6).

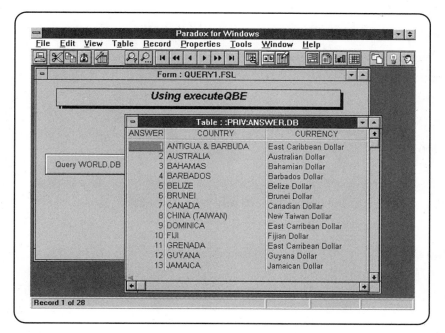

Figure 14.6. The QUERY1.FSL form.

Analysis

In step 4, lines 4 and 5 declare the Query and TableView variables. Lines 8–14 contain the query that is pasted in. Only line 8 has been altered. Line 9 specifies where the answer table should be created. If you leave out line 9, the default is `:PRIV:ANSWER.DB`. In this case, if you delete line 9, you will get the same result. Line 16 uses `executeQBE()` to execute the Query variable, and line 17 displays the table that results.

PASSING A VALUE TO A QUERY

You know how to execute a QBE file on disk and how to execute values stored in your code. The next step is to learn how to pass a value to a query. Often, you'll want to enable the user to enter values and to query the table for the values entered. In effect, you simulate the query Editor. Use a tilde variable whenever you want to pass a value to a query. This next tutorial demonstrates how to use a tilde variable to set values for a query.

Tutorial: Using a Tilde Variable

Suppose that you wish to pass a value to a query. The query then searches for that value.

On Disk: \ANSWERS\QUERY2.FSL

Quick Steps

1. Create a query interactively.
2. Paste the query into your ObjectPAL code.
3. Use the tilde character (~) to substitute a value.
4. Use `executeQBE()`.

Step By Step

1. Change your working directory to TUTORIAL. Create a new form. Place an unbound field named Enter_Language and labeled Enter search string. Also, place a button labeled Query World Table on the form (see Figure 14.7).

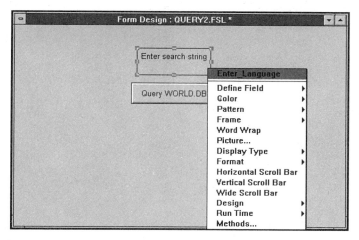

Figure 14.7. Set up form for tutorial.

2. Before entering the code in step 3, create a query like the one shown in Figure 14.8. Then paste the query and alter it.

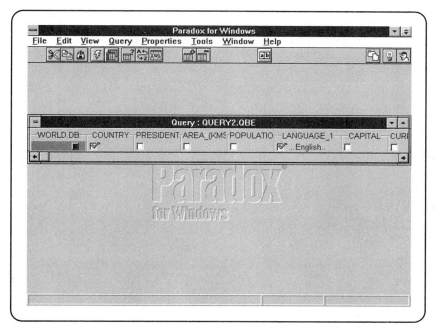

Figure 14.8. QUERY2.QBE.

3. The altered **pushButton** method of the Query WORLD Table button.

```
1:    ;Button :: pushButton
2:    method pushButton(var eventInfo Event)
3:       var
4:          q  Query
5:          tv TableView
6:          s  String
7:       endVar
8:
9:       s = Enter_Language.value
10:
11:      q = Query
12:
13:      ANSWER: :PRIV:ANSWER.DB
14:
15:      WORLD.DB ¦ COUNTRY ¦ LANGUAGE_1              ¦
16:               ¦ Check   ¦ Check ..~s..       ¦
17:
18:      EndQuery
19:
20:         executeQBE(q)
21:         tv.open(":PRIV:ANSWER.DB")
22:      endmethod
```

4. Check the syntax, save the form as QUERY2.FSL, and save it. Type a value—for example, English—and click the button. The value appears. If you don't type a value into the field, all records are displayed.

Analysis

In step 3, lines 4–6 declare the variables. Line 9 passes the value in the Enter search string field to the s variable. Lines 11–18 are the query that you pasted. Lines 11 and 16 have been altered from the value that was pasted in. Line 20 executes the Query variable, and line 21 displays the result.

Rather than bring the query Editor up for the user to use (as demonstrated previously), you can simulate the query Editor on a form with an interface that is more specific than File | Open | Query. Table 14.2 lists the operators you can use.

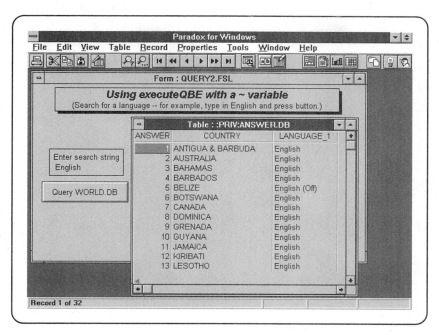

Figure 14.9. QUERY2.FSL.

TABLE 14.2. QUERY BY EXAMPLE OPERATORS.

Operator	Field Types	Meaning
,	All	Specifies the AND conditions in a field
!	All except BLOB	Displays all the values in a field, regardless of matches
( )	N, F, D, $, S	Groups arithmetic operations
*	N, F, $, S	Multiplication
+	A, C, N, F, D, $, S	Addition or alphanumeric string concatenation
-	N, F, D, $, S	Subtraction
. .	A, C, N, F, D, $, S, M, FM	Any series of characters
/	N, F, $, S	Division
<	All except BLOB	Less than

continues

	TABLE 14.2. CONTINUED	
Operator	Field Types	Meaning
<=	All except BLOB	Less than or equal to
=	All	Equal to (optional)
>	All except BLOB	Greater than
>=	All except BLOB	Greater than or equal to
@	A, C, N, F, D, $, S, M, FM	Any single character
ALL	All except BLOB	Calculates a summary based on all the values in a group
AS	All	Specifies the name of a field in the answer table
AVERAGE	N, F, $, S	The average of the values in a field
BLANK	All	No value
CALC	All	Calculates a new field
CHANGETO	All except BLOB	Changes specified values in fields
Check desc	All except BLOB	Displays a field with its values sorted in descending order
Check plus	All except BLOB	Displays a field and includes duplicate values
Checkmark	All	Displays a field in the answer table
COUNT	All except BLOB	The number of values in a field
DELETE	All except BLOB	Removes records with specified values
EVERY	All except BLOB	Displays the records that match every member of the defined set
EXACTLY	All except BLOB	Displays the records that match all members of the defined set and no others
GroupBy check	All except BLOB	Specifies one group of records for a comparison that uses set comparison operators

Operator	Field Types	Meaning
INSERT	All except BLOB	Inserts records with specified values
LIKE	A, C	Similar to
MAX	All except BLOB	The highest value in a field
MIN	All except BLOB	The lowest value in a field
NO	All except BLOB	Displays the records that match no members of the defined set
NOT	All	Doesn't match
ONLY	All except BLOB	Displays the records that match only members of the defined set
OR	All	Specifies the OR conditions in a field
SET	All except BLOB	Defines specific records as a set for comparisons
SUM	N, F, $, S	The total of all the values in a field
TODAY	D	Today's date
UNIQUE	All except BLOB	Calculates a summary based on the values that appear only once in a group

By default, SUM and AVERAGE operate on all the values in a field, whereas COUNT, MAX, and MIN operate on all values by default. You can override these default groupings by adding the word ALL or UNIQUE to a CALC statement.

In memo and formatted memo fields, you must use the .. operator. You can use the @ operator, too, but only if you use the .. operator as well.

Checkmark and check desc work like check plus in BLOB fields. You can type a CALC expression in a BLOB field. You can't calculate with BLOB values, however.

Executing a Query Stored in a String

If you wish, you can build a query in a string variable and then use `readFromString()` to read the string into a Query variable. Once the query string is in a Query variable, use `executeQBE()` to execute it. Because we have tilde variables, this technique is not really needed, but can be useful. Change your working directory to the TUTORIAL directory and type lines 3–21 into the **pushButton** method of a button.

```
 1:      ;Button :: pushButton
 2:      method pushButton(var eventInfo Event)
 3:          var
 4:              sQuery      String       ;Declare string variable.
 5:              q           Query        ;Declare query variable.
 6:              tv          TableView
 7:          endVar
 8:
 9:          errorTrapOnWarnings(Yes)
10:
11:          s1 = "Query\n"
12:          s2 = "ANSWER: :PRIV:ANSWER.DB\n"
13:          s3 = "WORLD.DB ¦ COUNTRY ¦ CURRENCY        ¦\n"
14:          s4 = "         ¦ Check   ¦ Check ..Dollar.. ¦\n"
15:          s5 = "EndQuery"
16:
17:          sQuery = s1 + s2 + s3 + s4 + s5
18:
19:          q.readFromString(sQuery)
20:          q.executeQBE()
21:          if not tv.open(":PRIV:ANSWER") then errorShow() endIf
22:      endmethod
```

Here is a tip if you are having problems with a query and you are not sure whether the problem is the query string itself or somthing else. Use `writeQBE()` to write the Query variable out to a file, and then try to run the query interactively.

Another debugging technique is to use the `errorShow()` procedure. For example:

```
1:  if not q.executeQBE() then errorShow() endIf
```

Points to remember about using `readFromString()` are as follows:

- End each line of the query with \n, which represents a line feed.
- A quoted string is limited to 255 characters.
- Use multiple quoted strings for quoted strings longer than 255.
- Use the `errorShow()` procedure to check whether the query executes.

> **NOTE FOR 1.0 & 4.5 USERS**
>
> *executeQBEString()* Is Now *readFromString()*
>
> In versions 1.0 and 4.5, you used `executeQBEString()` to execute a string as if it were a query block. Just as `executeQBEFile()` changed, so did `executeQBEString()`. For backward compatibility reasons, you can still use this undocumented feature. The new technique in version 5, however, is to use `readFromString()` and `executeQBE()` from the Query type as discussed previously.

WORKING WITH DYNASETS

A query is a means of extracting sets of information from a database or table. You can base forms and reports off a subset of your data by using a query as the first table in your data model. This technique is great for limiting the view of data. You can even use a live query—a dynaset—so you are working with the original data. The form ANSWERS\DYNASET1.FSL demonstrates this technique. It is always preferred to use a live query, but at times you can't. Use a non-live query when `setGenFilter()` or a live query in the data model does not filter out enough records—for example, when you need unique values.

You can even use these techniques—query, setGenFilter, and a live query—as a detail table. Although there is less of a need for this technique because of `setGenfilter()` and live queries, it is still useful because you can do a lot more with a query than you can do with either a live query or `setGenFilter()`.

CREATING A DESCENDING ORDER INDEX

Paradox, unlike dBASE, does not have a descending order feature in its indexes. You can use the dynaset technique to add a descending order to a Paradox table using a dBASE table. The form \ANSWERS\STATES.FSL demonstrates this technique (see Figure 14.10). In essence, the dBASE table controls the look of the Paradox table.

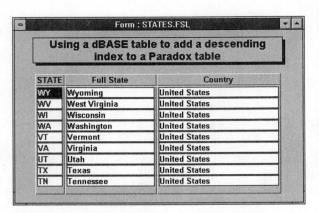

Figure 14.10. \ANSWERS\STATES.FSL.

Make sure that you include the added dBASE table in every data model that uses it, or copy the records from the Paradox table to the dBASE table before you use the combination of both tables.

A query is what you use to ask a table a question. These questions enable you analyze your data. After you analyze your data, you might want to print all or part of it. You use reports, discussed in the next chapter, to print data in Paradox.

HANDLING REPORTS

REPORTS AND DEVELOPING

A report is a tool for printing data. Reports are a way to get an organized, formatted hard copy of your data. You can communicate data with presentation-quality reports. Use this high-quality tool for the majority of your printouts. With the combination of reports and queries—and the ObjectPAL commands that enable you to use them—you can add printing capabilities to your applications.

Printing a report

Previewing and printing a report

Using queries with reports

Using a custom Toolbar with a report

USING REPORTS IN OBJECTPAL

The Report variable is a handle to a report window. With a report variable, you can attach to an already opened report, or you can open a report. Once the handle is established, you can manipulate the report. Table 15.1 lists the Report methods and procedures. As you can see by Table 15.1, many more Form type methods are inherited by the report type then by the TableView type. Version 4.5 users should note that the addition of methods to version 5 include data model methods and the addition of `menuAction()`.

TABLE 15.1. REPORT METHODS AND PROCEDURES.

attach	enumUIObjectProperties
bringToTop*	getFileName*
close	getPosition*
create*	getProtoProperty*
currentPage	getStyleSheet*
deliver*	getTitle*
design	hide*
dmAddTable*	isDesign*
dmBuildQueryString*	isMaximized*
dmEnumLinkFields*	isMinimized*
dmGetProperty*	isVisible*
dmHasTable*	load
dmLinkToFields*	maximize*
dmLinkToIndex*	menuAction*
dmRemoveTable*	minimize*
dmSetProperty*	moveTo*
dmUnlink*	moveToPage
enumDataModel*	open
enumSource*	print
enumTableLinks*	run
enumUIObjectNames	save*

saveStyleSheet*   setTitle*

selectCurrentTool*   show*

setPosition*   wait*

setProtoProperty*   windowClientHandle*

setStyleSheet*   windowHandle*

*Inherited from the Form type

Opening a Report

The next bit of code demonstrates opening a report and setting the title of the report. To achieve a smooth opening of the report, note that WinStyleDefault + WinStyleHidden is used along with the show() method. Change working directories to the TUTORIAL directory and type lines 3–9 into the **pushButton** method of a button.

```
1:  ;Button :: pushButton
2:  method pushButton(var eventInfo Event)
3:      var
4:          r Report
5:      endVar
6:
7:      r.open("REPORT", WinStyleDefault + WinStyleHidden)
8:      r.setTitle("New report title")
9:      r.show()
10: endMethod
```

Printing Reports

The first step in learning how to handle reports with ObjectPAL is learning how to print an existing report. The next two tutorials demonstrate how to use the print() and open() report methods.

Tutorial: Printing a Report from a Button

Suppose that you wish to create two buttons on a form. The first button directly prints an existing report with no interaction from the user. The second button previews the report and prompts the user with the Print File dialog box.

On Disk: \ANSWERS\REPORT1.FSL

Quick Steps

1. Declare a Report variable.

2. To print a report directly, use the `print()` command alone.

3. To preview and call the Print File dialog box, open the report and use the `print()` command.

Step By Step

1. Change your working directory to TUTORIAL. Create a new form and place two buttons on it. Label the first button Print Report and the second Open then Print Report (see Figure 15.1).

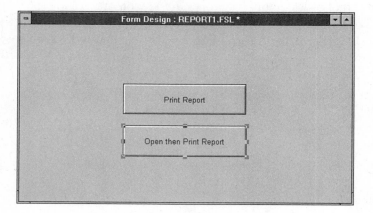

Figure 15.1. Set up form for the printing a Report tutorial.

2. Add lines 3–7 to the **pushButton** method of the Print Report button.

```
1:    ;Button :: pushButton
2:    method pushButton(var eventInfo Event)
3:       var
4:          r    Report
5:       endVar
6:
7:       r.print("REPORT")
8:    endmethod
```

3. Add lines 3–8 to the **pushButton** method of the Open then Print Report button.

```
1:    ;Button :: pushButton
2:    method pushButton(var eventInfo Event)
3:       var
4:          r  Report
5:       endVar
6:
7:       r.open("REPORT")
8:       r.print()
9:    endmethod
```

4. Check your syntax, save the form as REPORT1.FSL, run the form, and press the Open then Print Report button.

Analysis

In steps 2 & 3, line 4 in both declares r to be a Report variable. In this case, r is a temporary variable, alive only for the duration of the method. This is important to note because with display managers, the existence of the object—the report, in this case—does not close when the variable dies. This is not true with all objects. For example, OLE and TCursor objects automatically close when the variable dies. To optimize this form, you can combine these two declarations into a single declaration higher up in the containership path.

In step 2, line 7, `print()` is used to print the report without first previewing it. You do not need to open the report first.

In step 3, lines 7 and 8 on the second button use `open()` to open the report to preview it, and use `print()` to bring up the Print File dialog box (see Figure 15.2).

Q: Why do some printers have the multiple copies option grayed out? There seems to be a specific class of printer drivers to which Paradox prints no more than one copy of a report. For example, with the Generic print driver, the number of copies area is grayed out; with the LaserJet driver, it isn't. Moreover, other programs that use the Generic driver permit multiple copies. I have tried this in Notebook, Write, and Word for Windows. My customer is using an Epson driver that has the same problem. Why does Paradox or the driver permit only a single copy to be printed?

A: Paradox relies on the printer's capability to print multiple copies. Therefore, users may print multiple copies with page printers but not with dot-matrix printers. Because dot-matrix printers have no memory, they have no capacity for multiple copies. Perhaps Borland will add this extra capability in a future version. For now, though, use a loop in your ObjectPAL code to print the number of copies you need. For example:

```
 1:  method pushButton(var eventInfo Event)
 2:      Var
 3:          r          Report
 4:          nCopies    Number
 5:      enVar
 6:
 7:      nCopies=1
 8:      nCopies.view("How many copies?")
 9:      for Counter from 1 to nCopies
10:          r.print("REPORT")
11:      endFor
12:  endMethod
```

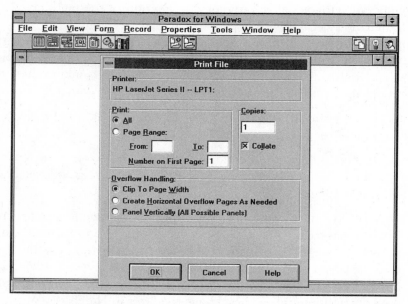

Figure 15.2. The Open then Print Report button previews a report and brings up the Print File dialog box.

PRINTING A REPORT BASED ON THE CURRENT RECORD

In general, reports deal only with a set of data. They step through the master table one record at a time and print the report information once for every record. Often, you need to print a report based on a subset of the table or even just a single record. This is possible in Paradox, but it takes two steps. First, execute a query. Then, print a report that is based on the answer table for the query. In the following tutorial, you print a report based on only the current record.

Tutorial: Printing a Report Based on the Current Record

Suppose that you wish to print a report based on the current record. This tutorial uses an embedded query to generate a table with a single record in it. It also demonstrates using a temporary table to control the report.

On Disk: \ANSWERS\REPORT2.FSL

Quick Steps

1. Create a query based on the master table of the data model and paste the query in your code, then alter it so that you can execute it with `executeQBE()`.

2. Create or alter a report so that the master table is based on the answer table that the query creates.

3. In code, execute the query before you print the report.

Step By Step

1. Change your working directory to TUTORIAL and create a new form with the :PRIV:ANSWERS.DB, ORDERS.DB, and LINEITEM.DB tables in the data model. Link the :PRIV:ANSWERS.DB table to the Orders table in a 1:1 relationship. Then, link the Orders table to the Lineitem table in a 1:M relationship. Place a button on the form, and label it Print Current Invoice. Note that you must initially create the :PRIV:ANSWER.DB table in order to link it.

2. Add lines 3–19 to the **pushButton** method of the Print Current
   Invoice button.

```
1:     ;Button :: pushButton
2:     method pushButton(var eventInfo Event)
3:        var
4:           r   Report
5:           q   Query
6:           s   String
7:        endVar
8:
9:        s = Order_No
10:       q = Query
11:         ANSWER: :PRIV:ANSWER.DB
12:
13:         ORDERS.DB ¦ Order No  ¦
14:                   ¦ Check  ~s ¦
15:
16:       EndQuery
17:
18:       executeQBE(q)
19:       r.print("REPORT")
20:    endmethod
```

3. Check your syntax, save the form as REPORT2.FSL, and run it. Move
   to the record that you want to print and click the button.

Analysis

In step 2, line 9 takes the value from the *Order_No* field and puts it in the *s*
variable. Lines 10–16 make up the query; line 14 uses the *s* variable. Line 18
executes the query, and line 19 prints the report. Because the report is based on
the table created by the query executed in line 19, it consists of only one record.

Fully Controlling a Report

On disk, The Invoicing System is included. It demonstrates an alternate—and
perhaps easier—technique to print the current record and maintain full control
of a report. It uses `setGenFilter()`, `setMenu()`, and `wait()`. `setGenFilter()` is
used to filter the data down to the current invoice. `setMenu()` is used to keep the
user from using other menu options. Finally, `wait()` is used so the user doesn't
stray from the report. Here is the code in full for you to study.

```
1:  ;btn :: pushButton
2:  method pushButton(var eventInfo Event)
3:      var
4:          r               Report
5:          m               Menu
6:          pop             PopUpMenu
7:          dynFilter       DynArray[] String
8:      endVar
9:
10:         ;Load the report hidden.
11:         if not r.load(":INVOICE:INVOICE", WinStyleDefault + WinStyleHidden) then
12:             errorShow()
13:             return
14:         endIf
15:
16:         ;Apply filter.
17:         dynFilter["Order No"] = string(Order_No.value)
18:         r.Order_No.setGenFilter(dynFilter)
19:         r.run()
20:
21:         ;Give the user only a simple menu.
22:         pop.addText("&Print...", MenuEnabled, MenuFilePrint)
23:         pop.addText("&Printer Setup...", MenuEnabled, MenuFilePrinterSetup)
24:         pop.addText("&Close", MenuEnabled, MenuControlClose)
25:         m.addPopUp("&File", pop)
26:         r.setMenu(m)
27:
28:         ;Show report and wait.
29:         r.maximize()
30:         r.wait()
31: endmethod
```

PRINTING TO A FILE

Sometimes printing a report to a file is useful. For example, you can upload the file to a mainframe or take it to a service for printing. Use a generic text printer driver for text. Or use a graphic printer driver for printer language files, and redirect the output to a file. Now, you can print a report to a file by setting PORT=FILE in the Windows Control Panel.

Follow these steps to print a report to a file:

1. If you want the file that you print to be a text-only file—no lines, frames, graphs, and so on—choose the Generic/Text Only printer driver. If it's not on the list of installed printers, install it.

> Viewing a report on-screen with the Generic/Text Only printer driver
> loaded might make your screen look irregular. The document, however,
> prints to a file correctly. To get rid of the irregular appearance, make sure
> that you design your report for the screen rather than the printer.
>
> The reason for this actually goes back to the Windows operating system
> itself. When Windows applications display fonts and graphics, they pull
> a lot of information from the printer driver. Because the Generic/Text
> Only printer driver has no font information, the report writer built in to
> Paradox does not know what to display.

If you want to keep the formatting for your report, however, choose
a graphics printer driver, such as the Hewlett Packard Series II or
PostScript printer drivers. These printer drivers send printer language
code to a file. This is useful for taking a printer file to an image setter.

2. From Control Panel, set up the driver to print to a file. Select the
   Connect button, and choose File from the ports list.

3. From Paradox, choose File | Printer Setup and select the printer
   driver that is set up to print to a file. When you print the report,
   Paradox prompts you for a filename.

MANIPULATING THE PRINTER BEFORE YOU PRINT

Version 1 users have been asking for the capability to manipulate the printer
with ObjectPAL and now, with version 5, you can. Version 5 added the
System Type procedures `printerGetInfo()`, `printerGetOptions()`,
`printerSetCurrent()`, `printerSetOptions()` and `enumPrinters()`. For example,
to get a listing of all the available printers, type lines 3-8 into the **pushButton**
method of a button.

```
1:  btn :: pushButton
2:  method pushButton(var eventInfo Event)
3:     var
4:        arPrinters      Array[] String
5:     endVar
6:
7:     enumPrinters(arPrinters)
8:     arPrinters.view("Available Printers")
9:  endmethod
```

In addition to these System Type procedures, the Report Type `print()` method
can control the printer.

Using the reportPrintInfo Variable

Another option for changing printer orientation is to set `reportPrintInfo.orient = PrintLandscape`. The following code prints a report called CUST94.RSL in landscape orientation.

```
1:      var
2:            r     Report
3:            rpi   ReportPrintInfo
4:      endVar
5:
6:      rpi.orient = PrintLandscape
7:
8:      ; Note -- the file extension is optional
9:      rpi.name = "CUST94.RSL"
10:     r.print( rpi )
```

Paper size cannot be set this way, but the number of copies, page incrementing, and starting and ending pages can be set, IF THE PRINTER DRIVER SUPPORTS THESE FEATURES. To find out whether your printer driver supports these features, select File | Printer Setup: <Modify Printer Setup> <Setup>. If the Printer Setup dialog box provides fields for you to specify the number of copies, starting and ending pages, or page incrementing, then your printer driver does handle these features; otherwise, it does not.

You also can use this technique to change the master table of a report. The following code demonstrates this.

```
1:      var
2:            r     report
3:            rpi   reportPrintInfo
4:      endVar
5:
6:      rpi.name = "MYREPORT"
7:
8:      rpi.masterTable = "OTHER.DB"
9:      r.print(rpi)
```

Using a Custom Toolbar with a Report

You can't use user-defined pull-down menus with a report, because reports don't have ObjectPAL. Specifically, reports don't have a **menuAction** built-in method to which you can add code. There is, however, an alternative solution. Create a small Toolbar-type dialog box, then open the dialog box over the report. That is, after you preview the report, open the dialog box. Because dialog boxes are always on top, the options that you put on the dialog box are always seen; therefore, they are always active. In the following tutorial, you launch a report and a dialog box from a button.

Tutorial: Adding a Toolbar to a Report

Suppose that you wish to launch a report and a dialog box from a button. Because the second form is a dialog box, it always stays on top of the report.

On Disk: \ANSWERS\REPORT3.FSL

Quick Steps

1. Create a form like a dialog box with the options you want to add.

2. From your main form, open the report and the second form—that is, the dialog box you created earlier.

Step By Step

1. Change your working directory to TUTORIAL. Create a new form or open an existing one, and place a button on it. Label the button Go and set the title of the form to Report Form and save the form as REPORT3.FSL (see Figure 15.3).

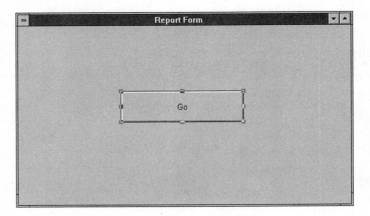

Figure 15.3. The Go button launches the report.

2. Now, create a small form with four buttons on it, set the form title to *Options*, and save it as REP–MENU.FSL. Label the four buttons Design, Maximize, Go to page 5, and Close (see Figure 15.4).

Figure 15.4. REP–MENU.FSL with its title changed to Options.

3. Add lines 3–19 to the **pushButton** method of the Go button on the main form and save it as REPORT3.FSL.

```
1:    ;Button :: pushButton
2:    method pushButton(var eventInfo Event)
3:       var
4:         f    Form
5:         r    Report
6:       endVar
7:
8:       if r.attach("Report 1") then
9:           r.bringToTop()
10:      else
11:          r.open("REPORT")
12:          r.setTitle("Report 1")
13:      endIf
14:
15:      if f.attach("Options") then
16:          f.moveTo()
17:      else
18:          f.open("REP-MNU2")
19:      endIf
20:    endmethod
```

4. Open the REP–MENU.FSL form you created in step 2 and add line 3 to its Var window.

```
1:    ;Page :: Var
2:    Var
3:        r   Report
4:    endVar
```

5. Add lines 3–8 to the **open** method of the REP–MENU.FSL form.

```
1:     ;Page :: open
2:     method open(var eventInfo Event)
3:         if r.attach("Report 1") then
4:             r.bringToTop()
5:         else
6:             msgStop("Startup Error!",
                        "This form is only for
                           use with Report3.fsl")
7:             close()
8:         endIf
9:     endmethod
```

6. Add line 3 to the **pushButton** method of the Design button on the REP–MENU.FSL form.

```
1:     ;Button :: pushButton
2:     method pushButton(var eventInfo Event)
3:         r.design()
4:     endmethod
```

7. Add line 3 to the **pushButton** method of the Maximize button on the REP–MENU.FSL form.

```
1:     ;Button :: pushButton
2:     method pushButton(var eventInfo Event)
3:         r.maximize()
4:     endmethod
```

8. Add line 3 to the **pushButton** method of the Move to Page 5 button on the REP–MENU.FSL form.

```
1:     ;Button :: pushButton
2:     method pushButton(var eventInfo Event)
3:         r.moveToPage(5)
4:     endmethod
```

9. Add lines 3 and 4 to the Close button on the REP–MENU.FSL form.

```
1:    ;Button :: pushButton
2:    method pushButton(var eventInfo Event)
3:        r.close()
4:        close()
5:    endmethod
```

10. Add lines 3–5 and 12–16 to the **depart** method of the REP–MENU.FSL form.

```
1:    ;Form :: depart
2:    method depart(var eventInfo MoveEvent)
3:        var
4:          f  Form
5:        endVar
6:
7:        if eventInfo.isPreFilter()
8:          then
9:            ;This code executes for each object on the form
10:         else
11:            ;This code executes only for the form
12:            if f.attach("Report Form") then
13:                f.moveTo()
14:            else
15:                f.open("REPORT3")
16:            endIf
17:        endif
18:    endmethod
```

11. Check your syntax and save both forms. Close the REP–MENU form and run the first REPORT3.FSL form. Click the Go button. The report opens first, and the dialog box opens on top of it. You can select either the pull-down menus or the buttons from the dialog box form you created. It doesn't matter whether the report or the dialog box is active (see Figure 15.5).

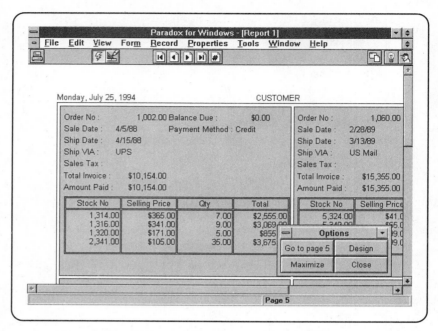

Figure 15.5. REP–MENU.FSL and a report. The form always stays above the report because it's a dialog box.

Analysis

In step 3, lines 4 and 5 on the Go button of the first form declare *f* as a Form variable and *r* as a Report variable. Lines 8–13 use a Report variable to either open the report or attach to it and bring it to the top if it's open. Line 12 specifically sets a title when the report is opened. This is done so that later you can attach a Report variable to the open report. Lines 15–19 either open the small dialog box form or attach a Form variable to it and move to the small dialog box.

In step 4, Line 3 on the dialog box form declares *r* as a Report variable. The *r* Report variable is used throughout the dialog box to deal with the open report.

For example, in step 5, lines 3–8 in the **open** method of the dialog box establish a handle to the open report. If the report isn't open, it's assumed that the user opened the form directly. A start-up error is displayed in line 6, and the form is closed in line 7. Once this form is delivered, the only way to use it is when a report named `Report 1` is open.

Steps 6, 7, 8 and 9 manipulate the report on their respective buttons.

In step 10 in the var block, line 4 declares *f* as a Form variable. That variable is used in the **depart** method of the form to attach and move to the calling form. If you closed the calling form, it's reopened in line 15.

> Q: I have a form with some hidden objects on it. I want to open this form as a report. What's the best way to keep these objects hidden in the report?
>
> A: There's no visible property for objects in a report. Therefore, objects can't be hidden on a report; they can be hidden only on a form. Try making the field, text, and frame of the objects white. An alternative is to open the form as a report in design mode, delete the hidden objects, and save the new report.

USEFUL FEATURE

Many of the `open()` and `load()` Commands Can Use

WinStyleConstants

Many of the methods that open a window are overloaded with the `WinStyleConstants`. Therefore, the `ReportVar.load()` method accepts the following syntax:

```
load("ReportName", WinStyleDefault + WinStyleHidden)
```

This capability enables you to open a form or a report in Design mode with no impact on the screen.

USING MENUS WITH REPORTS

You can now add a menu to a report using the new `setMenu()` method. Although it was briefly introduced in this chapter, Chapter 25, "Using Menus, Toolbars, and the File System," discusses this technique further.

Building a Report from Scratch

Version 5 introduced new ObjectPAL methods that allow you to create a report: `create()`, `deliver()`, `design()`, `dmAddTable()`, `dmBuildQueryString()`, `dmLinkFields()`, `dmLinkToIndex()`. These new methods along with the original ones let you create a report or form complete with a linked data model defined to UIObjects.

In this chapter, you learned about using reports and integrating them into your application.

In the previous two chapters, you learned how to use and manipulate large objects in ObjectPAL. In Chapter 21, "Manipulating Design Objects," you learn how to manipulate UIObjects on a form; these chapters give you control over objects.

USING TABLE AND TCURSOR VARIABLES

TABLES

A *table* is an object that consists of rows of records and columns of fields. In ObjectPAL, a Table variable is a handle to a table on disk. It's different from a TCursor variable. A TCursor variable looks at the data in a table, whereas a Table variable looks at the whole table. Table variables enable you to manipulate tables as a whole. For example, you can add records from one table to another, copy a table, and get the average value for a field. Table 16.1 lists the Table type methods and procedures. All the commands deal with the table as a whole. Version 4.5 users should note the absence of `setFitler()`, which went through a name change and is now known as `setRange()`.

Using table methods and procedures

What is a TCursor?

`attach()` *versus* `open()`

Dealing with restricted records

Getting the n *largest values*

TABLE 16.1. TABLE TYPES OF METHODS AND PROCEDURES.	
add	getGenFilter
attach	getRange
cAverage	index
cCount	isAssigned
cMax	isEmpty
cMin	isEncrypted
cNpv	isShared
compact	isTable
copy	lock
create	nFields
createIndex	nKeyFields
cSamStd	nRecords
cSamVar	protect
cStd	reIndex
cSum	reIndexAll
cVar	rename
delete	setExclusive
dropGenFilter	setGenFilter
dropIndex	setIndex
empty	setRange
enumFieldNames	setReadOnly
enumFieldNamesInIndex	showDeleted
enumFieldStruct	sort
enumIndexStruct	subtract
enumRefIntStruct	tableRights
enumSecStruct	type
familyRights	unAttach
fieldName	unlock
fieldNo	unProtect
fieldType	usesIndexes

Opening a Table Variable

An open() method is conspicuously absent from the table methods. The attach() method associates a Table variable with a table's filename. The extensions .DB and .DBF specify the type of table. To use a Table variable, you need to declare it:

```
1:   var
2:        tbl   Table
3:   endVar
```

After you have a Table variable with which to work, you open it by attaching directly to a table on disk:

```
1:   tbl.attach("CUSTOMER.DB")
```

Using Table Methods and Procedures

Many of the table methods deal with data in the table and are duplicated in the TCursor class. After you declare a Table variable and open it with attach(), you can use the table methods on it. For example, the following statements are valid:

```
1:   tbl.attach("DEST.DB")
2:   tbl.cMax("Total")
3:   tbl.delete()
```

The next tutorial puts the cAverage() method to work with a Table variable.

Tutorial: Using *cAverage( )* with a Table Variable

Suppose that you wish to find the average population for all the countries of the world. You can do this by using cAverage() and a Table variable.

On Disk: \ANSWERS\TABLE1.FSL

Quick Steps

1. Declare a Table variable.

2. Attach the Table variable to the table.

3. Use cAverage() to get the value. Display it in a message information box.

Step By Step

1. Change your working directory to TUTORIAL. Open a form or create a new one. Place a button labeled Average population of all the countries of the world on it.

2. Add lines 3–8 to the **pushButton** method of the Average population of all the countries of the world button.

```
1:   ;Button :: pushButton
2:   method pushButton(var eventInfo Event)
3:       var
4:            tbl   Table
5:       endVar
6:
7:       tbl.attach("WORLD.DB")
8:       msgInfo("Average population (millions)",
tbl.cAverage("POPULATION_(MIL)"))
9:   endmethod
```

3. Check the syntax, save the form as TABLE1.FSL, and run it. Click the button. After a short time, the answer is displayed (see Figure 16.1).

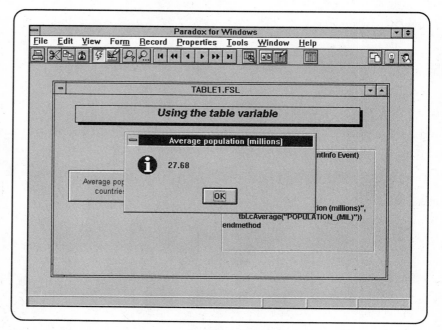

Figure 16.1. TABLE1.FSL. Using a Table variable with cAverage().

Analysis

Line 4 declares the Table variable. Line 7 attaches the Table variable to the WORLD.DB table. Line 8 displays the result of `cAverage()`.

TCURSORS

A TCursor (table cursor) is a pointer to a record in a table. A TCursor is a tool used to manipulate a table behind the scenes. A Table variable deals with the whole table. A TCursor variable deals with the data in a table. Specifically, a TCursor variable is a pointer to a record in a table. Once you declare a TCursor variable, you can open it to a table. Once open, you then have a handle to the data in the table. When you open a TCursor, it's already pointing at the first record in the table. Table 16.2 lists the TCursor class methods and procedures. In addition to the commands that deal with the table as a whole, many commands deal with a single record or a single field. Version 4.5 users should note that the addition of `setGenFiler()` is among the methods added to version 5.

TABLE 16.2. TCURSOR CLASS METHODS AND PROCEDURES.	
add	copy
atFirst	copyFromArray
atLast	copyRecord
attach	copyToArray
attachToKeyViol	createIndex
bot	cSamStd
cancelEdit	cSamVar
cAverage	cStd
cCount	cSum
close	currRecord
cMax	cVar
cMin	deleteRecord
cNpv	didFlyAway
compact	dmAttach

continues

TABLE 16.2. CONTINUED	

dmResync	insertAfterRecord
dropGenFilter	insertBeforeRecord
dropIndex	insertRecord
edit	instantiateView
empty	isAssigned
end	isEdit
endEdit	isEmpty
enumFieldNames	isEncrypted
enumFieldNamesInIndex	isInMemoryTCursor
enumFieldStruct	isOnSQLServer
enumIndexStruct	isOpenOnUniqueIndex
enumLocks	isRecordDeleted
enumRefIntStruct	isShared
enumSecStruct	isShowDeletedOn
enumTableProperties	isValid
eot	isView
familyRights	locate
fieldNo	locateNext
fieldRights	locateNextPattern
fieldSize	locatePattern
fieldType	locatePrior
fieldUnits2	locatePriorPattern
fieldValue	lock
forceRefresh	lockRecord
getGenFilter	lockStatus
getIndexName	moveToRecNo
getLanguageDriver	moveToRecord
getLanguageDriverDesc	nextRecord
getRange	nFields
home	nKeyFields
initRecord	nRecords

open	setRange
postRecord	showDeleted
priorRecord	skip
qLocate	sortTo
recNo	subtract
recordStatus	switchIndex
reIndex	tableName
reIndexAll	tableRights
seqNo	type
setBatchOn	unDeleteRecord
setBatchOff	unlock
setFlyAwayControl	unlockRecord
setFieldValue	update
setGenFilter	updateRecord

TCURSORS AND INVISIBLE ACCESS TO A TABLE

When you use a TCursor, you can't see the changes made to a table. You can manipulate a TCursor variable just like a Table variable, however. In fact, a TCursor has many of the same methods as a UIObject. The Table type doesn't have nearly as many methods as a TCursor does. Its functionality is more limited because it operates only for the table as a whole, whereas a TCursor works directly on the data.

Think of a TCursor as a channel you open to a table. Typically, you open a TCursor with

```
1:   tc.open("TABLE.DB")
```

tc is a TCursor class variable. All further references to the table can be represented by the TCursor:

```
1:   tc.FieldName = Today()
```

In this example, quotation marks aren't used around the field name in the table. Quotation marks aren't needed for field names that have no special characters. If a field name, however, contains a special character—such as a space or a hyphen—quotation marks are required. For the sake of consistency, you might put quotation marks around all field names when you use a TCursor. For example:

```
1:   tc."FieldName" = Today()
```

A TCursor works in the background. Therefore, when you manipulate a database, movement through the table doesn't appear on screen. Because the screen isn't refreshed, changes are made quickly.

> In many ways, using a TCursor in ObjectPAL is like using a table on the workspace with ECHO OFF in PAL (the programming language used in Paradox for DOS).

USING A TCURSOR

Treat a TCursor variable like other variables. Declare it in the Var window of the object. If the method executes only once—like **pushButton**—or if you need a private version of the variable, declare it within the method.

In general, opening and closing a TCursor can be time consuming because opening and closing a file on a disk is slower than leaving it open. Therefore, it's best to minimize the number of times you open and close these objects. If the method you use occurs once—like **pushButton**—it's okay to declare it inside the method:

```
1:      ;Button :: pushButton
2:      method pushButton(var eventInfo Event)
3:         var
4:            tc    TCursor
5:         endVar
6:
7:         tc.open("WORLD.DB")
8:         msgInfo("Current country", tc.COUNTRY)
9:      endMethod
```

REFERRING TO FIELDS IN A TABLE WITH A TCURSOR

```
1:   tc.Last_Name
2:   tc."Last_Name"
3:   tc.(2)
```

The preferred usage is to always use quotation marks.

The next tutorial gets data from the WORLD.DB table.

Tutorial: Using a TCursor

Suppose that you want to grab the name of a country and its capital from record 5. Then, position on the United States record and grab its capital. To do this, you can open a TCursor to the WORLD.DB table, grab some information, and display it to the user.

On Disk: \ANSWERS\TC1.FSL

Quick Steps

1. Declare a TCursor variable.
2. Open a TCursor.
3. Use `moveToRecord()` to position on record 5.
4. Display the information in a message box.
5. Use `locate()` to position the record pointer on the United States.
6. Display the information in a message box.
7. Close the TCursor.

Step By Step

1. Set your working directory to TUTORIAL. Create a new form and place a button labeled Display Capitals on it.
2. Add lines 3–12 to the **pushButton** method of the Display Capitals button.

```
1:  ;Button :: pushButton
2:  method pushButton(var eventInfo Event)
3:      var
4:          tc    TCursor
5:      endVar
6:
7:      tc.open("WORLD.DB")
8:      tc.moveToRecord(5)
9:      msgInfo("Capital of " + tc.COUNTRY, tc.CAPITAL)
10:     tc.locate("Country", "UNITED STATES")
11:     msgInfo("Capital of " + tc.COUNTRY, tc.CAPITAL)
12:     tc.close()
13: endmethod
```

3. Check the syntax, save the form as TC1.FSL, and run it. Click the button. The country and capital from record 5 are displayed first (see Figure 16.2). Click OK. The United States and its capital are displayed. Click OK again.

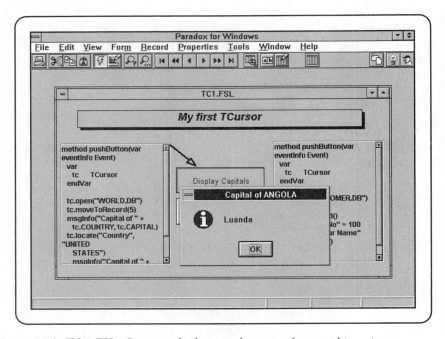

Figure 16.2. TC1.FSL. Opening, displaying information from, and inserting a new record with a TCursor.

Analysis

In step 2, line 4 declares *tc* as a TCursor variable. Because the **pushButton** method occurs only when the button is clicked, you can declare the TCursor variable inside the **pushButton** method. The variable is redeclared every time the button is clicked, however. Therefore, a better place to declare the variable is in the button's Var window. Line 7 opens the TCursor. Just as you can use a UIObject to move to a record, you can use a TCursor, too, as line 8 shows. Line 9 displays two values from record 5. Line 10 uses `locate()` to position on the record for the United States, and line 11 displays information from it. Because the data is stored in all capital letters, you must put *UNITED STATES* in all capitals for the `locate()` to succeed. As an alternative, you could use `ignoreCaseInLocate()` to tell Paradox to ignore the case of the letters. Line 12 closes the TCursor. This final step isn't necessary, as the TCursor will close automatically when the variable goes out of scope as the method ends. However, it's good programming to close any open TCursors when you're done with them.

EDITING DATA WITH A TCURSOR

With a TCursor, you can manipulate and add data directly to a table with no interaction on the form, just as you can use a UIObject to put the table connected to it into Edit mode, insert a record, and post a value. You can do the same tasks with a TCursor, as the following tutorial demonstrates.

Tutorial: Editing Data with a TCursor

Suppose that you wish to insert a new record into the CUSTOMER.DB table. To do this, open a TCursor to the CUSTOMER.DB table and insert a new record.

On Disk: \ANSWERS\TC1.FSL
Quick Steps

1. Declare a TCursor variable.
2. Open a TCursor.
3. Manipulate the TCursor by using the commands with which you're familiar: `edit()`, `insertRecord()`, `postRecord()`, and `endEdit()`.
4. Close the TCursor.

Step By Step

1. Set your working directory to TUTORIAL. Open the TC1.FSL form you created in the last tutorial and add a button labeled Add your Name.
2. Add lines 3–14 to the **pushButton** method of the Add your Name button.

```
1:  ;Button :: pushButton
2:  method pushButton(var eventInfo Event)
3:      var
4:          tc    TCursor
5:      endVar
```

```
 6:
 7:     tc.open("CUSTOMER.DB")
 8:     tc.edit()
 9:     tc.insertRecord()
10:     tc."Customer No" = 100
11:     tc.Name = "Your Name"
12:     tc.postRecord()
13:     tc.endEdit()
14:     tc.close()
15: endmethod
```

3. Check the syntax, save the form, run the form, and click the button. Nothing seems to happen. Open the CUSTOMER.DB table. Now the first record is 100, and it displays your name.

Analysis

In step 2, line 4 declares *tc* as a TCursor variable. Line 7 opens the CUSTOMER.DB table. Line 7 uses the `open()` method to open the TCursor. Line 8 puts the TCursor into Edit mode. Line 9 inserts a new record. Lines 10 and 11 set two values in the new record. Line 12 posts the new record. Line 13 ends Edit mode. Line 14 closes the TCursor.

USING *SWITCHINDEX( )* WITH A TCURSOR

When you wish to change the active index on a TCursor, use the `switchIndex()` method. The `switchIndex()` is in both the UIObject and TCursor types. The syntax for `switchIndes()` is the same:

> **switchIndex(** [const ***IndexName***_String][, const_***stayOnRecord***
> Logical] **)** Logical

For example, to switch a table frame to a secondary index named *secCity*, use the following:

```
1:   CUSTOMERS.switchIndex("secCity")
```

To switch back to the primary key, leave out the secondary index. For example:

```
1:   CUSTOMERS.switchIndex()
```

You can use `switchIndex()` on a TCursor just like on a UIObject. You can even synchronize a UIObject connected to the same table with `resync()`. The next tutorial demonstrates the technique of switching an index on a TCursor using ObjectPAL, then resyncing it to the UIObject.

Tutorial: Using *switchIndex( )*

Suppose that you wish to sort the records in a table frame by using the primary key and the secondary index. The twist in this case is that you wish to do this using a TCursor, and then synchronize it to the UIObject.

On Disk: \ANSWERS\SEC-IND.FSL

Quick Steps

1. Use the TCursor `switchIndex()`.
2. Open the TCursor and specify the secondary index in the `open()` method.
3. Use `resync()` to sync the UIObject to the TCursor variable.
4. Use `switchIndex()` to switch back to the primary key.

Step By Step

1. Change your working directory to the TUTORIAL directory. Create a new form with the WORLD.DB table in the data model. Choose Tabular in the Style panel in the Design Layout dialog box. Place two buttons on the form, and label them Sort by Country and Sort by Currency (see Figure 16.3).

2. Add lines 3–8 to the **pushButton** method of the Sort by Currency button.

```
1:   ;Button :: pushButton
2:   method pushButton(var eventInfo Event)
3:      var
4:           tc    TCursor
5:      endVar
6:
7:   tc.open("WORLD", "secCurrency")
8:   WORLD.resync(tc)
9:   endmethod
```

3. Add lines 3–9 to the **pushButton** method of the Sort by Country button.

```
1:   ;Button :: pushButton
2:   method pushButton(var eventInfo Event)
```

```
3:      var
4:          tc    TCursor
5:      endVar
6:
7:      tc.attach(Sec_Ind)
8:      tc.switchIndex()
9:      WORLD.resync(tc)
10: endmethod
```

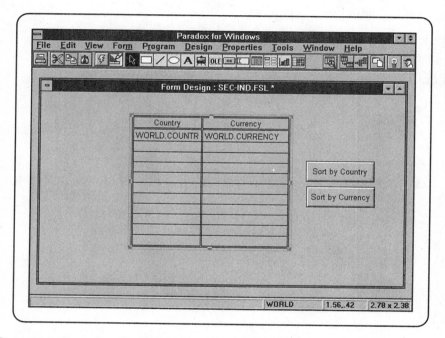

Figure 16.3. Setup form for the `switchIndex()` *tutorial.*

4. Check your syntax, save the form as SEC-IND.FSL, and run the form. Click the Sort by Currency button; the table is now sorted by Currency, as shown in Figure 16.4. (This figure is a dressed-up version of the form you create in the "Using `switchIndex` with a TCursor" tutorial.) Click the Sort by Country button to return the sort order to the primary key.

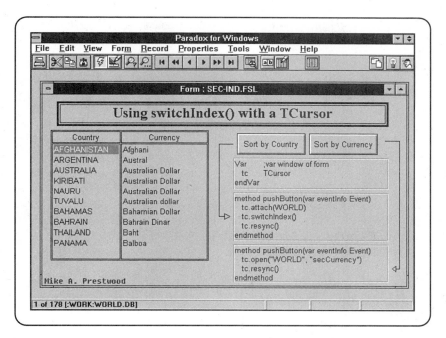

Figure 16.4. The table sorted by Currency.

Analysis

In step 2, line 4 declares *tc* as a TCursor. Line 7 opens and switches the index in one step by using the alternative syntax for the TCursor `open()` method. Line 8 updates the screen with `resync()`.

In step 3, line 4 declares *tc* as a TCursor. Lines 7–9 switch the index to the primary key. Line 8 uses `switchIndex()` without any parameters to switch to the primary key. These two routines can be optimized. For example, declaring and opening the TCursor in a higher container is more elegant.

TCURSORS CAN GET IN THE WAY

Sometimes you need to be wary of your own programming. An open TCursor acts like another user or session. Therefore, if an open TCursor points to or edits the same record that you are trying to edit, the error message "Record already locked by this session" will appear. To resolve this situation, you must move or post the TCursor. If the data you want to reach is part of the current record on the current form, always use `dmget()` to receive the values and `dmput()` to write the values. Use a TCursor only for noncurrent records.

DECLARING AND REDECLARING TCURSORS

Let's analyze the following code:

```
1:   var
2:        tc TCursor
3:   endVar
4:
5:   tc.open(t1)
6:   tc.open(t2)
```

In this simple example, a TCursor is declared and used twice in a row without ever closing the first TCursor. The question is, does the first instance of *tc* close when you reopen it? Yes.

attach() VERSUS *open()*

Many people confuse attaching and opening. You can attach a TCursor to a table window, to a UIObject, or to a TCursor variable that is already attached. This establishes an association between a new TCursor variable and an already open channel. This new TCursor variable inherits all the characterists that apply from the attached variable. This includes edit mode, record number, and range.

When you open a TCursor, its view is the whole table. When you attach a TCursor, its view is restricted. In a multitable form, the first table in the data model is the master and controlling table. All other linked tables are detail tables. The second table shows only those records that match the current master record and are said to have a **restricted view**. When you attach a TCursor to a detail table, the TCursor inherits the restricted view of the detail table.

A TCURSOR CAN RESPECT A RESTRICTED VIEW

A table is in restricted view when it is filtered down to a subset of records. When you establish a 1:M relationship between the order numbers in the ORDERS.DB table and the records in the LINEITEM.DB table, the subset of records in the LINEITEM.DB table is restricted or filtered.

In addition to opening a TCursor in the background, you can attach a TCursor to a UIObject, which forces the TCursor to respect the restricted view of the object. For example, in a 1:M relationship, or in an active `setRange()`, you can attach a TCursor variable to any UIObject, and the TCursor will be restricted, just as the original UIObject is, and on the same record that the UIObject is.

The next tutorial shows you how to open a TCursor by attaching it to an object already connected to the table.

Tutorial: Using *attach()* to Open a TCursor

Suppose that you wish to display the corresponding capital of the current country. One technique for doing this is to open a TCursor to the WORLD.DB table by attaching it to a UIObject on the form and using it to grab the value. You also can use `dmGet()` to do this type of operation.

On Disk: \ANSWERS\TC2.FSL

Quick Steps

1. Declare a TCursor variable.
2. Attach the TCursor to the UIObject.
3. Use the TCursor to display some data.
4. Close the TCursor.

Step By Step

1. Set your working directory to TUTORIAL. Create a new form that has WORLD.DB in the data model. Display only the country field. Place a button labeled Display Capital on the form (see Figure 16.5).

2. Add lines 3–9 to the **pushButton** method of the Display Capital button.

```
1:  ;Button :: pushButton
2:  method pushButton(var eventInfo Event)
3:     var
4:          tc    Cursor
5:     endVar
6:
7:     tc.attach(COUNTRY)
8:     msgInfo("Capital of " + tc.COUNTRY, tc.CAPITAL)
9:     tc.close()
10: endmethod
```

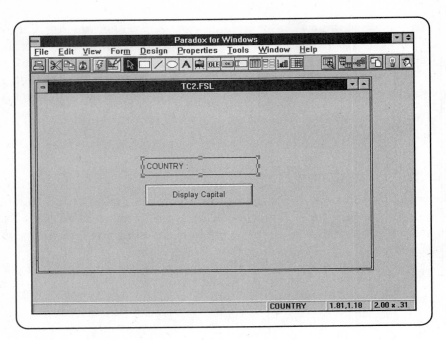

Figure 16.5. Set up form.

3. Check the syntax, save the form as TC2.FSL, and run it. Position on any country you want and click the button. The capital of the country you chose is displayed (see Figure 16.6). Click OK and choose another country.

Analysis

In step 2, line 4 declares *tc* as a TCursor variable. Line 7 opens the TCursor by attaching it to the *COUNTRY* field. This technique associates the TCursor variable with the table that is bound to the field. The record number of the UIObject is inherited. Therefore, it's not necessary to use `locate()` to position the TCursor on the same record. Line 8 displays the capital of the current record. Line 9 closes the TCursor.

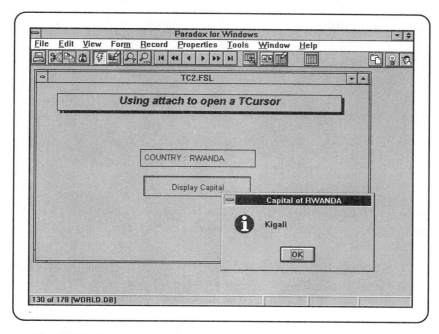

Figure 16.6. TC2.FSL. Opening, displaying information from, and inserting a new record with a TCursor.

Implementing Cascade Delete Using ObjectPAL

A cascade delete is a setting you can set with many database products, including Borland's simpler database product, ObjectVision. Cascade Delete deletes all the child records of a parent record. Because Paradox doesn't support cascade deletes, you must delete the child records. In a 1:1 relationship, this isn't a big deal. Simply delete both records in each table with something like

```
1:  ObjectConnectedToTableTwo.deleteRecord()
2:  ObjectConnectedToTableOne.deleteRecord()
```

This technique works quite well. You just have to remember to do it.

In a 1:M relationship, deleting child records is trickier. You have to loop through the children and delete them one at a time. As mentioned in

Chapter 10, "Control Structures," you shouldn't use a `scan` loop to delete records from a table. Instead, use a `for` loop with `nRecords()`:

```
1:  var
2:        Counter    Number
3:        tc TCursor
4:  endVar
5:
6:  tc.attach(ChildUIObjectName)
7:  tc.edit()
8:
9:  For Counter from 1 to tc.nRecords()
10:       tc.deleteRecord()
11: endFor
```

In this code, you attach the TCursor to the UIObject, which ensures that the TCursor will have the same restricted view that the object has. Therefore, `tc.nRecords()` returns the number of records in the restricted view—not the whole table.

Another technique is to use a `while` loop with `eot()`. For example, the following code worked great in versions 1.0 and 4.5:

```
1:  method pushButton(var eventInfo Event)
2:      var
3:            tc        TCursor
4:          siCounter SmallInt
5:      endVar
6:
7:      errorTrapOnWarnings(Yes)
8:
9:      tc.attach(LINEITEM)       ;Attach to detail table.
10:     tc.edit()
11:
12:     ;Delete all children records.
13:     while not tc.eot()
14:         tc.deleteRecord()
15:     endWhile
16:
17:     edit()                    ;Make sure form is in edit mode.
18:     Order_No.deleteRecord()   ;Then delete the parent record.
19: endmethod
```

The preceding technique is no longer logically correct with version 5.0 because of the new interactive filter settings. The following represents the correct way to implement cascade delete in version 5:

```
1:  ;btnCascadeDelete :: pushButton
2:  method pushButton(var eventInfo Event)
3:      var
4:            tc                TCursor
5:          siCounter SmallInt
6:      endVar
7:
```

```
 8:        tc.attach(LINEITEM)      ;Attach to detail table.
 9:        tc.dropGenFilter()       ;Drop any user set filters.
10:        tc.home()                ;Put TCursor on first record.
11:        tc.edit()
12:
13:        while not tc.eot()       ;If there are any child
14:            tc.deleteRecord()    ;records, delete all of them.
15:        endWhile
16:
17:        edit()                   ;Make sure form is in edit mode.
18:        Order_No.deleteRecord()  ;Delete the parent record.
19: endmethod
```

The next tutorial shows you how to implement cascade deletes using ObjectPAL.

Tutorial: Cascade Delete

Suppose that you wish to delete all the children records when a user deletes their parent record. This technique is particularly important when you have implemented Prohibit referential integrity.

On Disk: \ANSWERS\D-CHILD.FSL

Quick Steps

1. Attach a TCursor to a UIObject used in the child table in the **action** method of an object above the parent field's.

2. Use a for loop with the TCursor and nRecords() to loop through the child table and delete each record.

3. Close the TCursor.

Step By Step

1. Set your working directory to TUTORIAL. Create a new form with ORDERS.DB and LINEITEM.DB in the data model. Link them in a 1:M relationship from ORDERS.DB to LINEITEM.DB. Group all the fields connected to the Orders table (see Figure 16.7).

2. Add lines 3–18 to the **action** method of the group object that is made up of all the fields from the parent table. This code deletes all the children records.

```
1:  ;Group :: action
2:  method action(var eventInfo ActionEvent)
3:     var
4:          liCounter      LongInt
5:          tc                 TCursor
6:     endVar
```

```
 7:
 8:        if eventInfo.id() = DataDeleteRecord and isEdit() then
 9:             ;Open TCursor with UIObject restricted view.
10:             tc.attach(LINEITEM)
11:
12:             ;Loop through child table until all records are gone.
13:             For liCounter from 1 to tc.nRecords()
14:                 tc.deleteRecord()
15:             endFor
16:
17:             tc.close()
18:        endIf
19:        ;The default behavior occurs here and
20:        ;deletes the parent record.
21: endmethod
```

3. Check the syntax, save the form as D-CHILD.FSL, and run it. Move to a record that has several child records and delete the parent record.

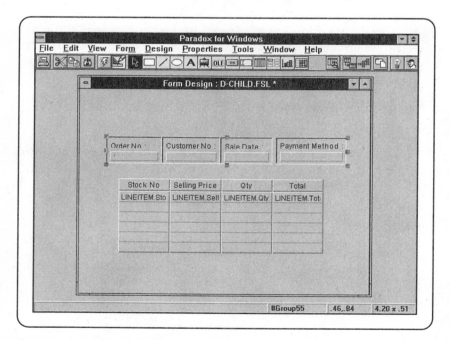

Figure 16.7. D-CHILD.FSL, which shows an elegant technique for deleting all the children records of a parent record.

Analysis

In step 2, the var block in lines 3–6 declares *liCounter* and *tc* as LongInt and TCursor variables, respectively. Line 8 watches for the constant `DataDeleteRecord` to bubble up through the **action** method of the group object. Line 10 opens the TCursor with a restricted view by attaching to the LINEITEM table frame. Note that the *tc* TCursor variable inherits many characteristics of the LINEITEM table frame, including its restricted view of the table and its edit mode. The `for` structure in lines 13–15 deletes every record in the restricted view. The `for` loop knows how many records are in the restricted view because of `tc.nRecords()` in line 13 (`nRecords()` returns the number of records in the table). Line 17 closes the TCursor. In this case, you don't have to close the TCursor because the TCursor variable is declared inside the `method` block. This means that the TCursor's instance exists only for the duration of the **action** method. It's a good programming practice, however, to get in the habit of closing any TCursor that you open.

In place of the `for` loop in lines 8–10, you could have used a `while` loop. For example:

```
1:   while tc.nRecords() > 0
2:        tc.deleteRecords()
3:   endWhile
```

Yet another variation on this exercise is to use the TCursor `eot()` method. For example:

```
1:   while not tc.eot()
2:        tc.deleteRecords()
3:   endWhile
```

Why do I show you three different ways to accomplish the same task? For several reasons. First, to get you acquainted with the various ObjectPAL commands; and second, to show you that in ObjectPAL, there are often many ways to accomplish a single task. Which one is best? The best technique is usually the fastest or the one that uses the smallest amount of code. In this case, I believe all three are about equal.

Using *setRange()*

In versions 1 and 4.5, Borland provided the programmer with a handy but confusing method called `setFilter()`. `setFilter()` did not set a filter; it specified a range of values. This unfortunate name confused many programmers. Now with version 5, Borland provides true filters with the `setGenFilter()`

(discussed next) and renamed `setFilter()` to `setRange()`. All your old code that uses `setFilter()` still works; you just will not see `setFilter()` documented in the manuals, in the online help, or even when you use `enumRTLMethods()`. In other words, although you can use either `setFilter()` or `setRange()`, for the sake of clarity, only `setRange()` is documented.

`setRange()` is always preferred over `setGenFilter()` because `setRange()` uses the active index (either primary or secondary). This makes `setRange()` faster than `setGenFilter()`.

Tutorial: Using *setRange()* with a TCursor

Suppose that you wish to allow the user to specify a range of records they wish to see, kind of like a live query. The technique presented in this tutorial uses `setRange()` on a TCursor with the `resync()` method.

On Disk: \ANSWERS\SETRANGE.FSL

Quick Steps

1. Open a TCursor to the table.
2. Switch the active index and use `setRange()` to specify a range of values.
3. Use `resync()` to sync the UIObject back to the TCursor.

Step By Step

1. Change your working directory to the TUTORIAL directory and create a new form with the Customer table in the data model and displayed in a table frame. Add two buttons labeled All Cities and Set Range of Cities (see Figure 16.8).

2. In the **pushButton** method of the Set Range of Cities, type lines 3–13.

```
1:   ;btnRange :: pushButton
2:   method pushButton(var eventInfo Event)
3:       var
4:           tc TCursor
5:       endVar
6:
7:       if not tc.open("CUSTOMER") then      ;Open TCursor.
8:           errorShow()
9:       endIf
10:
11:      tc.switchIndex("City")               ;Switch index.
```

```
12:    tc.setRange(startField, endField)   ;Set range.
13:    CUSTOMER.resync(tc)                 ;Update table frame.
14: endmethod
```

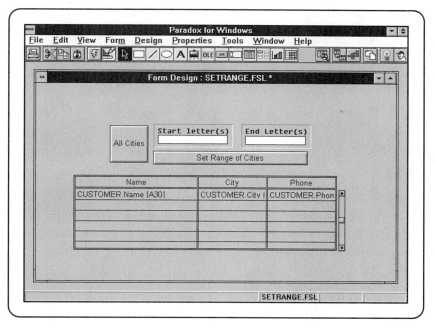

Figure 16.8. Set up form for the tutorial.

3. In the **pushButton** method of the All Cities button, type line 3.

```
1:  ;btnAll :: pushButton
2:  method pushButton(var eventInfo Event)
3:     CUSTOMER.switchIndex()
4:  endmethod
```

4. Check the syntax, save the form as SETRANGE.FSL, and run it (see Figure 16.9).

Analysis

In step 2, line 4 declares a TCursor variable for use in line 7 to open a second channel to the Customer table. This *tc* TCursor is used to switch the index in line 11 and set the range of records in line 12. Finally, after the TCursor has set the correct range behind the scenes, the CUSTOMER table frame is synchronized with the TCursor.

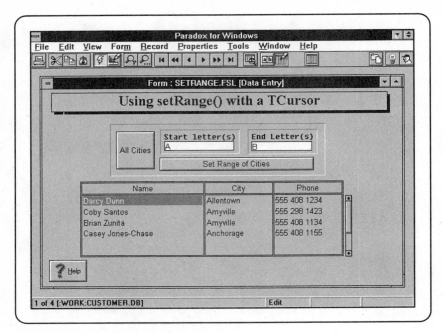

Figure 16.9. SETRANGE.FSL.

USING *setGenFilter()*

Using `setGenFilter()` requires two steps. First you declare a DynArray variable and populate it with the filtering data, and then you pass the DynArray to `setGenFilter()`. Once you declare a DynArray, you assign values to it specifying the field and the values. Here are some examples of the types of formulas you can use with `setGenFilter()`:

```
1:  var
2:       dyn  DynArray[] String
3:  endVar
4:
5:  dyn["State"] = "CA"              ;State field equals 'CA'.
6:  dyn["Total"] = "< 0"             ;Negative numbers in Total field.
7:  dyn["Total"] = "> 100, < 1000"   ;Greater then 100 & less then 1000.
8:  dyn["Total"] = ">= 4, <= 8"
```

For example, to view all Orders with a Balance Due over $100.00 and less than $1,000.00, type the following on the **pushButton** method of a button on a form bound to the Orders table. Figure 16.10 shows what your form will look like.

```
1:  btnShowMiddle :: pushButton
2:  pushButton (var eventInfo Event)
3:  var
4:      dyn  DynArray[] String          ;Declare DynArray.
5:  endVar
6:
7:  dyn["Balance Due"] = "> 100, <1000" ;Assign filter to it.
8:  ORDERS.setGenFilter(dyn)            ;Use it with setGenFilter().
```

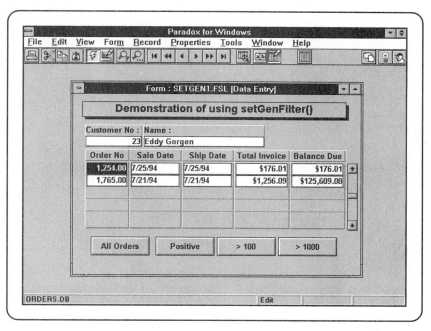

Figure 16.10. \ANSWERS\SETGEN1.FSL *demonstrates using* setGenFilter().

Grabbing the *n* Largest Values

How do you grab the three largest values in a field? This problem often stumps database programmers. With ObjectPAL, this problem can be solved easily with a TCursor and a secondary index. You can create a secondary index based on the field you want to grab the largest three values from, activate the index, go to the end of the table, put the value in a variable, do a priorRecord(), and store the value in a variable. You also can use this technique to grab the *n* smallest values in a table.

Tutorial: Displaying the 10 Largest Countries

Suppose that you wish to display the records for the ten largest or smallest values in a field. In this tutorial you use a TCursor and a secondary index to display the 10 largest countries in the world—actually, what were the 10 largest countries when WORLD.DB table was created.

On Disk: \ANSWERS\TC3.FSL

Quick Steps

1. Create a secondary index interactively or with ObjectPAL.
2. Open the TCursor with the secondary index.
3. Move to the end of the table.
4. Store the value in a variable.
5. Move to the prior record and store the value.

Step By Step

1. Set your working directory to TUTORIAL. Create a new form and place a button labeled 10 Largest Countries on it.
2. Add lines 4–19 to the **pushButton** method of the button.

```
1:  ;Button :: pushButton
2:  method pushButton(var eventInfo Event)
3:     var
4:         tc                 TCursor
5:         ar                 Array[10] String
6:         siCounter    SmallInt
7:     endVar
8:
9:     tc.open("WORLD.DB", "secArea")
10:    tc.end()
11:
12:    for siCounter from 1 to 10
13:        ar[siCounter] = tc.COUNTRY + " (" + tc."Area_(KMSQ)" + ")"
14:        tc.priorRecord()
15:    endFor
16:
17:    tc.close()
18:    ar.view("10 Largest Countries (Square Kilometers)")
19: endmethod
```

3. Check the syntax, save the form as TC3.FSL, run the form, and click the button. After a moment, the results are displayed in a dynamic-array viewer (see Figure 16.11).

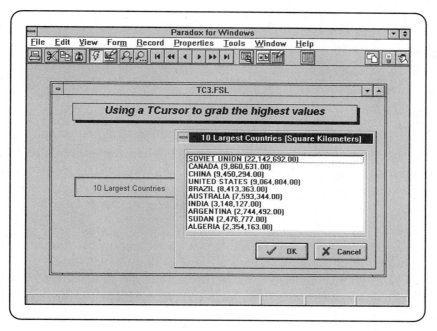

Figure 16.11. TC3.FSL. Getting the largest values from a nonkey field using a secondary index.

Analysis

Lines 4–6 declare the variables used for this routine. Line 4 declares a TCursor variable. Line 38 declares a static array that is ready to receive 10 elements. Line 6 declares the *Counter* variable, which is used with the for loop later in line 12.

Line 9 opens the TCursor variable and passes it the name of the optional secondary index. Line 10 gets ready to store the values by moving to the end of the table. Because the *Area* secondary index is active, the end of the table is the record that has the largest number in its *Area_(KMSQ)* field.

Line 12 sets up the for loop to loop 10 times. Line 13 puts the first value in the first element of the array. Line 10 set the correct record. Line 14 moves the record pointer backward one record. The loop continues for a total of 10 occurrences. Line 17 closes the TCursor—always a good idea—and line 18 displays the results.

Using Temporary Files

Sometimes, you need to create temporary tables to store information. Temporary tables are temporary because the data is needed only while the program is running. When you're done, you can delete them. One technique for deleting the tables is to use the **canDepart** of the form.

A better technique is to use a little-known feature built into Paradox. Whenever you quit Paradox, it deletes all the tables in the private directory whose names start with two underscores and stores them in your private directory. You can use this feature to your advantage. Whenever you create tables for temporary use in ObjectPAL, give them names that start with two underscores. Paradox takes care of deleting them for you. As a further benefit, the tables are hidden from the file browser.

This technique isn't limited to tables. In fact, it isn't limited to Paradox files. Whenever it exits, Paradox deletes all files in the private directory whose names start with two underscores. Use this feature to your advantage. Put all scratch files into your private directory, and give them filenames that start with two underscores.

Manipulating Data in a Table

There are four basic approaches to manipulating tables and records with ObjectPAL:

- Attach a Table variable to a table on disk. Then use the Table type methods to manipulate the table. Synchronize them with `resync()`, if necessary. (The table methods deal with the table as a whole).

- Open a TCursor or attach it to a UIObject. Then use the TCursor class methods to manipulate the table. No manipulations are updated to the screen. If you want to update the screen, use `resync()`.

- Use the UIObject methods to manipulate the data. Each manipulation updates the screen as it occurs.

- Send action commands to the UIObjects—for example, `active.action(DataNextRecord)`. The action commands simulate what a user does.

> ### Speeding up TCursors
>
> You can speed up a TCursor in three ways: `update()`, `setBatchOn()`, and `copyToArray()`. If you use `setBatchOn()`, make sure to follow it with `setBatchOff()` every time you use it.

Copying an Entire Record with a TCursor

Q: I know I can "ditto" the previous field, but is there a way to "ditto" an entire record in a tableFrame?

A: Yes, by using the ObjectPal method `copyToArray()`. For the sake of simplicity, create a button on the form. In the **pushButton** method, use the following code:

```
1:   method pushButton(var eventInfo Event)
2:      var
3:          recArr    array[]    anyType
4:      endVar
5:
6:      tFrameObject.edit()
7:      tFrameObject.copyToArray(recArr)
8:      tFrameObject.insertAfterRecord()
9:      tFrameObject.copyFromArray(recArr)
10: endMethod
```

In doing this, a complete duplicate of the record will be entered after the current record. Another approach would be to attach the preceding code to the tableframe object using the **keyPhysical** method to monitor which key was pressed.

Autoincrementing

So far, this chapter has only touched on the power and capabilities of Table and TCursor variables. A whole book could be devoted to just these two variable types. This final section of this chapter addresses autoincrementing with the TCursor.

Paradox does have a field type to easily create an autoincrementing field. This feature was introduced with version 5. You may have reasons to use ObjectPAL to create autoincrementing fields, however.

In this section, you learn how to autoincrement using ObjectPAL. First, you autoincrement a simple field. Second, you autoincrement a nonkey field. Third, for the most elegant solution, you add locking to the routine. By studying simple and elegant methods, you learn how to implement different routines under different situations and functional programming.

Autoincrementing a field involves inserting a new record, finding the highest value, adding 1 to it, and storing the new value. You already know how to insert a new record. For example:

```
1:  active.insertRecord()
2:  Line_Item.insertRecord()
3:  self.action(DataInsertRecord)
4:  tc.insertRecord()
```

To get the current highest value, either move to the end of the table and put the value in a variable, or use the cMax() method. Either way, once you get the highest value, you need to put it into a variable.

AUTOINCREMENTING A KEY FIELD

Suppose that you want to get the current highest value by moving to the end of the table and putting the value in a variable. First, declare a long integer variable that will hold the new number:

```
1:  var
2:       n    LongInt
3:  endVar
```

Next, move to the end of the table. Grab the current highest value and place it in the waiting variable:

```
1:  Customer_No.end()
2:  n = Customer_No
```

Now that you have the current highest value, you need to insert a new record, add 1 to the number, put the value into the field, and post the record:

```
1:  Customer_No.edit()
2:  Customer_No.insertRecord()
3:  Customer_No = n + 1
4:  Customer_No.postRecord()
```

The last line posts the record. It is important. If you don't include this line of code, the next person who tries to get the highest value won't get an accurate value.

> ANSWERS\AUTO1.FSL demonstrates a simple way to autoincrement
> by using UIObject methods and procedures (see Figure 16.12).

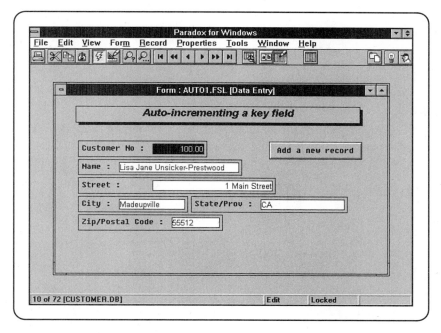

Figure 16.12. AUTO1.FSL.

Here is the complete code:

```
 1:  ;Button :: pushButton
 2:  method pushButton(var eventInfo Event)
 3:      var
 4:          n    LongInt
 5:      endVar
 6:
 7:      Customer_No.end()
 8:      n = Customer_No
 9:      Customer_No.edit()
10:      Customer_No.insertRecord()
11:      Customer_No = n + 1
12:      Customer_No.postRecord()
13:      Name.moveTo()
14: endmethod
```

This simple example illustrates the basic steps of autoincrementing. It has many holes, however. For example, the code doesn't allow for users who press the Insert key (an often-used way of inserting a record). It also is possible for two users to end up with the same number, and one user will end up with a key violation.

The next tutorial on autoincrementing shows you how to tackle the problem of the user's not being able to press the Insert key. It's intended only for a single-user application.

Tutorial: Autoincrementing for a Single User

Suppose that you wish to automatically autoincrement the *Customer_No* field. One technique to do this is to use the **action** method to trap for when a user inserts a record, and increment the value at that time.

On Disk: \ANSWERS\AUTO2.FSL

Quick Steps

1. Declare a TCursor.
2. In the **action** method, trap for `DataInsertRecord`.
3. Put the form into Edit mode.
4. Use `DoDefault`.
5. Take the highest value from the TCursor and add 1 to it with `cMax() + 1`. Put the result into the *Customer_No* field.
6. Post the record.

Step By Step

1. Set your working directory to TUTORIAL. Create a new form with the CUSTOMER.DB table in the data model (see Figure 16.13).
2. In the Var window of the page, add line 3.

```
1:   ;Page :: Var
2:   Var
3:      tc TCursor
4:   endVar
```

3. In the **action** method of the page, add lines 3–10.

```
1:   ;Page :: action
2:   method action(var eventInfo ActionEvent)
3:      if eventInfo.id() = DataInsertRecord then
```

```
 4:    Customer_No.edit()
 5:        DoDefault
 6:        tc.open("CUSTOMER.DB")
 7:        Customer_No = tc.cMax("Customer No") + 1
 8:        Customer_No.postRecord()
 9:        Name.moveTo()
10:    endIf
11: endmethod
```

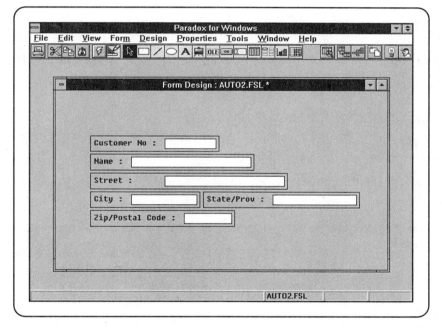

Figure 16.13. Set up form for the tutorial.

4. Check the syntax, save the form as AUTO2.FSL, and run the form. Insert a record however you want.

Analysis

In step 2, line 3 declares a TCursor in the Var window of the page. This is important. If the TCursor were declared in the **action** method, it might be redeclared thousands of times in a session—a potential problem.

In step 3, line 3 checks the event packet for DataInsertRecord every time an action goes to the page. Once DataInsertRecord is detected, line 4 puts the whole form into Edit mode if it isn't in Edit mode already. Line 5 executes the default behavior. Line 6 opens a TCursor—another gateway—to the same table. Line 7 uses the TCursor with the cMax() method to get the highest value plus 1, and it places the new value into the *Customer_No* field. Line 8 posts the record. Line 9 moves the focus to the *Name* field as a convenience to the user.

Autoincrementing and Locking

Now you have just one more loophole to close. Theoretically, it's still possible for two users to end up with the same number. You can use autoincrementing with locks to make sure that this doesn't happen. A **lock** is a feature of the IDAPI database engine that prevents other users from viewing, changing, or locking a table or a record while one user has a lock on it. The next tutorial uses autoincrementing with locks.

Tutorial: Autoincrementing with Locks

Suppose that you wish to autoincrement a field in a multiuser environment. To do this, you need to work with locks.

On Disk: \ANSWERS\AUTO3.FSL

Quick Steps

1. Create a separate table used only for keeping track of the highest number.
2. Use a TCursor to lock the INCREMNT.DB table.
3. After the table is locked, use the number to generate a new highest number. Store the new number.

Step By Step

1. Set your working directory to TUTORIAL. Create a new form with the CUSTOMER.DB table in the data model.
2. Add lines 3 and 4 to the Var window of the page.

```
1:  ;Page :: Var
2:  Var
3:    tc              TCursor
4:    siCounter    SmallInt
5:  endVar
```

3. In the **action** method of the page, type lines 3–25.

```
 1:  ;Page :: action
 2:  method action(var eventInfo ActionEvent)
 3:      if eventInfo.id() = DataInsertRecord then
 4:          tc.open("INCREMNT.DB")
 5:          siCounter = 0
 6:          while not tc.lock("Full")
 7:              siCounter = siCounter + 1
 8:              message("Attempting to establish lock: " +
string(siCounter))
 9:              sleep(100)
10:              If siCounter = 100 then
11:                  DisableDefault
12:                  msgStop("Warning", "Could not establish lock.")
13:                  return
14:              endIf
15:          endWhile
16:          edit()
17:          DoDefault
18:          tc.edit()
19:          tc."Customer No" = tc."Customer No" + 1
20:          tc.postRecord()
21:          Customer_No = tc."Customer No"
22:          tc.unLock("Full")
23:          Name.moveTo()
24:          tc.close()
25:      endIf
26: endmethod
```

4. Check the syntax, save the form as AUTO3.FSL, and run the form. Insert a record.

Analysis

In step 2, lines 3 and 4 declare a TCursor and SmallInt variables for use in the **action** method.

In step 3, line 3 checks the event packet for DataInsertRecord every time an action goes to the page. When DataInsertRecord is detected, the elaborate autoincrementing routine begins. Line 4 opens a TCursor. Lines 6–15 attempt to put a lock on the increment table 100 times. If the program is successful, the execution skips to line 16. Otherwise, line 7 increments the counter, line 8 displays a message, and line 9 causes the program to sleep for one-tenth of a second. Lines 10–14 check whether it is the hundredth attempt. Line 16 puts the form into Edit mode. Line 17 executes the default behavior. Lines 18–20 generate a new number. Line 21 uses the new number. Line 22 releases the incrementing table. It is important to note that this routine has two exit points. Control will leave this routine either in line 13 with the `return` keyword or at `endMethod` in line 26.

The technique you use to autoincrement your applications depends on the application and the amount of time and energy you have.

HANDLING THE DATA MODEL

DM METHODS AND PROCEDURES

The dm in dm methods stands for *data model*. With the dm methods and procedures, you can deal directly with the data model. Table 17.1 lists the dm methods and procedures.

Using dm methods and procedures

Using unlinked tables in the data model

Using enum methods and procedures

Enumerating fonts

TABLE 17.1. DM METHODS AND PROCEDURES.	
dmAddTable	dmLinkToFields
dmAttach	dmLinkToIndex
dmBuildQueryString	dmPut
dmEnumLinkFields	dmRemoveTable
dmGet	dmResync
dmGetProperty	dmSetProperty
dmHasTable	dmUnlink

Using *dmGet()* and *dmPut()*

Sometimes, you need values from a table in the data model for a field for which you didn't have room on your form. In those cases, `dmGet()` and `dmPut()` come in handy.

Tutorial: Using *dmGet()* and *dmPut()*

Suppose that you wish to grab some values from fields in a table from the current record for which you did not have room on a form. To do this, use `dmGet()` and `dmPut()`.

On Disk: \ANSWERS\DMGETPUT.FSL

Quick Steps

1. Use `dmGet()` to get a value and put it into a variable to show the user.
2. Use `dmPut()` to put a value into a field in the data model. You must be in Edit mode.

Step By Step

1. Change your working directory to TUTORIAL. Create a new form with the WORLD.DB in its data model, but define only the COUNTRY field. Add a button and two undefined fields to the form. Label the button Change Value. Change the label of the first undefined field to *Value*, and change its name to *VField*. Change the display type of the second undefined field to the Radio Buttons field type, and add

the following four values to its item list: *PRESIDENT, POPULATION_(MIL), CURRENCY,* and *LANGUAGE_1.* Figure 17.1 shows how your form should look. Change its name to *Table_Field.*

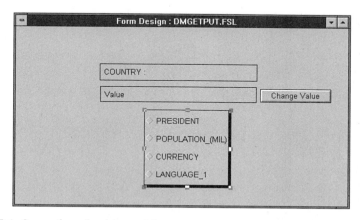

Figure 17.1. Set up form for the tutorial.

2. In the Var window of the page, add line 3.

```
1:    ;Page :: Var
2:    Var
3:        data AnyType
4:    endVar
```

3. In the **newValue** method of the *Table_Field* field, add lines 3–6.

```
1:    ;Table_Field :: newValue
2:    method newValue(var eventInfo Event)
3:        if not self.isBlank() then
4:            dmGet("WORLD.DB", Table_Field, data)
5:            VField.value = data
6:        endIf
7:    endmethod
```

4. Add line 3 to the **newValue** method of the COUNTRY field.

```
1:    ;COUNTRY :: newValue
2:    method newValue(var eventInfo Event)
3:        if not Table_Field.isBlank() then
4:            dmGet("WORLD.DB", Table_Field, data)
```

```
5:                VField.value = data
6:            endIf
7:        endmethod
```

5. Add lines 3–7 to the **pushButton** method of the Change Value
   button.

```
1:     ;Button :: pushButton
2:     method pushButton(var eventInfo Event)
3:         if not Table_Field.isBlank() then
4:             edit()
5:             dmPut("WORLD.DB", Table_Field, VField)
6:             endEdit()
7:         endIf
8:     endmethod
```

6. Check the syntax, save the form as DMGETPUT.FSL, and run the
   form. Try out the various features of this form. For example, search for
   United States. You might change the name of the president from
   Ronald Reagan to *Bill Clinton*. (This shows how out-of-date the *United
   States* record is.) Figure 17.2 shows how the form looks when you
   use it.

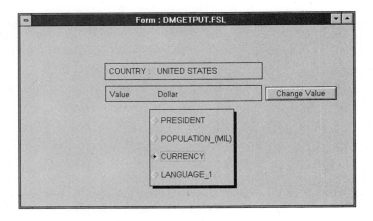

Figure 17.2. DMGETPUT.FSL.

Analysis

In step 2, line 3 declares *data* as an AnyType variable at the page level. This is important because *data* is used in both the *Table_Field* and *COUNTRY* fields. The page is the lowest container above both of these fields.

In step 3, lines 3–6 check whether the *Table_Field* field is blank. If it isn't, line 4 gets the appropriate value directly from the table and puts it first into the *data* variable and then into the *Vield* field.

In step 4, lines 3–6 duplicate this routine for the *COUNTRY* field.

In step 5, lines 3–5 change the value. Line 3 makes sure that a field has been selected. Line 4 puts the form into Edit mode. Line 5 puts the changed value into the field in the table. The value isn't posted yet; pressing Alt+Backspace undoes the change.

USING UNLINKED TABLES IN THE DATA MODEL

Almost all of the time you are going to want to use the luxury of the data model. Sometimes, however, you may need to not link the tables in it. Why? One reason is that in a multiuser situation such as Customer to Orders to Lineitem, you may have a need to have multiple data entry on customer. The problem is that the data model will lock the Customer table when you enter an order into the Order table, effectively forcing your application to be a single customer application. The trick is to emulate the data model's restricting of records without duplicating its locking scheme.

Emulate the data model by using the record object. If you have fields on the form, then surround it with a 1-by-1 MRO. Once this is done, use the **arrive** method of the record object and use `doDefault` and and `setFilter()` on the child table or tables. Study the form NO_LINK.FSL to see this technique in detail (see Figure 17.3).

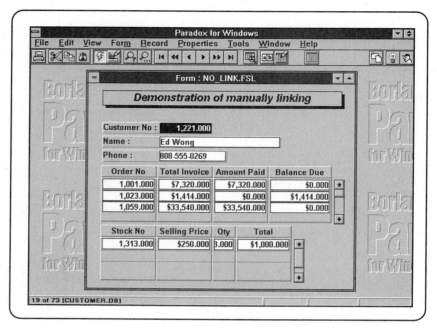

Figure 17.3. NO_LINK.FSL.

THE ENUM CATEGORY

Let's finish off this small chapter with an interesting way to study a subject; that is, to put it in a category. If you were studying procedures, all the procedures that give or enumerate information could be grouped in a category. This section takes a brief look at the enum methods and procedures. An **enum procedure** is a procedure that enumerates information and puts it in a table.

Using an enum Method

You use enum methods and procedures the same way you use other methods and procedures. If the enum command you want to use is a procedure, simply call it with little or no setup. For example, to create a table on disk of all the files in a folder, use

```
1:  enumFolder("FILES.DB")
```

Many enum methods enable you to fill an array instead of a table on disk. For example, to fill an array with all the files in a folder, use

```
1:  var
2:        ar   Array[] Anytype
3:  endVar
4:  enumFolder(ar)
5:  ar.view()
```

Finally, if the enum command is a method, you have to set up the appropriate variable first.

The following code defines *tv* as a TableView variable, creates a table of the current sessions in your private directory, and shows that table.

```
1:  var
2:        tv   TableView
3:  endVar
4:  enumDesktopWindowNames(":priv:sessions.db")
5:  tv.open(":priv:sessions.db")
```

The next tutorial demonstrates using one of the enum procedures—enumFonts().

Tutorial: Enumerating Fonts

Suppose that you wish to enumerate all your fonts and display the resulting table in a TableView. This tutorial also acquaints you with setMouseShape().

On Disk: \ANSWERS\FONTS.FSL

Quick Steps

1. Use enumFonts() to list all the fonts to a table.
2. Open the resulting table as a table view.

Step By Step

1. Create a new form or open an existing one. Place a button labeled List Fonts on it (see Figure 17.4).
2. Add lines 3–12 to the **pushButton** method of the List Fonts button.

```
1:      ;Button :: pushButton

2:      method pushButton(var eventInfo Event)

3:          var

4:              tv   TableView

5:          endVar

6:

7:          message("This may take a while, searching for fonts.")

8:          setMouseShape(MouseWait)
```

```
9:          enumFonts(":PRIV:__FONTS.DB")
10:             setMouseShape(MouseArrow)
11:             message("")
12:             tv.open(":PRIV:__FONTS.DB")
13:          endmethod
```

Figure 17.4. Set up form for the tutorial.

3. Check the syntax and save your work as FONTS.FSL. Run the form and click the button. While the fonts are being enumerated, the mouse pointer turns into the waiting mouse, and a message is displayed in the status bar (see Figure 17.5).

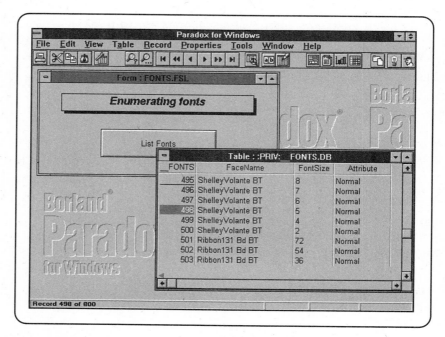

Figure 17.5. FONTS.FSL. Listing and displaying all your system fonts.

Analysis

In step 2, line 4 declares a TableView variable for use in line 12. Line 7 displays a message letting the user know that the routine might take a long time. This message is important. The more fonts you have, the longer the routine takes, and some users have many fonts.

Line 8 reinforces the message by changing the mouse pointer to the waiting mouse. Line 9 enumerates the fonts to a table in the private directory. The two underscores preceding the name of the table are important, because Paradox will automatically erase the table when it exits.

Line 10 sets the mouse pointer back to the pointer mouse, and line 11 clears the message in the status bar. Line 12 displays the TableView.

FIELDS, TABLE FRAMES, AND MROS

AUTOMATICALLY ENTERING MEMO VIEW

Memo view allows you to easily edit fields defined to a memo field. For example, the return key takes you to the next line in a memo field when in Memo view. To manually enter Memo, view and then select Shift+F2. To automatically enter memo view, put the following code in the **arrive** method of a standard or formatted memo field:

```
1:    method arrive (var eventInfo MoveEvent)
2:       doDefault
3:       self.action(EditEnterMemoView)
4:    endMethod
```

The following code can be used in a **pushButton** method to move to a memo field and put the memo field into memo view:

Setting the tab order of a form

Using list and drop-down edit fields

Preventing the user from going past the end of a record on a table frame

Highlighting an inactive table frame

Redefining a table frame

```
1:    method pushButton (var eventInfo Event)
2:        MyMemoField.moveto()
3:        MyMemoField.action(EditEnterMemoView)
4:    endmethod
```

SETTING THE TAB ORDER OF A FORM

There are three commonly used techniques to set the tab stop order of a form: setting the Next Tab Stop property, using ObjectPAL, and using the concept of containership. The most elegant of these three solutions is the Next Tab Stop feature (new to 5.0). The Next Tab Stop is an interactive—and easy—solution. For the sake of demonstrating containership and because it is very useful, however, I'll show you the third technique here: using containership.

Paradox has containership, which enables you to put a smaller object inside a larger object. You can say that the larger object contains the smaller object. You can use containership to dictate the tab order of fields by grouping them or putting them inside another object. Suppose that you have a two-column form—a form with fields on the left and right. You put a box around the fields on the left; the box will contain those fields. Likewise, you can select all the fields and group them by selecting Design | Group. The form \ANSWERS\DM_1-1.FSL demonstrates this technique (see Figure 18.1). In this case, when you tab to the first field in the group on the left, the tab order goes through all the other fields in the group before it exits to the fields on the right.

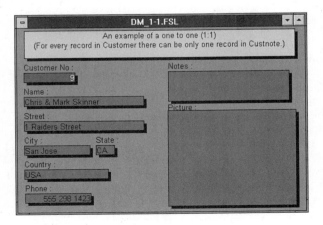

Figure 18.1. Screen shot of form \ANSWERS\DM_1-1.FSL.

You can create a box with or without a border or group the objects. It might be a good idea to put a box around the fields on the right side of the form, too. This way the user goes through all the fields on the right even if some of the fields on the left are empty.

The last technique for controlling tab order is to use the **depart** method of the object, and use `objectName.moveto()` to move the focus to the new object. Because version 5 introduces the new Next Tab Stop property, however, I do not recommend this technique.

On a similar note, you can set the `errorCode()` to `CanNotDepart` for the page to prevent the user from getting to the next page except through your code. To do this, you must set flags.

Drop-Down Edit Lists

Often, you want to have a pick list or a drop-down edit field available in your form when you're editing. A list field enables you to restrict the values entered into a field to those on the list. Table 18.1 lists the pertinent properties of the list object.

TABLE 18.1. LIST PROPERTIES FOR FILLING A LIST.

Property	Description
datasource	Fills a list object with the values in a field in a table
list.count	Specifies the number of elements in the list
list.selection	Use to specify the currently selected item in list
list.value	Sets the value of an item in a list

With the properties in Table 18.1, you can control a list object. Suppose that a user needs ID numbers or items of a specific kind in a list and doesn't want to have to type hundreds of ID numbers. To fill a list object, use the `dataSource` property. You can place this line of code on the list object of the drop-down edit box:

```
1:  self.DataSource = "[tablename.fieldname]"
```

If you use the .DB file extension when you describe your table name, you need to embed the table name in quotation marks. Because the expression is already in quotation marks, you need to use \" to represent a quotation mark. The backslash character means that the next character is taken literally. For example:

```
1:   self.DataSource = "[\"tablename.db\".fieldname]"
```

To reach the list object, select the field and open the Object Tree by using the Toolbar. Right-click the list object listed on the Object Tree, and place the code on the **open** method.

This technique changes the actual value of the field when you're in Edit mode. It doesn't move to the record that matches that value. The list is a list of choices that changes the value of the current field to which the drop-down edit box is attached.

Emptying a List

A list can be blanked by setting its count to 0. For example, the following code empties the list object called lst1:

```
1:   lst1.list.count = 0
```

Using a drop-down edit list to move to a new record—rather than change the value of the current record in that field—requires a few extra steps:

1. Make the drop-down field an undefined field. Name it *DROP*.

2. Add the `self.DataSource` code to the list object.

3. On the drop-down edit object—not the list object—change two methods as follows:

```
1:       ;lst1 :: open
2:       self.value = fieldname.value   ;This sets the
3:                                      ;initial value

1:       ;lst :: newValue
2:       if eventInfo.reason() = EditValue then
3:            fieldName.locate("fieldname", DROP.value)
4:       endIf
```

4. Save and execute this code. Now the drop-down edit list acts as a data navigator for your table. I don't recommend this technique for large tables because a drop-down edit list with more than a few hundred

options is unmanageable. In addition, ObjectPAL limits the number of items in a list to 2,500.

The next tutorial demonstrates how to populate a drop-down edit list.

Tutorial: Populating a Drop-Down Edit List

Suppose that you wish to populate a drop-down edit list and to activate it whenever the user arrives on the field.

On Disk: \ANSWERS\LIST1.FSL

Quick Steps

1. Use the `DataSource` property to populate the list.
2. Use the `EditDropDownList` constant to drop the list.

Step By Step

1. Set your working directory to TUTORIAL. Create a new form with three undefined fields on it. Make the middle field a drop-down edit list, and name the list object *list* (see Figure 18.2). This tutorial uses only the middle undefined field. The other two fields are on the form so that you can move on and off the middle field.

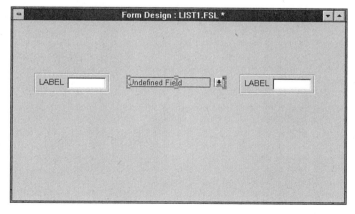

Figure 18.2. Set up form for the tutorial.

2. Add line 3 to the **open** method of the list object of the field.

```
1:    ;fldList :: open
2:    method open(var eventInfo Event)
```

```
3:              self.list.DataSource="[WORLD.COUNTRY]"
4:       endmethod
```

3. Add lines 3–5 to the **arrive** method of the field.

```
1:     ;fldList :: Arrive
2:     method arrive(var eventInfo MoveEvent)
3:         if self.isBlank() then
4:             action(EditDropDownList)
5:         endIf
6:     endmethod
```

4. Check the syntax, save the form as LIST1.FSL, and run it. Use the
   Tab key to move from field to field. When you arrive on the field that
   has the code, its drop-down edit list is displayed (see Figure 18.3).
   Select a value from the list, and tab. The list no longer drops down.

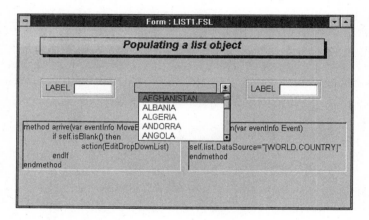

Figure 18.3. LIST1.FSL.

Analysis

In step 2, line 3 populates the *list* object of the field. In step 3, line 3 checks
whether it has a value. If the field object is blank, line 4 drops the list for the
user.

The next tutorial demonstrates how to add automatically to a drop-down list.

Tutorial: Adding Automatically to a Drop-Down List

Suppose that you wish to populate a drop-down edit list and automatically add new entries to it.

On Disk: \ANSWERS\LIST2.FSL

Quick Steps

1. Use the DataSource property to populate the list.
2. Use a TCursor to check for the entry and to add the entry to the table.

Step By Step

1. Set your working directory to TUTORIAL. Create a new form with two undefined fields on it. Make the first field a drop-down edit list, and name the list object *list* (see Figure 18.4). This tutorial uses only the first undefined field. The other field is on the form so that you can move on and off the first field.

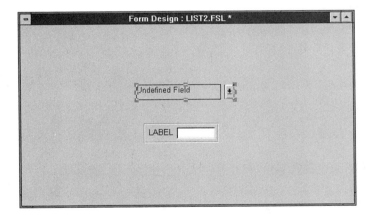

Figure 18.4. Set up form for the tutorial.

2. In the **arrive** method of the *list* object of the field add line 3.

```
1:      ;fldList :: arrive
2:      method arrive(var eventInfo MoveEvent)
3:          self.list.DataSource="[CUSTOMER.Name]"
4:      endmethod
```

3. In the **canDepart** method of the field add lines 3–18.

```
1:      ;fldList :: canDepart
2:      method canDepart(var eventInfo MoveEvent)
3:           var
4:                tc   TCursor
5:           endVar
6:
7:           ;Add a value if necessary.
8:           if not self.isBlank() then
9:                tc.open("CUSTOMER.DB")
10:               if not tc.locate("Name", self.value) then
11:                    tc.edit()
12:                    tc.insertRecord()
13:                    tc."Name" = self.value
14:                    tc.(1) = tc.cMax("Customer No") + 1
15:                    tc.postRecord()
16:               endIf
17:               tc.close()
18:          endIf
19:     endmethod
```

4. Check the syntax, save the form as LIST2.FSL, and run it. Add a new entry to the drop-down edit list. Move off the field. Move back and drop down the edit list. Your entry has been added to the list (see figure 18.5).

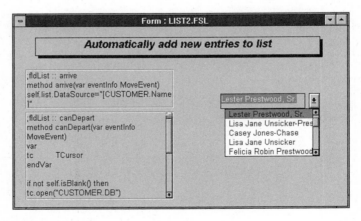

Figure 18.5. LIST2.FSL.

Analysis

In step 2, line 3 populates the *list* object of the field. The **arrive** method was selected for this task because we need the list to repopulate with the latest information every time it is selected.

In step 3, line 4 declares a TCursor variable. (A better place to declare the variable is before the method or in the Var window. To keep the code visually close together, the code in this tutorial puts the variable inside the method.) Line 8 tests whether the field has a value in it. If it does, line 9 opens a TCursor that will be used in lines 10–15. Line 10 tests whether the value is already in the table. If it isn't, line 11 puts the TCursor into Edit mode. Line 12 inserts a new record. Lines 13 and 14 set the values, and line 15 posts the record. Line 17 closes the TCursor.

VERIFYING VALIDITY CHECKS

If you want to prevent the user from moving off a field when a validity check fails or when a key violation occurs within a field, use the following code:

```
1:  ;Field :: depart
2:  doDefault
3:  if self.edit() then
4:     if not self.postRecord() then
5:        errorShow()
6:        self.moveTo()
7:     endif
8:  endif
```

TABLE FRAMES

This section discusses how you can manipulate table frames.

Preventing the User from Going Past the End of a Table

You can use the auto-append feature of the data model to always restrict the user from going past the last record in a table frame.

Suppose that you want to prevent new records from being inserted into a table that is being accessed by means of a table frame embedded in a form. You can prevent a new record from being inserted by first trapping the DataInsertRecord action constant and then disabling the code of the default built-in method. If you just want to stop the user from inserting a new record by moving past the last record, however, then uncheck the auto-append property of the table in the data model.

Selecting Multiple Records from a Table Frame

Sometimes it is useful to mark a set of records permanently. dBASE does this when you delete a record. The record is marked for deletion, and it is permanently deleted when you pack the table. When you program, you often want to mark a set of records permanently. I call this mechanism a *marked list*.

To implement a marked list, include a field in the database structure called *Marked*. Make the field type A1. With code, you enable the user to select the record—perhaps with the Spacebar or by clicking it. In turn, you place a character into the marked field of the record—perhaps the letter Y for Yes or X for marked.

At this point, you can do a variety of things with queries. For example, by interrogating the *Marked* field and looking for your character that signifies that the field is marked, you can save the answer query in another directory or do simple housekeeping chores. This is an important technique for permanently marking records. It has a broad range of uses in your applications. For example:

```
1:   ;Routine to mark field.
2:   ;Field :: mouseDown
3:   disableDefault
4:   if self.isBlank() then
5:       self.value = "X"
6:   else
7:       self.value = ""
8:   endIf
```

Once a user marks records, you can query for the "X" or you can use a scan loop to loop through the table and do something with each record marked. For example:

```
1:   ;Routine to handle marked field.
2:   var
3:       tc    TCursor
4:   endVar
5:
6:   tc.open("TABLE.DB")
7:   scan tc for tc."Field" = "X":
8:       ;Do something here.
9:   endScan
```

Remember, you also need to clear out the *Marked* field at some point. For example:

```
1:   ;Routine to clear marked field.
2:   var
3:       tc    TCursor
4:   endVar
5:
```

```
 6:   tc.open("TABLE.DB")
 7:   tc.edit()
 8:   scan tc:
 9:        tc."Marked" = ""
10:   endScan
```

You can highlight an inactive table frame. In the next tutorial you highlight the current record of a table frame that no longer has focus.

Tutorial: Highlighting an Inactive Table Frame

Suppose that you wish to highlight the current record of a table frame that no longer has focus.

On Disk: \ANSWERS\HIGHLIT1.FSL

Quick Steps

1. Name the record object of the table frame so that you can refer to it with code.

2. On the **canArrive** method of the table frame, set the color to transparent.

3. On the **canDepart** method of the table frame, set the color to yellow or to any highlight color.

4. Put a 1-by-1 MRO around the master table fields and set the color of the record object to transparent in **canDepart**.

Step By Step

1. Change your working directory to the TUTORIAL directory. Create a new form with CUSTOMER.DB, ORDERS.DB, and LINEITEM.DB in the data model set up as a 1:M:M relationship. Add a 1-by-1 MRO around the master table fields as Figure 18.6 shows. Name the record object of the *ORDERS* table frame *recOrders*. Without any code, you can't tell to what record records appearing in the second table frame belong.

2. In the **canDepart** method of the *ORDERS* table frame add line 3.

```
1:      ;ORDERS :: canDepart
2:      method canDepart(var eventInfo MoveEvent)
3:          recOrders.color = Yellow
4:      endmethod
```

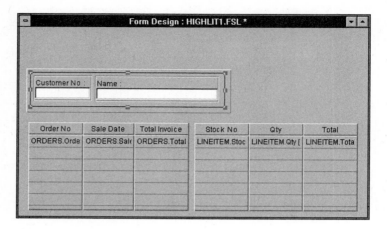

Figure 18.6. Set up form for the tutorial.

3. In the **canArrive** method of the ORDERS table frame add line 3.

```
1:      ;ORDERS :: canArrive
2:      method canArrive(var eventInfo MoveEvent)
3:          recOrders.color = Transparent
4:      endmethod
```

4. Add line 3 to the **canDepart** method of the 1-by-1 MRO.

```
1:      ;mroOneByOne :: canDepart
2:      method canDepart(var eventInfo MoveEvent)
3:          recOrders.color = Transparent
4:      endmethod
```

5. Check the syntax, save the form as HIGHLIT1.FSL, and run it.
   Nothing seems different. Click any record in the ORDERS table
   frame, then click the Name field. You still have a visual indication of
   which record the second table frame is on. Figure 18.7 shows that
   record 1,202.00 is highlighted even when the focus is on the Name
   field.

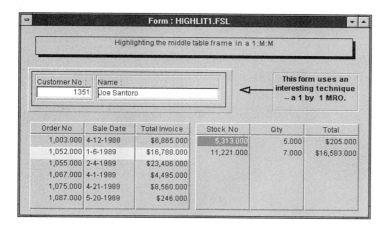

Figure 18.7. HIGHLIT1.FSL.

Analysis

The technique used in this routine is interesting because of how it uses the event model. The next tutorial shows you how to make the highlight consistent when the table frame has the focus and when it doesn't.

Tutorial: Highlighting a Table Frame

Suppose that you wish to highlight the current record of a table frame when it has the focus and when it loses the focus.

On Disk: \ANSWERS\HIGHLIT2.FSL

Quick Steps

1. Name the record object of the table frame.
2. On the **canArrive** method of the table frame, set the color to Transparent.
3. On the **canDepart** method of the table frame, set the color to yellow or to any highlight color.
4. Put a 1-by-1 MRO around the master table fields and set the color of the record object to transparent in **canDepart**.

Step By Step

1. Change your working directory to TUTORIAL. Create a new form with CUSTOMER.DB, ORDERS.DB, and LINEITEM.DB in the data model set up as a 1:M:M relationship (see Figure 18.8).

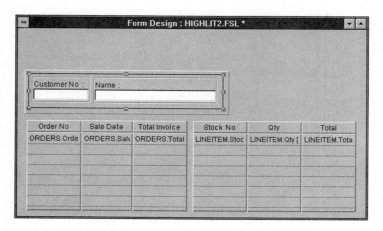

Figure 18.8. Set up form for the tutorial.

2. Add line 3 to the **canArrive** method of the *ORDERS* table frame.

```
1:      ;ORDERS :: canArrive
2:      method canArrive(var eventInfo MoveEvent)
3:          recOrders.color = Transparent
4:      endmethod
```

3. Add line 3 to the **canDepart** method of the *ORDERS* table frame.

```
1:      ;ORDERS :: canDepart
2:      method canDepart(var eventInfo MoveEvent)
3:          recOrders.color = Yellow
4:      endmethod
```

4. Add line 3 to the **canDepart** method of the *recOrders* record object.

```
1:      ;recOrders :: canDepart
2:      method canDepart(var eventInfo MoveEvent)
3:          self.color = Transparent
4:      endmethod
```

5. Add line 3 to the **arrive** method of the *recOrders* record object.

```
1:      ;recOrders :: arrive
2:      method arrive(var eventInfo MoveEvent)
3:          self.color = Yellow
4:      endmethod
```

6. Add line 3 to the **canDepart** method of the 1-by-1 MRO.

```
1:      ;mroOneByOne :: canDepart
2:      method canDepart(var eventInfo MoveEvent)
3:          recOrders.color = Transparent
4:      endmethod
```

7. Check the syntax, save the form as HIGHLIT2.FSL, and run it. Nothing seems different. Click any record in the *ORDERS* table frame, then click the *Name* field. You still have a visual indication of which record the second table frame is on. Now, move the cursor up and down the table frame. The table frame highlight moves with the pointer (see Figure 18.9).

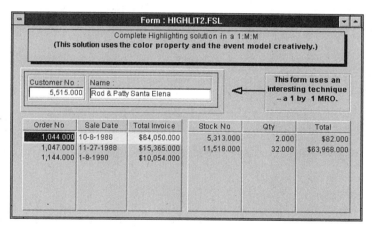

Figure 18.9. HIGHLIT2.FSL.

Analysis

In step 2, line 3 sets the color of the record object named *recOrders* to Transparent. This code occurs whenever the focus moves to the *ORDERS* table frame. Without this code, the highlight doesn't clear, and you end up with multiple records highlighted.

In step 3, line 3 sets the color of the current record to yellow whenever the focus leaves the table frame. In this example, nothing but the default behavior occurs when you're actually on the table frame.

In step 4, line 3 sets the record that you are leaving to Transparent. In step 5, line 3 sets the record on which you are arriving to Yellow. In step 6, line 3 changes the color of the record object to Transparent whenever it changes the master records.

The previous two tutorials compensate for the lack of a table frame marker in Paradox. Borland left out this much-needed feature. TableView objects in Paradox underline the current record. ObjectVision offers a pointer to the table object—a little arrow on the left side of an object resembling a table frame. Borland needs to add this feature in a future version of Paradox.

Selectively Highlighting Records in a Table Frame

Sometimes it is useful to highlight records of a table frame based on certain criteria. The following tutorial demonstrates one technique for doing this.

Tutorial: Selectively Highlighting Records in a Table Frame

Suppose that you wish to highlight all the records in a table frame with a positive value in a certain field.

On Disk: \ANSWERS\HIGHLIT3.FSL

Quick Step

On the **newValue** method of the field that you want to be the controlling field, use an `if` statement to set the field's container to a highlight color or to Transparent.

Step By Step

1. Change your working directory to TUTORIAL. Create a new form with ORDERS.DB in the data model and displayed in a table frame (see Figure 18.10).

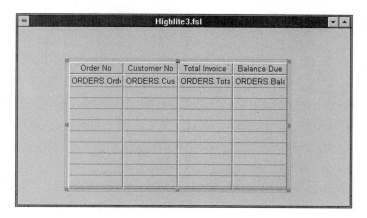

Figure 18.10. Set up form for the tutorial.

2. Add lines 3–7 to the **newValue** method of the *Balance_Due* field.

```
1:      ;Field :: newValue
2:      method newValue(var eventInfo Event)
3:          if self.value > 0 then
4:                self.container.color = Red
5:          else
6:                self.container.color = Transparent
7:          endIf
8:      endmethod
```

3. Check the syntax, save the form as HIGHLIT3.FSL, and run it. Scroll through the table frame. The records are colored red when *Balance_Due* is positive (see Figure 8.11).

Analysis

In step 2, line 3 checks whether the value in the *Balance_Due* field is positive. If it is, line 4 sets the container's color to red. If it isn't, line 6 sets the color to white.

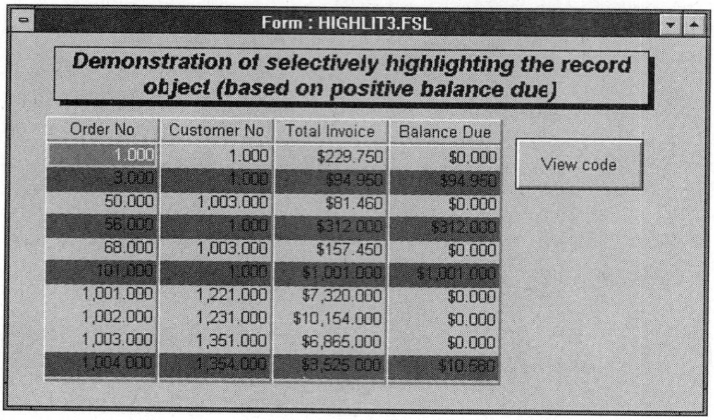

Figure 18.11. HIGHLIT3.FSL. *Highlighting certain records based on a condition.*

Redefining a Table Frame with the *TableName* and *FieldName* Properties

This section discusses redefining table frames in Run mode. The next tutorial demonstrates how to define which table is bound to a table frame.

Tutorial: Defining the Table for a Table Frame

Suppose that you wish to define an undefined table frame when the user presses a button.

On Disk: \ANSWERS\DMADD1.FSL

Quick Step

Set the table frame's `TableName` property to the table you want.

Step By Step

1. Change your working directory to TUTORIAL. Create a new form with no tables in its data model. Place a button labeled Set on the form. Add an undefined table frame to the form (see Figure 18.12).

2. Add line 3 to the **pushButton** method of the Set button.

```
1:    ;Button :: pushButton
2:    method pushButton(var eventInfo Event)
```

```
3:          Table_Frame.TableName = "WORLD.DB"
4:      endmethod
```

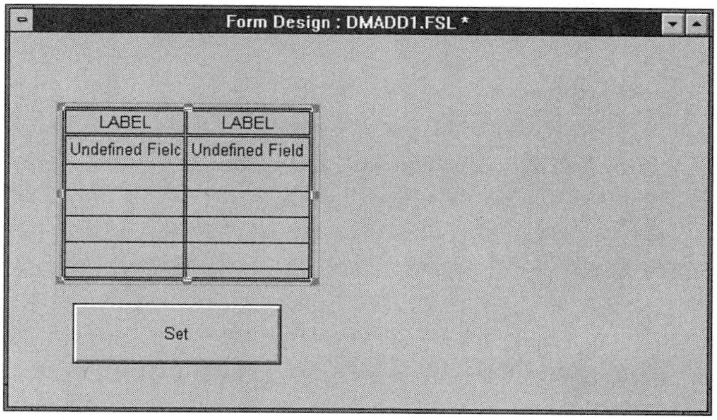

Figure 18.12. Set up form for the tutorial.

3. Check the syntax, save the form as DMADD1.FSL, and run it. Click the Set button. The table frame has exploded from one column to all the fields in the table, as Figure 18.13 shows.

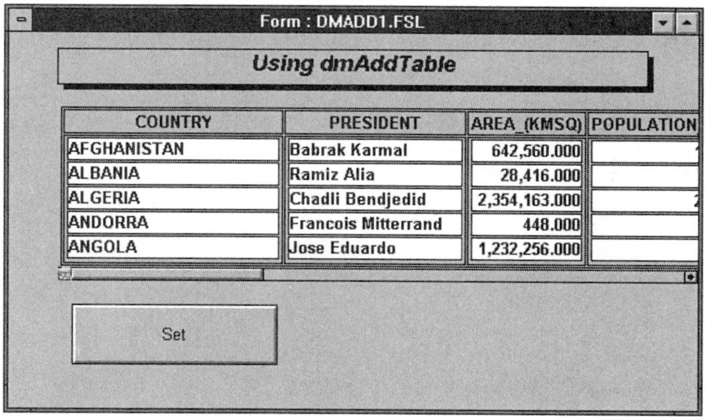

Figure 18.13. DMADD1.FSL after the table frame has exploded from one column to all the fields in the table.

Analysis

Table_Frame is the name of the table frame on the form. `TableName` is a property of the table frame object. This code doesn't rely on `dmAddTable()` to add the table to the data model. Simply setting the property does that.

DEFINING THE COLUMNS OF A TABLE FRAME

The technique used in the preceding tutorial is useful in some situations—for example, when you want the table frame redefined. In many cases, however, you want to define just a few columns. The next tutorial shows you a technique for doing that.

Tutorial: Defining the Columns of a Table Frame

Suppose that you wish to define three columns of an undefined table frame without affecting its size.

On Disk: \ANSWERS\DMADD2.FSL

Quick Step

Set each field's `FieldName` property to the table and field you want.

Step By Step

1. Change your working directory to TUTORIAL. Create a new form with no tables in its data model. Place a button labeled Set on the form. Add an undefined table frame to the form with three columns named *Col1*, *Col2*, and *Col3* (see Figure 18.14).

2. Add lines 3–5 to the **pushButton** method of the Set button.

```
1:    ;Button :: pushButton
2:    method pushButton(var eventInfo Event)
3:        Col1.FieldName = "WORLD.COUNTRY"
4:        Col2.FieldName = "WORLD.PRESIDENT"
5:        Col3.FieldName = "WORLD.CAPITAL"
6:    endmethod
```

3. Check the syntax, save the form as DMADD2.FSL, and run it. Click the Set button. Now the columns of the table frame are defined.

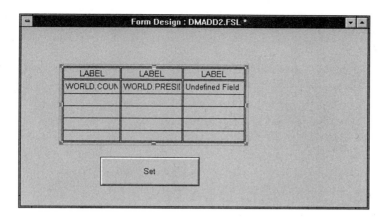

Figure 18.14. DMADD2.FSL. Using the `FieldName` property of a table frame to define the columns of the table frame.

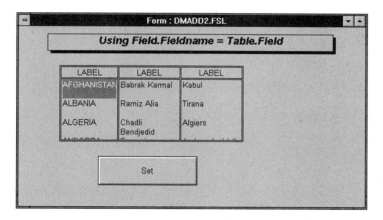

Figure 18.15. DMADD2.FSL. Using the `FieldName` property of a field to define the columns of a table frame.

Analysis

In step 2, lines 3–5 set the `FieldName` property of all three columns. Figure 18.15 shows how the DMADD2.FSL form uses the `FieldName` property of a field to define the columns of a table frame. This technique doesn't alter the properties of the table. In this figure, the undefined labels and the first column are too narrow.

You can use this technique to redefine a table, too. The trick is to redefine the table frame to the null character. In the following code, *WORLD* is the name of the table frame.

```
1:  WORLD = ""
```

Then you can redefine the columns without a problem. For example:

```
1:  Col1.FieldName = "LINEITEM.Order No"
2:  Col2.FieldName = "LINEITEM.Stock No"
3:  Col3.FieldName = "LINEITEM.Total"
```

The final level of control is the character level. Chapter 19, "Manipulating Strings and Handling the Keyboard," discusses adding control at the keyboard and character level.

Validating Fields at the Record Level of a Table Frame

Chapter 8, "Where to Put Code," briefly discussed using the record level of a table frame to validate fields. The next tutorial demonstrates how to use this important technique.

Tutorial: Validating Fields at the Record Level of a Table Frame

Suppose that you wish to make sure that the user hasn't entered a date beyond today's date in the *Contact Date* field of the customer table.

On Disk: \ANSWERS\RECORD1.FSL

Quick Step

On the record object of a table frame, check whether the field has an appropriate value. If it doesn't, set the error code to `CanNotDepart`.

Step By Step

1. Set your working directory to TUTORIAL. Create a new form with the ORDERS.DB table in the data model (see Figure 18.16).

2. Add lines 3–9 to the **canDepart** method of the record object of the table frame bound to ORDERS.DB.

```
1:      ;TableFrame.Record :: canDepart
2:      method canDepart(var eventInfo MoveEvent)
3:          if Sale_Date > today() then
```

```
4:                    eventInfo.setErrorCode(CanNotDepart)
5:                    msgStop("Invalid Date!", "Sale date is invalid.")
6:                    moveTo(Sale_Date)
7:            endIf
8:        endmethod
```

Figure 18.16. Set up form for the tutorial.

You also can use a validity check at the table structure level. When you restructure a table, you can use today in the maximum validity check field. In fact, this should be your first choice for data validity.

3. Check the syntax, save your work, and run the form. Press F9 to enter Edit mode, and try to change the *Sale Date* field to tomorrow's date. You get a message indicating that the date is invalid, and the record turns yellow while the message is displayed (see Figure 18.17).

Analysis

In step 2, line 3 checks whether the date entered in the *Sale_Date* field is later than today's date. If it is, line 4 sets the CanNotDepart error code. Lines 5–8 notify the user of the inaccurate date by changing the color of the box to yellow, displaying a warning, and moving back to the field. You can customize your own warning system if you like.

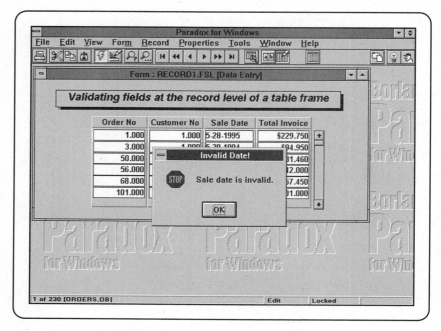

Figure 18.17. RECORD1.FSL. Using the record object of a table name to validate values.

Fly Away

Fly Away is the default behavior that occurs in a TableView and table frame when you add a new record or change the key of a record. The new or altered record moves to its ordered location in the table and appears to fly away. You can disable Fly Away with ObjectPAL. I recommend that you use the following code to disable Fly Away:

```
1:  ;Record :: action
2:  method action(var eventInfo ActionEvent)
3:    ;This code is attached to a TableFrame or MRO
4:      if eventInfo.id() = DataUnlockRecord then
5:        self.action(DataPostRecord)
6:      endIf
7:  endmethod
```

This code tells the default Paradox behavior to stay with the record as it flies away. If the record flies away as the code executes, Paradox flies with it because that's the default behavior for `DataPostRecord`. First, the record takes its new location. Then, Paradox moves off the record. In effect, Paradox has followed the record to its new location.

Using a 1-By-1 Multirecord Object

Using the record object of a table frame to manipulate data at a record level is great, but what do you do when you have several fields? You use a 1-by-1 multirecord object (MRO) and surround the fields, which causes the MRO to bind to the underlying table. A *multirecord* object (MRO) is an object that displays several records at once in a box. It is used with forms and reports. You can use a 1-by-1 MRO to add a record object to fields on a form. This enables you to do field validation by using the record object of the MRO in a way similar to how you use the record of a table frame. This is because the fields in the MRO are contained by a record object. Having a record object means that you can use the **canDepart** built-in method to trap for record departs, among other record-oriented tasks.

The first step in using this technique is to place an MRO over the fields you want to validate (see Figure 18.18). Don't panic as your screen becomes jumbled. Next, change the MRO to a 1-by-1 MRO and resize it so that the fields fit within it. This cleans up your screen and automatically binds the record object to the underlying table (see Figure 18.19). After you set up the record object, you can use the MRO record object's methods to manipulate the data at the record level.

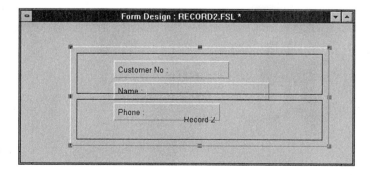

Figure 18.18. The first step in using the record object of an MRO to manipulate data at the record level.

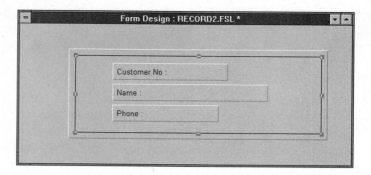

Figure 18.19. The second step in using the record object of an MRO to manipulate data at the record level.

The next tutorial demonstrates the important technique of using a 1-by-1 MRO.

Tutorial: Validating Fields at the Record Level by Using a Multirecord Object

Suppose that you wish to make sure that the user doesn't leave the telephone number field of the customer table empty.

On Disk: \ANSWERS\RECORD2.FSL

Quick Step

On the record object of a table frame, check whether the field has an appropriate value. If it doesn't, set the error code to CanNotDepart.

Step By Step

1. Set your working directory to TUTORIAL. Create a new form with the CUSTOMER.DB table in the data model. Create field objects and define them to *Customer No, Name,* and *Phone,* respectively (refer to Figures 18.18 and 18.19 to help set up the 1-by-1 MRO).

2. Add lines 3–9 to the **canDepart** method of the record object in the Multirecord object.

```
1:    ;MRO.Record :: canDepart
2:    method canDepart(var eventInfo MoveEvent)
3:        if Phone.isBlank() then
```

```
4:            eventInfo.setErrorCode(CanNotDepart)
5:            self.color = Yellow
6:            msgStop("Warning!", "Phone number required on this
               form.")
7:            self.color = Transparent
8:            moveTo(Phone)
9:        endIf
10:   endmethod
```

3. Check the syntax, save your work as RECORD2.FSL, and run the form. Press F9 to enter Edit mode, and try to leave the *Phone* field blank. You get a message indicating that the phone number is required, and the record turns yellow while the message is displayed (see Figure 18.20).

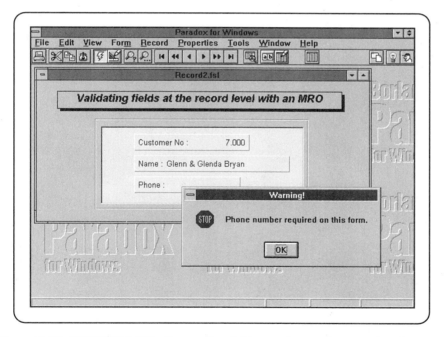

Figure 18.20. RECORD2.FSL. Surrounding fields on a form with an MRO and using the record object of the MRO to validate field values.

Analysis

Line 3 checks whether the Phone field is blank. If it is, line 4 sets the
`CanNotDepart` error code. Lines 5–8 notify the user by turning the box yellow,
displaying a warning, and moving back to the field. You can customize these
warnings to your own liking.

Normally, you do field validation at the table restructure level; you don't use
ObjectPAL at all. Proper field validation must be at the table level. Otherwise,
your users could open the table directly and enter bad data. If you want to
restrict input only on a particular form, however, you can use the techniques
discussed in the previous two tutorials.

MANIPULATING STRINGS AND HANDLING THE KEYBOARD

MANIPULATING STRINGS

It's important to be familiar with string manipulation. For example, most programming and macro languages have left and right string functions—that is, a single step returns the left or right *n* characters of a string. You can accomplish both these actions with the subStr() method, but the syntax is a little tricky. To assign the left three characters of a string variable *s1* to the string variable *s2*, type the following into the **pushButton** method of a button:

Using KeyEvent *methods and procedures*

Using **keyPhysical**

Character sets

```
 1:   ;Button :: pushButton
 2:   method pushButton(var eventInfo Event)
 3:       var
 4:              s1, s2     String
 5:       endVar
 6:
 7:       s1 = "Felicia"
 8:       s2 = s1.subStr(1, 3)
 9:       s2.view() ;Displays "Fel".
10:   endMethod
```

Doing the similar procedure with the right three characters is trickier. To assign the last three characters of *s1* to *s2*, use

```
 1:   ;Button :: pushButton
 2:   method pushButton(var eventInfo Event)
 3:       var
 4:              s1, s2     String
 5:       endVar
 6:
 7:       s1 = "Felicia"
 8:       s2 = s1.subStr(s1.size()-3, 3)
 9:       s2.view() ;Displays "cia".
10:   endMethod
```

By using the subStr() method with the size() method, you can extract from a string all the combinations of values that you need.

THE PATH OF A KEY PRESS

A *keycode* is a code that represents a keyboard character in ObjectPAL. A keycode can be an ASCII number, an IBM extended keycode number, or a string that represents a keyname known to Paradox. When a user presses a key on the keyboard, one of two things occurs. Either Windows processes it, or Paradox processes it. For example, Windows processes it when the sequence Ctrl+Esc is used. When Paradox processes it, **keyPhysical** always sees it, and in the case of a character, **keyPhysical** passes the event to **keyChar** (see Figure 19.1).

The steps to trapping a keypress are as follows:

1. Decide whether you need to trap for a character or virtual key. If you wish to trap for a character such as a, A, b, B, 1, !, or @, then use either **keyPhysical** or **keyChar**. If you wish to trap for virtual keys such as F1 or Esc, then you must use **keyPhysical**.

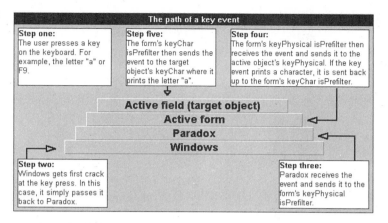

Figure 19.1. The path of a key event.

2. Decide at what level you need to trap for the key press. The two usual places are the form's prefilter or directly on the field.

3. Inspect the *eventInfo* packet with either char() or vChar() to trap for the key press. If case does not matter, then use vChar(). If case does matter, then use char().

As long as a field has focus, key presses do not bubble because the key press is used up by the field. Therefore, the two best choices to trap for key presses is the form's prefilter or on the field itself.

Using KeyEvent Methods and Procedures

You can use the KeyEvent methods and procedures to allow you to get and set information about keystroke events. Both **keyChar** and **keyPhysical** methods are triggered by KeyEvents. Table 19.1 lists the KeyEvent methods and procedures.

TABLE 19.1. KeyEvent class methods and procedures.	
char	reason*
charAnsiCode	setAltKeyDown
errorCode*	setChar
getTarget*	setControlKeyDown
isAltKeyDown	setErrorCode*
isControlKeyDown	setReason*
isFirstTime*	setShiftKeyDown
isFromUI	setVChar
isPreFilter*	setVCharCode
isShiftKeyDown	vChar
isTargetSelf*	vCharCode

*Inherited from the Event type

INTERRUPTING A LOOP

You can use form's prefilter with vChar() to trap a key press. For example, sometimes you may want to give the user the option of interrupting a loop. This type of control adds a touch of professionalism to your application. The following tutorial demonstrates how you can enable the user to interrupt a loop by pressing the Esc key.

Tutorial: Interrupting a Loop

Suppose that you wish to loop to 1000 and display the counter in the status bar as the loop increments. The twist on this tutorial is that you need to allow the user to press Esc to interrupt the loop.

On Disk: \ANSWERS\QUITLOOP.FSL

Quick Steps

1. Set up a loop to count to 1000.
2. In the `isPreFilter()` portion of the form's **keyPhysical**, check for virtual character *VK_Escape* with `vChar()`. See Appendix H for a complete list of virtual keys.
3. If the user presses Esc, set a flag variable to true.
4. Inside the loop, sleep for 1 millisecond to yield to Windows. Then, check whether the flag is set to true.

Step By Step

1. Create a new form and place a button labeled Count to 1000 on it (see Figure 19.2).

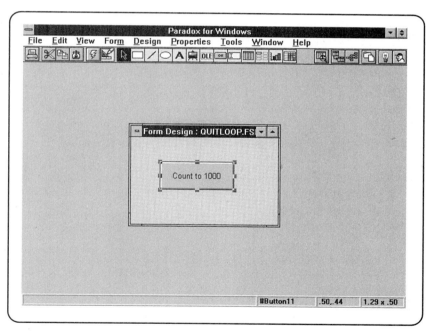

Figure 19.2. Set up form for quit loop tutorial.

2. Add line 3 to the Var window of the form.

```
1:     ;Form :: Var
2:     Var
3:         lFlag Logical
4:     endVar
```

3. Add lines 5–7 to the **keyPhysical** method of the form.

```
1:     ;Form :: keyPhysical
2:     method keyPhysical(var eventInfo KeyEvent)
3:     if eventInfo.isPreFilter() then
4:         ;This code executes for each object on the form
5:         if eventInfo.vchar() = "VK_ESCAPE" then
6:             lFlag = True
7:         endIf
8:     else
9:         ;This code executes only for the form
10:    endif
11:    endmethod
```

4. Add lines 3–16 to the **pushButton** method of the Count to 1000 button.

```
1:     ;Button :: pushButton
2:     method pushButton(var eventInfo Event)
3:         var
4:             siCounter SmallInt
5:         endvar
6:
7:         lFlag = False
8:
9:         for siCounter from 1 to 1000
10:            message(siCounter)
11:            sleep(1)
12:            if lFlag = True then
13:                message("Counting interrupted")
14:                quitloop
15:            endIf
16:        endFor
17:    endmethod
```

5. Check the syntax, run the form, and click the button. As the computer counts to one thousand, the counter is shown in the status bar. Press Esc to interrupt the loop (see Figure 19.3).

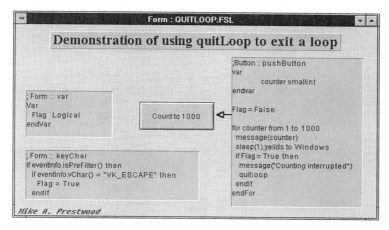

Figure 19.3. QUITLOOP.FSL.

Analysis

In step 2, line 3 declares a variable global to the form.

In step 3, line 5 checks whether the user presses the Esc key. If the user does, line 6 sets the logical *lFlag* to true.

In step 4, line 4 declares a variable private to a method for use in the `for` loop (lines 9–16). Line 7 sets the flag to false in case the user presses Esc, setting the flag to true. Line 10 displays the value of `counter` in the status bar. Line 11 sleeps for one millisecond, which is plenty of time to yield to Windows. This enables the Esc key to sneak in. Line 12 checks whether the flag has changed to true. If the flag is true, line 13 displays a message, and line 14 quits the loop.

> In place of `sleep(1)`, you can use `sleep()` without a parameter—`sleep()`. In that case, Windows automatically permits two events to occur.

USING KEYPHYSICAL

As already discussed, use **keyPhysical** when you want to trap for all keyboard keys. Use **keyChar** when you want to trap for only characters that are printable to the screen.

ECHOING KEYBOARD INPUT FROM ONE FIELD TO ANOTHER

Suppose that you created two field objects—*field1* and *field2*. You want *field2* to echo whatever you type into *field1*—including Backspace, Delete, and Enter—just as though you were typing directly into *field2*. How do you do this?

A problem that often confronts users is that values aren't committed to the field until endMethod. Remember that the default behavior occurs last in a method. Therefore, when you use **keyPhysical** and **keyChar**, invoke the default behavior to commit the last keystroke. For example:

```
1:  ;Field1 :: keyPhysical
2:  doDefault
3:  field2.value = self.value
```

HIDING USER INPUT

Sometimes you need to hide user input, such as passwords or sensitive data. One technique is to make the background color the same as the text color. Showing an asterisk for each character as the user enters it, however, requires ObjectPAL. The following tutorial shows you how to hide user input.

Tutorial: Hiding User Input

Suppose that you wish to hide user input by displaying an asterisk for each character the user types.

On Disk: \ANSWERS\PASSWORD.FSL

Quick Steps
1. Invoke the default behavior to commit the character to the field.
2. Add the character most recently typed to the password field or variable.
3. Fill the input field with asterisks.
4. Provide a way to reset or clear the password.

Step By Step

1. Create a new form with two fields and a button on it (see Figure 19.4). Name the first field *Input_Field* and label it *Input*. Name the second field *Password* and label it *Password*. Label the button Reset.

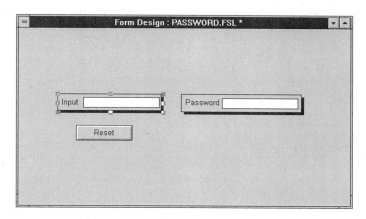

Figure 19.4. Set up form for the hiding user input tutorial.

2. Add lines 3–5 to the **keyChar** method of the *Input_Field* field.

```
1:    ;Field :: keyChar
2:    method keyChar(var eventInfo KeyEvent)
3:       doDefault
4:       Password = Password +
          ➥Input_Field.subStr(size(Input_Field))
5:       Input_Field = fill("*", size(Password))
6:    endmethod
```

3. Add lines 3 and 4 to the **pushButton** method of the Reset button.

```
1:    ;Button :: pushButton
2:    method pushButton(var eventInfo Event)
3:       Password = ""
4:       Input_Field = ""
5:    endmethod
```

4. Check the syntax, save the form as PASSWORD.FSL, and run the form. Type some values into the field. Click the button to reset the field (see Figure 19.5).

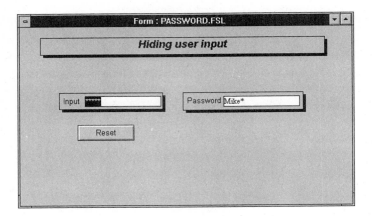

Figure 19.5. PASSWORD.FSL. One technique for hiding user input.

Analysis

In step 2, line 3 invokes the default behavior to commit the character to the field. Line 4 adds the last character to the *Password* field. Line 5 fills the input field with one asterisk for each character in the *Password* field.

In step 3, lines 3 and 4 on the **pushButton** method of the button provide a way to clear the password.

This tutorial is a beginning technique for hiding user input. For example, the user's input is echoed to a field called *Password* instead of directly to a variable. To make this routine work without the field, delete the field and declare a *Password* String variable. Remember to initiate the variable—perhaps when you open the form.

Another technique is to use the noEcho property on the password field and to send each keystroke there by using the UIObject keyPhysical() method on the input field's built-in **keyPhysical** method.

USE THE *KEY*PHYSICAL METHOD OF ANY OBJECT TO ECHO KEYBOARD INPUT TO THE STATUS BAR

*Put the following two lines of code into the **keyPhysical** method of an active object:*

```
message(eventInfo.vChar())
sleep(250)
```

When you run the form and press the keys on your keyboard, the vChar() name of each key is echoed to the status bar.

To try this out, create a new form and put the two lines of code in the built-in **keyPhysical** method of the page. Run the form and press some keys.

LIMITING KEYBOARD INPUT

If you want to limit the user's input, use either the **keyChar** or **keyPhysical** methods of the input object. If you want to limit the user's input to characters, use **keyChar**. If you want to control all keystrokes, use **keyPhysical**. The next tutorial shows you how to limit the user's input.

Tutorial: Limiting a User's Input

Suppose that you wish to limit the user's input to uppercase, lowercase, and numbers. In addition, you wish to allow a few editing keys. The technique presented here can be used to control any keys.

On Disk: \ANSWERS\ONLYKEYS.FSL

Quick Steps

1. Declare a String variable.
2. Use the isPreFilter() portion of the **keyPhysical** method of the form.
3. Trap for unwanted characters, or use disableDefault to trap for the characters you want.

Step By Step

1. Create a form with a single undefined field (see Figure 19.6).
2. Add line 3 to the Var window of the form.

```
1:    ;Form :: Var
2:    Var
3:        ans  String
4:    endVar
```

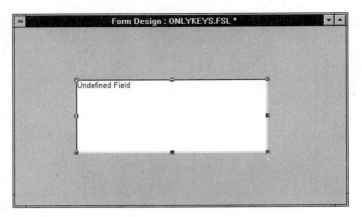

Figure 19.6. Set up form for limiting a user's input tutorial.

3. Add lines 7–18 to the **keyPhysical** of the form.

```
1:  ;Form :: keyPhysical
2:  method keyPhysical(var eventInfo KeyEvent)
3:     if eventInfo.isPreFilter()
4:     then
5:        ; This code executes for each object on the form.
6:
7:     ans = eventInfo.char()
8:
9:     switch
10:       case eventInfo.vCharCode() = VK_DELETE : doDefault
          ➥return
11:       case eventInfo.vCharCode() = VK_BACK    : doDefault
          ➥return
12:       case eventInfo.vCharCode() = VK_LEFT    : doDefault
          ➥return
13:       case eventInfo.vCharCode() = VK_RIGHT   : doDefault
          ➥return
14:       case ans >="A" and ans <="z"  : doDefault return
15:       case ans >="0" and ans <="9"  : doDefault return
16:       case ans = " "                : doDefault return
17:       otherwise                     : disableDefault
18:     endSwitch
```

```
19:
20:    else
21:        ; This code executes only for the form.
22:
23:        endif
24: endmethod
```

4. Check the syntax, save the form as ONLYKEYS.FSL, and run it. Type some characters. Be sure sure to try numbers, letters, and special characters (see Figure 19.7).

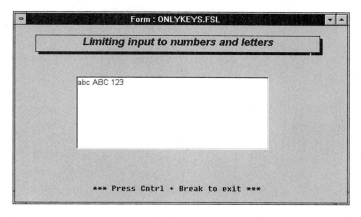

Figure 19.7. ONLYKEYS.FSL. Limit the user's input to numbers, letters, and spaces.

Analysis

In step 2, line 3 declares a String variable that is used in step 3, line 7 to capture the Windows virtual character. Because char() returns a null character if a nonprintable character is detected, line 17 disables the default behavior and returns control. (In this case, returning control is a way of exiting the method.) If the character is a printable character, line 7 puts its virtual character into the String variable. It will be used in lines 9–18. Line 14 checks for letters. Line 15 checks for numbers. Line 16 checks for the space character. Line 17 disables all other characters.

This a good routine to turn into a custom method that you can call whenever you need to limit user input. If you don't want to enable the user to enter a space, delete line 16. This technique is useful when you want input for a filename. Alter this routine in other ways to suit your needs. You can't trap for everything, however. Some keys and key combinations are reserved by Windows—for example, Ctrl+F4.

The FELICIA.FSL form in Figure 19.8 uses a technique similar to the one in this tutorial. It adds pictures and sound routines to create a game that introduces an infant to the keyboard.

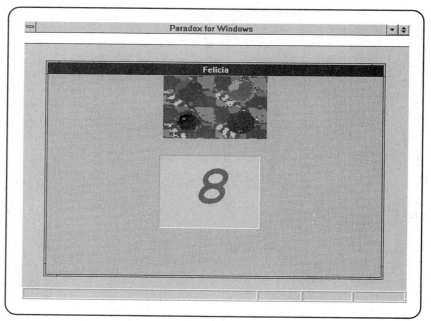

Figure 19.8. FELICIA.FSL.

CHARACTER SETS

You can't store all characters in a Paradox table. This is a limitation of current computer technology. The issue is what Paradox should store to a table. For example, should it store Windows ANSI characters or OEM DOS characters?

ANSI is an acronym for American National Standards Institute. The ANSI set consists of eight-bit codes that represent 256 standard characters—letters, numbers, and symbols. The ANSI set is used by Windows applications. *extended ASCII* is a character set designed by IBM. IBM extended the standard ASCII set from seven-bit codes to eight-bit codes and added more characters. The extended ASCII set contains 256 characters.

As a Windows product, the Paradox table structure has to be able to store Windows ANSI characters. Paradox supports dBASE and Paradox tables, however, and traditionally these table structures store OEM DOS characters. Therefore, Paradox must be able to deal with both character sets: the character set traditionally used by other products that used the table structures before Paradox for Windows and the character set used by Windows. In Paradox for Windows, the character set is determined by the table language driver. The problem is that although Microsoft controls both DOS and Windows, the two character sets, OEM and ANSI, are incompatible. You must decide between the two when you create your table.

One solution is to use the strict translation option of the Link tool. When strict translation is checked (the default), only the first 128 characters are stored. If you uncheck it, you enable your users to add characters that may not be supported by a different table language. There are disadvantages, however. Read the online help on strict translation for further information.

USING SENDKEYS()

This procedure introduced in version 4.5 sends keystrokes to the Windows message loop. The syntax for sendKeys() is as follows:

sendKeys(const **keyText** String [, const **wait** Logical]) Logical

The **wait** argument indicates whether to send the keys immediately (TRUE), or to wait until the current method has finished (FALSE). In most cases, FALSE is the preferred setting.

Table 19.2 lists the keys used with sendKeys().

Table 19.2. Using sendKeys().

Key	Code
Shift	+
Control	^
Alt	%
Backspace	{BACKSPACE}, {BS}, {BKSP}, {VK_BACK}
Break	{BREAK}, {VK_BREAK}
Caps Lock	{CAPSLOCK}, {VK_CAPTIAL}
Clear	{CLEAR}, {VK_CLEAR}
Del	{DELETE}, {DEL}, {VK_DELETE}
Down Arrow	{DOWN}, {VK_DOWN}
End	{END}, {VK_END}
Enter	{ENTER}, {RETURN}, {VK_RETURN} (the character ~)
Esc	{ESCAPE}, {ESC}, {VK_ESCAPE}
Help	{HELP}, {VK_HELP}
Home	{HOME}, {VK_HOME}
Ins	{INSERT}, {VK_INSERT}
Left Arrow	{LEFT}, {VK_LEFT}
Num Lock	{NUMLOCK}, {VK_NUMLOCK}
Page Down	{PGDN}, {VK_NEXT}
Page Up	{PGUP}, {VK_PRIOR}
Print Screen	{PRTSC}, {VK_SNAPSHOT}
Right Arrow	{RIGHT}, {VK_RIGHT}
Scroll Lock	{SCROLLLOCK}, {VK_SCROLL}
Tab	{TAB}, {VK_TAB}
Up Arrow	{UP}, {VK_UP}
F1	{F1}, {VK_F1}
F2	{F2}, {VK_F2}
F3	{F3}, {VK_F3}

Key	Code
F4	{F4}, {VK_F4}
F5	{F5}, {VK_F5}
F6	{F6}, {VK_F6}
F7	{F7}, {VK_F7}
F8	{F8}, {VK_F8}
F9	{F9}, {VK_F9}
F10	{F10}, {VK_F10}

20

CHAPTER

PROPERTIES

READ-ONLY PROPERTIES

There are two categories of properties: read/write
and read-only. Figure 20.1 shows the Display Objects and Properties dialog box. You're familiar with
the read/write properties. The read-only properties
include Arrived, BlankRecord, Class, ContainerName,
FieldNo, FieldSize, FieldType, Focus, FullName,
FullSize, IndexField, Locked, and Required. The
following statement assumes that an object named
theBox is on a form:

```
1:  ;Button :: pushButton
2:  message("Full containership path is " +
        ➥theBox.fullName)
```

Read-only properties

Using the first property

*Playing tricks with
properties*

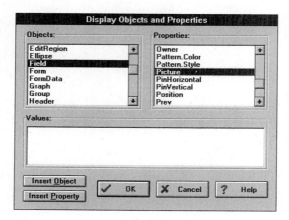

Figure 20.1. The Display Objects and Properties dialog box.

If you're having trouble with scope or the containership hierarchy and you need to know the full containership path of an object, use the preceding statement.

Only UIObjects have properties. Objects such as TCursors and strings do not.

Refer to Appendix E, "Properties," for a complete list of properties grouped by class, complete with a sample value. You read and set properties in ObjectPAL by means of dot notation, just as you do with the other aspects of ObjectPAL syntax. You are familiar with the basic syntax for properties. The following two examples should look familiar:

```
1:   Last_Name.value = "Homann"
2:   theBox.color = Red
```

Here are examples of setting the value for a read/write property. If you have a box named theBox on a form, you could put the following code on a button:

```
1:   ;Button :: pushButton
2:   method pushButton(var eventInfo Event)
3:        theBox.color = Red
4:        theBox.Frame.Color = Blue
5:        theBox.Frame.Style = DashDotFrame
6:        theBox.Frame.Thickness = LWidth3Points
7:        theBox.Pattern.Color = Yellow
8:        theBox.Pattern.Style = LatticePattern
9:   endmethod
```

No matter which property is set, the syntax is the same: *objectName.property = constant*. Use this syntax whenever you set the value of a read/write property.

The previous examples set the values of properties. The syntax for reading an object's property value is similar. When you get the current value of a read/write or read-only property, you use the syntax *objectName.property*, which returns the current value of the object's specified property.

The following code displays the current color of the object named theBox in the status bar. Usually, you use this technique to add logic to your application:

```
1:   ;Button :: pushButton
2:   method pushButton(var eventInfo Event)
3:         message(theBox.color)
4:   endmethod
```

In the following code, the value property of the field named GotoPage is used to determine whether it should display a message and move to Page2:

```
1:   ;Button :: pushButton
2:   method pushButton(var eventInfo Event)
3:        if GotoPage.value = "Page2" then
4:             message("Moving to page two")
5:             Page2.moveTo()
6:        endIf
7:   endmethod
```

USING THE *FIRST* PROPERTY OF AN OBJECT

The first property returns the full containership path of the first contained object. You can display the string it returns in a message information dialog box. For example, type the following code in the **pushButton** method of a button. It displays the full path of the label the button contains.

```
1:   ;Button :: pushButon
2:   method pushButton(var eventInfo Event)
3:        msgInfo("Button label", self.first)
4:   endMethod
```

A more practical use of first is to write generic routines. For example, suppose that you wish to change the font color of the label of a button. You could rename the button's label and use the font.color property of the object. This technique, however, uses up more of the symbol table which is limited to 64K. If you change the name of an object, name and its 4-byte address are stored in the symbol table. Therefore, use the following code instead.

```
1:   ;Button :: pushButon
2:   method pushButton(var eventInfo Event)
3:        var
```

```
4:             f     Form
5:        endVar
6:
7:        f.attach()
8:        f.(self.first).font.color = Red
9:   endMethod
```

Note in the above code two things: the use of `attach()` and parentheses. `first` returns a string, not an object. In order to use the string in ObjectPAL, you need to dereference it. Dereferencing in ObjectPAL requires two rules: an object and the use of parentheses. You need to start back in the containership path one object and then put the string in parenthesis (see the preceding line 7). The following tutorial puts this technique to work.

Tutorial: Toggling the Font Color of the Label of a Button

Now you'll see a full example. Suppose that you wish to toggle the font color of the label of a button between red and black.

On Disk: \ANSWERS\TOGGLE3.FSL

Quick Steps

1. Check the font color of the label on the font.
2. Switch the font color to the other color.

Step By Step

1. Change your working directory to TUTORIAL and create a new form. Place a button on it.

2. Add lines 2 through 15 to the **pushButton** method. (As always, typing the comments is optional.)

```
1:          ;Button :: pushButton
2:   method pushButton(var eventInfo Event)
3:     var
4:        f Form      ;Declare a Form variable.
5:     endVar
6:
7:      f.attach()    ;Attach to current form.
8:
9:     ;Notice the use of the Form variable and
10:     ;the use of parantheses to dereference
11:     ;the string.
12:     if f.(self.first).font.color = Red then
```

```
13:        f.(self.first).font.color = Black
14:    else
15:        f.(self.first).font.color = Red
16:    endIf
17: endmethod
```

3. Check the syntax, save the new form as TOGGLE3.FSL, and run it (see Figure 20.2).

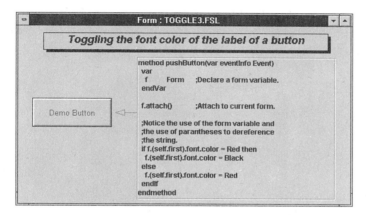

Figure 20.2. TOGGLE3.FSL.

Analysis

In step 2, line 4 declares *f* as a Form variable, which line 6 uses to attach to the current form. Lines 12–16 use the form variable with the object variable `self` and the `first` property to inspect and alter the `color` property of the button label's text.

ADDING SCROLL BARS TO A GRAPHIC FIELD

A fun exercise is to use a property that you normally set interactively in your code. The next tutorial toggles the horizontal and vertical scroll bars on a field.

Tutorial: Adding Scroll Bars to a Graphic Field

Suppose that you wish to add scroll bars to a Graphic field when the user double-clicks it.

On Disk: \ANSWERS\SCROLL.FSL

Quick Steps

1. Use delayScreenUpdates() to prevent the image from displaying twice.
2. Use an if structure to check whether the scroll bars are on or off.
3. Based on the result of the if statement, toggle both scroll bars on or off.

Step By Step

1. Create a new form bound to the GRAPHICS.DB table. If you prefer, alter it so that it looks similar to the form in Figure 20.3.

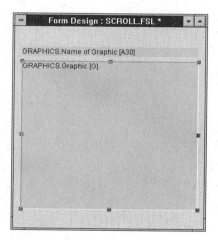

Figure 20.3. Set up form for adding scroll bars tutorial.

2. Add lines 3–15 to the **mouseDouble** method of the *Graphic* field.

```
1:    ;Field :: doubleClick
2:    method mouseDouble(var eventInfo MouseEvent)
3:       delayScreenUpdates(Yes)
4:       if self.HorizontalScrollBar = On then
5:         message("Removing scroll bars...")
6:         self.HorizontalScrollBar = Off
7:         self.VerticalScrollBar = Off
8:         message("")
9:       else
10:        message("Adding scroll bars...")
```

```
11:        self.HorizontalScrollBar = On
12:        self.VerticalScrollBar = On
13:        message("")
14:     endIf
15:     delayScreenUpdates(No)
16:  endmethod
```

3. Check your syntax and run the form. Click the graphic several times and watch the scroll bars come and go (see Figure 20.4).

Figure 20.4. The form from SCROLL.FSL.

Analysis

In step 2, line 3 turns on a feature that delays the drawing of the screen until the operation is complete. Without this line of code, the graphic would refresh twice, once for each scroll bar added. To see this for yourself, put a semicolon in front of line 3. This disables the line of code. Run the form. Line 4 determines whether you need to add or remove both scroll bars by checking whether the horizontal scroll bar is on.

GRAPHIC2.FSL demonstrates toggling scroll bars by using a custom method called `toggleScrollBars()` on the form.

If the horizontal scroll bar is on in line 3, lines 4–7 remove both scroll bars. Line 4 tells the user that the scroll bars are being removed. Lines 5 and 6 turn off the horizontal and vertical scroll bars. Line 7 clears the status bar.

If the horizontal scroll bar isn't on in line 3, lines 9–12 add both scroll bars. Line 9 tells the user that the scroll bars are being added. Lines 10 and 11 turn on the horizontal and vertical scroll bars. GRAPHIC2.FSL on disk uses this routine in a custom method on the form (see Figure 20.5).

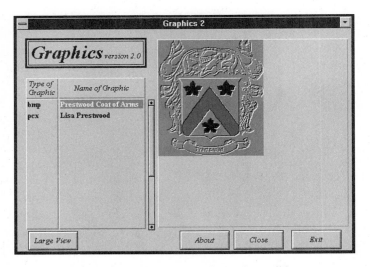

Figure 20.5. GRAPHIC2.FSL. This form uses the toggle scroll bars routine in a custom method on the form.

Playing Tricks with Properties

With all the various properties of objects in ObjectPAL, it is easy to do tricks and add interesting effects to your applications. You can place a box on a form, add a little code to the **mouseEnter** and **mouseExit** of the box, and watch the box fade in and out when you move over it. For example:

```
1:  ;Box :: mouseEnter
2:  method mouseEnter(var eventInfo MouseEvent)
3:    box.visible = False
4:  endmethod
```

```
1:   ;Box :: mouseExit
2:   method mouseExit(var eventInfo MouseEvent)
3:     box.visible = True
4:   endmethod
```

On disk is the form BOX.FSL, which demonstrates the preceding technique (see Figure 20.6).

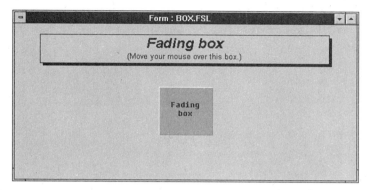

Figure 20.6. BOX.FSL.

AN IMPORTANT TECHNIQUE FOR MODIFYING RUNNING FORMS

Sometimes you need to open another form, alter it, and close it. When you do, you are prompted to save the changes to the form; this is a very undesirable feature for a finished application. You could deliver the form and the problem would go away, or you could use the designModified property of the form. For example:

```
1:   f.designModified = False
```

In essence, you are telling the form that nothing was changed, when in fact it was.

DEMONSTRATION OF USER-SELECTABLE COLORS

Some Windows applications let the user adjust the colors of objects to the user's own liking. For an extra bit of professionalism, you can add this feature to your own applications. On disk is the form SETTINGS.FSL, which demonstrates a technique to allow users to select their own colors for the form (see Figure 20.7).

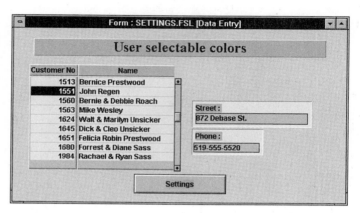

Figure 20.7. SETTINGS.FSL.

The interesting bit of code in this form is in the form's Var window and **open** method. This code first opens a TCursor in the then portion of the **open** method, and then uses the TCursor to locate color values in the SETTINGS.DB table. You can edit the SETTINGS.DB table to change colors or add objects whose color is to be changed.

```
1:  ;Form :: Var
2:  Var
3:    tcSettings    TCursor
4:    uiSettings    UIObject
5:  endVar

1:  ;Form :: open
2:  method open(var eventInfo Event)
3:  if eventInfo.isPreFilter() then
4:    ; This code executes for each object on the form.
5:    eventInfo.getTarget(uiSettings)
6:    if tcSettings.locate("Object Class", uiSettings.class) then
7:        uiSettings.color = tcSettings."Color"
```

```
 8:     endIf
 9:   else
10:     ; This code executes only for the form.
11:     tcSettings.open("SETTINGS.DB")
12:
13:   endif
14: endmethod
```

The other interesting bit of code is in the **changeValue** method of the *Property_Value* field on the second page. It checks to make sure that the user enters a valid color by trying to set the `color` property of the *boxSample* box (see Figure 20.8).

```
1:   ;fld :: changeValue
2:   method changeValue(var eventInfo ValueEvent)
3:     try
4:         boxSample.color = eventInfo.newValue()
5:     onFail
6:         DisableDefault
7:         msgStop("Warning", "Invalid color")
8:     endTry
9:   endmethod
```

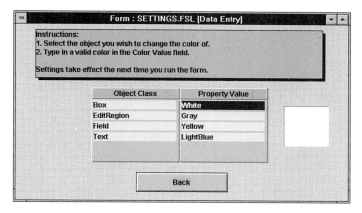

Figure 20.8. The second page of SETTINGS.FSL.

MANIPULATING DESIGN OBJECTS

MANIPULATING UIOBJECTS IN RUN MODE

A *pixel* is an abbreviation for picture element. Pixels vary in size depending on your monitor. One physical pixel is one dot on your screen, regardless of resolution. Contrast this with a *twip,* which is a physical unit where 1,440 twips are equal to one inch, regardless of resolution. Most ObjectPAL properties that manipulate size are in twips, not pixels.

GLOSSARY TERM

Using variables for UIObjects

Keeping a button pressed

Using switchIndex

Adding scroll bars to an object during runtime

USING THE UIOBJECT VARIABLE

Objects that you place on forms and reports are UIObjects (User Interface Objects). Only UIObjects that you place on forms contain built-in methods. The form itself is also a UIObject—it has built-in methods and responds to events.

ObjectPAL offers tremendous flexibility in manipulating UIObjects during runtime. Table 21.1

lists the UIObject methods and procedures. As noted earlier in the TCursor type, version 4.5 users should note that setFilter() was replaced with setRange().

Table 21.1. UIObject methods and procedures.

action	enumUIObjectProperties
atFirst	execMethod
atLast	forceRefresh
attach	getBoundingBox
bringToFront	getGenFilter
broadcastAction	getPosition
cancelEdit	getProperty
convertPointWithRespectTo	getPropertyAsString
copyFromArray	getRange
copyToArray	getRGB
copyToToolBar	hasMouse
create	home
currRecord	insertAfterRecord
delete	insertBeforeRecord
deleteRecord	insertRecord
dropGenFilter	isContainerValid
edit	isEdit
empty	isEmpty
end	isLastMouseClickedValid
endEdit	isLastMouseRightClickedValid
enumFieldNames	isRecordDeleted
enumLocks	keyChar
enumObjectNames	keyPhysical
enumSource	killTimer
enumSourceToFile	locate
enumUIClasses	locateNext
enumUIObjectNames	locateNextPattern

locatePattern	nKeyFields
locatePrior	nRecords
locatePriorPattern	pixelsToTwips
lockRecord	postAction
lockStatus	postRecord
menuAction	priorRecord
methodDelete	pushButton
methodGet	recordStatus
methodSet	resync
mouseClick	rgb
mouseDouble	sendToBack
mouseDown	setGenFilter
mouseEnter	setPosition
mouseExit	setProperty
mouseMove	setRange
mouseRightDouble	setTimer
mouseRightDown	skip
mouseRightUp	switchIndex
mouseUp	twipsToPixels
moveTo	unDeleteRecord
moveToRecNo	unlockRecord
moveToRecord	view
nextRecord	wasLastClicked
nFields	wasLastRightClicked

Dereferencing a UIObject

You can create, move, size, and generally change any property of a UIObject. But how do you reference a UIObject with a variable? You do so through dot notation and the use of parentheses. Referencing objects without hard-coding their names in the application adds flexibility to your routines.

When you work with several objects on a form, you might want to perform the same actions on each of the objects at different points in the code. One technique that saves many lines of code is to use a variable to reference an object. Remember the following three rules when you use a variable to reference an object:

- The statement that references an object must include a containership path. In the example that follows, *Page* refers to the name of the actual page in which the (Y) object resides.
- The first object in the path must *not* be a variable.
- Parentheses should surround the name of the variable.

Here is an example of how these rules are applied:

```
1:   for X from 1 to 10
2:   Y = "Box" + strVal(X) ;This evaluates Y = "Box1" for
3:   Page.(Y).color = Blue ;the first iteration of the
4:                         ;for loop
5:   endFor
```

This code changes the color of the objects named *Box1* through *Box10* to the color blue. Remember that it's easier to access the objects if you rename them yourself. If the name of the object is the previous name suffixed by a number—for example, *Box1*—you can use code. The sample form UIObject.FSL demonstrates this technique (see Figure 21.1).

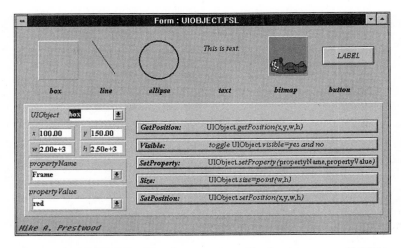

Figure 21.1. UIOBJECT.FSL. This form uses variables for the names of UIObjects.

TIME SAVER

Object Tree Is Best for Renaming Many Objects

If you need to rename many objects, use the Object Tree. By selecting and inspecting each object, you can quickly rename many objects.

READ-ONLY PROPERTIES AND DEREFERENCING

On disk is the form READONLY.FSL, which demonstrates two important features: read-only properties and dereferencing a UIObject. This form uses dereferencing to allow you to browse the various read-only properties of a field.

The interesting bit of code in this form is on the **pushButton** method of the Display property result button (see line 3 that follows).

```
1:   ;Button :: pushButton
2:   method pushButton(var eventInfo Event)
3:   message(pge1.(fldName.value).getProperty(fldProperty.value))
4:   endmethod
```

Line 3 uses dereferencing to use the value in the *fldName* field as an object. When the SS# is selected, the line evaluates to the following:

```
1:   message(pge1.SS#.getProperty(fldProperty.value))
```

Once again, to dereference in ObjectPAL requires two steps:

1. Start back in the containership path at least one object. In this case, *pge1* contains the *fldName* field.

2. Surround the field with parentheses. This tells the compiler to evaluate what is in the parentheses first.

USING TIMERS

Timers in ObjectPAL offer a powerful way to manipulate your environment. A timer enables you to execute an event every so many milliseconds. To set a timer, use setTimer():

```
1:   setTimer(milliSeconds [,repeat])
```

For example, on the **open** method of any object, you can set a timer to trigger every ten seconds:

```
1:  self.setTimer(10000)
```

ANSWERS\TIMER1.FSL demonstrates the above line of code.

After you set the timer, add the code that you want to execute on the **timer** method of the object. For example:

```
1:  method timer(var eventInfo TimerEvent)
2:    msgInfo("10 second timer", "Press OK")
3:  endmethod
```

Windows timers operate at a minimum of 55 milliseconds even if you specify less than 55 in `sleep()` or with **Timer**. Therefore, the fastest timer that you can have is every 55 milliseconds.

You can use timers for a multitude of tasks, such as

- Executing a set of commands every *n* milliseconds
- Checking the system time or date to set scheduled events
- Looping every *n* milliseconds for a multitasking looping technique
- Animating objects by moving and resizing them

ANIMATING A BOX ACROSS THE SCREEN

The following tutorial demonstrates how to move an object across the screen. It uses the **timer** method and the `position` property.

Tutorial: Animating a Box Across the Screen

Suppose that you wish to animate a box moving across a form.

On Disk: \ANSWERS\TIMER2.FSL

Quick Steps

    1. On the box to be animated, set a timer of 100 milliseconds.

2. On the **timer** method of the box, get its current position and move it.

Step By Step

1. Create a new form with a box measuring approximately one inch by one inch (see Figure 21.2).

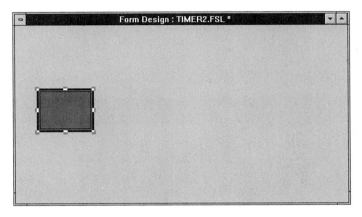

Figure 21.2. Set up form for the tutorial.

2. Add lines 3 and 4 to the Var window of the box

```
1:     ;Box :: Var
2:     Var
3:         posPt   Point
4:         x,y     LongInt
5:     endVar
```

3. Add lines 3–6 to the **open** method of the box.

```
1:     ;Box :: open
2:     method open(var eventInfo Event)
3:         self.setTimer(100)
4:         posPt = self.position
5:         x = posPt.x()
6:         y = posPt.y()
7:     endmethod
```

4. Add lines 3–7 to the **timer** method of the box.

```
1:     ;Box :: timer
2:     method timer(var eventInfo TimerEvent)
```

```
3:        x = x + 50
4:        self.position = Point(x, y)
5:        if x > 5800 then
6:            x = 200
7:        endIf
8:    endmethod
```

5. Check your syntax and run the form. The pull-down menus still work even though the code is executing (see Figure 21.3).

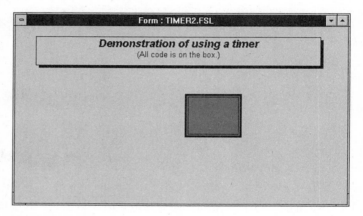

Figure 21.3. TIMER2.FSL.

Analysis

In step 4, line 3 starts the timer so that the code will execute ten times a second (100/1000 = 10). Line 4 from step 2 declares *posPt* a point variable so that you can get the position of the box in line 7. Line 4 in step 2 declares *x* and *y* long integers to store the values in lines 5 and 6.

Line 3 in step 4 increments *x* by 50 for use in line 4 to move the box horizontally to the right by 50 twips. Lines 5–6 check whether the box has traveled as far as you want to the right. If it has, line 6 repositions it to the left.

You can have a lot of fun animating your forms with timers. As an exercise, add objects to this form. You could even introduce a random moving of objects. Timers have two basic uses: for timed events and for multitasking. Use timers when you need to execute a set of commands repeatedly, or when you need to multitask one task with another.

APPS\FELICIA\FELICIA.FSL uses a similar technique to the one just demonstrated to animate a bitmap picture moving across the screen.

LOOPING WITH A TIMER

Suppose that you wish to allow a user to continue using his computer during a `while` loop that will take a long time to complete. To do this, you need to return control to Windows because Windows 3.1 is a nonpreemptive operating system. You won't see function calls in ObjectPAL that are equivalent to `WaitMessage` in Windows SDK. How do you handle this situation? Because it's part of the Windows API, you can call `WaitMessage` directly. To do this, declare it in a Uses statement, and call it. There are, however, two better and easier techniques.

You can use two techniques, depending on how much control you want to give back to Windows. You can insert a `sleep()` statement in your `while` loop, which yields to Windows events. Depending on how complicated the `while` loop is, this might give you enough of a yield. You can add more `sleep()` statements to your code, or you can recode it to use the built-in **timer** method.

Set a **timer** event on a UIObject to fire every x milliseconds. You set x. Then, place one iteration of the `while` loop on the **timer** built-in method. The iteration of the loop will process. You can vary how much you do on each **timer** event; a single iteration is the simplest example. Of course, you'll remove the `while` statement because the **timer** event controls the repetitive processing.

Table 21.1 lists the TimerEvent methods and procedures. Notice that TimerEvent has no unique methods or procedures; all of them are inherited from the base Event type.

TABLE 21.1. TIMEREVENT METHODS AND PROCEDURES.	
errorCode*	isTargetSelf*
getTarget*	reason*
isFirstTime*	setErrorCode*
isPreFilter*	setReason*
*Inherited from the Event type	

Tutorial: Looping with Timers

Suppose that you wish to add three fields to a form that count up while still allowing the user to use the form and Windows. You can use this technique to create loops that allow the user to continue their work. In this tutorial, you set up three independent loops that use timers and three buttons that control the three loops as a set. The first button starts the looping process. The second button causes the three loops to pause. The third button kills all three loops. To show that these three loops are multitasking, you add a table frame connected to a table. That way, you can add records while the three loops count.

On Disk: \ANSWERS\LOOP-T.FSL

Quick Steps

1. Set up three objects, each with its own timer.
2. Use the buttons to start and kill the timers. To implement the pause effect, kill the timers without reinitializing the counter variables.

Step By Step

1. Set your working directory to TUTORIAL. Create a new form, based on the WORLD.DB table, with three buttons on it. Label the buttons Start Timers, Pause Timers, and Kill Timers. Add three unlabeled, undefined fields. Name them *Field1*, *Field2*, and *Field3*. Figure 21.4 shows how the form should look. In this figure, the three undefined fields and each font size have been enlarged, and most of the columns have been deleted.

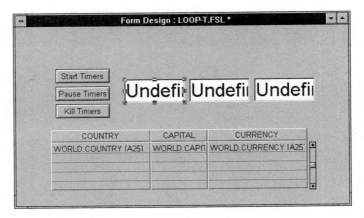

Figure 21.4. Set up form for the tutorial.

2. Type line 3 in the Var window of the form.

```
1:    ;Form :: Var
2:    Var
3:        Counter1, Counter2, Counter3 SmallInt
4:    endVar
```

3. Type lines 3–5 in the **open** method of the form.

```
1:    ;Page :: open
2:    method open(var eventInfo Event)
3:        Counter1 = 0
4:        Counter2 = 0
5:        Counter3 = 0
6:    endmethod
```

4. Add lines 3–10 to the **timer** method of the *Field1* field.

```
1:    ;Field :: timer
2:    method timer(var eventInfo TimerEvent)
3:        if Counter1 < 100 then
4:            Counter1 = Counter1 + 1
5:            self = Counter1
6:        else
7:            Counter1 = 0
8:            self = 0
9:            self.killTimer()
10:       endIf
11:   endmethod
```

5. Add lines 3–10 to the **timer** method of the *Field2* field.

```
1:    ;Field :: timer
2:    method timer(var eventInfo TimerEvent)
3:        if Counter2 < 200 then
4:            Counter2 = Counter2 + 1
5:            self = Counter2
6:        else
7:            Counter2 = 0
8:            self = 0
9:            self.killTimer()
10:       endIf
11:   endmethod
```

6. Add lines 3–10 to the **timer** method of the *Field3* field.

```
1:    ;Field :: timer
2:    method timer(var eventInfo TimerEvent)
3:       if Counter3 < 1000 then
4:          Counter3 = Counter3 + 1
5:          self = Counter3
6:       else
7:          Counter3 = 0
8:          self = 0
9:          self.killTimer()
10:      endIf
11:   endmethod
```

7. Add lines 3–5 to the **pushButton** method of the Start Timers button.

```
1:    ;Button :: pushButton
2:    method pushButton(var eventInfo Event)
3:       field1.setTimer(1000)
4:       field2.setTimer(250)
5:       field3.setTimer(50)
6:    endmethod
```

8. Add lines 3–5 to the **pushButton** method of the Pause Timers button.

```
1:    ;Button :: pushButton
2:    method pushButton(var eventInfo Event)
3:       field1.killTimer()
4:       field2.killTimer()
5:       field3.killTimer()
6:    endmethod
```

9. Add lines 3–13 to the **pushButton method** of the Kill Timers button.

```
1:    ;Button :: pushButton
2:    method pushButton(var eventInfo Event)
3:       field1.killTimer()
4:       Counter1 = 0
5:       Field1 = 0
6:
7:       field2.killTimer()
8:       Counter2 = 0
9:       Field2 = 0
10:
```

```
11:        field3.killTimer()
12:        Counter3 = 0
13:        Field3 = 0
14:     endmethod
```

10. Check the syntax, save the form as LOOP-T.FSL, and run the form. Click the Start Timers button and let it run a while. All three loops run at different speeds. You can use this effect to prioritize tasks. Click on the Pause Timers button; all three loops pause. When you press the Start Timers button a second time, the loops continue from where they paused. Now, use the table frame. For example, scroll a few records up and down, insert a record, and so on. Click the Kill Timers button to stop and reset all three loops. Figure 21.5 shows how the form should look after you've finished this tutorial.

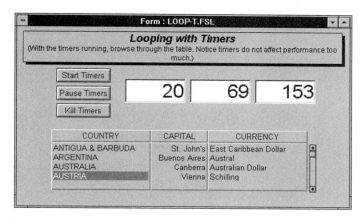

Figure 21.5. LOOP-T.FSL. Using timers to create multitasking loops that can be paused.

Analysis

In step 2, line 3 declares the three variables used in the three timers.

In step 3, lines 3–5 initialize them when the form is opened.

Except for the number of times that they loop, the three timers are the same. In step 4, line 3, the first loop checks whether the counter variable is less than 100. If it is, line 4 increments it by 1. Line 5 sets the value of self to the value of the counter variable. This shows progress through the loop; normally, you would do something more productive. If the counter variable in line 3 isn't less than 100, line 7 sets it to 0. Line 8 sets the value of the field to 0 to indicate visually that the loop is over. Line 16 destroys the timer.

In step 7, lines 3–5 on the Start Timer button start the looping process. They dictate which loop has priority—that is, the loop speed. Line 3 sets the first timer to fire once every second, and starts it. Line 4 sets the second timer to fire once every quarter-second, and starts it. Line 5 sets the third timer to fire once every one-twentieth of a second, and starts it.

In step 8, lines 3–5 on the Pause Timer button kill the timers but don't reset the counter variables. This enables the three loops to pause and restart.

In step 9, lines 3–13 kill and reset the timers, counter variables, and field values. Using timers to multitask and pause loops is an important technique. It will often come in handy.

Toggle Buttons

How do you keep a button down? Simply disable the event prior to the **pushButton** method with `disableDefault`. For example, use the following code on the button's **mouseUp** method:

```
1:  disableDefault
2:  buttonName.value = true
```

Because `value` is assumed, you can shorten the second line of code to

```
1:  buttonName = true
```

Keeping a Button Pressed

`doDefault` doesn't cause a button to pop up. It simply causes Paradox to immediately execute the internal code associated with a **pushButton** event. The button's popping up isn't part of this. The button's popping up signals the change of the button's value from True to False. If you want a button to pop up immediately, set its value to False. Having the button remain pressed, however, is a good way to signal to users that an operation stemming from the button is proceeding. The next tutorial demonstrates how to keep a button pressed.

Tutorial: Toggling a Button Down and Up

Suppose that you wish to toggle a button between down and up, and to set its label's text color to dark gray when the button is down. To the user, this has the effect of the button being off when it is up, and on when it is down.

On Disk: \ANSWERS\TOGGLE.FSL

Quick Steps

1. Use only the **mouseUp** method of the button, disabling the default behavior with `disableDefault`.
2. Check whether the button is up or down by checking its value.
3. For a more professional look, change the button's label to black when the button is up and to dark gray when it's down.

Step By Step

1. Create a new form and place a button on the form, name the label on the button textObject, and change the value of the label to Toggle me.
2. Add lines 3–12 to the **mouseUp** method of the Toggle me button.

```
1:    ;Button :: mouseUp
2:    method mouseUp(var eventInfo MouseEvent)
3:       DisableDefault
4:       if self = False then
5:          self = True
6:          self.textObject.font.Color = DarkGray
7:          ;Put down code here
8:       else
9:          self = False
10:         self.textObject.font.color = Black
11:         ;Put up code here
12:      endIf
13:   endmethod
```

3. Check your syntax, save the form as TOGGLE.FSL, run the form, and click the button. Notice that the button goes down and its label turns gray. Click it again. The button comes up and its label turns black (see Figure 21.6).

Analysis

In step 2, line 3 disables the default behavior. In this case, the call to **pushButton** is prevented. Line 4 checks whether the button is up. If the button is up, line 5 puts it down, and line 6 changes its label to dark gray. If the button is down, line 9 puts it up, and line 10 changes its label to black.

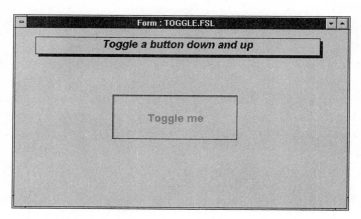

Figure 21.6. TOGGLE.FSL.

The next tutorial shows you how to toggle among a number of buttons. While one button is down, all the other buttons are up.

Tutorial: Toggling Between Two Buttons

Suppose that you wish to put two buttons on a form and toggle between them. If the user presses button 1, and button 2 is down, it will come up, and vice versa. In addition, you want to change a value in a field, depending on which button is down.

On Disk: \ANSWERS\TOGGLE2.FSL

Quick Steps
1. Put two buttons on a form. This time, put all the code in both buttons' **mouseDown** methods.
2. Disable the default behavior and set the button up and down by setting its value.

Step By Step
1. Open an existing form or create a new one. Place two buttons and a field on the form. Name the two buttons Option1 and Option2, and name the field *Choice_Selected* (see Figure 21.7).

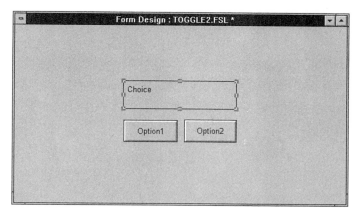

Figure 21.7. Set up form for the tutorial.

2. Add lines 3–6 to the **mouseUp** method of the Option1 button.

```
1:    ;Button :: mouseUp
2:    method mouseUp(var eventInfo MouseEvent)
3:        DisableDefault
4:        Option1Name = True
5:        Option2Name = False
6:        Choice_Selected = "Option one is down"
7:    endmethod
```

3. Add lines 3–6 to the **mouseUp** method of the Option2 button.

```
1:    ;Button :: mouseUp
2:    method mouseUp(var eventInfo MouseEvent)
3:        DisableDefault
4:        Option1Name = False
5:        Option2Name = True
6:        Choice_Selected = "Option two is down"
7:    endmethod
```

4. Check your syntax, save the form as TOGGLE2.FSL, run the form, and click the Option1 button. The button goes down. Now click the Option2 button. Option1 pops up, and Option2 stays down (see Figure 21.8).

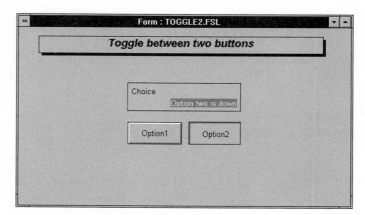

Figure 21.8. TOGGLE2.FSL. This form toggles between the two buttons.

Analysis

The code for both buttons is similar. The key to holding the button down is to disable the default behavior on the **mouseUp** method of the button (step 2, line 3 and step 3, line 3) and to explicitly set it up or down by making its value True or False (step 2, lines 4–5 and step 3, lines 4–5). In this simple tutorial, the only code executed controls the buttons and sets the value of the *Choice_Selected* field. No code is put on the **pushButton** method.

CREATING UIOBJECTS

ObjectPAL enables you to create objects in runtime. To create objects on the fly, you need to use the `create()` method, and you need to know about things such as points and twips. As stated earlier, a twip is what you use to measure points on the screen. A point has an *x* value and a *y* value, both of which are measured in twips. A twip is 1/1440 of an inch—or 1/20 of a printer's point. The following two tutorials use the `create()` command and a point variable to create and delete a line. `create()` does just what its name implies—creates objects. The type of object, where the object is created, and the dimensions of the object are all specified as part of the parameters for `create()`.

The properties (frame, color, font, and so on) of the object produced by `create()` default to whatever the object defaults happen to be at the time the object is created. To modify the properties, each must be changed individually after the object has been created. The notation and properties specific to graphs will be discussed later.

The constants that correspond to the types of objects that one can create with UIObject `Create()` are as follows:

BoxTool	LineTool
ButtonTool	OleTool
ChartTool	RecordTool
EllipseTool	TableFrameTool
FieldTool	TextTool
GraphicTool	XtabTool

For example, graphs are created with ChartTool.

The parameters for `Create()` are as follows:

objectType	This corresponds to the type of object being created. For graphs, this will be ChartTool.
x	The x coordinate (in twips) of the upper-left corner of the object.
y	The y-coordinate (in twips) of the upper-left corner of the object.
w	The width (in twips) of the object to be created.
h	The height (in twips) of the object to be created.
container	This is an optional parameter. If present, container must be a UIObject capable of containing the created object. In other words, you cannot place a 1000×1000 object within a 500×500 container.

Working with Groups

Normal object creation goes from the outside to inside. For example, first the page is created, then you place a box on the page. Within the box, you place a table frame. Obviously, you cannot create the box without first creating the page. Likewise, you cannot create the frame without first creating the box. Unfortunately, groups work the opposite way. You cannot place a group on the page and then place objects within the group. You must first place the two objects and then place a group around these two objects.

Working with Frames

Because frames can vary in thickness, you need to allow for a border on the containing object. As a general rule of thumb, it is a good idea to give 15 twips distance between the inner object and its containing object.

Tutorial: Creating a Line the Same Size as the Page

Suppose that you wish to allow the user to create and delete a line. To do this, you use two buttons on a form. One button creates a line, and the other deletes it.

On Disk: \ANSWERS\CREATE2.FSL

Quick Steps

1. Declare a UIObject variable in a container higher than the buttons—perhaps at the page level.
2. On the Create Line button, declare the form and point variables and attach to the current form with the Form variable, and put the size of the form in the point variable.
3. Use the create() method to create the line and set the visible property of the new object to true.
4. On the Delete Line button, use the delete() method to delete the line.

Step By Step

1. Create a new form and place two buttons on it. Label the buttons Create Line and Delete Line (see Figure 21.9).
2. Add line 3 to the Var window of the page.

```
1:      ;Page :: Var
2:      Var
3:          ui UIObject
4:      endVar
```

3. Add lines 3–12 to the **pushButton** method of the Create Line button.

```
1:      ;Button :: pushButton
2:    method pushButton(var eventInfo Event)
3:      var
4:          p Point
5:      endvar
```

```
6:    p = container.size    ;size of page
7:
8:    ui.create(LineTool, 15, p.y()-15, 0, -1000, self.container)
9:    ui.end = point(p.x(), 0)
10:   ui.visible = True
11: endmethod
```

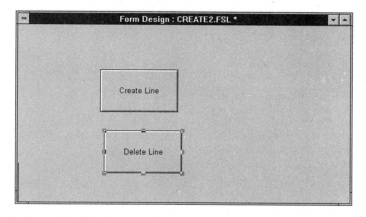

Figure 21.9. Set up form for the tutorial.

4. Add line 3 to the **pushButton** method of the Delete Line button.

```
1:    ;Button :: pushButton
2:    method pushButton(var eventInfo Event)
3:        ui.delete()
4:    endmethod
```

5. Check your syntax, save the form as CREATE2.FSL, run the form, and click the Create Line button. After the line is created, click the Delete Line button to get rid of it (see Figure 21.10).

Analysis

In step 2, line 3 declares a UIObject variable named *ui*. Once you declare a UIObject variable, you can use it to create new objects and to manipulate existing objects. In this case, the UIObject variable is created at the page level. Therefore, both buttons have access to it.

In step 3, line 3 declares *p* as a point variable for use in line 9. Lines 8–10 create the line, set its end point, and make it visible.

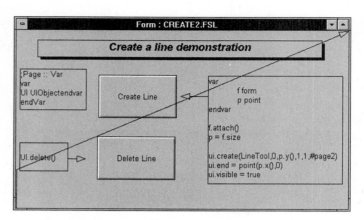

Figure 21.10. CREATE2.FSL. A line is created and deleted.

In step 4, line 3 on the second button uses the `delete()` method to delete the UIObject. The `delete()` method isn't new to you, but the UIObject version is. Earlier, you learned why many of ObjectPAL's commands are polymorphic—that is, why they behave in context. This is a good example of polymorphism. The `delete()` method in line 3 knows that it's working on a UIObject and handles it accordingly.

CREATING A GRAPH FROM SCRATCH

Now that you've seen how easy the `create()` method is, type the following code into the **pushButton** method of a button:

```
1:  ;Button :: pushButton
2:  method pushButton(var eventInfo Event)
3:    var
4:      ui    UIObject          ;Declare a UIObject variable.
5:    endVar
6:
7:    ui.create( ChartTool, 100, 100, 3000, 3000 ) ;Create the graph.
8:    ui.tableName = "ORDERS.DB" ;Set graph properties.
9:    ui.visible = True          ;Display graph.
10: endMethod
```

The preceding code creates a graph from scratch on a form. ObjectPAL is powerful; it allows you to create all kinds of objects while the object the code is attached to is running. You can also alter the properties of graphs already created.

A SIMPLE EXAMPLE OF MANIPULATING A GRAPH PROPERTY

Here is another example you can type into the **pushButton** method of a button:

```
1:  method pushButton(var eventInfo Event)
2:    var
3:       ui   UIObject
4:    endVar
5:
6:    ui.create( ChartTool, 20, 20, 3000, 3000 )
7:    ui.bindType = GraphTabular
8:    ui.graphType = Graph2DPie
9:    ui.tableName = "ORDERS.DB"
10:   ui.visible = True
11: endMethod
```

USING *designModified* TO SAVE A FORM OR REPORT WITHOUT PROMPTING

Sometimes it is necessary to alter an existing form or report with ObjectPAL, designing a form or report on the fly. If you do, however, the user will be prompted to save the form or report. The question is, is it possible to close unsaved forms and reports without being prompted to save them? Yes, set the designModified property to False. For example, the following code snippet from the Paradox Desktop opens a report and alters it:

```
1:   var
2:      r    Report            ;Declare r as a report variable.
3:      ri   ReportOpenInfo    ;Declare ri as a ReportOpenInfo variable.
4:   endVar
5:
6:   ri.name = "SOURCE"        ;Specify report name.
7:   ri.masterTable = "SOURCE.DB"   ;Set master table for report.
8:   r.open(ri)                ;Open report.
9:
```

```
10:   ;Set the value property of a text object.
11:   r.txtTitle.value = "Source Code for " + fldFileName.value
12:   r.show()
13:   r.designModified = False         ;Tell report it has not changed.
14:   r.wait()
```

ADDING PUSHBUTTON TO A BOX

Sometimes, you want a box or another UIObject to have a built-in method that it normally doesn't have, such as **pushButton**. In those cases, simply add the method as a custom method. When you view the Method Inspector the next time, Paradox recognizes the custom method as a built-in method and adds it to the list of built-in methods. This happens even though, normally, some built-in methods are omitted because boxes don't have **pushButton** methods.

After you add a **pushButton** method to an object that normally doesn't have one, you must call it. For example, if you have the following code on an added **pushButton** method of a box:

```
1:   ;box :: pushButton
2:   method pushButton(var eventInfo Event)
3:     msgInfo("From box", "This is the pushButton method")
4:   endmethod
```

you need to call this new method from one of the normal built-in methods, such as **MouseClick**:

```
1:   ;box :: mouseClick
2:   method mouseClick(var eventInfo MouseEvent)
3:   self.pushbutton()
4:   endmethod
```

THE FORM STYLE CREATOR

Type the following code into a script or the **pushButton** method of a button. It automatically creates style sheets from your favorite forms. Follow the comments to see how it works.

```
1:   var
2:     f          Form
3:     fbi        FileBrowserInfo
4:     sFilename  String
5:     sSheet     String
6:     ar         Array[] Anytype
7:     siCounter  SmallInt
8:   endVar
9:
```

```
10:   msgInfo("The Style Sheet Creater", "version 1\nby Mike
      Prestwood\n\nSelect an undelivered form to create style sheet from.")
11:
12:   fbi.allowableTypes =  fbForm
13:
14:   if fileBrowser(sFileName, fbi) then
15:   else                                ;If no file is selected,
16:      return                           ;then abort.
17:   endIf
18:
19:   ;Find path of file.
20:   switch
21:      case isDir(fbi.alias)
22:         : sFilename = fbi.alias + fbi.path + sFilename
23:      case sFilename.subStr(1,6) = ":PRIV:"
24:         : sFilename = sFilename.subStr(7, sFilename.size() - 6)
25:           sFilename = getAliasPath(":PRIV:") + "\\" + sFilename
26:      otherwise
27:         : sFilename = getAliasPath(fbi.alias) + "\\" + fbi.path + sFilename
28:   endSwitch
29:
30:   f.load(sFilename, WinStyleHidden)    ;Attach to form.
31:   f.enumObjectNames(ar)                ;Populate array with object names.
32:
33:   ;Prompt user for name of new style sheet.
34:   sSheet = "Style sheet name"
35:   sSheet.view("Enter name of style sheet")
36:
37:   if sSheet = "Style sheet name" then  ;If variable was not changed then
38:      beep()                            ;beep, display a message, and
39:      message("Operation aborted")      ;quit the operation.
40:      return
41:   endIf
42:
43:   for siCounter from 1 to ar.size()    ;Cycle through ar and
44:      copyToSpeedBar(f.(ar[siCounter])) ;copy the object properties to
45:   endFor                               ;the toolbar.
46:
47:   if not f.saveStyleSheet(sSheet, True) then
48:      errorShow("Error saving style sheet", "Check path & filename")
49:   endIf
50:
51:   f.designModified = False             ;Tell loaded form it didn't change
52:   f.close()                            ;Close form.
```

You can use the two style sheets, S-SHEET1.SSL and S-SHEET2.SSL, to automatically create form and report style sheets. Simply run the S-SHEET1.SSL or S-SHEET2.SSL script included in the ANSWERS directory and select a form or report.

IMPORTING AND EXPORTING DATA

AN OVERVIEW OF ASCII FILES

ASCII is an acronym for American Standard Code for Information Interchange. The ASCII set consists of 7-bit codes that represent 128 standard characters—letters, numbers, and symbols. The characters in the ASCII set are the same as the first 128 characters in the extended ASCII and ANSI sets.

The meaning of the term *ASCII file* has expanded from its strict technical definition to something more generic. Today, ASCII can refer to any file that is composed of readable characters, even if it contains characters other than the 128 of the original set. Most programmers still restrict the definition of ASCII, however. They use the term *text file* when they need a more generic term.

ASCII files are important because they are the means by which programs and computer platforms exchange data. More and more programs can import and export dBASE tables. More and more

GLOSSARY TERM

ASCII files and formats

Exporting ASCII files

Importing ASCII files

applications are adding Paradox to their list of import and export routines. If the program you want to bring data from or port data to supports either Paradox or dBASE, use either of those formats. You might have to work with programs that can't import or export, however. In those cases, you fall back on ASCII text files. ASCII text files are the one format that nearly all applications on all platforms can use. Text files are the common thread that enables applications and platforms to share data.

WHAT YOU CAN AND CAN'T DO

In version 1.0, you couldn't import or export Quattro, Excel, or Lotus spreadsheets with ObjectPAL. Many users expressed an interest. Borland agreed and introduced in version 4.5 both import and export procedures. You pass these new procedures a few parameters, and it takes over. In version 4.5, you can use the `importASCIIFix()`, `importASCIIVar()`, and `importSpreadSheet()`.

EXPORTING

To *export* a file is to convert it from a native format—either Paradox or dBASE—to a foreign format, such as ASCII. When you need data stored in either a Paradox or dBASE table in a text file, you export it. In the next two tutorials, you will build two of the routines used in EXPORT.FSL, which is on the disk that comes with this book (see Figure 22.1). The form demonstrates how to export standard and nonstandard ASCII files.

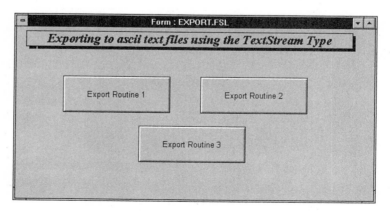

Figure 22.1. EXPORT.FSL.

You can use the following procedures to export data:

- `exportASCIIFix()`
- `exportASCIIVar()`
- `exportParadoxDOS()`
- `exportSpreadSheet()`

EXPORTING WITH TEXTSTREAM

With the TextStream methods, you can export and import ASCII files in any format you want. Often, your code contains fewer than 15 lines—no big deal. Take a look at Table 22.1, which lists the TextStream methods and procedures.

TABLE 22.1. TEXTSTREAM METHODS AND PROCEDURES.
advMatch
close
commit
create
end
eof
home
isAssigned
open
position
readChars
readLine
setPosition
size
writeLine
writeString

The following tutorial demonstrates exporting a table to an ASCII file.

Tutorial: Exporting Fields to an ASCII File

Suppose that you wish to export two fields of a table to an ASCII file with the fields separated by a comma.

On Disk: \ANSWERS\IMPORT\EXPORT.FSL

Quick Steps

1. Declare a TCursor variable and a TextStream variable.
2. Open both variables to the appropriate files. The text file doesn't need to exist.
3. Scan through the table. As you loop, write out whatever values you want.
4. Close both variables.

Step By Step

1. Change your working directory to TUTORIAL\IMPORT. Create a new form. Place a button labeled Export routine 1 on it.
2. Add lines 3–15 to the **pushButton** method of the Export routine 1 button.

```
1:    ;Button :: pushButton
2:    method pushButton(var eventInfo Event)
3:       var
4:          tc    TCursor
5:          ts    TextStream
6:       endVar
7:
8:       tc.open("EXPORT.DB")
9:       ts.open("EXPORT1.TXT", "NW")   ;N=new, W=write
10:
11:      scan tc:
12:        ts.writeLine(tc."First Name", ", ", tc."Last Name")
13:      endScan
14:      tc.close()
15:      ts.close()
16:    endmethod
```

3. Check the syntax and save the form as EXPORT.FSL. Run it and click the button. The button stays down momentarily while the table is exported. You can use any Editor—for example, Notepad—to view the EXPORT1.TXT text file (see Figure 22.2).

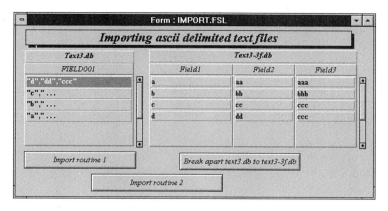

Figure 22.2. IMPORT.FSL.

Analysis

In step 2, lines 4 and 5 declare the TCursor and TextStream variables *tc* and *ts*. Line 8 opens the TCursor, and line 9 opens the TextStream. Lines 11–13 scan through the table. Line 12 writes each record to the text file. Line 12 adds a comma and a space between the two fields. You could use a tab—chr(9)— instead. Lines 14 and 15 close both variables.

SDF is an acronym for *standard delimited format*. An SDF is a text file formatted in a particular style. Each field is enclosed in quotation marks and separated by a comma. Each line ends with a carriage return and a linefeed. The next tutorial shows you how to import a whole table in SDF format.

Tutorial: Exporting a Table to ASCII

Suppose that you wish to export a Paradox table to an ASCII file in SDF format.

On Disk: \ANSWERS\IMPORT\EXPORT.FSL

Quick Steps

1. Declare a TCursor variable and a TextStream variable and open both variables to the appropriate files. The text file doesn't need to exist.
2. Scan through the table. As you loop, write out whatever values you want. Use the appropriate syntax to get the resulting text file into SDF.

3. Close both variables.

4. For a professional touch, set the mouse shape to the waiting mouse icon before the import and back to the arrow mouse icon after the import.

Step By Step

1. Change your working directory to IMPORT. Create a new form. Place a button labeled Export routine 2 on it. This label is different from the label in EXPORT.FSL (Refer to Figure 22.1).

2. Add lines 3–20 to the **pushButton** method of the Export routine 2 button.

```
1:    ;Button :: pushButton
2:    method pushButton(var eventInfo Event)
3:        var
4:            tc       TCursor
5:            ts       TextStream
6:            s1,s2    String
7:        endVar
8:
9:        setMouseShape(MouseWait)
10:       tc.open("EXPORT.DB")
11:       ts.open("EXPORT3.TXT", "NW")   ;N=new, W=write
12:       s1 = "\""
13:       s2 = "\","
14:
15:       scan tc:
16:           ts.writeLine(s1+tc."First Name"+s2, s1+tc."Last Name"+s2,
          s1+tc."City"+s2, s1+tc."Hobby"+s1)
17:       endScan
18:       tc.close()
19:       ts.close()
20:       setMouseShape(MouseArrow)
21:   endmethod
```

3. Check the syntax and save the form. Run it and click the button. The button stays down momentarily while the table is exported. You can use any Editor—for example, Notepad—to view the EXPORT1.TXT text file.

Analysis

In step 2, lines 4–6 declare the TCursor, TextStream, and String variables *tc*, *ts*, *s1*, and *s2*. Line 9 sets the mouse pointer to a waiting mouse icon so that the user clearly understands to wait. Line 10 opens the TCursor, and line 11 opens the TextStream. Lines 12 and 13 define the two String variables declared in line 6. Lines 15–17 scan through the table. Line 16 writes each record to the text file.

Line 16 uses the two String variables instead of the separators. This technique has two benefits. You save effort by not having to type all the extra commas, slashes, and quotation marks. You also can easily change the separator later if you want.

Lines 18 and 19 tidy up and close both variables. Line 20 notifies the user that the routine is done by switching back to the arrow mouse icon.

Importing

When you **import** a file, you convert the data from a foreign format, such as ASCII, to a native format—either Paradox or dBASE. Importing data is the process of bringing data into dBASE, Paradox, or a variable. Normally, you can import just about anything into ObjectPAL. At the least, you can read in a file and dump it into a memo field.

You can use any of the easy-to-use procedures to import files:

- `dlgImportAsciiFix()`
- `dlgImportAsciiVar()`
- `dlgImportSpreadsheet()`
- `importASCIIFix()`
- `importASCIIVar()`
- `appendASCIIFix()`
- `appendASCIIVar()`

> Both `appendASCIIFix()` and `appendASCIIVar()` were added just before
> Paradox 5 shipped. These two procedures were added to dramatically
> increase the importing of text files to existing tables. Although they are
> not documented in the Paradox manuals or the online help, they are
> mentioned in the README.TXT text file.

Using TextStream

Sometimes, however, a client or another user will give you a table whose format
isn't consistent and expect you to translate it to Paradox or dBASE. Usually,
you can use a `while` loop to loop through the text file and convert the text.
Occasionally, however, the data won't permit this. When you run into this kind
of data, don't waste your time. Return the table and tell the person to give you
consistent data. If he pushes, explain the specifics of why the data cannot be
imported.

For example, suppose that you have a text field with a date field and dates such
as 1193, 121293, 42593, and 12193. If the text has four or six characters, you
can easily break it into 1/1/93 and 12/12/93. If the text file has five characters,
you might not be able to tell what the date is supposed to be. Clearly, 42593 is
4/25/93, but 12193 could be 1/21/93 or 12/1/93. There's no way to know. The
moral of the story is to make sure that the original program exports data
properly.

To import data, follow these steps:

1. Open a TextStream to the text file. It can be read-only.
2. Use a `while` loop to loop through the text file. You can use `eof` to
    check for the end of the file.
3. Use `readLine()` to read one line at a time to a String variable.
4. Use the `match()` method to look for the names of fields, or use the
    `breakApart()` method to break each line into logical components.
5. Close the TCursor and TextStream variables.

The next two tutorials demonstrate routines from the IMPORT.FSL program, which is on the disk that comes with this book (refer to Figure 22.2). The form demonstrates how to import text files into ObjectPAL, manipulate them, and store them in a Paradox table.

> Rather than use `eof()` to check for the end of the file, you can check whether `readLine()` was successful. If `readLine()` returns false, you're at the end of the file.

In the next tutorial, you import a text file to a memo field and update the screen.

Tutorial: Importing a Text File to a Memo Field

Suppose that you wish to import a text file to a Paradox memo field—one record for each line of text—and to update the screen.

On Disk: \ANSWERS\IMPORT\IMPORT.FSL

Quick Steps

1. Declare a TCursor and a TextStream variable.
2. Open both variables to the appropriate files.
3. Use a `while` loop with `eof()` to loop through the TextStream.
4. In each increment of the loop, insert a record. Read in the line of text with `readLine()`, and post the new record.
5. Update the screen with `UIObjectName.resync(TableCursorName)`.
6. Close both variables.

Step By Step

1. Change your working directory to IMPORT. Create a new form. Place a table frame named *Text3* and a button labeled Import routine 1 on it.
2. Add lines 3–20 to the **pushButton** method of the Import routine 1 button.

```
1:    ;Button :: pushButton
2:    method pushButton(var eventInfo Event)
3:       var
```

```
 4:        tc  TCursor
 5:        ts  TextStream
 6:      endVar
 7:
 8:      tc.open("text3.db")
 9:      ts.open("text3.txt","R")
10:      tc.edit()
11:
12:      while not ts.eof()
13:        tc.insertRecord()
14:        ts.readline(tc.field1)
15:        tc.postrecord()
16:      endWhile
17:
18:      Text3.resync(tc)
19:      tc.close()
20:      ts.close()
21:    endmethod
```

3. Check the syntax and save the form as IMPORT.FSL. Run it and click the button. The button stays down momentarily while the table is imported. Because TEXT3.TXT is such a small ASCII file, the table frame populates almost immediately.

Analysis

In step 2, lines 4 and 5 declare the TCursor and TextStream variables *tc* and *ts*. Line 8 opens the TCursor, and line 9 opens the TextStream. Line 10 puts the TCursor into Edit mode so that it can be used in the loop in lines 12–16. Line 12 sets up the loop and in effect says, "While not at the end of the file connected to the Textstream variable, do the following." Line 13 inserts a new blank record into the TCursor, and line 14 reads from the TextStream directly into the TCursor. Line 15 posts the new record. Line 18 updates the screen. Lines 19 and 20 tidy up and close both variables.

USING *breakApart( )*

The next tutorial adds the breakApart() method to the routine. breakApart() is a ª powerful method. It can split a string into substrings based on a separator. This tutorial also sets the mouse pointer to the waiting mouse while the import takes place.

Tutorial: A More Sophisticated Import Routine

Suppose that you wish to import a text file, break it apart, put the parts into the appropriate Paradox fields, and update the screen.

On Disk: \ANSWERS\IMPORT\IMPORT.FSL

Quick Steps

1. Declare a TCursor variable and a TextStream variable.
2. Open both variables to the appropriate files.
3. Use a while loop with eof() to loop through the TextStream.
4. In each increment of the loop, insert a record. Read in the line of text with readLine(), and post the new record.
5. Update the screen with UIObjectName.resync(TableCursorName) if you want to see the changes.
6. Close both variables.

Step By Step

1. Change your working directory to IMPORT. Create a new form. Place a table frame named *Table_Frame* on it. Bind *Table_Frame* to the TEXT3.DB table. Also place a button labeled Import routine 2 on the form.
2. Add lines 3–29 to the **pushButton** method of the Import routine 2 button.

```
1:    ;Button :: pushButton
2:    method pushButton(var eventInfo Event)
3:       var
4:          tc   TCursor
5:          ts   TextStream
6:          s    String
7:          ar array[]   String
8:       endVar
9:
10:       setMouseShape(MouseWait)
11:       ts.open("text3.txt","R")
12:       tc.open("text3-3f.db")
13:       tc.edit()
14:
15:       while not ts.eof()
16:          ts.readline(s)
17:          s.breakApart(ar,",")
18:          tc.insertRecord()
19:          tc."Field1"=ar[1].subStr(2,size(ar[1])-2)
20:          tc."Field2"=ar[2].subStr(2,size(ar[2])-2)
21:          tc."Field3"=ar[3].subStr(2,size(ar[3])-2)
22:          tc.postRecord()
23:       endWhile
24:
25:       tc.endEdit()
26:       Table_Frame.resync(tc)
27:       tc.close()
28:       ts.close()
29:       setMouseShape(MouseArrow)
30:    endmethod
```

3. Check the syntax and save the form. Run it and click the button. The button stays down momentarily while the table is imported. Because TEXT3.TXT is such a small ASCII file, the table frame populates almost immediately.

Analysis

Lines 4–7 declare the variables needed to import and break apart an ASCII file: a TCursor, a TextStream, a String, and a resizeable Array. Line 8 sets the mouse pointer to the waiting mouse icon. Line 11 and 12 open the TCursor and the TextStream. Line 13 puts the TCursor into Edit mode so that it can be used in the loop in lines 15–23. Line 15 sets up the loop and in effect says, "while not at the end of the file connected to the TextStream variable, do the following." Lines 16 and 17 read in a line of text and separate it into a resizeable array. Line 17 indicates that the separation uses single commas. Line 18 inserts a new blank record. Lines 19–21 strip away excess characters and use the powerful breakApart() method to put the values into this blank record. Line 22 posts the new record. Line 25 ends Edit mode, and line 26 updates the screen. Lines 27 and 28 tidy up and close both variables. Line 29 sets the mouse pointer back to an arrow.

Now that you've practiced importing and exporting ASCII files, you can import or export almost any ASCII file that has consistent data. Chapter 23, "Storing and Centralizing Code," discusses how you can reuse and compartmentalize your code.

STORING AND CENTRALIZING CODE

CUSTOM METHODS AND CUSTOM PROCEDURES

In ObjectPAL, custom methods and procedures are equivalent to subroutines. A *subroutine* is a sequence of instructions that performs a specific task, usually more than once in a program. The sequence may be invoked many times by the current program or by multiple applications. Although ObjectPAL doesn't have *actual* subroutines, you can think of custom methods and custom procedures as subroutines.

GLOSSARY
TERM

ObjectPAL comes with a set of methods and procedures called the runtime library. A custom method consists of methods and procedures from the runtime library, as well as registered functions from dynamic link libraries (DLLs). Think of the set of custom methods and custom procedures that you develop as your own private runtime library.

A *custom method* is a method that you create. It consists of methods and procedures from the runtime library and from other custom methods and procedures. Custom methods are subroutines that objects can access. A *custom procedure* is similar to a custom method, except that the scope for a custom procedure is much more limited. Scope determines the availability of a custom procedure to other objects.

Global Versus Private

A custom method is always global to the object. The object to which the custom method is attached and all the objects contained by it can call the custom method directly. With dot notation, objects can use the custom methods of other objects. For example, if a button has a custom method called cmMsg() on it, it can be called from another button.

```
1:   ;Button1 :: cmMsg
2:   method cmMsg()
3:      message("Paradox tables can have up to 255 secondary indexes.")
4:   endMethod
```

```
1:   ;Button2 :: pushButton
2:   method pushButton(var eventInfo Event)
3:      Button1.cmMsg()
4:   endmethod
```

Custom procedures, on the other hand, are more limited in scope. Custom procedures have the same scope as variables. Only the object on which the custom procedure is created can call the custom procedure directly. In addition, dot notation doesn't work with custom procedures. A custom procedure in the Proc window of an object is global to the object. That is, an object can access its own procedure and the procedures defined in the objects that contain it. Remember, the scope of a variable depends on where it is declared; the same applies to custom methods and custom procedures.

```
1:  ;Button :: proc
2:  proc cpMsg()
3:      message("A BLOB field type is limited to 256 MB")
4:  endProc
5:
6:  ;Button :: pushButton
7:  method pushButton(var eventInfo Event)
8:       cpMsg()
9:  endmethod
```

A custom procedure can be private to a method. When a custom procedure is private to a method, no other objects can call it. Likewise, no other built-in methods within the object can call it. The following is an example of a private custom procedure. The `proc` structure goes above the normal `method` block.

```
1:  ;Button :: proc
2:  proc cpMsg()
3:      message("A primary index can consist of up to 255 fields")
4:  endProc
5:
6:  method pushButton(var eventInfo Event)
7:       cpMsg()
8:  endmethod
```

Passing by Value versus Passing by Reference

Custom methods can receive and return values. You can pass a value by value or by reference. When you pass a value to a custom method by value, you pass a copy of the value. If the custom method alters the copy, nothing happens to the original. When you pass a value to a custom method by reference, you pass a reference to the location where the value is currently stored. In other words, you are actually referring to the original value. If the custom method alters it, it is altering the original value.

Passing by value and passing by reference are common to custom methods and procedures. Take a look at the following custom method prototypes.

```
1:  method cmCode(var s String)    ;Pass by reference.
2:  method cmCode(s String)        ;Pass by value.
3:  method cmCode(Const s String)  ;Pass by reference,
4:                                 ;but not changeable.
```

If you're familiar with Pascal programming, you can see that examples 1 and 2 correspond to how you pass values to subroutines in Pascal. Example 1 has s as a `var` parameter that can be altered by the `cmCode()` method. In example 2, s is a value parameter.

In example 1, the value of s is changed. When you leave the cpCode() custom method, the value to which you changed s stays. In example 2, s is passed by value: A copy of s is given to cpCode(), and any change doesn't affect the original value. In example 3, the value is passed by reference. Because the value is a constant, the custom method can't change it. The following tutorials demonstrate these concepts. The form shown in Figure 23.1 demonstrates the six types of custom procedures created in this chapter's first six tutorials.

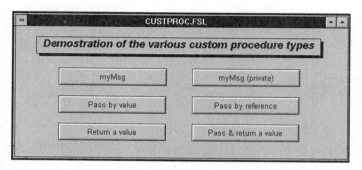

Figure 23.1. CUSTPROC.FSL.

In the next tutorial, you create and use a simple custom procedure.

Tutorial: My First Custom Procedure

This tutorial demonstrates creating and using a simple custom procedure that doesn't receive or return a value.

On Disk: \ANSWERS\CUSTPROC.FSL

Quick Steps

1. In the Proc window of the object, set up a procedure.
2. Call the procedure from a built-in method on the object.

Step By Step

1. Create a new form and place a button labeled myMsg on it.
2. Alter the proc window of the myMsg button to look like the following.

```
1:    ;Button :: Proc
2:    proc cpMsg()
3:       msgInfo("PDoxWin Trivia",
                 "You can use up to 24 tables in a query.")
4:    endProc
```

3. Add line 3 to the **pushButton** method of the myMsg button.

```
1:    ;Button :: pushButton
2:    method pushButton(var eventInfo Event)
3:        cpMsg()
4:    endmethod
```

4. Check the syntax and save your work. Run the form and click the myMsg button. When the message is displayed, click OK (see Figure 23.2).

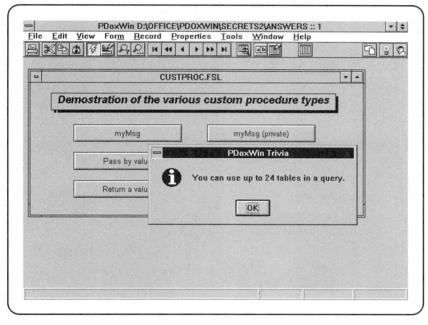

Figure 23.2. CUSTPROC.FSL showing the myMsg button.

Analysis

Step 2, line 2 prototypes (sets up) the custom procedure. Nothing is in the parentheses, which indicates that the custom procedure expects to be passed nothing. The lack of code after the closing parenthesis indicates that the custom procedure returns nothing. Line 3 does the actual work.

In step 3, line 3 calls the custom method. The call passes the custom method nothing, as the lack of code in parentheses indicates.

In the next tutorial, you create and use a private custom procedure.

Tutorial: My First Private Custom Procedure

This tutorial demonstrates creating and using a simple custom procedure that doesn't receive or return a value and is private to the built-in method.

On Disk: \ANSWERS\CUSTPROC.FSL

Quick Steps

1. Set up a procedure structure before the method structure in the built-in method that will use the private custom procedure.
2. Call the procedure from within the method block.

Step By Step

1. Open an existing form or create a new one. Place a button labeled myMsg (private) on it. In this code example, the proc structure comes before the method block.

2. In the **pushButton** method of the myMsg button, add lines 2–4 above the method and line 6 below.

```
1:      ;Button :: pushButton
2:      proc cpMsg()
3:         msgStop("PDoxWin Trivia",
        "A Paradox table is limited to 256 MB")
4:      endProc
5:      method pushButton(var eventInfo Event)
6:         cpMsg()
7:      endmethod
```

3. Check the syntax and save your work. Run the form and click the myMsg (private) button. When the message is displayed, click OK (see Figure 23.3).

Analysis

In step 2, line 2 prototypes the custom procedure exactly as it does in the previous tutorial. Nothing is in the parentheses, which indicates that the custom procedure expects to be passed nothing. The lack of code after the closing parenthesis indicates that the custom procedure returns nothing. Line 3 does the actual work of the custom procedure. Line 6 calls the custom method. Line 6 passes the custom method nothing, again as the lack of code in the parentheses indicates.

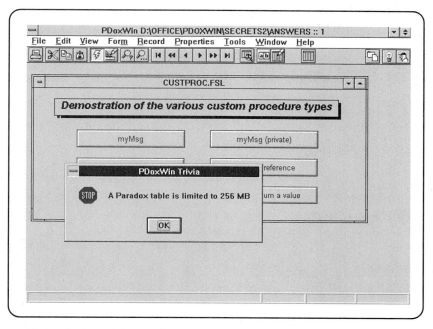

Figure 23.3. CUSTPROC.FSL showing the myMsg button.

Tutorial: Passing By Value to a Custom Procedure

This tutorial demonstrates creating and using a custom procedure that receives, but doesn't return, a value.

On Disk: \ANSWERS\CUSTPROC.FSL

Quick Steps

1. In the Proc window of the object, set up the procedure so that it is ready to receive a value.

2. Call the procedure from a built-in method on the object that passes a value to the custom method.

Step By Step

1. Open an existing form or create a new one. Place a button labeled Pass by value on it.

2. Add line 3 to the Proc window of the Pass by value button.

```
1:    ;Button :: Proc
2:    proc cpMsg(s String)
```

```
3:        msgInfo("PDoxWin Trivia", s)
4:     endProc
```

3. Add lines 3–7 to the **pushButton** method of the Pass by value button.

```
1:     ;Button :: pushButton
2:     method pushButton(var eventInfo Event)
3:        var
4:          s    String
5:        endVar
6:
7:        cpMsg("Numeric fields are accurate to 15 significant digits")
8:     endmethod
```

4. Check the syntax and save your work. Run the form and click the Pass by value button. When the message is displayed, click OK (see Figure 23.4).

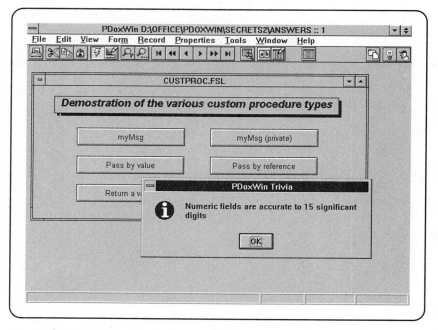

Figure 23.4. CUSTPROC.FSL showing the Pass by value button.

Analysis

The custom procedures are starting to get interesting. I'll begin this discussion with the **pushButton** method in step 3. Line 4 declares s as a String variable, and line 7 calls the custom method. This time, a string is passed to it.

In step 2, line 2 prototypes the custom procedure. s String, which is between the parentheses, indicates that the custom procedure expects to be passed a string. The lack of code after the closing parenthesis indicates that the custom procedure returns nothing. Line 3 does the actual work of the custom procedure. It uses the variable s.

In this example, both the calling code and the custom procedure use a String variable called s. This shows the connection between the two. In reality, both variables need only to be of the same type; they don't need to have the same name.

Tutorial: Passing By Reference to a Custom Procedure

This tutorial demonstrates creating and using a custom procedure that receives a reference to a variable but doesn't return a value.

On Disk: \ANSWERS\CUSTPROC.FSL

Quick Steps

1. In the Proc window of the object, set up the procedure so that it is ready to receive a reference to a variable.
2. Call the procedure from a built-in method on the object that passes a variable name to the custom method.

Step By Step

1. Open an existing form or create a new one. Place a button labeled Pass by reference on it.
2. Add line 3 to the Proc window of the Pass by reference button.

```
1:    ;Button :: Proc
2:    proc cpMsg(var s String)
3:        msgInfo("Windows limit", s)
4:    endProc
```

3. Add lines 3–8 to the the **pushButton** method of the Pass by reference button.

```
1:    ;Button :: pushButton
2:    method pushButton(var eventInfo Event)
```

```
3:      var
4:        x      String
5:      endVar
6:
7:      x = "INI files are limited to 64k in Windows 3.1"
8:      cpMsg(x)
9:    endmethod
```

4. Check the syntax and save your work. Run the form and click the Pass by reference button. When the message is displayed, click OK (see Figure 23.5).

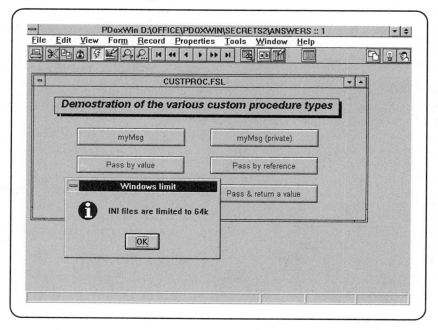

Figure 23.5. CUSTPROC.FSL showing the Pass by reference button.

Analysis

I'll start this discussion with the **pushButton** method in step 3. Line 4 declares *x* as a String variable. Line 8 calls the custom method that uses the variable *x*. This time, a variable is passed to the custom procedure.

In step 2, line 2 prototypes the custom procedure. In this case, var s String in parentheses indicates that the custom procedure expects to be passed a variable. The lack of code after the closing parenthesis indicates that the custom procedure returns nothing. Line 2 does the actual work of the custom procedure. It uses the variable s.

In this example, the calling code and the custom procedure use different variable names—s and x. This shows that, although the two variables have a direct connection, the connection is by reference to the same value. You could have used the same variable name.

Tutorial: Returning a Value from a Custom Procedure

This tutorial demonstrates how to create and use a custom procedure that doesn't receive a value by reference but does return a value. After the procedure is created, the return value is used in a message information dialog box.

On Disk: \ANSWERS\CUSTPROC.FSL

Quick Steps

1. In the Proc window of the object, set up the procedure so that it is ready to return a value.

2. Call the procedure from within msgInfo().

Step By Step

1. Create a new form and place a button labeled Return a value on it.

2. In the Proc window of the Return a value button, add line 3.

```
1:    ;Button :: Proc
2:    proc cpNever() String
3:        return "Never duplicate a line of code!"
4:    endProc
```

3. In the **pushButton** method of the Return a value button, add line 3.

```
1:    ;Button :: pushButton
2:    method pushButton(var eventInfo Event)
3:        msgInfo("Message from guru", cpNever())
4:    endmethod
```

4. Check the syntax and save your work. Run the form and click the Return a value button. When the message is displayed, click OK (see Figure 23.6).

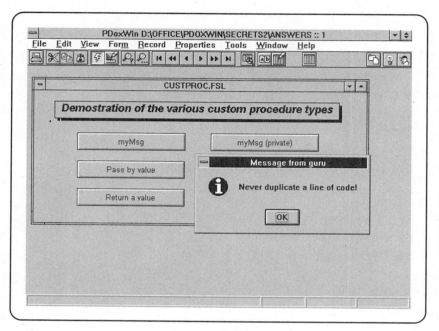

Figure 23.6. CUSTPROC.FSL showing the Return a value button.

Analysis

Line 2 of step 2 prototypes the custom procedure. The lack of code in the parentheses indicates that the custom procedure expects to be passed nothing. The data declaration after the closing parenthesis indicates that the custom procedure returns a string. Line 3 does the actual work of the custom procedure. It uses the `return` keyword and passes back a string.

In step 3, line 3 calls the custom procedure and passes it nothing. Because the runtime library procedure `msgInfo()` expects a string, the custom procedure must return a value.

Tutorial: Sending and Returning a Value from a Custom Procedure

This tutorial demonstrates how to create and use a custom procedure that receives a value by a reference and returns a value. After the procedure is created, the return value is used in a message information dialog box.

On Disk: \ANSWERS\CUSTPROC.FSL

Quick Steps

1. In the Proc window of the object, set up the procedure so that it is ready to return a value.

2. Call the procedure from within `msgInfo()`.

Step By Step

1. Open an existing form or create a new one. Place a button labeled Pass & return a value on it.

2. Add lines 3–8 to the Proc window of the Pass & return a value button.

```
1:    ;Button :: Proc
2:    proc cpAge(var d Date) Number
3:       var
4:          n    Number
5:       endVar
6:
7:          n = year(today()) - year(d)
8:       return n
9:    endProc
```

3. Add lines 3–9 to the **pushButton** method of the Pass & return a value button.

```
1:    ;Button :: pushButton
2:    method pushButton(var eventInfo Event)
3:       var
4:          dBorn     date
5:       endVar
6:
7:       dBorn = date("01/08/65")
8:       dBorn.view("Enter your birthdate")
9:       msgInfo("Your age", cpAge(dBorn))
10:   endmethod
```

4. Check the syntax and save the form as CUSTPROC.FSL. Run the form and click the Pass & return a value button. When the first dialog box is displayed, type your birthdate and click OK. When the message displays your age, click OK (see Figure 23.7).

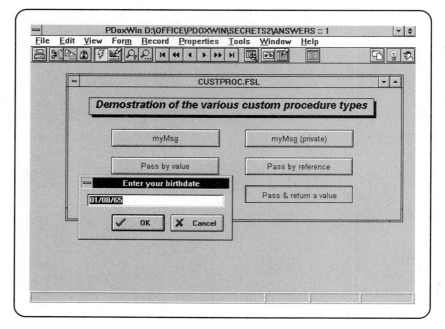

Figure 23.7. CUSTPROC.FSL showing the Pass & return a value button.

Analysis

In step 2, line 2 prototypes the custom procedure. `var d Date` in parentheses indicates that the custom procedure expects to be passed a reference to a Date variable. The data declaration after the closing parenthesis indicates that the custom procedure returns a number. Line 4 declares *n* as a Number variable. It is used in line 7 to accept the result of the calculation of the number of years between today and the date passed to the custom procedure. Line 8 returns *n*.

In step 3, line 4 declares *dBorn* as a Date variable. *dBorn* is given a value in line 7. Line 8 enables the user to change the value with a Date View dialog box. Line 9 calls the custom procedure inside a `msgInfo()` procedure.

The previous six tutorials represent the various types of custom procedures. In a nutshell, a custom procedure can be private to the method or global to the object. Values can be passed to the custom procedure by value or by reference. Custom procedures can return a value, or not. Once you master these elements, you can begin optimizing your code. Try never to duplicate a line of code. If you need to duplicate code on two objects, then consider putting the common code in a custom method or procedure and call it from both objects.

CUSTOM METHODS

Custom methods don't differ from custom procedures in any way except for scope. Whereas custom procedures can be private to a method or global to an object, custom methods are always global to an object. A custom method on an object can be called directly from any built-in method on the object or from any built-in method lower in the containership hierarchy. With dot notation, any object can call another object's custom method. The form shown in Figure 23.8 demonstrates custom methods. The three buttons on it are the buttons you create in the next three tutorials.

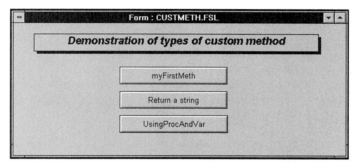

Figure 23.8. CUSTMETH.FSL.

Tutorial: My First Custom Method

This tutorial demonstrates how to create and use a custom method that asks a question.

On Disk: \ANSWERS\CUSTMETH.FSL

Quick Steps

1. On the form, create a custom method that asks a question.
2. Call the custom method from a button.

Step By Step

1. Change your working directory to the TUTORIAL directory, create a new form and place a button labeled myFirstMeth on it.
2. Create a new custom method called *cmQuestion* at the form level and add lines 3–7 to it.

```
1:    ;Form :: cmQuestion
```

```
2:    method cmQuestion()
3:       if msgQuestion("Question?",
             "Is ObjectPAL full of features?")= "Yes" then
4:         message("When you're right, you're right!")
5:       else
6:          message("How much more do you want?")
7:       endIf
8:    endmethod
```

3. Add line 3 to the **pushButton** method of the MyFirstMeth button.

```
1:    ;Button :: pushButton
2:    method pushButton(var eventInfo Event)
3:       cmQuestion()
4:    endmethod
```

4. Check the syntax and save the form as CUSTMETH.FSL. Run the form and click the myFirstMeth button. When the first dialog box is displayed, answer the question. When the message is displayed in the status bar, you're done (see Figure 23.9).

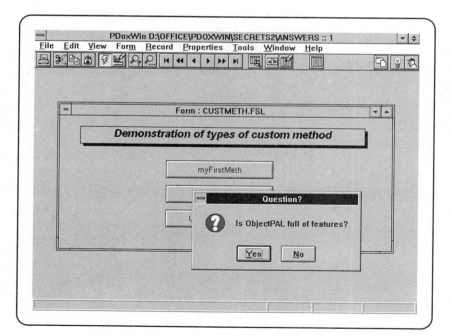

Figure 23.9. CUSTMETH.FSL showing the MyFirstMeth button.

Analysis

In step 2, line 3 uses the message question dialog box to ask a question. If the user clicks Yes, the condition of the `if` structure is satisfied, and the message in line 4 is displayed in the status bar. If the user clicks No, the message in line 6 is displayed.

In step 3, line 3 starts the whole procedure. The syntax for calling a custom method is the same as the syntax for calling a custom procedure. Therefore, you can't use the same name for a custom procedure and for a custom method in the same object. You can, however, use the same name for both as long as they are in different objects; the scope determines whether the procedure or method is called. For example, if you put a custom procedure named *cmQuestion* on the page level of the form created in this tutorial, it's called from the button instead of the *cmQuestion* form-level custom method. If you look at the Object Tree by selecting Tools | Object Tree, you'll notice that the page is closer to the button than the form is.

The next tutorial demonstrates how to return a string from a custom method.

Tutorial: Returning a String from a Custom Method

This tutorial demonstrates that returning a value from a custom method is the same as returning a value from a custom procedure.

On Disk: \ANSWERS\CUSTMETH.FSL

Quick Steps

1. Create a custom method that returns a string.
2. Call the custom method.

Step By Step

1. Create a new form or open an existing one. Place a button labeled Return a string on it.
2. Create a custom method on the form level called `cmHelloWorld` and add line 3 to it.

```
1:    ;Form :: cmHelloWorld
2:    method cmHelloWorld() String
3:       return "Hello world!"
4:    endmethod
```

3. Add line 3 to the **pushButton** method of the Return a string button.

```
1:    ;Button :: pushButton
2:    method pushButton(var eventInfo Event)
3:        message(cmHelloWorld())
4:    endmethod
```

4. Check the syntax and save your work. Run the form (see Figure 23.10).

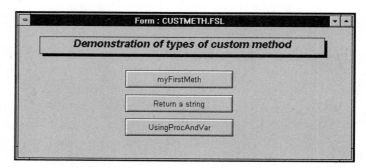

Figure 23.10. CUSTPROC.FSL showing the Return a string button.

Analysis

In step 2, line 2 prototypes the custom method. As with a custom procedure, if you're going to receive or return a value, you prototype it in the first line. When you create a custom method, you prototype it as you would a custom procedure. The only difference is that a custom procedure resides in a `proc` block, whereas a custom method resides in a `method` block. Line 3 returns the string, and line 3 in step 3 calls the custom method.

Tutorial: Adding *proc* and *var* Structures to Custom Methods

Suppose that you need to add `proc` and `var` structures to a custom method. This tutorial demonstrates how to add `proc` and `var` structures to a custom method.

On Disk: \ANSWERS\CUSTMETH.FSL

Quick Steps

1. Create a custom method that uses local `var` and `proc` structures.
2. Call the custom method.

Step By Step

1. Create a new form or open an existing one. Place a button labeled UsingProcAndVar on it.

2. Create a custom method at the form level named cmUsingProc and add lines 2–13 to it.

```
1:    ;Form :: cmUsingProc
2:    var
3:        siCounter    SmallInt
4:    endVar
5:
6:    Proc cpCounter()
7:        siCounter = siCounter + 1
8:    endProc
9:
10:   method cmUsingProc()
11:       siCounter = 9
12:       cpCounter()
13:       siCounter.view()
14:   endmethod
```

3. Add line 3 to the **pushButton** method of the UsingProcAndVar button.

```
1:    ;Button :: pushButon
2:    method pushButton(var eventInfo Event)
3:        cmUsingProc()
4:    endmethod
```

4. Check the syntax and save your work. Run the form and click the button. Only the number 10 is displayed (see Figure 23.11).

Analysis

Step 2, lines 2–4 add a var structure to the custom method, which creates a variable private to the method. Line 3 in the var structure declares *siCounter* as a small integer. Lines 6–8 add a proc structure to the custom method. Line 6 prototypes the new custom procedure. Note the use of the *siCounter* variable. Lines 10–14 make up the actual custom method. Line 10 prototypes it. Line 11 sets the initial value for *siCounter*. Line 12 calls the custom procedure that increments the value. Line 13 views the variable.

In step 3, line 3 in the **pushButton** method of the button starts the custom method.

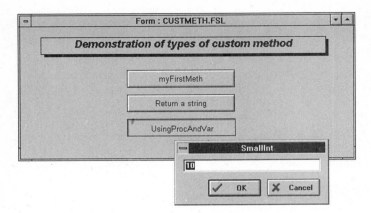

Figure 23.11. CUSTPROC.FSL showing the UsingProcAndVar button.

PASSING A SUBJECT TO A CUSTOM METHOD

You can pass a subject to a custom method. With dot notation, you can tell a custom method to act on another object. To do this, you use the keyword `subject`. This next tutorial demonstrates how to use `subject` and dereference an object.

Tutorial: Using *subject* to Dereference an Object

Suppose that you wish to toggle the pattern of one of two ellipses, depending on the value in a field.

On Disk: \ANSWERS\SUBJECT.FSL

Quick Steps

1. Pass another object to a custom method, use `subject` in the custom method, and call the custom method by using dot notation.
2. Refer to the value in a field as an object name, include the field in parentheses, and precede it with the name of its container.

Step By Step

1. Create a new form with two ellipses on it named *Ellipse1* and *Ellipse2*. Add a radio button field named *choice* with the two values *Ellipse1* and *Ellipse2*. Also add a button labeled Toggle pattern. The form in Figure 23.12 uses `subject` with a custom method and dereferences an object.

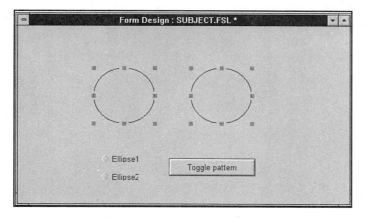

Figure 23.12. Set up form for the tutorial.

2. Create a custom method at the form level called cmToggleBackground()
   and add lines 3–7 to it.

```
1:    ;Form :: cmToggleBackground
2:    method cmToggleBackground()
3:        if subject.Pattern.Style = BricksPattern then
4:           subject.Pattern.Style = WeavePattern
5:        else
6:           subject.Pattern.Style = BricksPattern
7:        endIf
8:    endmethod
```

3. Add lines 3–7 to the **pushButton** method of the button.

```
1:    ;Button :: pushButton
2:    method pushButton(var eventInfo Event)
3:        if choice.isBlank() then
4:           return
5:        else
6:           pge1.(choice).cmToggleBackground()
7:        endIf
8:    endmethod
```

4. Check the syntax and save your work. Run the form. Select an ellipse
   from the *choice* field and click the button. Experiment with this form
   (see Figure 23.13).

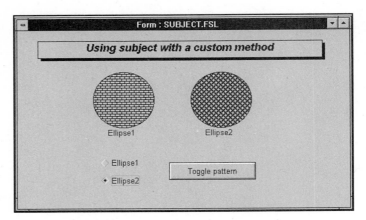

Figure 23.13. SUBJECT.FSL.

Analysis

In step 2, line 2 prototypes the custom method. Line 3 checks whether the pattern of subject is a bricks pattern. If it is, line 4 changes it to a weave pattern. If it isn't, line 6 sets it to a bricks pattern. Note the use of subject. By not hard-coding the name of the object, you can make your routines more generic and flexible.

In step 3, line 3 makes sure that the *choice* field has a value. Otherwise, an error would occur whenever the field is left blank. If the *choice* field is blank, the method returns control. If a choice was made, line 6 calls the custom method. Parentheses are used around the field name, and an object is specified before the first parenthesis.

PASSING ARRAYS AND DYNARRAYS

To pass an Array or a DynArray to a custom method or procedure, you need to set up a Type statement. The syntax checker doesn't enable you to declare an array directly, so you have to use a trick. The next tutorial demonstrates how to pass an array to a custom method.

Tutorial: Passing an Array to a Custom Method

Suppose that you need to pass an array with two elements in it to a custom method for display.

On Disk: \ANSWERS\PASS-AR.FSL

Quick Steps

1. Create a custom type for an array.
2. In the prototype of the custom method, use the new custom type. The custom method should simply display the array.
3. Call the custom method from a button.

Step By Step

1. Create a new form and put a button labeled Pass Array on it.
2. Add line 3 to the Type window of the Pass Array button.

```
1:    ;Button :: Type
2:    Type
3:        ctPassAr = Array[2] String
4:    endType
```

3. Create a custom method called `cmDisplayArray()` on the Pass Array button and add line 3 to it.

```
1:    ;Button :: cmDisplayArray
2:    method cmDisplayArray(var ar ctPassAr)
3:        ar.view("Childhood friend")
4:    endmethod
```

4. Add lines 3–9 to the **pushButton** method of the Pass Array button.

```
1:    ;Button :: pushButton
2:    method pushButton(var eventInfo Event)
3:        var
4:          arName Array[2] String
5:        endVar
6:
7:        arName[1] = "Grant"
8:        arName[2] = "Winship"
9:        cmDisplayArray(arName)
10:   endmethod
```

5. Check the syntax and save your work. Run the form and click the button. The name *Grant Winship* is displayed in an array view dialog box, as Figure 23.14 shows.

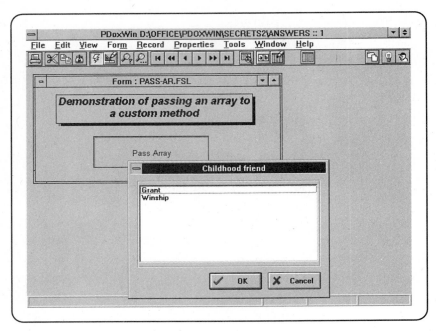

Figure 23.14. PASS-AR.FSL.

Analysis

In step 2, line 3 declares a new data type: a two-element array that is ready to receive string elements.

In step 3, line 2 uses the new data type in the custom method's prototype. The var keyword indicates that the array is passed by reference. If you leave out the var keyword, the array is passed by value. Line 3 displays the array.

In step 4, line 4 declares *arName* as a two-element private array that is ready to receive string values. Lines 7 and 8 populate the array. Line 9 passes the array to the custom method.

With the knowledge you gained in this chapter, you can start to reuse and compartmentalize your code. Remember to try never to duplicate a line of code and to put often used-code into custom procedures. These techniques work well for reusing code in a form. For reusing code across forms, ObjectPAL provides an object that is used only for storing code—the library.

LIBRARIES

A *library* is a Paradox object that stores custom ObjectPAL code. A library is useful for storing and maintaining frequently used routines and for sharing custom methods and variables among forms, scripts, and other libraries.

In a library, you can store custom methods, custom procedures, variables, constants, and user-defined types. Think of a library as a place to store often-used routines. It's the key to reusing your code and therefore is a time saver. The more you use libraries, the more time and energy you will save. You code a library similar to how you code a form. Select File | New | Library and add custom methods. You don't run a library. Instead, from your forms, you access the custom methods that you create in a library.

CHARACTERISTICS OF A LIBRARY

A library is never run. With ObjectPAL, you open and use the custom methods in a library, but you never run a library. A library doesn't contain objects. It can contain up to 64K of compiled code stored in custom methods and custom procedures.

The object variable *self* has different meanings, depending on when it's used. When it's used in a library, `self` refers to the calling object. When it's used in a form, `self` refers to the object to which the code is attached.

`self` refers to the calling object, not the library. This makes sense, although it's different than when another object's custom methods use `self`.

The scope of a library is determined by where you declare its variable and by how you open it (with or without the constant `PrivateToForm`). Although you can open a library from any point in the containership path, the placement of the Library variable determines which objects can see it. The form's Var window is a good place to declare a library's variable.

Every library has a built-in **open**, **close**, and **error** method. The **open** and **close** work just like a form's **open** and **close** methods. **open** is a good place to initialize variables. **error** is called when code in the library generates an error. The **error** method is a good place to trap for errors that the library itself might generate. By default, the **error** method calls the built-in **error** method of the form that called that particular custom method.

A library is a complete unit, just like a form. With a library, however, external objects have access only to the library's custom methods. Although a library can't contain objects, it has Var, Const, and Type windows for declaring, setting, and defining variables. A library also has Procs and Uses windows for writing procedures and accessing other libraries and DLLs. You access all these items by writing custom methods that utilize them.

The custom methods you write in a library can be self-contained. That is, each method contains all the commands within its own code. By using custom methods, you can access variables, constants, types, and procedures inside a library. You can even get to a library's Uses window to call functions from other libraries or DLLs. Table 23.1 lists the Library methods and procedures.

TABLE 23.1. LIBRARY METHODS AND PROCEDURES.

```
close

create

deliver*

enumSource

enumSourceToFile

execmethod

load*

methodDelete*

methodGet*

methodSet*

open

save*
```
*Inherited from the Form type

Libraries enable you to do the following:

- Reuse your code
- Centralize your code
- Set and retrieve variables in the Var window
- Call custom procedures in the Procs window

When should you use a library? Whenever you repeat code, create a custom method. Whenever you want to use a custom method on more than one form, put it in a library.

Opening a Library with *open()*

Use open() to give access to a library. You must declare a library first. As soon as you declare a variable, you use the open() command to open it. The syntax is as follows:

LibVar.open(*Library*, [*GlobalToDesktop* | *PrivateToForm*]) Logical

Here are two examples:

```
1:  lib.open("LIBRARY")
2:  lib.open("LIBRARY", PrivateToForm)
```

Closing a Library with *close()*

Although it's not necessary, you can close a library. The syntax is simple:

LibVar.close()

For example:

```
1:  lib.close()
```

STEPS IN USING A LIBRARY

1. Create a custom method in a library. By means of custom methods, you can access all the various components of a library.
2. Declare the Library variable. You need to declare a Library variable on every form you want to use a particular library with. A good place to declare a Library variable is on the Var window of the form:

   ```
   1:  var
   2:      lib Library
   3:  endVar
   ```

3. Open the library. After you declare the Library variable, you can use it to open the library. The syntax for opening a library is as follows:

   library.open(*Filename*)

   Note that if you leave the second parameter blank, Paradox assumes that it is GlobalToDesktop.

A good place to open a form's library is in the form's **open** method:

```
1:   lib.open("LIBRARY")
```

Note that this statement doesn't specify an extension. Paradox automatically looks for LIBRARY.LSL first and then for LIBRARY.LDL.

> Use the open() command on all the forms in an application. Libraries don't have an attach() command. It is implied by open().

4. Declare the custom method or methods in the Uses window. Every method you want to use from a library must be declared in the Uses window of the object you want to use it in. The syntax to do this is as follows:

Uses **ObjectPAL**
    methodName([[var | const] *argList*]) [*returnType*]
EndUses

A good place for this is in the form's Uses window:

```
1:     Uses ObjectPAL
2:        cmMsg()
3:     endUses
```

5. Use the custom method. After the custom method is set up for use, you must use proper dot notation to call it. The syntax for using a custom method from a library is as follows:

library**Variable**.*customMethod*([*argList*]).

For example:

```
1:   lib.cmMsg()
```

> The syntax of *container.method*() is consistent throughout ObjectPAL. If an object with the name box has code on its built-in mouseClick method, you can access that code with box.mouseClick() from any other object. When this code executes the UIObject method mouseClick() calls the built-in **mouseClick** method for a UIObject. How do you know when you can call the code in a built-in method of an object? Easy, if the runtime library has a method equivalent, then you can use it. For example, mouseClick() and pushButton().

The form LIBRARY.FSL demonstrates how to open and use a library with dot notation. It uses two libraries—LIBRARY.FSL and LIBRARY2.FSL.

LIBRARIES ARE SELF-DOCUMENTING

Use enum Procedures to Help Document Your Code

You can use `enumSource()` and `enumSourceToFile()` to send all the code from a library to a table or a text file. The syntax for these two procedures is as follows:

```
LibVar.enumSource("TABLE.DB")
```

and

```
LibVar.enumSourceToFile("FILE.TXT")
```

After you use an enum procedure, it's easy to create a form or a text file that documents your library. This technique also works with forms.

Tutorial: Your First Library

This tutorial demonstrates how to create a new library, put a simple custom method in it that displays a message, and then use it.

On Disk: \ANSWERS\LIB-TUT1.FSL

Quick Steps

1. Create a library with a custom method in it.
2. Declare a Library variable, and open the library.
3. Declare the custom method in the Uses window and use the custom method by means of proper dot notation.

Step By Step

1. Create a new library by selecting File | New | Library. A new Library object is displayed (see Figure 23.15).

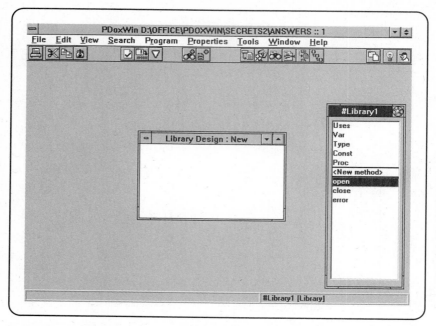

Figure 23.15. LIB-TUT1.LSL in development. Note that a library has only three built-in methods.

2. Bring up the methods dialog box by selecting Language | Methods. Type **errorMsg** in the New Custom Method edit region and click OK.

3. Edit the newly created `errorMsg()` custom method to look like this:

```
1:    ;LIB-TUT :: errorMsg
2:    method errorMsg()
3:      msgStop("Warning", "Execution stopped,
              press OK to continue")
4:    endmethod
```

4. Check the syntax, exit the edit window, and save the library as LIB-TUT.LSL. You can close the library if you want, but you don't have to.

5. Create a new form. Edit the form's Var window to look like this:

```
1:    ;Form :: Var
2:    var
3:      lib  Library
4:    endVar
```

6. Open the library on the **open** method of the form with the following:

```
1:     ;Form :: open
2:     lib.open("LIB-TUT")
```

7. Prototype the custom method in the Uses window of the form as follows:

```
1:     ;Form :: Uses
2:     Uses ObjectPAL
3:        errorMsg()
4:     endUses
```

8. Place a button on the form, and alter its **pushButton** method as follows:

```
1:     ;Button :: pushButton
2:     lib.cmMsg()
```

9. Save your work and run the form (see Figure 23.16).

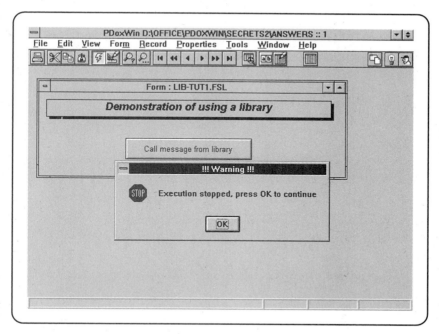

Figure 23.16. LIB-TUT1.FSL. This form demonstrates how to use a library—namely, LIB-TUT.LSL.

Analysis

In step 3, lines 2–4 make up the actual custom method. In step 5, line 3 declares the *lib* variable. The *lib* variable is used in step 6, line 2 to open the library. In step 7, lines 2 and 3 prototype the custom method. In step 8, line 2 calls the custom method.

PASSING VARIABLES THROUGH A LIBRARY

Passing variables from form to form and from form to library comes close to making up for the lack of a true global variable in ObjectPAL. Occasionally, you need a system-wide control mechanism, or you need to store a piece of data from a form in a library for later use. A variable in a library enables you to emulate a true global variable. The next tutorial shows you how to put variables into and get variables from a library.

Tutorial: Passing a Variable Between Forms

Suppose that you wish to pass a value from one form to another through a library. Because you are using a library, both forms don't have to be open at the same time.

On Disk: \ANSWERS\LIB1.FSL, ANSWERS\LIB2.FSL, and ANSWERS\LIB.LSL

Quick Steps

1. Create a custom method in a library that puts a value that is sent to it into a variable.
2. Create a second custom method in the library that gets a value from a variable and passes it back to the calling routine.
3. On one form, call the custom method that puts a value into the library.
4. On another form, call a custom method that gets the value from the library.

Step By Step

1. Change the working directory to a directory other than TUTORIAL. Create two forms. Put a button labeled Put on the first form and a button labeled Get on the second. Create a library and save it as LIB.LSL (see Figure 23.17). Note that if you close LIB1.FSL before

you open LIB2.FSL, the library is closed and reopened, losing any variables that were set.

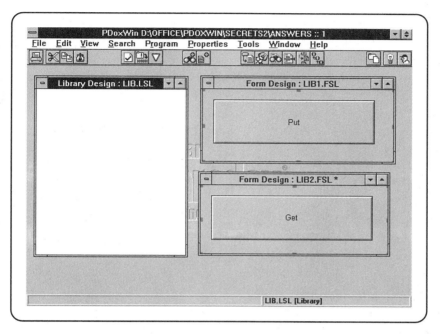

Figure 23.17. Passing a variable from one form to another form by means of a library.

2. Create a new library and line 3 to the Var window of the library.

```
1:    ;Library :: Var
2:    Var
3:       s1,s2 String
4:    endVar
```

3. Create a new custom method in the library called cmPutString1() and add line 3 to it.

```
1:    ;Library :: cmPutString1
2:    method cmPutString1(s string)
3:       s1 = s
4:    endmethod
```

4. Create a new custom method in the library called cmPutString2() and add line 3 to it.

```
1:    ;Library :: cmPutString2
```

```
2:      method cmPutString2(s string)
3:         s2 = s
4:      endmethod
```

5. Create a new custom method in the library called cmGetString1() and add line 3 to it.

```
1:      ;Library :: cmGetString1
2:      method cmGetString1() String
3:         return s1
4:      endmethod
```

6. Create a new custom method in the library called cmGetString2() and add line 3 to it. Save the library as LIB.LSL.

```
1:      ;Library :: cmGetString2
2:      method cmGetString2() String
3:         return s2
4:      endmethod
```

7. Create a new form and add lines 3 and 4 to the Uses window of the first form.

```
1:      ;Form :: Uses
2:      Uses ObjectPal
3:         cmPutString1(s String)
4:         cmPutString2(s String)
5:      endUses
```

8. Add line 3 to the Var window of the first form.

```
1:      ;Form :: Var
2:      Var
3:         lib Library
4:      endVar
```

9. Add lines 3–5 to the **pushButton** method of the Put button on the first form. Save the form as LIB1.FSL.

```
1:      ;Button :: pushButton
2:      method pushButton(var eventInfo Event)
3:         lib.open("LIB")
4:         lib.cmPutString1("Keith")
5:         lib.cmPutString2("Kinnamont")
6:      endmethod
```

10. Add lines 3 and 4 to the Uses window of the second form.

```
1:    ;Form :: Uses
2:    Uses ObjectPal
3:       cmGetString1() string
4:       cmGetString2() string
5:    endUses
```

11. Add line 3 to the Var window of the second form.

```
1:    ;Form :: Var
2:    Var
3:       lib Library
4:    endVar
```

12. Add lines 3 and 4 to the **pushButton** method of the Get button on the second form. Save the form as LIB2.FSL.

```
1:    ;Button :: pushButton
2:    method pushButton(var eventInfo Event)
3:       lib.open("lib.lsl")
4:       msgInfo("Childhood friend", lib.cmGetString1() + " " +
          ➥lib.cmGetString2())
5:    endmethod
```

13. Check the syntax and save all the various elements (the forms and the library). Close the library and run both forms. Click the Put button on the first form, then click the Get button on the second form (see Figure 23.18).

Analysis

In step 2, line 3 declares two String variables in the library Var window. The variables are global to the library.

Line 2 in steps 3, 4, 5, and 6 prototypes the four custom methods. Line 3 in steps 3, 4, 5, and 6 either sets or returns a variable.

In step 7, lines 3 and 4 prototype the library's custom methods in the Uses window of the first form.

In step 8, line 3 declares *lib* as a Library variable that is used to open the library in step 9, line 3.

In step 9, lines 4 and 5 call two of the four custom methods in the library.

In step 10, lines 3 and 4 prototype the other two custom methods in the library.

In step 11, line 3 declares *lib* as a Library variable that is used in step 12.

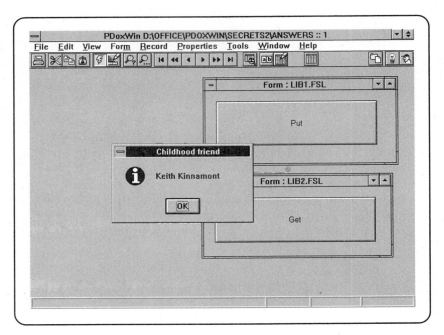

Figure 23.18. LIB1.FSL, LIB2.FSL, and LIB.LSL.

In step 12, line 3 opens the library for the second form. Line 4 uses the two cmGetString1() and cmGetString2() custom methods in a message information dialog box.

Calling a Library Custom Method from Another Library

A library can access the custom methods in other libraries, as the next tutorial demonstrates. This tutorial is a good example of reusing code. Although it often takes more time to reuse code than to copy and paste, the benefits are significant. By reusing as much code as possible, you will make your applications more powerful. They will contain fewer bugs and should be smaller, too.

Tutorial: Calling a Library Custom Method from Another Library

Suppose that you need to call a custom method in a library that calls another custom method in another library.

ADVANCED
TUTORIAL

On Disk: \ANSWERS\LIB-TUT2.FSL, \ANSWERS\LIB-TUT2.LSL, \ANSWERS\LIB-TUT3.LSL

Quick Steps

1. Create a custom method in a library that uses a custom method in another library.

2. From a form, call the first library's custom method.

Step By Step

1. Create a new form and place on it a button labeled as follows: Call Lib-Tut2, which calls Lib-Tut3. After you complete steps 1 through 5, create a new library for steps 6 through 9; save it as LIB-TUT2.LSL. Create another library for step 10; save it as LIB-TUT3.LSL.

2. Add line 3 to the Var window of the Call Lib-Tut2 button.

```
1:    ;Button :: Var
2:    Var
3:        lib  Library
4:    endVar
```

3. Add line 3 to the **open** method of the Call Lib-Tut2 button.

```
1:    ;Button :: open
2:    method open(var eventInfo Event)
3:        lib.open("LIB-TUT2.LSL")
4:    endmethod
```

4. Add line 3 to the Uses window of the Call Lib-Tut2 button.

```
1:    ;Button :: Uses
2:    Uses ObjectPal
3:        cmFromLib2()
4:    endUses
```

5. Add line 3 to the **pushButton** method of the Call Lib-Tut2 button.

```
1:    ;Button :: pushButton
2:    method pushButton(var eventInfo Event)
3:        lib.cmFromLib2()
4:    endmethod
```

6. Add line 3 to the Var window of the LIB-TUT2 library.

```
1:    ;Library :: Var
2:    Var
3:        libLIB-TUT3  Library
4:    endVar
```

7. Add line 3 to the **open** method of the LIB-TUT2 library.

```
1:      ;Library :: open
2:      method open(var eventInfo Event)
3:          libLIB-TUT3.open("LIB-TUT3")
4:      endmethod
```

8. Add line 3 to the Uses window of the LIB-TUT2 library.

```
1:      ;Library :: Uses
2:      Uses ObjectPAL
3:          cpMsg()
4:      endUses
```

9. Create a custom method called `cmFromLib2()` in the LIB-TUT2 library.

```
1:      ;Library :: cmFromLib2
2:      method cmFromLib2()
3:          LibLIB-TUT3.msg()
4:      endmethod
```

10. Create a custom method called `cpMsg()` in the LIB-TUT3 library and add line 3 to it.

```
1:      ;Library :: cmMsg
2:      method cmMsg()
3:          msgInfo("From LIB-TUT3", "Reuse as much code as possible")
4:      endmethod
```

11. Check the syntax and save your work. Run the form and click the Call Lib-Tut2 which calls Lib-Tut3 button. When the message is displayed, click on OK (see Figure 23.19).

Analysis

All the code that opens the first library is on the same object—the button. Because the Library variable is declared on the button in step 2, line 3, no other objects on the form can use the library. This keeps all the code for this tutorial together. In actual practice, however, you will want to move the Library variable up the containership path to a more accessible location.

In step 3, line 3 opens the library on the **open** method of the button. It doesn't matter where the library is opened. The only thing that matters is that the library *is* opened.

In step 4, line 3 prototypes the custom method *cmFromLib2* called in the **pushButton** method in step 5 line 3.

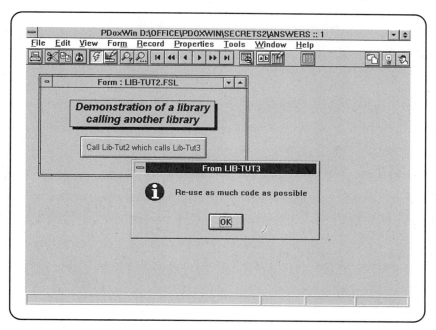

Figure 23.19. LIB-TUT2.FSL.

Steps 6, 7, and 8 from the first library are similar to the code from the button. I purposefully have kept this tutorial simple. The first library, however, usually does much more than what it does here. Take the message in step 10, line 3 to heart. It's the reason for this tutorial.

USING LIBRARIES TO DEVELOP LARGE PROGRAMS EFFICIENTLY

With larger applications, you might want to move most—but not all—of the code from the form to a library. This technique offers two benefits.

- It enables you to understand the relationship between forms and libraries.
- It enables you to change the code easily.

Use this technique when you develop a large application with many forms. You can change the way a routine behaves, and instantly change it for all the forms connected to it. This technique gives you an edge in maintaining an application. Application maintenance is the one part of development that most people want to avoid. Programmers love to create new things, but they hate modifying old ones. You probably won't develop all your applications this way; that would be foolish. When you develop a large application, however, consider using this technique. The more you use this technique, the more you will get used to creating general-purpose custom methods at the form and library levels.

CREATING A LIBRARY FROM SCRATCH

The form LIB-CR.FSL demonstrates creating a library from scratch and then using it. This capability is new to version 5 (see Figure 23.20). The following is the pertinent code:

```
 1:   ;Button :: pushButton
 2:   method pushButton(var eventInfo Event)
 3:      var
 4:          lib   Library
 5:      endVar
 6:
 7:      ;Create library.
 8:      lib.create()
 9:      lib.methodSet("cmMessage", "method cmMessage() msgInfo(\"From new
         ➡library\", \"Hello World!\") endMethod")
10:      lib.save("test")
11:      lib.close()
12:
13:      ;Use library.
14:      lib.open("test")
15:      lib.cmMessage()
16:   endmethod
```

```
 1:   ;Button :: Uses
 2:   Uses ObjectPAL
 3:      cmMessage()
 4:   endUses
```

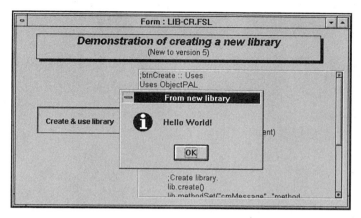

Figure 23.20. LIB-CR.FSL demonstrates creating and using a library.

SCRIPTS

A *script* is a Paradox object that consists of ObjectPAL code that can be run independently of a form or called from ObjectPAL. Unlike a form or a report, a script doesn't have any objects. Unlike a library, a script can be run without ObjectPAL.

The code for a script isn't attached to a form. Libraries exist. So why would you need or want scripts? Scripts are used to store code. Also, sometimes it's useful to give users a way to run code by selecting File | Open | Script without displaying a UIObject. Scripts are excellent when you aren't using a UIObject, such as a form. Because libraries require a UIObject (you can't open and run a library from Interactive mode), scripts are a way to give users the capability to run code interactively. You can run a script with the ObjectPAL procedure `play()`. The syntax for `play()` is as follows:

```
play(ScriptName) AnyType
```

Use `play()` to play a script from ObjectPAL. In this example, `play()` searches first for ENUM.SSL and then for ENUM.SDL. After the correct file is found, the statements in the script are executed. For example:

```
1:  Play("ENUM")
```

> **INSTANT SCRIPTS HAVE ARRIVED**
>
> *You've Had Them All Along!*
>
> The DOS version of Paradox has *instant scripts*. The Windows version has no exact counterpart, but, in effect, you've had them all along. Just right-click the Scripts icon on the Toolbar and select New. If the Toolbar doesn't contain the Scripts icon, select File | New | Script. Type some code into the Editor window and click the Run icon—that is, the lightning bolt—on the Toolbar. Now, your script will run.

The next tutorial shows you how to write and run a script. You run the script by either selecting File | Open | Script or playing it from a button.

> Here are some notes to keep in mind when developing a script.
>
> • No menus are possible with scripts.
>
> • Do not use the form type `wait()` as in `f.wait()`.

Tutorial: Writing a Script

Suppose that you wish to create four tables of ObjectPAL information to disk.

On Disk: \ANSWERS\ENUM.SSL

Quick Steps

1. Select File | New | Script.
2. Type the code and save it.
3. Use `play("FileName")` on a method.

Step By Step

1. Set your working directory to the TUTORIAL directory. Select File | New | Script. The Edit window for the built-in **run** method is displayed (see Figure 23.21).

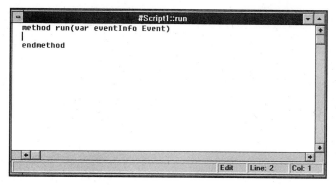

Figure 23.21. The **run** method of the script.

2. Add lines 3–13 to the **run** method of the script.

```
1:    ;Script :: run
2:    method run(var eventInfo Event)
3:        message("Sending RTL constants to RTLCONST.DB ...")
4:        enumRTLConstants("RTLCONST.DB")
5:
6:        message("Sending RTL class names to RTLCLASS.DB ...")
7:        enumRTLClassNames("RTLCLASS.DB")
8:
9:        message("Sending RTL methods to RTLMETH.DB ...")
10:       enumRTLMethods("RTLMETH.DB")
11:
12:       message("Sending UIObject classes to CLASSES.DB ...")
13:       enumUIClasses("CLASSES.DB")
14:   endmethod
```

3. Check the syntax, save the script as ENUM.SSL, and run it. You also could run the script from a form. To do this, place a button on a form and use the `play()` procedure to run the script. For example:

```
1:    ;Button :: pushButton
2:    method pushButton(var eventInfo Event)
3:        play("ENUM")
4:    endmethod
```

Analysis

In step 2, lines 3, 6, 9, and 12 send messages to the status line. Lines 4, 7, 10, and 13 enumerate information to their respective tables.

SENDING TABLE STRUCTURES TO TEXT FILES

Paradox lacks an easy way to grab the structure of all the tables in a directory. A feature that does this would be very useful. After all, a directory full of tables is considered a database in Paradox. This tutorial demonstrates how to grab the structure for all the tables in a directory. Specifically, it creates a text file of the structure with the same name as each table.

Tutorial: Sending Structures to Text Files

Suppose that you wish to create a text file of the structure of every Paradox table in a directory.

On Disk: \ANSWERS\STRUCT.SSL

Quick Steps

1. Use `enumFileList()` to fill the elements of an array with all the tables in a directory.

2. Use a `for` loop to scan through the array. For each element in the array, open a TCursor and use `enumFieldStruct()`. Open the table that results with another TCursor.

3. Open a text stream variable and use `scan` to loop through the second TCursor. Write the first four fields of every record to the open text file.

4. Close both TCursors after the `scan` loop.

Step By Step

1. Select File | New | Script and type lines 3–50 into the **run** method of the script.

```
1:    ;Script :: Run
2:    method run(var eventInfo Event)
3:      var
4:        sDir, s1, s2, s3, s4, S      String
5:        fs              FileSystem
6:        arTable         Array[]    String
7:        siCounter       SmallInt
8:        tc1, tc2        TCursor
9:        ts              TextStream
10:     endVar
```

```
11:
12:        ;Get path of tables
13:        sDir = getAliasPath("work")
14:        sDir.view("Enter path of tables")
15:
16:        ;Make sure "\" is at end of sDir variable (the path)
17:        if sDir.subStr(size(sDir)) <> "\\" then
18:          sDir = sDir + "\\"
19:        endIf
20:
21:        ;Get all .db tables from directory
22:        fs.enumFileList(sDir + "*.db", arTable)
23:        arTable.view("Cancel button does nothing")
24:
25:        ;Process each table
26:        setMouseShape(MouseWait)
27:        for siCounter from 1 to arTable.size()
28:         ;Display message in status bar
29:         message("Processing: " + arTable[siCounter])
30:
31:         ;Create struct.db in private directory
32:         tc1.open(sDir + arTable[siCounter])
33:         tc1.enumFieldStruct(":PRIV:STRUCT.DB")
34:
35:         ;Open text file
36:         splitFullFileName(sDir + arTable[siCounter], s1, s2, s3, s4)
37:         ts.open(s1 + s2 + s3 + ".TXT","NW")
38:
39:         ;Write table to text file")
40:         TC2.open(":PRIV:STRUCT.DB")
41:         scan tc2:
42:             ts.writeLine(TC2."Field Name", chr(9), TC2."Type", chr(9),
43:             tc2."size", chr(9), TC2."Key")
44:         endScan
45:
46:         tc1.close()
47:         tc2.close()
48:         ts.close()
49:        endFor
```

```
50:        setMouseShape(MouseArrow)
51:        message("All done.")
52:    endmethod
```

2. Check the syntax and save your work. Run the script. As each structure is written, a message is displayed in the status bar.

Analysis

In step 1, lines 3–10 make up the var block, which declares all the variables used in the script. Lines 13 and 14 set the directory. Line 13 uses getAliasPath() to get the path of the current working directory and assigns it to the *sDir* variable. The user sees the initial path in line 14, where he or she can change it. Lines 17–19 make sure that "\" appears at the end of the path. In line 22, enumFileList() uses the path to put all the Paradox tables into the resizable *arTable* array. Line 23, which isn't required for this routine, displays the list of tables.

Lines 25–48 loop through the list of tables stored in *arTable* and write out the ASCII files. Lines 25 and 49 set the mouse pointer to the waiting mouse and back.

This routine is great, but it can be improved. For example, you could add a print option to each table. Also, view() is not the best option to use because it might mislead the user into thinking that he or she can cancel the process. To make the code more interesting, add a feature that creates tables with the same name as the table in a subdirectory of the destination directory.

Although a script has limited use, it enables a user to select File | Open | Script to do a set of chores. Likewise, a script is a good place to store code. Occasionally, it is useful to start off an application with a script.

ObjectPAL offers many ways to reuse and compartmentalize your code by means of custom methods in forms, custom methods in libraries, and scripts. It might not always seem as though you have time to use these code-saving features. A few extra minutes now will save you hours later, however.

Returning a Value from a Script to a Form

Q: How do you have a script return a value back to a form?
A: One way to return a value from a script back to a form is to use formReturn().

```
1:  method run(var eventInfo Event)
2:      var
```

```
3:        n Number
4:     endVar
5:
6:     n = 5
7:     formReturn(n)
8:   endMethod
```

Here is an example in the **pushbutton** method of a button playing a script:

```
1:  method pushbutton(var eventInfo Event)
2:     var
3:        any   AnyType
4:     endvar
5:
6:     any = play("scriptname")
7:  endmethod
```

Running a Script from a Form

Q: When I run a script from within a form the form won't close until the script is done running. Why?

A: The script uses a method called **run** to handle execution of ObjectPAL code when it opens. The script is considered by the form to be one of its own methods running. Because no form can close while a method is being executed, it will remain open until the script finishes execution.

Using *executeString()*

The executeString() procedure is similar to a script in that it lets you execute a bit of code. The syntax is as follows:

executeString(const **scriptText** String) AnyType

This procedure was introduced in version 4.5 and provides a way to build and execute dynamic methods. There are a few quirks to be aware of concerning executeString(). These quirks are related to the fact that executeString() generates and executes a temporary script at runtime.

- You can declare types, constants, and variables within the string, but you cannot use the Uses clause.

- To return a value from `executeString`, you must use `formReturn()`.
- If the string contains syntax errors, the Script window is left on the Desktop.

EXPLORING ACTION AND MENUACTION

Whenever you interact with Paradox, you generate either an Action or MenuAction constant. For example, when you select a menu item a constant is sent to the built-in **menuAction** method. If the constant maps to an Action constant, an equivalent Action constant is then sent to the built-in **action** method. For example, when you select File | Print, the constant `MenuFilePrint` is sent to the form's **menuAction** method. Since `MenuFilePrint` maps to the action constant `DataPrint`, `DataPrint` is sent to **action**. In the built-in methods **action** and **menuAction**, you can trap for nearly every user interaction. In addition, using the `action()` and `menuAction()` methods you can invoke or imitate nearly any user interaction by sending Action and MenuAction constants to the built-in **action** and **menuAction** methods.

Categories of ActionEvents

Time stamping a Memo field

*Using **action***

*Using **menuAction***

CATEGORIES OF ACTIONEVENTS

As you can see by Table 24.1, most action events do not bubble. In fact, only ActionDataCommands bubble.

TABLE 24.1. CATEGORIES OF ACTIONEVENTS.		
ActionEvent	*Bubble?*	*Description of Action*
ActionDataCommands	Yes	Deal with the whole form
ActionEditCommands	No	Deal with editing data
ActionFieldCommands	No	Move from field to field
ActionMoveCommands	No	Move the cursor within a field
ActionSelectCommands	No	Select data within a field

MANIPULATING A MEMO FIELD

On disk is the form CONSTANT.FSL, which demonstrates using the ActionSelectCommands and ActionMoveCommands (see Figure 24.1). Use this technique to alter the font attributes and text of a memo field.

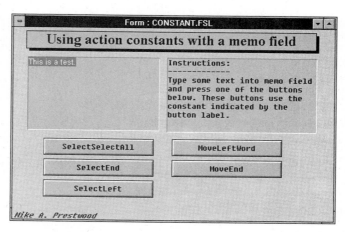

Figure 24.1. CONSTANT.FSL.

The basic technique is the same for all the buttons:

```
field.action( ActionConstant )
```

For example, the following is from the SelectSelectAll button.

```
1:  ;Form :: Var
2:  method pushButton(var eventInfo Event)
3:    fldMemo.action(SelectSelectAll)
4:  endmethod
```

TIME AND DATE STAMPING A MEMO FIELD

On disk is the form ANSWERS\STAMP-IT.FSL, which demonstrates using the ActionEditCommands and ActionMoveCommands (see Figure 24.2).

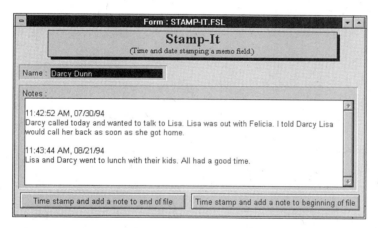

Figure 24.2. STAMP-IT.FSL.

To time stamp and add a note to end of the memo field, use lines 3–7.

```
1:  ;Button :: pushButton
2:  method pushButton(var eventInfo Event)
3:    edit()
4:    Notes.moveTo()
5:    Notes.value = Notes.value + chr(13) + String(DateTime()) + chr(13)
6:    Notes.action(EditEnterMemoView)
7:    Notes.action(MoveEnd)
8:  endmethod
```

To time stamp and add a note to the beginning of the memo field, use lines 3–8.

```
1:  ;Button :: pushButton
```

```
2:  method pushButton(var eventInfo Event)
3:    edit()
4:    Notes.moveTo()
5:    Notes.value = String(DateTime()) + chr(13) + chr(13) + Notes.value
6:    Notes.action(EditEnterMemoView)
7:    Notes.action(MoveBegin)
8:    Notes.action(MoveDown)
9:  endmethod
```

Using the action Built-In Method

Using constantValueToName() allows you to extract the name of a constant from a number. The syntax for constantValueToName() is as follows:

> constantValueToName (const *groupName* String, const *value*
> AnyType, var *constName* String) Logical

This method is very helpful in developing an application when you want to know which actions are being triggered. The one weakness of this method is that you have to specify the group type. For example, you have to specify ActionDataCommand, ActionMoveCommand, Error, or some other group. Type the following code into the **action** method of the form; this code displays every action generated and every error generated.

```
1:  ;#Form1 :: action
2:  method action(var eventInfo ActionEvent)
3:  var
4:    s String
5:  endVar
6:  if eventInfo.isPreFilter()
7:    then
8:      ; This code executes for each object on the form.
9:    dodefault
10:   s="a"
11:   constantValueToName("Errors",eventInfo.errorCode(),s)
12:   if s <> "a" and s <> "peOk" then
13:      msgInfo("Errors",s)
14:      s="a"
15:   endif
16:   constantValueToName("ActionDataCommands",eventInfo.id(),s)
17:   if s <> "a" then
18:      msgInfo("ActionDataCommands",s)
19:      s="a"
20:
21:   endif
22:   constantValueToName("ActionEditCommands",eventInfo.id(),s)
23:   if s <> "a" then
24:      msgInfo("ActionEditCommands",s)
25:      s="a"
26:   endif
27:   constantValueToName("ActionMoveCommands",eventInfo.id(),s)
```

```
28:    if s <> "a" then
29:        msgInfo("ActionMoveCommands",s)
30:        s="a"
31:    ndif
32:    constantValueToName("ActionFieldCommands",eventInfo.id(),s)
33:    if s <> "a" then
34:        msgInfo("ActionFieldCommands",s)
35:        s="a"
36:    ndif
37:    constantValueToName("ActionSelectCommands",eventInfo.id(),s)
38:
39:    if s <> "a" then
40:        msgInfo("ActionSelectCommands",s)
41:        s="a"
42:    ndif
43:
44:    else
45:        ; This code executes only for the form.
46:
47: endif
48: endmethod
```

SEND A LIST OF ALL THE CONSTANTS TO A TABLE!

Create and run the following one-line script:

```
enumRTLConstants("RTLC50.DB")
```

This script creates a table that has all 1,326 constants, including all the error constants. Use this table to create reports in any order you like.

USING MENUACTION()

Not all the menu constants are enabled in version 5. For example, `MenuFileOpen` does not display the Form Open dialog box. However, many more do work in version 5. For example, the following failed in versions 1.0 and 4.5, but in version 5, it works.

```
1:    menuAction(MenuWindowCloseAll)
```

You can use the form \ANSWERS\MENUID.FSL to browse and test menu constants (see Figure 24.3).

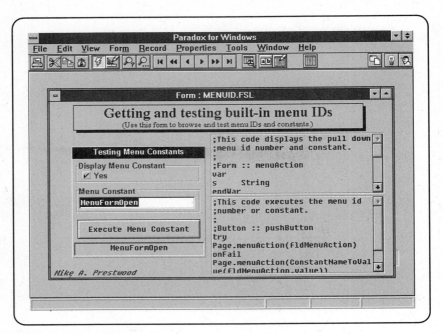

Figure 24.3. MENUID.FSL.

Steps to using the MENUID form:

1. Select a menu option to generate a menu constant.
2. Put the constant or number in the MenuAction field (the constant is always preferred). You can just click on the constant displayed below the Execute Menu Constant button.
3. Press the button to make sure it works.

The interesting bit of code is in the page's **menuAction** method and in the **pushButton** method of the button. The code in **menuAction** traps the menu constants and the **pushButton** uses a `try` block to first try to execute a MenuCommand number, then a constant.

```
;page :: menuAction
method menuAction(var eventInfo MenuEvent)
method menuAction(var eventInfo MenuEvent)
   var
      s    String
   endVar

   if eventInfo.isPreFilter() then
      ;// This code executes for each object on the form:
```

```
else
   ;// This code executes only for the form:
   switch
      case eventInfo.id() = MenuInit
         :    ;Occurs when the menu option is selected.
              ;Do nothing.
      case eventInfo.id() = MenuBuild
         :    ;Occurs when the menu is first built.
              ;Do nothing.
      case eventInfo.id() = MenuControlKeyMenu
         :    ;Menu selected via a key press.
              ;Do nothing.
                    otherwise
         :    if fldDisplay.value = "Yes" then
                 constantValueToName("MenuCommands", eventInfo.id(), s)
                 msgInfo(eventInfo.id(), s)
              endIf
   endSwitch
   constantValueToName("MenuCommands", eventInfo.id(), s)
   fldStatus.value = s
endmethod
```

You can imitate nearly any user interaction by sending Action and MenuAction
constants to the built-in **action** and **menuAction** methods with action() and
menuAction() . In addition, you can trap for most user interactions in the built-
in **action** and **menuAction** methods.

Using Menus, Toolbars, and the File System

Pop-Up Menus

A *pop-up menu* is the vertical list of options that gets attached to a menu, but it doesn't have to be attached. In other words, you can use pop-up menus without a menu. Most Borland applications use pop-up menus heavily. When you right-click an object in Paradox, the Property Inspector that appears is a pop-up menu. This section explores how to use pop-up menus with a menu variable.

Pull-down menus

Pop-up menus

Pull-down menus on a form

Using the Toolbar

Developing a custom Toolbar

You can use some of the methods and procedures from the Menu type in addition to the PopUpMenu methods and procedures. Table 25.1 lists the PopUpMenu class methods and procedures.

TABLE 25.1. POPUPMENU CLASS METHODS AND PROCEDURES.
addArray
addBar
addBreak
addPopUp
addSeparator
addStaticText
addText
contains*
count*
empty*
isAssigned**
remove*
show
switchMenu

*Inherited from the Menu type   **Inherited from the AnyType type

USING A POP-UP MENU

Stand-alone pop-up menus do not trigger **menuAction**. That is, when a user selects an option from a stand-alone pop-up menu, no event is sent to **menuAction**. Therefore, you cannot trap for stand-alone pop-up menus with

menuAction. How, then, do you trap for the user's selection? You use `show()` to display the pop-up menu. Fortunately, `show()` returns the user's selection in a string. Therefore, use the following syntax:

```
1:  s = pop1.show()
2:  if s = "Option1" then
3:     ;Execute option1 code here.
4:  endIf
```

Pull-Down Menus

A *menu* is a set of options. Typically, a menu is a list that appears horizontally across the menu bar of an application. Menus in ObjectPAL also can take the form of buttons on a form, pull-down menus, or pop-up menus. A ***pull-down menu*** is a list of items that appears when you choose a menu item from the horizontal menu list. A pull-down menu displays further options for you to choose.

Maneuvering within Windows applications has become quite elaborate. With Paradox, the user can use the built-in pull-down menus, the Toolbar, and the Property Inspector. As a programmer, you can leave the Paradox default menu in place, trap for the menu constants in the **menuAction** method, and execute your own code in place of the default behavior. You also can remove the Toolbar with `hideToolbar()`. You even can get rid of the built-in menus and use your own menus instead. You can't add to the Toolbar or menus, however.

You can add pop-up menus that are similar to the Property Inspector, and the menus can pop up anywhere on screen. Although Paradox doesn't support a custom Toolbar or balloon help—which is just now becoming popular—it does offer the programmer much control. Table 25.2 lists the Menu methods and procedures.

TABLE 25.2. MENU CLASS METHODS AND PROCEDURES.

addArray

addBreak

addPopUp

addStaticText

addText

contains

count

empty

getMenuChoiceAttribute

getMenuChoiceAttributeById

hasMenuChoiceAttribute

isAssigned*

remove

removeMenu

setMenuChoiceAttribute

setMenuChoiceAttributeById

show

*Inherited from the AnyType type

WHERE TO PUT CODE

When you use custom menus in ObjectPAL, you must do two things: build the menu and process the user's input. The usual place to define a menu is in the **arrive** method of the form or page.

If you plan to change the menus in a particular form when you move from one page to another, however, create your menus on the **arrive** method of each page. In fact, a good rule of thumb is always to build and show menus on the **arrive** method of the page. That way, if you ever need to add a menu to the form, you can add it to another page—the most logical breaking point.

To process user input, use the **menuAction** method of the page. The following steps outline a good technique for capturing and processing user input:

1. Declare a String variable that catches **menuAction** constants in step 2.
2. Use `sAns = eventInfo.menuChoice()`.
3. Use a `switch` structure to process the user's choice.

UNIQUE ENTRY MENUS

It's simple to set up a menu that always has a unique entry. For example, File | Save and Record | Save selections wouldn't work together, because Save is duplicated in two pull-down menus. If you need duplicate menu options, use a menu ID number.

To set up a unique entry menu, follow these steps:

1. Define your variables. You need to define a Menu variable for the menu itself and a PopUpMenu variable for each pull-down menu you want. For example, you might use the following code on the Var window of the page:

```
1:   var
2:     m    Menu
3:      pop  PopUpMenu
4:   endVar
```

2. Build the menu. Construct the pull-down menus, attach them to entries in the menu, and show the menu. Use the `addText()` method to add entries to the PopUpMenu variable. For example, you might use the following code on the **arrive** method of the page:

```
1:   pop.addText("Cut")
2:   pop.addText("Copy")
3:   pop.addText("Paste")
```

3. Add PopUpMenu to a menu bar item. Attach the constructed PopUpMenu variable to an entry on the Menu variable. For example, you might use the following code immediately after the code shown in step 2:

```
1:   m.addPopUp("Edit", pop)
```

4. Display the menu. You display the Menu variable with the show() method:

```
1:   m.show()
```

5. Trap for user responses. After you construct the menu, you must decide what each menu option does. In the **menuAction** method—usually the **menuAction** method of the page—you trap for the selection and act on that selection. For example, you can declare a String variable, trap for menuChoice() with eventInfo.menuChoice(), and use the switch statement to act on that selection.

```
 1:     var
 2:        sAns String      ;Declare sAns as a String variable.
 3:     endVar
 4:
 5:     sAns = eventInfo.menuChoice() ;Capture user selection.
 6:
 7:     ;Process user selection.
 8:     Switch
 9:        case sAns = "Cut"   : active.action(EditCutSelection)
10:        case sAns = "Copy"  : active.action(EditCopySelection)
11:        case sAns = "Paste" : active.action(EditPaste)
12:     endSwitch
```

The next tutorial uses the CUSTOMER.DB table from the files that come with Paradox.

Duplicating the Paradox Menu

There are times you need to create your own menu system, yet retain a few of the Paradox menu options. You can duplicate the Paradox menu and send the correct constant to the built-in **menuAction** method in one step.

```
1:   pop.addText("&Tile", MenuEnabled, MenuWindowTile)
```

This technique is particularly important now that you can add a menu to a report because menus can respond only to menu constants. More on this later in the chapter.

Tutorial: Building a Unique Entry Menu

Suppose that you wish to build a functional, two-entry, pull-down menu. File | Exit closes the form, and Edit | Cut, Edit | Copy, and Edit | Paste cuts, copies, and pastes text.

On Disk: \ANSWERS\MENU-1.FSL

Quick Steps

1. Build the menu with `addText()` and `addPopUp()`. Then display the menu with `show()`.
2. Trap for the menu selections with `eventInfo.menuChoice()`.
3. Use a `Switch` statement to process the menu selections.

Step By Step

1. Create a form based on the CUSTOMER.DB table located in the \TUTORIAL directory. You can make it as fancy as you want, but a simple form is all that you need (see Figure 25.1).

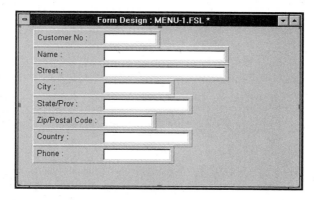

Figure 25.1. Set up form for the tutorial.

2. Define the variables in the Var window of the page.

```
1:    ;Page :: Var
2:    Var
3:       m                    Menu
4:       sAns                 String
5:       popFile, popEdit  PopUpMenu
6:    endVar
```

3. Build and show the menu in the **arrive** method of the page.

```
1:    ;Page :: arrive
2:    method arrive(var eventInfo MoveEvent)
3:       ;Build File menu.
4:       popFile.addText("Exit")
5:       m.addPopUp("File", popFile)
6:
7:       ;Build Edit menu.
8:       popEdit.addText("Cut")
```

```
 9:         popEdit.addText("Copy")
10:         popEdit.addSeparator()
11:         popEdit.addText("Paste")
12:         m.addPopUp("Edit", popEdit)
13:
14:         ;Display menu.
15:         m.show()
16:     endMethod
```

4. Trap for user selections in the **menuAction** of the page.

```
 1:     ;Page :: menuAction
 2:     method menuAction(var eventInfo MenuEvent)
 3:         sAns = eventInfo.menuChoice()
 4:
 5:       switch
 6:          case sAns = "Exit"  : close()
 7:          case sAns = "Cut"   : active.action(EditCutSelection)
 8:          case sAns = "Copy"  : active.action(EditCopySelection)
 9:          case sAns = "Paste" : active.action(EditPaste)
10:       endSwitch
11:     endmethod
```

5. Check the syntax, save the form as MENU-1.FSL, and run it (see Figure 25.2).

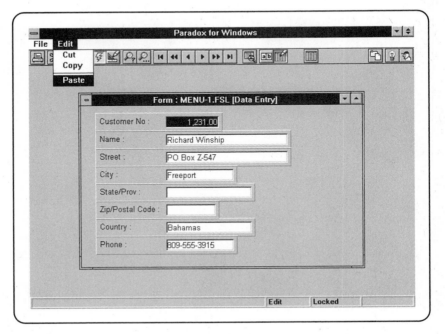

Figure 25.2. MENU-1.FSL.

Analysis

In step 2, lines 3–5 declare the variables. A good place in which to declare the menu variables is in the Var window of the page. If you declare the String variable *sAns* in the **menuAction** method, it is redeclared every time a user chooses a menu option. It makes only a minor difference here, but it can make a significant difference in a large application. It is slightly more elegant to declare the variable static; for example, in the Var window of the page.

Step 3 builds and shows the menu. Line 4 adds text to the *popFile* variable, and line 5 attaches *popFile* to the menu variable. Lines 8–11 add text to the *popEdit* variable. Line 10 adds a line to the menu between Copy and Paste with the `addSeparator()` method. Line 12 attaches the *popEdit* variable to the *m* menu variable. Now, two pop-up menus are attached to *m*. Line 15 uses the show method.

Step 4 processes the user's selection. Line 3 grabs the user's selection and puts it into the *sAns* String variable. Lines 5–10 check which selection the user has selected and respond accordingly.

DRESSING UP A MENU

Most programs use hot keys, bars, and other features to enhance the look of their menus. Use the following to dress up a menu:

```
& = accelerator (underlines character)
\008 = all the way to the right like Help
\009 = tab use only on a sub menu
addSeperator()
addBreak()
addBar()
```

USING MENU ID NUMBERS

Menu IDs allow you to have identical menu options. The next tutorial shows you how to build a menu by using menu IDs.

Tutorial: Using Menu ID Numbers

This tutorial demonstrates using menu IDs. In this tutorial, you build a menu that is identical to the one in the previous tutorial, but this time the menu uses menu IDs.

On Disk: \ANSWERS\MENU-2.FSL

Quick Steps

1. Use the third syntax variation of `addText()` to build pop-up menus that use IDs.
2. Add the pop-up menus to the menu variable by using `addPopUp()`.
3. Display the menu with `show()`.
4. Trap for the menu selections with `eventInfo.id()`.
5. Use `Switch` statement to process the menu selections.

Step By Step

1. Change your working directory to the TUTORIAL directory and create a new form.
2. Define the variables in the Var window of the form.

```
1:     ;Page :: Var
2:     Var
3:         m                      Menu
4:         popFile, popEdit   PopUpMenu
5:         siAns                  SmallInt
6:     endVar
```

3. Build and show the menu in the page's **arrive** method.

```
1:     ;Page :: arrive
2:     method arrive(var eventInfo MoveEvent)
3:         ;Build File menu
4:         popFile.addText("Exit", MenuEnabled, UserMenu + 101)
5:         m.addPopUp("File", popFile)
6:
7:         ;Build Edit menu
8:         popEdit.addText("Cut", MenuEnabled, UserMenu + 201)
9:         popEdit.addText("Copy", MenuEnabled, UserMenu + 202)
10:        popEdit.addSeparator()
11:        popEdit.addText("Paste", MenuEnabled, UserMenu + 203)
12:        m.addPopUp("Edit", popEdit)
13:
14:        ;Display menu
15:        m.show()
16:    endMethod
```

4. Trap for the menu selection in the page's **menuAction** method.

```
1:     ;Page :: menuAction
2:     method menuAction(var eventInfo MenuEvent)
3:         siAns = eventInfo.id()
4:
5:         Switch
6:           case siAns = UserMenu + 101
7:               :  close()
8:           case siAns = UserMenu + 201
9:               :  active.action(EditCutSelection)
```

```
10:          case siAns = UserMenu + 202
11:              : active.action(EditCopySelection)
12:          case siAns = UserMenu + 203
13:              : active.action(EditPaste)
14:       endSwitch
15:    endmethod
```

5. Check the syntax, save the form as MENU-2.FSL, and run it (see Figure 25.3).

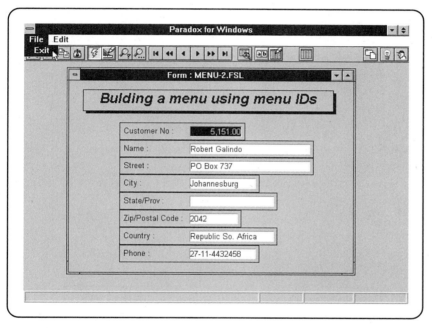

Figure 25.3. MENU-2.FSL.

Analysis

The only lines analyzed here are those that deal with using menu IDs. For analysis of the other lines, refer to the Analysis section in the preceding tutorial.

In step 2, line 5 declares a SmallInt variable for use in step 4.

In step 3, line 4 and lines 8–11 use the third syntax variation to assign return values to the menu options. They use the UserMenu built-in constant, which gives you the base value allowed in this version of Paradox. The numbering system used here and in the manuals is only by convention; with this version, you can use any numbers up to 2000 that you like. To verify the maximum number you can use with the constant UserMenu, type line 3 into the **pushButton** method of a button.

```
1:     ;Button :: pushButton
2:     method pushButton(var eventInfo Event)
3:             view(UserMenuMax - UserMenu)        ;Displays 2000.
4:     endmethod
```

It's a good idea to use the first digit of the menu ID for its left-to-right position and the next two digits for its top-to-bottom position. MenuEnabled is used because syntax 3 of addText() requires a MenuChoiceAttributes constant.

In step 4, lines 5–14 process the user's selection in the **menuAction** method. Lines 6–12 must use UserMenu because UserMenu was used earlier.

USING THE *MenuInit* CONSTANT

When you activate a menu, the first event isn't MenuChoice(); it's MenuInit. This occurs just before the item or pull-down menu is displayed. It's your last-minute chance to change the status of the menu items. You might want to add the following code:

```
1:  if eventinfo.id() <> MenuInit then
2:      sChoice = eventInfo.menuChoice()
3:      view(sChoice)
4:  endif
```

Use MenuEnabled only when you're creating menus. Use setMenuChoiceAttributes() later to modify them.

Table 25.3 lists the menu choice attributes.

TABLE 25.3. MENU CHOICE ATTRIBUTES.

Attribute	Description
MenuChecked	Displays a checkmark before the menu option
MenuDisabled	Disables the menu option
MenuEnabled	Activates the menu option

Attribute	Description
MenuGrayed	Grays a menu option and deactivates it
MenuHilited	Highlights the menu option
MenuNotChecked	Removes a checkmark
MenuNotGrayed	Displays the item normally
MenuNotHilited	Turns off an option's highlight

CASCADING MENUS

A *cascading menu* is the object that pops up when a pull-down menu or a pop-up menu displays another pop-up menu. The next tutorial shows you how to build a cascading menu.

TUTORIAL: CASCADING PULL-DOWN MENUS

Suppose that you need to build a cascading menu.

On Disk: \ANSWERS\MENU-3.FSL

Quick Steps

1. Build the menus and submenus with addText.
2. Use addPopUp to add the pop-up submenu to the pop-up menu.
3. Display the menu with show.
4. Trap for the menu selections with eventInfo.menuChoice.
5. Use Switch and case to process the menu selections.

Step By Step

1. Change your working directory to the TUTORIAL directory and create a new form.
2. Define the variables in the page's Var window.

```
1:    ;Page :: Var
2:    Var
3:       m                            Menu
4:       popFile, popEdit, popCut     PopUpMenu
5:       sAns                         String
6:    endVar
```

3. Build the menus in the page's **arrive** method.

```
 1:    ;Page :: arrive
 2:    method arrive(var eventInfo MoveEvent)
 3:        ;Build File menu
 4:        popFile.addText("Exit")
 5:        m.addPopUp("File", popFile)
 6:
 7:        ;Build Cut sub menu
 8:        popCut.addText("Text")
 9:        popCut.addText("Record")
10:        popEdit.addPopUp("Cut", popCut)
11:
12:        ;Build Edit menu
13:        popEdit.addText("Copy")
14:        popEdit.addSeparator()
15:        popEdit.addText("Paste")
16:        m.addPopUp("Edit", popEdit)
17:
18:        ;Display menu
19:        m.show()
20:    endMethod
```

4. Trap for user input in the page's **menuAction** method.

```
 1:    ;Page :: menuAction
 2:    method menuAction(var eventInfo MenuEvent)
 3:        sAns = eventInfo.menuChoice()
 4:
 5:        Switch
 6:          case sAns = "Exit"
 7:              : close()
 8:          case sAns = "Text"
 9:              : active.action(EditCutSelection)
10:          case sAns = "Record"
11:              : active.action(DataDeleteRecord)
12:          case sAns = "Copy"
13:              : active.action(EditCopySelection)
14:          case sAns = "Paste"   : active.action(EditPaste)
15:        endSwitch
16:    endmethod
```

5. Check the syntax, save the form as MENU-3.FSL, and run it. Figure 25.4 shows how the MENU-3.FSL form looks.

Analysis

The only lines analyzed here are those that deal with using cascading menus. For analysis of the other lines, refer to the Analysis sections in the previous two tutorials.

In step 2, line 4 uses an extra pop-up menu variable, *popCut*.

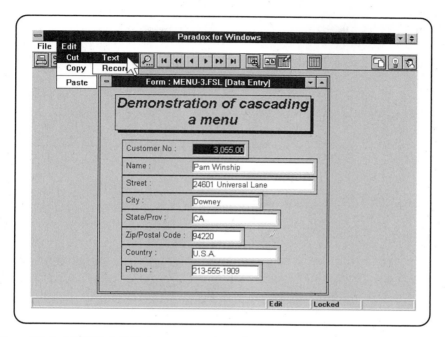

Figure 25.4. MENU-3.FSL demonstrates cascading menus.

In step 3, lines 8 and 9 add two entries to the pop-up menu variable *popCut*. Line 10 adds *popCut* to *popEdit*. Lines 13–15 construct the rest of the *popEdit* pop-up menu. Line 16 adds this cascaded menu to the *m* menu variable. Line 19 displays the results.

Step 4 processes the user's menu choice.

You can use this technique to cascade as many times as you need. Don't overuse cascading menus. You can use one or two cascades, but anything more becomes cumbersome for the user and takes up a lot of memory.

MENU CONSTANTS HAVE DUPLICATES

ObjectPAL is a very rich language. In fact, there are often two or three ways to accomplish a single task. Many menu constants have duplicate constants in other classes. For example, the menu constant MenuFilePrint has a DataAction constant `DataPrint`. Because Borland might change the menu constant in the future, use the other class constants whenever possible. For example, rather than print your form with `menuAction(MenuFilePrint)`, use `action(DataPrint)`.

> Don't confuse the `menuAction()` procedure with the **menuAction** built-in method.

Overcoming the Pop-Up Menu Limit

When you display more items than what will fit on the screen, the pop-up menu keeps going, and you can't see the options off the screen. You can use the `mod()` method to determine how many columns you need to display, and build the pop-up menu accordingly.

You can use Paradox as a model. Paradox displays many fonts by using a two-step approach. When there are too many fonts to display on a pop-up, Paradox displays *n* items with the string *More* as the last option. When the user selects that item, a dialog box that displays all the fonts in a table frame object appears. This solution is easy for the user to use, and it's straightforward to implement. An alternative is to write code that wraps the menu items to multiple columns.

The number of items is limited to 35. You can change this limit, however. Although Borland imposed this limit, it actually comes from Windows. Windows creates menus in the USER segment, which is limited to 64K. Many other objects must share this same segment of memory. If the USER segment is nearly full, don't create a new ObjectPAL menu. If the USER segment becomes too full, Windows will crash in ways and places over which Paradox has no control.

UNDOCUMENTED `menuSetLimit()` PROCEDURE

Borland set a limit of 35 options for each pop-up menu that you build. If you want to create a single pop-up with more than 35 options, use the undocumented `menuSetLimit()` procedure. For example:

```
menuSetLimit(NumberOfItems)
```

During the testing of the product, when ObjectPAL programmers tried to create menus with hundreds of items, they got GPFs from Windows. As a rule of thumb for user interfaces, don't create menus or pop-up menus with a large number of items. It's too difficult to select one from the list. For this reason, Borland put an artificial limit of 35 items for each top-level menu, pop-up menu, and submenu. If you need to increase this limit, use **menuSetLimit** (*NumberOfItems*)

This gets you past the artificial limit, but it opens up the possibility of Windows crashing if you include too many options. How many is too many? That depends on your system and the applications that are currently running. Use `menuSetLimit()` at your own risk for two reasons: first, you could end up with an unstable application, and second, Borland may take out any undocumented software in the future.

The form ANSWERS\POPUP100.FSL demonstrates using `menuSetLimit()` (see Figure 25.5).

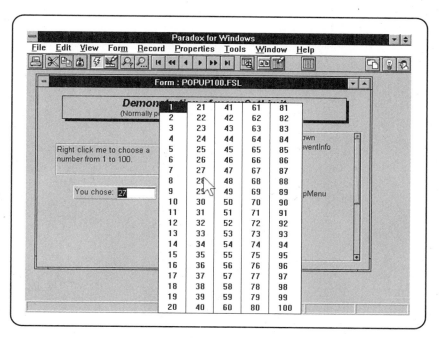

Figure 25.5. POPUP100.FSL.

The following is the pertinent code from POPUP100.FSL from the **mouseRightDown** method of the *txtInstruction* text object.

```
 1:  ;txtInstruction :: mouseRightDown
 2:  method mouseRightDown(var eventInfo MouseEvent)
 3:    var
 4:       si1Counter   SmallInt
 5:       si2Counter   SmallInt
 6:       popChose     PopUpMenu
 7:    endVar
 8:
 9:    si2Counter = 0
10:
11:    menuSetLimit(200)
12:
13:    for si1Counter from 1 to 100
14:       popChose.addText(si1Counter)
15:
16:       si2Counter = si2Counter + 1
17:       if si2Counter = 20 then
18:         popChose.addBar()
19:         si2Counter = 0
20:       endIf
21:    endFor
22:
23:    fldChose = popChose.show()
24: endmethod
```

PULL-DOWN MENUS ON A FORM

Although ObjectPAL doesn't have an explicit command for putting pull-down menus on a form, you can simulate one by using PopUpMenu, a box, and a text object.

Tutorial: Creating Pull-Down Menus on a Form

This tutorial shows you how to create a pull-down menu on a form.

On Disk: \ANSWERS\MENU-4.FSL

Step By Step

1. Create a form with a long white box at the top that resembles a menu bar. Add two text objects labeled *File* and *Quit* (see Figure 25.6).

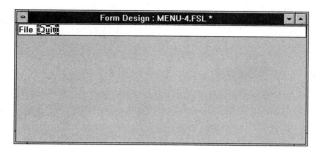

Figure 25.6. MENU-4.FSL.

2. Create a custom method called `cmFileMenu()` at the form level and add lines 3–23 to it.

```
1:    ;FileText :: cmFileMenu
2:    method cmFileMenu()
3:       var
4:          p          PopUpMenu
5:          sChoice    String
6:       endVar
7:
8:       oldforgroundcolor=self.font.color
9:       oldbackgroundcolor=self.color
10:      subject.color=DarkBlue
11:      subject.font.color=White
12:
13:      p.addtext("Option1")
14:      p.addtext("Option2")
15:
16:      sChoice=p.show(20,300)
17:      subject.color=oldbackgroundcolor
18:      subject.font.color=oldforgroundcolor
19:
20:      switch
21:        case sChoice = "Option1" : msgInfo("", "Option 1")
22:        case sChoice = "Option2" : msgInfo("", "Option 2")
23:      endSwitch
24:   endmethod
```

3. Call the custom method for the first time by adding line 3 to the **mouseDown** method of the FileText object.

```
1:    ;FileText :: mouseDown
2:    method mouseDown(var eventInfo MouseEvent)
3:       cmFileMenu()
4:    endmethod
```

4. Call the custom method for the second time by adding line 3 to the **mouseClick** method of the FileText object.

```
 1:   ;FileText :: mouseClick
 2:   method mouseClick(var eventInfo MouseEvent)
 3:       cmFileMenu()
 4:   endmethod
```

5. Add lines 3-13 to the **mouseClick** method.

```
 1:   ;QuitText :: mouseClick
 2:   method mouseClick(var eventInfo MouseEvent)
 3:       oldforgroundcolor=self.font.color   ;Original colors.
 4:       oldbackgroundcolor=self.color
 5:       self.color=DarkBlue   ;Sets new colors
 6:       self.font.color=White
 7:
 8:       if msgQuestion("Quit?", "Are you sure?") = "Yes" then
 9:          close()
10:       endIf
11:
12:       self.color=oldbackgroundcolor   ;Back to original.
13:       self.font.color=oldforgroundcolor
14:   endmethod
```

6. Save the form as MENU-4.FSL and run it. Select the three options set up in this tutorial. Figure 25.7 shows that there are two sets of pull-down menus.

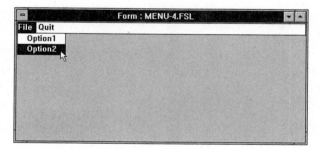

Figure 25.7. MENU-4.FSL. There are two sets of pull-down menus.

In the above tutorial, notice that the custom method is at the form level. It was placed at the form level only for convenience of this tutorial. An even better technique would be to move the custom methods to the box that contains the text boxes instead of all the way up at the form level. This would make the form menu object a self-contained object that can be pasted from form to form.

The form shown in Figure 25.8, PULLDOWN.FSL, demonstrates a technique for simulating pull-down menus on a form. It was developed for this book by Dave Orriss Jr. when Dave worked at Borland.

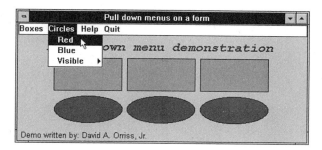

Figure 25.8. PULLDOWN.FSL. Simulating pull-down menus on a form.

The *BuildMenu* and *MenuInit* Constants

You can trap for all MenuCommand constants in the **menuAction** method, including MenuBuild and MenuInit. The MenuBuild constant reports when the Desktop is building a menu. The MenuInit constant reports when the user selects a menu option from a pull-down menu. With these two constants, you can trap for when a menu is built or when a user selects a menu option.

Tutorial: Using *setMenu( )* with a Report

The default menus that display with a report allow the user to do many tasks you may not wish—for example, opening a table. Suppose that you wish to use just a limited set of menu options.

On Disk: \ANSWERS\SETMENU.FSL

Quick Steps

1. Build a menu.
2. Open the report and use setMenu() to attach the menu to the report using the report variable with which you opened it.

Step By Step

1. Change your working directory to the TUTORIAL directory, create a new form, and place a button on it.

2. In the **pushButton** method, type lines 3–17:

```
1:     ;theBox :: mouseClick
2:     method pushButton(var eventInfo Event)
3:        var
4:           r     Report
5:           m     Menu
6:          pop   PopUpMenu
7:        endVar
8:
9:        r.open("REPORT", WinStyleDefault + WinStyleMaximize)
10:
11:       pop.addText("&Print...", MenuEnabled, MenuFilePrint)
12:       pop.addText("&Printer Setup...", MenuEnabled,
          ➥MenuFilePrinterSetup)
13:       pop.addText("&Close", MenuEnabled, MenuControlClose)
14:       m.addPopUp("&File", pop)
15:
16:       r.setMenu(m)
17:    endmethod
```

3. Check the syntax, save the form as SETMENU.FSL, and run it (see Figure 25.9).

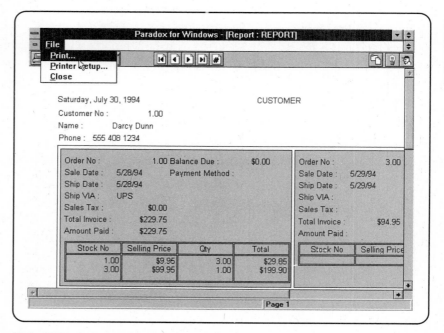

Figure 25.9. SETMENU.FSL adding a menu to a report.

Analysis

In step 2, line 9 opens the REPORT.RSL with the *r* Report variable declared in line 4. Lines 11–14 build the menu and line 16 attaches it to the report using the *r* Report variable. It is important to note the use of menu constants in lines 11–13. You can add menu options only to reports that call existing menu constants. Therefore, using menus on reports is somewhat limited.

SIMULATING A TOOLBAR ON A FORM

Toolbars don't exist at the form level, but you can simulate one. One technique is to make a screen shot of the Paradox Desktop (with the Toolbar). Open Paintbrush and cut out Paradox's Toolbar. Add it to your form, and add methods to each button. To create a form-level Toolbar, follow these steps:

1. Press the Print Screen button on your keyboard while Paradox is showing. This sends a bitmap to the Clipboard.
2. Launch Paintbrush and paste the image into it.
3. Cut out only the Toolbar—or only the parts that you want.
4. Paste the image into your form.
5. Add a transparent box over every Toolbar option.
6. Add code to the **mouseClick** method of each transparent box.

This technique works, but no option on the Toolbar depresses. If you want to go through the trouble, you can use two bitmaps and toggle their visible properties or place a bitmap inside a real button. One final technique is to use a graphic as a button by toggling its frame between `Inside3DFrame` and `Outside3DFrame`. This technique is demonstrated in the Paradox Desktop and since the form is a delivered form, the following is the pertinent code. Add a bitmap to a form and type the following code:

```
1: ; Bitmap :: mouseDown
2: method mouseDown(var eventInfo MouseEvent)
3:    self.Frame.Style = Inside3DFrame    ;Make frame pop in.
4: endmethod
```

```
1: ;Bitmap :: mouseUp
2: method mouseUp(var eventInfo MouseEvent)
3:    self.Frame.Style = Outside3DFrame   ;Make frame pop out.
4: endmethod
```

The interesting thing about using **mouseDown**, **mouseUp**, and **mouseClick** is that **mouseClick** is called only when the pointer is inside the boundary of the object for both the **mouseDown** and **mouseUp** methods. This behaves just like a real button. You can execute any code you wish in the **mouseClick**, but here is the code that is executed in the **mouseClick** method of the light bulb bitmap in Paradox Desktop:

```
1:;Bitmap :: mouseClick
2: var
3:    siQuestion    SmallInt
4: endVar
5: method mouseClick(var eventInfo MouseEvent)
6:    if not siQuestion.isAssigned() then
7:        siQuestion = 1
8:    endIf
9:
10:    switch
11:        case siQuestion = 1
12:        :  msgInfo("About this screen", "This screen is the main screen.")
13:            siQuestion = 2
14:        case siQuestion = 2
15:        :  msgInfo("Keyboard Short Cuts", "Ctrl+M = Paradox Desktop Menu")
16:            siQuestion = 3
17:        case siQuestion = 3
18:        :  msgInfo("Tip / Hint", "Run multiple instances to increase your
           productivity.")
19:            siQuestion = 1
20: endSwitch
21: endmethod
```

Floating

You also can use a separate form to simulate a floating Toolbar. Create a form that is long and thin like the Paradox floating Toolbar. Put buttons or pictures on it. Then, make the form a dialog box. If the form isn't a dialog box, it's hidden every time the user selects the main form. Chapter 15, "Handling Reports," contains an example of this technique: the sample Toolbar.

FileSystem Methods and Procedures

With the FileSystem commands, you can change your working directory, manipulate files on a disk, get the time and date of a file, and do many other things. Table 25.4 lists the FileSystem methods and procedures.

TABLE 25.4. FileSystem methods and procedures.	
accessRights	isRemote
clearDirLock	isRemovable
copy	makeDir
delete	name
deleteDir	privDir
drives	rename
enumFileList	setDir
existDrive	setDirLock
findFirst	setDrive
findNext	setFileAccessRights
freeDiskSpace	setPrivDir
fullName	setWorkingDir
getDir	size
getDrive	splitFullFileName
getFileAccessRights	startUpDir
getValidFileExtensions	time
isAssigned	totalDiskSpace
isDir	windowsDir
isFile	windowsSystemDir
isFixed	workingDir

Changing Your Working Directory

To change working directories, use the setWorkingDir() method. This is particularly useful when you open a form. On the **open** of the form, do the following:

```
1:    var
2:      f        Form
```

```
3:      dynPath  DynArray[] String
4:   endVar
5:
6:   f.attach()
7:   splitFullFileName(f.getFileName(), dynPath)
8:   setWorkingDir(dynPath["Drive"] + dynPath["Path"])
```

The default behavior when you change working directories is to close all the objects that are open on the Paradox desktop. If you wish to prevent the currently opened objects from closing, use the following in the form's **menuAction**:

```
1:   if eventInfo.id() = MenuChangingWork then
2:       eventInfo.setErrorCode(1)
3:   endIf
```

It is important to note that you cannot execute any code after calling setWorkingDir() in the **open** method. If you wish to execute code after changing working directories, then trap for the MenuChangedWork constant in **menuAction**.

```
1:   if eventInfo.id() = MenuChangedWork then
2:       ;Execute more code here.
3:   endIf
```

Both setWorkingDir() and setPrivDir() are posted actions. Therefore, the logical value returned by them reports whether the action was posted (placed in the event que)—not whether the directory was changed. Instead, use a try block to see whether the directory changed; do not depend on the return value.

Tutorial: Changing the Working Directory of a Form

Suppose that you wish to automatically change working directories when a form opens. In this case, you wish to change the working directory to the same directory the form is in.

On Disk: \ANSWERS\WORK1.FSL

Quick Steps
1. Use setWorkingDir() in the **open** of the form.
2. Check for the constant MenuChangingWork in the **action** of the form and set a nonzero error.

Step By Step
1. Change your working directory to TUTORIAL and create a new form.

2. Add lines 3–6 and 14–21 to the **open** method of the form.

```
 1:    ;Form :: open
 2:    method open(var eventInfo Event)
 3:       var
 4:          f      Form
 5:          dyn1 DynArray[] String
 6:       endVar
 7:
 8:       if eventInfo.isPreFilter() then
 9:          ;// This code executes for each object on the form:
10:
11:    else
12:       ;// This code executes only for the form:
13:
14:       ;Set working directory to this directory.
15:       f.attach()
16:       if not isFile(":WORK:WORK1.FSL") then
17:          splitFullFileName(f.getFileName(), dyn1)
18:          if not setWorkingDir(dyn1["Drive"] + dyn1["Path"]) then
19:            errorShow()
20:          endIf
21:       endIf
22:
23:    endif
24:
25:    endmethod
```

3. Add lines 9–11 to the **open** method of the form.

```
 1:    ;Form :: menuAction
 2:    method menuAction(var eventInfo MenuEvent)
 3:
 4:       if eventInfo.isPreFilter() then
 5:          ;// This code executes for each object on the form:
 6:
 7:    else
 8:       ;// This code executes only for the form:
 9:       if eventInfo.id() = MenuChangingWork then ;Do not close this
              ➥form.
10:          eventInfo.setErrorCode(1) ;When the working directory
              ➥changes.
11:       endIf
12:
13:    endif
14:
15:    endmethod
```

4. Check the syntax, save the new form as WORK1.FSL, and close it.
   Change your working directory to some other directory and open up
   the form by browsing for it. When it opens, notice what your working
   directory is set to (see Figure 25.10).

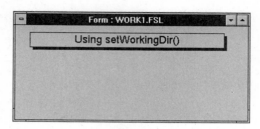

Figure 25.10. WORK1.FSL.

Analysis

In step 2, line 15 attaches to the current form with the Form variable declared in line 4. Line 16 checks to see whether the current file is in the working directory, and if it is not, proceeds with lines 17–20. Line 17 grabs the current path and puts it into the *dyn1* DynArray that was declared in line 5. Line 18 uses the DynArray to set the working directory and displays an error in line 19 if it fails.

In step 3, line 9 checks the *eventInfo* id for the constant MenuChangingWork. If the current id is MenuChangingWork, then a nonzero error code is set in line 10.

One other constant of interest when you're changing working directories is MenuChangedWork. This constant flows through **menuAction** after the working directory has successfully changed. You can use this, for example, to let the user know what the new working directory is whenever the working directory has changed. For example:

```
1: ;Form :: menuAction
2: if eventInfo.id() = MenuChangedWork then
3:    message("New working directory: " + workingDir())
4: endIf
```

Tutorial: Finding the Path of a File

Suppose that you wish to have a button open up the Paradox browser, browse for a file, select a file, and place it and its full path in a field. (This task is harder than it should be.)

On Disk: \ANSWERS\FINDPATH.FSL

Quick Steps

1. Use the fileBrowser() procedure with the FilebrowserInfo variable to find a file.
2. Use isDir() along with subStr() to determine the path of the file.

Step By Step

1. Change your working directory to the TUTORIAL directory and create a new form with a field and a button on it. Name the field *fldFile* and label the button Browse (see Figure 25.11).

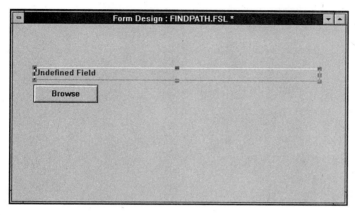

Figure 25.11. Set up form for the tutorial.

2. In the **pushButton** method, type lines 3–23:

```
1:   ;Button :: pushButton
2:   method pushButton(var eventInfo Event)
3:     var
4:       sFilename   String
5:       fbi         FileBrowserInfo
6:     endVar
7:
8:     if fileBrowser(sFileName, fbi) then
9:             ;A File was selected.
10:    else      ;If no file is selected,
11:      return  ;then return.
12:    endIf
13:
14:    ;Find path of file.
15:    switch
16:      case isDir(fbi.alias)
17:        : fldFile.value = fbi.alias + fbi.path + sFilename
18:      case sFilename.subStr(1,6) = ":PRIV:"
19:        : sFilename = sFilename.subStr(7, sFilename.size() - 6)
20:          fldFile.value = getAliasPath(":PRIV:") + "\\" + sFilename
21:      otherwise
22:        : fldFile.value = getAliasPath(fbi.alias) + "\\" + fbi.path
                ➥+ sFilename
23:    endSwitch
24:  endmethod
```

3. Check the syntax, save the form as FINDPATH.FSL, and run it (see Figure 25.12). Click the Browse button and choose a file. Try choosing files from the current working directory and from another directory using an alias.

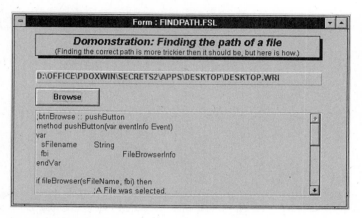

Figure 25.12. FINDPATH.FSL.

Analysis

In step 2, lines 3–6 declare an *sFilename* string variable to receive the name of the file in line 8 and an *fbi* FileBrowserInfo variable for use with `fileBrowser()`, also in line 8. Lines 15–23 determine the path of the file.

In the next tutorial, you set up a way to launch a file by double-clicking on its filename.

Tutorial: Finding a File

Suppose that you wish to create a form that lists all the files in a directory and enables the user to launch a file by double-clicking its filename.

On Disk: \ANSWERS\FINDFILE.FSL

Quick Steps

1. Create a form with two fields on it. Make one of the fields a list field.
2. Use `findFirst()` and `findNext()` to populate the list field.
3. Use `execute()` to execute one of the values.

Step By Step

1. Create a new form with two undefined fields. Label the first undefined field *Search For*, and change its name to *SearchForField* (see Figure 25.13). Make the second undefined field a list field; change its name to *fldResult* and its list to *FileList*. Figure 25.14 shows the Object Tree of the list field. The list object is inside the field object.

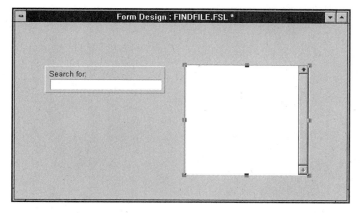

Figure 25.13. Set up form for the tutorial.

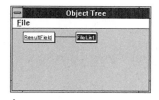

Figure 25.14. The Object Tree of the list field.

2. Place a text object above the *fldResult* field with the text *Double click to execute*. Figure 25.15 shows how your form should now look.

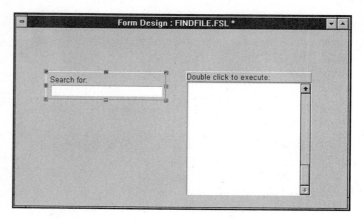

Figure 25.15. Add instructions via a text object.

3. Add line 3 to the Var window of the *Search for* field.

```
1:     ;SearchForField :: Var
2:     Var
3:        fs FileSystem
4:     endVar
```

4. Add lines 3 and 4 to the **open** method of the *Search for* field.

```
1:     ;SearchForField :: open
2:     method open(var eventInfo Event)
3:        doDefault
4:        self.value = windowsDir() + "\\*.EXE"
5:     endmethod
```

5. Add lines 3–17 to the **newValue** method of the *Search for* field.

```
1:     ;SearchForField :: newValue
2:     method newValue(var eventInfo Event)
3:        if not SearchForField.isBlank() then
4:           if fs.findFirst(SearchForField) then
5:              fldResult.FileList.list.count = 0
6:              fldResult.FileList.list.selection = 1
7:              fldResult.FileList.list.value = FS.name()
8:              while FS.findNext()
9:                 fldResult.FileList.list.selection =
                    ↪fldResult.FileList.list.selection +1
10:                fldResult.FileList.list.value = FS.name()
11:             endWhile
12:          else
13:             fldResult.FileList.list.count = 0
14:             fldResult.FileList.list.selection = 1
15:             fldResult.FileList.list.value = "File not found"
16:          endIf
17:       endIf
18:    endmethod
```

6. Add lines 3–7 to the **mouseDouble** method of the *fldResult* field.

```
1:    ;fldResult :: mouseDouble
2:    method mouseDouble(var eventInfo MouseEvent)
3:       try
4:          execute(fldResult.value)
5:       onFail
6:          msgStop("Warning", "Could not launch file")
7:       endTry
8:    endmethod
```

7. Check the syntax and save the form. Run the form. All the .EXE files from your Windows directory are listed. If you double-click a file, it will execute (see Figure 25.16). Change the extension to .HLP. If .HLP is associated with WINHELP.EXE like the Windows default, you can double-click any Help file to launch it. Now, type in an invalid extension—for example, .XYZ. The words *File not found* appear.

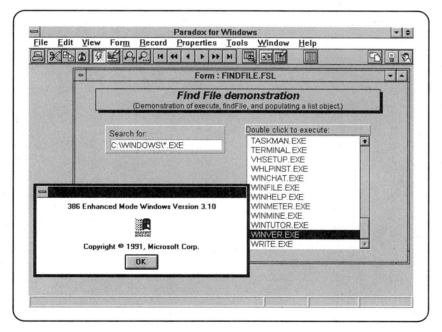

Figure 25.16. FINDFILE.FSL.

Analysis

In step 3, line 3 sets up *fs* as a FileSystem variable. It's used later in step 5.

In step 4, line 4 populates the *Search for* field after invoking the default behavior.

In step 5, line 3 checks the value, and line 9 uses it and the *fs* system variable to find the first occurrence of the search criteria. If nothing is found, the execution skips to line 14. Lines 14–16 clear the list and set the first value to *File not found.* If line 3 finds a file, lines 5–7 clear the list and set the initial value, and lines 8–12 loop through and populate the rest of the list.

In step 6, lines 3–7 attempt to launch the value that you double-click. These lines use a try block. If you don't use a try block, ObjectPAL will display abstract errors when the file isn't found. In other words, many ObjectPAL errors are meant for the programmer. You might want to use a try structure to test your code. If it fails, display a more meaningful message to the end user.

Pull-down menus, Toolbars, and the FileSystem give the user a sense of control. With the techniques you learned in this chapter, you can give your users control over your applications. Remember to be consistent within an application. If you develop a particularly attractive look and feel for one application, you might want to use it with all your applications.

LAUNCHING THINGS

UNLIMITED EXPANSIBILITY

This chapter shows you how to add more power to Paradox through the use of and communication with other applications. You'll learn how to quickly and easily add other applications to your application —true object-oriented programming (plug and go).

The open architecture of Paradox means that there are very few limits to the kinds of applications you can create. Through DLLs, Paradox supports direct access to functions written in traditional programming languages. Paradox also offers full support for DDE and OLE. In addition, you can execute commands to launch anything Windows can launch (discussed in this chapter). This includes Windows and DOS applications and batch files. You can use the execute() procedure (see Table 26.1 for the commands) to easily include other applications in the applications you develop. Doing so gives the user easy access to those applications and increases the functionality of your applications.

Executing Windows applications

Executing DOS applications

Using switchMenu to build fast and easy pop-up menus

Getting the most out of batch files

Command	Class	Description
execute	DDE	Sends a command via a DDE link
execute	System	Executes an application

TABLE 26.1. THE TWO execute() COMMANDS.

EXECUTING WINDOWS APPLICATIONS

Sometimes it's useful to start another application from within a form, such as the Windows Notepad or Calculator. Many applications, such as Quicken for Windows, give the user such access to other programs through icons or pushbuttons. Paradox makes it easy to implement this type of feature; it takes just one line of code that uses the execute() procedure. The following example starts the Solitaire program from the **pushButton** method of a button object:

```
1:  ;Button :: push Button
2:  method pushButton(var eventInfo Event)
3:    if not execute("CALC.EXE") then
4:      msgStop("Error", "Unable to start application.")
5:    endif
6:  endmethod
```

Remember that two backslashes (\ \ ) take the place of a single backslash (\ ) whenever you need to include a single backslash in a string. When you use the execute() command, you pass it a string to execute—for example, C:\ \IDAPI\ \IDAPICFG.EXE.

EXECUTING DOS APPLICATIONS

In addition to executing Windows applications, you can execute anything Windows can execute, including DOS applications. For example, to start a DOS session, you could execute a Windows .PIF file or the COMMAND.COM directly:

```
1:  ;Button :: pushButton
2:  method pushButton(var eventInfo Event)
3:    execute("COMMAND.COM")
4:  endmethod
```

USING *execute( )* WITH *switchMenu*

The following tutorial adds the most useful Windows and DOS applications to a button. As soon as these four buttons are created, you can simply copy and paste from them into any application you develop.

A **desk accessory** is a term usually used in the Macintosh world to refer to a small application that adds functionality to an application. You can create or use small Windows or Paradox applications with your application.

Tutorial: Using *execute( )* with *switchMenu*

Suppose that you wish to set up four buttons. The first button will launch some common Windows applications. The second will launch the Paradox accessory applications. The third will launch the Paradox help files, and the fourth will launch some common DOS applications.

On Disk: \ANSWERS\DA.FSL

Quick Steps

For each button, use a switchMenu structure along with the execute() command to show the user options and to execute the commands.

Step By Step

1. Create a form with four buttons on it. Label them WinApp Desk Accessories, DOS Desk Accessories, PDoxWin Desk Accessories, and PDoxWin Info (see Figure 26.1).

Figure 26.1. Set up form for tutorial.

2. Add lines 3–7 to the **pushButton** method of the DOS Desk Accessories button.

```
1:    ;Button :: pushButton
2:    method pushButton(var eventInfo Event)
3:       switchMenu
4:          case "DOS" : execute("COMMAND.COM")
5:          case "Edit" : execute("EDIT.COM")
6:          case "DOS Shell" : execute("DOSSHELL.COM")
7:       endSwitchMenu
8:    endmethod
```

3. Add lines 3–6 to the **pushButton** method of the PDoxWin Desk Accessories button.

```
1:    ;Button :: pushButton
2:    method pushButton(var eventInfo Event)
3:       switchMenu
4:          case "IDAPI Config" : execute("IDAPICFG.EXE")
5:          case "Local Settings" : execute("PWLOCAL.EXE")
6:       endSwitchMenu
7:    endmethod
```

4. Add lines 3–12 to the **pushButton** method of the PDoxWin Info button.

```
1:    ;Button :: pushButton
2:    method pushButton(var eventInfo Event)
3:       switchMenu
4:          case "PDoxWin Help"
5:             : execute("WINHELP.EXE PDOXWIN.HLP")
6:          case "OPal Help"
7:             : execute("WINHELP.EXE PAL.HLP")
8:          case "IDAPI Help"
9:             : execute("WINHELP.EXE IDAPICFG.HLP")
10:         case "Read Me"
11:            : execute("NOTEPAD.EXE README.TXT")
12:      endSwitchMenu
13:   endmethod
```

5. Add lines 3–10 to the **pushButton** method of the WinApps Desk Accessories button.

```
1:    ;Button :: pushButton
2:    method pushButton(var eventInfo Event)
```

```
 3:        switchMenu
 4:            case "Calculator" : execute("CALC.EXE")
 5:            case "Clock" : execute("CLOCK.EXE")
 6:            case "Control Panel" : execute("CONTROL.EXE")
 7:            case "File Manager" : execute("WINFILE.EXE")
 8:            case "Notepad" : execute("NOTEPAD.EXE")
 9:            case "Sysedit" : execute("SYSEDIT.EXE")
10:        endSwitchMenu
11:    endmethod
```

6. Check the syntax, save your work, and run the form. Click any of the buttons to display its pop-up menu and make a selection (see Figure 26.2). If the selection you choose doesn't execute, make sure that it is on your DOS path.

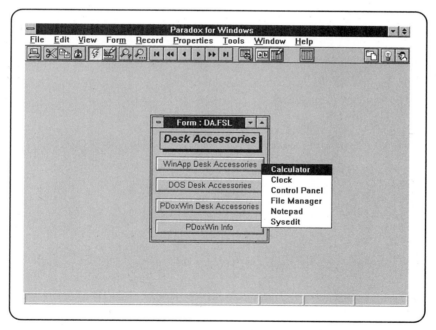

Figure 26.2. DA.FSL. Using execute() *and* switchMenu *to simulate four desk accessory-style buttons.*

Analysis

This tutorial demonstrated an easy way to build pop-up menus and process the user's choice. All four switchMenu statements are basically the same, so I'll analyze just the first one in step 2. Line 3 uses the keyword `switchMenu` to start the switch menu block. This is similar to how you start a `switch` block. Lines 4–6 build and display the menu options and launch the appropriate DOS application.

> When using `execute()`, the path that is searched is Paradox's startup directory, the Window's directory, the Window's system directory then the DOS path.

EXECUTING DOS BATCH FILES

A *batch file* is a text file that contains one or more DOS commands. A batch file always has an extension of .BAT. The commands in a batch file are executed sequentially. In Chapter 4, "Your First ObjectPAL Experience," you learned that you can use all you know about computers with Paradox. For example, maybe you're familiar with batch files and feel comfortable writing them. If you have the following batch file saved as BATCH.BAT:

```
1:   echo.
2:   CLS
3:   echo *** Listing of files ***
4:   echo.
5:   dir  C:\ ¦more
6:   echo.
7:   pause
```

you could execute the batch file with the following:

```
1:   execute("BATCH.BAT")
```

Most of the time, you won't find batch files too useful, mainly because of the many and broad features of ObjectPAL. Occasionally, however, you'll find that batch files are convenient, easy, and a fast way to accomplish a set of tasks. For example, you could use a batch file to run a set of DOS back-up programs and use a timer in ObjectPAL to start the whole process.

Tutorial: Using DOS Batch Files in ObjectPAL

You also can use batch files to redirect the output of a DOS application to a text file on a disk, then use Notepad to view it. The next tutorial demonstrates the technique of integrating a batch file into ObjectPAL. Use a batch file to redirect the output of the DOS DIR command to a text file, then view the text file in an Editor.

On Disk: \ANSWERS\BATCH.FSL

Quick Steps

1. Create the batch file.
2. Use the execute() command to launch the batch file.
3. Use the execute() command again to view the resulting file.

Step By Step

1. Change your working directory to TUTORIAL and create a new form with two buttons on it. Label them Create Directory Tree and View Directory Tree (see Figure 26.3). In this tutorial, the batch file, ANSWERS\TREE.BAT, is already created and on disk.

Figure 26.3. Set up form for executing a batch file tutorial.

2. Add lines 3–10 to the **pushButton** method of the Create Directory Tree button.

```
1:    ;Button :: pushButton
2:    method pushButton(var eventInfo Event)
3:       var
4:          s1,s2      String
5:       endVar
```

```
6:
7:        s2 = "C:\\"
8:        s2.view("Enter a path to view")
9:        s1 = getAliasPath("work")
10:       execute(s1 + "\\TREE.BAT " + s2 + " " + s1 + "\\TREE.TXT")
9:          endmethod
```

3. Add line 3 to the **pushButton** method of the View Directory Tree button.

```
1:      ;Button :: pushButton
2:      method pushButton(var eventInfo Event)
3:          execute("WRITE.EXE " + getAliasPath("work") +"\\TREE.TXT")
4:      endmethod
```

4. Check the syntax, save your work, and run the form. Click the Create Directory Tree button, then either click OK or change the path and click OK. Press any key to continue the batch file. When your disk light goes out, click the View Directory Tree button (see Figure 26.4).

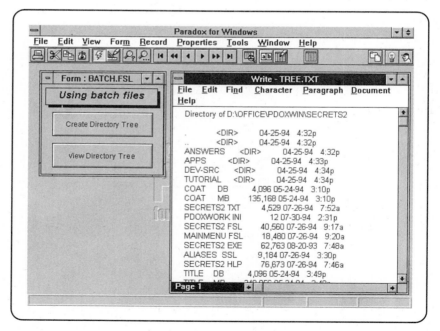

Figure 26.4. BATCH.FSL. Using `execute()` *to integrate DOS batch files into your application.*

Analysis

In step 2, line 4 declares two String variables for use in lines 7–10. Line 7 sets the initial directory path that will be passed to the batch file in line 10. Line 8 offers the user a chance to change the default path. Line 9 sets the path for the location of the batch file and the destination of the resulting text file. Line 10 executes the batch file and passes it the parameters you built.

In step 3, line 3 on the **pushButton** method of the other button enables the user to view the resulting text file using Microsoft Write (see Figure 26.4). Write is used instead of Notepad because Notepad can't handle large files, and the directory tree often is very large.

USING DDE AND OLE

DDE VERSUS OLE

Dynamic data exchange (DDE) and *object linking and embedding* (OLE) are two protocols, or standards, that Microsoft asks makers of Windows applications to support. Both provide easy ways to exchange data with another Windows application. Although DDE and OLE are primarily interactive user features, you can carry out some interesting tasks with them in ObjectPAL.

Except for some common questions and their answers at the end of the DDE and OLE sections, this chapter deals with using DDE and OLE in ObjectPAL.

The primary difference between DDE and OLE has to do with what each one sends. DDE sends data and commands between two applications. OLE either embeds data directly into another application, or stores information about a link to a specific piece of data. You can store OLE data in an OLE field type of a table. You can't store DDE links in a table.

What Is DDE?

DDE is a powerful tool for Windows programmers. DDE in ObjectPAL enables you to do three things: send values to another application, get values from another application, and send commands to another application.

Just as you have a client and a server in a network environment, you have a DDE client and a DDE server when you establish a DDE link between two applications. The application that is the source—that is, the provider—of the data is the *server*. The application that receives the data is the *client*. Paradox is only a DDE client with ObjectPAL. Therefore, you can send and receive values, but Paradox must be the application that does the sending and receiving. In other words, another application can't tell Paradox to send or receive data.

DDE Basics

The term **DDE** stands for *Dynamic Data Exchange*, which is a way for two or more applications to share data. A DDE link is distinctly different from an OLE link. Use DDE to exchange bits of data and execute DDE commands. Use OLE to embed objects from one application into another. The application that receives data from the server application is the **DDE client**. The **DDE server** is the application that responds to the calling application—that is, the client—in a DDE or OLE conversation, usually by sending data. The client application is responsible for starting the DDE or OLE conversation. A **DDE topic** is the subject of a DDE conversation. Usually, it is the name of a data file of the application. A **DDE item** is the piece of data sent between applications.

What DDE Can Do for You

DDE sends and receives one piece of data or a command at a time. This means that you can use DDE to send the value of a single field or a complete table. You can send several single values one after another. With DDE, you can send text, field information, or even a bitmap. For example, you can put a button on a form that tells your word processor to open a document. Then you can send it values and tell it to print.

Not every application can exchange data with Paradox. For example, DOS applications don't support DDE. Most—but not all—Windows applications support DDE. Applications that support DDE include Quattro Pro for Windows, Excel, Word for Windows, WordPerfect for Windows, ObjectVision, and Quicken for Windows. Small utilities often don't support DDE.

Most programmers stay away from DDE because they think that it's difficult. The funny thing, though, is that DDE isn't difficult. In fact, only four commands in ObjectPAL deal with DDE. Table 27.1 lists the DDE methods and procedures.

Method	Description
TABLE 27.1. DDE METHODS AND PROCEDURES.	
Method	*Description*
close	Closes a DDE link
execute	Sends a command by means of a DDE link
open	Opens a DDE link to another application
setItem	Specifies an item in a DDE conversation

THE WINDOWS REGISTRATION DATABASE

The Windows *registration database* is a systemwide source of information listing the server applications that support the DDE/OLE protocol, the names of the executable files for these applications, the verbs for classes of objects, and whether an object-handler library exists for a given class of object (see Figure 27.1).

> The registration database updates the embedding section of the win.ini file. This is done only for compatibility with Windows 3.0 applications.

When a DDE or an OLE server is installed, the correct information about the server is stored in the registration database. Get used to this idea, because the registration database is a big part of the upcoming Windows 4. This can sometimes be done manually by double-clicking on a file in File manager that has a .REG extension in the servers system directory. If a program is merely copied to a workstation, problems with DDE and OLE can occur. A DDE server must be in the DOS PATH.

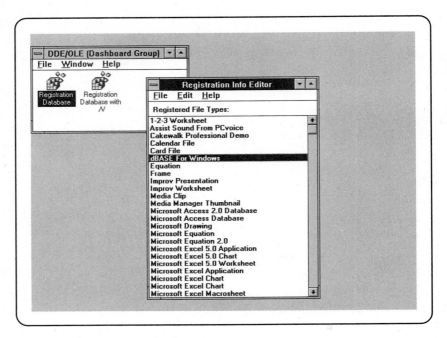

Figure 27.1. The registration database.

You can view the registration database in its verbose form by entering "REGEDIT /V" in Program Manager's | File | Run. In Figure 27.2, the pointer is pointing to the "verb" SoundRec can use for playing an OLE object with edit. For example:

```
1:  o.edit("", 0)
```

HOW TO USE DDE FROM OBJECTPAL

You must establish all DDE and OLE links for a form from Paradox. You can do this interactively or through ObjectPAL. You can't use another application's macro or a programming language to establish a link with a form.

To establish a DDE link with another application through ObjectPAL, you need to know three things: the name of the other application, what the other application uses as a DDE topic, and what the other application uses as a DDE item. The name of the application almost always is the name of the executable. For example, Word for Windows uses WINWORD, and ObjectVision uses VISION.

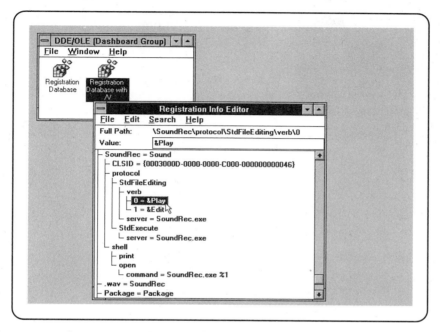

Figure 27.2. The registration database with the /V option.

The DDE topic almost always is the name of the document with which you want to establish the link. For example, Word for Windows uses the document name, such as README.DOC, and ObjectVision uses the application name, such as ORDER.OVD. When using the document name, remember to include the path to the document.

The DDE item is trickier. In most cases, you must consult the manual of the other application to find out what it uses for the DDE item. Usually, the DDE item is an element of the document—in other words, an element of the DDE topic. For example, Word for Windows uses the document's bookmarks, and ObjectVision uses the application's field names.

USING THE DDE *open()* METHOD

You can think of DDE links as conversations between two applications. One application must ask the other application if it wants to talk about a particular subject or topic. You do this with the open() method. You can use three syntax models:

DDEVariable.open (*server*)

DDEVariable.open (*server*, *topic*)

DDEVariable.open (*server*, *topic*, *item*)

As always, first you must declare a variable. For example:

```
1:   var
2:        ddeVar      DDE
3:   endVar
```

As soon as you have a variable to work with, you can use one of the three syntax models to establish a link. With syntax 1, you ask the other application whether it wants to talk. You can use the following techniques to establish links with most DDE-compatible applications.

The following line of code asks Word for Windows whether it can talk:

```
1:   ddeVar.open("WINWORD")
```

If Word for Windows isn't open already but it's in your path, this command launches it. After a conversation, or link, is established, you can use the `execute()` method to execute a command in the other application.

In most cases, however, you won't use syntax 1 because it doesn't establish a topic. The following command uses syntax 2. It opens a link and establishes a topic with Word for Windows.

```
1:   ddeVar.open("WINWORD", "C:\\WINWORD\\DATA\\README.DOC")
```

EXECUTING DDE COMMANDS

To enable you to control other applications with DDE, ObjectPAL offers the `execute()` command. You can use ObjectPAL to send commands to other applications. You use the same macro command structure that the controlled application understands. For Word for Windows version 2.0, this is WordBasic. You can search the Word for Windows help screen to find the WordBasic commands.

If the only thing you want to do is to print the document, you don't need to establish an item. The following line of code uses the `execute()` command to tell Word for Windows to print the document:

```
1:   ddeVar.execute("[FilePrintDefault]")
```

> Do not confuse the DDE type `execute()` with the system type `execute()`. The DDE `execute()` sends the string command to an application via a DDE link. The system `execute()` executes or runs a Windows or DOS application. The nature of the DDE `execute()` command will vary from one application to another. Commands sent to Excel probably won't work in Quattro or in a word processor.

USING *setItem()*

If you want to exchange data, you must send (or in DDE terminology, poke) the data into another application or get information from it. To do this, open a DDE channel, use the `setItem()` method, and assign the data as a value to the DDE variable. If the README.DOC document has a `LastName` bookmark, you can set the item of conversation to it with this statement:

```
1:  ddeVar.setItem("LastName")
```

Otherwise, you can use syntax 3. It opens a conversation and sets both the topic and the item in one line of code:

```
1:  ddeVar.open("WINWORD", "C:\\WINWORD\\DATA\\README.DOC", "LastName")
```

After you establish the link, or gateway, you can use regular dot notation to manipulate the data in the open document. For example, to get a value from the established DDE item and to put it in a variable, you can use the following code:

```
1:  var
2:       Last_Name String
3:  endVar
4:
5:  Last_Name = ddeVar
```

Setting the value in the other application is just as easy. For example, the following statement sets the item in the other application to the value in the variable named `Last_Name`:

```
1:  ddeVar = Last_Name
```

Now, put all these statements together. The code looks like this:

```
1:  ;button :: pushButton
2:      method pushButton(var eventInfo Event)
3:  var
```

```
 4:         ddeVar      DDE
 5:         Last_Name String
 6: endVar
 7:
 8: ddeVar.open("WINWORD", "C:\\WINWORD\\DATA\\README.DOC", "LastName")
 9: Last_Name = ddeVar
10:  Last_Name.view("Value in Word")
11: ddeVar = "Ault"
12: Last_Name = ddeVar
13: Last_Name.view("New value in Word")
14:     endMethod
```

EXCHANGING MULTIPLE VALUES

So far, I've talked about sending and receiving only single values. You might be wondering how you send multiple values. To do so, first use the `setItem()` method to set the item. Next, send or receive the value. Then, use `setItem()` again to establish a new item of discussion. In DDE terminology, that is a new item within the current topic.

The following code builds on the README.DOC example. It sends three different values to three different bookmarks. It assumes that you already have established the three bookmarks in Word for Windows:

```
1:  ddeVar.setItem("LastName")
2:  ddeVar = Last_Name
3:
4:  ddeVar.setItem("FirstName")
5:  ddeVar = First_Name
6:
7:  ddeVar.setItem("PhoneNumber")
8:  ddeVar = Phone_Number
```

Paradox makes asynchronous transmissions. This means that Paradox waits for the other program to respond. This waiting doesn't always occur correctly. This means you might need to put a `sleep()` command in your code to wait for the server to respond to certain requests. As a rule of thumb, if a DDE command fails when it sends or gets values or when it sends commands, put a `sleep(100)` command between the two lines of code. This tells Paradox to sleep for one-tenth of a second. In computer time, this is usually plenty of time for the other application to return a message.

Starting the Other Application Ahead of Time

If you want, you can launch an application before you establish the DDE link. For example, you can launch Word for Windows ahead of time with code such as this:

```
1:  ;Button :: pushButton
2:  method pushButton(var eventInfo Event)
3:      execute("WINWORD.EXE C:\\WINWORD\\README.DOC")
4:  endmethod
```

This approach offers no real advantage. Sometimes, however, you want to enable the user to open the application ahead of time without doing any DDE exchanges.

The form in Figure 27.3 demonstrates how to link to Word for Windows, send and get values, and print. You must have Word for Windows in your path for this form to work. When you tell Word for Windows to print, the system doesn't switch to Word for Windows. Instead, the Printing dialog box from Word for Windows appears over Paradox.

Sometimes, you might want to send a large text field to Word for Windows for spell checking. When the spell checking is done, you retrieve the text file. The form in Figure 27.3 demonstrates how you can do this.

Table 27.2 lists sample DDE applications, names, topics, and items. For the applications, case doesn't matter.

TABLE 27.2. SAMPLE DDE APPLICATIONS, NAMES, TOPICS, AND ITEMS.

Program	Application	DDE Topic	DDE Item
ObjectVision	Vision	OVD filename	Field name
Paradox	PDoxWin	Table filename	Field name
Word for Windows	WinWord	Document	Bookmark
WordPerfect for Win. v5	WPWin	Document	not supported
WordPerfect for Win. v6	WPWin60_Macros	Document	not supported

continues

TABLE 27.2. CONTINUED			
Program	Application	DDE Topic	DDE Item
Quicken for Windows	Quicken	System	SysItems, ReturnMessage, Key

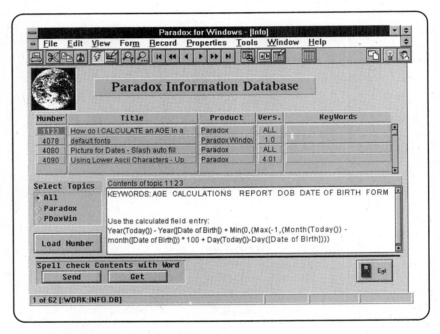

Figure 27.3. APPS\INFO\INFO.FSL.

You can use DDE to spell check a field with Winword. Take a look at The Information Database (\APPS\INFO\INFO.FSL) for an example of this technique. Also note that you can use this technique to grammar check.

LIMITATIONS OF DDE

DDE in Paradox is limited. You can't send values from another application to a Paradox form. You must use ObjectPAL to get the values from the other application. This is simply a matter of what has control. Paradox must have control—except when you use a TableView object.

Another limitation is that Paradox doesn't support the system topic—a general-purpose topic that some applications support. Paradox can't exchange data through the system topic.

DDE QUESTIONS AND ANSWERS

This section contains a series of general questions and answers about DDE in general and specifically about using DDE in interactive mode. First are questions you might have about Paradox as a DDE client:

> *Q:* Why do I get the message "Unable to launch" when I press Shift+F2?
>
> *A:* The server application needs to be in the DOS path.
>
> *Q:* How do I view data paste linked into a table?
>
> *A:* Press Shift+F2 to launch the server application from a Table window. Make sure that you aren't in Field view.
>
> *Q:* Why can't I paste link into a form?
>
> *A:* You can paste link only in alphanumeric fields in a Table window and in query forms.
>
> *Q:* Why do I get the message "Link information will not fit in field" when I paste link?
>
> *A:* The field must be large enough to contain the server (application) name; the document (topic) name, including the complete path to it from the root directory; the reference (item) name; and nine additional characters.
>
> *Q:* Why do I get the message "Only one DDE link allowed" when I run a query?
>
> *A:* You may paste link only once into a query form.

The following are questions that you might have about Paradox as a DDE server:

Q: How can I use Paradox as a DDE server application?

A: You can copy data only from a Table window. The data can be from one field in one record, or it can be the entire table. Likewise, the data can be from any field type. The data must not be in Field view or Memo view, however.

Q: Why does the data from a memo field appear as `<BLOB Memo>` when I paste link into another application?

A: This is how a *binary large object* appears to the clipboard as text. You should paste link as a bitmap to see the format you expect.

Q: How can I copy more than one line of a memo field so that I can paste link it into another application?

A: Resize the height of the row to give the maximum view in that record. Make sure that you aren't in Memo view. Select Edit | Copy. You can copy only what's displayed. It is paste linked as a graphic into the client application.

Q: How can I establish a cold link or a hot link?

A: By default, Windows establishes a hot link (automatic updates) when you paste link into applications. The client application (the target) usually controls the updates. Some clients enable you to change a link so that you must do manual updates—in other words, a cold link.

Paradox permits this control as the server from a TableView. After you establish a link, select Table | Notify On. When you uncheck this option, the client's request for an update is ignored until Notify On is checked again. This option enables you to control whether the link is hot or cold. As a server, Paradox doesn't support the warm link function. In a warm link, the server sends a message that asks the client if it wants an update. You might have difficulty finding an application that supports this, because it's not commonly implemented.

Q: Can other applications send commands to Paradox through DDE?

A: If you want to control an application through DDE, that application must contain a predefined set of macro commands to which it can respond. Paradox uses only ObjectPAL to control itself automatically. When ObjectPAL is executed, ObjectPAL is compiled into another Paradox application that can be controlled only by external events such as user input. ObjectPAL isn't a macro language that can be sent through a DDE channel. It's a compiled programming language.

Q: Why doesn't data update in a link from Paradox?

A: PDOXWIN.EXE might not be in the DOS path. You must put PDOXWIN.EXE in the path and reboot to use Paradox as a DDE server.

Q: Can other applications poke data into Paradox?

A: The table is the only Paradox object that has DDE functionality. Because of performance constraints, the function that enables users to poke isn't included. Likewise, because Paradox has no macro language, you can't use DDE to force changes.

Q: Can I do a DDE link from WordPerfect for Windows to a Paradox table?

A: No. WordPerfect 5.2/6.0 for Windows is a DDE client but not a DDE server. You can create a DDE link from Paradox to WordPerfect for Windows, however, because Paradox is both a DDE client and a DDE server.

OLE Basics

The term **OLE** stands for Object linking and embedding. You use OLE to insert files from OLE servers into a Paradox table using the OLE field type or to an OLE object on a form or report. An **OLE client** is an application that uses the documents provided by an OLE server. Paradox is both an OLE server and client. An **OLE server** is an application that can provide access to its documents by means of OLE. An **OLE object** is the object the server shares. This object is similar to the document that an OLE server can save. An OLE object is stored in the OLE client much as a document is stored on a disk. An **OLE variable** is a handle to an OLE object. You use an OLE variable in ObjectPAL to manipulate an OLE object.

Using OLE

OLE is another tool that enables you to take advantage of another application. OLE enables you to insert objects created by OLE servers into forms and reports, or you can use them in fields of a table. You can use OLE to manage large numbers of files on disk. For example, you might browse through a database of AutoCAD drawings, which is actually a Windows metafile snapshot of a data file. Then, double-click on the drawing you want. The OLE link automatically brings up AutoCAD and feeds it the correct file. OLE fields enable you to store objects from other Windows applications in your database. You can create a database of your word processing documents or spreadsheets and manage them with Paradox.

OLE Version One

Currently, two types of OLE are on the market: object linking and object embedding. Can Paradox OLE embed, link, or both? You can link to files using the command-line option in Windows Object Packager or through DDE Paste Link into a table's alphanumeric field.

OLE Version Two

Paradox now supports version two of OLE. With OLE 2, you can use the other application right in your database application; including its menus.

ObjectPAL and OLE

Through ObjectPAL, you can use Paradox as a client or server. You can use ObjectPAL to send data from Paradox to another application or to get values from another application. In ObjectPAL, you can retrieve data in two ways: from a table or from the clipboard.

OLE Methods and Procedures

You can use the OLE methods and procedures and most of the methods and procedures from the AnyType type. Table 27.3 lists the OLE class of procedures and methods.

TABLE 27.3. OLE METHODS AND PROCEDURES.	

```
blank*
canLinkFromClipboard
canReadFromClipboard
dataType*
edit
enumServerClassNames
enumVerbs
getServerName
insertObject
isAssigned*
isBlank*
isFixedType*
isLinked
linkFromClipboard
readFromClipboard
writeToClipboard
unAssign*
updateLinkNow
```

*Inherited by the Anytype type

Table 27.4 describes some of the more important OLE methods.

TABLE 27.4. OLE METHODS AND PROCEDURES DESCRIPTIONS.	

Method	Description
canReadFromClipboard	Reports whether an OLE object can be pasted from the clipboard into an OLE variable
edit	Launches the OLE server and enables the user to edit the object or take another action

continues

TABLE 27.4. CONTINUED	
Method	Description
enumVerbs	Creates a DynArray that lists the actions supported by the OLE server
getServerName	Returns the name of the OLE server for an OLE object
readFromClipboard	Pastes an OLE object from the clipboard into an OLE variable
writeToClipboard	Copies an OLE variable to the clipboard

USING *enumServerClassNames()*

Using enumServerClassNames() to find the OLE servers on your system—specifically, the OLE verbs. For example, a Microsoft Word for Windows Server name is either Microsoft Word 6.0 Document or Microsoft Word 6.0 Picture. The corresponding OLE verb you use in ObjectPAL to refer to the OLE server is either Word.Document.6 or Word.Picture.6. You find this information with the following code:

```
1:  ;btnServers :: pushButton
2:  method pushButton(var eventInfo Event)
3:    var
4:        dyn  DynArray[] AnyType
5:        o    OLE
6:    endVar
7:
8:    o.enumServerClassNames(dyn)
9:    dyn.view("OLE Servers on system")
10: endmethod
```

Go ahead and type the preceding code into the **pushButton** method of a button on a form. Run the form and press the button.

USING *insertObject()*

You can use insertObject() to insert a linked or embedded OLE object into an OLE variable. The following is the syntax for insertObject().

insertObject ( ) Logical

insertObject (const *fileName* String , const *link* Logical) Logical

insertObject (const *className* String) Logical

The first syntax is just like choosing Edit | Insert Object. In the second syntax, you insert the name of a file. Finally, in the third syntax, you specify the class of the object to insert. For example, place a button and an OLE object on a form and type the following into the **pushButton** method of a button.

```
 1:  ; btnInsertOLE :: pushButton
 2:  var
 3:    o  OLE
 4:  endVar
 5:  method pushButton(var eventInfo Event)
 6:    if not o.insertObject() then
 7:      errorShow()
 8:      fldOLE.value = o
 9:    endIf
10: endMethod
```

USING OLE TYPE *edit()*

The edit() method launches the OLE server application and gives control to the user when used with an OLE object. The argument *oleText* is a string that Paradox passes to the server application. Many server applications can display *oleText* in the title bar.

o.edit (const *oleText* String, const *verb* SmallInt) Logical

edit passes verb to the application server to specify an action to take. *verb* is an integer that corresponds to one of the OLE server's action constants. The meaning of *verb* varies from application to application, so a *verb* that is appropriate for one application may not be for another. Usually, you can pass an OLE server the number 1 to play or display the OLE object.

USING *CanReadFromClipboard()*

With ObjectPAL you can read OLE data directly off the Windows clipboard.
You can use `canReadFromClipboard()` to test if anything is on the clipboard. The
syntax is as follows:

o.canReadFromClipboard ( ) Logical

This method is useful in a routine that informs the user whether an operation
is possible. `canReadFromClipboard()` returns True if an OLE object can be read
from the Clipboard into an OLE variable; otherwise, it returns False. For
example, type the following into the **pushButton** method of a button.

```
1:   ;Button :: pushButton
2:   method (var eventInfo Event)
3:      var
4:          o OLE
5:      endVar
6:
7:      view(o.canReadFromClipboard)
8:   endMethod
```

OLE QUESTIONS AND ANSWERS

Here are the answers to some questions you might have about Paradox as an
OLE client and server:

Q: Why do I see only an icon of the application my document came
   from in an OLE table field?

A: The OLE server—that is, the application you're pasting from—
   presents itself to the Clipboard as an icon picture. Some servers,
   such as paint and spreadsheet applications, present themselves as
   a graphic. All OLE clients paste in the same way.

Q: Why is the Paste Link option grayed out in Paradox when I paste
   an OLE object from Microsoft Word?

A: One reason could be that Microsoft Word hasn't been registered
   for OLE. Microsoft recommends that you use the Registration
   Info Editor to register applications. A quick way to accomplish
   the same result is to add the following line to the embedding
   section of the WIN.INI file:

```
1:   WordDocument = word document,word document,
2:                      C:\WINWORD\WINWORD.EXE,picture
```

Replace `c:\WINWORD\WINWORD.EXE` with the directory in which you installed Word.

Q: Why doesn't anything happen when I use the `EditLaunchServer` action constant in a **pushButton** method?

A: You first must set the OLE object in focus.

Q: Why don't changes appear when I use the OLE `edit()` method to edit and save an OLE object in which the OLE variable gets assigned to another OLE object in the same method? For example:

```
1:  ;Button :: pushButton
2:  method pushButton(var eventInfo Event)
3:      var
4:          o OLE
5:      endVar
6:
7:      o = ole1.value    ;The first OLE object
8:      o.edit("Testing", 0)
9:      ole2.value = o    ;The second OLE object
10: endmethod
```

A: The OLE `edit()` method executes synchronously. You can't wait for an OLE server to close. Therefore, the variable gets destroyed if you declare it locally, because the method finishes executing before the server closes. To solve this problem, declare the variable in the Var windows of the object so that the instance of the variable stays around for the duration of the OLE edit. Then, create a separate button to assign the second OLE object to the variable. Push that button after the server closes.

In Chapter 28, "Multimedia and ObjectPAL," you'll learn more about how Paradox interacts with other applications.

MULTIMEDIA AND OBJECTPAL

GENERATING SOUND

This chapter discusses two ways in which you can add sound to your Paradox applications—with built-in ObjectPAL methods and procedures, and with the Windows multimedia DLL. The `beep()` command in ObjectPAL enables you to beep your PC's speaker; it sounds the Windows default beep. The `sound()` command enables you to play sounds by using a sound card. It creates a sound of a specified frequency and duration. You use the Windows multimedia DLL to play .WAV files and other MCI files.

Using ObjectPAL to generate sound

Playing .WAV files

Manipulating graphics

OBJECTPAL SOUND ROUTINES

You can use the beep() command to beep almost any computer—except for one that doesn't have even a little speaker. You can use the sound() procedure to play melodies.

USING *beep()*

A *beep* in computer programming terms is an audible sound produced by a computer speaker. beep() is a command in some computer languages, including ObjectPAL. One way in which you can add sound to your applications is with the simple beep() procedure. beep() belongs to the System class of procedures. For example, to make every button in your application beep, use the beep() procedure in the isPreFilter of the form:

```
1:   ;Form :: pushButton
2:   method pushButton(var eventInfo Event)
3:   if eventInfo.isPreFilter()
4:        then
5:              ;This code executes for each object on the form
6:              beep()
7:        else
8:              ;This code executes only for the form
9:
10: endif
11:  endmethod
```

You can expand this technique and set it up as a configuration option.

> If beep() ever fails to sound a beep, check the [windows] section of the WIN.INI file to make sure that beep = Yes.

Tutorial: Using *beep()* in *isPrefilter*

Suppose that you wish to use the beep() procedure globally so that every button beeps when a setup field has the value Yes in it.

On Disk: /ANSWERS\BEEP.FSL

Quick Steps

1. In the isPreFilter of the **pushButton** method on the form, test for Yes in the configuration field, and beep.

2. Set up a field to toggle from Yes to No.

Step By Step

1. Create a new form with a checkbox field named *Beep* that has the values *Yes* and *No*. Add two buttons to the form. You don't need to label them; they are used only for demonstration (see Figure 28.1).

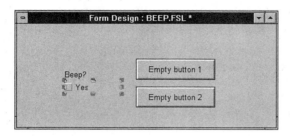

Figure 28.1. Set up form for tutorial.

2. Add line 5 to the Form's **pushButton** method.

```
 1:    ;Form :: pushButton
 2:    method pushButton(var eventInfo Event)
 3:    if eventInfo.isPreFilter() then
 4:        ;This code executes for each object on the form
 5:        if Beep = "Yes" then beep() endIf
 6:    else
 7:        ;This code executes only for the form
 8:
 9:    endif
10:    endmethod
```

3. Check the syntax, run the form, and click the buttons. In this case, the dummy buttons do nothing but beep (see Figure 28.2).

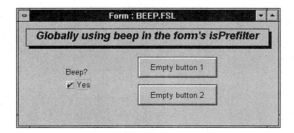

*Figure 28.2. BEEP.FSL. Using beep in the `isPreFilter` section of the **pushButton** method of the form to globally make every button beep.*

Analysis

In step 2, line 5 checks whether the field named *Beep* is set to *Yes*. If it is, line 5 causes the computer to beep. What is powerful about this tutorial is not this one line of code but rather the placement of this one line of code. Whenever a button is clicked, the method is sent first to the form's prefilter and then to the target object.

THE *sound()* PROCEDURE

`sound()` belongs to the System class of procedures. It creates a sound of a specified frequency and duration. The syntax for the sound procedure is as follows:

> sound (*freqHertz*, *durationMilliSecs*)

`sound()` creates a sound of a specified frequency in Hertz—*freqHertz*—for a specified length of time in milliseconds—*durationMilliSecs*. The frequency values can range from 1 to 50,000 Hz. The audible limit for the human ear is approximately 16Hz to 20,000 Hz.

Table 28.1 lists eight tones that you can use to construct your own melodies.

TABLE 28.1. COMMON TONES.

Tone	Description
sound(130,240)	130 is C1
sound(146,240)	146 is D1
sound(164,240)	164 is E1
sound(174,240)	174 is F1
sound(195,240)	195 is G1
sound(220,240)	220 is A2
sound(249,240)	249 is B2
sound(265,240)	265 is C2

> In MIDI terminology, each note is given a number. For example, C2 is the same note as C1, but an octave higher.

Table 28.2 lists a duration for each type of note. Use the values when you create melodies.

TABLE 28.2. COMMON DURATIONS.

Note	Duration in Milliseconds
Whole note	960
Half note	480
Quarter note	240
Eighth note	120
Sixteenth note	60

The following code plays a C major scale in eighth notes except for the final C, which is a half note. Type lines 3–10 in the **pushButton** method of a button.

```
1:  ;Button :: pushButton
2:  method pushButton(var eventInfo Event)
3:       sound(130,120)
4:       sound(146,120)
5:       sound(164,120)
6:       sound(174,120)
7:       sound(195,120)
8:       sound(220,120)
9:       sound(249,120)
10:      sound(265,480)
11: endmethod
```

You can use other elements of ObjectPAL to create interesting effects. See the following tutorial for an example.

ANOTHER *sound()* EXAMPLE

The following tutorial uses the ObjectPAL method rand() with the sound() procedure to play a random melody.

Tutorial: Creating Sounds of Random Duration

Suppose that you need to create a random note played for a random duration. To do this, use the rand() method to play a random note for a random duration. You should make sure that the note is within hearing range and has at least a certain minimum duration.

On Disk: \ANSWERS\SOUNDS.FSL

Quick Steps

1. Use rand() in a while loop to generate a random tone that is greater than 60 Hz and longer than 60 milliseconds.

2. Use the randomly generated tone and duration with sound().

Step By Step

1. Create a new form and place a button on it. Label it Using sound() with rand().

2. The Using sound() with rand() button.

```
1:    ;Button :: pushButton
2:    method pushButton(var eventInfo Event)
3:       var
4:          freq, dur Number
5:       endVar
6:
7:       freq = 0
8:       dur = 0
9:
10:      while freq < 110
11:         freq = rand()*1000
12:      endWhile
13:
14:      while dur < 60
15:         dur = rand()*300
16:      endWhile
17:
18:      sound(freq,dur)
19:      sound(freq+65,dur)
20:      sound(freq+70,dur*2)
21:   endmethod
```

3. Check the syntax, save the form as SOUNDS.FSL, run the form, and click the button. Figure 28.3 shows the SOUNDS.FSL form with three ways to add sound to your applications using beep(), sound(), and .WAV files.

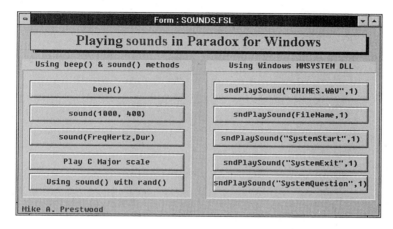

```
Form : SOUNDS.FSL

Playing sounds in Paradox for Windows

Using beep() & sound() methods          Using Windows MMSYSTEM DLL

beep()                              sndPlaySound("CHIMES.WAV",1)

sound(1000, 400)                    sndPlaySound(FileName,1)

sound(FreqHertz,Dur)                sndPlaySound("SystemStart",1)

Play C Major scale                  sndPlaySound("SystemExit",1)

Using sound() with rand()           sndPlaySound("SystemQuestion",1)

Mike A. Prestwood
```

Figure 28.3. SOUNDS.FSL. Using beep(), sound(), and .WAV files.

Analysis

In step 2, line 4 declares Number variables that will be used with rand() and sound(). Lines 7–8 set the variables you need. All variables must be set to a value before you can use them. Lines 10–12 generate a number that produces an audible tone. Lines 14–16 generate a reasonable duration. Anything shorter than 60 milliseconds is too short to be used in the routine in lines 18–20. Lines 18–20 play the first, third, and fifth notes of a major scale. These are the same notes in a major chord.

USING WINDOWS TO PLAY SOUNDS

A **.WAV file** is a sound file format that is the standard on the Windows platform. Paradox can use the Microsoft Windows multimedia DLL to play sounds directly. MSYSTEM.DLL is a multimedia DLL that comes with Windows. It provides high-level audio services with which you can play audio files. It is located in the Windows system directory. To use this DLL, you need to configure Windows to use your sound card or PC Speaker. PC Speaker—SPEAKER.DRV—is a Windows sound driver available free of charge from sources such as CompuServe.

MMSYSTEM.DLL provides high-level audio services that enable applications to play audio files directly; Windows manages audio playback. Use the `sndPlaySound` function to play memory-resident waveform sounds specified by filename, system-alert level, or WIN.INI entries.

To play sounds, follow these steps:

1. Configure Microsoft Windows to play sounds.
2. Find some sound files you want to play.
3. Define the DLL function in the Uses window—perhaps at the form level so that you can use sounds anywhere:

```
1:    ;Form :: Uses
2:    Uses MMSYSTEM
3:        sndPlaySound(fileName CPTR, parameter CWORD) CWORD
4:    endUses
```

4. As soon as you have registered the `sndPlaySound` function from the MMSYSTEM DLL, you can use it in your code to play sounds:

```
1:    ;Button :: pushButton
2:    method pushButton(var eventInfo Event)
3:        sndPlaySound("MYSOUND.WAV",1)
4:    endmethod
```

5. MMSYSTEM is the DLL that is accessed. The `sndPlaySound` function plays a waveform sound specified by a filename or by an entry in the `[sounds]` section of WIN.INI. The sound must fit in available physical memory, and an installed waveform audio device driver must be able to play it. The following code plays the sound file that is defined as the Question in the Sound applet in Control Panel:

```
1:  sndPlaySound("SystemQuestion",1)
```

`SystemQuestion` is how the path to this sound is stored in the WIN.INI file. You can create your own system sounds in the WIN.INI and play them, which enables you to change the sounds easily by using Control Panel. Other Sound applets in the Control Panel that you can try are as follows:

```
SystemAsterisk
SystemQuestion
SystemExclamation
SystemExit
SystemStart
SystemAsterisk
```

If the .WAV file isn't found, the sndPlaySound function returns False. The directories searched are the current directory, the Windows directory, the Windows system directory, and your path. The following tutorial demonstrates playing .WAV files.

Tutorial: Playing .WAV Files

Suppose that you wish to use the built-in multimedia capabilities of Windows to play wave sound files. To do this, use the MMSYSTEM.DLL from Windows.

On Disk: \ANSWERS\API-WAV.FSL

Quick Steps

1. Use the FileSystem class of methods to populate a list field with all the .WAV files from a directory.

2. Prototype the sndPlaySound function from the MMSYSTEM DLL in the Uses window of the form.

3. Use the sndPlaySound function to play the sounds.

Step By Step

1. Create a new form with a list field, a labeled field, and a button on it. Name the list field *WavField* and its list object *FileList*. Name the labeled field *SearchForField*. Label the button Play WAV file (see Figure 28.4).

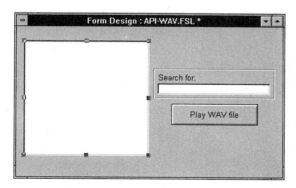

Figure 28.4. Set up form for playing a .WAV file tutorial.

2. Add line 3 to the Var window of the *SearchForField*.

```
1:    ;Field :: Var
2:    Var
3:        fs FileSystem
4:    endVar
```

3. Add line 3 to the **open** method of the *SearchForField*.

```
1:    ;Field :: open
2:    method open(var eventInfo Event)
3:        self = windowsDir() + "\\*.WAV"
4:    endmethod
```

4. Add lines 3–18 to the *SearchForField* list field.

```
1:    ;Field :: newValue
2:    method newValue(var eventInfo Event)
3:        if not SearchForField.isBlank() then
4:          if fs.findFirst(SearchForField) then
5:            WavField.FileList.list.count = 0
6:            WavField.FileList.list.selection = 1
7:            WavField.FileList.list.value = FS.name()
8:            while fs.findNext()
9:              WavField.FileList.list.selection =
10:                WavField.FileList.list.selection +1
11:              WavField.FileList.list.value = FS.name()
12:            endWhile
13:          else
14:            WavField.FileList.list.count = 0
15:            WavField.FileList.list.selection = 1
16:            WavField.FileList.list.value = "File not found"
17:          endIf
18:        endIf
19:    endmethod
```

5. Add line 3 to the Uses window of the form.

```
1:    ;Form :: Uses
2:    Uses MMSYSTEM
3:        sndPlaySound(fileName CPTR, parameter CWORD) CWORD
4:    endUses
```

6. Add lines 3–5 to the Play WAV file button.

```
1:    ;Button :: pushButton
2:    method pushButton(var eventInfo Event)
3:       if sndPlaySound(String(WavField), 1) <> 1 then
4:          message("Not able to play sound.")
5:       endIf
6:    endmethod
```

7. Check the syntax, save the form as API-WAV.FSL, and run the form. Select a .WAV file to play, and click the Play WAV file button. Figure 28.5 shows how the form should look when you're done.

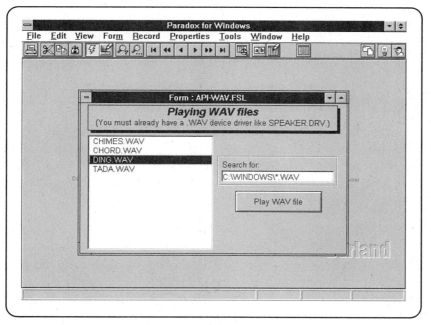

Figure 28.5. API-WAV.FSL. Listing and playing .WAV files.

Analysis

You're already familiar with steps 2, 3, and 4. They were used in the tutorial called "Finding a File." To refresh your memory as to what these lines do, refer to that tutorial in Chapter 25.

In step 5, line 2 tells ObjectPAL which DLL to search for the functions listed in the following lines. In this case, only one function from the multimedia DLL is needed. `sndPlaySound` is prototyped in line 3.

In step 6, line 3 plays the sound file and checks whether it returns 1. If `sndPlaySound` returns something other than 1, line 4 displays a message indicating that the sound can't be played.

MIDI

The term **MIDI** is an acronym for *musical instrument digital interface*. MIDI is a standard protocol that computers and musical instruments use to communicate with and control one another. Currently, Paradox doesn't support MIDI. If you need MIDI support, you have to call a DLL. Another, less elegant solution is to use an OLE field with a media player to play MIDI files.

Displaying Graphics

Graphics add flair and visual excitement to your forms. Pasting static graphics is fairly straightforward. In fact, in Chapter 3, "Forms and Developing," I encouraged you to use graphics this way. Switching graphics while a form is running adds even more visual excitement to your applications and makes them more fun to use.

Graphics Methods and Procedures

ObjectPAL offers several methods you can use to read and write graphics from the clipboard or directly from a file. Table 28.3 lists the Graphic class methods and procedures.

TABLE 28.3. THE GRAPHIC METHODS AND PROCEDURES.

```
blank*
dataType*
isAssigned*
isBlank*
isFixedType*
readFromClipboard
```

```
readFromFile

writeToClipboard

writeToFile
```

*Inherited from AnyType

Bringing Bitmaps from Disk Directly into a Form

If a table is too large because too many graphics have been pasted into it, you can use the graphic readFromFile() method in a form.

Tutorial: Displaying Bitmaps

This tutorial demonstrates listing files on a disk and selectively reading them in with readFromFile(), and then displaying them on a form.

On Disk: \ANSWERS\BMP.FSL

Quick Steps

1. Use the FileSystem class of methods to populate a list field with all the .BMP files from a directory.
2. Use splitFullFileName() and the fullName() method to get the path of the bitmap.
3. Read the bitmap into a graphics variable with readFromFile().
4. Set the value of the graphics object to the value of the graphics variable.

Step By Step

1. Create a new form with a list field, a labeled field, and a button. Label the button Display bitmap. Name the list field *BMPField* and its list object *FileList*. Name the labeled field *SearchForField* and change its label to *Search For*. (see Figure 28.6).
2. Add line 3 to the Var window of the form.

```
1:      ;Form :: Var
2:      Var
3:          fs    FileSystem
4:      endVar
```

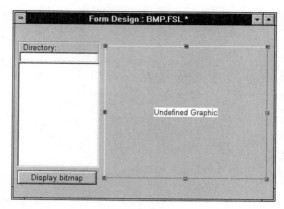

Figure 28.6. Set up form for displaying bitmaps tutorial.

3. Add line 3 to the **open** method of the *SearchForField* field.

```
1:    ;Field :: open
2:    method open(var eventInfo Event)
3:        self = windowsDir() + "\\*.BMP"
4:    endmethod
```

4. Add lines 3–18 to the **newValue** method of the *SearchForField* field.

```
1:    ;Field :: newValue
2:    method newValue(var eventInfo Event)
3:        if not SearchForField.isBlank() then
4:          if fs.findFirst(SearchForField) then
5:             BMPField.FileList.list.count = 0
6:             BMPField.FileList.list.selection = 1
7:             BMPField.FileList.list.value = fs.name()
8:             while fs.findNext()
9:                BMPField.FileList.list.selection =
10:               BMPField.FileList.list.selection +1
11:               BMPField.FileList.list.value = FS.name()
12:            endWhile
13:          else
14:             BMPField.FileList.list.count = 0
15:             BMPField.FileList.list.selection = 1
16:             BMPField.FileList.list.value = "File not found"
17:          endIf
18:        endIf
19:    endmethod
```

5. Add lines 3–10 to the **pushButton** method of the Display bitmap button.

```
1:     ;Button :: pushButton
2:     method pushButton(var eventInfo Event)
3:        var
4:          g Graphic
5:          s1, s2, s3, s4 String
6:        endVar
7:
8:        splitFullFileName(fs.fullName(),s1, s2, s3, s4)
9:        g.readFromFile(s1 + s2 + BMPField)
10:       GraphicField = g
11:    endmethod
```

6. Check the syntax, save your work, and run the form. Select a bitmap and click the button to display it. Your form should look similar to Figure 28.7 when you're done with this tutorial.

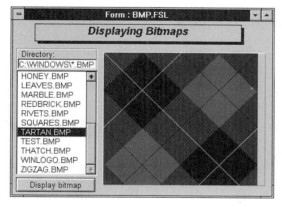

Figure 28.7. BMP.FSL. Listing and displaying bitmaps.

Analysis

You're already familiar with steps 2, 3, and 4. They were used in the tutorial called "Finding a File." To refresh your memory as to what lines do, refer to that tutorial in Chapter 25.

In step 5, line 4 declares a graphics variable for use in lines 9 and 10. Line 5 declares four `String` variables for use with `splitFullFileName()` in line 8. Line 8 splits the current file system variable into its four components: drive letter, path, filename, and file extension. Line 9 uses the drive letter—stored in s1—and the path—stored in s2—and the user's selection to read in a bitmap from a disk. Line 10 sets the value for the GraphicField object to the bitmap brought into g.

You can use the technique you learned in this tutorial to load files from a disk. You even can apply this technique to a table frame by following these steps:

1. Create a table with an alphanumeric field.
2. In each record, place the name of the graphics file with the full path.
3. Create a tabular form that is bound to the table that you created.
4. Place a graphics object.
5. In the **arrive** method of the *tableFrame* field object, place the following code:

```
1:   ;TableFrame.Field :: arrive
2:   method arrive(var eventInfo MoveEvent)
3:   var
4:      g Graphic
5:      s String
6:   endVar
7:
8:   s = tableframeFieldObjectName
9:   g.readFromFile(s)
10:  graphicObjectName = g
11:  endMethod
```

As you scroll through the records, the graphics file is read into the graphics object. You don't need to be in Edit mode. You also might check the read-only property of the tableFrame field object.

Sound and graphics add flair to your applications and make them fun to use. You might not always have the time to add these extra features to your applications, but your users will appreciate it when you do.

Another technique to read a file in from diskette is to use the value property of a graphic field. The form \APPS\FELICIA\FELICIA.FSL uses this technique. The interesting piece of code is a procedure that is part of the **timer** method of the bitmap. Note that line 6 below uses the value property of the graphic object.

```
1:  Proc cpFindBitmap()
2:    if not fs.findNext() then
3:      fs.findFirst(windowsDir() + "\\*.BMP")
4:    endIf
5:
6:    self.value = windowsDir() + "\\" + fs.name()
7:  endProc
```

Using *readFromClipboard()* and *writeToClipboard()*

On disk is the form GRAPHICS.FSL, which is a simple demonstration of using `readFromClipboard()` and `writeToClipboard()` (see Figure 28.8). It writes the graphic on the left to the clipboard and then reads it from the clipboard into the object on the right.

```
1:  ;Button :: pushButton
2:  method pushButton(var eventInfo Event)
3:    var
4:      bmpOriginal Graphic
5:      bmpTemp     Graphic
6:    endVar
7:
8:    bmpOriginal = bmp1.value
9:    bmpOriginal.writeToClipBoard()
10:
11:   bmpTemp.readFromClipboard()
12:
13:   bmp2.value = bmpTemp
14: endmethod
```

Figure 28.8. GRAPHICS.FSL.

ANIMATION

There are many ways to create and play animation in ObjectPAL. You can animate with a TCursor and a Graphic field by cycling through the table. You can animate using the visible property, making one picture or element visiable at a time. A similar technique is to use `bringToFront()`. Finally, you can use OLE to play AVI files (short movies). See the file ANSWERS\OLE2.FSL for an example of playing an AVI file (see Figure 28.9). Once you have embedded the OLE object, you can use the following code to play any Media Manager object. In this example, the user just clicks the object.

```
1:  ;Object :: Var
2:  Var
3:    o  OLE
4:  endVar
```

```
1:  ;Object :: mouseClick
2:  method mouseClick(var eventInfo MouseEvent)
3:    o = self.value
4:    o.edit("", 0)
5:  endmethod
```

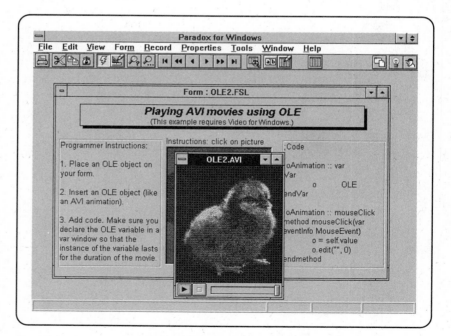

Figure 28.9. OLE2.FSL playing an .AVI animation file with Media player.

My favorite way to animate in ObjectPAL is to read in all the graphics from a table into an Array and then cycle through the graphics.

Tutorial: Using a Table to Animate

Suppose that you wish to add a spinning animation to your application to add that extra bit of flare.

On Disk: \ANSWERS\ANIMATE.FSL

Quick Steps
1. Add pictures to a table.
2. Load all the pictures into an array.
3. Cycle through the graphics in the array.

Step By Step
1. Change your working directory to the TUTORIAL directory and create a new form with an undefined graphic field on it (see Figure 28.10).

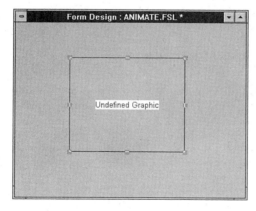

Figure 28.10. Set up form for using table to animate tutorial.

2. In the **open** method of the undefined graphic field, type lines 3–18:

```
1:    ;fldGraphic :: open
2:___Var
3:        lDirectionFlag          Logical
4:        lPosition               SmallInt
5:        arAnimation             Array[] Graphic
6:     endVar
```

3. In the **open** method of the undefined graphic field, type lines 3–18:

```
1:    ;fldGraphic :: open
2:    method open(var eventInfo Event)
3:       var
4:         tc TCursor
5:       endVar
6:
7:       DoDefault                ;Finish opening object.
8:
9:       tc.open("ANIMATE.DB")
10:
11:      scan tc:
12:        arAnimation.setSize(arAnimation.size() + 1)
13:        arAnimation[tc.recNo()] = tc.(2)
14:      endScan
15:
16:      lPosition = 1            ;Set starting position.
17:      lDirectionFlag = True ;Set start direction.
18:      self.setTimer(100)      ;Set speed of animation.
19:    endmethod
```

4. In the **timer** method of the undefined graphic field, type lines 3–18:

```
1:    ;fldGraphic :: timer
2:    method timer(var eventInfo TimerEvent)
3:       switch
4:          case lDirectionFlag = True :              ;Forward
    ➡direction.
5:            if lPosition = arAnimation.size() then;If at end,
6:              lDirectionFlag = False                ;move backward.
7:            else
8:              self = arAnimation[lPosition]
9:              lPosition = lPosition + 1
```

```
10:          endIf
11:
12:          case lDirectionFlag = False :   ;Backward direction.
13:          if lPosition = 1 then
14:              lDirectionFlag = True        ;Next time move
   ➡forward.
15:          else
16:            self = arAnimation[lPosition]
17:            lPosition = lPosition - 1
18:          endIf
19:        endSwitch
20:   endmethod
```

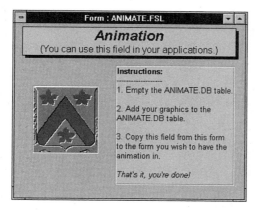

5. Check the syntax, save the form as ANIMATE.FSL, and run it (see Figure 28.11).

Figure 28.11. The ANIMATE.FSL form.

Analysis

Step 3 uses a TCursor and a scan loop to read in all the graphics into an array ready to receive graphics.

Step 4 cycles through the Array forward and then backward. This gives the images a sense of animation.

PART IV

SPECIAL TOPICS

DEALING WITH ERRORS

THE OBJECTPAL DEBUGGER

Until now, it's been assumed that you are an excellent typist. Occasionally, you might have typed a routine incorrectly. In those cases, you either spotted the typo and debugged the routine or ran the program from the ANSWERS directory. This next section formally introduces the Debugger. It gives you the tools you need to debug your code with confidence.

ObjectPAL offers an advanced debugging tool called the ObjectPAL Debugger. The Debugger is a set of features built into the ObjectPAL Editor that helps you debug your application. With the Debugger, you can inspect variables, list the methods called, step through code, and monitor various elements of your application.

Debugging techniques

Debugging without the Debugger

Types of errors

Warning and critical errors

Handling syntax errors

Handling runtime errors

The ObjectPAL Debugger

Using the Debugger

The debugger for version 5 of Paradox is much more powerful. You can view your running application using the following debugger windows: Breakpoints, Call Stack, Watches, Tracer, and Debugger (see Figure 29.1).

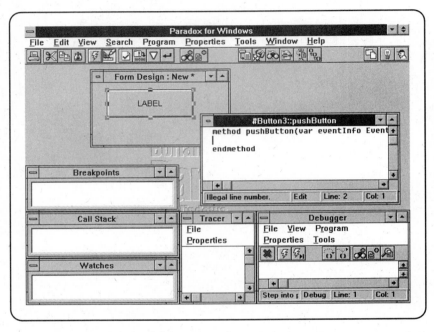

Figure 29.1. The new enhanced debugger.

Entering and Exiting the Debugger

Any time you are in the ObjectPAL Editor, you can open any of the five ObjectPAL Debugger windows from the View menu or with the appropriate Toolbar icons.

If your form or script is running, you can enter the Debugger in three ways:

- If Compile with Debug is checked, add a debug() procedure to your code and run the form.
- If Enable Ctrl+Break is checked, use Ctrl+Break when the form is running.

- Set a breakpoint and run the form.

Placing a `debug()` statement in a method has the same effect as setting a breakpoint at a line. The advantage of `debug()` is that it is saved with the source code, so you don't have to keep resetting it as you would with a breakpoint. The setting for Compile with Debug is saved with the form. When this option isn't checked, `debug()` statements are ignored. There is no need to uncheck this option before you deliver a form because the compiler strips out all `debug()` statements before it compiles. Using the debug statement will not interrupt execution when the user runs the form.

To use the `debug()` procedure, follow these steps:

1. Place `debug()` in your code.
2. Make sure that Compile with Debug is checked.
3. Run the form.

One advantage of using the `debug()` procedure instead of setting a breakpoint is the ability to use it conditionally. For example:

```
1:    if siCounter > 100 then
2:        ;Execute code.
3:    else
4:        debug()
5:    endIf
```

> When using a `debug()` statement in a library, the Compile with Debug option must be selected from within the library for it to take effect.

THE BREAKPOINTS WINDOW

A **breakpoint** is a flag you can set in your code that stops a form during runtime and enters the Debugger. The Debugger enables you to inspect variables, step through your code, and much more. The most common way of entering the Debugger is by setting a breakpoint. When you choose Program | Toggle Breakpoint, the visual minus sign appears next to the active line (see Figure 29.2). Go ahead and type the code you see in Figure 29.2, put the cursor on the second `msgStop()`, and select Program | Toggle Breakpoint. In addition to selecting Toggle Breakpoint, you can double-click the line of code where you wish to place a breakpoint.

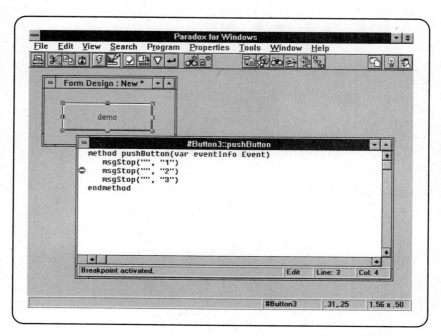

Figure 29.2. Setting a breakpoint.

To see the currently set breakpoints, toggle the Breakpoints window open by selecting View | Breakpoints (see Figure 29.3). Right-click the Breakpoints window to gain access to its menu.

When you run the form, execution stops at the second `msgInfo()`—right where you placed the breakpoint (see Figure 29.4). Note that the pointer turns into a stop sign while you are in debug mode.

Once in debug mode, you have many options. For now, just select Program | Run or press F8 to continue execution.

To use breakpoints, follow these steps:

1. Select the method in which you want to put a breakpoint—for example, **pushButton**, **newValue**, and so on.

2. Place the cursor on the line on which you want the breakpoint to occur.

3. Select Program | Toggle Breakpoint.

4. Run the form.

5. To view the current breakpoints, select View | Breakpoints to display the Breakpoints windows.

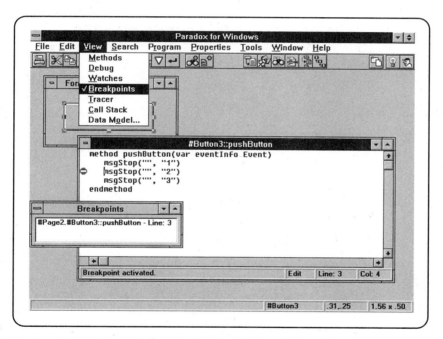

Figure 29.3. Open the Breakpoints window by selecting View | Breakpoints.

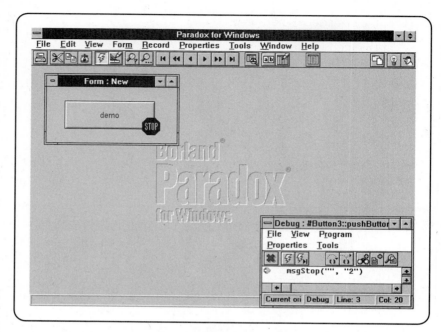

Figure 29.4. Stopping at a breakpoint opens the Debugger window.

THE CALL STACK WINDOW

The Call Stack window is used after execution stops at a breakpoint. Select View | Call Stack to toggle the Call Stack window open. The Call Stack window lists all the methods and procedures called since the form started running. The most recently called routine and its caller are listed first. This process continues all the way back to the first method or procedure.

The Call Stack window is most useful when you want to know where you are. For example, if you've called several custom methods in your code and you want to verify that a certain custom method was called, use View | Call Stack.

To use the Call Stack window, follow these steps:

1. Set a breakpoint at the place in your code from which you want to start viewing the stack.

2. Run the form.

3. When the breakpoint occurs, select View | Call Stack. A list of all the called methods appears. Right-click the Call Stack window to view its menu.

ATTENTION, PAL PROGRAMMERS

Stack Backtrace Is Similar to the where command in Paradox for DOS!

Setting a breakpoint and using Stack Backtrace is similar to using the Paradox for DOS where command in the Debugger. View | Call Stack in the Paradox Debugger tells you where you are.

THE WATCH WINDOW

The Watch window allows you to watch variables as your form executes. To toggle the Watches window open, select View | Watches. To add a watch, select Program | Add Watch, or right-click on the Watch window (see Figure 29.5).

Figure 29.5. The Watch window.

THE TRACER WINDOW

ObjectPAL offers a powerful tracing utility that enables you to view the behind-the-scenes activity of your application. You can start the tracer before you run your form while in the Editor. A window that logs all the activity of your code and the built-in methods pops up.

The Properties | Tracer On option in the Tracer window toggles the tracer on. When the form is open, a window opens that traces the form, script, or report.

The Properties | Show Code option in the Tracer window toggles on and off whether the Tracer lists each line of code as it executes.

The Properties | BuiltIns option in the Tracer window allows you to select any built-in methods you wish to trace. If you check the Properties | Tracer On option and you haven't selected any built-in methods to trace, the ObjectPAL tracer opens a window and lists each line of code as it executes. Use this method to trace only the code you write. This is a wonderful way to find the location of a problem.

To trace your code, follow these steps:

1. Make sure that Properties | Compile with Debug is checked.
2. Select Properties | Tracer On. Make sure that no built-in methods are checked.
3. Make sure that Properties | Show Code is checked.
4. Run the form.

> The tracer requires that you have Properties | Compile with Debug checked in order to trace your code. This is different than version 4.5, and is undocumented. Properties | Compile with Debug has no effect on tracing built-methods.

TRACING BUILT-IN METHODS

In addition to tracing only your code, you can trace your code and the built-in methods. If you check the View | Tracer option and select some built-in methods to trace, the ObjectPAL tracer opens a window and lists each line of code and each built-in method as it executes.

Checking a built-in method indicates that you want that method traced; unchecked methods are not traced. It doesn't matter whether the method has code attached to it. If you check the method, it will be traced. Figure 29.6 shows the Select BuiltIn Methods for Tracing dialog box with the **action** method select. The action method is perhaps the most important built-in method to trace.

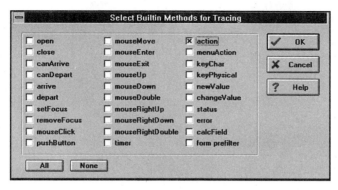

Figure 29.6. The Select BuiltIn Methods for Tracing dialog box.

When the box labeled Form Prefilter is checked, methods are traced as they execute for the form and for the intended target object. Otherwise, methods are traced only for the target object. Your settings for these options are saved with the form, so you don't have to check them every time you want to trace execution. When the Tracer is open, execution proceeds normally. ObjectPAL provides procedures for controlling the tracer. To trace your code and the built-in methods, follow these steps:

1. Select Properties | Builtins. Choose the built-in methods that you want to trace (see Figure 29.6 shown previously). You can check any combination of methods, but the fewer you check, the better. It will be easier to follow.

2. Make sure that Properties | Trace On is checked.

3. Run the form.

You also can use the `tracerOn()` procedure in your ObjectPAL code, but you still have to manually select the combination of methods you wish to trace.

THE DEBUGGER WINDOW

You can get into and out of the Debugger, but what can you do with it? When execution stops at a breakpoint, you can inspect variables. Paradox has a built-in way to check a variable's value at a certain point in your code. To check a value, set a break at the point in your code where you want to check a variable, and run the form. When your program breaks, select Program | Inspect to inspect as many different variables as you want.

There are three steps in inspecting a variable:

1. Set a breakpoint at the place in your code where you want to view a variable.
2. Run the form.
3. When the breakpoint occurs, select Program | Inspect from the Debug window and type the name of the variable you want to see.

The options in the Debugger window fall into these four categories:

- Entering and exiting the Debugger
- Inspecting variables
- Stepping through the application
- Monitoring the application

The following paragraphs describe the more important options in the Debugger.

Program | Run—You can select this option before or after you set breakpoints or while you're in the Debugger. Using this option is equivalent to selecting View | View Data. If you haven't set any breakpoints, Run does nothing extra. After you set breakpoints, select Program | Run to run the form. Paradox saves all attached methods, compiles the code, and runs the form. When Paradox encounters a breakpoint, execution halts and a Debugger window opens. In effect, this is how you enter the Debugger. When you're in a Debugger window, this option enables you to continue execution from the breakpoint.

Program | Step Over—Select Program | Step Over to step through your code line by line. You can use this option after execution stops at a breakpoint.

Program | Step Into—Select Program | Step Into to step through every line in a custom procedure. You can use this option after execution stops at a breakpoint.

Program | Stop Execution—Select Program | Stop Execution to exit the Debugger. This option halts execution and closes any Debugger windows. You can use this option after execution stops at a breakpoint.

Program | Inspect—Select Program | Inspect to display and change the value of a variable. You can use this option when execution stops at a breakpoint.

Program | Origin—Select Program | Origin to return to the method that contains the current breakpoint. The cursor will appear on the line that contains the breakpoint. You can use this convenient feature when execution suspends at a breakpoint and your screen becomes cluttered.

Properties | Enable DEBUG—Check Properties | Enable DEBUG Statement to stop execution whenever the debug() statement is encountered. Placing a debug() statement in a method has the same effect as setting a breakpoint at that line. Unlike a breakpoint, the debug() procedure can be saved as part of your code. This option tells Paradox to provide more detailed error information. Therefore, I recommend that you always leave it on—even if you never use the debug() statement.

Enable Ctrl+Break—If you check Enable Ctrl+Break, pressing Ctrl+Break in the ObjectPAL Preferences dialog box, execution suspends and opens a Debugger window that contains the active method or procedure. This operation is similar to setting a breakpoint. If Enable Ctrl+Break to Debugger isn't checked, pressing Ctrl+Break still works, but it only halts execution. Although Ctrl+Break halts the execution of ObjectPAL methods and procedures, other operations, such as queries, are not affected.

It is also important to note that Enable Ctrl+Break will stop execution when Ctrl+Break is pressed, but you must also check Compile with Debug in order for Ctrl+Break to enter the Debugger.

GET BETTER ERROR MESSAGES

The Compile with Debug option Is for More Than Just Setting Breakpoints!

Here is an undocumented tip. If you're like most programmers, the default error messages make sense most of the time, but not always. Select Properties | Compile with Debug to get better error messages from the compiler. This applies even if you don't use the debug() procedure.

The Enable Ctrl+Break Option

To get into the Debugger easily, use the Enable Ctrl+Break option and press Ctrl+Break. This technique suspends execution when your form is running. It enables you to decide on the fly whether—and where—you want to interrupt execution. Although this technique is less precise than setting a specific breakpoint or using the `debug()` procedure, you'll like its flexibility.

To use Ctrl+Break, follow these steps:

1. Select the Properties | ObjectPAL and check the Enable Ctrl+Break option.
2. Run the form.
3. Press Ctrl+Break when you want to move into the Debugger.

Stepping Through Your Application

Selecting Program | Step Over enables you to step through your code line by line. Selecting Program | Step Into enables you to step through every line in a method and through every line in a custom procedure that it calls.

To step through your code, follow these steps:

1. Set a breakpoint at the place in your code you want to start stepping through.
2. Run the form.
3. When the breakpoint occurs, select Program | Step Into or Program | Step Over to execute the next piece of code.

If you want to try this, make sure that Compile with Debug is checked. Place the following code on a button and run the form:

```
1:    ;Button :: pushButton
2:    method pushButton(var eventInfo Event)
3:       debug()
4:
5:       message("1")
6:       message("2")
7:       message("3")
8:       message("4")
9:    endmethod
```

After you run the form, click the button. The Debugger window opens. Select Program | Step Into repeatedly to step through the messages.

DEBUGGING WITHOUT THE DEBUGGER

The Debugger is wonderful. Often, however, it's just as easy to debug code without the Debugger as it is to set a breakpoint and go into the Debugger. This section discusses general debugging techniques.

Debugging means locating the places where your application or routine doesn't work—but also the places where it does. If you're debugging, you're at a place where your application doesn't work, and you need to get to a place where it does work. One popular technique is to strip code and objects until something works, and then rebuild. ObjectPAL offers several ways to debug without the Debugger.

TYPES OF ERRORS

A *logic error* is an error in thinking. Often, you try to code something that doesn't make sense because it's a logic error. Logic errors are among the most difficult types of errors to diagnose. If you knew that your thinking was wrong, you wouldn't try to implement the code in the first place! A *runtime error* is an error that occurs while a form is being run, even though the routine has passed a syntax check. A *syntax error* is an error that occurs because of an incorrectly expressed statement. Syntax errors usually occur when you mistype a command or when you attempt to use a command that doesn't exist.

OPTIONAL COMPILER WARNINGS

Turn On Compiler Warnings to Get Better Error Checking

If you want tighter, cleaner code, turn on the Compiler Warnings option. It gives you better control over your code. For example, not declaring variables slows down your code. The Compiler Warnings option catches undeclared variables and warns you. To turn on this option, go into the ObjectPAL Editor and select Properties | Show Compiler Warnings is now Properties | Compiler Warnings.

USE AN *IF* STATEMENT TO SEE WHETHER A ROUTINE IS SUCCESSFUL

A technique commonly used for error checking is to use an `if` statement. Many methods and procedures return a Logical and display or do one thing when a routine succeeds and another when it fails. For example, type the following into the **pushButton** method of a button.

```
1:  ;Button :: pushButton
2:  method pushButton(var eventInfo Event)
3:    if isFile("AUTOEXEC.BAT") then    ;If exists, then
4:      message("File exists")          ;display "File exists".
5:    else                              ;If not,
6:      message("File does not exist")  ;dislplay "File does not".
7:    endIf
8: endMethod
```

I used a variation of the preceding error-checking routine in the form **open** routines in an earlier chapter:

```
1:  if f.attach("MYFORM") then  ;MYFORM is a title.
2:    f.moveTo()
3:  else
4:    f.open("MYFORM")          ;MYFORM is a filename.
5:  endIf
```

You can use an `if` structure for many methods and procedures to give the user a better user-oriented message than the programmer-oriented, built-in error messages. For example, type the following code into the **pushButton** method of a button.

```
1:  ;Button :: pushButton
2:  method pushButton(var eventInfo Event)
3:    var
4:        tbl  Table
5:    endVar
6:
7:    if isTable("WORLD.DB") then
8:      if not tbl.attach("WORLD.DB") then
9:        msgStop("Oops!", "Could not find WORLD.DB. Check your working
directory")
10:     endIf
11:   endIf
12: endMethod
```

`Table.attach()` returns True if the Table variable is associated with the table name. It doesn't report if it is a valid table, or even that the file exists!

USE ERRORSHOW() IN AN IF STATEMENT

With Paradox, you can utilize its built-in error stack. To do this, you use the errorShow() procedure. The errorShow() procedure displays the error dialog box with the current error information from the error stack. For example:

```
1:  if not tc.open("LINEITEM") then errorShow() endIf
```

If the **open** method fails for any reason, an error message is displayed. You won't see benefits of this type of error checking while you develop. Instead, the benefits come when users use your program. Without this extra code, you might get a telephone call from a user who says, "The program doesn't work. When I click this button, nothing happens." With the extra code, the user would get a specific message—for example, an error saying that a table doesn't exist (see Figure 29.7). The user could check whether the table exists on the disk, and you would be spared the telephone call.

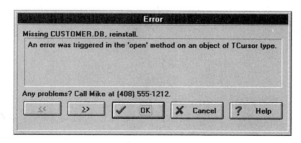

Figure 29.7. Using the errorShow() *procedure.*

The errorShow() procedure also can accept two optional string parameters you can use to add text to the error box. When you use hundreds of errorShow() procedures in a large project, adding text to the error box can really help. The following is the complete syntax for errorShow():

```
1:  errorShow( [const topHelp String, [const bottomHelp String]] )
```

You can use *topHelp* and *bottomHelp* for anything you wish, but here is a suggestion. Use the the *topHelp* for the name of the object followed by the path to the code and *bottomHelp* for extra information. For example:

```
1:  if not tc.open("LINEITEM") then
2:    errorShow("Secrets.fsl :: button1 :: pushButton", "Open routine failed")
3:  endIf
```

USE VIEW() TO VIEW A VARIABLE

Sometimes it's convenient to use view() to view a variable in your code. view() also provides a stopping point that can help you narrow down a problem. For example, type the following into the **pushButton** method of a button.

```
1:  ;Button :: pushButton
2:     method pushButton(var eventInfo Event)
3:     var
4:        s1, s2, s3 String
5:     endVar
6:
7:     s1 = "Tim"
8:     s1.view()
9:     s2 = "Keely"
10:    s2.view()
11:    s3 = s1 + " " + s2
12:    s3.view()
13:    Name.value = s3
14: endMethod
```

This code doesn't shed light on any problems because it has no bugs. The code demonstrates, however, how view(), heavily used, breaks a large piece of code into smaller parts. If a problem existed, you might get a view box before the problem appeared. That would enable you to get closer to the problem. The closer you are to a problem, the easier it is to fix. You also can turn on the Compile with Debug option to receive better error messages.

Table 29.1 describes many methods and procedures you can use to deal with errors.

TABLE 29.1. METHODS AND PROCEDURES USED FOR DEALING WITH ERRORS.

Method or Procedure	Description
errorCode	Reports the status of the error flag
getTarget	Returns the name of the target of an event
isFirstTime	Reports whether the form is handling an event for the first time before it dispatches it
isPreFilter	Reports whether the form is handling a form event
isTargetSelf	Reports whether an object is the target of an event

Method or Procedure	Description
reason	Reports why an event occurred
setErrorCode	Sets the error code for an event
setReason	Specifies a reason for generating an event
constantNameToValue	Returns the numeric value of a constant
constantValueToName	Returns the name of a constant
debug	Halts execution of a method and invokes the Debugger
errorClear	Clears the error stack
errorCode	Returns a number that lists the most recent runtime error or error condition
errorLog	Adds information to the error stack
errorHasErrorCode	Check the error stack for a specific error
errorHasNativeErrorCode	Checks the error stack for a specific SQL error
errorMessage	Returns the text of the most recent error message
errorNativeCode	Returns the error code from an SQL server
errorPop	Removes the top layer of information from the error stack
errorShow	Displays an error dialog box
errorTrapOnWarnings	Specifies whether ObjectPAL handles warning errors as critical errors
isErrorTrapOnWarnings	Specifies whether errorTrapOnWarnings is toggled on
fail	Causes a method to fail
tracerClear	Clears the Tracer window
tracerHide	Hides the Tracer window
tracerOff	Closes the Tracer window
tracerOn	Activates code tracing
tracerSave	Saves the contents of the Tracer window to a file
tracerShow	Makes the Tracer window visible

continues

TABLE 29.1. CONTINUED	
Method or Procedure	*Description*
tracerToTop	Makes the Tracer window the top window
tracerWrite	Writes a message to the Tracer window

USE MSGINFO() AND SLEEP() TO OVERCOME TIMING PROBLEMS

You can use msgInfo(), msgStop(), or any procedure that stops execution to fix or at least test for timing problems. Occasionally, timing problems interfere with your code. For example, you might open a TCursor too close to a running query. Or you might have too many forms closing too quickly for Windows to handle, and a GPF (general protection fault) results. Whenever you suspect that timing might be causing a problem, use msgInfo() to stop execution as a test. If using msgInfo() solves the problem, use sleep(100) to put the code to sleep for one-tenth of a second between the tasks.

USE THE FULLNAME PROPERTY

If you're having trouble with scope or the containership hierarchy and you need to know the full containership path of an object, use the following example. It assumes that an object named theBox is on a form:

```
1:  ;Button :: pushButton
2:      method pushButton(var eventInfo Event)
3:      message("Full containership path is " + theBox.fullName)
4:  endMethod
```

Sometimes you'll be surprised about the full path of an object. Using the fullName property involves checking yourself. Some people call this type of debugging a reality check because you test your own perception of what's going on. If you're absolutely positive that an object has a certain path, do a reality check with fullName.

USE THE OBJECT TREE

Another way to check an object's path is to use the Object Tree inspector. The Object Tree is a visual hierarchical display of a form and its containers. The Object Tree is most valuable when you come back to your own old code or analyze someone else's application. It's also a valuable everyday tool for opening many methods and for accessing stacked objects more easily. New with version 5, you can now print the Object Tree (see Figure 29.8).

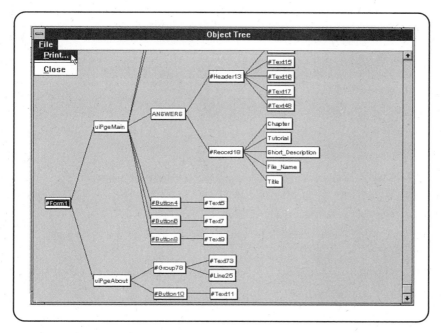

Figure 29.8. The Object Tree allows you to see all the objects.

WARNING AND CRITICAL ERRORS

In ObjectPAL, two levels of errors occur: warning errors and critical errors. Because warning errors aren't critical errors, they display nothing during runtime, or, at most, a message in the status bar. A key violation error is an example of this type of error. If you want to include a higher level of error trapping in your applications, use one of the following techniques:

- If the method or procedure returns a Logical, use it in an `if` statement.
- Use `errorShow()` to display the built-in error messages.
- Use a `try` structure to trap for errors.

Warning errors do not stop execution, whereas critical errors do. To illustrate, type the following code into the **pushButton** method of a button.

```
 1:  ;btn1 :: pushButton
 2:  method pushButton(var eventInfo Event)
 3:     var
 4:        tc  TCursor
 5:     endVar
 6:
 7:     errorTrapOnWarnings(No)     ;Make sure warning errors
 8:                                 ;stay warning errors.
 9:
10:     msgInfo("", "Before error")
11:     tc.open("123xyz")          ;123xyz does not exist.
12:     msgInfo("", "After error")  ;This message does appear.
13:  endmethod
```

Now let's raise the warning error to a critical error. Type the following:

```
 1:  method pushButton(var eventInfo Event)
 2:     var
 3:        tc  TCursor
 4:     endVar
 5:
 6:     errorTrapOnWarnings(Yes)    ;Raise warning errors to
 7:                                 ;critical errors.
 8:
 9:     msgInfo("", "Before error")
10:     tc.open("123xyz")          ;123xyz does not exist.
11:     msgInfo("", "After error")  ;Note that this message never appears.
12:  endmethod
```

This is an important part of dealing with errors. Note that warning errors do not stop execution of code, whereas critical errors do (see Figure 29.9).

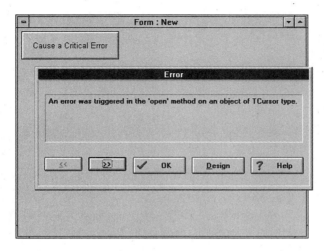

Figure 29.9. Critical errors stop execution.

RAISING WARNING ERRORS TO CRITICAL

To deal with errors yourself, you can place a try structure around your code. If an error is detected, you can use reTry, execute optional code, or display an error message that's better or more complete than the built-in error message. The following code uses a variation of this technique. It displays the built-in error messages, which normally wouldn't be triggered:

```
1:  ErrorTrapOnWarnings(yes)
2:  try
3:    ;Your code here
4:  onFail
5:    msgStop( errorCode(), errorMessage() )
6:    ;You could also use errorShow()
7:  endTry
```

Use errorTrapOnWarnings(Yes) to raise warning errors to critical. If you wish to write really tight ObjectPAL code, do the following three things:

- Use errorTrapOnWarnings(Yes) in the **open** method of every form.
- Make sure that Properties | Show Compiler Warnings is checked for every form.
- Make sure that Properties | Compile with Debug is checked for every form.

Sometimes, however, you will want to turn off `errorTrapOnWarnings()`. The most common time is when you are using the warning error in an `if` statement.

Another technique to raise warning errors to critical is with `setReason()`. Suppose that you wish to use `setReason()` to raise warning errors to critical. You might wish to use this technique when filtering out reasons. Add lines 2–4 to the **error** method of the form.

```
1:  ;Form :: Error Prefilter
2:     method pushButton(var eventInfo Event)
3:    if eventInfo.reason() = ErrorWarning then
4:      eventInfo.setReason(ErrorCritical)
5:    endIf
6:  endMethod
```

The `errorTrapOnWarnings(Yes)` makes warning errors critical errors. Specifically, it has the effect of the following:

- The built-in **error** method will be called.
- The standard error dialog box will be shown.
- `onFail` will be called in a `try` structure.
- The next line of code will not execute.

ERROREVENT

Table 29.2 lists the ErrorEvent methods and procedures.

TABLE 29.2. ERROREVENT METHODS AND PROCEDURES.

errorCode*

getTarget*

isFirstTime*

isPreFilter*

isTargetSelf*

reason

setErrorCode*

setReason

*Inherited from the Event type

USING THE BUILT-IN error METHOD

So far, I haven't discussed the built-in **error** method. Despite what you might think, the built-in **error** method is not the preferred place to put code. The reason is that the built-in error method is always called after the error occured. Most of the time, you are going to want to know before the error occurs so that you can take appropriate steps. Sometimes, however, you will want to simply add to or alter an error message.

USING *errorHasErrorCode()*

You can use `errorHasErrorCode()` to check whether a specific error code is in the error stack. The syntax is as follows:

```
errorHasErrorCode(const errorCode SmallInt) Logical
```

This procedure was introduced in version 4.5 and is very useful, because a test like this:

```
1:  if errorCode() = peKeyViol then
2:     ;Your code here.
3:  endIf
```

would fail if another error occurred after the key violation. The following code would detect the key violation, no matter where the error code is in the error stack:

```
1:  if errorHasErrorCode(peKeyViol) then
2:     ;Your code here.
3:  endIf
```

UNDOCUMENTED ERRORS

The `error()` method is available for UIObjects. You can use the `eventInfo.errorCode()` method to determine whether a referential integrity violation took place.

The actual `LongInt` codes aren't listed in the documentation or online. Therefore, you might have to experiment to find the correct one. Use `view( eventInfo.errorCode() )` to display the codes.

Overcoming a "Cannot Modify Data During Refresh" Error

If you attempt to put a value into a field while the field is updating, you get a runtime error. The following code is supposed to enable the user to type into either column, and the other column should calculate automatically. This sounds easy, but the code generates an error.

```
1:  ;Total_Column :: newValue
2:  method newValue(var eventInfo Event)
3:      x2 = self * 2
4:  endmethod
5:
6:  ;Calculated_Column :: changeValue
7:  method changeValue(var eventInfo ValueEvent)
8:      Total = self * .5
9:  endmethod
```

Like many obstacles in ObjectPAL, a "Cannot modify data during refresh" error seems insurmountable, but it isn't. The following tutorial shows a way to overcome this error. Although a more elegant solution to this problem might exist, the technique illustrated in this tutorial works well. It's a good example of working with the event model instead of against it. This technique uses flags to overcome conditional problems. It also demonstrates that nearly any problem in ObjectPAL can be overcome.

Tutorial: Overcoming a "Cannot Modify Data During Refresh" Error

Suppose that you want to work around the "Cannot modify data during refresh" error. In this case, the specific goal is to enable the user to type into either the Total or the x2 columns. The x2 column is a calculation based on data in the Total column.

On Disk: /ANSWERS\ERROR2.FSL

Quick Steps

1. Declare a variable in a container higher than the two objects. Use this variable as a flag.

2. In the **newValue** method of the first field that changes the value of the second field, set the flag to false. Do the calculation and call the default behavior. Then, set the flag to true.

3. On the second field that changes the first field, check the flag. If it's true, call the default behavior and do the calculation.

Step By Step

1. Set the working directory to TUTORIAL. Create a new form that has LINEITEM.DB in the data model. Add a column labeled x2 (see Figure 29.10).

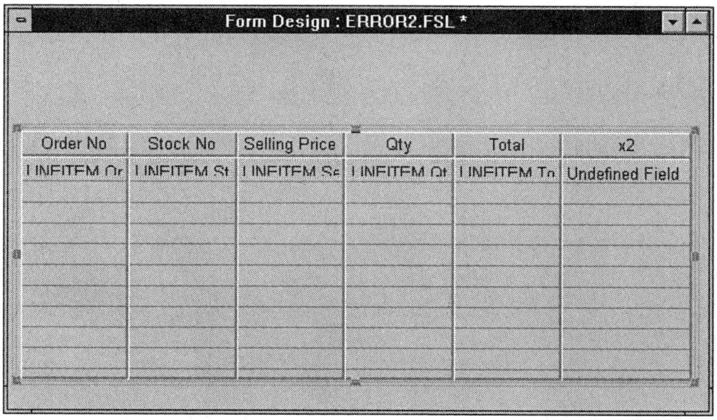

Figure 29.10. Set up form for tutorial.

2. Add line 3 to the Var window of the page.

```
1:     ;Page :: Var
2:     Var
3:         Flag Logical
4:     endVar
```

3. Add lines 3–5 to the **newValue** method of the *x2* field in the column.

```
1:     ;Field :: newValue
2:     method newValue(var eventInfo Event)
3:         Flag = False
4:         x2 = self * 2
5:         Flag = True
6:     endmethod
```

4. Add lines 3–6 to the **changeValue** method of the *Total* field in the column.

```
1:     ;UndefinedField :: changeValue
2:     method changeValue(var eventInfo ValueEvent)
```

```
3:          if Flag = True then
4:              DoDefault
5:              Total = self * .5
6:          endIf
7:      endmethod
```

5. Check the syntax, save the form as ERROR2.FSL, and run the form. Scroll the table frame up and down. Then, change the values in both the *Total* and *x2* columns. Figure 29.11 shows that the cursor is in the last column. Using a calculated field wouldn't have worked because the user couldn't have edited the value.

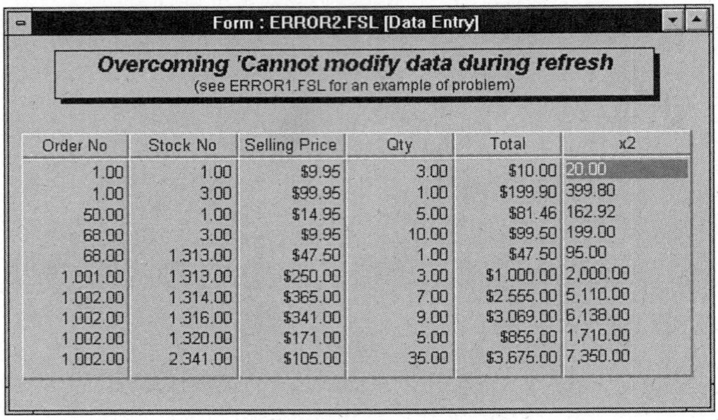

Figure 29.11. Overcoming the "Cannot modify data during refresh" error.

Analysis

Step 2, line 3 declares a logical Flag variable for use with both methods. This flag enables the methods to communicate with each other. In effect, the *Total* field tells the *x2* field not to execute its code at key moments.

Steps 3 and 4 are intertwined. Let's look at them twice. The first time, assume that the user changes the value in the *x2* field. In step 3, line 3 sets the flag to false. Line 4 changes the value in *x2*. Because line 3 in step 4 checks the flag and sets it to false, the **newValue** code is skipped. Line 5 sets the flag back to true in case the user wants to change the value in *x2*.

Now assume that the user changes the value in the *Total* field. Line 3 in step 4 checks whether the flag is set to true; at this point, it is. Line 4 implements the default behavior (commits the displayed value). Line 5 changes the `Total` field to the new value by implementing the same code just discussed.

This tutorial is a good example of how to use the tools that are available to overcome an obstacle. This process is often difficult to carry out, and it sometimes requires creative thinking. If you are racking your brain trying to figure out how to do something, take a break. Go fishing, play table tennis, or do something. When you come back to the problem later, your mind will be fresh.

The built-in **newValue** method has three reasons to execute, refreshing the displayed value in the object:

- `FieldValue`: The **newValue** method executes when the user types in a new value. Note: There's no way to tell the difference between a refresh across the network or a refresh in which the user changed the value of a field.

- `EditValue`: The **newValue** method executes when the user selects a value from a drop-down list.

- `StartupValue`: If a value was specified when the form was opened, **newValue** will execute.

Basically, data should never be changed in a **newValue**. You can almost always use **changeValue** to get the desired effect after a `doDefault`. If you *must* use **newValue**, use the following technique to deal with the error message:

```
1:   ;fld :: newValue
2:   if eventInfo.reason() = FieldValue then
3:      postAction(UserAction + 1)
4:   endIf
```

```
1:   ;fld :: action
2:   if eventInfo.id() = UserAction + 1 then
3:      x2 = self * 2
4:   endIf
```

This posts a custom action using Paradox's internal "flags" (actions), thus dealing with the problem more elegantly. Now that you understand using flags to overcome an error, next you'll learn about using ObjectPAL's built-in flags to accomplish the same thing more elegantly.

ROUNDING ERRORS

The blame for another type of runtime error, rounding errors, can definitely be assigned to the computer. Take, for example, the following three rounding errors.

- Compare .35 entered in a numeric field to see whether it is less than .35. You'll find out that Paradox thinks it is.

- `message(.1+.1+.1+.1+.1+.1+.1+.1+.1+.1=1)` returns `False`.

- Add .7 in one numeric field to .3 in another number field. Then compare them to 1. You'll find they don't equal. For example, `view((a.value + b.value) = 1)` returns False.

These examples are typical of floating-point number handling in C, C++, and other low-level programming languages. Paradox for DOS, however, handles it correctly. Also, Paradox for DOS does provides a consistent, predictable value when the `round()` function is used; that is, banker's rounding (rounding to two significant digits).

USING COMPILEINFORMATION()

To find out whether your form is close to the 64K compiled code or 64K symbol table limits, use `compileInformation()`. For example, type the following code on the **pushButton** method of a button.

```
1:  ;Button :: pushButton
2:  method pushButton(var eventInfo Event)
3:      var
4:          dyn  DynArray[] Anytype
5:      endVar
6:
7:      CompileInformation(dyn)
8:      dyn.view()
9:  endmethod
```

Note that `compileInformation()` reports on the last form to compile. Therefore, either put a button on the form in question or open the form in second after you open the form with the button on it. Figure 29.12 shows the Paradox Desktop compiler information. As you can see, the form is nearly to the 64K code limit. In fact, whenever I add a feature, I first have to go through and optimize my code before I can add any significant amount of code.

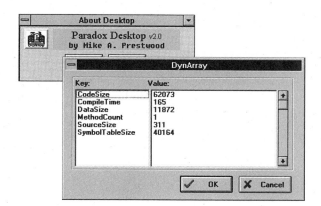

Figure 29.12. `compileInformation()` *allows you to see how close you are to the 64K code limit.*

All programmers have their own ways of debugging. Now that you have the basics down, you can develop a style of your own. When problems arise, you'll be able to isolate them quickly. You'll be able to correct your mistakes, straighten out your logic, or find a solution that works around the problem.

THE EVENT
MODEL
REVISITED

Now that you have explored ObjectPAL in depth, it's time to revisit the event model. As discussed earlier, built-in methods are triggered by internal, external, and special events. Let's review the three categories of built-in methods and the paths they follow.

Built-in methods

Moving a text box

*Redirecting status
messages*

The path of events

INTERNAL BUILT-IN METHODS

Internal built-in methods are events generated by Paradox. A good case study example of an internal event is **open**. The **open** built-in method occurs from outer container inward. The form is opened, then the page, then the objects in the page. The **canArrive**, **arrive**, and **setFocus** methods also trigger from outer container inward.

Internal events are generated by ObjectPAL. Like external events, internal events go first to the form and then to the target object. Unlike external and special events, internal events do not bubble. In simple terms, the event dies at the target. In other words, the complete path for an internal event is sent to the form and back to the object.

Take a closer look at the default behavior of each internal built-in method. Internal methods are always called either from other internal methods or from an external built-in event. There is much built-in default behavior in Paradox. The following paragraphs describe the internal built-in methods and their default behavior.

The open and close Built-In Methods

Every object has to be opened and is eventually closed. The **open** event is called only once for every object, starting with the form, then the page, then the objects contained by the page, and finally the objects contained within that container. After the first page is completely open, the process starts over with the next page in the form. Remember that the prefilter of the form sees the **open** event before the target object sees it.

> **Default behavior:** The default code for **open** calls the **open** method for each of the objects it contains. Then, the **open** method for each one of those objects calls the **open** method for the objects it contains, and so on. If you use DisableDefault in the **open** of an object, the object and the objects it contains are still opened; the appearance is that DisableDefault has no effect, however it does. DisableDefault in the **open** method prevents the code in the **open** method of the objects it contains from executing. If a table is bound to the object, the object also opens the table.
>
> The default behavior for the **close** method acts in the same way.

Effect of errors: Any errors will abort the **open** process and put the object in design mode. For example, `eventInfo.setErrorCode(1)` will prevent an object from opening and put the object in design mode.

The canArrive **Built-In Method**

The **canArrive** method is interesting. It occurs before movement to an object is permitted. Think of **canArrive** as asking permission to move to the object. Contrary to what is implied in the manuals, **canArrive** is not used just for restricting entrance to a field. You can use this method to execute almost any kind of code just before arriving on an object.

Default behavior: The **canArrive** method blocks arrival for records beyond the end of a table—except, of course, when you are in Edit mode and the Auto-Append data model property is checked. Any object whose tab stop property is unchecked also is blocked. You can't disable the default behavior with DisableDefault. Instead use

```
eventInfo.setErrorCode(CanNotArrive).
```

EventInfo: The *eventInfo* packet for the **canArrive** method is type MoveEvent. The reasons for a MoveEvent are PalMove, RefreshMove, ShutDownMove, StartupMove, and UserMove. Suppose that you wish to know whether a move was made by ObjectPAL or by a user. You could use the following in **canArrive:**

```
1:  Switch
2:    case eventInfo.reason() = PalMove
3:       : message("ObjectPAL move")
4:    case eventInfo.reason() = UserMove
5:       : message("move by user")
6:  endSwitch
```

The MoveEvent *eventInfo* packet has a unique method called `getDestination()`. `getDestination()` allows you to know what object the user is trying to move to. Suppose that you wish to know whether a user is going to move to either of two fields, say *Last_Name* or *First_Name*, and you wish to do this at the form level.

```
1:  ;Form :: canArrive prefilter
2:  var
3:    ui UIObject
4:  endVar
5:
6:  ;then
7:  eventInfo.getDestination(ui)
8:  if  ui.name = "Last_Name" or  ui.name = "First_Name" then
9:    ;Execute code here.
10: endIf
```

Effect of errors: Any error denies permission to arrive on the object. Suppose that you wish to stop movement to a field. You could use the following code in the `canArrive` built-in method.

```
eventInfo.setErrorCode(1)
```

ObjectPAL does provides the constant `CanNotArrive` to humanize the language a bit. As an alternative to using any nonzero value, you could use the following:

```
eventInfo.setErrorCode(CanNotArrive)
```

The arrive Built-In Method

The **arrive** method is executed after movement has arrived on an object. An **arrive** method can be called only after a **canArrive** method. You can use the properties `inserting` and `blankRecord` properties to tell when a record is being inserted and when a record is blank.

Default behavior: Arrive calls the **arrive** method of the objects it contains. This occurs inward; that is, from the outer container in—the form, the page, the objects in the page, and so on. Pages, table frames, and multirecord objects move to the first tab stop object they contain. When you arrive on a field or a record, the object is made current; if you're in Edit mode, an editing window is displayed when the field is touched, in FieldView or MemoView. If the object is a drop-down edit list, the focus moves to the list. If the object is a radio button, the focus moves to the first button.

EventInfo: The *eventInfo* packet for **arrive** is type MoveEvent. See *eventInfo* for canArrive.

Effect of error: Any error prevents arriving on the object. Visually, this means no highlight. DisableDefault seems to have the same effect as setting an error. As usual, the preferred way to stop the behavior is to set an error.

The setFocus Built-In Method

The **setFocus** method occurs every time an object gets the focus.

Default behavior: If the object getting the focus is contained in another object, **setFocus** is called for each container—from the outer-most container inward. For example, if a page contains a box, which contains a field, **setFocus** is triggered first for the page, next for the box, and then for the field. In an edit field, the default code highlights the currently selected edit region and causes the insertion point to blink. The focus property is set to True, and the status message reports the number of the current record and the total number of records. For buttons, if the tab stop property is set, a dotted rectangle is displayed around the label.

The canDepart **Built-In Method**

The **canDepart** method is triggered before a move off an object.

> **Default behavior:** Field objects try to post their contents and trip **changeValue**. If the record is a changed record, the object tries to commit the current record. If the record is locked, the form tries to unlock it.

> **EventInfo:** The *eventInfo* packet for **canDepart** is type MoveEvent. See *eventInfo* for **canArrive**.

The removeFocus **Built-In Method**

The **removeFocus** method occurs when an object loses the focus.

> **Default behavior:** On field objects, the flashing insertion point and highlight are removed. On a button, the dotted rectangle is removed. The object's **focus** property is set to false. This is called for the active object and its containers.

> **EventInfo:** The *eventInfo* packet for **removeFocus** is type Event. The reasons for an Event are `EditValue`, `FieldValue`, and `StartupValue`.

The depart **Built-In Method**

After **canDepart** and **removeFocus** have executed successfully, the **depart** method is called.

> **Default behavior:** Field objects close their edit windows, then repaint and clean up the screen.

> **EventInfo:** The *eventInfo* packet for **depart** is type MoveEvent. The reasons for a MoveEvent are `PalMove`, `RefreshMove`, `ShutDownMove`, `StartupMove`, and `UserMove`. All of these event reasons are self explanatory except perhaps for RefreshMove. An example of when a `RefreshMove` reason is generated is when data is updated by scrolling through a table.

Effect of error: Any nonzero value will stop the departure from a field or a page. For example, `eventInfo.setErrorCode(CanNotDepart)` in the **depart** method of a field or page keeps focus on the current field or page. In the case of a page, however, focus is lost. Therefore, a better location to execute this code for all objects is in the **canDepart**. Setting the error code in the **depart** method of the form does not stop the form from closing.

The mouseEnter **Built-In Method**

The **mouseEnter** method is generated whenever the mouse pointer enters an object.

Default behavior: Form, page, and button objects set the pointer to an arrow. Field objects set the pointer to an I-beam. If a button has received a **mouseDown**, but not a **mouseUp**, and is still down, its value toggles from False to True. You can disable this default behavior with `DisableDefault` in **mouseEnter**.

The mouseExit **Built-In Method**

The **mouseExit** method is generated whenever the mouse pointer exits an object.

Default behavior: Field objects set the pointer back to the arrow. If a button has received a **mouseDown**, but not a **mouseUp**, and is still down, its value toggles from True to False. You can disable this default behavior with `DisableDefault` in **mouseEnter**.

External Built-In Methods

External built-in methods are events generated by the user interacting with a form. Keep in mind, however, that some external built-in methods can be triggered by ObjectPAL.

Now take a closer look at the default behavior of each external built-in method. Both internal and external events go first to the form and then to the target object. External events, however, unlike internal events, bubble back up to the form. There is much built-in default behavior in Paradox. The default behavior for an external method is to pass the event to its container, which is how it bubbles up to the form. The following explains the default behavior of the external built-in methods that do something in addition to bubbling their events.

The mouseDown Built-In Method

The **mouseDown** method occurs when the left mouse button is pressed.

> **Default behavior:** If the object is a field that is active, the field is put into Field View. If the object is a button with its TabStop property set to True, the button will become active. A button's value is toggled from False to True. You can verify this by typing the following code into the **pushButton** method of a button.

```
1:   ;Button :: pushButton
2:   method mouseDown(var eventInfo MouseEvent)
3:       message(self.value)
4:       sleep(500)
5:       DoDefault
6:       message(self.value)
7    endmethod
```

> **EventInfo:** The event packet for **mouseDown** contains the mouse coordinates in twips relative to the last object that executed a **mouseEnter** method.

The mouseRightDown Built-In Method

The **mouseRightDown** method occurs when the right mouse button is pressed. It is the same as the **mouseDown** method, except that it uses the right mouse button instead.

> **Default behavior:** If the object is a formatted memo, a graphic, OLE, or an undefined field, a pop-up menu is displayed.

The mouseUp Built-In Method

The **mouseUp** method occurs when the left mouse button is released. **mouseUp** is called for the last object that received a **mouseDown** method. Therefore, an object always sees the **mouseDown** and **mouseUp** methods in a pair.

> **Default behavior:** If you select text, **mouseUp** ends the selection. If the object is a button and the pointer is still inside the button, **mouseUp** calls the **pushButton** method. The **mouseRightUp** method is the same as the **mouseUp** method, except that it uses the right mouse button instead.

The mouseDouble Built-In Method

The **mouseDouble** method occurs when the left mouse button is double-clicked.

> **Default behavior:** A field object enters Field View. The **mouseRightDouble** method is the same as the **mouseDouble** method, except that it uses the right mouse button.

The mouseMove Built-In Method

The movement of the mouse is tracked with the **mouseMove** method. Whenever the pointer is moved within an object, the **mouseMove** method is triggered.

> **Default behavior:** An active edit field checks the state of the Shift key; if the Shift key is down, the selection is extended. If necessary, an active graphic field scrolls the graphic. When you press and hold the mouse button inside an object, the **mouseMove** method of the object is called until you release it (even when the pointer moves outside the object).

The keyPhysical Built-In Method

The **keyPhysical** method occurs whenever any key is pressed and each time a key is autorepeated. **keyPhysical** includes all the physical keys on the keyboard, including the character keys, the function keys, and the Alt, Ctrl, and Esc keys.

> **Default behavior:** A keystroke goes first to Windows and then to Paradox, which gives it to the form's prefilter. The form sends it to the active object for processing. The object determines whether the keystroke represents an action or a display character. Actions are passed to the **action** method, and display characters are passed to **keyChar**.

The keyChar Built-In Method

The **keyChar** method occurs whenever a character key is pressed. Actually, the **keyPhysical** method for the active object sends action events such as nextRecord() to the **action** method, and it sends characters such as *a* to **keyChar**; if a **keyPhysical** does not map to an action, then it calls **keyChar**.

Default behavior: If the active object is a field in Edit mode, a lock is put on the record before the first character is inserted.

If the active object is a button and the character is a Spacebar, the button's **pushButton** method is called without calling **mouseDown** or **mouseUp**. In other words, your code in **mouseDown** and **mouseUp** does not execute! (Remember, a button can be active only if its tab stop is set to True.)

The action **Built-In Method**

The **action** method is called frequently. It executes when it is sent an action keystroke **KeyEvent** from **keyPhysical**, when a MenuEvent from **menuAction** maps to a menu option, or when a method calls for an action. An example of a method calling for an action is `UIObject.postRecord()`. In this case, the `postRecord()` calls for a `DataPostRecord`. The constant `DataPostRecord` is sent to the built-in method **action**. You can send Action commands to **action** with the `action()` method.

Default behavior: The default behavior for **action** is extensive because all actions go through it. For example, Page Down moves to the next record, F9 toggles Edit mode, and Alt+Tab task-switches to another application.

The menuAction **Built-In Method**

The **menuAction** method occurs when a menu option or Toolbar icon is selected. You can send MenuCommands to **menuAction** with the `menuAction()` method.

Default behavior: The option is sent first to the form's **menuAction** method for processing, and then to the active object.

The error **Built-In Method**

The **error** method occurs after an error is encountered. Because error is always triggered after an error, trap for errors in the **action** method.

Default behavior: An error is passed to its container until it gets to the form. The form might or might not display a message, depending on the severity of the error; that is, depending on whether the error is a Warning or Critical level. You can trap for errors and alter this default behavior in the form's **action** method.

The status **Built-In Method**

The **status** method occurs whenever a message is displayed in the status bar.

> **Default behavior:** The default behavior of **status** is too extensive to be described here. In short, any time you see a message in one of the four status areas, it has gone through the built-in **status** method. For example, whenever a key violation occurs, a message is sent to the StatusWindow.

SPECIAL BUILT-IN METHODS

Special built-in methods are specific to a few objects, such as a field's **newValue** method. The following paragraphs explain the default behavior of the special built-in methods.

The pushButton **Built-In Method**

Only button objects and the form have a **pushButton** method. Some field display types are actually composite objects that include buttons; fields themselves never have a **pushButton**. For example, a field displayed as a check box is composed of a field, a button, and a text object.

The form, which has all the built-in methods, acts like a dispatcher. The **pushButton** method occurs when the pointer is inside an object for both the **mouseDown** and **mouseUp** methods. In fact, **mouseUp** calls **mouseClick** which then calls **pushButton**.

> **Default behavior:** Button objects visually depress and pop out. Check boxes check or uncheck. Radio buttons push in or pop out. If the tab stop property is set to True, the focus moves to it.

The newValue **Built-In Method**

Only fields and the form have a **newValue** method. The **newValue** method is triggered after the value in a field changes. **newValue** is triggered even if the value is changed only on screen. The form's **open** method also triggers **newValue** for each field object in the form. The **changeValue** method, on the other hand, is triggered by a change in a table.

The changeValue Built-In Method

The **changeValue** method is triggered before a value in a table is changed. If you have code on both **changeValue** and **newValue**, the code on **changeValue** occurs first—that is, before the value changes. **newValue** is triggered after the value changes. Therefore, if you want to do validity checks on a field, do them in **changeValue**. To fully understand the relationship between `DoDefault`, `self.value`, and `eventInfo.newValue()`, enter the following code into the **changeValue** method of a field bound to a table and then change the value.

```
1:  ;Field :: changeValue
2:  method changeValue(var eventInfo ValueEvent)
3:    ;Before default behavior.
4:    view(self.value, "self before DoDefault")
5:    view(string(eventInfo.newValue()), "newValue before DoDefault")
6:
7:    DoDefault
8:
9:    ;After default behavior.
10:   view(self.value, "self after DoDefault")
11:   view(string(eventInfo.newValue()), "newValue after DoDefault")
12:  endmethod
```

MOVING A TEXT BOX DURING RUN MODE

Enabling the user to move objects around during Run mode is very useful. In ObjectPAL, you can enable the user to move an object around to reveal something behind it, or you can enable the user to move an object to a new location. The following tutorial shows you how to move an object around. When you let go (mouse up), the object snaps back to its original position. You could use this technique for many things. For example, you could use this technique in a game to reveal answers or offer clues.

Tutorial: Moving a Text Box During Run Mode

Suppose that you wish to enable the user to move text fields around, but not place them, while the form is in View Data mode.

On Disk: \ANSWERS\MOVER.FSL

Quick Steps

1. Declare a UIObject, a String, and six small integer variables.
2. When the form is opened, initialize the String variable.
3. On the form mouse down, get and store the object's initial position.

4. On the form mouse move, get and set the object's position. This happens continually as the mouse moves.

5. On the form's **mouseDown** method, set the object's position back to the initial position.

Step By Step

1. Create a form with several text boxes on it. Give them various frames and colors (see Figure 30.1).

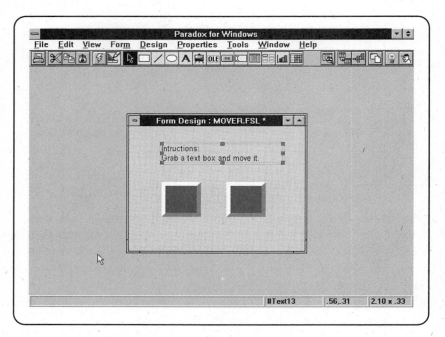

Figure 30.1. Set up form for the tutorial.

2. Add lines 3–5 to the Var window of the form.

```
1:    ;Form :: Var
2:    Var
3:        x,y,x1,y1,w,h  SmallInt
4:        ui             UIObject
5:        targetclass    String
6:    endVar
```

3. Add line 8 to the **Open** method of the form.

```
1:      ;Form :: open
2:      method open(var eventInfo Event)
3:          if eventInfo.isPreFilter() then
4:              ;This code executes for each object on the form
5:
6:          else
7:              ;This code executes only for the form
8:              targetclass=""
9:          endif
10:     endmethod
```

4. Add lines 8–10 to the **mouseDown** of the form.

```
1:      ;Form :: mouseDown
2:      method mouseDown(var eventInfo MouseEvent)
3:          if eventInfo.isPreFilter() then
4:              ;This code executes for each object on the form
5:
6:          else
7:              ;This code executes only for the form
8:              eventinfo.getTarget(ui)
9:              ui.getPosition(x1,y1,w,h)
10:             targetClass=ui.class
11:         endif
12:     endmethod
```

5. Add lines 8–14 to the **mouseMove** of the form.

```
1:      ;Form :: mouseMove
2:      method mouseMove(var eventInfo MouseEvent)
3:          if eventInfo.isPreFilter() then
4:              ;This code executes for each object on the form
5:
6:          else
7:              ;This code executes only for the form
8:              if eventinfo.isLeftDown() and
9:                  targetclass="Text" then
10:                 u=eventinfo.x()
11:                 v=eventinfo.y()
12:                 ui.getPosition(x,y,w,h)
13:                 ui.setPosition(x+u-400,y+v-400,w,h)
```

```
14:          endif
15:        endif
16:      endmethod
```

6. Add line 8 to the **mouseUp** of the form.

```
1:    ;Form :: mouseUp
2:    method mouseUp(var eventInfo MouseEvent)
3:        if eventInfo.isPreFilter() then
4:            ;This code executes for each object on the form
5:
6:        else
7:            ;This code executes only for the form
8:            ui.setPosition(x1,y1,w,h)
9:        endif
10:    endmethod
```

7. Check the syntax, save the form as MOVER.FSL, and run the form. Click and drag any text box you placed on the form to move it. When you let go (mouse up), the object snaps back to its original location (see Figure 30.2).

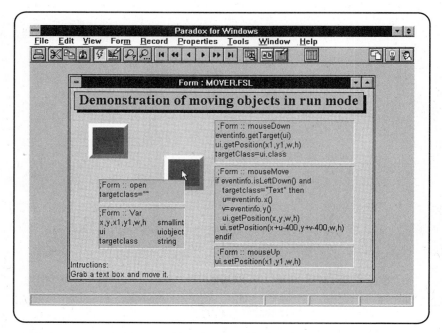

Figure 30.2. MOVER.FSL. Moving objects during runtime.

Analysis

In step 2, lines 2–5 declare all the variables needed in the Var window of the form.

When the form is opened, line 8 in step 3 initializes the *targetclass* variable for use later.

In step 4, lines 8–10 get the original size and location of the object that the user clicks. This information is used later to set the object back to its original position in **mouseUp** (the snapping-back effect).

Step 5 executes the fun code. Lines 8–14 move the object with the pointer. Lines 8 and 9 check to see whether the left mouse button is down and whether the target is the object you want (in this case, a text object). If both conditions are satisfied, lines 10 and 11 get the current position of the pointer. Line 12 gets the current position of the object. Line 13 uses the two values to set the new position of the object. Lines 8–14 are what create the "glued to the pointer" effect.

In step 6, line 8 activates when the mouse button is released and sets the object back to its old position. An interesting effect is to remark out line 8 and run the form. Notice that when you move all the objects around, they stay in the new location! You aren't prompted to save your changes when you exit the form, however. This means that you can't design a form while it's running. This is logical because forms are compiled.

REDIRECTING STATUS MESSAGES

You can use `reason()` in the **status** built-in method to trap for a particular category of messages and redirect either with `setReason()` or `statusValue()` (see Table 30.1).

TABLE 30.1. SECTIONS OF THE STATUS BAR.	
Constant	Description
StatusWindow	The left largest area on the status bar
ModeWindow1	First small window right of the status area
ModeWindow2	Second small window right of the status area
ModeWindow3	Third small window right of the status area (right-most window)

To redirect status messages to a field, use the following code in the prefilter of the **status** method:

```
1:  if eventInfo.reason() = StatusWindow then
2:    fldStatus.value = eventInfo.statusValue()
3:  endIf
```

THE PATH OF EVENTS

Figure 30.3 shows the path of a user pressing a key. As you can see, a single press of a key has two paths, either printable to the screen or not. If it is printable to the screen, the event goes through **keyPhysical** and **keyChar**. If not, it just goes through **keyPhysical**.

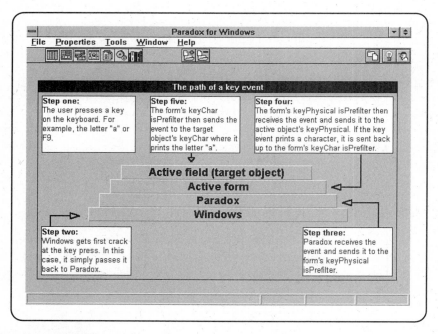

Figure 30.3. The path of events.

CASE STUDY: TRAPPING FOR THE DOWN ARROW IN KEYPHYSICAL

Trapping for the down arrow in **keyPhysical** presents some interesting problems when combined with `doDefault` and `disableDefault`. For example, suppose that you put the following code on the **keyPhysical** method of a field named *Name* (see Figure 30.4).

```
1:  ;fldName :: keyPhysical
2:  method keyPhysical(var eventInfo KeyEvent)
3:    if eventInfo.vCharCode() = VK_DOWN then
4:        Total_Invoice.moveTo()
5:    endIf
6:  endmethod
```

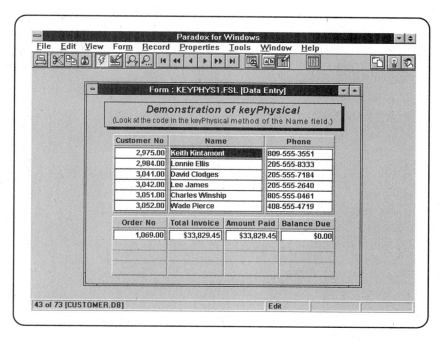

Figure 30.4. KEYPHYS1.FSL.

What do you think will happen when the user presses the down arrow while on the *Name* field? The goal is to jump from the *Name* field to the *Total_Invoice* field when the user presses the down key. The code, however, appears to have no effect. What actually happens is the focus does move to the *Total_Invoice* field, but immediately—in a flash—moves back to the *Name* field (this time on the next record down). This occurs because the default behavior executes after our move.

Now consider the following code.

```
1:   ;fldName :: keyPhysical
2:   method keyPhysical(var eventInfo KeyEvent)
3:     if eventInfo.vCharCode() = VK_DOWN then
4:        doDefault
5:        Total_Invoice.moveTo()
6:     endIf
7:   endmethod
```

Now, what do you think will happen when the user presses the down arrow while on the *Name* field? What happens is that our code appears to do the job. The focus is indeed on *Total_Invoice*. What actually occurs, however, is that focus moves first to the *Name* field of the next record and then to our destination; this is invoked by the `doDefault`. What if you have code on the **arrive** of *Name*? It, of course, would execute.

Finally, consider the following code.

```
1:   ;fldName :: keyPhysical
2:   method keyPhysical(var eventInfo KeyEvent)
3:     if eventInfo.vCharCode() = VK_DOWN then
4:        disableDefault
5:        Total_Invoice.moveTo()
6:     endIf
7:   endmethod
```

Now the code works just the way we wanted. Why? Because in this case, we disabled the default behavior and in essence pretended the key stroke never occurred.

Passing eventInfo

Just like you can pass variables to a custom method, you can pass the *eventInfo* variable to a custom method. You can use this technique to further centralize your code. For example, you can pass the *eventInfo* up to a library routine to handle all errors.

Inspecting eventInfo

You can use the technique of passing *eventInfo* to inspect the *eventInfo* by creating your own custom method. For example, the following custom method displays information about an ActionEvent when passed *eventInfo*. Create a form based on the customer table (see Figure 30.5). Type it into a custom method named `cmActionEvent()` at the form level.

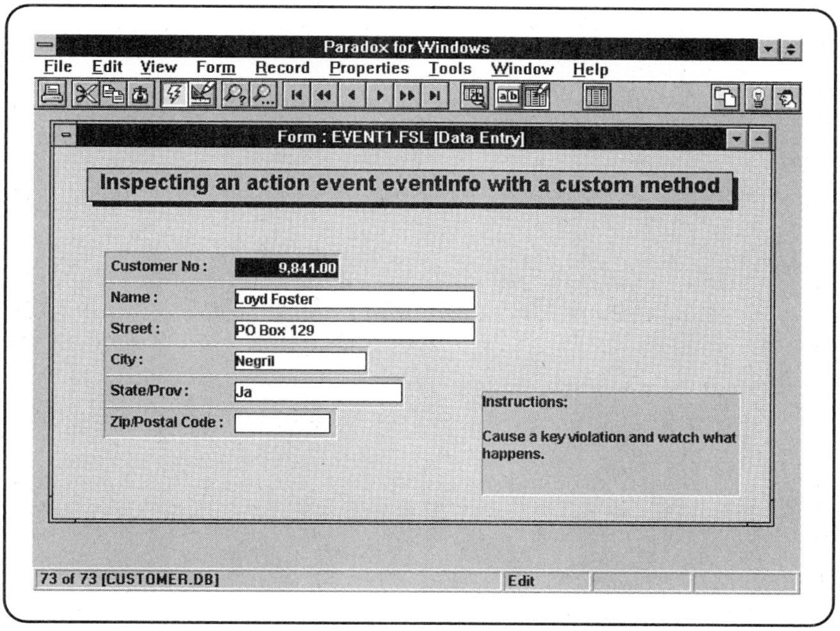

Figure 30.5. EVENT1.FSL.

```
1:   Form :: cmActionEvent
2:   method cmActionEvent(var eventInfo ActionEvent)
3:     var
4:         ui  UIObject
5:     endVar
6:
7:     eventInfo.getTarget(ui)
8:
9:     dynEventInfo["actionClass"] = eventInfo.actionClass()
10:    dynEventInfo["errorCode"] = eventInfo.errorCode()
11:    nEventInfo["getTarget Name"] = ui.name
12:    dynEventInfo["getTarget Value"] = ui.value
13:    dynEventInfo["getTarget Container Name"] = ui.container.name
14:    dynEventInfo["id"] = eventInfo.id()
15:    dynEventInfo["isFirstTime"] = eventInfo.isFirstTime()
16:    dynEventInfo["isPreFilter"] = eventInfo.isPreFilter()
17:    dynEventInfo["isTargetSelf"] = eventInfo.isTargetSelf()
18:    dynEventInfo["Reason"] = eventInfo.reason()
19:
20:    dynEventInfo.view("View Eventinfo")
21:  endmethod
```

Next, pass it an ActionEvent *eventInfo* variable. For example, type the following code into the **action** method of the form.

```
 1:  ;Form :: action
 2:  method action(var eventInfo ActionEvent)
 3:  if eventInfo.isPreFilter()
 4:     then
 5:        ; This code executes for each object on the form.
 6:        if eventInfo.id() = DataUnlockRecord or
 7:          eventInfo.id() = DataPostRecord then
 8:          DoDefault
 9:          if eventInfo.errorCode() = peKeyViol then
10:             msgStop("Warning", "Key violation\n\nLet's inspect the action
event eventInfo.")
11:             cmActionEvent(eventInfo)
12:          endIf
13:       endIf
14:  endMethod
```

Next, run the form and cause a key violation (see Figure 30.6).

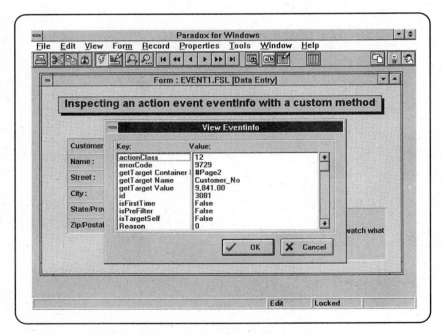

Figure 30.6. EVENT1.FSL showing the contents of eventInfo.

CREATING AND SENDING YOUR OWN EVENTS

You have already learned about `action()` and `menuAction()` to generate built-in Action and MenuAction constants. Now it is time to introduce `postAction()` and `broadcastAction()`. `broadcastAction()` and `postAction()` work similar to `action()`, they send Action constants to the **action** method. `broadcastAction()` sends an Action constant to the **action** method of an object *and* all the objects it contains! `postAction()`sends the Action constant to a queue for delayed execution. `postAction()` is most useful when working with **newValue**.

In general, avoid placing code in **newValue** except when using `postAction()`. The **newValue** built-in method is called when the data underneath a field changes, or when you click a list member (such as a radio button or listbox). While you are in a **newValue** method, you are coming out of the heart of a recalc/repaint loop inside the **newValue** method. Therefore, you may not modify the value of a bound field. The solution is to use **newValue** sparingly, and when you do use it, use `postAction()`. For example:

```
1:   self.postAction(UserAction + 1)
```

This has the effect of queueing up a user-defined action call to the object receiving the **newValue**. As soon as the **newValue** is done executing and the system has completed the refresh loop, the `action()` built-in will fire, and you can trap for this action with the following:

```
1:   If eventInfo.id() = UserAction + 1 then
2:     ;Do here what you would have done in newValue.
3:   endif
```

The end effect is the same, but the code is much safer and easier to debug.

If you have a common set of code (such as a calculation), which you were putting in **newValue**, then you can trigger this calculation from anywhere in your application simply by calling the `action()` or `postAction()` method for this object, thus making your code more re-useable.

There are many things you can write in a **newValue** that are harmless, such as writing to unbound fields or changing display properties; but many programmers try to do "database stuff" inside a **newValue**, and this isn't good. When in doubt, use `postAction()` to send a custom action ID to `self` and trap for the custom action ID in the **action** method. Your safety will be guaranteed, because the **action** code can NOT execute until the recalc/repaint cycle is complete.

Events Can Cause Events

In an event-driven environment such as Paradox for Windows, an event often creates another event before the first event finishes. In effect, you can have several events occurring at the same time. (Some developers have mistakenly called this a secondary event stream. Furthermore, they have mistakenly referred to the first event as the primary event stream. I will not do that here, for it just confuses the issue.) Suffice it to say, just as Windows sends messages from application to application, Paradox sends messages from object to object.

Using the Built-In Error Codes

Rather than always just setting the error code to a nonzero value, try to use built-in error constants whenever possible. The next example enforces uniqueness in a table and checks whether the field is a required field. What is interesting is that it uses the peReqdErr and peKeyViol constants instead of just a nonzero value.

```
1:   ;Record :: action
2:   var
3:      tc TCursor
4:   endvar
5:
6:   ;check for required field
7:   if isBlank(Ship_Via) and self.locked then
8:      eventinfo.setErrorCode(peReqdErr)
9:      return
10: endif
11:
12: ;Key violation check
13: tc.attach(ORDERS)
14: if tc.locate("Order_No", Order_No.value) then
15:    if tc.recNo()<> self.recNo then
16:       eventinfo.setErrorCode(peKeyViol)
17:    endif
18: endIf
```

It is interesting to note the above code works for both Paradox and dBASE tables; it works even though dBASE tables do not use the concept of keys and therefore cannot have a key violation.

Moving Focus to a Box

One final note for this chapter. It is interesting to note that although only fields and buttons have tab stop properties, it is possible to move focus to an object other than a field or a button; for example, a box. ObjectPAL has the flexibility to move focus to any object. Suppose that you have a box on your form named *box1*. You can move focus to it with `box1.moveTo()`. To the user, the only visual difference is that no object on the screen appears to have focus.

USING AND WRITING DLLS

This chapter provides a general overview of how to register and use a DLL in Paradox for Windows.

DYNAMIC LINK LIBRARIES

The term **DLL** is an acronym for *dynamic link library*. A DLL is a type of application used by other applications. It usually contains a library of functions. A DLL is a module of executable Windows code that other applications can use. Typically, a DLL has several functions or modules that can be called. Just as you can run Windows .EXE applications within Windows, a Windows application can run or use a function in a DLL. The function is loaded on demand and linked at runtime. If the DLL is a good Windows DLL, the function is unloaded when you no longer need the code.

WHAT'S IN A DLL?

Your hard drive has many DLLs with thousands of functions in them—all the files with a .DLL extension. The problem with using DLLs on your hard drive is that they were never designed for any other program except the original to call. So how do you find out what commands or functions are in them? Some utilities dump the header of a DLL into a file, but they usually aren't worth the time that it takes to reverse-engineer a DLL. If you're writing a DLL, you know what the calls are. If you purchase a DLL, its documentation tells you.

In general, the DLL interface is intended for people who already know how to write DLLs or who are willing to invest the time and effort to learn. The DLL interface also is intended for people who know how to hook into third-party DLLs written explicitly for this purpose. It's difficult—and in many cases, impossible—to use a DLL that has no documentation or that is written for a particular application. For example, many DLLs on the Borland BBS and CompuServe were written specifically and only for ObjectVision. Some of these DLLs do things that simply don't apply to any other application. That doesn't mean that none of the ObjectVision DLLs work with Paradox—some do. It does mean, however, that there are two categories of DLLs—specific and general. With proper documentation, most of the general DLLs will work within ObjectPAL. All the Paradox-specific DLLs will work. As for the rest, you have to try them on a case-by-case basis.

Most DLLs designed to be called from another product come with documentation that lists the available functions, parameter data types, and return values. Once you have this information, you can link and call the DLLs from Paradox. Without this information, you'll have a hard time figuring out how to call those DLLs.

WHERE DO YOU GET DLLS?

You can write your own DLLs, download them for free from BBSs, or buy them. You also can ask the producers of the products on your hard disk to let you use the DLLs and provide you with documentation. This is a reliable and reasonable way to get access to the DLLs in which you're interested. If you want to write your own DLL, the template later in this chapter will be helpful.

USING A DLL

To use a function in a DLL, you first must register it. In ObjectPAL, you register DLLs in the Uses window of an object. You call the code in the Uses window from the object or the object's containership path. Use the following template:

```
1:  Uses DLLName
2:     FunctionName(Parameters) ReturnType
3:  endUses
```

For example, suppose that you have a DLL with the filename STRINGS.DLL. It has a function in it called scramble. You register it with code like this:

```
1:  Uses Strings
2:     scramble(text cptr) cptr
3:  endUses
```

Once you register a DLL function, you can call it just like any runtime library method or procedure. In the next tutorial, you pass a number to a DLL. The DLL returns the number and some characters. In other words, you send a value to a DLL and receive an altered value. Our goal is to use ObjectPAL to pass a number to a DLL that will pass back a string and the same number. Make sure to use the correct parameters.

Tutorial: Using a DLL

This tutorial demonstrates how to use a DLL—specifically, to pass a number to a DLL that will pass back a string and the same number.

On Disk: \ANSWERS\DLL\HELLO.FSL

Quick Steps

1. Prototype the function in the Uses window of the button.
2. Call the function in the **pushButton** method.

Step By Step

1. Change your working directory to TUTORIAL\DLL. Create a new form and place a button labeled Use DLL on it.
2. Alter the Uses window of the form to look like lines 2–4.

```
1:     ;Form :: Uses
2:     Uses Hello
3:         getHelloString(text cWord) cptr
4:     endUses
```

3. Add lines 3–8 to the **pushButton** method of the Use DLL button.

```
1:    ;Button :: pushButton
2:    method pushButton(var eventInfo Event)
3:       var
4:          s   String
5:       endVar
6:
7:       s = getHelloString(3)
8:       s.view()
9:    endmethod
```

4. Check the syntax, save the form as HELLO.FSL, run it, and click the Use DLL button. Almost immediately, a string dialog box is displayed. Click OK. Figure 31.1 shows how the HELLO.FSL form should look when you're done.

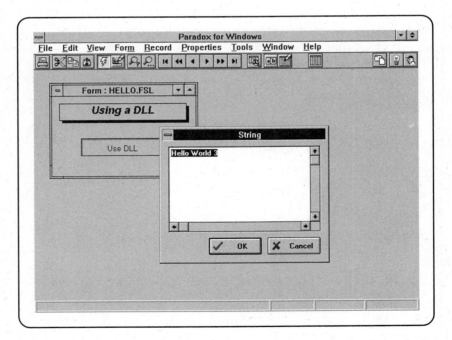

Figure 31.1. HELLO.FSL.

Analysis

Line 2, step 2 tells ObjectPAL which function is in HELLO.DLL. No path or extension is used. ObjectPAL automatically searches the current directory, the Windows directory, and all the directories on the path for the DLL. Line 3 prototypes the function in the DLL. You prototype DLLs similarly to custom methods. In this case, the DLL function is called `getHelloString`. It takes a single parameter and returns a string.

In step 3, line 4 declares a String variable so that there is a place in which to store the string returned by the DLL in line 7. Line 8 shows you the result in a String View dialog box.

DLLS AND DATA TYPES

When you use or register DLLs with another application, you need to know how the other application deals with data types. The following table lists the names of the different data types for the Uses window in ObjectPAL, C, and Pascal.

TABLE 31.1. THE DLL DATA TYPES.			
Data Type	Uses Window	C	Pascal
16-bit integer	CWORD	int	Integer
32-bit integer	CLONG	long	Longint
64-bit floating-point number	CDOUBLE	double	Double
80-bit floating-point number	CLONGDOUBLE	long double	Extended
Pointer	CPTR	char far*	String
Binary or graphic data	CHANDLE	handle	THandle

The only place these special ObjectPAL data types are valid is in the uses Window. Use CWORD, CLONG, CDOUBLE, DLONGDOUBLE, CPTR, and CHANDLE in the Uses window to prototype functions in DLLs.

- CWORD corresponds to SmallInt
- CLONG corresponds to LongInt
- CDOUBLE and CLONGDOUBLE correspond to Number
- CPTR corresponds to String
- CHANDLE corresponds to Binary or Graphic

PASSING BY VALUE

Just as custom methods have the concept of passing by value versus passing by reference, so do DLLs. Here is an example of passing by value:

C data type:	Long Int
C syntax:	void pascal far _loadds cproc(long int value)
In Uses block:	cproc(value CLONG)
ObjectPAL call:	cproc(si) or cproc(li)

PASSING BY REFERENCE

Here is an example of passing by reference. Note that the DLL data type used in the Uses windows is CPTR, which is a C pointer. A C pointer points to a memory location.

C data type:	Long Int *
C syntax:	void pascal far _loadds cproc(long int * value)
In Uses block:	cproc(value CPTR)
ObjectPAL call:	cproc(li)

COMMON ERROR MESSAGES

When you misspell a DLL or function, or the DLL is not found, you get the error message displayed in Figure 31.2 when you try to run the form.

When you try to pass a DLL the wrong data type, you get the synax error message illustrated in Figure 31.2. This error message also occurs if you try to pass by value and you mean to pass by reference (or vice versa). This is known as a reference mismatch. In particular, this error message occurs when you try to pass a constant and you prototype to pass by reference (see Figure 31.3).

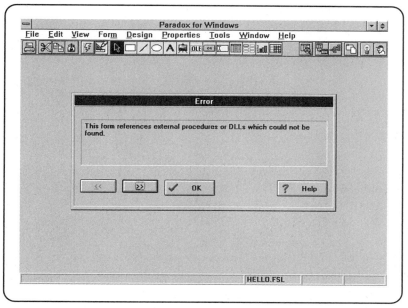

Figure 31.2. The error message displayed when the DLL or DLL function cannot be found.

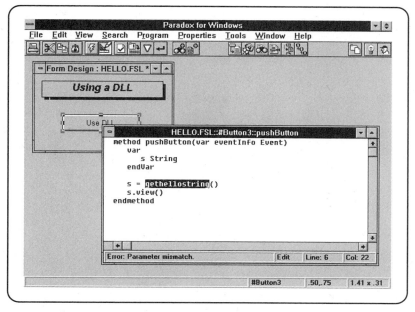

Figure 31.3. The error message displayed when you try to pass a function something other than what it is prototyped for.

QUESTIONS AND ANSWERS

Q. How can I use a DLL if I do not know the parameters?

A. You don't. Although some third party utilities to pry into DLLs are available, they are generally considered hard to use and not worth the time.

Q. The DLL I wish to use needs to pass an array back to PDoxWin. How is this accomplished?

A. Because you cannot pass an array to a DLL or back to PDoxWin, you need to write an intermediate DLL that can then pass the data one element at a time to the DLL and back to PDoxWin. This type of intermediate DLL is known as a wrapper because, in a sense, it wraps itself around the DLL.

Q. Why does Paradox cause a GPF when I pass a string of one size to a DLL, make it larger in the DLL, and return the larger string?

A. You need to set the maximum size of the string ahead of time. Be careful to set the maximum length of the variable in your ObjectPAL code. For example:

```
1:    var
2:       x    String
3:    endVar
4:
5:    x = "12345678901234567890"
```

Q. How do I pass a window handle to a DLL?

A. The data type for a window handle is a small integer. Therefore, use the ObjectPAL data type SmallInt in your ObjectPAL code and CWORD in your Uses window. Do not confuse this with a Binary or graphic data type.

Q. How do you pass a null to a DLL?

A. Use the CWORD data type and pass a 0 (zero).

Q. How do you pass a logical to a DLL?

A. Use a CWORD and pass a 0 for false and a 1 for true (any nonzero value represents a true).

Q. Why do I get a GPF when I try to use a DLL?

A. One possible reason is that you are trying to pass an invalid data type. Make sure that you are passing it the correct parameter data types and valid data.

TIPS FOR WRITING YOUR OWN DLLs

This section contains information essential to the C or Pascal programmer who is interested in writing DLLs. I provide you with a template written in C++ that you can use as a prototype for writing your own DLL. This template is the DLL that you registered in the first tutorial in this chapter.

DLLs AND DATA TYPES

When you use or register DLLs with another application, you need to know how the other application deals with data types. Table 31.2 lists the names of the different data types that ObjectPAL, C, Pascal, and ObjectVision support.

TABLE 31.2. DATA TYPES.

Date Type	ObjectPAL	C	Pascal	ObjectVision
16-bit integer	CWORD	int	Integer	I, H, or A
32-bit integer	CLONG	long	Longint	J
64-bit floating-point number	CDOUBLE	double	Double	B
80-bit floating-point number	DLONGDOUBLE	long double	Extended	none
Pointer	CPTR	char far	String	C
Binary or graphic data	CWORD	handle	THandle	y

Page 160 of the ObjectVision reference guide lists all 19 data types that ObjectVision supports when it deals with DLLs. You can't use an ObjectVision DLL with Paradox if it uses a data type other than the seven data types listed for ObjectVision in Table 31.2.

Notes on Writing a DLL

I recommend that you use the large memory model so that everything is far. It makes many details of writing a DLL easier and automatic.

A string null pointer in ObjectPAL is not the same as a null pointer in C. If you need to pass a null string to a DLL, use CWORD set as 0. If you pass a string by reference—that is, by CPTR—don't modify the length of the string with the DLL.

CPTR Is a Pointer to a Location in Memory

A DLL with a return value of a string actually is a pointer to a memory address that defines the beginning of the string that is returned. You might have to define the maximize size of the string in ObjectPAL before you call this DLL. Here's an example. Suppose that the DLL function takes an Integer as an argument, and returns a string no longer than 30 characters.

```
1:  ;Button :: Uses statement
2:  Uses MYDLL
3:      MyFunction(const MyNum CWORD) CPTR
4:  endUses
```

```
1:  ;ObjectPAL Method
2:  Method pushButton(var eventInfo MouseEvent)
3:     var
4:        sMyString string
5:        siMyInteger smallInt
6:     endVar
7:
8:     ;Initialize variables
9:     siMyInteger = 10
10:     sMyString = "12345678901234567890123456789 0"
11:
12:     ;Call DLL function
13:     sMyString=MyFunction(iMyInteger)
14:
15:     ;Examine results
16:     sMyString.view("Result")
17: endMethod
```

A DLL Template Written in C++ for Use with ObjectPAL

If you're an experienced C++ programmer, you can use the following template. If you're a beginner at writing DLLs, then I suggest you pick up a good book dedicated to writing Windows DLLs.

CREATING YOUR FIRST DLL

Often, doing a tutorial is worth 20 pages of text. The following is a template for experienced C++ programmers. You can use this prototype for writing your own DLL. This template doesn't teach you how to write a DLL. It simply provides those who know C with a template for writing a DLL for use with Paradox.

Tutorial: Creating Your First DLL with Borland C++

Suppose that you wish to create and use your first DLL. This tutorial uses Borland's Turbo C++. Make the appropriate changes if you're using a different compiler.

On Disk: DLL\HELLO.CPP

Quick Steps

1. Type and compile the DLL template.
2. Use the newly created DLL in a form.

Step By Step

1. Launch BCW.EXE.
2. Select File | New. This brings up a new blank Edit window.
3. Select Options | Application and click the Windows DLL button.
4. Select Options | Compiler | Code Generation. This brings up the Code Generation Options dialog box. From the Model panel, select Large and click OK.
5. Type the following code (don't type the line numbers):

```
1:  // Sample program used to demonstrate writing DLLs
2:  #define  STRICT
3:  #include <windows.h>
4:
5:  // Turn off warning: Parameter '' is never used
6:  #pragma argsused
7:
8:  // Every DLL has an entry point, LibMain, and an exit point, WEP
9:     int FAR PASCAL LibMain( HINSTANCE hInstance, WORD wDataSegment,
10:    WORD wHeapSize, LPSTR lpszCmdLine )
11:    {
```

continues

```
12:    // The startup code for the DLL initializes the
13:  // local heap (if there is one) with a call to
14:  // LocalInit, which locks the data segment
15:   if ( wHeapSize != 0 )
16:      UnlockData( 0 );
17: return 1;   // Indicate that the DLL was initialized successfully
18: }
19:
20: // Turn off warning: Parameter '' is never used
21: #pragma argsused
22:
23: int FAR PASCAL WEP ( int bSystemExit )
24: {
25: return 1;
26: }
27:
28: char theString[80];
29:
30:
31: extern "C" {
32: char far * FAR PASCAL _export GetHelloString (int x)
33: {
34:  wsprintf (theString,"Hello World %d",x);
35:  return theString;
36:  }
37:
38:  }
```

6. Save the code by selecting File | Save As. You can save the file under any name you want—HELLO.CPP, for example.

7. Select Compile | Build All. This does all the work needed to use your DLL. If you don't have any syntax errors, you should be able to use the DLL with ObjectPAL.

USING THE NEWLY CREATED DLL WITH OBJECTPAL

1. Copy the DLL to your working directory. Alternatively, you can put it in any directory in the path—including the Windows system directory.

2. Launch Paradox and change working directories to the directory with the DLL.

3. Create a new form with a button on it.

4. Alter the Uses window to look like this:

```
1: ;Button :: Uses
2:    Uses Hello
3:       getHelloString(text CWORD) CPTR
4:    endUses
```

5. Alter the **pushButton** method of the button to look like this:

```
1: ;Button :: pushButton
2:    method pushButton(var eventInfo Event)
3:       var
4:         s String
5:       endVar
6:
7:       s = gethellostring(3)
8:       s.view()
9:    endmethod
```

6. Save the form as HELLO.FSL, run it, and click the button. A dialog box shows you the string *Hello World 3*.

Although this simple example doesn't do much, it does show the proper way to send a value to and receive a value from a DLL.

COMMON QUESTIONS AND ANSWERS ABOUT WRITING DLLS

Here are the answers to some questions you might have about writing DLLs:

Q: Which memory model is recommended for writing DLLs for Paradox?

A: Use the large memory model so that everything is far. It makes many details of writing DLLs easier and automatic.

Q: Why doesn't my DLL work correctly?

A: You must use the correct cw library to link. A small model DLL uses cwc—not cws. A medium model DLL uses cwl—not cwm. Compact and large models use cwc and cwl, respectively. I recommend the large memory model for developing DLLs for Paradox.

To learn more about writing DLLs for Paradox, consult *Paradox Programmer's Guide* (Sams Publishing, 1993) and the Windows API reference guides. In Chapter 32, "Using the Windows API," you build on your knowledge of DLLs with a study of the Windows API.

USING THE
WINDOWS API

The term **API** is an acronym for *application pro-gramming interface*. The Windows API is the set of DLLs that makes up Windows. It comprises all the functions, messages, data structures, data types, statements, and files that a programmer needs for developing Windows applications.

GLOSSARY
TERM

Windows itself is just several big DLLs, including USER.EXE and KRNL386.EXE. The DLLs that Windows uses don't end with the customary .DLL extension. The set of Windows DLLs is referred to as the Windows *application programming interface* (API). The API is full of functions of which you can take advantage. How do you know what functions are in there, and how do you figure out how to use them?

Many companies, including Borland, offer a set of API reference guides. These guides describe the Microsoft Windows API and list all the functions, messages, data structures, data types, statements, and files that a programmer needs for developing Windows applications. You can buy an API refer-ence guide for about $35.

COMMON WINDOWS DLLS

This section tells you about some of the more common Windows DLLs and what is in them. The following is a list of the DLLs that comprise the majority of Windows 3.1:

- COMMDLG.DLL—Common dialog box functions
- DDEML.DLL—Library used in Windows 3.1 for DDE
- GDI.EXE—Graphic Device Interface
- LZEXPAND.DLL—Used since Windows 3.0 to compress and decompress files
- MMSYSTEM.DLL—Library of Windows 3.1 multimedia functions
- OLECLI.DLL—Object linking and embedding client functions
- OLESVR.DLL—Object Linking and embedding server functions

THE FIVE STEPS TO USING A WINDOWS API FUNCTION

When dealing with a large subject, it is nice sometimes to be given clear-cut goals. The following is an overview of the five steps needed when you wish to use an API function:

1. Set a goal.
2. Check ObjectPAL. Make sure that the function is not already duplicated in ObjectPAL.
3. Find the API function. You can use any source you wish; the online help for BCW 3.x and 4.0 are perhaps the easiest. Open up BCW 3.1 or 4.0 and go to its help. In 3.x, go to Contents, then go to Windows API. In 4.0, click the API button. Try to find exitWindows and how to play a sound.
4. Find the name of the DLL from which the function comes. In BCW 3.x help, go to *Types and Modules*.
5. Prototype the function. Use a Uses Window in ObjectPAL to prototype a function in a DLL. Use the special ObjectPAL data types to choose an appropriate data type to map to. Refer to the online help or the header file for the appropriate typedef definition to find valid data.

HUNGARIAN NOTATION

The API consists of Hungarion notation for variable names. All variables of a given type should start with the prefix:

b	BOOL (int)
by	BYTE (unsigned char)
c	char
cx, cy	short (used as x or y length, c stands for count)
dw	DWORD (unsigned long)
h	Handle
i	int
l	LONG (long)
n	short or int
p	point
s	string
sz	String terminated by a zero
u	unsigned
w	WORD (unsigned int)
x,y	short (used as x or y coordinate)

API CALLS

To call an API function that shuts down Windows, you call a Windows function from USER.EXE:

```
1:  Uses User
2:    exitWindows(reserved CDOUBLE, returncode CWORD) Number
3:  endUses
```

Let's start by seeing an example. To call an API function that shuts down Windows, you call a Windows function from USER.EXE called exitWindows.

API Syntax

BOOL ExitWindows(dwReturnCode, reserved)

Parameters:

```
DWORD dwReturnCode; /* return or restart code    */
UINT  reserved    ; /* reserved; must be zero    */
```

Description:

The ExitWindows function can restart Windows, terminate Windows and return control to MS-DOS, or terminate Windows and restart the system.

Windows sends the WM_QUERYENDSESSION message to notify all applications that a request has been made to restart or terminate Windows. If all applications "agree" to terminate, Windows sends the WM_ENDSESSION message to all applications before terminating.

> In C, a /*   */ combination remarks out the characters between the asterisks.

The following is a translated Uses Statement:

```
1:   Uses User
2:     exitWindows(reserved CDOUBLE, returncode CLONG)
3:   endUses
```

The following is the ObjectPAL Call to API:

```
1:   method pushButton(var eventInfo Event)
2:     if msgQuestion("Exit Windows?", " ") = "Yes" then
3:       exitWindows(0,0)
4:     endIf
5:   endmethod
```

TRANSLATING FROM HEX TO DECIMAL

Version 5 of Paradox introduced two new ObjectPAL procedures for translating to and from hexidecimal: toHex() and fromHex(). Of these two, fromHex() is of particular interest in our discussion of DLLs because API functions are most often documented using hexidecimal numbers. To convert a hexidecimal number to a decimal number, type the following code into the **pushButton** method of a button.

```
1:   ;Button :: pushButton
2:   method pushButton(var eventInfo Event)
3:     var
4:       s    String
5:       li   LongInt
6:     endVar
7:
8:     ;Hexadecimal value to convert (for example "0x00010")
9:     s = "Enter Hex number"
10:    s.view("Hex value to convert")
11:    li = fromHex(s)
12:    li.view(s)
13: endMethod
```

EXITING WINDOWS

The next tutorial shows you that once you register a function in a DLL, you can use it just like any ObjectPAL procedure. It uses the exitWindows function. For more options on using this function, refer to the Windows SDK or API reference guides.

Tutorial: Exiting Windows

Suppose that you wish to exit Windows when a user presses a button on a form.

On Disk: \ANSWERS\WIN-EXIT.FSL

Quick Steps

1. Prototype the function in the Uses window of the button.
2. Call the function in the **pushButton** method.

Step By Step

1. Set your working directory to the TUTORIAL directory, create a new form, and place a button on it. Label it Exit Windows.
2. Add line 5 to the Uses window of the Exit Windows button.

```
1:    ;Button :: Uses
2:    Uses User
3:       ;The return value is zero if one or more applications
4:       ;refuse to terminate.
5:       exitWindows(reserved cdouble, returncode cword) Number
6:    endUses
```

3. Add lines 3–5 to the **pushButton** method of the Exit Windows button.

```
1:    ;Button :: pushButton
2:    method pushButton(var eventInfo Event)
3:       if msgQuestion("Exit Windows?",
      "Are you sure you wish to exit Windows?") = "Yes" then
4:          exitWindows(0,0)
5:       endIf
6:    endmethod
```

4. Check the syntax and save form as WIN-EXIT.FSL. Run the form and click the Exit Windows button. You exit not only Paradox but also Windows itself (see Figure 32.1).

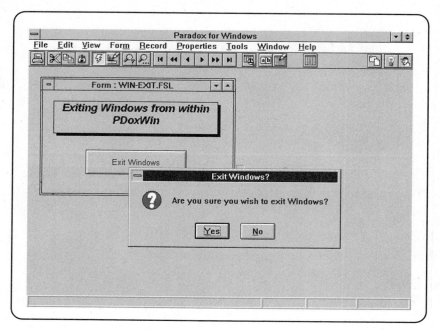

Figure 32.1. WIN-EXIT.FSL.

Analysis

In step 2, line 2 tells ObjectPAL which function is in the USER.EXE DLL. No path or extension is used. ObjectPAL automatically searches the current directory, the Windows directory, and all the directories on the path. Line 5 prototypes the function in the DLL. You prototype DLLs similarly to custom methods. In this case, the DLL function is called `exitWindows`. It takes two parameters and returns a number.

In step 3, line 3 prompts the user with a message question dialog box. If the answer to the question is yes, line 4 calls the function, which exits Windows. This button is completely self-contained; all the code is in it. Now that you have created it, you can copy and paste the button into any application that you want.

DIALING A TELEPHONE NUMBER WITH THE API

Sometimes it's useful to be able to dial a number and hang up the phone. This capability is especially handy with contact manager systems. The next tutorial requires that you have a modem ready to use.

Tutorial: Dialing a Telephone Number with the API

Suppose that you wish to use the Windows API to dial and hang up the phone.

On Disk: \ANSWERS\DLL\API-DIAL.FSL

Quick Steps

1. Register the Windows API functions `OpenComm`, `WriteComm`, and `CloseComm` from USER.EXE.

2. In the Dial Phone and Hang Up buttons, use the three functions to open a connection to the port, to send the command to the modem, and to close—that is, flush—the connection.

Step By Step

1. Create a new form and place two buttons labeled Dial Phone and Hang Up on it (see Figure 32.2).

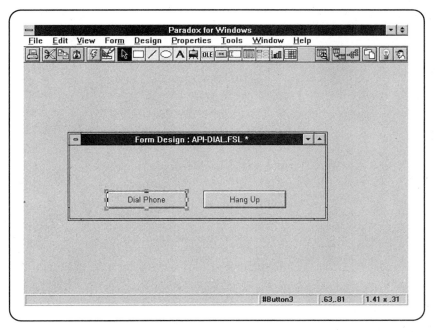

Figure 32.2. API-DIAL.FSL.

2. Add lines 3–5 to the Uses window of the form.

```
1:    ;Form :: Uses
2:    Uses USER
3:       OpenComm(ComPort CPTR, InQueue cWord, OutQueue cWord) cWord
4:       WriteComm(Cid CWORD, Buf CPTR, Size CWORD) CWORD
5:       CloseComm(Cid CWORD) CWORD
6:    endUses
```

3. Add line 3 to the Var window of the form.

```
1:    ;Form :: Var
2:    Var
3:       Cid  SmallInt
4:    endVar
```

4. Add lines 3–15 to the **pushButton** method of the Dial Phone button.

```
1:    ;Button :: pushButton
2:    method pushButton(var eventInfo Event)
3:       var
4:         SendStr    String
5:       endVar
6:
7:       SendStr = "1234567"
8:       SendStr.view("Enter phone number to dial")
9:
10:      if SendStr = "1234567" then return endIf
11:      SendStr = "ATDT" + SendStr + chr(13)
12:
13:      Cid = openComm("COM1", 32, 32)
14:      WriteComm(Cid, SendStr, SmallInt(size(SendStr)))
15:      CloseComm(Cid)
16:   endmethod
```

5. Add lines 3–5 to the **pushButton** method of the Hang Up button.

```
1:    ;Button :: pushButton
2:    method pushButton(var eventInfo Event)
3:       Cid = openComm("COM1", 32, 32)
4:       WriteComm(Cid, "H" + chr(13), 2)
5:       CloseComm(Cid)
6:    endmethod
```

6. Check the syntax, save the form as API-DIAL.FSL, run the form, and click the Dial Phone button (see Figure 32.3). If you entered a dummy number, click the Hang Up button immediately. Otherwise, click the Hang Up button when you're done talking.

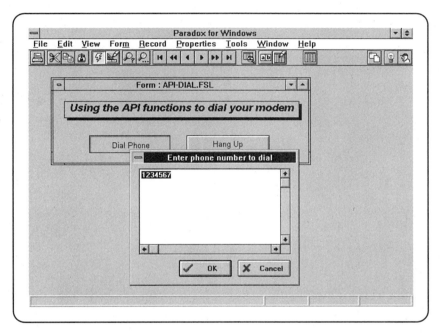

Figure 32.3. API-DIAL.FSL.

Analysis

In step 2, line 2 tells ObjectPAL which functions are in the USER.EXE DLL we wish to use. Lines 3–5 prototype the functions in the DLL. You'll find the API reference guides invaluable when you prototype Windows functions in ObjectPAL.

In step 3, line 3 declares a small integer variable in the form's Var window. This variable is used with both buttons.

In step 4, lines 7 and 8 set up the *SendStr* string for use in line 14. Line 4 declares the String variable, and line 7 initializes it. Line 8 enables the user to change the phone number. If the user doesn't change the phone number, the code assumes that he or she no longer wants to dial the phone, and the return keyword stops the routine. Line 11 concatenates the phone number to the string used for touch-tone phones—namely, *ATDT*. If you have a pulse phone, use *ATDP*. The manual that comes with your modem tells you the commands you can send to it. Lines 13–15 do the actual dialing. Line 13 opens the COM1 port and puts the a value into the small integer variable that you declared. This variable is used by `WriteComm` and `CloseComm` in lines 14 and 15. Line 14 writes the string to the communication port, and line 15 closes—flushes—the port.

In step 5, lines 3–5 use the H command. They are similar to previous lines except that they tell the modem to hang up rather than to dial.

The code in this tutorial makes a useful custom method. You might want to enhance it to check for errors. If you have touch-tone banking, you can use a speaker phone with this technique to develop your own custom touch-tone banking application.

Reading the Windows API Manuals

To use a Windows API function, you need to know several things: the function name, the name of the DLL containing the function, the parameters the function requires, and the parameters the function returns. Remember, part of the parameter information you need is what type of data it is. More on this in the next section. For now, let's discuss how to read a Windows API manual (Borland's in this example). You might, for example, find the following in a Windows API manual.

When you see WIN30, WIN3.1, and WIN32 in the API manuals, this is letting you know when the function was introduced. Any functions marked WIN32 cannot be used with ObjectPAL.

Example 1 (A Complete Example)

This example is provided only as an exercise. With version 5, Borland added the procedure `resourceInfo()` to ObjectPAL that calls the following API calls for you.

API Syntax:

UINT GetFreeSystemResources(fuSysResource)

Parameters:

UINT fuSysResource; /* type of resource to check */

Description:

The GetFreeSystemResources function returns the percentage of free space for system resources. The fuSysResource parameter specifies the type of resource to be checked. This parameter can be one of the following values:

Value	*Meaning*
GFSR_SYSTEMRESOURCES	Returns the percentage of free space for system resources.
GFSR_GDIRESOURCES	Returns the percentage of free space for GDI resources. GDI Resources include device-context handles, brushes, pens, regions, fonts, and bitmaps.
GFSR_USERRESOURCES	Returns the percentage of free space for USER resources. These resources include window and menu handles.

The return value specifies the percentage of free space for resources, if the function is successful.

> **Type Definition**—In C++, typedef is a keyword that assigns a symbol name (identifier) to the data type definition (type definition). The C++ syntax is as follows:

Syntax:

```
typedef <type definition> <identifier>
```

Examples:

```
typedef unsigned char byte;
typedef char str40[41];
```

Example 2

API Syntax:

BOOL sndPlaySound(lpszSoundName, fuOptions)

Parameters:

LPCSTR lpszSoundName; /* name of sound to play */

UINT fuOptions; /* options flags */

Description:

The `sndPlaySound` function plays a waveform sound specified by a filename or by an entry in the [sounds] section of the registry. If the sound cannot be found, the function plays the default sound specified by the `SystemDefault` entry in the [sounds] section of the registry. If there is no `SystemDefault` entry or if the default sound can't be found, the function makes no sound and returns FALSE.

The following is a translated Uses Statement:

```
1:   Uses MMSYSTEM
2:     sndPlaySound(fileName CPTR, parameter CWORD) CWORD
3:   endUses
```

The following is the ObjectPAL Call to API:

```
1:   method pushButton(var eventInfo Event)
2:     sndPlaySound("CHIMES.WAV",1)
3:   endmethod
```

DLLs AND DATA TYPES

When you use or register DLLs with another application, you need to know how the other application deals with data types. Table 32.1 later in this chapter lists the names of the different data types that ObjectPAL, C, and Pascal use.

Note that not all of the data types a DLL may use are listed in Table 32.1. If the DLL (or Windows API call) you wish to use needs to receive or pass back a variable other than the data types listed in Table 32.1, a wrapper DLL needs to be used. A wrapper DLL is an intermediate DLL that can communicate on behalf of Paradox for Windows with the DLL. For example, if you need to pass an array to a DLL, you could use a wrapper DLL. The wrapper DLL can take several strings from ObjectPAL, convert them to an array, and pass the array to the DLL. This also holds true for a C structure.

COMMON WINDOWS API CALLS

This next section is a reference of some of the more common Windows API calls users use in their ObjectPAL applications.

Playing .WAV files with MMSYSTEM.DLL

```
1:  Uses MMSYSTEM
2:    sndPlaySound(fileName CPTR, parameter CWORD) CWORD
3:  endUses
4:
5:  method pushButton(var eventInfo Event)
6:    if sndPlaySound(String(WavField), 1) <> 1 then
7:        message("Not able to play sound.")
8:    endIf
9:  endMethod
```

Checking the State of the Numlock Key with User.exe

```
1:  Uses User
2:    getkeystate(vkey CWORD) CWORD
3:  endUses
4:
5:  method pushButton(var eventInfo Event)
6:    if getkeystate(VK_NUMLOCK) = 1 then
7:        msgInfo("Numkey is...", "locked")
8:        else
9:          msgInfo("Numkey is...", "unlocked")
10:     endIf
11: endmethod
```

Switching to Another Application Using User.exe

```
1:  Uses User
2:    BringWindowToTop(WinHandle CWORD)
3:  endUses
4:
5:  method pushButton(var eventInfo Event)
6:    var
7:        tc TCursor
8:        s SmallInt
9:    endVar
10:
11:    enumWindowNames("WinNames.db")
12:
13:    tc.open("WinNames.db")
14:
15:    If tc.locate("WindowName", "Notepad - (Untitled)") Then
16:        s = tc.handle
```

```
17:        BringWindowToTop(s)
18:        else
19:          execute("notepad.exe")
20:     endIf
21: endmethod
```

Exiting Windows with User.exe

```
1:  Uses User
2:     exitWindows(reserved cdouble, returncode cword) Number
3:  endUses
4:
5:  method pushButton(var eventInfo Event)
6:     if msgQuestion("Exit Windows?", "Are you sure?") = "Yes" then
7:         exitWindows(0,0)
8:     endIf
9:  endmethod
```

Getting the Free System Resources with User.exe

```
1:  Uses User
2:     GetFreeSystemResources( gfsrResourceType CWORD ) CWORD
3:  endUses
4:
5:  method pushButton(var eventInfo Event)
6:     var
7:         System, GDI, User SmallInt
8:     endVar
9:
10:    System = GetFreeSystemResources( 0 )
11:    GDI = GetFreeSystemResources( 1 )
12:    User = GetFreeSystemResources( 2 )
13:
14:    msgInfo("Free Resources", "System: " + String(System) +
15:          "\n   GDI: " + String(GDI) +
16:          "\n   User: " + String(GDI) )
17: endMethod
```

Sending a File Directly to the Printer

```
1:  ;This example sends a file to a printer
2:  ;Printer is the name of the printer, may be any name
3:  ;Port is the name of the printer port
4:  ;Job is the name of the printer job
5:  ;File is the file being printed
6:  Uses GDI
7:     Spoolfile(Printer CPTR, Port CPTR, Job CPTR, File CPTR) CWORD
8:  endUses
9:
10:   SpoolFile("Diablo","LPT3","Labels","myfile.txt")
11:
12:   Uses Kernel
13:     GetTempFileName(Drive CWORD,Prefix CPTR,Uniq CWORD,File CPTR)CWORD
14: enduses
```

```
15:
16: var
17:    textfile string
18: endvar
19: ;This example gets a unique filename in the Windows temp directory
20: ;When done, textfile will have the filename (including the path)
21: textfile=fill(" ",144)
22: getTempFileName(0,"",0,textfile)
```

Dialing a Modem with User.exe

```
1:  Uses USER ; -- on form
2:     OpenComm(ComPort CPTR, InQueue cWord, OutQueue cWord) cWord
3:     WriteComm(Cid cWord, Buf CPTR, Size cWord) cWord
4:     CloseComm(Cid cWord) cWord
5:  endUses
6:
7:  Var ; -- on form
8:    Cid   SmallInt
9:  endVar
10:
11: ;The following code dials the phone.
12: method pushButton(var eventInfo Event)
13:    var
14:       SendStr    String
15:    endVar
16:
17:    SendStr = "1234567"
18:    SendStr.view("Enter phone number to dial")
19:
20:    if SendStr = "1234567" then return endIf
21:
22:    SendStr = "ATDT" + SendStr + chr(13)
23:
24:    Cid = openComm("COM1", 32, 32)
25:    WriteComm(Cid, SendStr, SmallInt(size(SendStr)))
26:    CloseComm(Cid)
27:  endmethod
28:
29: ;The following code hangs up the modem.
30: method pushButton(var eventInfo Event)
31:    Cid = openComm("COM1", 32, 32)
32:    WriteComm(Cid, "H" + chr(13), 2)
33:    CloseComm(Cid)
34: endmethod
```

TABLES

This final section privides some tables for use when prototyping Windows API calls. Table 32.1 gives you more information on the special DLL data types. Table 32.2 lists the ranges of the special DLL data types. Table 32.3 lists some of the common API function data types.

TABLE 32.1. OBJECTPAL SPECIAL DLL DATA TYPES.				
Date Type	Uses keyword	ObjectPAL	C	Pascal
16-bit integer	CWORD	SmallInt	int	Integer
32-bit integer	CLONG	LongInt	long	Longint
64-bit floating-point number	CDOUBLE	Number	double	Double
80-bit floating-point number	DLONGDOUBLE	Number	long double	Extended
Pointer	CPTR	String	char far*	String
Binary or graphic data	CHANDLE	Binary or Graphic		THandle

TABLE 32.2. OBJECTPAL SPECIAL DATA TYPES DATA RANGES.			
Date Type	Uses Keyword	ObjectPAL	ObjectPAL Range
16-bit integer	CWORD	SmallInt	−32,768 to 32,767
32-bit integer	CLONG	LongInt	−2,147,483,648 to 2,147,483,647
64-bit floating-point number	CDOUBLE	Number	$+\text{-}3.4 * 10\text{-}4930$ to $+ -1.1 * 10\ 4930$
80-bit floating-point number	DLONGDOUBLE	Number	same
Pointer	CPTR	String	32,767 (quoted up to 255)
Binary or graphic data	CHANDLE	Binary or Graphic	

Table 32.3. Common API Function Data Types.

API	Uses	OPAL	C Data Type	Length	C Range
	CWORD	SmallInt	unsigned char	8 bits	0 to 255
	CPTR	String	char	8 bits	−128 to 127
	CWORD	SmallInt	enum	16 bits	−32,768 to 32,767
UINT	CLONG	LongInt	unsigned int	16 bits	0 to 65,535
	CWORD	SmallInt	short int	16 bits	−32,768 to 32,767
INT	CWORD	SmallInt	int	16 bits	−32,768 to 32,767
	CDOUBLE	Number	unsigned long	32 bits	0 to 4,294,967,295
Word	CLONG	Long Integer		long	32 bits −2,147,483,648 to 2,147,483,647
	CDOUBLE	Number		float	32 bits 3.4 * (10**-38) to 3.4 * (10**+38)
	CDOUBLE	Number		double	64 bits 1.7 * (10**−308) to 1.7 * (10**+308)
	CLONGDOUBLE	Number		long double	80 bits 3.4 * (10**−4932) to 1.1 * (10**+4932)
LONG	CLONG	Long Integer		LONG	
BOOL	CWORD				Pass 0 or 1
DWORD					
NULL	CWORD				Pass a 0
HANDLE	CHANDLE				

The System, Session, and Binary Types

System Methods and Procedures

The System commands add functional programming power to ObjectPAL. For example, you can use them to beep the system speaker or read from and write to .INI files. Table 33.1 lists the System methods and procedures.

System methods and procedures

Using INI files

Using aliases

Using the Windows clipboard

TABLE 33.1. SYSTEM METHODS AND PROCEDURES.

appendASCIIFix	dlgSort
appendASCIIVar	dlgSubtract
beep	dlgTableInfo
close	enableExtendedCharacters
compileInformation	enumDesktopWindowNames
constantNameToValue	enumEnvironmentStrings
constantValueToName	enumFonts
cpuClockTime	enumFormats
debug	enumFormNames
desktopMenu	enumPrinters
disablePreviousError	enumReportNames
dlgAdd	enumRTLClassNames
dlgCopy	enumRTLConstants
dlgCreate	enumRTLErrors
dlgDelete	enumRTLMethods
dlgEmpty	enumWindowNames
dlgExport	errorClear
dlgImportASCIIFix	errorCode
dlgImportASCIIVar	errorHasErrorCode
dlgImportSpreadsheet	errorHasNativeErrorCode
dlgNetDrivers	isErrorTrapOnWarnings
dlgNetLocks	errorLog
dlgNetRefresh	errorMessage
dlgNetRetry	errorNativeCode
dlgNetSetLocks	errorPop
dlgNetSystem	errorShow
dlgNetUserName	errorTrapOnWarnings
dlgNetWho	exportParadoxDOS
dlgRename	execute
dlgRestructure	executeString
	exit

exportASCIIFix
exportASCIIVar
exportSpreadsheet
fail
fileBrowser
formatAdd
formatDelete
formatExist
formatGetSpec
formatSetCurrencyDefault
formatSetDateDefault
formatSetDateTimeDefault
formatSetLogicalDefault
formatSetLongIntDefault
formatSetNumberDefault
formatSetSmallIntDefault
formatSetTimeDefault
formatStringToDate
formatStringToNumber
getDefaultPrinterStyleSheet
getDefaultScreenStyleSheet
getLanguageDriver
getMouseScreenPosition
getUserLevel
helpOnHelp
helpQuit
helpSetIndex
helpShowContext
helpShowIndex
helpShowTopic
helpShowTopicInKeywordTable
importASCIIFix

importASCIIVar
importSpreadsheet
message
msgAbortRetryIgnore
msgInfo
msgQuestion
msgRetryCancel
msgStop
msgYesNoCancel
pixelsToTwips
play
printerGetInfo
printerGetOptions
printerSetCurrent
printerSetOptions
projectViewerClose
projectViewerIsOpen
projectViewerOpen
readEnvironmentString
readProfileString
resourceInfo
sendKeys
sendKeysActionID
setDefaultPrinterStyleSheet
setDefaultScreenStyleSheet
setMouseScreenPosition
setMouseShape
setUserLevel
sleep
sound
sysInfo
tracerClear

continues

TABLE 33.1. CONTINUED	
tracerHide	twipsToPixels
tracerOff	version
tracerOn	winGetMessageID
tracerSave	winPostMessage
tracerShow	winSendMessage
tracerToTop	writeEnvironmentString
tracerWrite	writeProfileString

USING .INI FILES

ObjectPAL offers a convenient way to read and write .INI files. Although you can read from and write to the WIN.INI file directly, I recommend that you don't, because it's restricted to 64K. A better technique is to write to your own custom .INI file in the working directory:

> **writeProfileString(*FileName*, *Section*, *Key*, *Value*)** Logical
> **readProfileString(*FileName*, *Section*, *Key*)** String

For example, to set a value in an INI file called MYAPP.INI, type the following code in the **pushButton** method of a button.

```
1:   writeProfileString("MYAPP.INI", "Colors", "Background",  "White")
2:   writeProfileString("MYAPP.INI", "Colors", "Foreground",  "Black")
```

You could then use this information to customize your application. When you open the application, read in the following values and set the foreground and background colors. For example, type the following code into the **pushButton** method of a button.

```
1:   var
2:      sBG, sFG String
3:   endVar
4:
5:   sBG = readProfileString("MYAPP.INI", "Colors", "Background")
6:   sFG = readProfileString("MYAPP.INI", "Colors", "Foreground")
7:
8:   sBG.view("Background Color")
9:   sFG.view("Forground Color")
```

Then, use these two variables to set colors in your application. For example, the following code uses the two variables defined above to set the colors of a box.

(Do not type this one in; the variable above is declared private to the **pushButton** method and is out of scope from the box.)

```
1:  box1 :: open
2:  doDefault
3:  self.color = sBG
4:  self.frame.color = sFG
```

The Paradox Desktop (\APPS\DESKTOP\DESKTOP.FDL) demonstrates using .INI files. It also shows you how to use a custom DESKTOP.INI file for storing settings from one session to another and for passing to the startup directory the next occurrence of DESKTOP.FSL. Since the form is delivered, here is the pertinent code.

```
1:  var app Application endVar
2:
3:  if isfile(":work:desktop.fsl") then
4:      writeProfileString(windowsDir()+"\\desktop.ini","Launch","DesktopPath",
                   getAliasPath("work")+"\\desktop.fdl")
5:      app.hide()
6:      DesktopInstance = 1
7:  else
8:      DesktopInstance = 2
9:  endIf
10:
11: ;sDesktopPath is declared in the Var window of the form.
12: sDeskTopPath = readProfileString(windowsDir()+"\\desktop.ini",
                   "Launch","DesktopPath")
```

.INI files are convenient because they don't rely on another form or library. They also are an excellent way to store configuration settings from one session to another.

SESSION METHODS AND PROCEDURES

With the Session methods and procedures, you can check for, list, add, and save aliases. Table 33.2 lists the Session methods and procedures.

TABLE 33.2. SESSION METHODS AND PROCEDURES.	
addAlias	close
addPassword	enumAliasLoginInfo
addProjectAlias	enumAliasNames
advancedWildcardsInLocate	enumDataBaseTables
blankAsZero	enumDriverCapabilities

continues

TABLE 33.2. CONTINUED	
enumDriverInfo	loadProjectAliases
enumDriverNamesenumDriverTopics	lock
enumEngineInfo	open
enumFolder	removeAlias
enumOpenDatabases	removeAllPasswords
enumUsers	removePassword
getAliasPath	removeProjectAlias
getAliasProperty	retryPeriod
getNetUserName	saveCFG
ignoreCaseInLocate	saveProjectAliases
isAdvancedWildcardsInLocate	setAliasPassword
isAssigned	setAliasPath
isBlankZero	setAliasProperty
isIgnoreCaseInLocate	setRetryPeriod
	unLock

Using Aliases

As an ObjectPAL programmer, you probably have dealt with aliases already. This involves checking for the existence of the alias, adding it if it does not exist, and saving the IDAPI configuration file. If you're really ambitious, you might add error-checking routines to make sure that the alias has a valid directory.

For example, you can use getAliasPath() to check whether an alias exists. You can use addAlias() to create a new alias. You can use setAliasPath() to set the path for an existing alias; this isn't needed if you use addAlias(). You also can use saveCFG() to save the alias permanently. The next tutorial shows you how to check for and add an alias in the current session.

Tutorial: Using the Alias in the Current Session

Suppose that you wish to create a button on a form that checks whether an alias exists and that adds the alias if it doesn't exist.

On Disk: \ANSWERS\ALIAS.FSL

Quick Steps

1. Use `getAliasPath()` to check whether the alias exists.
2. Use `addAlias()` if the alias doesn't exist.

Step By Step

1. Create a new form and place a button on it. Label the button Go.
2. Add lines 3–11 to the **pushButton** method of the Go button.

```
1:    ;Button :: pushButton
2:    method pushButton(var eventInfo Event)
3:        if getAliasPath("yyy") = blank() then
4:          if isFile("ALIAS.FSL") then
5:            addAlias("yyy", "Standard", getAliasPath(":work:"))
6:            msgInfo("yyy alias added", getAliasPath("yyy"))
7:          else
8:            msgStop("Startup Error!", "This form is not in the current
working directory")
9:            close()
10:         endIf
11:       endIf
12:   endmethod
```

3. Check the syntax, save the form as ALIAS.FSL, run the form, and click the button. If the yyy alias doesn't exist, it's added and a message information box is displayed. If the form isn't in your working directory, a stop message box pops up and the form closes (see Figure 33.1).

Analysis

Line 3 checks whether the yyy alias exists by checking whether its path is empty. For an alternative, you could use `enumAliasNames()` to write all the alias names to a table on a disk and scan the table for the name. That's too much work, though. (You can use or omit the colons.)

Line 4 makes sure that the form is in the current working directory. This is important because line 5 adds an alias based on the current working directory. That way, if a user attempts to open the form from a different directory, a bad alias won't be added. Instead, line 8 displays an error message, and line 9 closes the form.

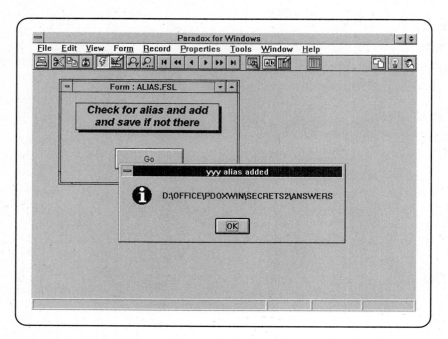

Figure 33.1. ALIAS.FSL.

Tutorial: Adding a Permanent Alias

This tutorial demonstrates how to add a permanent alias automatically when
the form opens. To do this, you need to check whether an alias exists and add
it if it doesn't exist.

On Disk: \ANSWERS\ALIAS2.FSL

Quick Steps

1. Use `getAliasPath()` to check whether the alias exists.
2. Use `AddAlias()` if the alias doesn't exist.

Step By Step

1. Create a new blank form.
2. Add line 3 to the Var window of the form.

```
1:    ;Form :: Var
2:    Var
3:       sys  DynArray[] AnyType
4:    endVar
```

3. Add lines 8–24 to the **open** method of the form.

```
 1:   ;Form :: open
 2:   method open(var eventInfo Event)
 3:   if eventInfo.isPreFilter() then
 4:       ;This code executes for each object on the form
 5:
 6:   else
 7:       ;This code executes only for the form
 8:       sysInfo(Sys)
 9:       if getAliasPath("zzz") = blank() then
10:         if isFile("ALIAS.FSL") then
11:           AddAlias("zzz", "Standard", getAliasPath(":work:"))
12:           saveCFG(Sys["ConfigFile"])
13:         else
14:           msgStop("Startup Error!", "This form is not in
                             the current working directory")
15:           close()
16:         endIf
17:       else
18:         if getAliasPath("zzz") <> getAliasPath(":work:") then
19:           if isFile("ALIAS.FSL") then
20:             AddAlias("zzz", "Standard", getAliasPath(":work:"))
21:             saveCFG(Sys["ConfigFile"])
22:           endIf
23:         endIf
24:       endIf
25:     endif
26:   endmethod
```

4. Check the syntax and run the form. If the *zzz* alias doesn't exist, it's added and a message information box is displayed. If the form isn't in your working directory, a stop message box pops up and the form closes. If the *zzz* alias exists and its path needs to be changed to the new current working directory, the path is changed and the configuration file is saved (see Figure 33.2).

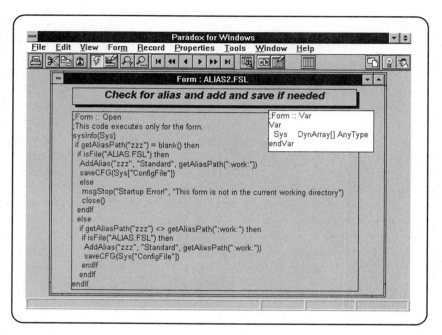

Figure 33.2. ALIAS2.FSL.

Analysis

In step 2, line 3 declares *sys* as a DynArray that is ready to accept data of any type. You declare this variable at the form-level Var window so that you can use it throughout the form.

In step 3, line 8 in the `else` portion of the form's **open** method populates *sys* with system information. If you're interested in all of this information, you can use the DynArray view box on a line after line 8 to view its data. Like the previous tutorial, this tutorial has a line that checks whether the alias exists by checking whether its path is empty. This is done in line 9. Line 10 makes sure that the form is in the current working directory. If a user attempts to open the form from a different directory, a bad alias isn't added. Instead, line 14 displays an error message, and line 15 closes the form. Lines 17–23 occur only if the *zzz* alias exists in line 9. Line 18 checks whether the path of the *zzz* alias is the same as the path of the current working directory. If it isn't, the program assumes that the current path of the *zzz* alias is incorrect. The path is set to the current working directory if the form *ALIAS.FSL* exists in it.

This example of checking for an alias and adding or updating it is elegant programming. It isn't elegant because of its simplicity, but rather because of its thoroughness. If the user forgets to create an alias, the alias is created for him. If the user moves the application directory, the alias is updated for him. Although you might not want to implement this routine on all your applications, you should if you're designing for sale an application that uses an alias.

STORING OBJECTS USING THE CLIPBOARD VIEWER

You can use the Clipboard Viewer that comes with Windows to store code. This technique of storing code is better than saving files to a disk as individual text files. Plus, you can store objects and code listings in the same place. You can read and write to the clipboard with writeToClipboard() and readFromClipboard().

CREATING A DATA DICTIONARY

A *data dictionary* is a set of tables that describes a database. A database in Paradox is roughly defined as all the files in a directory. Suppose that you wish to create a data dictionary for all the files in a directory. On disk is a script that builds a data dictionary of your application. The script is \ANSWERS\DD_BUILD.SSL. Especially handy is the table that stores all the source code: DD_SRC.DB. You can use this table to globally search the source code of all the forms, scripts, and libraries of an entire directory. Run this script on the files in the ANSWERS directory, then create a quick form based on the DD_SRC.DB table and browse all the source code.

TABLE 33.3. PRESTWOOD'S DATA DICTIONARY.	
Table	Description
DD_F.DB	Listing of forms
DD_FILES.DB	Listing of all files (including non-Paradox files)
DD_L.DB	Listing of libraries
DD_Q.DB	Listing of queries
DD_R.DB	Listing of reports
DD_S.DB	Listing of scripts
DD_SQL.DB	Listing of SQL source files
DD_SRC.DB	Listing of source code for forms, scripts, & libraries
DD_T.DB	Listing of tables

Although this data dictionary is useful, currently it does have limitations. The following are the limitations of DD_BUILD.SSL:

- Supports only Paradox tables.
- Only deals with files in the same directory (does not recurse subdirectories).
- Generates tables in the same directory as files.
- Does not scan through each table and delete the references to the data dictionary files. If you do not wish to have the data dictionary take up room in the data dictionary, then use a `scan` loop to go through each table that starts with *DD_* and delete every entry that starts with *DD_*.

> I am upgrading this Data Dictionary all the time. Refer to the SECRETS2.TXT text file for information on how to contact me for the latest version.

THE DLG CATEGORY

All 18 system dialog procedures start with dlg. These dialog procedures interactively bring up many—but not all—of the dialog boxes available. The next tutorial looks at six of them.

Tutorial: Using dlg Procedures (DLG.FSL)

This tutorial demonstrates how to use the system dialog procedures by studying six of them—`dlgDelete()`, `dlgCreate()`, `dlgCopy()`, `dlgSort()`, `dlgNetSetLocks()`, and `dlgNetWho()`.

On Disk: \ANSWERS\DLG.FSL

Quick Steps

1. Create a form and put six buttons on it.
2. Use `dlgDelete`, `dlgCreate`, `dlgCopy`, `dlgSort`, `dlgNetSetLocks`, and `dlgNetWho` on the **pushButton** method of each button.

Step By Step

1. Change your working directory to TUTORIAL. Create a new form with six buttons. Label the buttons Create TEMP table, Delete TEMP

table, Copy WORLD.DB, Sort World table, Lock/Unlock a table, and Show Current Users (see Figure 33.3).

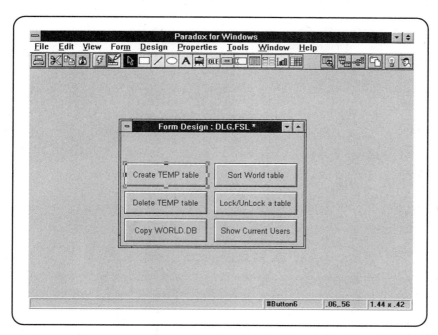

Figure 33.3. Set up form for the tutorial.

2. Add line 3 to the **pushButton** method of the Delete TEMP table button.

```
1:    ;Button :: pushButton
2:    method pushButton(var eventInfo Event)
3:        dlgDelete("TEMP")
4:    endmethod
```

3. Add line 3 to the **pushButton** method of the Create TEMP table button.

```
1:    ;Button :: pushButton
2:    method pushButton(var eventInfo Event)
3:        dlgCreate("TEMP")
4:    endmethod
```

4. Add the Copy WORLD.DB button.

```
1:    ;Button :: pushButton
2:    method pushButton(var eventInfo Event)
```

```
3:        dlgCopy("WORLD")
4:     endmethod
```

5. Add line 3 to the **pushButton** method of the Sort World table button.

```
1:     ;Button :: pushButton
2:     method pushButton(var eventInfo Event)
3:        dlgSort("WORLD")
4:     endmethod
```

6. Add line 3 to the **pushButton** method of the Lock/Unlock a table button.

```
1:     ;Button :: pushButton
2:     method pushButton(var eventInfo Event)
3:        dlgNetSetLocks()
4:     endmethod
```

7. Add line 3 to the **pushButton** method of the Show Current Users button.

```
1:     ;Button :: pushButton
2:     method pushButton(var eventInfo Event)
3:        dlgNetWho()
4:     endmethod
```

8. Check the syntax and save the form. Run the form. Click all six buttons in any order to see how they work. Figure 33.4 shows the Sort Table dialog box.

Analysis

The dialog procedures are fairly straightforward. The only interesting thing is that they have two types of syntax. One type of syntax requires a table name; the other one does not.

You should explore the other 12 system dialog procedures. Add the ones of interest to you to the form that you created in this tutorial.

THE BINARY TYPE

Use the binary data type for data that only the computer understands; Paradox does not know how to interpret the data. The Binary variable is a handle you can establish to a binary object. Table 33.4 lists the Binary methods and procedures.

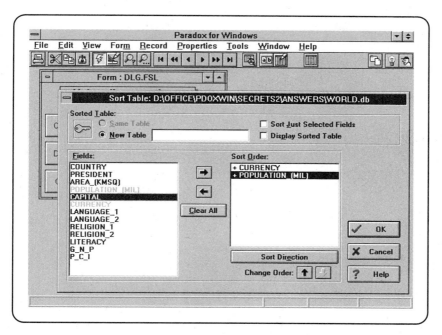

Figure 33.4. DLG.FSL and the Sort Table dialog box.

TABLE 33.4. THE BINARY METHODS AND PROCEDURES.

blank*	isFixedType*
clipboardErase	readFromClipboard
clipboardHasFormat	readFromFile
dataType*	size
enumClipboardFormats	writeToClipboard
isAssigned*	writeToFile
isBlank*	*Inherited from the Anytype Type

On disk, the form ANSWERS\BINARY.FSL demonstrates many of the Binary methods and procedures (see Figure 33.5).

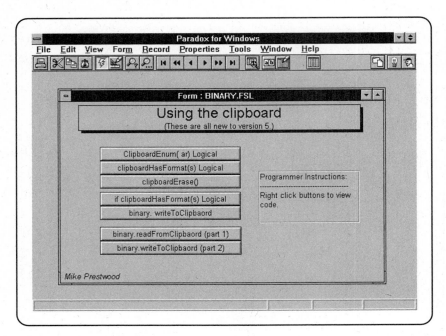

Figure 33.5. BINARY.FSL

For example, type lines 3–9 into the **pushButton** method of a button to display
the formats currently in the Windows clipboard.

```
1:  ;Button :: pushButton
2:  method pushButton(var eventInfo Event)
3:     var
4:        b    Binary
5:        ar   Array[] String
6:     endVar
7:
8:     b.clipboardEnum( ar )
9:     ar.view("Formats in Windows clipboard")
10: endmethod
```

This chapter was a catch-all for the System, Session, and Binary types and just
touched on the power in these three types. Of particular interest are the use of
aliases and the data dictionary; these two items will probably become part of
your everyday use.

NETWORKING

NETWORKING WITH PARADOX

A *network* is a system of interconnected computer systems and terminals that share software and data. Communicating with other applications enables you to increase the functionality and usability of your applications. This chapter teaches you how to create multiuser applications.

GLOSSARY
TERM

Installation and setup

Peer-to-peer networks

Multiapplication considerations

Paradox and other applications

Sending messages over a network

Network programming features enable you to create multiuser applications easily. And Paradox offers the best data connectivity available to Paradox and dBASE tables. Each major release of Paradox since version 2.0 has improved table structures. Paradox for Windows is compatible with Paradox for DOS versions 3.5, 4.0, and 4.5.

CONVERTING YOUR APPLICATION TO A NETWORK APPLICATION

The central, or controlling, computer in a local area network is the *server*. Although it could be used like a regular computer, a server usually is dedicated to sending and receiving data from devices that are connected to a network. A *client* is a device that receives data from the server in a local area network.

Any application you create in Paradox is fully networkable—automatically. It doesn't matter whether you use Paradox or dBASE table structures. Paradox for Windows obeys all the rules of networking for both Paradox and dBASE.

You still need to be concerned about multiple users, but you don't have to do anything other than properly install and set up Paradox in order to network your application. Most problems that come up in a network environment deal with users who step on or run into other users. This is almost always an issue about conflicting locks. Your first and main task when establishing a network application is to install it and set it up properly. Half the battle to networking successfully with Paradox is installing and setting up Paradox correctly. After you correctly install and set up all your applications, networking is transparent—and painless.

INSTALLING PARADOX ON A NETWORK

This section gives you an overview of the three possible configurations you can use to install Paradox on a network.

The worst and slowest configuration is to install everything on the network. With this setup, the only files you install locally are the boot files on your local hard drive—or even worse, on a single floppy disk. All other files—including utilities, Windows, Paradox, your application, net files, and data files—are on the server, susceptible to network traffic and breakdowns. This setup is called a diskless workstation. I don't recommend it. Given that the price for hard drives has plummeted, no company should use this setup.

The best and fastest configuration is to install everything locally, if you can. This includes DOS, Windows, Paradox, and your application. The only files that go on the network are the net files and data files. This setup requires the most hard drive space, but it offers the most convenience and speed of the three setups.

A compromise solution is to install some necessary files on the network and some files locally. If you use this setup, I recommend that you keep DOS, Windows, and Paradox local and put just your application, the data files, and the net files on the network. For a further compromise, you could keep DOS, Windows, and the IDAPI files local and put the rest of the files—Paradox, your application, the data files, and the net files—on the network. This setup requires less hard-drive space and offers moderate speed.

The best place to put files is in the place that gives you the most convenience and speed. Therefore, you should install DOS, Windows, Paradox, and your application files locally and store only the net files and data tables on the network. Paradox does run in all three configurations, however. You can install the Paradox files either locally or on a network hard drive (perhaps F:\WINAPPS\PDOXWIN). Each user must have read, open, scan, and execute rights to the directory in which you install Paradox (or its equivalent on networks that aren't Novell networks).

WINDOWS ON THE NETWORK, SHARE.EXE, AND NOVELL

If you're using a Novell network and you need to run Windows over the network and load DOS SHARE.EXE locally, you will run into problems. Novell's built-in share and the DOS share conflict. You can overcome this easily, however. Set the `Files=` line in CONFIG.SYS to a special number based on a formula provided by Novell:

1. Start with the maximum number of file handles: 255.

2. Subtract 2 for DOS.

3. Subtract the number of file handles indicated by the `Files=` line in SHELL.CFG.

For example, if you don't have a `Files=` line in your SHELL.CFG file, the default is 48. In that case, the formula would be 255–2–48 = 205. Then you would go into the CONFIG.SYS file and change the `Files=` line to `Files=205`.

WHERE TO INSTALL IDAPI FILES

IDAPI is an acronym for Integrated Database Application Programming Interface. IDAPI is the engine of the Windows versions of Paradox and dBASE. Without it, you can't access any database tables. Borland's decision to separate the engine from the application enables Borland to upgrade both independently and use the engine in other applications. Just as the DOS Paradox engine is available separately for C and Pascal programmers, the IDAPI engine is available for C and Pascal programmers and goes by the name of the Borland Database Engine.

You can put the IDAPI files in either the default Windows system directory or in another directory (perhaps F:\WINAPP\IDAPI). If Paradox is the only application on your network that is aware of Paradox, you may install the IDAPI files in the Paradox directory. I advise that you don't, however. Each user should have read, open, scan, and execute rights to the directory that contains the IDAPI files.

AFTER INSTALLATION

After you've installed all the files in their appropriate places, you still must deal with setup and configuration.

CONFIGURING IDAPI

The IDAPI Engine configuration file holds network-specific configuration information. Its default name is IDAPI.CFG. This file stores the location of the network control file and the list of database aliases, among other things.

To set the network control file, run the Configuration Utility program,

IDAPICFG.EXE, in the Paradox group (see Figure 34.1). Type the location of the Paradox network control file and click OK. As soon as you specify a network control file, Paradox is ready to access data over the network. Users who want or need their own IDAPI.CFG file can copy it from this location.

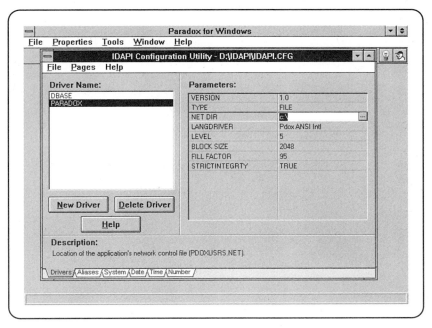

Figure 34.1. The IDAPI Configuration Utility dialog box.

You also use the IDAPI Configuration Utility program to set whether IDAPI shares local tables with other programs that use the Paradox 4.0 locking protocol.

THE NETWORK CONTROL FILE

The **network control file** is a file that controls items such as table and directory access. A network control file is often called a *net file*. The Paradox network control file, PDOXUSRS.NET, serves as the reference point for all the lock files created by Paradox. Each lock file references the network control file. Therefore, all the users must map to the same network control file using the same path but not necessarily the same drive letter. For example, one machine can use T:\NETFILES\PARADOX and another machine can use G:\NETFILES\PARADOX. The drive letter does not matter as long as the path is the same.

LOCAL SETTINGS

The Local Settings utility is one of the icons Paradox installs in the Paradox group when you install Paradox. Double-click this icon to run the Local Settings utility. Use the Local Settings Utility program to alter the name and location of the IDAPI.CFG file (see Figure 34.2). Alternatively, you can use any text Editor to change these designations in the WIN.INI file. The name and location of the IDAPI configuration file are in the [IDAPI] section of WIN.INI. For example:

```
1:   CONFIGFILE01=C:\WINDOWS\SYSTEM\IDAPI.CFG
```

The private and working directories are stored in the [PDOXWIN] section.

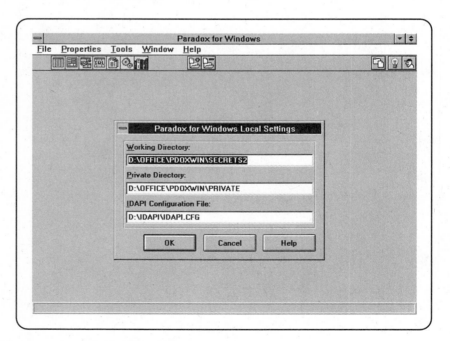

Figure 34.2. Paradox Local Settings dialog box.

WINDOWS FOR WORKGROUPS AND OTHER PEER-TO-PEER NETWORKS

Paradox works with Windows for Workgroups. You need to deal with a few problems, however. In a normal LAN environment, a server is dedicated to setting up the network drives. Everybody can map to at least one drive with the same drive letter and use that drive letter and path for the net file. In a peer-to-peer network, the server—in addition to the clients—often needs to access the same data. Therefore, make sure to map the same net file for the client and server. They can use different drive letters, but the paths have to be the same.

SETTING UP A PEER-TO-PEER NETWORK

When you set up a peer-to-peer network, keep these points in mind:

- Load SHARE.EXE in the AUTOEXEC.BAT.
- Turn Local Share on in IDAPI Configuration utility.
- Every user who wants to use the same data needs to map to the same location.
- If the server is going to share any files other than data files, mark them read-only.

These suggestions apply to any peer-to-peer network; they aren't limited to only Windows for Workgroups. When you set up a Lantastic network, you need to follow the same guidelines.

THE PARADOX STARTUP SEQUENCE

When Paradox starts, it attempts to access the network control file specified in the IDAPI configuration file. If a PDOXUSRS.NET file is available, Paradox opens it. If Paradox doesn't find a PDOXUSRS.NET file, it creates a new PDOXUSRS.NET file and continues with the startup process.

After Paradox successfully opens the PDOXUSRS.NET file, it places an exclusive PARADOX.LCK file in a designated directory for temporary files. If it can't place that exclusive PARADOX.LCK file, Paradox shuts itself down. After it secures a directory for temporary files, Paradox places a shareable

PARADOX.LCK file in a directory with data files. The initialization is complete, and Paradox is ready to open its first table.

Concurrency

Application *concurrency* is the simultaneous use of applications. It can be confusing with all the different applications—especially when the various versions of the programs support different locking protocols and, therefore, different levels of concurrency. The following section lists the issues involved in multiuser environments. You'll learn how to configure applications that are aware of Paradox.

Paradox Locking Protocols

A *lock* is a device that prevents other users from viewing, changing, or locking a table while one user is working with it. One networking feature of Paradox is locking. Powerful record-locking technology increases your productivity in multiuser performance and functionality. Multiuser locking is mostly automatic for both the end user and the programmer. Paradox also offers screen refresh. Changes made by other multiple users are immediately refreshed on screen.

Paradox has two locking protocols—namely, the protocol introduced with Paradox 2.0 and the protocol introduced with Paradox 4.0. These two protocols are incompatible with each other. The locking protocol has no bearing on the type of table a program can work with. A few programs can support both locking protocols. These programs can support only one protocol at a time, however. Table 34.1 lists which products support each locking protocol.

TABLE 34.1. THE PARADOX LOCKING PROTOCOLS AND THE PROGRAMS THAT SUPPORT EACH ONE.

Paradox 2.0	Paradox 4.0	Both Protocols
Paradox 2.0–3.5	Paradox 4.0	Quattro Pro 4.0
Paradox Runtime 2.0–3.5	Paradox Runtime 4.0	Quattro Pro
Quattro Pro 2.0–3.0	Database Desktop	
ObjectVision 1.0–2.0	Paradox	ObjectVision 2.1
Paradox Engine 1.0–2.0	ODAPI/IDAPI Engine	Paradox Engine 3.0
SideKick 2.0	Quick Reports 1.0	Crystal Reports 1.1–2.0

Four versions of the Paradox Engine are in wide use—namely, Paradox Engine 2.0, Paradox Engine 3.0, ODAPI, and the new IDAPI Engine. Versions 2.0 through 3.5 of Paradox use version 2.0 of the Paradox Engine. Paradox 4.0 uses version 3.0 of the Paradox Engine. Paradox 5 for Windows uses the new IDAPI Engine. In addition to the Paradox line of products, other products use versions of the Paradox Engines. When you implement a network application, it's important to understand which products use which engine.

THE PARADOX 2.0 LOCKING PROTOCOL

The Paradox 2.0 locking protocol is the older protocol. It's used in Paradox for DOS and Paradox Runtime versions 2.0–3.5 and Paradox Engine versions 1.0 and 2.0. As Table 34.1 indicates, many Borland applications—such as Quattro Pro 2.0–4.0, Object Vision 1.0–2.0, and SideKick 2.0—use this locking protocol. The designation *Paradox 2.0 locking protocol* represents this level of concurrency. In today's network environment, it's somewhat dated.

THE PARADOX 4.0 LOCKING PROTOCOL

As Table 34.1 shows, Paradox for Windows doesn't support the Paradox 2.0 locking protocol. This means that Paradox for Windows can't network with the products in the first column. Usually, you simply need to upgrade. For example, users of ObjectVision 2.0 must upgrade to version 2.1 to network with both ObjectVision and Paradox.

The Paradox 4.0 locking protocol is the only protocol available for the IDAPI Engine. Applications written with version 3.0 of the Paradox Engine library can switch the locking protocol that they use. The designation *Paradox 4.0 locking protocol* represents this style of locking and concurrency.

In a multiuser environment, the Paradox 4.0 locking protocol maintains concurrency through the PDOXUSRS.NET file. All users who want to share Paradox tables must map to the same PDOXUSRS.NET file in the same way by using the same path; they don't necessarily have to use the same drive letter. Paradox places a PDOXUSRS.LCK and an exclusive PARADOX.LCK file in each directory in which tables are being accessed. This prevents previous versions of Paradox from accessing files in the same directory. Each user who wants to share tables in that directory must map that directory in the same way by using the same path but not necessarily the same drive letter. Then, Paradox places all the locking information for that table in the PDOXUSRS.LCK file. This reduces the number of files that are needed.

TABLE LOCKS USED BY ENGINE 3.0, ODAPI, AND IDAPI

Paradox 4.0 places each table lock in the directory locking file, PDOXUSRS.LCK. It no longer uses the separate table lock file of previous versions. For example, suppose that three users are viewing the CUSTOMER.DB table, and one user is restructuring the ORDERS.DB table. The PDOXUSRS.LCK file will list a shareable lock for each of the three users who are viewing the CUSTOMER.DB table and an exclusive lock on ORDERS.DB for the user who is restructuring that table.

WHAT GETS A DIRECTORY LOCK

Because Paradox, the Paradox Engine, and ODAPI/IDAPI place a lock file in the directory that contains the tables, the first locking protocol to get to the directory owns it. If that locking protocol is compatible with Paradox 2.0, any version of Paradox 2.0–3.5 or Paradox Engine 1.0–2.0 or 3.0 in compatible locking mode has concurrent access to the directory and to all files in that directory. If the first locking protocol to use a directory is Paradox with ODAPI/IDAPI, only Engine 3.0 and ODAPI/IDAPI applications have access to the tables in that directory.

PRIVATE DIRECTORY

Paradox for Windows and Paradox for DOS require a directory for storing temporary files, such as the answer tables from queries. When Paradox starts, it places exclusive PDOXUSRS.LCK and PARADOX.LCK files in the private directory and designates that directory as the location for temporary files. This designation means that other Paradox users can't access tables in that directory. This occurs only if SHARE.EXE is loaded and Local Share is turned on in the IDAPI Configuration file.

BENEFITS OF THE PARADOX 4.0 LOCKING PROTOCOL

The Paradox 4.0 locking protocol replaces the form lock with a new locking protocol called a group lock. The Paradox 4.0 locking protocol also removes separate table lock files, thus reducing the number of files needed to maintain concurrent access. These improvements increase table concurrency, reduce network access time, and reduce downtime.

Table 34.2 lists the methods and procedures that deal with locks.

TABLE 34.2. METHODS AND PROCEDURES THAT DEAL WITH LOCKS.		
Method or Procedure	Class	Description
enumLocks	TCursor	Creates a Paradox table that lists the locks currently applied to a TCursor
enumLocks	UIObject	Creates a Paradox table that lists the locks currently applied to a UIObject and returns the number of locks
lock	Session	Locks one or more tables
lock	Table	Locks a specified table
lock	TCursor	Places specified locks on a specified table
lockRecord	TCursor	Puts a write lock on the current record
lockRecord	UIObject	Puts a write lock on the current record
lockStatus	TCursor	Returns the number of times that a lock has been placed on a table
lockStatus	UIObject	Returns the number of locks on a table
unLock	TC/TBL	Removes a specified lock
unLockRecord	TC/UI	Removes the current lock

Table 34.3 compares the locks in Paradox for DOS to the locks in Paradox.

TABLE 34.3. LOCKS IN PARADOX FOR DOS AND PARADOX FOR WINDOWS.	
Paradox 4.0	*Paradox for Windows*
write lock	read lock
prevent write lock	No equivalent; Paradox displays Unknown but respects it
group lock	Equivalent to a lock on the referential integrity master
Equivalent to write lock and prevent write lock	write lock
full lock	exclusive lock
prevent full lock	open lock

A Paradox image lock is a lock placed on the Table View (.TV file) so that a second user sharing the table can't modify any properties.

CONFIGURING SPECIFIC APPLICATIONS

As the person in charge of developing a network application, you need to know how to configure Paradox-compatible applications. The sections that follow explain how to configure different Borland applications that are aware of Paradox.

PARADOX ENGINE 3.0 AND WINDOWS APPLICATIONS

You define the network configuration of Windows applications that use the Paradox Engine with the Paradox Configuration Utility program. This utility is a Windows application whose filename is PXENGCFG.EXE. You use it to define the location of the network control file, the locking protocol, and the user name. You also use PXENGCFG.EXE to specify whether you want to share local tables. All this information is written into your WIN.INI file.

The Paradox Engine 3.0 has two locking modes: standard and compatible. The Paradox Engine 3.0 is capable of operating in either Paradox 2.0 locking or Paradox 4.0 locking. For non-Windows applications, you choose the locking protocol by calling the appropriate engine function. For Windows applications, you call `PXWinInit()` and write it into the WIN.INI file by using PXENGCFG.EXE. Quattro Pro 4.0, ObjectVision 2.1, and Quattro Pro for Windows all use Paradox Engine 3.0.

NETWORKING WITH PARADOX 4.0

You configure Paradox for a multiuser environment during installation or with NUPDATE.EXE (short for *network update*). NUPDATE.EXE enables you to designate the type of network and the location of the network control file. When you finish, this information is written into the PARADOX.SOM file.

Some command-line options, such as `-share` and `-net`, override the settings in PARADOX.SOM. The `-share` command-line option forces Paradox to treat the local hard disk as a network drive. You must load the MS-DOS SHARE.EXE program into memory before you start Paradox with this command-line option. The `-net` command-line option forces Paradox to use or create a network control file in the location specified after `-net`. A trailing backslash is required. For example:

```
1:   PARADOX -NET C:\DATA\ -SHARE
```

The User Interface compatibility mode of Paradox 4.0 causes it to emulate the look and feel of Paradox 3.5. This compatibility mode doesn't make Paradox's locking protocol compatible with Paradox 3.5. It's impossible to force Paradox 4.0 to use the older-style locking protocols. The User Interface compatibility mode also doesn't force Paradox 4.0 to create compatible tables.

NETWORKING WITH QUATTRO PRO

Quattro Pro for DOS uses the Paradox Engine. Quattro Pro 2.0–4.0 uses versions 1.0–2.0 of the Paradox Engine. Quattro Pro 4.0 with files dated

9/12/92 or later uses version 3.0 of the Paradox Engine. You set the location of the Paradox network control file by selecting Options | Other | Paradox Access | Paradox Net File.

Quattro Pro 4.0 for DOS can use Paradox tables and network locking protocols. You determine the location of the Paradox network control file that Quattro Pro 4.0 for DOS uses by selecting Options | Other | Paradox | Directory from the Quattro Pro 4.0 menu. The information should be placed in step 5 of the worksheet.

Networking with ObjectVision 2.1

ObjectVision 2.1 uses Paradox Engine 3.0 to connect to Paradox tables. You can determine the location of the Paradox network control file that ObjectVision 2.1 uses by running the PXENGCFG.EXE program, which was installed in the ObjectVision directory. When PXENGCFG.EXE is running, choose File | Network Configuration. This window specifies the Paradox network control file path and the locking protocol. If the locking protocol is set to Paradox 4.0, write the Paradox network control file path in step 7 of the worksheet.

Networking with dBASE

The DOS dBASE locking mechanism is different from Paradox's. Generally, you install dBASE IV on a server. It carries an access control file—DBASE415.ACC or DBASE420.ACC—for user counts. You can purchase an additional LAN PACK to increment the user count in the .ACC file. Whenever you load dBASE, the program transfers to your workstation's memory. dBASE's multiuser functionality relies on NETBIOS-compatible protocol for all certified network operating systems. This is why you don't need to load DOS SHARE. Local file sharing isn't supported in dBASE.

The operating system and dBASE IV attend to the mechanics of data integrity behind the scenes. The network operating systems supported by dBASE IV provide the means to lock an entire file or a single record in a multiuser session. dBASE IV can tap into these file- and record-locking capabilities, either automatically or by means of programming commands. The database engine provides the logic for Exclusive mode or Shared mode, depending on the option selected. For example, to modify a structure, you must activate Exclusive mode. After the file is locked exclusively by the network operating system, the other workstations can't access .DBF files at the server level. Paradox uses the Interbase Engine for advanced referential integrity without any programming, however. This option isn't available in dBASE yet.

What happens to record locks if the power fails or your workstation crashes? Suppose that two users are editing two different records; therefore, they have established two different records. In the event of a power failure, the database isn't corrupted because the record locks are released by the operating system. The next time you log in, you can access the same database file without a problem. You don't need to delete network lock files as you would if the same crash had occurred in Paradox. dBASE doesn't use lock files. The unsaved records are in the previous unchanged state. This is a minor hazard compared to Paradox lock or net files.

Paradox and DOS dBASE can network. The new IDAPI Engine fully supports the dBASE IV and V locking protocol. You can indeed have dBASE for DOS, dBASE for Windows, and Paradox for Windows all editing the same dBASE table. Likewise, you can have Paradox 4.5, Paradox for Windows and dBASE for Windows editing the same Paradox 4 table. This applies to a single machine or a network.

For example, when editing a dBASE table on the same record, dBASE will notice that the record has changed and prompt the user to press the Spacebar to update the screen.

Paradox also allows locking of dBASE files locally. dBASE does not.

SENDING MESSAGES OVER A NETWORK

You often use a network to communicate with other users connected to it. Two types of communicating systems are regularly used: messaging systems and mailing systems. In a messaging—or broadcasting—system, the other user must be logged onto the network. A mail system stores messages for later use; the other user doesn't have to be logged onto the network. If you don't already have a messaging system or if you want to include a messaging feature in your application, you can use ObjectPAL. Often, it's useful to include a way to send messages from one user to another in your application.

The next tutorial demonstrates a technique for sending messages across a network. It uses a common table with a timer. You use the timer to check whether the table has a message for you. If it does, you display the message, then delete it. You don't need to be connected to a network to go through this tutorial.

Tutorial: Sending Messages Over a Network

Suppose that you wish to add the capability to your application to send messages across the network to another user.

On Disk: \ANSWERS\NET-MSG.FSL

Quick Steps

1. Create a table to store the messages.

2. In the form with which you want to implement the messaging, set a timer that will fire every five seconds (or however often you like).

3. Use `getNetUserName()` or prompt the user to establish a name to use for message transfers.

4. With the custom methods, open a TCursor. Check the table for a message directed to you or to "All." If you find a message, read it.

5. Messages are deleted every five seconds (or however often you've specified).

6. Delete personal messages after you read them.

Step By Step

1. Create a new form and place a field and a button on it (see Figure 34.3). Change the field's label to *FromNetUserName*, and name the field *FromField*. Label the button Send a message.

2. Add lines 3 and 4 to the Var window of the form.

```
1:     ;Form :: Var
2:     Var
3:       toStr, msg  String
4:       tc          TCursor
5:     endVar
```

3. Add lines 7 and 8 to the **open** method of the form.

```
1:     ;Form :: open
2:     method open(var eventInfo Event)
3:     if eventInfo.isPreFilter() then
4:       ;This code executes for each object on the form
5:     else
```

```
 6:        ;This code executes only for the form
 7:        self.setTimer(5000)
 8:        tc.open("NET-MSG.DB")
 9:     endif
10:    endmethod
```

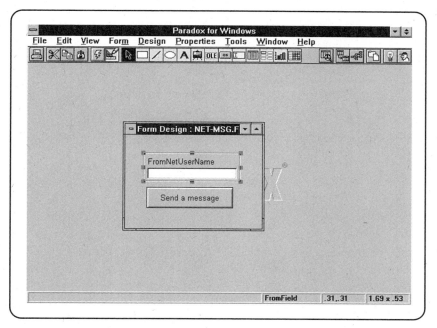

Figure 34.3. Set up form for the tutorial.

4. Add line 3 to the **open** method of the *FromField* field.

```
1:    ;Field :: open
2:    method open(var eventInfo Event)
3:        self = getNetUserName()
4:    endmethod
```

5. Add line 8 to the **timer** method of the form.

```
 1:    ;Form :: timer
 2:    method timer(var eventInfo TimerEvent)
 3:    if eventInfo.isPreFilter() then
 4:        ;This code executes for each object on the form
 5:
 6:    else
 7:        ;This code executes only for the form
 8:        checkMsg()
 9:    endif
10:    endmethod
```

6. Create a custom method called `sendMsg()` at the form level and add lines 3–22 to it.

```
1:      ;Form :: sendMsg
2:      method sendMsg()
3:         toStr = "All or username"
4:         toStr.view("Send message to?")
5:         if toStr = "All or username" then
6:            return
7:         endIf
8:
9:         msg = "Enter up to 30 characters"
10:        msg.view("Enter message")
11:        if msg = "Enter up to 30 characters" then
12:           return
13:        endIf
14:
15:        tc.edit()
16:        tc.insertRecord()
17:        tc."DateTime Stamp" = DateTime()
18:        tc."To" = toStr
19:        tc."From" = FromField
20:        tc.message = msg
21:        tc.postRecord()
22:        tc.endEdit()
23:     endmethod
```

7. Create another custom method at the form level, this time called `checkMsg()`, and add lines 3–20 to it.

```
1:      ;Form :: checkMsg
2:      method checkMsg()
3:         var
4:            s1, s2, s3 String
5:         endVar
6:
7:         if FromField.isBlank() then
8:            return
9:         endIf
10:
11:        if tc.locate("To", FromField) then
12:           s1 = tc."To"
13:           s2 = tc."From"
14:           s3 = tc."Message"
15:           tc.edit()
16:           tc.deleteRecord()
17:           msgInfo("*** Broadcast Message ***", "To: " + s1 +
           ➥   chr(13) + "From: " + s2 + chr(13) + chr(13) + s3)
18:           tc.endEdit()
19:        endIf
20:        checkAll()
21:     endmethod
```

8. Create one more custom method at the form level, this time called `checkAll()`, and add lines 3–11 to it.

```
1:      ;Form :: checkAll
2:      method checkAll()
3:         if tc.locate("To", "All") then
4:           if tc."DateTime Stamp" < DateTime() - (1000*5) then
5:             tc.edit()
6:               tc.deleteRecord()
7:               tc.endEdit()
8:           else
9:               msgInfo("*** Broadcast Message ***", "To: " +
       ➥       tc."To" + chr(13) + "From: " + tc."From" +
       ➥       chr(13) + chr(13) + tc."Message")
10:         endIf
11:       endIf
12:     endmethod
```

9. Add line 3 to the **pushButton** method of the *Send a message* button.

```
1:      ;Button :: pushButton
2:      method pushButton(var eventInfo Event)
3:         sendMsg()
4:      endmethod
```

10. Check the syntax, save your work, and run the form. If the wrong name or no user name shows up in the *FromField* field, type a user name. The customary user name is your first initial and last name. Send yourself a message. Click the Send a message button and type your network user name—in other words, the value in the *FromField* field. Click OK. When the Enter Message dialog box appears, enter a message and click OK. Within five seconds, your message should be displayed. Figure 34.4 shows how the form looks when you are done with this tutorial.

Analysis

In step 2, line 3 declares the two String variables used to store the name of the "To" user and the message. Line 4 declares a TCursor variable.

In step 3, line 7 sets the timer to trip every five seconds. Line 8 opens the TCursor. The TCursor is left open for the duration of the form to minimize how often a TCursor is opened. You might want to put error checking on line 8. That way, if the user is unable to open the table, the user gets an error. For example, if two users pointing to different net files try to access the table at the same time, the second user gets an appropriate error message.

In step 4, line 3 attempts to get the name of the current network user and store it in *FromField*—that is, the field labeled *FromNetUserName*.

In step 5, line 8 on the **timer** method of the form calls the checkMsg() custom method.

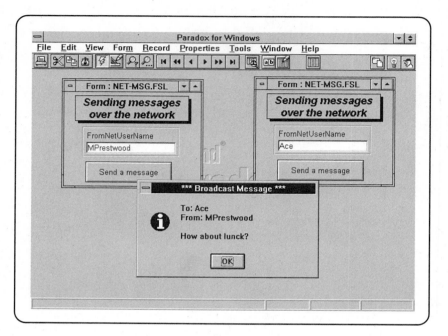

Figure 34.4. NET-MSG.FSL. Sending a message by means of a table and a timer through the network with Paradox.

In step 6, line 2 prototypes the sendMsg() custom method. This custom method is passed no value and returns no value. Lines 3 and 4 set the value for *toStr* and prompt the user to enter the network user name of the individual or the word "All." Line 5 makes sure that the user changed the value. If the user didn't, line 6 aborts the routine with return. Lines 9 and 10 set the value for *msg* and prompt the user to enter a message of up to 30 characters. Line 11 makes sure that the user changed the value. If he didn't, the routine is aborted in line 12. Note that there is no error checking to make sure that the user types 30 characters or less. Lines 15–22 place the TCursor into Edit mode, insert a record, date and timestamp the new record, set the values, post the record, and end Edit mode.

In step 7, line 2 prototypes the checkMsg() custom method. This custom method is passed no value and returns no value. Line 4 declares three String variables used to store the complete message. Line 7 makes sure that a current network user is defined. If a user isn't defined, line 8 aborts the routine. Line 11 checks whether a message for the user exists in the table. If one does, lines 12–14 grab the values and place them into String variables. Lines 15 and 16 delete the record so that the user doesn't get the same message more than once. Line 17 displays the message. Line 18 ends Edit mode.

In step 8, line 2 prototypes the checkAll() custom method. This custom method is passed no value and returns no value. Except for line 4, this routine is similar to the checkMsg() routine. Line 4 checks whether the All message is older than five seconds. If it is, line 6 deletes it without displaying it. Line 4 uses 5*1000 rather than 5000. This illustrates a technique for using milliseconds. It's difficult to think in terms of milliseconds. It's easier if you break the milliseconds into an equation. For example, how long is 3,600,000 milliseconds? (Where's Rain Man when you need him?) One thousand milliseconds—that is, one second—times 60 equals one minute. One minute times 60 equals an hour. You can see that 1000*60*60 is clearer than 3,600,000.

In step 9, line 3 calls the sendMsg() custom method, which starts the whole process.

You can simplify this routine so that it only sends a broadcast to everyone, or you can add to it to make it do more. If you want to include a way to display a message on all the terminals in your application without establishing the "To" and "From" users, you can strip this routine down. You also can add more groups than only "All." You can add a configuration that enables users to set things such as their personal user names or how often messages are checked. To take this technique to its limits, blow it up into a full-fledged mail system complete with storage—in other words, copy the message to a private table.

The complete Mail application \APPS\MAIL.FSL was inspired by the preceding broadcast tutorial.

QUESTIONS AND ANSWERS ON NETWORKING

Q: Does Paradox work with ObjectVision?

A: Paradox can read and write ObjectVision 1.0, 2.0, and 2.1 data.

Q: Can ObjectVision access Paradox data?

A: ObjectVision 2.1 is required to read and write Paradox 4 data. ObjectVision 2.1 cannot read the new Paradox for Windows 5 table structure. Paradox for Windows can read ObjectVision 1.0 and 2.0 data and can run concurrently with ObjectVision 2.1.

Q: Does Paradox for Windows run under OS/2 2.1 and Windows NT?

A: Paradox does run under OS/2 2.1 and Windows NT.

Q: Can I run Paradox 4.0 and Paradox on a network at the same time?

A: Yes. Paradox 4.0 and Paradox for Windows can work on a network simultaneously. You need the most recent version of Paradox to do this, however. Paradox supports the Paradox 4.0 file-locking protocol, which enables the two applications to share data concurrently.

Q: Can I run Paradox 3.5 and Paradox on a network at the same time?

A: No. Paradox 3.5 and Paradox for Windows don't have the same locking protocol. Therefore, they can't work concurrently.

Q: Does Paradox support SQL linking?

A: Yes, currently Paradox for Windows supports Borland's Interbase, Microsoft SQL, Sybase, Oracle 6 and 7, Informix, and, through the new IDAPTOR interface, ODBC.

Q: Does Paradox run in a Novell 3.11 environment?

A: Yes.

Q: Do I need a database server to use Paradox?

A: No.

The main point of this chapter was that Paradox comes ready to use a network. Whether you buy a single version or a network license, you get the same functionality. This functionality extends to your applications; all your applications are ready for the network. The only real issues left are configuration, setup, and multiuser considerations.

USING PARADOX WITH SQL

This chapter focuses on using Paradox as a client server development tool. It does not talk about connecting; it is assumed you have already connected. If you are having trouble connecting to a particular SQL server, then refer to the *Connection Guide* for that particular server. This chapter does review what a user can do interactively with Paradox and how to use ObjectPAL with SQL servers.

Who should read this chapter? Anyone interested in getting started with SQL. This includes using SQL on local tables—Paradox and dBASE tables. Do you need to be connected to a server? No, the first part of this chapter talks about SQL concepts and what you can do with SQL on local tables. Everybody can use the first part of this chapter up to the section titled, "Interactive SQL".

SQL

Structured Query Language (SQL) is an attempt to develop a standard for accessing database information. The ANSI standard for SQL allows a user to become familiar with the commands needed to query many different types of data. Once you learn ANSI SQL, you then have the core ability to query many different databases.

Is SQL a solid standard? Yes and no. Yes, the core ANSI SQL commands are solid and consistent from vendor to vendor. Every vendor, however, adds capability to its version of SQL. This is expected because ANSI SQL does not go far enough to cover every feature of every high-end DBMS.

The SQL standard is used by many companies for their high-end products. These include Oracle, Sybase, Microsoft SQL, Informix, and Borland's Interbase. With the release of version 5 of Paradox, Borland also provided the capability to use standard ANSI SQL commands on local Paradox and dBASE tables.

USING SQL ON LOCAL TABLES

Although SQL by definition is a standard, there are various flavors on the market. Borland, too, has its own flavor of SQL. Local SQL is built upon a modified version of the InterBase SQL parser. The parser turns the SQL statements into QBE syntax, and then executes or translates it into IDAPI function calls. Because the SQL statements are translated to QBE, only a subset of SQL can be supported, because QBE does not support the equivalent syntax for all SQL functionality. Even though local SQL syntax is limited to what QBE can execute, it is still fairly powerful. Refer to Table 35.1 for SQL syntax that is supported with local SQL.

TABLE 35.1. SQL SYNTAX SUPPORTED WITH LOCAL SQL.*			
Clauses	Aggregates	Operators	Misc.
select	sum	+	Update
where	avg	–	Insert
order by	min	*	Delete

Clauses	Aggregates	Operators	Misc.
group by	max	/	Create table
	count	=	index
		<	
		>	
			is null

*SQL views are not supported

As previously mentioned, Local SQL supports aliases when referencing table names. This allows you to execute heterogeneous joins; that is, joins of more than one table type. For example, you could create an SQL statement that joins Paradox, Oracle, and Informix tables in a single SQL query.

An SQL Tutorial

This section introduces you to ANSI SQL as it applies to local Paradox and dBASE tables. ANSI SQL is a very rich query language. Each command has many different keywords and parameters supported. To really learn SQL, you need to get a good ANSI SQL book and connect to a server. You can get started with just Paradox and local tables, however. Once you learn this core syntax, you can use it with any SQL DBMS (for example, Oracle, Sybase, and Gupta).

Using select

Your first step into SQL teaches you how to query your local Paradox tables with SQL; you will query the Customer and Orders tables using the SQL select command. The syntax for select is quite elaborate. For now, the basic syntax you will use is as follows:

```
select criteria
from tablename
[where whereCriteria]
[order by orderBy]
```

1. Change your working directory to the TUTORIAL directory and select File | New | SQL File. This brings up the SQL Editor ready for you to type and execute a single SQL statement. Your screen should now look like Figure 35.1.

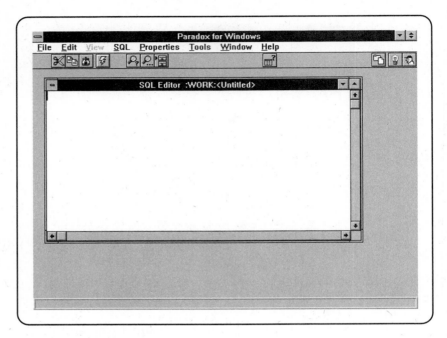

Figure 35.1. The SQL Editor.

2. In place of *criteria*, you can place the names of columns or an *, which signifies all columns. Type the following SQL statement and save it as SQL-LS1.SQL.

```
1:  select *
2:  from Customer
```

3. Run the SQL query by pressing F8. Your screen should look similar to Figure 35.2.

4. Next, specify the names of the columns you wish to see separated by commas and ending with a space. Type the following, save it as SQL-LS2.SQL, and run the SQL statement. Your screen should look similar to Figure 35.3.

```
1:  select Name, Phone
2:  from Customer
```

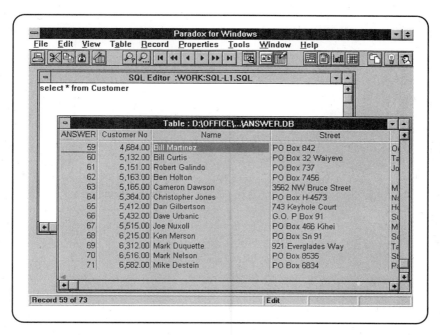

Figure 35.2. Using the select *command.*

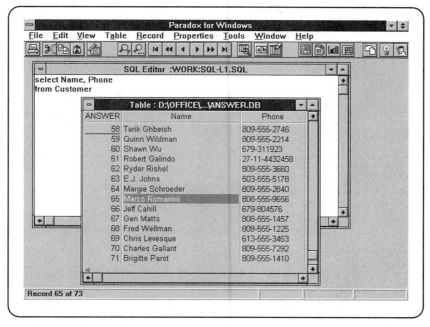

Figure 35.3. Specifying columns with select*.*

5. The where clause allows you to narrow down your search criteria. This is similar to specifying example elements in Paradox's QBE. Refer back to Table 35.1 to see which of the many aggregates and operators are supported by local SQL. Next, use the where clause to specify that you wish to see only the records where *City* is equal to *Madeupville*. To do this, type the following, save it as SQL-LS3.SQL, and run it. Your screen should look similar to Figure 35.4.

```
1:  select *
2:  from Customer
3:  where City = "Madeupville"
```

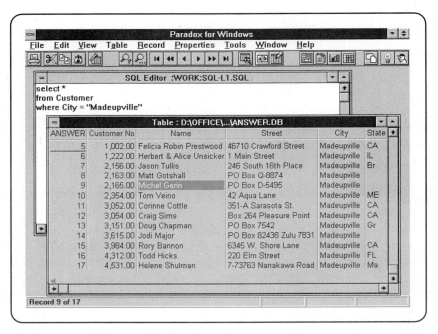

Figure 35.4. Using the where *clause with* select.

6. The where clause can also be used to link tables similar to how the Data Model does. For example, the following links the Customer and Orders tables. Type, save as SQL-LS4.SQL, and run the following SQL statement. Your screen should look similar to Figure 35.5. Note the use of the table name and quotation marks around the fields in line 1. Any field name that contains spaces requires quotation marks.

```
1:   select Customer."Customer No", Customer."Name",
     ➥Orders."Order No"
2:   from Customer, Orders
3:   where Customer."Customer No" = Orders."Customer No"
```

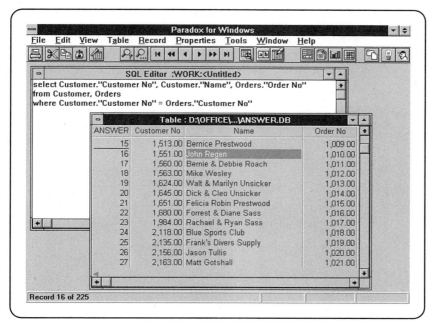

Figure 35.5. Joining tables with `select`.

Finally, here are some more select statements you can try. Keep your working directory set to the TUTORIAL directory and type and run any or all of them.

\ANSWERS\SQL-LS5.SQL links the Customer and Orders table on *Customer No* and displays the five columns (some from each table) where the *Balance Due* is not 0.

```
1:   select Customer."Customer No", Customer."Name",
2:       Customer."Phone", Orders."Order No", Orders."Balance Due"
3:   from Customer, Orders
4:   where Customer."Customer No" = Orders."Customer No"
5:       and Orders."Balance Due" <> 0
```

\ANSWERS\SQL-LS6.SQL introduces the order clause, which allows you to sort the answer table.

```
1:   select Customer."Customer No", Customer."Name",
2:   Customer."Phone"
3:   from Customer
4:   order by Name
```

\ANSWERS\SQL-LS7.SQL demonstrates linking two tables and ordering by one of the fields.

```
1:   select Orders."Order No", Orders."Balance Due",
2:       Lineitem."Stock No"
3:   from Orders, Lineitem
4:   where Orders."Order No" = Lineitem."Order No"
5:   order by Orders."Balance Due"
```

\ANSWERS\SQL-LS8.SQL demonstrates sorting in a descending order. When you use descending, you must also use distinct.

```
1:   select distinct Orders."Order No", Orders."Balance Due",
2:       Lineitem."Stock No"
3:   from Orders, Lineitem
4:   where Orders."Order No" = Lineitem."Order No"
5:   order by Orders."Balance Due" descending
```

USING *insert*

The syntax for `insert` is not nearly as elaborate as the syntax for `select`, but is still fairly substantial. Paradox supports only a small subset, however. For now, the basic syntax you will use is as follows:

```
insert into tableName
([columnName1 [, columnName2] [, columnName3]...])
values ([value1 [, value2] [, value3]...])
```

1. The next SQL statement uses `insert` to insert a new record into the Customer table. Type the following, save it as SQL-LI2.SQL, run the SQL statement, and then open the table. Your screen should look similar to Figure 35.6.

```
1:   insert into Customer
2:   (Customer."Customer No", Customer."Name")
3:   values (0, 'Aurora Cortez')
```

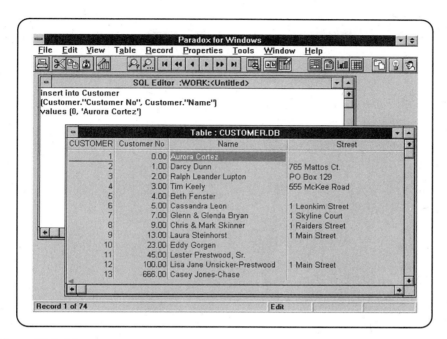

Figure 35.6. Using *insert*.

Using *update*

The syntax for *update* also is not as elaborate as the syntax for *select*, but is still fairly substantial. For now, the basic syntax you will use is as follows:

```
update tableName
set setcriteria
where wherecriteria
```

The *update* command is very powerful, so be cautious when using it. One mistyped word can change all the data in your table.

1. For your first example, suppose that Sandy Jones and her husband got a divorce and she now wishes to use her maiden name. The *update* command allows you to change the Customer table. Type the following SQL statement, save it as SQL-LU1.SQL, and execute it.

```
1:   update Customer
2:   set Name = "Sandy Kowalski"
3:   where Name = "Sandy Jones"
```

2. The next `update` statement assumes the entire town of *Madeupville* was magically moved to Illinois. Type the following SQL statement, save it as SQL-LU2.SQL, and execute it.

```
1:   update Customer
2:   set State = "IL"
3:   where City = "Madeupville"
```

3. This next `update` statement accomplishes a similar task as step 2, but this SQL statement demonstrates how to specify and update multiple columns. Type the following SQL statement, save it as SQL-LU3.SQL, and execute it.

```
1:   update Customer
2:   set City = "SJ", State = "IL"
3:   where City = "San Jose" and State = "CA"
```

Using *delete*

The syntax for `delete` is fairly straightforward. The basic syntax you will use is as follows:

delete from *tableName*
where *whereCriteria*

1. Suppose that you wish to delete a record or set of records from a database. The `delete` command allows you to do this. Type the following SQL statement, save it as SQL-LD1.SQL, and execute it.

```
1:   delete from Customer
2:   where Name = 'Aurora Cortez'
```

Using *create table* and *drop table*

The syntax for `create table` is as follows:

create table *tableName* (*fieldName fieldType* [, *fieldName fieldType...*])

Use the following field types: SMALLINT, INT, DECIMAL(x,y), NUMERIC(x,y), FLOAT(x,y), CHAR(n), DATE, BOOLEAN, BLOB(n,s), TIME, TIMESTAMP, MONEY, AUTOINC, and BYTES(n).

1. First, create a table.

```
1:   create table test
2:   ( field1 char(20))
```

2. Then, delete it.

```
1:  drop table test
```

3. Now, create one more for use with the following `index` examples.

```
1:  create table Contacts
2:  ( Name char(20), Phone char(15), Age SmallInt)
```

Using *create index* and *drop index*

1. To add a secondary index, execute the following SQL statement.

```
1:  create index secAge
2:  on Contacts (Age)
```

2. To delete the newly created secondary index, execute the following SQL statement.

```
1:  drop index Contacts.secAge
```

3. To delete the primary index, execute the following SQL statement.

```
1:  drop index Contacts.primary
```

Embedded SQL Also Works on Local Tables

Just as you can embed query code into your ObjectPAL code and execute it with `executeQBE()`, you can embed SQL code and execute it with `executeSQL()`. What is interesting is that embedded SQL statements work on local tables, too. For example, type the following code into the **pushButton** method of a button.

```
1:   ;Button :: pushButton
2:   method pushButton(var eventInfo Event)
3:      var
4:              q     SQL
5:              tc    TCursor
6:              db    Database
7:              tv    TableView
8:      endVar
9:
10:     q = SQL
11:         select Customer."Customer No", Customer."Name", Customer."Phone"
12:         from Customer
13:         where not Phone is null
14:     endSQL
15:
16:     db.open("WORK")
17:     q.executeSQL(db, ":PRIV:ANSWER.DB")
18:     tv.open(":PRIV:ANSWER.DB")
19:  endmethod
```

THE CLIENT/SERVER MODEL

In a client/server model, the database processes are shared between the client and the server. This is called *distributed processing*. In the case of Paradox, Paradox is the client and any of the SQL servers that IDAPI can use can be the server. Oracle, Sybase, Informix, and Borland's Interbase are examples of SQL servers. For example, when connecting Paradox to an Oracle server, the database processes are divided between the server and Paradox.

Paradox provides access to SQL servers through Borland's SQL Link for Windows. When Paradox communicates with an SQL server, queries—commands—from Paradox need to be in the dialect of the particular server. The link provides this translation and sends the appropriate commands to the server (see Figure 35.7). Because the link is fairly transparent, you do not have to learn SQL.

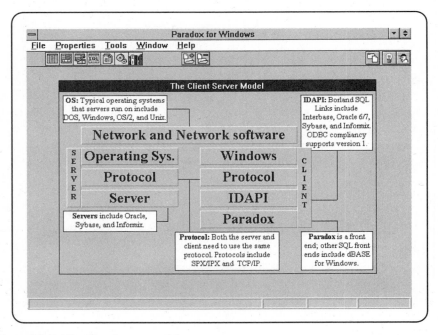

Figure 35.7. The client/server model.

BACK-END/FRONT-END

In a client server model, the SQL server is referred to as the **back-end**. A client application, such as Paradox, is referred to as the **front-end**. When you set up a very large database, generally there are two software buying considerations: the back-end and the front-end. Typical back-end servers include Borland's Interbase, Oracle, Sybase, Microsoft SQL, and Informix. Typical front-end servers include Paradox for Windows, Paradox for DOS, Access, and dBASE for Windows.

COLUMNS AND ROWS

Sometimes, just getting used to the terminology of a new subject helps to understand it. In SQL server terms, a **column** is the same as a Paradox table field's name and a **row** is the same as a record.

COMMIT AND ROLLBACK OVERVIEW

The term **commit** is part of a concept for entering data. The idea is to enter data into a temporary table and commit—that is, copy—the data to a main table. The term **rollback** is also part of a concept for entering data. The idea is to enter data into a temporary table with the opportunity to empty the temporary table and to leave the main table untouched. The term **two phase commits** applies this idea over a wide area network. With two phase commits, you can have data entry from anywhere in the world.

INTERACTIVE SQL

Before we jump into SQL and ObjectPAL, let's review what Paradox for Windows can do interactively with SQL. As a front-end for SQL, Paradox for Windows rivals anything on the market. Your first experience will lead you to the same conclusion. When you access SQL tables, you'll notice a few differences from using Paradox tables. The following are some of the obvious features to note.

- Open an SQL in a table window using File | Open | Table. Note that you can directly edit the data in the table. This is new to version 5.

- Next, create a quick form based on an SQL table. Note that you can press F9 to go into Edit mode. The default setting for Read-Only for all tables in the data is unchecked. This is new for version 5. Leave this option off to edit data. Also worth mentioning is that you need to execute `forceRefresh()` with table frames to update data altered by other users, but not with fields.

- When querying SQL tables with the QBE, note that the SQL button shows you the equivalent QBE query in SQL. If you are familiar with Borland's Query by Example (QBE), then you might wish to always use it—rather than SQL—to query both local and SQL tables. If you know SQL, or have an interest in learning it, however, you can use the SQL Editor built into Paradox.

- When using the SQL File (or querying SQL tables with SQL), note that you do not put a semicolon at the end of an SQL statement as you do with other SQL editors. Also note that you can execute only a single line of SQL at a time.

- You can use SQL statements with local tables.

- You can base a report on an SQL table. By now, you are probably noticing that the link to SQL tables is nearly transparent. No other SQL front-end is easier! Reports are no exception.

SQL TABLES ARE NO LONGER READ ONLY BY DEFAULT

The default of having the table always marked read only in version 1.0/4.5 was changed in version 5. In version 4.5, the default for SQL tables was Read-Only. You could allow writes to the remote table by right-clicking the remote table in the data model and unchecking the "Read Only" property. Note that you will be allowed to write to the table only if you have the privileges necessary to do so on the SQL server.

ANSWER SET

Whenever you access data on an SQL server, you create an answer set. When you open a table in an SQL database in a table window, you could refer to the data you are currently viewing as an answer set. When you execute a specific SQL query—either through a QBE query or an SQL file—you refer to the data returned by the server as an *answer set*.

TIP FOR SYBASE/MS SQL NLM USERS

Make sure that you use the URGENT command in your WIN.INI file for smooth access to your Sybase or Microsoft SQL server. For example, if you're connecting to a server called SERVER1, then the SQLSERVER section of your WIN.INI might look like the following:

```
[SQLSERVER]

SERVER1 = WDBNOVSP, 12345678, 1, 12AB, URGENT
```

The preceding WIN.INI entry uses the following syntax template:

```
ServerName = Connection DLL, Novell Network number, Node address,
Novell Socket [,URGENT]
```

Two of the symptoms users may experience if they are not using the optional URGENT command are extremely slow retrieving of records and failure of calculated fields on forms.

OBJECTPAL AND SQL (AN OVERVIEW)

With ObjectPAL, you can establish a connection to an SQL server. You can use TCursors and Table variables almost exactly the same way you do with local tables. You can embed SQL code in your ObjectPAL code; this includes any server-specific extensions. For example, you can have ObjectPAL, QBE, SQL, and Oracle's PL/SQL all in one built-in method. ObjectPAL also supports the use of transactions. You can even trap for errors.

Connecting via an Existing Alias

To connect to an existing alias, use the Database open method. The syntax for the Database open method is as follows:

open (const *aliasName* String) Logical

The following is a simple example:

```
1:  ;Button :: pushButton
2:  method pushButton(var eventInfo Event)
3:     var
4:        dbSQL        Database
5:     endVar
6:
7:        dbSQL.open(":Godzilla2:")
8:  endMethod
```

In the preceding example, the user will be prompted to enter his or her password. To provide the user's password for the user, use the following syntax:

open ([const *aliasName* String,] [const *ses* Session,] [const *parms* DynArray]) Logical

The following is another simple example of using the Database open method passing the alias a username and password.

```
1:  ;Button :: pushButton
2:  method pushButton(var eventInfo Event)
3:     var
4:        dbSQL        Database
5:        dynAlias     DynArray[]  AnyType
6:     endVar
7:
8:     dynAlias["USER NAME"]  = "guest"
9:     dynAlias["PASSWORD"]   = "guest"
10:    dbSQL.open(":Godzilla2:", dynAlias)
11: endMethod
```

Connecting via a New Alias

This next example demonstrates connecting to an Oracle server without a pre-existing alias.

```
1:  ;Button :: pushButton
2:  method pushButton(var eventInfo Event)
3:    var
4:       tv           TableView
5:       dbSQL        Database
6:       dynAlias     DynArray[]  String
7:    endVar
```

```
 8:
 9:  dynAlias["SERVER NAME"]        = "Godzilla2"
10:  dynAlias["USER NAME"]          = "guest"
11:  dynAlias["OPEN MODE"]          = "READ/WRITE"
12:  dynAlias["SCHEMA CACHE SIZE"]  = "8"
13:  dynAlias["NET PROTOCOL"]       = "SPX/IPX"
14:  dynAlias["LANGDRIVER"]         = ""
15:  dynAlias["SQLQRYMODE"]         = ""
16:  dynAlias["PASSWORD"]           = "guest"
17:
18:  addAlias("Godzilla2_guest", "Oracle", dynAlias)
19:  dbSQL.open("Godzilla2_guest", dynAlias)
20:  tv.open(":godzilla2_guest:ksmith.customer")
21: endmethod
```

Disconnecting is actually quite simple. Like so many other objects in ObjectPAL, you simply close it. Assuming that the SQL Database variable *DbSQL* from the above example is within scope, the following line of code closes the connection:

```
1:  dbSQL.close()
```

USING TCURSORS AND TABLE VARIABLES

The preceding example used a TableView variable to open up a TableView of an SQL table. The following code shows that you can use TCursors and Table variables with the same techniques with which you are already familiar. A *cursor* is a pointer to a row in an SQL answer set. Cursors are implemented in ObjectPAL as a TCursor object. This next example shows you how to copy a table from the server to a local hard drive.

```
 1:  ;Button :: pushButton
 2:  method pushButton(var eventInfo Event)
 3:      var
 4:          tc   TCursor    ;Declare a TCursor variable.
 5:      endVar
 6:
 7:      tc.open(":Godzilla2:rspitz.customer")  ;Open table on server.
 8:      tc.copy(":work:customer")              ;Copy table.
 9:      tc.close()                             ;Close table.
10: endmethod
```

The next example shows how to copy a table from your local hard drive to the server.

```
 1:  ;Button :: pushButton
 2:  method pushButton(var eventInfo Event)
 3:      var
 4:          tc   TCursor
 5:      endVar
 6:
```

```
7       errorTrapOnWarnings(Yes)
8:      try
9:          tc.open(":work:customer.db")
10:         tc.copy(":godzilla2:rspitz.test")
11:         tc.close()
12:     onFail
13:         errorShow()
14:     endTry
15:  endmethod
```

> Although TCursors and Table variables work with SQL data, for the sake
> of speed, it is always better to use an SQL query. Therefore, try to do what
> you want with a query first, then fall back to using a TCursor only when
> an SQL query is not possible.

EXECUTING AN SQL QUERY IN OBJECTPAL

The executeSQL() method works just like the Query equivalent executeQBE().
Once you define the SQL variable, then you execute it with executeSQL(). The
next example shows how to execute an existing SQL file. In ObjectPAL, the
technique is very similar to executing an existing QBE file.

```
1:  ;Button :: pushButton
2:  method pushButton(var eventInfo Event)
3:     var
4:        sqlEXESQL    SQL
5:        tvAnswer     TableView
6:     endVar
7:
8:     sqlEXESQL.readFromFile(":WORK:EXECSQL.SQL")
9:     sqlEXESQL.executeSQL(db, ":PRIV:ANSWER.DB")
10:
11:    tvAnswer.open(":PRIV:ANSWER.DB")
12: endmethod
```

You assign an SQL variable to an SQL string in any of the following three ways:
embedding SQL in ObjectPAL, reading it in from a string, or reading it in from
a file. We used readFromFile() previously to read in an SQL file and execute
it. The next three examples use embedded SQL, embedded SQL with a tilde
variable, and readFromString() to assign an SQL variable an SQL statement
and then use executeSQL() to execute it.

Embedded SQL

The capability to place SQL commands within another programming language allows you to extend that language. This is known as **embedding SQL**, and it means that you can actually embed SQL commands inside ObjectPAL. The next example shows how to embed SQL statements into your ObjectPAL code. Again, just as you can embed query code, you can embed ObjectPAL code.

```
 1:    ;Button :: pushButton
 2:    method pushButton(var eventInfo Event)
 3:       var
 4:            sqlVar    SQL
 5:            tvLike    TableView
 6:       endVar
 7:
 8:       ;Define SQL variable.
 9:       sqlVar = SQL
10:
11:       select * from ksmith.customer
12:
13:       endSQL
14:
15:       ;Execute SQL variable.
16:       executeSQL(db, sqlVar, ":PRIV:__LIKE")
17:
18:       ;View answer table.
19:       tvLike.open(":PRIV:__LIKE")
20:    endmethod
```

The next SQL query example demonstrates how to use a tilde variable to pass an SQL statement some data. You guessed it—this is just like passing a tilde variable to an embedded Query.

```
 1:    ;Button :: pushButton
 2:    method pushButton(var eventInfo Event)
 3:       var
 4:            sqlVar    SQL
 5:            tvLike    TableView
 6:            s         String
 7:       endVar
 8:
 9:       s = "ksmith.customer"
10:       s.view("Enter SQL table name")
11:
12:       sqlVar = SQL
13:
14:           select * from ~s
15:
16:       endSQL
17:
18:       executeSQL(db, sqlVar, ":PRIV:__LIKE")
19:       tvLike.open(":PRIV:__LIKE")
20:    endmethod
```

This final SQL query example demonstrates how to use an SQL string. It goes without saying that this is just like using a query string.

```
1:    ;Button :: pushButton
2:    method pushButton(var eventInfo Event)
3:       var
4:            s          String     ;Declare a String variable.
5:            sTilde     String
6:            sqlVar     SQL         ;Declare an SQL variable
7:            tv         TableView ;Declare a TableView variable.
8:       endVar
9:
10:       ;Assign string values.
11:       sTilde = "Dive"
12:
13:       s = "SELECT LAST_NAME, FIRST_NAME, COMPANY, PHONE " +
14:              "FROM    CONTACTS " +
15:              "WHERE   COMPANY LIKE '%" + sTilde + "%'"
16:
17:       ;Read string values into an SQL variable.
18:       sqlVar.readFromString(s)
19:
20:       ;Execute SQL statement.
21:       sqlVar.executeSQL(db, ":PRIV:ANSWER.DB")
22:
23:       ;Open answer table.
24:       tv.open(":PRIV:ANSWER.DB")
25:    endmethod
```

TRANSACTIONS ARE THE PROTOCOL FOR COMMUNICATION

Client applications such as Paradox communicate with SQL database servers with a unit of work called a transaction. Although a transaction is perceived as a single operation, a transaction may consist of a number of operations. For example, a single transaction could update multiple records. If you want to have some control over undeleting changes to your data, then use the following methods and procedures.

beginTransaction()	Starts a transaction on a server
commitTransaction()	Commits all changes within a transaction
rollbackTransaction()	Rolls back all changes within a transaction (undo feature)

```
1:    ;Button :: pushButton
2:    method pushButton(var eventInfo Event)
3:        var
```

```
4:            dbSQL      Database
5:            tc         TCursor
6:        endVar
7:
8:        dbSQL.open(":Server1:")
9:        dbSQL.beginTransaction()
10:        tc.open(":Server1:guest.customer")
11:        tc.insertRecord()
12:        tc.(1) = 1001
13:        tc.(2) = "Mike Prestwood"
14:        tc.postRecord()
15:        dbSQL.rollbackTransaction()    ;Un-inserts record 1001.
16:        dbSQL.begintransaction()
17:        tc.(1) = 1002
18:        tc.(2) = "Lisa Prestwood"
19:        dbSQL.commitTransaction()      ;Commits record 1002.
20:        tc.close()
21: endMethod
```

In the preceding example, the first record 1001 is posted to the table and then undone with the rollback.

STATEMENT ATOMICITY

In ObjectPAL, all database commands are committed immediately. For example, a single QBE query, a single ObjectPAL table append, and a single edit operation are all examples of commands that are executed and committed to the database immediately.

EXECUTING LOCALLY OR ON THE SERVER

If a QBE query generates SQL code, the query executes on the server; otherwise, the query executes locally. A query that executes on the server may take a long time, so it can be useful to know beforehand where it will execute. It is also important to note that a local SQL query may take longer than on the server. As the programmer, it is your job to experiment and use the best choice. Use the following methods to find out whether your SQL code will execute locally or on the server.

```
isExecuteQBELocal()
```

reports whether a QBE query will be executed locally or on a server. The syntax is as follows:

```
isExecuteQBELocal(const qbeVar Query) Logical
```

The next example displays one of two messages in a message stop dialog box, depending on whether the SQL query is to be executed locally or on the server.

```
 1:  ;Button :: pushButton
 2:  method pushButton(var eventInfo Event)
 3:      var
 4:          qAnswer    Query
 5:      endVar
 6:      qAnswer = Query
 7:
 8:              ANSWER: :PRIV:ANSWER.DB
 9:
10:              :IB_ALIAS:CONTACTS ┆ LAST_NAME  ┆ FIRST_NAME      ┆ COMPANY    ┆
11:                                 ┆ CheckPlus  ┆ CheckPlus Ron   ┆ CheckPlus  ┆
12:                                 ┆ CheckPlus  ┆ CheckPlus Phil  ┆ CheckPlus  ┆
13:
14:              EndQuery
15:      if isExecuteQBELocal(qAnswer) then
16:          beep()
17:          msgStop("WARNING", "Query Will Run Locally, This May Take Longer.")
18:      else
19:          msgInfo("Query Status", "This Query Will Run Remotely.")
20:      endIf
21: endmethod
```

VIEWS

A view is a virtual table that represents a part of the database or the whole database. The following is a list of various types of views.

- A vertical subset of columns from a single relation. This type of view limits the columns displayed.

- A horizontal subset of records from a single relation. This type of view limits the records displayed.

- A combined vertical and horizontal subset of records from a single relation. This type of view limits the number of records displayed.

- A subset of records from many relations. This type of view usually performs a join operation.

Why use a view? A view can ensure security—allow users to see only columns/ values necessary. Views can also allow users to see the bigger picture—simplify a complex join into a manageable package. You create a view using the SQL command CREATE VIEW. The syntax is as follows:

```
create view [<owner.>]<view name>
            [(<column name>[, <column name>...])
            as <SELECT statement>
```

A Note on Transactions and Informix

Because Informix support is new to Paradox for Windows, the following sidebar is provided. The following are some notes on Informix and Paradox.

Implicit/Explicit Transactions

Each of the three Informix database types supports different rules for implicit and explicit transaction starting.

ANSI Compliant Databases

Starts an implicit transaction. You can start a transaction only after a COMMIT WORK, CREATE DATABASE, DATABASE, ROLLBACK WORK, OR START DATABASE statement (these probably auto-commit a transaction). If you attempt to Close a database without ending the transaction, an error may occur.

AutoCommit Transactions

The following classes of SQL statements will automatically commit a transaction in Informix. You are guaranteed that there is no active transaction after one of the following statements has been executed:

```
COMMIT WORK, ROLLBACK, CREATE DATABASE, START DATABASE,

DATABASE (select a db for use).
```

As far as Data Definition statements are concerned, it appears that if they are executed inside a transaction, they will not be committed unless you commit the transaction. If there is no transaction, they will be committed when completed. For example, there is no autocommit for DDL statements.

For INFORMIX-SE, DDL statements are auto-committed when a transaction is started. They do not end an active transaction, however.

USING errorHasNativeErrorCode()

errorHasNativeErrorCode() checks the error stack for a specific SQL error code. This is equivalent to errorHasErrorCode(), except that it checks for SQL error codes. The syntax is as follows:

```
errorHasNativeErrorCode(const errCode LongInt) Logical
```

TRIGGERS AND STORED PROCEDURES

Triggers are procedures stored in the database that help you enforce both business and data relationship rules. With a trigger, you can keep summary data up to date, take actions based on what data a user enters, and enforce business rules such as no out-of-state checks accepted.

A trigger can occur when you either update, insert, or delete values. A trigger is like a Paradox validity check that you could put code in. In a way, triggers are analogous to built-in methods in a form and stored procedures are analogous to custom methods.

CREATING AND USING A SYBASE TRIGGER

The following is a simple example of how you might create and use a trigger in Sybase to ensure data integrity. On the SQL side, create an update trigger on a table's column. For example:

```
1:      create trigger updatetrigger on sqlTableName
2:      for update as
3:      if update(columnName)
4:         begin
5:            raiserror 30000 'Cannot change values in this.  Changes have been
               ➡discarded.'
6:            rollback transaction
7:         end
```

To raise or see the error in Paradox, use the **error** method. For example:

```
1:      ;tableframe :: error
2:      method error(var eventInfo ErrorEvent)
3:         if eventinfo.reason() = ErrorWarning then
4:            eventinfo.setReason(ErrorCritical)
5:         endIf
6:      endmethod
```

This is a very rudimentary example that should help you get started using triggers.

WHICH ODBC DRIVERS CAN YOU USE?

Because of the many flavors of ODBC drivers, it is impossible to provide a complete up-to-date list. Various ODBC drivers from various vendors give support for ODBC version 1 or 2 and level 1 or 2. Discovering even if the driver should work can be a chore. IDAPI was certified with the Q+E ODBC drivers by Pioneer; contact them for certified drivers that do work with the IDAPI ODBC socket.

If you have an ODBC driver you wish to test, follow these steps to find out if it is compatible:

1. Try it. If it works, fine; you're done.

2. If it doesn't, then try the driver with another ODBC-compliant software package (perhaps the one with which it was shipped).

3. If it doesn't work with other ODBC-compliant software, then get it to work and try again in Paradox.

4. If it does work, try Paradox one more time. If Paradox still cannot connect, then assume that the driver is not compatible and try another.

Although the ODBC socket requires the ODBC Manager version 2, you can use ODBC version 1 or 2 drivers.

QUESTIONS AND ANSWERS

Q. Why does the button on the vertical scrollbar in a table frame behave differently than with Paradox tables?

A. While viewing remote tables in Paradox, the data is cached. Unlike a local table, Paradox reads only part of a remote table. Performance would suffer if the SQL Link had to ask the server for the table size and record position while scrolling through the table.

Q. Why does Paradox have occasional delays when accessing data?

A. Paradox is fairly fast at retrieving data if the data is within the set of cached data. If, however, Paradox has to request a new set of records, then the SQL Link will slow down because Paradox has to either generate a fetch or select for the new data. Using indexes, for example, a primary key on Oracle tables, greatly speeds up performance and this issue is no longer a concern.

Q. Why does the SQL hourglass hang around after I exit a form?

A. When Paradox closes an SQL link, the IDAPI engine database connection and the server need to be engaged. If many users are connected to the server, then the act of closing will be shared with other users' transactions. Sybase has an URGENT parameter that can offset this delay.

Q. Why is more than one connection used when I log in?

A. A multitable form with remote tables in the data model can require multiple user connections, which are used in place of cursors to keep track of the link among tables. This method was used for performance reasons and could, understandably, be an issue if your license allowed a limited number of connections. Sybase 4.2, for example, does not include the concept of multiple cursors.

Q. Does the new link package support Oracle 7?

A. Yes. The Oracle link supports Oracle 6 and 7.

DELIVERING YOUR APPLICATION

FINAL TOUCHES

So far, this book has taught you elements of developing an application. At this point, you have all the knowledge you need to write a complete application. This final chapter deals with finishing your application and the future of Paradox for Windows.

WHAT ARE BUGS?

Many ObjectPAL programmers assume that when they reuse bug-free code in object-oriented programming, it will still work. If all the elements are bug-free, the code remains bug-free when it's reused. This assumption sometimes holds true, but often it does not. Because you are using the code within a new container, it might not work. You must test the code and debug it again. Therefore, although the components can work fine, the application might be buggy or poorly pasted together. Bug-free doesn't necessarily mean well designed.

You can accomplish complicated and sophisticated tasks by using Paradox interactively. If Paradox is bug-free, the applications that you develop also will be bug-free. This doesn't mean that your applications are well designed, however. It is Borland's job to make Paradox as free of bugs as possible. It's your job to make sure that the applications you develop with Paradox are well designed.

WHAT IS AN ANOMALY?

An error or mistake in a program is a **bug**. An **anomaly** is a nice way to say *bug*. Is Paradox a bug-free program? Of course not. Paradox isn't without its problems; no software company could make that claim about any product. Paradox has so few bugs, however, it is a testimony to the quality of its overall design and its use of object-oriented technology. The anomalies I'm about to discuss are documented in the SECRETS2.HLP help file that comes with the support files for this book.

HOW DO YOU ADDRESS ANOMALIES?

Anomalies are a fact of computing—and especially programming. As much as you might try, it often is difficult to avoid them. By the time you read this chapter, Borland might have already released the next version, which could take care of many of its anomalies. The next version might even address anomalies that you never have—and never will—run into.

There are three kinds of anomalies: configuration anomalies, gotchas, and WADs. A *configuration anomaly* is a conflict between Paradox and another application or the hardware. A *gotcha* is an anomaly that both you and Borland think shouldn't happen. A *WAD*—short for *works as designed*—refers to product behavior that you dislike, even though it was designed intentionally.

GPFs

A *GPF* is an acronym for *general protection fault*. A GPF is a special type of error that Windows catches. Windows displays the name of the application that caused the error in an error box. GPFs usually occur when two programs collide in memory. Sometimes they are caused by a mistake in programming. In Windows 3.0, a GPF is called a UAE, which is short for *unknown application error*. Microsoft renamed them in Windows 3.1.

If you get a GPF, follow these steps:

1. Try to reproduce the GPF. If the GPF is reproducible, go to step 2. If it isn't, don't worry about it. Computers have tiny circuits; the smallest disturbance can cause a one-time crash. If the problem occurs again, go to step 2.

2. Run a utility to check your hard drive media. Hard drive media are rarely at fault. The test is quick, however, and it eliminates one potential cause of the GPF. DOS comes with a utility called Check Disk. To run it, exit Windows and type

   ```
   CHKDSK /f
   ```

   If you own Norton Disk Doctor or PCTools DiskFix, run it instead. Either utility is better at recovering files than Check Disk. Be sure to observe the Norton or PC Tools warnings about running their diskfix programs with caches and other TSR programs.

3. If you use Paradox tables, exit Paradox and delete all the stranded .LCK files. If you are on a network, tell everyone who uses the same net file as you to exit Paradox—as well as any program that accesses the tables. Because no one is in Paradox, there shouldn't be any .LCK files on your system. Find and delete all the .LCK files. Typically, they are in the data directory and private directory. Use a global search utility to ensure that you find all of them, however.

4. If you find stranded .LCK files, delete them and retest for the GPF. If your machine works, the cause of the problem probably was a corrupt stranded .LCK file. A corrupt stranded .LCK file can occur whenever the Paradox system is exited abruptly, such as when a power outage

happens, the program crashes with another program or the user turns off his machine without exiting Paradox first. This last reason is common in large companies that do data entry. It is important to train users to exit Paradox and Windows properly. It is a good idea to put CHKDSK /f in the AUTOEXEC.BAT file of every inexperienced user.

> I test the software of thousands of users. I have used CHKDSK /f in my AUTOEXEC.BAT for the past year and I have lost no data. Before, I would occasionally lose data.

5. If you still get the GPF, rebuild the tables with the Table Repair utility. This might seem like a drastic step, but it takes only a few minutes, and it eliminates table damage as a possibility. It is important to rebuild all the tables involved; don't just verify their header information.

6. Simplify your system. Often, GPFs are caused by conflicts between programs. Simplifying your system might lead to the offensive program. See Appendix A, "Installation and Setup," for steps in simplifying your system. If you still get the GPF after you've simplified your system, go to step 7.

7. Ask yourself whether you should be able to do what you are trying to do. In ObjectPAL, the language is so rich that some combinations of methods and procedures can cause a GPF. Always ask yourself, "Is this the right way to do what I'm trying to do?" If you think that you should be able to do what you are doing, call Technical Support at Borland International. If they can reproduce the problem, they will pass it on to Quality Assurance. More important, Borland can suggest a work-around—that is, another way to accomplish the same task.

In general, you can fix a GPF by reconfiguring your system or by avoiding a particular sequence of steps. If you get a more serious error—for example, the computer freezes or Windows exits to DOS—the situation is more serious. In that case, you might have to reinstall DOS, Windows, or Paradox in addition to following the previous steps.

> Bugs, gotchas, anomalies—whatever you wish to call them—are part of any program. Paradox for Windows is no exception. For the latest on development issues, see the SECRETS2.HLP Windows help file on disk. It contains up to date information on bugs, WADs, and other such anomalies.

ANOMALIES THAT ARE WADS

WAD stands for *works as designed*. A WAD is behavior that a product's designers intended. For example, some users don't like the way in which the bands within a report are adjusted. It feels awkward to them. Many of them have called Borland and notified the company that the report section was broken. The problem, of course, is that these users don't understand how the product works. The report doesn't have a bug; the users simply need some guidance on how to use it.

In the computer industry, there are always several ways of looking at a feature. Companies put in some features and take out others for a multitude of reasons. If you disagree with Borland International on a particular feature, write a product suggestion letter to let the company know how you feel. Then, forget about it. There's no possible way that a major feature in Paradox will get changed overnight. You can, however, affect how the product is changed and enhanced in the long run.

PROTECTING YOUR APPLICATION

Protecting your application means that users can't edit your application, even if they own Paradox. In addition, you want to restrict the user's movement through your application. You don't want the user to exit without your permission. Also, you don't want users to be able to alter your applications. To protect your applications, you need to do only two things: password-protect your data tables and deliver your forms, reports, libraries, and scripts.

TESTING

The *alpha test* cycle is the preliminary testing of a new product in which research and development are still in progress. The *beta test* is a stage in product testing in which testing is done with actual users in the users' environment. Before you deliver your forms and put your application into production, you need to test it. Borland, for example, has a large team of engineers who test Paradox. The series of tests each quality-assurance engineer puts Paradox through can take up to three days to complete—and this is for just one small section of the product. You don't have to go through such extensive testing, but you owe it to your users to do at least some testing. The following are some hints and tips on testing your completed application.

Find Someone Else to Run Your Program

If possible, find someone else to exercise your program. As the programmer, you have certain ideas of how a user will use your application. These ideas probably apply to about half the users.

Run Every Feature Three Times

Test each feature three times. Sometimes, errors in logic don't show up until the second or even the third time through a sequence of events.

Test the Boundaries

Try your application with very large tables and empty tables. Run it on systems with the least amount of memory Paradox will run on—4MB. Log any errors you come across for final testing. Finally, play a game of "what if." For example:

- What if the user uses a corrupt table?
- What if the table gets moved or deleted?
- What if the user starts up using the wrong working directory?

Try to add your own questions to this list.

DELIVER YOUR FORMS

The final step in the development cycle is to *Deliver* all the forms, scripts, libraries and reports. In ObjectPAL, it's the process of compiling an object for a special Paradox-only dynamic link library. I recommend that you deliver your forms occasionally as you develop for testing. If you haven't been doing this, you should start.

> The Delivery System is on disk. This script, \ANSWERS\DELIVER.SSL, delivers all the forms, scripts, libraries, and reports in a directory

PACKAGING A COMPLETE APPLICATION

The first step in getting ready to deliver your application to a client is to gather all the files. You can create an icon in Program Manager for a form that contains your main menu. Make sure that you have associated .FSL and .FDL files with PDOXWIN.EXE. When you double-click on the form's icon, Paradox will load with that form open. To get rid of the Toolbar, you can put `HideToolbar()` in the **open** or **arrive** method of the form.

Some users, especially those who've purchased a custom application from a programmer, don't know enough about Windows to set up an icon. The more you try to make your applications foolproof, the better.

COMPILING TO AN EXECUTABLE FILE

I bet this section's title got your attention. To be honest, currently you can't compile your entire application into an .EXE. Even if you could compile all your forms, reports, queries, libraries, and scripts and somehow bind them to the runtime version of Paradox, you would end up with a huge executable of 2000K to 8000K, and you still couldn't compile your tables.

Get used to the idea of distributing a directory full of stuff as your application. Most Windows applications consist of a directory full of files. Word for Windows, WordPerfect, and Winfax are all Windows applications that consist of a directory full of files. Today's software market is so complex that the days of old when you could count on many of your applications being a single .EXE are gone. PDOXWIN.EXE itself is a 138K file that launches the entire 13MB Paradox experience. The problem is that users expect to see an .EXE file, not an .FDL or an .FSL. This idea of starting the whole process with an executable file, rather than a form, is what the next section is about.

THE LAUNCH.EXE PROGRAM

Although you can't compile your whole application into a single .EXE, you can use an .EXE to start the process. You can create a small .EXE using C or Pascal that accomplishes several things. First, it gives the application the look and feel of a "real" nonruntime application. Second, the .EXE is a storage place for a custom icon. Third, if the user to whom you give an application messes up his or her program groups, the user would look for an .EXE in the directory (not an .FDL, .FSL, .SDL, or .SSL). You can create this .EXE that starts your application very easily with LAUNCH.EXE.

The program design for LAUNCH.EXE is by Mike Prestwood, and the original LOADER.EXE was written by Rich Jones for the first edition of this book. Joe Nuxoll updated it to LAUNCH.EXE for the second edition.

This program was designed to launch a Paradox for Windows form (.FSL or .FDL) from an icon. LAUNCH.EXE automatically finds Paradox for Windows (or Paradox for Windows Runtime), sets the DOS working directory to the location of PDOXWIN.EXE (or PFWRUN.EXE), sets the Paradox working directory based on the location of LAUNCH.EXE (even after you rename it), and automatically locates and sets a new private directory for each session it launches. SHARE.EXE is required to launch multiple sessions of Paradox for Windows, and local share must be set to True in the IDAPI configuration utility for this utility to work.

To use LAUNCH.EXE, place it in the same directory as the form (.FSL or .FDL) that you wish to launch. Rename LAUNCH.EXE to the name of your form with an .EXE extension. For example, to launch MYFORM.FDL in the C:\PDOXWIN\MYDIR directory, copy LAUNCH.EXE to the C:\PDOXWIN\MYDIR directory. Rename LAUNCH.EXE to MYFORM.EXE. Create an icon for MYFORM.EXE in any group in Program Manager. To launch the form, just double-click MYFORM.EXE.

Tutorial: Using LAUNCH.EXE

The goal of this tutorial is to use LAUNCH.EXE to make the \APPS\PROPERTY application seem just like a regular Windows application.

On Disk: LAUNCH.EXE
Quick Steps

1. Copy LAUNCH.EXE to the directory that has your forms.
2. Rename LAUNCH.EXE to the name of the form you want to load. Keep the .EXE extension.
3. This step is optional: Use an icon Editor to customize the icon.

Step By Step

1. Copy LAUNCH.EXE to the directory where the PROPERTY.FSL file is located. You can do this with a DOS command such as

   `COPY LAUNCH.EXE \SECRETS2\APPS\PROPERTY\LOADER.EXE`

2. Change to the \ANSWERS\APPS\PROPERTY directory.

   `CD PROPERTY`

3. Rename LAUNCH.EXE to the name of the form you want it to load.

   `REN LAUNCH.EXE PROPERTY.EXE`

4. This step is optional: Launch your favorite icon Editor and edit the icon in PROPERTY.EXE. Both Norton Desktop for Windows and Borland's Resource Workshop come with an icon Editor. In addition, several are available in the public domain.

5. Go into File Manager and double-click PROPERTY.EXE. As soon as you've set up this file, your application is complete. Optionally, you can install the PROPERTY.EXE program into the Secrets2 Program Manager group (see Figure 36.1).

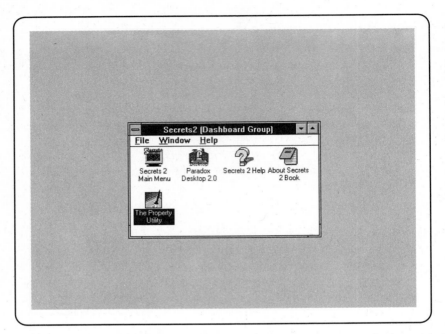

Figure 36.1. The Secrets2 group with the Property utility added using LAUNCH.EXE.

WRITING YOUR OWN LAUNCH PROGRAM

In case you want to take the idea of writing your own loader program and run with it, the source code is provided in Pascal on the disk that comes with this book. The following is the essence of a C version of a loader program.

```
1:  #include  <windows.h>;
2:
3:  main()
4:  {
5:      WinExec("PDOXWIN.EXE SECRETS2.FSL",SW_SHOWMAXIMIZED);
6:      return 0;
7:  }
```

ON THE
DISK

The Pascal source code for LAUNCH.EXE is on disk in
\DEV-SRC\LAUNCH\LAUNCH.PAS.

IDEAS FOR IMPROVEMENT

Have any ideas for improvement? The source code provided in this book and on disk is for you to run with. With the runtime package, Borland introduced RTLAUNCH.EXE, which had some of the functionality of the original LOADER.EXE. Hopefully, Borland will catch up in the future and provide this type of functionality (and more) for all of us.

CUSTOMIZING PARADOX

Many programmers want to give their Paradox applications a custom look and feel. Using an icon Editor, you can change the custom icon that Paradox uses. Use the PDOXWIN.EXE file. In addition, you can open many of the DLLs that Paradox uses and alter its resources. You do this with Borland's Windows Resource Workshop or another resource Editor. You can edit splash screens and bitmaps, menus and string tables, and dialog boxes.

UNDOCUMENTED WIN.INI SETTING

Add the following to the [PDOXWIN] section in your WIN.INI to load a custom bitmap in place of Paradox's normal startup screen. This is great when you have several versions installed (such as version 4.5 and 5.0).

```
MyOwnSplashScreen=BITMAP.BMP
```

THE FUTURE OF PARADOX FOR WINDOWS

What's in store next for Paradox? I think we all agree that Paradox has a wonderful and rich set of features. However, as humans, we always want more. This section talks about some of the features I would like to see in the product and some of the frequently requested features.

VBX, OCX, and VCL Support

Access, dBASE for Windows, and many other applications offer VBX support, which enables you to add custom objects to forms (OCX and VCL are two other versions of this technology). To some deveopers, Paradox needs this support to compete with Access and dBASE for Windows.

Should Paradox Offer an Undelete Feature As dBASE Does?

It would be nice if Paradox for Windows offered an undelete record function similar to the one dBASE has. When you delete a Paradox record, it's not actually deleted—it's marked for deletion. It's not packed until a restructure, or it could be reused (overwritten) automatically. This would make using the two databases a little more consistent. Here's a project for all you hackers out there.

An Easy Way to Print a Table Structure

In version 1.0/4.5, you could generate a STRUCT.DB table in your private directory just by using either the Info Structure or Restructure option. In version 5, Borland made it even harder to print a structure. Hopefully, this fairly easy-to-implement feature will be in the next version.

OBJECT VISION HAS SOMETHING OVER PARADOX FOR WINDOWS?

What record am I on? ObjectVision has a little blue triangle next to each table frame that points to the active record. Paradox desperately needs this feature, especially since both ObjectVision and Paradox are Borland products.

Support for cascade delete. Although you can fairly easily implement cascade delete with ObjectPAL, this feature really demands to be a part of the referential integrity scheme.

True OOP: Create Subclasses

Imagine having the capability to create subclasses (or more precisely, subtypes) from the existing types. Imagine creating a new object based on the form type. This new object inherits all of the features of the old type, but allows you to modify it as needed. If Borland implements subtypes, I can imagine selecting File | New | Other and selecting my new type from a list of user defined subtypes. Perhaps there could be a form-like object with added pull-down menus, a status bar, and code on it that automatically hides and shows the Paradox desktop when it is opened and closed.

More Speed

Borland made great headway with version 5. In fact, the speed of Paradox for many developers is no longer a sore point. All developers agree, however, that any improvements in screen refreshes, database access, or load time would be a great improvement.

More SQL Connections

Currently, the list of supported IDAPI connections includes Paradox, dBASE, Borland's Interbase, Microsoft SQL, Sybase, Oracle, Informix, and ODBC version 1.1. Although the connectivity is growing very fast, more in this case is better.

More SQL Speed

There are two types of SQL drivers: interpreters and native. An SQL interpreter driver translates all commands into their own commands. A native driver does not. The IDAPI engine currently is an interpreter and is therefore slightly slower than a native driver. If it is possible, IDAPI needs to convert over to native drivers for all SQL connections. If it is not possible, then the IDAPI developers need to find ways to speed up the SQL connections even more.

Miscellaneous

Of course, when dreaming of a wish list like this, I could probably go on for another five pages, but let me finish with a few less significant wishes:

- Easily add bitmap images to buttons from a provided library.
- Editable speed bars as Quattro Pro has.
- Allow expressions in a query.
- Add ObjectPAL capability to the desktop, reports, and tableviews.
- A menu expert would be nice (anyone can write this one, how about you?).
- Lookup tables need to take advantage of aliases.
- The SQL tools need to be integrated into the regular menus (why is this a separate, anyway?).
- Heck, while I'm dreaming, why not allow us to compile to an .EXE?

THAT'S A WRAP

Most of the examples that you went through in this book were geared toward accomplishing a specific task, learning a particular technique, or explaining a concept. Now that you have finished this book, it's up to you to put what you've learned in this book and elsewhere to work. You're ready to take on a whole project. Remember to keep this book and support software handy.

One of the reasons why I got into programming—and the reason why I wrote this book—is that I love to create. Creating things gives us all a sense of accomplishment and the feeling that we have added something to this world. Paradox is one of the best tools that you can use to create applications. Use it.

APPENDIXES

APPENDIX A

INSTALLATION AND SETUP

This appendix is provided for the developer. Its intention is not to help you install the product; it is assumed that you have already installed it and learned about interactive Paradox. This appendix is for after you distribute your Paradox application to your clients and to address some particularly interesting features.

REQUIREMENTS

The following are the minimum system requirements:

- 80386 or higher microprocessor.
- 6MB is Borland's official recommendation. However, it does run on a well configured 4MB system, although slowly. Performance will increase dramatically with more memory. I recomend a minimum of 8MB for a well configured system.
- Hard disk with at least 20MB of free disk space. You need 20MB to use Paradox for Windows effectively.
- EGA video card. VGA or higher is recommended.

- Microsoft Windows 3.1 or later. Version 3.0 isn't supported.
- A mouse. Some design features can be accessed only by a mouse.

The following lists optional equipment:

- Any Windows-compatible printer.
- Extended memory (the more the better).
- Network adapter card and communications software appropriate for the network.

The following networks are supported:

- Any Microsoft Windows 3.1-compatible network. This includes the following:

  OS/2 2.1
  Novell Netware
  3COM 3Plus/3Plus Open
  Microsoft LAN Manager
  Windows for Workgroups 3.11
  Windows NT 3.11
  Any network that is 100 percent Windows compatible

For a current list of supported networks, view the NETWORKS.WRI file in the WINDOWS directory.

INSTALLATION NOTES

Because you are a developer who might distribute your applications, you need to be familiar with installation problems. If one of your clients is having problems installing Paradox for Windows, read this section.

Hard Disk Notes

- Because the installation program uses the Windows drive to expand compressed files, you need about 3MB free on the drive where Windows resides. Therefore, you need at least 3MB free on the Windows drive, and approximately 18MB on the drive where Paradox will be installed.
- Check your hard drive media with CHKDSK, NDD, or any other media-checking utility. Bad media can be responsible for installation failure.

Errors should be repaired using an appropriate data recovery tool such as Norton Disk Doctor.

- If you use a hard disk compression utility, such as Stacker, be aware that hard disk space might not be correctly evaluated. Compression programs assume a particular ratio of compression, usually 2 to 1, which isn't appropriate for some Paradox files. To avoid problems with insufficient disk space, assume that you need approximately 25MB free on a compressed drive.

System Configuration

Conflicts with memory-resident software and device drivers can prevent the installation program from executing successfully. To keep this from happening, simplify your system configuration:

1. Disable all lines in your CONFIG.SYS files (by typing REM before each line) that aren't necessary for your system to run Windows, and keep only the following lines:

```
DEVICE = C:\WINDOWS\HIMEM.SYS
FILES = 80
BUFFERS = 40
STACKS = 9,256
SHELL = C:\DOS\COMMAND.COM C:\DOS /p /e:2048
```

2. Do the same for your AUTOEXEC.BAT:

```
PROMPT $P$G
PATH=C:\;C:\DOS;C:\WINDOWS
SET TEMP=C:\WINDOWS\TEMP
```

3. Reboot your computer.
4. Launch Windows in standard mode with WIN /S.
5. After Paradox installs, take out the REM remarks from AUTOEXEC.BAT and CONFIG.SYS. If you still can't install Paradox, use the steps in the following section to complete installation.

Installing Manually

If the installation program still fails to complete, you must install Paradox manually:

1. Copy PDOXINST.LZ from the first Paradox disk to your Windows directory:

```
COPY A:\PDOXINST.LZ C:\WINDOWS
```

2. Change directories to your Windows directory and unpack the Paradox installation program:

```
EXPAND PDOXINST.LZ PDOXINST.EXE
```

3. Now that the installation is unpacked on your drive, you can load Windows and run it. Load Windows, select File | Run from Program Manager, and type PDOXINST.

4. After the installation program successfully installs Paradox, you can delete PDOXINST.EXE from your Windows directory.

What If I Get a General Protection Fault?

If you get a general protection fault (GPF), follow these steps:

1. Make sure that your media is okay by running CHKDSK /F or NDD or any other media-checking utility. If you get errors, correct those errors and recheck. Keep in mind that you might need to reinstall DOS, Windows, or Paradox.

2. Exit Paradox and search and delete *.LCK, PARADOX.NET, and PDOXUSRS.NET files. Retest.

3. Check your CONFIG.SYS for the following and retest:

```
Files = 80 (or higher)
Buffers = 40 (or higher)
Stacks = 9,256
no FCBS
```

4. If these steps don't work, you're in the unlucky minority. At this point, the problem could be caused by configuration or corrupt files (or both). Because corrupt files are rare, stick with configuration and try to weed out all unknown variables. Take out any TSRs, screen savers, virus protectors, and any other nonessential software.

5. Try testing on someone else's system. If it works on that system and not yours, you have a configuration problem. Go back to step 4.

6. Try adding the following line to the [386 Enhanced] section of your SYSTEM.INI file.

```
MaxBPs=768
```

7. If none of these steps works, you can either continue simplifying your system or you can reinstall DOS, Windows, and Paradox. You can retest between each installation.

LAUNCHING PARAMETERS

Paradox for Windows enables you to specify command-line options when starting up. You can set up many different icons to start up Paradox for Windows in different ways. One great benefit is that you will be able to launch several sessions of Paradox. To change an icon, select File | Properties in Program Manager. The syntax for the command-line option is `[[Drive:] Path]` `PDOXWIN.EXE [Command-line options] [Startup file]`.

Table A.1 describes the launching parameters.

TABLE A.1. THE LAUNCHING PARAMETERS.

Parameter	Description
`-b`	Prevents Paradox from launching a second instance. Attempting to run a second instance will switch to the first instance.
`-c`	Starts Paradox with a clear Desktop. If you prefer to start with a clear desktop, use this option. Also, if you cannot start Paradox for any reason, try using `-c` to start without opening any objects.
`-d Filename`	Use `-dfilepath + filename` to specify an alternative PDOXWORK.INI file. You can use this to hard code a single PDOXWORK.INI file, even if you change working directories by specifying a complete path. In addition, this option allows you to create different folders/Project Viewers for each user.
`-e`	Prevents Paradox from writing all changes to PDOXWIN.INI and PDOXWORK.INI. This option is useful when you have your environment set up the way you like it (that is, when you've set your title, maximized, opened a folder or form, and so on).

continues

TABLE A.1. CONTINUED

Parameter	Description
-f	Allows changes to PDOXWIN.INI and PDOXWORK.INI that have been prevented by -e. This option overrides -e, even if it's placed in the FLAGS= line in the [PDOXWIN] section of WIN.INI.
-i Filename	Use -ifilepath + filename to specify an alternative PDOXWIN.INI file. This is very useful for keeping separate environment settings.
-m	Runs Paradox minimized. This is useful if you wish to load Paradox but not work with it right away.
-n	Doesn't write changes to WIN.INI. Use this option if you use the -p and -w command-line options to set your private and working directories. You can place -n in the FLAGS= line of the [PDOXWIN] section of WIN.INI. If you do this, you can override the -n option by starting Paradox with the -y option.
-o Filename	Use -ofilepath + filename to specify an alternative IDAPI.CFG file. This can be useful for maintaining separate lists of aliases.
-p Path	Use -pfilepath to specify an alternative private directory. Use this to set up more than one instance of Paradox on each system. You may wish to do this, for example, if you are installing several applications on a single system.
-q	Starts Paradox without displaying the title screen.
-s	Prevents users from resizing the Desktop. This option starts Paradox without a resizable window border. It doesn't prevent the window from being resized by ObjectPAL applications.

Parameter	Description
-t	Enables users to resize the Desktop. This option can be used to override -s if it's placed in the FLAGS= line in the [PDOXWIN] section of WIN.INI.
-w Path	Use -wfilepath to specify an alternative working directory. Use this to set up more than one application on each system.
-y	Overrides the -n command line option.
filename	Use filepath + filename to load any valid Paradox file. Valid filenames include MYFORM.FSL, MYFORM.FDL, MYREPORT.RSL, MYSCRIPT.SSL, etc.

When starting a second instance of Paradox, use the -n, -p, and -w command-line options. -n prohibits Paradox from saving private and working directory settings in the WIN.INI. The -p and -w options set different private and working directories. If you set up icons using these parameters, you'll be able to launch many different Paradox for Windows sessions and use more than one application at a time. For developers, copying and pasting from other forms becomes easier.

EXAMPLES OF USING PARAMETERS

Use this line when you have your environment the way you want it:

```
PDOXWIN.EXE -e
```

Use this line for launching a particular form in an extra instance:

```
PDOXWIN.EXE -n -pC:\PDOXWIN\DIVEPLAN -wC:\PDOXWIN\DIVEPLAN DIVEPLAN.FSL
```

Use this line to set up an application:

```
PDOXWIN.EXE -e -pD:\PDOXWIN\LIBRARY -wD:\PDOXWIN\LIBRARY
-iLIBRARY.INI LIBRARY.FSL
```

SPEEDING UP PARADOX FOR WINDOWS

As a developer, you need to optimize Windows for yourself and perhaps for your clients. Browse through the following section for suggestions on improving your machine and your clients' machines.

Memory

Windows requires at least 1MB of extended memory. This means a minimum of 2MB of memory. The first megabyte is used by conventional memory, and the second is used by Windows. Paradox for Windows requires that a minimum of 2MB of memory be available after you start Windows. This combines to a minimum requirement of 4MB to run both Windows and Paradox. By optimizing, you help both Windows and Paradox run more efficiently. The following are some memory suggestions:

- Use a permanent swap file. Windows uses either a temporary or permanent swap file for virtual memory to help with memory demand. If you use enhanced mode, use a permanent swap file set to at least half your physical RAM.

- Add memory. With today's low prices, it makes sense to add RAM to a 4MB system (especially a system with huge, powerful applications such as Paradox). This long-term solution will improve performance of all Windows applications. By increasing physical RAM, you decrease the use of the slower virtual memory.

- Run with a smaller SmartDrive, the disk cache program for Windows. For example:

  ```
  SMARTDRV 2048 256
  ```

  sets up SmartDrive to use 2048K when you're in DOS and only 256K while Windows is running. If you have more than 4MB of RAM, you can increase the second number slightly.

- Keep your hard drive optimized. Running a compression utility such as PC Tools COMPRESS or Norton SpeedDisk weekly or monthly will help Windows' performance. Some users have reported a tremendous increase in speed when they performed a File | Sort | By Extension with the extensions .DLL, .EXE, and .COM.

- Disable expanded memory. Windows does not use expanded memory (EMS), and any RAM set aside as EMS is taken away from Windows.

If you use EMM386.EXE, use the following code line in your CONFIG.SYS file:

```
Device=C:\WINDOWS\EMM386.EXE NOEMS
```

- Use fewer fonts or move them to the end of the WIN.INI file. Using fewer fonts means a smaller WIN.INI. Moving the fonts to the end of the WIN.INI file improves performance because programs don't have to read as far into the file for their information.

- Adjust the Max Buffer Size in the IDAPI Configuration Utility. For best performance, set the maximum buffer size to two-thirds of your available extended memory.

SPECIFICATIONS OF PARADOX FOR WINDOWS

For some reason, Borland is a little reluctant to publish specifications for Paradox. This appendix is provided to try to make up for the lack of a centralized location on Paradox and dBASE table, ObjectPAL, and general Paradox limits.

BORLAND DATABASE ENGINE (IDAPI)

- Local table types supported: Paradox 3.5, 4, Paradox for Windows 1.0, Paradox for Windows 5.0, dBASE III Plus, dBASE IV, and dBASE for Windows.
- SQL Database Servers: Interbase Server, Oracle 6 & 7, Sybase SQL Server, Microsoft SQL Server, and Informix.

- ODBC support requires ODBC Driver Manager 2.0. ODBC drivers include: Text, Excel spreadsheets, Access, DB2, AS/400, Btrieve, Ingres, and HP ALBASE/SQL (many others are also available).

PARADOX STANDARD TABLE SPECIFICATIONS

The Paradox standard table format was introduced in Paradox for DOS version 4. Other products that use the standard format include Paradox for DOS version 4.5, ObjectVision 2.1, and Paradox for Windows versions 1.0 and 4.5.

Earlier versions of the Paradox table type are referred to as the Compatible table type. In the IDAPI Configuration Utility, the level option for the Paradox driver dictates what default table type is created by Paradox for Windows. Use 3 for Compatible tables, use 4 for Standard tables, or use the default of 5 for Paradox 5 table format.

- 256MB file size limit if the table is in Paradox format and using a 4K block size. Maximum number of fields is 255. Maximum number of validity checks is 64 per table.
- Up to 255 fields per record, and up to 1,350 bytes per record for indexed tables or 4,000 bytes per record for nonindexed tables.
- Up to 64 validity checks per table for Paradox for Windows version 1.0.
- A primary index can have up to 16 fields.
- Tables can have up to 127 secondary indexes.
- Up to two billion records per file. Because of the 256MB file size limit and other factors like block size, however, the limit is much smaller. Tables of 190,000 records are easily achievable (and you can have more if you don't use up the 1350-bytes-per-record limit for a keyed table). Tables with close to a million records are common.
- Block size can be 1024, 2048, 3072, or 4096. Paradox stores data in fixed records. Even if part or all of the record is empty, the space is claimed. Knowing the interworkings can save you disk space. Paradox stores records in fixed blocks of 1024, 2048, 3072, 4096 in size.

  Once a block size is set for a table, that size is fixed, and all blocks in the table will be of that size. To conserve disk space, you want to try to get your record size as close to a multiple of block size as possible (minus 6 bytes, which are used by Paradox to manage the table).

- Record size: 1350 for keyed tables, and 4000 for unkeyed tables. When figuring out the size (the number of bytes or characters) of a table, remember that Alpha fields take up their size (for example, an A10 = 10 bytes), numeric field types take up 8 bytes, short number field types take up 2 bytes, money takes up 8, and dates take up 4 bytes.

  Memos, BLOBs, and so on take 10 bytes plus however much of the memo is stored in the .DB. For example, M15 takes 25 bytes. Alphas take 1 byte per character allocated.

PARADOX 5 TABLE SPECIFICATIONS

- Up to two billion records per file. No limit on file size.
- Up to 255 fields per record.
- Record size: Up to 10,800 bytes per record for indexed tables or 32,750 bytes per record for nonindexed tables. When figuring out the size (the number of bytes or characters) of a table, remember that Alpha fields take up their size (for example, an A10 = 10 bytes), numeric field types take up 8 bytes, short number field types take up 2 bytes, money takes up 8, and dates take up 4 bytes.

  Memos, BLOBs, and so on take 10 bytes plus however much of the memo is stored in the .DB. For example, M15 takes 25 bytes. Alphas take 1 byte per character allocated.

- Up to 64 validity checks per table for Paradox for Windows tables.
- A primary index can have up to 16 fields.
- Tables can have up to 127 secondary indexes.
- Block size can be from 1k to 32k in steps of 1k. For example, 1024, 2048, 3072, 4096, 5120...32768.

DBASE IV TABLE SPECIFICATIONS

- 2GB file size.
- Two billion records per file.
- A maximum of 255 fields per record.
- Maintained indexes can have up to 47 indexes per file. Each index can be created using field expressions of virtually any combination, including conditional expressions of up to 255 characters per expression that result in an index of up to 100 bytes.

- Unlimited nonmaintained indexes can be stored on disk. You can use up to 47 of them simultaneously.

dBase V Table Specifications

- Up to one billion records per file.
- A maximum of 1,024 fields per record.
- Up to 32,767 bytes per record.
- Unlimited nonmaintained indexes can be stored on disk. You can use up to 47 of them simultaneously.
- Up to 10 master index files open per database. Each master index can have up to 47 indexes.
- Maintained indexes can have up to 47 indexes per file. Each index can be created using field expressions of virtually any combination, including conditional expressions of up to 255 characters per expression that result in an index of up to 100 bytes.

Paradox and dBASE Field Type Specifications

See Chapter 2 for additional information on the following field types.

- **Alpha** (A)—Paradox 3.5, 4, and 5 field type that can contain up to 255 letters and numbers. This field type was called Alphanumeric in versions of Paradox before version 5. It is similar to the Character field type in dBASE.
- **Character** (C)—dBASE III+, IV, and V field type that can contain up to 254 characters (including blank spaces). This field is similar to the Paradox Alpha field type.

- **Autoincrement** (+)—Paradox 5 field type that begins with the number 1 and adds one number for each record in the table up to 2,147,483,647. Deleting a record does not change the field values of other records.

- **BCD** (#)—Paradox 5 field type is provided only for compatibility with other applications that use BCD data. Paradox correctly interprets BCD data from other applications that use the BCD type. When Paradox performs calculations on BCD data, it converts the data to the numeric float type, then converts the result back to BCD. When this field type is fully supported, it will support up to 32 significant digits.

- **Binary** (B)—Paradox for Windows 1 and 5 field type that can store binary data up to 256 MB per file.

- **Bytes** (Y)—Paradox 5 field type for storing binary data up to 255 bytes. Unlike binary fields, bytes fields are stored in the Paradox table (rather than in the separate .MB file), allowing for faster access.

- **Date** (D)—Paradox 3.5, 4, and 5 as well as dBASE III+, IV, and V. dBASE tables can store dates from January 1, 100, to December 31, 9999. Paradox 5 tables can store from 12/31/9999 B.C. to 12/31/9999 A.D.

- **Float** (F)—dBASE IV and V floating-point numeric field type provides up to 20 significant digits.

- **Formatted Memo** (F)—Paradox for Windows 1, 4.5, and 5 field type is like a memo field except that you can format the text. You can alter and store the text attributes typeface, style, color, and size. This rich text document has a variable-length up to 256 MB per file.

- **Graphic** (G)—Paradox for Windows 1.0 and 5 field type can contain pictures in .BMP (up to 24-bit), .TIF (up to 256 color), .GIF (up to 256 color), .PCX, and .EPS file formats. Not all graphic variations are available. For example, currently you cannot store a 24-bit .TIF graphic. When you paste a graphic into a graphic field, Paradox converts the graphic into the .BMP format.

- **Logical** (L)—Paradox 5 and dBASE III+, IV, and V field type can store values representing True or False (yes or no). By default, valid entries include T and F (case is not important).

- **Long Integer** (I)—Paradox 5 field type that can store 32-bit signed integers that contain whole numbers in the range 2,147,483,647 to −2,147,483,647.

- **Memo** (M)—Paradox 4 and 5 as well as dBASE III+, IV, and V field. A Paradox field type is a Alpha variable-length field up to 256 MB per file. dBASE Memo fields can contain binary as well as memo data.

    The file is divided into blocks of 512 characters. Each block is referenced by a sequential number, beginning at zero. Block 0 begins with a four-byte number in hexadecimal format, in which the least significant byte comes first. This number specifies the number of the next available block. It is, in effect, a pointer to the end of the memo file. The remainder of Block 0 isn't used.

- **Money** ($)—Paradox 3.5, 4, and 5 field type, like number fields, can contain only numbers. They can hold positive or negative values. Paradox recognizes up to six decimal places when performing internal calculations on money fields. This field type was called Currency in previous versions of Paradox.

- **OLE** (O)— Paradox for Windows 1 and 5 as well as dBASE V field type that can store OLE data. Paradox for Windows 5 supports both OLE 1 and OLE 2. dBASE for Windows supports only OLE 1.

- **Number** (N)—Paradox 3.5, 4, and 5 as well as dBASE III+, IV, and V field type can store up to 15 significant digits -10^{307} to $+ 10^{308}$ with up to 15 significant digits.

  dBASE number fields contain numeric data in a Binary Coded Decimal (BCD) format. Use number fields when you need to perform precise calculations on the field data. Calculations on number fields are performed more slowly but with greater precision than are calculations on float number fields. The size of a dBASE number field can be from 1 to 20. Remember, however, that BCD is in Paradox for Windows version 5 only for compatibility and is mapped directly to the Number field type.

- **Short** (S)—Paradox 3.5, 4, and 5 field type that can contain integers from −32,767 through 32,767—no decimal.

- **Time** (T)—Paradox 5 field type that can contain time times of day, stored in milliseconds since midnight and limited to 24 hours.

> This field type does not store duration. For example, if you need to store the duration of a song, use an Alpha field. Whenever you need to store time, make a distinction between clock time and duration. The Time field type is perfect for clock time. Duration can be stored in an Alpha field and manipulated with ObjectPAL.

- **TimeStamp** (@)—Paradox 5 field type comprised of both date and time values. Rules for this field type are the same as those for date fields and time fields.

OBJECTPAL (APPLIES TO FORMS, SCRIPTS, AND LIBRARIES)

- **Calculated fields:** Calculated fields are limited to 850 characters.
- **Code:** Forms can have up to 64K of compiled p-code. P-code is an intermediate form of compiled code that requires a p-code interpreter to execute the object code. If you need more than 64K of compiled p-code, use a library.
- **Symbol table:** Forms can have up to 64K of variable names and named UIObjects. The noise name, the name you gave, and the four-byte address of the object are stored in the symbol table. For example, if you rename the page from its noise name of #page2 to Pge1, 13 bytes are stored in the symbol table. Five bytes for the noise name, four bytes for the name you gave it, and four more bytes for the page object address in memory.

  The following are placed into the symbol table: variables, constants (user-defined), procedure prototypes, Uses prototypes, types, records, object names, and custom method names/prototypes. Finally, if Compile with DEBUG is checked, more information is provided to you when a critical error occurs (including the object, method, and line of code that caused the error).

  If you need to use thousands and thousands of variables, then use arrays or DynArrays. The reason behind this is that only the array or DynArray name and the four-byte address are stored in memory. The Array and DynArray data are stored separately.

- **Variable length:** You can use variable names up to 64 characters.
- **Object name length:** You can use object names up to 64 characters.
- **Calculated fields:** Calculated fields are limited to just under 1000 characters.
- **Parameter limit:** Built-in and custom methods and procedures have a 29-parameter limit. Attempting to compile a form or script with more than 29 parameters gives the error "Error: Maximum number of parameters has been exceeded."
- **Built-in methods:** Built-in methods are limited to 32K. This matches the limit for a memo variable. This limit is important because of the method methodGet().

- **Quoted strings:** Quoted strings are limited to 255 characters. This applies to such expressions as the following:

```
x = "abc 123"        ;An example of a quoted string.
```

- **Arrays:** Arrays are limited to 65,535 elements.
- **DynArrays:** DynArrays are only limited by memory.

QUERIES

- Up to 32 tables in a single query.
- Unlimited number of lines in a query. This is limited by memory.

DATABASE QUICK REFERENCE

How many times have you been creating a database and not had any idea of how long a field should be, what type of fields to include in a table, or what the relationship between two tables might be? This appendix is an invaluable starting point and reference.

When you're deciding what fields to put in a database, it's nice to have a starting point. Table C.1 is a list of common field names, along with suggested field type and length. These are only suggestions and shouldn't be taken as gospel. Use this table as a starting point.

TABLE C.1. COMMON FIELD TYPES AND LENGTHS.

Field Name (Type)	Field Name (Type)
Accommodations (A15)	Band (A20)
Account No (A20)	Basement (A3)
ActionFieldView (A32)	Baths (N)
ActionInDesignWindow (A31)	Beam (ft) (N)
ActionInForm (A21)	Beam (m) (N)
ActionInQuery (A21)	Bedrooms (N)
ActionInTable (A21)	Bet ($)
ActionInTableWindow (A31)	Birthday (D)
ActionNonFieldView (A32)	Body of Water (A20)
Address (full) (A50)	Business (A30)
Address 1 (A25)	Campaign (A35)
Address 2 (A25)	Capacity (A20)
Affiliation (A25)	Capacity (N)
Age (S)	Carrier (A15)
Album Title (A40)	Cash Flow ($)
AMENITIES (A32)	Category (A15)
Amount ($)	Cause (A15)
Anniversary (D)	Certification (A15)
Appeal type (A12)	Check No (A12)
Application Description (A1)	City (A15)
Application ID (A8)	City/St/Zip (A28)
Application Name (A80)	Classification (A40)
Approval No (A20)	ClassName (A32)
Approved by (A25)	Clerical skills (A15)
Area Code (A3)	College Education (A20)
Attribute (A64)	Comments (A255)
Auto lib (A80)	Comments (F10)
Avery Label No (A6)	Comments (A10)
Balance ($)	Company Name (A30)

Field Name (Type)	Field Name (Type)
Condition (A12)	Default (A4)
ConstantName (A48)	Default Menu Style (A10)
Constellation (A4)	Default Percentage (N)
Contact (A30)	Delivery (A15)
Context ID (N)	Den (A3)
Cost ($)	Department (A25)
Count (N)	Dependents (A11)
Country (abbreviation) (A3)	Depth (ft) (N)
Country (full) (A24)	Depth (m) (N)
Create (A4)	Description (A255)
Credit ($)	Description (F10)
Credit Card Date (MMYY) (A4)	Description (fancy) (F10)
Credit Card No (no spaces) (A16)	Description (long) (A50)
Credit Card No (with spaces) (A19)	Description (short) (A25)
Credit rating (A20)	Description of Vehicle (A51)
Customer No (N)	Detail Steps (F10)
Customer No (integers) (S)	Died (D)
Customer No (letters and numbers) (A10)	Dimensions (A15)
Date (D)	Directory (A79)
D (D)	Distance (km) (N)
DateTime (Two Fields: D & T)	Distance (m) (N)
DateTime (@)	Division (A25)
DateTime (N)	Down Payment (N)
Day of Week (abbreviation) (A3)	Drive Designation (A1)
Day of Week (full name) (A9)	Drive type (A6)
DBName (A32)	DRIVER (A1)
DBPath (A82)	Driver's License (A10)
DBType (A32)	Driver Type (A32)
Debit ($)	Entry date (D)
Declination (N)	Equipment Class (A30)

continues

TABLE C.1. CONTINUED	
Field Name (Type)	*Field Name (Type)*
Estimated current value ($)	Last Name (A20)
Face Name (A64)	Last Paid (D)
Fall Temp (C) (N)	Length (N)
Fall Temp (F) (S)	Length (cm) (N)
FAX (A15)	Length-ft (N)
Fax Number (A15)	Length-in (N)
Field Name (A35)	Length-m (N)
Field Type (A32)	Length-minutes (N)
File Name (computer) (A12)	Letter (A1)
Film Name (A30)	Level (A15)
First Name (A15)	Line Note (A255)
FOB (A20)	Line Total ($)
fantasize (A8)	List Price ($)
Form Name (A8)	Location (A20)
Format (A4)	Logical (A3)
Format (A32)	Logical (L)
FORUM (A10)	Logo (G0)
Front Porch (A3)	Manual/Outdoor work (A25)
Graphic (G0)	Marital Status (A11)
Graphic (filename) (A12)	Market segment (A25)
Heat (A8)	Math chip (A10)
Hobbies (F240)	MaxRecSize (A6)
Hobby (A20)	Media (A12)
Home AC (A3)	Member (A1)
HS Education (A20)	MEMBER (A1)
Instrument (s) (A20)	Membership (A1)
Internal only (A15)	Messier Number (A4)
Key Combination (A13)	Meters (N)
keepers (A12)	MethodArgs (A255)

Field Name (Type)	Field Name (Type)
Method Name (A64)	Occupants (N)
Method Type (A8)	On Meridian (D (1)
Middle Initial (A1)	Operator (A10)
Middle Name (A15)	Origin (A10)
Miles (N)	Original cost ($)
Model (A20)	OS (A15)
Modulation (A20)	OS version (N)
Month (abbreviation) (A3)	Pager (A21)
Month (full) (A9)	Passengers/Crew (N)
Movie Rating (A5)	Payment Method (A11)
Musician (A30)	Payment Method (short) (A2)
Musician Notes (A10)	Percent (N)
Name (full) (A35)	Percentage (N)
Name (initials) (A3)	Percentage Rate (N)
Native Type (A6)	Peripheral Name (A25)
NGC Number (A8)	Phone (A12)
Notes (A255)	Phone (A15)
Notes (F10)	Phone (local) (A8)
Notes (long) (A60)	Phone Ext (A5)
Notes (short) (A30)	Picture (graphic) (G0)
Object (A20)	Position title (A25)
Object Code (A8)	Price ($)
Object ID (A35)	Primary Key (A4)
Object Memo (A10)	Processor (A10)
Object Name (A32)	Processor speed (A10)
Object Path (A100)	Qty (N)
Object Table (A40)	Query ID (S)
Object Type (A8)	RAM (N)
ObjectClass (A32)	Rate (N)
ObjectName (A128)	Rating (A10)

continues

TABLE C.1. CONTINUED	
Field Name (Type)	Field Name (Type)
ReadWrite (A4)	Species No (N)
Reason (A15)	Spouse (A13)
ReturnType (A32)	Spring Temp (C) (N)
ROM BIOS (A15)	Spring Temp (F) (S)
Routing (A20)	SquareFeet (N)
Salary ($)	Startup Proc (A32)
Schematic (A2)	State (A3)
School (A11)	State (full) (A21)
School Degree (A15)	State (US) (A2)
Security (A4)	State/Prov (A3)
Sex M/F (L)	State/Prov (full) (A20)
Sheet (G0)	Status of Residence (A11)
Shift (A8)	Street (A30)
Siding (A7)	Subtotal ($)
Signed (A15)	Summer Temp (C) (N)
Size (S)	Summer Temp (F) (S)
Skill Level (A12)	Supervisor (A25)
Slogan (A40)	Survivors (N)
Social Security Number (A11)	Symbol (A3)
Solicitations (S)	Table Name (A8)
Song Length (A10)	TableType (A32)
Song Notes (A100)	Task (A30)
Song Title (A30)	TaxValue (N)
Sound (OLE) (OLE0)	Telephone (A13)
Source (A15)	Term of Contract Months (N)
Special donor (A14)	Terms (A15)
Special Instructions (F240)	THREAD (A30)
Species Name (A40)	Time (T)

Field Name (Type)	Field Name (Type)
TIME (N)	Visibility (m) (N)
Time (HH:MM:SS AM/PM) (A11)	Width (N)
Title (A30)	WindowName (A32)
Tonnage (N)	Winter Temp (C) (N)
Topic (A32)	Winter Temp (F) (S)
Total ($)	Year (A4)
Trade for your vehicle ($)	Years at Residence (A6)
Transaction Type (A16)	Zip (A5)
Travel Cost ($)	Zip (full) (A10)
Trip Code (N)	Zip Ext (A4)
Type (A20)	Zip/Postal Code (A10)
TYPE UNIT (A5)	_Default Value (A255)
Unpaid Balance ($)	_Invariant Field ID (S)
User (A15)	_Max Value (A255)
VacationCost ($)	_Min Value (A255)
ValChecks (A4)	_Picture Value (A175)
Value (A64)	_Required Value (A1)
Vendor No (N)	_Table Lookup (A81)
Visibility (ft) (N)	_Table Lookup Type (A1)

Common Table Structures

The tables that follow list some common table structures. Use these suggested database structures when you're not inspired or when you need a hand. An asterisk after the field name indicates that the field is part of the primary key.

	Table C.2. Address book table.	
Field Name (Type)	Secondary Index(es)
SS# (A15)*	
Name (A30)	**

continues

TABLE C.2. CONTINUED

Field Name (Type)	Secondary Index(es)
Address (A30)	
City (A15)	
State/Province (A2)	
Zip (A10)	
Phone (A15)	
Born (D)	
Age (N)	
Notes (M10)	
Picture (G0)	

TABLE C.3. AREA CODE TABLE.

Field Name (Type)	Secondary Index(es)
Area Code (A3)*	
State (A2)	**
Full State (A21)	
Country (A30)	

TABLE C.4. ATM TRANSACTIONS.

Field Name (Type)	Secondary Index(es)
Transaction Number (N)*	
Date (D)	**
Amount ($)	
Transaction Type (A16)	

TABLE C.5. CUSTOMER TABLE.	
Field Name (Type)	Secondary Index(es)
Customer No (N)*	
Name (A30)	**
Street (A30)	
City (A15)	
State/Prov (A20)	
Zip/Postal Code (A10)	
Country (A20)	
Phone (A15)	
First Contact (D)	

TABLE C.6. EMPLOYEE TABLE.	
Field Name (Type)	Secondary Index(es)
SSN (A15)*	
Department (A30)	
Position (A30)	
Desk Phone (A15)	
Manager SSN (A15)	**
Start Date (D)	
Shift Start Time (T)	
Shift End Time (T)	
Salary (per year) ($)	
Notes (F)	
Picture (G)	

TABLE C.7. EXPENSES TABLE.

Field Name (Type)	Secondary Index(es)
Expense No (+)*	
Date (N)	**
Type (A20)	
Transaction Type (A20)	
Transaction Number (N)	
Comments (A20)	

TABLE C.8. CASSETTE LABEL TEMPLATE.

Field Name (Type)	Secondary Index(es)
Label Set (A15)*	
Label Number (S)*	
Header—one line (A70)	**
Songs—up to three lines (A255)	
Side (one character) (A1)	
Band name (or tape name) (A60)	
Note (one line) (A70)	
Inside label (A50)	

TABLE C.9. LOANS TABLE.

Field Name (Type)	Secondary Index(es)
Description (A20)*	
Date of first Payment (D)	

Field Name (Type)	Secondary Index(es)
Loan Amount ($)	
Interest Rate (N)	
Term of Loan In Years (N)	
Payments Per Year (N)	
Total Payments (N)	
Payment Amount ($)	

TABLE C.10. MAIL SYSTEM TABLE.

Field Name (Type)	Secondary Index(es)
Status (A1)*	
Time (T)*	
To (A20)*	**
Date (D)	**
From (A20)	
Subject (A50)	
Message (M10)	
FileName (A30)	

TABLE C.11. SECOND ADDRESS BOOK TABLE.

Field Name (Type)	Secondary Index(es)
Last Name (A20)*	
First Name (A15)*	
Middle Initial (A1)*	

continues

TABLE C.11. CONTINUED

Field Name (Type)	Secondary Index(es)
Title (A30)	
Company (A30)	**
Address1 (A30)	
Address2 (A30)	
City (A15)	
State (A3)	
Zip (A10)	
Phone Number (A15)	
Work Number (A15)	
Fax Number (A15)	
Notes (F10)	

TABLE C.12. FLEXIBLE PHONE NUMBER TABLE FOR USE WITH SECOND ADDRESS BOOK.

Field Name (Type)	Secondary Index(es)
Last Name (A20)*	
First Name (A15)*	
Middle Name (A15)*	
Phone # Name (A15)*	**
Phone Number (A15)	
Phone Ext (A5)	

Table C.13. Line items of an invoice.

Field Name (Type)	Secondary Index(es)
Order No (N)*	
Stock No (N)*	
Selling Price (M)	
Qty (N)	
Line Total (M)	

Table C.14. Line item look-up table.

Field Name (Type)	Secondary Index(es)
Stock No (N)*	
Desc (A20)	**

Table C.15. Orders table.

Field Name (Type)	Secondary Index(es)
Order No (N)*	
Customer No (N)	
Sale Date (D)	
Ship Date (D)	
Ship VIA (A7)	
Total Invoice ($)	
Amount Paid ($)	
Balance Due ($)	

continues

TABLE C.15. CONTINUED	
Field Name (Type)	*Secondary Index(es)*
Terms (A6)	
Payment Method (A7)	

TABLE C.16. STATES LOOK-UP TABLE.	
Field Name (Type)	*Secondary Index(es)*
State (A2)*	
Full State (A21)	
Country (A30)	

TABLE C.17. STOCK OR INVENTORY TABLE.	
Field Name (Type)	*Secondary Index(es)*
Stock No (N)*	
Vendor No (N)	
Equipment Class (A30)	
Model (A20)	
Part No (A15)	
Description (A30)	
Catalog Description (F10)	
Qty (N)	
List Price ($)	

TABLE C.18. VENDORS OR COMPANIES.

Field Name (Type)	Secondary Index(es)
Vendor No (N)*	
Vendor Name (A30)	
Street (A30)	
City (A20)	
State/Prov (A20)	
Country (A15)	
Zip/Postal Rt (A10)	
Phone (A15)	
FAX (A15)	
Preferred (A3)	

TABLE C.19. ZIP CODES LOOK-UP TABLE.

Field Name (Type)	Secondary Index(es)
Zip code (A5)*	
City (A25)	**
State (A2)	**

METHODS AND PROCEDURES

Table D.1 lists the methods and procedures, their syntax, return values, base class, whether it is a method or procedure, and what version the method or procedure was introduced in.

TABLE D.1. METHODS AND PROCEDURES SYNTAX.

Syntax	Base Class	M/P	Ver
abs() Number	Number	M	1.0
accessRights() String	FileSystem	M	1.0
acos() Number	Number	M	1.0
action(const *actionId* SmallInt) Logical	Form	M	1.0
action(const *actionId* SmallInt) Logical	Form	P	1.0
action(const *actionId* SmallInt) Logical	TableView	M	1.0
action(const *actionId* SmallInt) Logical	UIObject	M	1.0
actionClass() SmallInt	ActionEvent	M	1.0
add(const *destTable* Table [, const *append* Logical [, const *update* Logical]]) Logical	Table	M	1.0
add(const *destTable* Table [, const *append* Logical [, const *update* Logical]]) Logical	TCursor	M	1.0
add(const *destTableName* String [, const *append* Logical [, const *update* Logical]]) Logical	Table	M	1.0
add(const *destTableName* String [, const *append* Logical [, const *update* Logical]]) Logical	TCursor	M	1.0
add(const *destTCursor* TCursor [, const *append* Logical [, const *update* Logical]]) Logical	TCursor	M	1.0
add(const *tableName* String, const *destTableName* String) Logical	Table	M	1.0
add(const *tableName* String, const *destTableName* String, const *append* Logical, const *update* Logical) Logical	Table	P	1.0
addAlias(const *alias* String, const *existingAlias* String) Logical	Session	M	5.0
addAlias(const *alias* String, const *existingAlias* String) Logical	Session	P	5.0

Syntax	Base Class	M/P	Ver
addAlias(const *alias* String, const *type* String, const *params* DynArray[] String) Logical	Session	M	4.5
addAlias(const *alias* String, const *type* String, const *params* DynArray[] String) Logical	Session	P	4.5
addAlias(const *alias* String, const *type* String, const *path* String) Logical	Session	M	1.0
addAlias(const *alias* String, const *type* String, const *path* String) Logical	Session	P	1.0
addArray(const *items* Array[] String)	Menu	M	1.0
addArray(const *items* Array[] String)	PopUpMenu	M	1.0
addBar()	PopUpMenu	M	1.0
addBreak()	Menu	M	1.0
addBreak()	PopUpMenu	M	1.0
addKeys(const *keys* String) Logical	System	P	5.0
addLast(const *value* AnyType)	Array	M	1.0
addPassword(const *password* String)	Session	M	1.0
addPassword(const *password* String)	Session	P	1.0
addPopUp(const *menuName* String, const *cascadedPopUp* PopUpMenu)	Menu	M	1.0
addPopUp(const *menuName* String, const *cascadedPopUp* PopUpMenu)	PopUpMenu	M	1.0
addProjectAlias(const *alias* String, const *existingAlias* String) Logical	Session	M	5.0
addProjectAlias(const *alias* String, const *existingAlias* String) Logical	Session	P	5.0
addProjectAlias(const *alias* String, const *type* String, const *params* DynArray[] String) Logical	Session	M	5.0
addProjectAlias(const *alias* String, const *type* String, const *params* DynArray[] String) Logical	Session	P	5.0
addProjectAlias(const *alias* String, const *type* String, const *path* String) Logical	Session	M	5.0

continues

Table D.1. continued

Syntax	Base Class	M/P	Ver
addProjectAlias(const *alias* String, const *type* String, const *path* String) Logical	Session	P	5.0
addSeparator()	PopUpMenu	M	1.0
addStaticText(const *item* String)	Menu	M	1.0
addStaticText(const *item* String)	PopUpMenu	M	1.0
addText(const *menuName* String)	Menu	M	1.0
addText(const *menuName* String)	PopUpMenu	M	1.0
addText(const *menuName* String, const *attrib* SmallInt)	Menu	M	1.0
addText(const *menuName* String, const *attrib* SmallInt)	PopUpMenu	M	1.0
addText(const *menuName* String, const *attrib* SmallInt, const *id* SmallInt)	Menu	M	1.0
addText(const *menuName* String, const *attrib* SmallInt, const *id* SmallInt)	PopUpMenu	M	1.0
advancedWildcardsInLocate([const *yesNo* Logical])	Session	P	1.0
advMatch(const *pattern* String, ...) Logical	String	M	1.0
advMatch(var *startIndex* LongInt, var *endIndex* LongInt, const *pattern* String) Logical	TextStream	M	1.0
ansiCode(const *char* String) SmallInt	String	P	1.0
append(const *newArray* Array[] AnyType)	Array	M	1.0
asin() Number	Number	M	1.0
atan() Number	Number	M	1.0
atan2(const *x* Number) Number	Number	M	1.0
atFirst() Logical	TCursor	M	1.0
atFirst() Logical	UIObject	M	1.0

Syntax	Base Class	M/P	Ver
atLast() Logical	TCursor	M	1.0
atLast() Logical	UIObject	M	1.0
attach() Logical	Form	M	1.0
attach() Logical	Script	M	5.0
attach() Logical	UIObject	M	1.0
attach(const *form* Form) Logical	UIObject	M	1.0
attach(const *form* Form, const *objectName* String) Logical	UIObject	M	1.0
attach(const *formName* String) Logical	Form	M	1.0
attach(const *object* UIObject) Logical	TCursor	M	1.0
attach(const *object* UIObject) Logical	UIObject	M	1.0
attach(const *report* Report) Logical	UIObject	M	1.0
attach(const *report* Report, const *objectName* String) Logical	UIObject	M	1.0
attach(const *reportName* String) Logical	Report	M	1.0
attach(const *srcTCursor* TCursor) Logical	TCursor	M	1.0
attach(const *tableName* String) Logical	Table	M	1.0
attach(const *tableName* String, const *dB* Database) Logical	Table	M	1.0
attach(const *tableName* String, const *tableType* String) Logical	Table	M	1.0
attach(const *tableName* String, const *tableType* String, const *dB* Database) Logical	Table	M	1.0
attach(const *tv* TableView) Logical	TCursor	M	1.0
attachToKeyViol(const *oldTC* TCursor) Logical	TCursor	M	1.0
beep()	System	P	1.0

continues

	TABLE D.1. CONTINUED		
Syntax	Base Class	M/P	Ver
beginTransaction() Logical	Database	M	4.5
beginTransaction(const *isoLevel* String) Logical	Database	M	5.0
bitAND(const *value* LongInt) LongInt	LongInt	M	1.0
bitAND(const *value* SmallInt) SmallInt	SmallInt	M	1.0
bitIsSet(const *value* LongInt) Logical	LongInt	M	1.0
bitIsSet(const *value* SmallInt) Logical	SmallInt	M	1.0
bitOR(const *value* LongInt) LongInt	LongInt	M	1.0
bitOR(const *value* SmallInt) SmallInt	SmallInt	M	1.0
bitXOR(const *value* LongInt) LongInt	LongInt	M	1.0
bitXOR(const *value* SmallInt) SmallInt	SmallInt	M	1.0
blank()	AnyType	M	1.0
blank() AnyType	AnyType	P	1.0
blankAsZero(const *yesNo* Logical)	**Session**	M	1.0
blankAsZero(const *yesNo* Logical)	**Session**	P	1.0
bot() Logical	TCursor	M	1.0
breakApart(var *tokenArray* Array[] String, [const *separators* String])	String	M	1.0
bringToFront()	UIObject	M	5.0
bringToTop()	**Application**	M	1.0
bringToTop()	Form	M	1.0
bringToTop()	Form	P	1.0

Syntax	Base Class	M/P	Ver
bringToTop()	**Report**	M	1.0
bringToTop()	TableView	M	1.0
broadcastAction(const *actionId* SmallInt)	UIObject	M	1.0
cancelEdit() Logical	TCursor	M	1.0
cancelEdit() Logical	UIObject	M	1.0
canLinkFromClipboard() Logical	Ole	M	5.0
canReadFromClipboard() Logical	Ole	M	1.0
cAverage(const *fieldName* String) Number	Table	M	1.0
cAverage(const *fieldName* String) Number	TCursor	M	1.0
cAverage(const *fieldNum* SmallInt) Number	Table	M	1.0
cAverage(const *fieldNum* SmallInt) Number	TCursor	M	1.0
cAverage(const *tableName* String, const *fieldName* String) Number	Table	P	1.0
cAverage(const *tableName* String, const *fieldNum* SmallInt) Number	Table	P	1.0
cCount(const *fieldName* String) LongInt	Table	M	5.0
cCount(const *fieldName* String) LongInt	TCursor	M	5.0
cCount(const *fieldName* String) Number	Table	M	1.0
cCount(const *fieldName* String) Number	TCursor	M	1.0
cCount(const *fieldNum* SmallInt) LongInt	Table	M	5.0
cCount(const *fieldNum* SmallInt) LongInt	TCursor	M	5.0
cCount(const *fieldNum* SmallInt) Number	Table	M	1.0
cCount(const *fieldNum* SmallInt) Number	TCursor	M	1.0

continues

TABLE D.1. CONTINUED

Syntax	Base Class	M/P	Ver
cCount(const *tableName* String, const *fieldName* String) LongInt	Table	P	5.0
cCount(const *tableName* String, const *fieldName* String) Number	Table	P	1.0
cCount(const *tableName* String, const *fieldNum* SmallInt) LongInt	Table	P	5.0
cCount(const *tableName* String, const *fieldNum* SmallInt) Number	Table	P	1.0
ceil() Number	Number	M	1.0
char() String	KeyEvent	M	1.0
charAnsiCode() SmallInt	KeyEvent	M	1.0
chr(const *ansiCode* SmallInt) String	String	P	1.0
chrOEM(const *oemCode* SmallInt) String	String	P	1.0
chrToKeyName(const *char* String) String	String	P	1.0
clearDirLock(const *dirName* String) Logical	FileSystem	P	5.0
ClipboardEnum(var *formatNames* Array[] String) SmallInt	Binary	M	5.0
ClipboardErase()	Binary	M	5.0
ClipboardHasFormat(const *formatName* String) Logical	Binary	M	5.0
close()	Form	M	1.0
close()	Library	M	1.0
close()	Report	M	1.0
close()	TableView	M	1.0
close() Logical	Database	M	1.0
close() Logical	DDE	M	1.0
close() Logical	Form	M	4.5

Syntax	Base Class	M/P	Ver
close() Logical	Library	M	4.5
close() Logical	Report	M	4.5
close() Logical	Script	M	5.0
close() Logical	Session	M	1.0
close() Logical	TableView	M	4.5
close() Logical	TCursor	M	1.0
close() Logical	TextStream	M	1.0
close([const *returnValue* AnyType])	Form	P	1.0
close([const *returnValue* AnyType])	System	P	1.0
cMax(const *fieldName* String) AnyType	Table	M	5.0
cMax(const *fieldName* String) AnyType	TCursor	M	5.0
cMax(const *fieldName* String) Number	Table	M	1.0
cMax(const *fieldName* String) Number	TCursor	M	1.0
cMax(const *fieldNum* SmallInt) AnyType	Table	M	5.0
cMax(const *fieldNum* SmallInt) AnyType	TCursor	M	5.0
cMax(const *fieldNum* SmallInt) Number	Table	M	1.0
cMax(const *fieldNum* SmallInt) Number	TCursor	M	1.0
cMax(const *tableName* String, const *fieldName* String) AnyType	Table	P	5.0
cMax(const *tableName* String, const *fieldName* String) Number	Table	P	1.0
cMax(const *tableName* String, const *fieldNum* SmallInt) AnyType	Table	P	5.0
cMax(const *tableName* String, const *fieldNum* SmallInt) Number	Table	P	1.0

continues

TABLE D.1. CONTINUED

Syntax	Base Class	M/P	Ver
cMin(const *fieldName* String) AnyType	Table	M	5.0
cMin(const *fieldName* String) AnyType	TCursor	M	5.0
cMin(const *fieldName* String) Number	Table	M	1.0
cMin(const *fieldName* String) Number	TCursor	M	1.0
cMin(const *fieldNum* SmallInt) AnyType	Table	M	5.0
cMin(const *fieldNum* SmallInt) AnyType	TCursor	M	5.0
cMin(const *fieldNum* SmallInt) Number	Table	M	1.0
cMin(const *fieldNum* SmallInt) Number	TCursor	M	1.0
cMin(const *tableName* String, const *fieldName* String) AnyType	Table	P	5.0
cMin(const *tableName* String, const *fieldName* String) Number	Table	P	1.0
cMin(const *tableName* String, const *fieldNum* SmallInt) AnyType	Table	P	5.0
cMin(const *tableName* String, const *fieldNum* SmallInt) Number	Table	P	1.0
cNpv(const *fieldName* String, const *discRate* AnyType) Number	Table	M	1.0
cNpv(const *fieldName* String, const *discRate* Number) Number	TCursor	M	1.0
cNpv(const *fieldNum* SmallInt, const *discRate* AnyType) Number	Table	M	1.0
cNpv(const *fieldNum* SmallInt, const *discRate* Number) Number	TCursor	M	1.0
cNpv(const *tableName* String, const *fieldName* String, const *discRate* AnyType) Number	Table	P	1.0
cNpv(const *tableName* String, const *fieldNum* SmallInt, const *discRate* AnyType) Number	Table	P	1.0
commit()	TextStream	M	1.0

continues

Syntax	Base Class	M/P	Ver
commitTransaction() Logical	Database	M	4.5
compact([const *regIndex* Logical]) Logical	Table	M	1.0
compact([const *regIndex* Logical]) Logical	TCursor	M	1.0
compileInformation(var *info* DynArray[] AnyType)	System	P	5.0
compilerTimeInfo(var *info* DynArray[] AnyType)	System	P	5.0
constantNameToValue(const constantName String) AnyType	System	P	1.0
constantValueToName(const *groupName* String, const *value* AnyType, var constName String) Logical	System	P	1.0
contains(const *item* String) Logical	Menu	M	1.0
contains(const *item* String) Logical	PopUpMenu	M	1.0
contains(const *value* AnyType) Logical	Array	M	1.0
contains(const *value* AnyType) Logical	DynArray	M	1.0
convertFieldInfo(const *sourceDriver* String, var *srcFieldDesc* DynArray[] AnyType, const *destDriver* AnyType, var *destFieldDesc* DynArray[] AnyType) Logical	Session	M	5.0
convertPointWithRespectTo(const *otherUIObject* UIObject, const *oldPoint* Point, var *convertedPoint* Point)	UIObject	M	1.0
copy(const *destTable* Table) Logical	Table	M	1.0
copy(const *destTableName* String) Logical	Table	M	1.0
copy(const *srcName* String, const *dstName* String) Logical	FileSystem	M	1.0
copy(const *tableName* String) Logical	TCursor	M	1.0
copy(const *tableName* String, const *destTable* Table) Logical	Table	P	1.0
copy(const *tableName* String, const *destTableName* String) Logical	Table	P	1.0

TABLE D.1. CONTINUED

Syntax	Base Class	M/P	Ver
copy(const *tableVar* Table) Logical	TCursor	M	1.0
copyFromArray(const *ar* Array[] AnyType) Logical	TCursor	M	1.0
copyFromArray(const *ar* Array[] AnyType) Logical	UIObject	M	1.0
copyFromArray(const *ar* DynArray[] AnyType) Logical	TCursor	M	1.0
copyToArray(var *ar* Array[] AnyType) Logical	UIObject	M	1.0
copyToToolbar() Logical	UIObject	M	5.0
cos() Number	Number	M	1.0
cosh() Number	Number	M	1.0
count() SmallInt	**Menu**	M	1.0
count() SmallInt	PopUpMenu	M	1.0
countOf(const *value* AnyType) LongInt	Array	M	1.0
cpuClockTime() LongInt	**System**	P	1.0
create() Logical	Form	M	1.0
create() Logical	**Library**	M	5.0
create() Logical	**Report**	M	1.0
create() Logical	**Script**	M	5.0
create(const *fileName* String) Logical	**TextStream**	M	1.0
create(const *objectType* SmallInt, const *x* LongInt, const *y* LongInt, const *w* LongInt, const *h* LongInt)	UIObject	M	1.0
create(const *objectType* SmallInt, const *x* LongInt, const *y* LongInt, const *w* LongInt, const *h* LongInt, const *container* UIObject)	UIObject	M	1.0

Syntax	Base Class	M/P	Ver
createIndex(const *attrib* DynArray[] AnyType, const *fields* Array[] String) Logical	Table	M	5.0
createIndex(const *attrib* DynArray[] AnyType, const *fields* Array[] String) Logical	TCursor	M	5.0
cSamStd(const *fieldName* String) Number	Table	M	1.0
cSamStd(const *fieldName* String) Number	TCursor	M	1.0
cSamStd(const *fieldNum* SmallInt) Number	Table	M	1.0
cSamStd(const *fieldNum* SmallInt) Number	TCursor	M	1.0
cSamStd(const *tableName* String, const *fieldName* String) Number	Table	P	1.0
cSamStd(const *tableName* String, const *fieldNum* SmallInt) Number	Table	P	1.0
cSamVar(const *fieldName* String) Number	Table	M	1.0
cSamVar(const *fieldName* String) Number	TCursor	M	1.0
cSamVar(const *fieldNum* SmallInt) Number	Table	M	1.0
cSamVar(const *fieldNum* SmallInt) Number	TCursor	M	1.0
cSamVar(const *tableName* String, const *fieldName* String) Number	Table	P	1.0
cSamVar(const *tableName* String, const *fieldNum* SmallInt) Number	Table	P	1.0
cStd(const *fieldName* String) Number	Table	M	1.0
cStd(const *fieldName* String) Number	TCursor	M	1.0
cStd(const *fieldNum* SmallInt) Number	Table	M	1.0
cStd(const *fieldNum* SmallInt) Number	TCursor	M	1.0
cStd(const *tableName* String, const *fieldName* String) Number	Table	P	1.0
cStd(const *tableName* String, const *fieldNum* SmallInt) Number	Table	P	1.0
cSum(const *fieldName* String) Number	Table	M	1.0

continues

TABLE D.1. CONTINUED

Syntax	Base Class	M/P	Ver
cSum(const *fieldName* String) Number	TCursor	M	1.0
cSum(const *fieldNum* SmallInt) Number	Table	M	1.0
cSum(const *fieldNum* SmallInt) Number	TCursor	M	1.0
cSum(const *tableName* String, const *fieldName* String) Number	Table	P	1.0
cSum(const *tableName* String, const *fieldNum* SmallInt) Number	Table	P	1.0
currency(const *value* AnyType) Currency	Currency	P	1.0
currentPage() SmallInt	**Report**	M	1.0
currRecord() Logical	TCursor	M	1.0
currRecord() Logical	UIObject	M	1.0
cVar(const *fieldName* String) Number	Table	M	1.0
cVar(const *fieldName* String) Number	TCursor	M	1.0
cVar(const *fieldNum* SmallInt) Number	Table	M	1.0
cVar(const *fieldNum* SmallInt) Number	TCursor	M	1.0
cVar(const *tableName* String, const *fieldName* String) Number	Table	P	1.0
cVar(const *tableName* String, const *fieldNum* SmallInt) Number	Table	P	1.0
data() LongInt	**MenuEvent**	M	1.0
data Type() String	AnyType	M	1.0
date(dateString String, *formatSpec* String) **Date**	**Date**	P	5.0
date([const *value* AnyType]) **Date**	Date	P	1.0
dateTime([const *value* AnyType]) **DateTime**	DateTime	P	1.0

Syntax	Base Class	M/P	Ver
dateVal(const *value* AnyType) *Date*	**Date**	P	1.0
day() SmallInt	**Date**	M	1.0
day() SmallInt	**DateTime**	M	1.0
daysInMonth() SmallInt	**Date**	M	1.0
daysInMonth() SmallInt	**DateTime**	M	1.0
debug()	**System**	P	1.0
delayScreenUpdates(const *yesNo* Logical)	Form	P	1.0
delete()	UIObject	M	1.0
delete() Logical	Table	M	1.0
delete(const *name* String) Logical	**FileSystem**	M	1.0
delete(const *tableName* String [, const *tableType* String]) Logical	Database	M	1.0
delete(const *tableName* String [, const *tableType* String]) Logical	Table	P	1.0
delete(const *tableName* String[, const *tableType* String]) Logical	Database	P	1.0
delete(const *tableVar* Table) Logical	Database	M	1.0
delete(const *tableVar* Table) Logical	Database	P	1.0
deleteDir(const *name* String) Logical	**FileSystem**	M	1.0
deleteRecord() Logical	TCursor	M	1.0
deleteRecord() Logical	UIObject	M	1.0
deliver() Logical	Form	M	1.0
deliver() Logical	**Library**	M	5.0
deliver() Logical	**Report**	M	5.0

continues

TABLE D.1. CONTINUED

Syntax	Base Class	M/P	Ver
deliver() Logical	Script	M	5.0
design() Logical	Form	M	1.0
design() Logical	Report	M	1.0
desktopMenu()	System	P	5.0
didFlyAway() Logical	TCursor	M	1.0
disableBreakMessage(const *yesNo* Logical) Logical	Form	P	1.0
disablePreviousError(const *yesNo* Logical) Logical	Form	P	5.0
distance(const *p* Point) Number	Point	M	1.0
dlgAdd(const *tableName* String)	System	P	1.0
dlgCopy(const *tableName* String)	System	P	1.0
dlgCreate(const *tableName* String)	System	P	1.0
dlgDelete(const *tableName* String)	System	P	1.0
dlgEmpty(const *tableName* String)	System	P	1.0
dlgExport(const *tableName* String)	System	P	1.0
dlgImportASCIIFix(const *fileName* String)	System	P	4.5
dlgImportASCIIVar(const *fileName* String)	System	P	4.5
dlgImportSpreadSheet(const *fileName* String)	System	P	4.5
dlgNetDrivers()	System	P	1.0
dlgNetLocks()	System	P	1.0
dlgNetRefresh()	System	P	1.0
dlgNetRetry()	System	P	1.0

Syntax	Base Class	M/P	Ver
dlgNetSetLocks()	System	P	1.0
dlgNetSystem()	System	P	1.0
dlgNetUserName()	System	P	1.0
dlgNetWho()	System	P	1.0
dlgRename(const *tableName* String)	System	P	1.0
dlgRestructure(const *tableName* String)	System	P	1.0
dlgSort(const *tableName* String)	System	P	1.0
dlgSubtract(const *tableName* String)	System	P	1.0
dlgTableInfo(const *tableName* String)	System	P	1.0
dmAddTable(const *tableName* String) Logical	Form	M	1.0
dmAddTable(const *tableName* String) Logical	Form	P	1.0
dmAddTable(const *tableName* String) Logical	Report	M	5.0
dmAttach(const *dmTableName* String) Logical	TCursor	M	5.0
dmAttach(tc *tcursor*, const *tableName* String) Logical	Form	M	5.0
dmAttach(tc *tcursor*, const *tableName* String) Logical	Form	P	5.0
dmBuildQueryString(var *queryString* String) Logical	Form	M	5.0
dmBuildQueryString(var *queryString* String) Logical	Form	P	5.0
dmBuildQueryString(var *queryString* String) Logical	Report	M	5.0
dmEnumLinkFields(var *masterTable* String, var *masterFields* Array[] String, const *detailTable* String, var *detailFields* Array[] String, var *detailIndex* String) Logical	Form	M	5.0
dmEnumLinkFields(var *masterTable* String, var *masterFields* Array[] String, const *detailTable* String, var *detailFields* Array[] String, var *detailIndex* String) Logical	Form	P	5.0

continues

TABLE D.1. CONTINUED

Syntax	Base Class	M/P	Ver
dmEnumLinkFields(var *masterTable* String, var *masterFields* Array[] String, const *detailTable* String, var *detailFields* Array[] String, var *indexName* String) Logical	Report	M	5.0
dmGet(const *tableName* String, const *fieldName* String, var *datum* AnyType) Logical	Form	M	1.0
dmGet(const *tableName* String, const *fieldName* String, var *datum* AnyType) Logical	Form	P	1.0
dmGetProperty(const *TableName* String, const *PropertyName* String) AnyType	Form	M	4.5
dmGetProperty(const *TableName* String, const *PropertyName* String) AnyType	Form	P	4.5
dmGetProperty(const *TableName* String, const *PropertyName* String) AnyType	Report	M	5.0
dmGetProperty(const *TableName* String, const *PropertyName* String, var *Value* AnyType) Logical	Form	M	5.0
dmGetProperty(const *TableName* String, const *PropertyName* String, var *Value* AnyType) Logical	Form	P	5.0
dmGetProperty(const *TableName* String, const *PropertyName* String, var *Value* AnyType) Logical	Report	M	5.0
dmHasTable(const *tableName* String) Logical	Form	M	1.0
dmHasTable(const *tableName* String) Logical	Form	P	1.0
dmHasTable(const *tableName* String) Logical	Report	M	5.0
dmLinkToFields(const *masterTable* String, const *masterFields* Array[] String, const *detailTable* String, const *detailFields* Array[] String) Logical	Form	M	4.5
dmLinkToFields(const *masterTable* String, const *masterFields* Array[] String, const *detailTable* String, const *detailFields* Array[] String) Logical	Form	P	4.5
dmLinkToFields(const *masterTable* String, const *masterFields* Array[] String, const *detailTable* String, const *detailFields* Array[] String) Logical	Report	M	5.0

Syntax	Base Class	M/P	Ver
dmLinkToIndex(const *masterTable* String, const *masterFields* Array[] String, const *detailTable* String, const *detailIndex* String) Logical	Form	M	5.0
dmLinkToIndex(const *masterTable* String, const *masterFields* Array[] String, const *detailTable* String, const *detailIndex* String) Logical	Form	P	5.0
dmLinkToIndex(const *masterTable* String, const *masterIndex* Array[] String, const *detailTable* String, const *detailIndex* String) Logical	Form	M	4.5
dmLinkToIndex(const *masterTable* String, const *masterIndex* Array[] String, const *detailTable* String, const *detailIndex* String) Logical	Form	P	4.5
dmLinkToIndex(const *masterTable* String, const *masterIndex* Array[] String, const *detailTable* String, const *detailIndex* String) Logical	Report	M	5.0
dmPut(const *tableName* String, const *fieldName* String, const *datum* AnyType) Logical	Form	M	1.0
dmPut(const *tableName* String, const *fieldName* String, const *datum* AnyType) Logical	Form	P	1.0
dmRemoveTable(const *tableName* String) Logical	Form	M	1.0
dmRemoveTable(const *tableName* String) Logical	Form	P	1.0
dmRemoveTable(const *tableName* String) Logical	Report	M	5.0
dmResync(const *dmTableName* String, var *paltbl* TCursor) Logical	TCursor	P	5.0
dmResync(const *tableName* String, var *tc tcursor*) Logical	Form	M	5.0
dmResync(const *tableName* String, var *tc tcursor*) Logical	Form	P	5.0
dmSetProperty(const *TableName* String, const *PropertyName* String, *Value* AnyType) Logical	Form	M	5.0
dmSetProperty(const *TableName* String, const *PropertyName* String, *Value* AnyType) Logical	Form	P	5.0
dmSetProperty(const *TableName* String, const *PropertyName* String, *Value* AnyType) Logical	Report	M	5.0

continues

TABLE D.1. CONTINUED

Syntax	Base Class	M/P	Ver
dmSetProperty(const *TableName* String, const *PropertyName* String, var *Value* AnyType) AnyType	Form	M	4.5
dmSetProperty(const *TableName* String, const *PropertyName* String, var *Value* AnyType) AnyType	Form	P	4.5
dmUnlink(const *masterTable* String, const *detailTable* String) Logical	Form	M	4.5
dmUnlink(const *masterTable* String, const *detailTable* String) Logical	Form	P	4.5
dmUnlink(const *masterTable* String, const *detailTable* String) Logical	**Report**	M	5.0
dow() String	Date	M	1.0
dow() String	DateTime	M	1.0
dowOrd() SmallInt	Date	M	1.0
dowOrd() SmallInt	DateTime	M	1.0
doy() SmallInt	Date	M	1.0
doy() SmallInt	DateTime	M	1.0
drives() String	FileSystem	M	1.0
dropGenFilter() Logical	Table	M	5.0
dropGenFilter() Logical	TCursor	M	5.0
dropGenFilter() Logical	UIObject	M	5.0
dropIndex(const *indexName* String [, const *tagName* String]) Logical	Table	M	1.0
dropIndex(const *indexName* String [, const *tagName* String]) Logical	TCursor	M	1.0
edit() Logical	TCursor	M	1.0
edit() Logical	UIObject	M	1.0

Syntax	Base Class	M/P	Ver
edit(const *name* String, const *verb* SmallInt) Logical	Ole	M	1.0
empty()	Array	M	1.0
empty()	DynArray	M	1.0
empty()	**Menu**	M	1.0
empty()	PopUpMenu	M	1.0
empty() Logical	Table	M	1.0
empty() Logical	TCursor	M	1.0
empty() Logical	UIObject	M	1.0
empty(const *tableName* String) Logical	Table	P	1.0
EnableExtendedCharacters(const *yesNo* Logical) Logical	**System**	P	5.0
end()	**TextStream**	M	1.0
end() Logical	TCursor	M	1.0
end() Logical	UIObject	M	1.0
endEdit() Logical	TCursor	M	1.0
endEdit() Logical	UIObject	M	1.0
enumAliasLoginInfo(const *tableName* String, const *aliasName* String) Logical	Session	M	5.0
enumAliasLoginInfo(const *tableName* String, const *aliasName* String) Logical	Session	P	5.0
enumAliasLoginInfo(const *tableName* String, const *databaseName* String) Logical	Session	M	4.5
enumAliasLoginInfo(const *tableName* String, const *databaseName* String) Logical	Session	P	4.5
enumAliasNames(const *tableName* String [, const *LoginInfoTableName* String]) Logical	Session	M	4.5
enumAliasNames(const *tableName* String [, const *LoginInfoTableName* String]) Logical	Session	P	4.5

continues

TABLE D.1. CONTINUED

Syntax	Base Class	M/P	Ver
enumAliasNames(const *tableName* String) Logical	**Session**	M	1.0
enumAliasNames(const *tableName* String) Logical	**Session**	P	1.0
enumAliasNames(var *aliasNames* Array[] String) Logical	**Session**	M	5.0
enumAliasNames(var *tableNames* Array[] String) Logical	**Session**	P	5.0
enumCapabilities(const *TblCap_TblName* String, const *FldCap_TblName* String [,const *IndxCap_TblName*]) Logical	Database	M	5.0
enumClipboardFormats(var *formatNames* Array[] String) SmallInt	**Binary**	M	5.0
enumDatabaseTables(const *tableName* String, const *aliasName* String, const *fileSpec* String) Logical	**Session**	M	5.0
enumDatabaseTables(const *tableName* String, const *aliasName* String, const *fileSpec* String) Logical	**Session**	P	5.0
enumDatabaseTables(const *tableName* String, const *databaseName* String, const *fileSpec* String) Logical	**Session**	M	1.0
enumDatabaseTables(const *tableName* String, const *databaseName* String, const *fileSpec* String) Logical	**Session**	P	1.0
enumDatabaseTables(var *tableNames* Array[] String, const *aliasName* String, const *fileSpec* String) Logical	**Session**	M	5.0
enumDataModel(const *tableName* String) Logical	**Form**	M	5.0
enumDataModel(const *tableName* String) Logical	**Form**	P	5.0
enumDataModel(const *tableName* String) Logical	**Report**	M	5.0
enumDesktopWindowNames(const *tableName* String) Logical	**System**	P	1.0
enumDesktopWindowNames(var *windowNames* Array[] String)	**System**	P	1.0

Syntax	Base Class	M/P	Ver
enumDriverCapabilities(const *DrvCap*_TblName String, const *TblCap*_TblName String, const *FldCap*_TblName String [,const *IndxCap*_TblName]) Logical	Session	P	4.5
enumDriverCapabilities(const *DrvCap*_TblName String, const *TblCap*_TblName String, const *FldCap*_TblName String)	Session	P	1.0
enumDriverInfo(const *tableName* String) Logical	Session	P	1.0
enumDriverNames(const *tableName* String) Logical	Session	P	1.0
enumDriverTopics(const *tableName* String) Logical	Session	P	1.0
enumEngineInfo(const *tableName* String) Logical	Session	P	1.0
enumEnvironmentStrings(var *values* DynArray[] String) Logical	System	P	5.0
enumFamily(var *members* DynArray[] String, const *tableName* String) Logical	Database	M	5.0
enumFamily(var *members* DynArray[] String, const *tableName* String) Logical	Database	P	5.0
enumFieldNames(var *fieldArray* Array[] String) Logical	Table	M	1.0
enumFieldNames(var *fieldArray* Array[] String) Logical	TCursor	M	1.0
enumFieldNames(var *fieldNames* Array[] String) Logical	UIObject	M	1.0
enumFieldNamesInIndex([const *indexName* String, [const *tagName* String,]] var *fieldNames* Array[] String) Logical	Table	M	1.0
enumFieldNamesInIndex([const *indexName* String, [const *tagName* String,]] var *fieldNames* Array[] String) Logical	TCursor	M	1.0
enumFieldStruct(const *ansTbl* String) Logical	Query	M	5.0
enumFieldStruct(const *db* Database, const *ansTbl* String) Logical	Query	M	5.0
enumFieldStruct(const *db* Database, var *ansTbl* TCursor) Logical	Query	M	5.0
enumFieldStruct(const *tableName* String) Logical	Table	M	1.0

continues

TABLE D.1. CONTINUED

Syntax	Base Class	M/P	Ver
enumFieldStruct(const *tableName* String) Logical	TCursor	M	1.0
enumFieldStruct(inMem TCursor) Logical	Table	M	5.0
enumFieldStruct(inMem TCursor) Logical	TCursor	M	5.0
enumFieldStruct(var *ansTbl* TCursor) Logical	Query	M	5.0
enumFileList(const *fileSpec* String, const *tableName* String)	**FileSystem**	M	1.0
enumFileList(const *fileSpec* String, var Array[ ] String)	**FileSystem**	M	1.0
enumFileList(const *fileSpec* String, var *fileNames* Array[ ] String)	**FileSystem**	M	4.5
enumFolder(const *tableName* String [, const *fileSpec* String]) Logical	Session	P	1.0
enumFolder(var *result* Array[ ] String [, const *fileSpec* String]) Logical	Session	P	1.0
enumFonts(const *tableName* String) Logical	System	P	1.0
enumFonts(deviceType SmallInt, *fontList* Array[ ] String) Logical	System	P	5.0
enumFontSizes(fontName String, *fontSizes* Array[ ] **Smallint**) Logical	System	P	5.0
enumFontStyles(fontName String, *fontStyles* Array[ ] **Smallint**) Logical	System	P	5.0
enumFormats(const *formatType* String, *formats dynArray*[ ] String) Logical	System	P	5.0
enumFormNames(var *formNames* Array[ ] String)	System	P	1.0
enumIndexStruct(const *tableName* String) Logical	Table	M	1.0
enumIndexStruct(const *tableName* String) Logical	TCursor	M	1.0
enumIndexStruct(inMem TCursor) Logical	Table	M	5.0
enumIndexStruct(inMem TCursor) Logical	TCursor	M	5.0
enumLocks(const *tableName* String) LongInt	TCursor	M	1.0
enumLocks(const *tableName* String) LongInt	UIObject	M	1.0

Syntax	Base Class	M/P	Ver
enumObjectNames(var *objectNames* Array[ ] String)	UIObject	M	4.5
enumObjectNames(var *objectNames* Array[ ] String)	UIObject	P	4.5
enumObjectNames(var *objectNames* Array[ ] String) Logical	UIObject	M	1.0
enumObjectNames(var *objectNames* Array[ ] String) Logical	UIObject	P	1.0
enumOpenDatabases(const *tableName* String) Logical	Session	M	1.0
enumOpenDatabases(const *tableName* String) Logical	Session	P	1.0
enumOpenDatabases(var *tableNames* Array[ ] String) Logical	Session	M	5.0
enumOpenDatabases(var *tableNames* Array[ ] String) Logical	Session	P	5.0
enumPrinters(var *printers* Array[ ] String) Logical	System	P	5.0
enumRefIntStruct(const *tableName* String) Logical	Table	M	1.0
enumRefIntStruct(const *tableName* String) Logical	TCursor	M	1.0
enumRefIntStruct(inMem TCursor) Logical	Table	M	5.0
enumRefIntStruct(inMem TCursor) Logical	TCursor	M	5.0
enumReportNames(var *reportNames* Array[ ] String)	System	P	1.0
enumRTLClassNames(const *tableName* String) Logical	System	P	1.0
enumRTLConstants(const *tableName* String) Logical	System	P	1.0
enumRTLErrors(const *tableName* String) Logical	System	P	5.0
enumRTLMethods(const *tableName* String) Logical	System	P	1.0
enumSecStruct(const *tableName* String) Logical	Table	M	1.0
enumSecStruct(const *tableName* String) Logical	TCursor	M	1.0
enumSecStruct(inMem TCursor) Logical	Table	M	5.0

continues

TABLE D.1. CONTINUED

Syntax	Base Class	M/P	Ver
enumSecStruct(inMem TCursor) Logical	TCursor	M	5.0
enumServerClassNames(var *classes* DynArray[ ] String) Logical	Ole	M	5.0
enumSource(const *tableName* String [, const *recurse* Logical]) Logical	Form	M	1.0
enumSource(const *tableName* String [, const *recurse* Logical]) Logical	Form	P	1.0
enumSource(const *tableName* String [, const *recurse* Logical]) Logical	**Library**	M	1.0
enumSource(const *tableName* String [, const *recurse* Logical]) Logical	**Script**	M	5.0
enumSource(const *tableName* String [, const *recurse* Logical]) Logical	UIObject	M	1.0
enumSourceToFile(const *fileName* String [, const *recurse* Logical]) Logical	Form	M	1.0
enumSourceToFile(const *fileName* String [, const *recurse* Logical]) Logical	Form	P	1.0
enumSourceToFile(const *fileName* String [, const *recurse* Logical]) Logical	**Library**	M	1.0
enumSourceToFile(const *fileName* String [, const *recurse* Logical]) Logical	**Script**	M	5.0
enumSourceToFile(const *fileName* String [, const *recurse* Logical]) Logical	UIObject	M	1.0
enumTableLinks(const *tableName* String) Logical	Form	M	1.0
enumTableLinks(const *tableName* String) Logical	Form	P	1.0
enumTableLinks(const *tableName* String) Logical	**Report**	M	5.0
enumTableProperties(const *tableName* String) Logical	TCursor	M	1.0
enumUIClasses(const *tableName* String) Logical	UIObject	P	1.0
enumUIObjectNames(const *tableName* String) Logical	Form	M	1.0
enumUIObjectNames(const *tableName* String) Logical	**Report**	M	1.0
enumUIObjectNames(const *tableName* String) Logical	UIObject	M	1.0

Syntax	Base Class	M/P	Ver
enumUIObjectNames(const *tableName* String) Logical	UIObject	P	1.0
enumUIObjectProperties(const *tableName* String) Logical	Form	M	1.0
enumUIObjectProperties(const *tableName* String) Logical	**Report**	M	1.0
enumUIObjectProperties(const *tableName* String) Logical	UIObject	M	1.0
enumUIObjectProperties(const *tableName* String) Logical	UIObject	P	1.0
enumUIObjectProperties(properties DynArray[] String) Logical	UIObject	M	5.0
enumUsers(const *tableName* String) LongInt	**Session**	P	1.0
enumUsers(var *userNames* Array[] String) LongInt	**Session**	P	5.0
enumVerbs(var *verbs* DynArray[] SmallInt) Logical	**Ole**	M	1.0
enumWindowNames(const *tableName* String) Logical	System	P	1.0
enumWindowNames(var *windowNames* Array[] String)	System	P	1.0
eof() Logical	**TextStream**	M	1.0
eot() Logical	TCursor	M	1.0
errorClear()	**System**	P	1.0
errorCode() LongInt	**ActionEvent**	M	1.0
errorCode() LongInt	**ErrorEvent**	M	1.0
errorCode() LongInt	Event	M	1.0
errorCode() LongInt	**KeyEvent**	M	1.0
errorCode() LongInt	**MenuEvent**	M	1.0
errorCode() LongInt	**MouseEvent**	M	1.0
errorCode() LongInt	**MoveEvent**	M	1.0

continues

TABLE D.1. CONTINUED

Syntax	Base Class	M/P	Ver
errorCode() LongInt	StatusEvent	M	1.0
errorCode() LongInt	TimerEvent	M	1.0
errorCode() LongInt	ValueEvent	M	1.0
errorCode() SmallInt	ActionEvent	M	5.0
errorCode() SmallInt	ErrorEvent	M	5.0
errorCode() SmallInt	Event	M	5.0
errorCode() SmallInt	MenuEvent	M	5.0
errorCode() SmallInt	MoveEvent	M	5.0
errorCode() SmallInt	StatusEvent	M	5.0
errorCode() SmallInt	System	P	1.0
errorCode() SmallInt	TimerEvent	M	5.0
errorCode() SmallInt	ValueEvent	M	5.0
errorHasErrorCode(const *errorCode* SmallInt) Logical	System	P	4.5
errorHasNativeErrorCode(const *errorCode* LongInt) Logical	System	P	4.5
errorIsTrapOnWarnings() Logical	System	P	5.0
errorLog(const *errorCode* SmallInt, const *errorMessage* String)	System	P	1.0
errorMessage() String	System	P	1.0
errorNativeCode() LongInt	System	P	4.5
errorPop() Logical	System	P	1.0
errorShow() Logical	System	P	1.0

Syntax	Base Class	M/P	Ver
errorShow(const *topHelp* String) Logical	System	P	4.5
errorShow(const *topHelp* String, const *bottomHelp* String) Logical	System	P	1.0
errorShow(const *topHelp*) Logical	System	P	1.0
errorTrapOnWarnings(const *yesNo* Logical)	System	P	1.0
exchange(const *index1* LongInt, const *index2* LongInt)	Array	M	1.0
execMethod(const *methodName* String)	Library	M	1.0
execMethod(const *methodName* String)	UIObject	M	1.0
execMethod(const *methodName* String)	UIObject	P	1.0
execute(const *command* String) Logical	DDE	M	1.0
execute(const *programName* String) Logical	System	P	1.0
execute(const *programName* String, const *wait* Logical) Logical	System	P	1.0
execute(const *programName* String, const *wait* Logical, const *displayMode* SmallInt) Logical	System	P	1.0
executeQBE( ) Logical	Query	M	1.0
executeQBE(const *ansTbl* String) Logical	Query	M	1.0
executeQBE(const *ansTbl* Table) Logical	Query	M	1.0
executeQBE(const *db* Database, const *qbeVar* Query) Logical	Query	P	4.5
executeQBE(const *db* Database, const *qbeVar* Query, const *ansTbl* String) Logical	Query	P	4.5
executeQBE(const *db* Database, const *qbeVar* Query, const *ansTbl* Table) Logical	Query	P	4.5
executeQBE(const *db* Database, const *qbeVar* Query, var *ansTbl* TCursor) Logical	Query	P	4.5
executeQBE(const *qbeVar* Query) Logical	Database	M	1.0
executeQBE(const *qbeVar* Query) Logical	Database	P	1.0

continues

TABLE D.1. CONTINUED

Syntax	Base Class	M/P	Ver
executeQBE(const *qbeVar* Query, const *ansTbl* String) Logical	Database	M	1.0
executeQBE(const *qbeVar* Query, const *ansTbl* String) Logical	Database	P	1.0
executeQBE(const *qbeVar* Query, const *ansTbl* Table) Logical	Database	M	1.0
executeQBE(const *qbeVar* Query, const *ansTbl* Table) Logical	Database	P	1.0
executeQBE(const *qbeVar* Query, var *ansTbl* TCursor) Logical	Database	M	1.0
executeQBE(const *qbeVar* Query, var *ansTbl* TCursor) Logical	Database	P	1.0
executeQBE(var *ansTbl* TCursor) Logical	Query	M	1.0
executeQBEFile(const *fileName* String) Logical	Database	M	1.0
executeQBEFile(const *fileName* String) Logical	Database	P	1.0
executeQBEFile(const *fileName* String, const *ansTbl* String) Logical	Database	M	1.0
executeQBEFile(const *fileName* String, const *ansTbl* String) Logical	Database	P	1.0
executeQBEFile(const *fileName* String, const *ansTbl* Table) Logical	Database	M	1.0
executeQBEFile(const *fileName* String, const *ansTbl* Table) Logical	Database	P	1.0
executeQBEFile(const *fileName* String, var *ansTbl* TCursor) Logical	Database	M	1.0
executeQBEFile(const *fileName* String, var *ansTbl* TCursor) Logical	Database	P	1.0
executeQBEFile([const *db* Database,] const *fileName* String) Logical	Query	P	4.5
executeQBEFile([const *db* Database,] const *fileName* String, const *ansTbl* String) Logical	Query	P	4.5
executeQBEFile([const *db* Database,] const *fileName* String, const *ansTbl* Table) Logical	Query	P	4.5

Syntax	Base Class	M/P	Ver
executeQBEFile([const *db* Database,] const *fileName* String, var *ansTbl* TCursor) Logical	Query	P	4.5
executeQBEString(const qbeString String) Logical	Database	M	1.0
executeQBEString(const qbeString String) Logical	Database	P	1.0
executeQBEString(const qbeString String, const *ansTbl* String) Logical	Database	M	1.0
executeQBEString(const qbeString String, const *ansTbl* String) Logical	Database	P	1.0
executeQBEString(const qbeString String, const *ansTbl* Table) Logical	Database	M	1.0
executeQBEString(const qbeString String, const *ansTbl* Table) Logical	Database	P	1.0
executeQBEString(const qbeString String, var *ansTbl* TCursor) Logical	Database	M	1.0
executeQBEString(const qbeString String, var *ansTbl* TCursor) Logical	Database	P	1.0
executeQBEString([const *db* Database,] const qbeString String) Logical	Query	P	4.5
executeQBEString([const *db* Database,] const qbeString String, const *ansTbl* String) Logical	Query	P	4.5
executeQBEString([const *db* Database,] const qbeString String, const *ansTbl* Table) Logical	Query	P	4.5
executeQBEString([const *db* Database,] const qbeString String, var *ansTbl* TCursor) Logical	Query	P	4.5
executeSQL(const *db* Database) Logical	SQL	M	4.5
executeSQL(const *db* Database, const *ansTbl* String) Logical	SQL	M	4.5
executeSQL(const *db* Database, const *ansTbl* Table) Logical	SQL	M	4.5
executeSQL(const *db* Database, const *qbeVar* SQL) Logical	SQL	P	4.5
executeSQL(const *db* Database, const *qbeVar* SQL, const *ansTbl* String) Logical	SQL	P	4.5

continues

TABLE D.1. CONTINUED

Syntax	Base Class	M/P	Ver
executeSQL(const *db* Database, const *qbeVar SQL*, const *ansTbl* Table) Logical	SQL	P	4.5
executeSQL(const *db* Database, const *qbeVar SQL*, var *ansTbl* TCursor) Logical	SQL	P	4.5
executeSQL(const *db* Database, var *ansTbl* TCursor) Logical	SQL	M	4.5
executeSQLFile(const *db* Database, const *fileName* String) Logical	SQL	P	4.5
executeSQLFile(const *db* Database, const *fileName* String, const *ansTbl* String) Logical	SQL	P	4.5
executeSQLFile(const *db* Database, const *fileName* String, const *ansTbl* Table) Logical	SQL	P	4.5
executeSQLFile(const *db* Database, const *fileName* String, ar *ansTbl* TCursor) Logical	SQL	P	4.5
executeSQLString(const *db* Database, const *sqlString* String) Logical	SQL	P	4.5
executeSQLString(const *db* Database, const *sqlString* String, const *ansTbl* String)	SQL	P	4.5
executeSQLString(const *db* Database, const *sqlString* String, const *ansTbl* Table) Logical	SQL	P	4.5
executeSQLString(const *db* Database, const *sqlString* String, var *ansTbl* TCursor) Logical	SQL	P	4.5
executeString(const *scriptText* String) AnyType	System	P	4.5
existDrive(const *driveLetter* String) Logical	FileSystem	M	1.0
exit()	System	P	1.0
exp() Number	Number	M	1.0
exportASCIIFix(const *tableName* String, const *fileName* String, const *specTableName* String [, const *ANSI* Logical]) Logical	System	P	4.5

Syntax	Base Class	M/P	Ver
exportASCIIVar(const *tableName* String, const *fileName* String [, const *separator* String, const *delimiter* String, const *allFieldsDelimited* Logical, const *ANSI* Logical]) Logical	System	P	4.5
exportParadoxDOS(const *tableName* String, const *fileName* String) Logical	System	P	5.0
exportSpreadSheet(const *tableName* String, const *fileName* String [, const *makeRowHeaders* Logical]) Logical	System	P	4.5
fail()	System	P	1.0
fail(const *errorNumber* SmallInt, const *errorMessage* String)	System	P	1.0
familyRights(const *rights* String) Logical	Table	M	1.0
familyRights(const *rights* String) Logical	TCursor	M	1.0
familyRights(const *tableName* String, const *rights* AnyType) Logical	Table	P	1.0
familyRights(const *tableName* String, const *rights* String) Logical	Table	P	5.0
fieldName(const *fieldNum* SmallInt) String	Table	M	1.0
fieldName(const *fieldNum* SmallInt) String	TCursor	M	1.0
fieldName(const *tableName* String, const *fieldNum* SmallInt) String	Table	P	1.0
fieldNo(const *fieldName* String) SmallInt	Table	M	1.0
fieldNo(const *fieldName* String) SmallInt	TCursor	M	1.0
fieldNo(const *tableName* String, const *fieldName* String) SmallInt	Table	P	1.0
fieldRights(const *fieldName* String, const *rights* String) Logical	TCursor	M	1.0
fieldRights(const *fieldNum* SmallInt, const *rights* String) Logical	TCursor	M	1.0
fieldSize(const *fieldName* String) SmallInt	TCursor	M	1.0
fieldSize(const *fieldNum* SmallInt) SmallInt	TCursor	M	1.0
fieldType(const *fieldName* String) String	Table	M	1.0

continues

TABLE D.1. CONTINUED

Syntax	Base Class	M/P	Ver
fieldType(const *fieldName* String) String	TCursor	M	1.0
fieldType(const *fieldNum* SmallInt) String	Table	M	1.0
fieldType(const *fieldNum* SmallInt) String	TCursor	M	1.0
fieldType(const *tableName* String, const *fieldName* String) String	Table	P	1.0
fieldType(const *tableName* String, const *fieldNum* SmallInt) String	Table	P	1.0
fieldUnits2(const *fieldName* String) SmallInt	TCursor	M	1.0
fieldUnits2(const *fieldNum* SmallInt) SmallInt	TCursor	M	1.0
fieldValue(const *fieldName* String, var *result* AnyType) Logical	TCursor	M	1.0
fieldValue(const *fieldNum* SmallInt, var *result* AnyType) Logical	TCursor	M	1.0
fileBrowser(var *selectedFile* String) Logical	**System**	P	1.0
fileBrowser(var *selectedFile* String, var *browserInfo* FileBrowserInfo) Logical	**System**	P	1.0
fileBrowser(var *selectedFiles* Array[ ] String) Logical	**System**	P	1.0
fileBrowser(var *selectedFiles* Array[ ] String, var *browserInfo* FileBrowserInfo) Logical	**System**	P	1.0
fill(const *fillCharacter* String, const numberOfRepetitions SmallInt) String	String	P	1.0
fill(const *value* AnyType)	Array	M	1.0
findFirst(const *pattern* String) Logical	**FileSystem**	M	1.0
findNext() Logical	**FileSystem**	M	1.0
floor() Number	Number	M	1.0
forceRefresh() Logical	TCursor	M	4.5
forceRefresh() Logical	UIObject	M	4.5
format(const *formatSpec* String, const *value* AnyType) String	String	P	1.0

Syntax	Base Class	M/P	Ver
formatAdd(const *formatName* String, const *formatSpec* String) Logical	System	P	5.0
formatAdd(const *formatName* String, const *formatSpec* String) String	System	P	1.0
formatDelete(const *formatName* String) Logical	System	P	1.0
formatExist(const *formatName* String) Logical	System	P	1.0
formatGetSpec(const *formatName* String) String	System	P	5.0
formatSetCurrencyDefault(const *formatName* String) Logical	System	P	1.0
formatSetDateDefault(const *formatName* String) Logical	System	P	1.0
formatSetDateTimeDefault(const *formatName* String) Logical	System	P	1.0
formatSetLogicalDefault(const *formatName* String) Logical	System	P	1.0
formatSetLongIntDefault(const *formatName* String) Logical	System	P	1.0
formatSetNumberDefault(const *formatName* String) Logical	System	P	1.0
formatSetSmallIntDefault(const *formatName* String) Logical	System	P	1.0
formatSetTimeDefault(const *formatName* String) Logical	System	P	1.0
formatStringToDate(DateString String, *FormatSpec* String) *Date*	System	P	5.0
formatStringToNumber(NumberString String, *FormatSpec* String) Number	System	P	5.0
formCaller(var *caller* Form) Logical	Form	P	1.0
formReturn()	Form	P	1.0
formReturn(const *returnValue* AnyType)	Form	P	1.0
fraction() Number	Number	M	1.0
freeDiskSpace(const *driveLetter* String) LongInt	FileSystem	M	1.0
fromHex(const *value* String) LongInt	AnyType	P	5.0
fullName(const *fileName* String) String	FileSystem	P	5.0

continues

TABLE D.1. CONTINUED

Syntax	Base Class	M/P	Ver
fullName() String	**FileSystem**	M	1.0
fv(const *interestRate* Number, const *periods* Number) Number	Number	M	1.0
getAliasPath(const *aliasName* String) String	**Session**	M	1.0
getAliasPath(const *aliasName* String) String	**Session**	P	1.0
getAliasProperty(const *aliasName* String, const *property* String) String	**Session**	M	4.5
getAliasProperty(const *aliasName* String, const *property* String) String	**Session**	P	4.5
getBoundingBox(var *topLeft* Point, var *bottomRight* Point)	UIObject	M	1.0
getDefaultPrinterStyleSheet() String	**System**	P	5.0
getDefaultScreenStyleSheet() String	**System**	P	5.0
getDestination(var *dest* UIObject)	MoveEvent	M	1.0
getDir() String	**FileSystem**	M	1.0
getDrive() String	**FileSystem**	M	1.0
getFileAccessRights(const *fileName* String) String	**FileSystem**	P	1.0
getFileName() String	Form	M	1.0
getFileName() String	Form	P	1.0
getFileName() String	**Report**	M	5.0
getGenFilter(filters Array[ ] String) Logical	Table	M	5.0
getGenFilter(filters Array[ ] String) Logical	TCursor	M	5.0
getGenFilter(filters Array[ ] String) Logical	UIObject	M	5.0
getGenFilter(filters Array[ ] String, *names* Array[ ] AnyType) Logical	Table	M	5.0

Syntax	Base Class	M/P	Ver
getGenFilter(filters Array[ ] String, *names* Array[ ] AnyType) Logical	TCursor	M	5.0
getGenFilter(filters Array[ ] String, *names* Array[ ] AnyType) Logical	UIObject	M	5.0
getGenFilter(filters DynArray[ ] String) Logical	Table	M	5.0
getGenFilter(filters DynArray[ ] String) Logical	TCursor	M	5.0
getGenFilter(filters DynArray[ ] String) Logical	UIObject	M	5.0
getGenFilter(fltr String) Logical	Table	M	5.0
getGenFilter(fltr String) Logical	TCursor	M	5.0
getGenFilter(fltr String) Logical	UIObject	M	5.0
getIndexName(String *indexName*) *logical*	TCursor	M	5.0
getIndexName(String *indexName*, String *TagName*) *logical*	TCursor	M	5.0
getKeys(var *keyNames* Array[ ] String)	DynArray	M	1.0
getLanguageDriver() String	System	P	5.0
getLanguageDriver() String	TCursor	M	1.0
getLanguageDriverDesc() String	TCursor	M	1.0
getMenuChoiceAttribute(const *menuChoice* String) SmallInt	Menu	P	1.0
getMenuChoiceAttributeById(const *menuId* SmallInt) SmallInt	Menu	P	1.0
getMousePosition(var *p* Point)	MouseEvent	M	1.0
getMousePosition(var *xPosition* LongInt, var *yPosition* LongInt)	MouseEvent	M	1.0
getMouseScreenPosition() Point	System	P	1.0
getNetUserName() String	Session	M	1.0
getNetUserName() String	Session	P	1.0

continues

	TABLE D.1. CONTINUED			
Syntax		Base Class	M/P	Ver
getObjectHit(var **target** UIObject) Logical		**MouseEvent**	M	1.0
getPosition(var **x** LongInt, var **y** LongInt, var **w** LongInt, var **h** LongInt)		**Application**	M	1.0
getPosition(var **x** LongInt, var **y** LongInt, var **w** LongInt, var **h** LongInt)		Form	M	1.0
getPosition(var **x** LongInt, var **y** LongInt, var **w** LongInt, var **h** LongInt)		Form	P	1.0
getPosition(var **x** LongInt, var **y** LongInt, var **w** LongInt, var **h** LongInt)		**Report**	M	1.0
getPosition(var **x** LongInt, var **y** LongInt, var **w** LongInt, var **h** LongInt)		TableView	M	1.0
getPosition(var **x** LongInt, var **y** LongInt, var **w** LongInt, var **h** LongInt)		UIObject	M	1.0
getProperty(const **propertyName** String) AnyType		UIObject	M	1.0
getPropertyAsString(const **propertyName** String) String		UIObject	M	1.0
getProtoProperty(const **ObjType** SmallInt, **propertyName** String) AnyType		Form	M	5.0
getProtoProperty(const **ObjType** SmallInt, **propertyName** String) AnyType		Form	P	5.0
getProtoProperty(const **ObjType** SmallInt, **propertyName** String) AnyType		**Report**	M	5.0
getQueryRestartOptions() SmallInt		Database	M	1.0
getQueryRestartOptions() SmallInt		Database	P	1.0
getQueryRestartOptions() SmallInt		Query	M	5.0
getQueryRestartOptions() SmallInt		**SQL**	M	5.0
getRange(var **result** Array[ ] AnyType) Logical		UIObject	M	5.0
getRange(var **result** Array[ ] AnyType) Logical		UIObject	P	5.0
getRange(var **result** Array[ ] String) Logical		Table	M	5.0
getRange(var **result** Array[ ] String) Logical		TCursor	M	5.0

Syntax	Base Class	M/P	Ver
getRGB(const **rgb** LongInt, var **red** SmallInt, var **green** SmallInt, var **blue** SmallInt)	UIObject	P	1.0
getSelectedObjects(var **objects** Array[ ] UIObject) SmallInt	Form	P	5.0
getServerName() String	Ole	M	1.0
getStyleSheet() String	Form	M	5.0
getStyleSheet() String	Form	P	5.0
getStyleSheet() String	Report	M	5.0
getTarget(var **target** UIObject)	ActionEvent	M	1.0
getTarget(var **target** UIObject)	ErrorEvent	M	1.0
getTarget(var **target** UIObject)	Event	M	1.0
getTarget(var **target** UIObject)	KeyEvent	M	1.0
getTarget(var **target** UIObject)	MenuEvent	M	1.0
getTarget(var **target** UIObject)	MouseEvent	M	4.5
getTarget(var **target** UIObject)	MoveEvent	M	1.0
getTarget(var **target** UIObject)	StatusEvent	M	1.0
getTarget(var **target** UIObject)	TimerEvent	M	1.0
getTarget(var **target** UIObject)	ValueEvent	M	1.0
getTarget(var **target** UIObject) Logical	MouseEvent	M	1.0
getTitle() String	Application	M	1.0
getTitle() String	Form	M	1.0
getTitle() String	Form	P	1.0
getTitle() String	Report	M	1.0

continues

TABLE D.1. CONTINUED

Syntax	Base Class	M/P	Ver
getTitle() String	TableView	M	1.0
getUserLevel() String	System	P	5.0
getValidFileExtensions(const *objectType* String) String	FileSystem	P	1.0
grow(const *increment* LongInt)	Array	M	1.0
hasMenuChoiceAttribute(const *menuAttribute* SmallInt, const *testAttributes* SmallInt) Logical	Menu	P	1.0
hasMouse() Logical	UIObject	M	1.0
helpOnHelp() Logical	System	P	1.0
helpQuit(const *helpFileName* String) Logical	System	P	1.0
helpSetIndex(const *helpFileName* String, const *indexId* LongInt) Logical	System	P	1.0
helpShowContext(const *helpFileName* String, const *helpId* LongInt) Logical	System	P	1.0
helpShowIndex(const *helpFileName* String) Logical	System	P	1.0
helpShowTopic(const *helpFileName* String, const *topicKey* String) Logical	System	P	1.0
helpShowTopicInKeywordTable(const *helpFileName* String, const *keyTableLetter* String, const *topicKey* String) Logical	System	P	1.0
hide()	Application	M	1.0
hide()	Form	M	1.0
hide()	Form	P	1.0
hide()	Report	M	1.0
hide()	TableView	M	1.0
hideSpeedBar()	Form	P	1.0

Syntax	Base Class	M/P	Ver
hideToolBar()	Form	P	5.0
home()	TextStream	M	1.0
home() Logical	TCursor	M	1.0
home() Logical	UIObject	M	1.0
hour() SmallInt	DateTime	M	1.0
hour() SmallInt	Time	M	1.0
id() SmallInt	ActionEvent	M	1.0
id() SmallInt	MenuEvent	M	1.0
ignoreCaseInLocate([const *yesNo* Logical])	Session	P	1.0
ignoreCaseInStringCompares(const *yes_no* Logical)	String	P	1.0
importASCIIFix(const *fileName* String, const *tableName* String, const *specTableName* String [, const *ANSI* Logical]) Logical	System	P	4.5
importASCIIVar(const *fileName* String, const *tableName* String [, const *separator* String, const *delimiter* String, const *allFieldsDelimited* Logical, const *ANSI* Logical]) Logical	System	P	4.5
importSpreadSheet(const *fileName* String, const *tableName* String, const *fromCell* String, const *toCell* String [, const *getFieldNames* Logical]) Logical	System	P	4.5
indexOf(const *value* AnyType) LongInt	Array	M	1.0
initRecord() Logical	TCursor	M	1.0
insert(const *index* LongInt)	Array	M	1.0
insert(const *index* LongInt, const numberOfElements LongInt)	Array	M	1.0
insertAfter(const *keyItem* AnyType, const *insertedItem* AnyType)	Array	M	1.0

continues

Syntax	Base Class	M/P	Ver
TABLE D.1. CONTINUED			
insertAfterRecord() Logical	TCursor	M	1.0
insertAfterRecord() Logical	UIObject	M	1.0
insertAfterRecord(const *cursor* TCursor) Logical	TCursor	M	1.0
insertBefore(const *keyItem* AnyType, const *insertedItem* AnyType)	Array	M	1.0
insertBeforeRecord() Logical	TCursor	M	1.0
insertBeforeRecord() Logical	UIObject	M	1.0
insertBeforeRecord(const *cursor* TCursor) Logical	TCursor	M	1.0
insertFirst(const *value* AnyType)	Array	M	1.0
insertObject() Logical	Ole	M	5.0
insertObject(const *className* String) Logical	Ole	M	5.0
insertObject(const *fileName* String, const *link* Logical) Logical	Ole	M	5.0
insertRecord() Logical	TCursor	M	1.0
insertRecord() Logical	UIObject	M	1.0
insertRecord(const *cursor* TCursor) Logical	TCursor	M	1.0
instantiateView(const *tableName* String) Logical	TCursor	M	5.0
instantiateView(const *tableVar* Table) Logical	TCursor	M	5.0
int(const *value* AnyType) SmallInt	SmallInt	P	1.0
isAbove(const *p* Point) Logical	Point	M	1.0
isAdvancedWildcardsInLocate() Logical	Session	P	1.0
isAltKeyDown() Logical	KeyEvent	M	1.0
isAssigned() Logical	AnyType	M	1.0

Syntax	Base Class	M/P	Ver
isAssigned() Logical	Database	M	1.0
isAssigned() Logical	FileSystem	M	5.0
isAssigned() Logical	Form	M	5.0
isAssigned() Logical	Library	M	5.0
isAssigned() Logical	Menu	M	5.0
isAssigned() Logical	PopUpMenu	M	5.0
isAssigned() Logical	Query	M	1.0
isAssigned() Logical	Report	M	5.0
isAssigned() Logical	Script	M	5.0
isAssigned() Logical	Session	M	1.0
isAssigned() Logical	SQL	M	4.5
isAssigned() Logical	Table	M	1.0
isAssigned() Logical	TableView	M	5.0
isAssigned() Logical	TCursor	M	1.0
isAssigned() Logical	TextStream	M	5.0
isBelow(const *p* Point) Logical	Point	M	1.0
isBlank() Logical	AnyType	M	1.0
isBlankZero() Logical	Session	M	1.0
isBlankZero() Logical	Session	P	1.0
isContainerValid() Logical	UIObject	P	1.0
isControlKeyDown() Logical	KeyEvent	M	1.0

continues

TABLE D.1. CONTINUED

Syntax	Base Class	M/P	Ver
isControlKeyDown() Logical	**MouseEvent**	M	1.0
isDesign() Logical	Form	M	5.0
isDesign() Logical	**Report**	M	5.0
isDir(const **dirName** String) Logical	**FileSystem**	P	1.0
isEdit() Logical	TCursor	M	1.0
isEdit() Logical	UIObject	M	1.0
isEmpty() Logical	Table	M	1.0
isEmpty() Logical	TCursor	M	1.0
isEmpty() Logical	UIObject	M	1.0
isEmpty(const **tableName** String) Logical	Table	P	1.0
isEncrypted() Logical	Table	M	1.0
isEncrypted() Logical	TCursor	M	1.0
isEncrypted(const **tableName** String) Logical	Table	P	1.0
isErrorTrapOnWarnings() Logical	**System**	P	5.0
isExecuteQBEFileLocal(const **fileName** String) Logical	Database	M	4.5
isExecuteQBEFileLocal(const **fileName** String) Logical	Database	P	4.5
isExecuteQBELocal() Logical	Query	M	5.0
isExecuteQBELocal(const **db database**, const **qbeVar** Query) Logical	Query	P	5.0
isExecuteQBELocal(const **qbeVar** Query) Logical	Database	M	4.5
isExecuteQBELocal(const **qbeVar** Query) Logical	Database	P	4.5
isExecuteQBEStringLocal(const **qbeString** String) Logical	Database	M	4.5

Syntax	Base Class	M/P	Ver
isExecuteQBEStringLocal(const *qbeString* String) Logical	Database	P	4.5
isFile(const *fileName* String) Logical	FileSystem	P	1.0
isFirstTime() Logical	ActionEvent	M	1.0
isFirstTime() Logical	ErrorEvent	M	1.0
isFirstTime() Logical	Event	M	1.0
isFirstTime() Logical	KeyEvent	M	1.0
isFirstTime() Logical	MenuEvent	M	1.0
isFirstTime() Logical	MouseEvent	M	1.0
isFirstTime() Logical	MoveEvent	M	1.0
isFirstTime() Logical	StatusEvent	M	1.0
isFirstTime() Logical	TimerEvent	M	1.0
isFirstTime() Logical	ValueEvent	M	1.0
isFixed(const *driveLetter* String) Logical	FileSystem	M	1.0
isFixedType() Logical	AnyType	M	1.0
isFromUI() Logical	KeyEvent	M	1.0
isFromUI() Logical	MenuEvent	M	1.0
isFromUI() Logical	MouseEvent	M	1.0
isIgnoreCaseInLocate() Logical	Session	P	1.0
isIgnoreCaseInStringCompares() Logical	String	P	1.0
isInMemoryTCursor() Logical	TCursor	M	5.0
isInside() Logical	MouseEvent	M	1.0

continues

TABLE D.1. CONTINUED

Syntax	Base Class	M/P	Ver
isLastMouseClickedValid() Logical	UIObject	P	1.0
isLastMouseRightClickedValid() Logical	UIObject	P	1.0
isLeapYear() Logical	Date	M	1.0
isLeapYear() Logical	DateTime	M	1.0
isLeft(const p Point) Logical	Point	M	1.0
isLeftDown() Logical	MouseEvent	M	1.0
isLinked() Logical	Ole	M	5.0
isMaximized() Logical	Application	M	1.0
isMaximized() Logical	Form	M	1.0
isMaximized() Logical	Form	P	1.0
isMaximized() Logical	Report	M	1.0
isMaximized() Logical	TableView	M	1.0
isMiddleDown() Logical	MouseEvent	M	1.0
isMinimized() Logical	Application	M	1.0
isMinimized() Logical	Form	M	1.0
isMinimized() Logical	Form	P	1.0
isMinimized() Logical	Report	M	1.0
isMinimized() Logical	TableView	M	1.0
isOnSQLServer() Logical	TCursor	M	4.5
isOpenOnUniqueIndex() Logical	TCursor	M	4.5

Syntax	Base Class	M/P	Ver
isPreFilter() Logical	ActionEvent	M	1.0
isPreFilter() Logical	ErrorEvent	M	1.0
isPreFilter() Logical	Event	M	1.0
isPreFilter() Logical	KeyEvent	M	1.0
isPreFilter() Logical	MenuEvent	M	1.0
isPreFilter() Logical	MouseEvent	M	1.0
isPreFilter() Logical	MoveEvent	M	1.0
isPreFilter() Logical	StatusEvent	M	1.0
isPreFilter() Logical	TimerEvent	M	1.0
isPreFilter() Logical	ValueEvent	M	1.0
isRecordDeleted() Logical	TCursor	M	1.0
isRecordDeleted() Logical	UIObject	M	1.0
isRemote(const *driveLetter* String) Logical	FileSystem	M	1.0
isRemovable(const *driveLetter* String) Logical	FileSystem	M	1.0
isResizeable() Logical	Array	M	1.0
isRight(const *p* Point) Logical	Point	M	1.0
isRightDown() Logical	MouseEvent	M	1.0
isShared() Logical	Table	M	1.0
isShared() Logical	TCursor	M	1.0
isShared(const *tableName* String) Logical	Table	P	1.0
isShiftKeyDown() Logical	KeyEvent	M	1.0

continues

TABLE D.1. CONTINUED

Syntax	Base Class	M/P	Ver
isShiftKeyDown() Logical	MouseEvent	M	1.0
isShowDeletedOn() Logical	TCursor	M	1.0
isSpace() Logical	String	M	4.5
isSpace(const string String) Logical	String	M	1.0
isSpeedBarShowing() Logical	Form	P	1.0
isSQLServer() Logical	Database	M	4.5
isTable() Logical	Table	M	1.0
isTable(const *tableName* String) Logical	Table	P	1.0
isTable(const *tableName* String, const *tableType* String]) Logical	Database	M	1.0
isTable(const *tableName* String, const *tableType* String]) Logical	Database	P	1.0
isTable(const *tableVar* Table) Logical	Database	M	1.0
isTable(const *tableVar* Table) Logical	Database	P	1.0
isTargetSelf() Logical	ActionEvent	M	1.0
isTargetSelf() Logical	ErrorEvent	M	1.0
isTargetSelf() Logical	Event	M	1.0
isTargetSelf() Logical	KeyEvent	M	1.0
isTargetSelf() Logical	MenuEvent	M	1.0
isTargetSelf() Logical	MouseEvent	M	1.0
isTargetSelf() Logical	MoveEvent	M	1.0
isTargetSelf() Logical	StatusEvent	M	1.0
isTargetSelf() Logical	TimerEvent	M	1.0

Syntax	Base Class	M/P	Ver
isTargetSelf() Logical	**ValueEvent**	M	1.0
isToolBarShowing() Logical	Form	P	5.0
isValid(const *fieldName* String, const *value* AnyType) Logical	TCursor	M	1.0
isValid(const *fieldNum* SmallInt, const *value* AnyType) Logical	TCursor	M	1.0
isView() Logical	TCursor	M	5.0
isVisible() Logical	**Application**	M	1.0
isVisible() Logical	Form	M	1.0
isVisible() Logical	Form	P	1.0
isVisible() Logical	**Report**	M	1.0
isVisible() Logical	TableView	M	1.0
keyChar(const *aChar* SmallInt, const *vChar* SmallInt, const *state* SmallInt) Logical	Form	M	1.0
keyChar(const *ansiKeyValue* SmallInt) Logical	UIObject	M	1.0
keyChar(const *ansiKeyValue* SmallInt, const *vChar* SmallInt, const *state* SmallInt) Logical	UIObject	M	1.0
keyChar(const *characters* String) Logical	Form	M	1.0
keyChar(const *characters* String) Logical	UIObject	M	1.0
keyChar(const *characters* String, const *state* SmallInt) Logical	Form	M	1.0
keyChar(const *characters* String, const *state* SmallInt) Logical	UIObject	M	1.0
keyNameToChar(const *keyName* String) String	String	P	1.0
keyNameToVKCode(const *keyName* String) SmallInt	String	P	1.0
keyPhysical(const *aChar* SmallInt, const *vChar* SmallInt, const *state* SmallInt) Logical	Form	M	1.0

continues

TABLE D.1. CONTINUED

Syntax	Base Class	M/P	Ver
keyPhysical(const *ansiKeyValue* SmallInt, const *vChar* SmallInt, const *state* SmallInt) Logical	UIObject	M	1.0
killTimer()	UIObject	M	1.0
linkFromClipboard() Logical	**Ole**	M	5.0
ln() Number	Number	M	1.0
load(const *formName* String) Logical	Form	M	1.0
load(const *formName* String,[const *windowStyle* LongInt [, const *x* LongInt, const *y* LongInt, const *w* LongInt, const *h* LongInt]]) Logical	Form	M	5.0
load(const *libName* String,[const *windowStyle* LongInt [, const *x* LongInt, const *y* LongInt, const *w* LongInt, const *h* LongInt]]) Logical	**Library**	M	5.0
load(const *reportName* String) Logical	**Report**	M	1.0
load(const *reportName* String,[const *windowStyle* LongInt [, const *x* LongInt, const *y* LongInt, const *w* LongInt, const *h* LongInt]]) Logical	**Report**	M	5.0
load(const *scriptName* String) Logical	Script	M	5.0
loadProjectAliases(const *fileName* String) Logical	Session	M	5.0
loadProjectAliases(const *fileName* String) Logical	Session	P	5.0
locate(const *fieldName* String, const *exactMatch* AnyType, ...) Logical	UIObject	M	1.0
locate(const *fieldName* String, const *exactMatch* String, ...) Logical	TCursor	M	1.0
locate(const *fieldNum* SmallInt, const *exactMatch* AnyType, ...) Logical	UIObject	M	1.0
locate(const *fieldNum* SmallInt, const *exactMatch* String, ...) Logical	TCursor	M	1.0
locateNext(const *fieldName* String, const *exactMatch* AnyType, ...) Logical	UIObject	M	1.0

Syntax	Base Class	M/P	Ver
locateNext(const *fieldName* String, const *exactMatch* String, ...) Logical	TCursor	M	1.0
locateNext(const *fieldNum* SmallInt, const *exactMatch* AnyType, ...) Logical	UIObject	M	1.0
locateNext(const *fieldNum* SmallInt, const *exactMatch* String, ...) Logical	TCursor	M	1.0
locateNextPattern([const *fieldName* String, const *exactMatch* AnyType, ...] const *fieldName* String, const *pattern* String) Logical	TCursor	M	1.0
locateNextPattern([const *fieldName* String, const *exactMatch* AnyType, ...], const *fieldName* String, const *pattern* String) Logical	UIObject	M	1.0
locateNextPattern([const *fieldNum* SmallInt, const *exactMatch* AnyType,...] const *fieldNum* smallInt, const *pattern* String) Logical	TCursor	M	1.0
locateNextPattern([const *fieldNum* SmallInt, const *exactMatch* AnyType, ...], const *fieldNum* SmallInt, const *pattern* String) Logical	UIObject	M	1.0
locatePattern([const *fieldName* String, const *exactMatch* AnyType, ...] const *fieldName* String, const *pattern* String) Logical	TCursor	M	1.0
locatePattern([const *fieldName* String, const *exactMatch* AnyType, ...], cost *fieldName* String, const *pattern* String) Logical	UIObject	M	1.0
locatePattern([const *fieldNum* SmallInt, const *exactMatch* AnyType, ...] cost *fieldNum* smallInt, const *pattern* String) Logical	TCursor	M	1.0
locatePattern([const *fieldNum* SmallInt, const *exactMatch* AnyType, ...], const *fieldNum* SmallInt, const *pattern* String) Logical	UIObject	M	1.0
locatePrior(const *fieldName* String, const *exactMatch* AnyType, ...) Logical	UIObject	M	1.0
locatePrior(const *fieldName* String, const *exactMatch* String, ...) Logical	TCursor	M	1.0
locatePrior(const *fieldNum* SmallInt, const *exactMatch* AnyType, ...) Logical	UIObject	M	1.0
locatePrior(const *fieldNum* SmallInt, const *exactMatch* String, ...) Logical	TCursor	M	1.0

continues

TABLE D.1. CONTINUED

Syntax	Base Class	M/P	Ver
locatePriorPattern([const *fieldName* String, const *exactMatch* AnyType, ...] const *fieldName* String, const *pattern* String) Logical	TCursor	M	1.0
locatePriorPattern([const *fieldName* String, const *exactMatch* AnyType, ...], const *fieldName* String, const *pattern* String) Logical	UIObject	M	1.0
locatePriorPattern([const *fieldNum* SmallInt, const *exactMatch* AnyType, ...] const *fieldNum smallInt*, const *pattern* String) Logical	TCursor	M	1.0
locatePriorPattern([const *fieldNum* SmallInt, const *exactMatch* AnyType, ...], const *fieldNum* SmallInt, const *pattern* String) Logical	UIObject	M	1.0
lock(const *lockType* String) Logical	Table	M	1.0
lock(const *lockType* String) Logical	TCursor	M	1.0
lock(const *tableName* [Table | TCursor], const *lockType* String, ...) Logical	**Session**	P	1.0
lockRecord() Logical	TCursor	M	1.0
lockRecord() Logical	UIObject	M	1.0
lockStatus(const *statusType* String) SmallInt	TCursor	M	1.0
lockStatus(const *statusType* String) SmallInt	UIObject	M	1.0
log() Number	Number	M	1.0
logical(const *value* AnyType) Logical	Logical	P	1.0
longInt(const *value* AnyType) LongInt	LongInt	P	1.0
lower() String	String	M	1.0
lTrim() String	String	M	1.0
makeDir(const *name* String) Logical	**FileSystem**	M	1.0

Syntax	Base Class	M/P	Ver
match(const *pattern* String, ...) Logical	String	M	1.0
max(const *x1* AnyType, const *x2* AnyType) AnyType	Number	P	1.0
maximize()	**Application**	M	1.0
maximize()	Form	M	1.0
maximize()	Form	P	1.0
maximize()	**Report**	M	1.0
maximize()	TableView	M	1.0
memo(const *value* AnyType, ...) *Memo*	**Memo**	P	1.0
menuAction(const *menuId* SmallInt) Logical	Form	M	1.0
menuAction(const *menuId* SmallInt) Logical	Form	P	1.0
menuAction(const *menuId* SmallInt) Logical	**Report**	M	5.0
menuAction(const *menuId* SmallInt) Logical	UIObject	M	1.0
menuChoice() String	**MenuEvent**	M	1.0
menuSetLimit(const *limit* SmallInt)	**Menu**	P	5.0
message(const *message* String, ...)	**System**	P	1.0
methodDelete(const *methodName* String) Logical	Form	M	1.0
methodDelete(const *methodName* String) Logical	**Library**	M	5.0
methodDelete(const *methodName* String) Logical	Script	M	5.0
methodDelete(const *methodName* String) Logical	UIObject	M	1.0
methodGet(const *methodName* String) String	Form	M	1.0
methodGet(const *methodName* String) String	**Library**	M	5.0

continues

TABLE D.1. CONTINUED

Syntax	Base Class	M/P	Ver
methodGet(const *methodName* String) String	Script	M	5.0
methodGet(const *methodName* String) String	UIObject	M	1.0
methodSet(const *methodName* String, const *methodText* String) Logical	Form	M	1.0
methodSet(const *methodName* String, const *methodText* String) Logical	Library	M	5.0
methodSet(const *methodName* String, const *methodText* String) Logical	Script	M	5.0
methodSet(const *methodName* String, const *methodText* String) Logical	UIObject	M	1.0
milliSec() SmallInt	DateTime	M	1.0
milliSec() SmallInt	Time	M	1.0
min(const *x1* AnyType, const *x2* AnyType) AnyType	Number	P	1.0
minimize()	Application	M	1.0
minimize()	Form	M	1.0
minimize()	Form	P	1.0
minimize()	Report	M	1.0
minimize()	TableView	M	1.0
minute() SmallInt	DateTime	M	1.0
minute() SmallInt	Time	M	1.0
mod(const *modulus* Number) Number	Number	M	1.0
month() SmallInt	Date	M	1.0
month() SmallInt	DateTime	M	1.0
mouseClick() Logical	UIObject	M	1.0
mouseDouble(const *x* LongInt, const *y* LongInt, const *state* SmallInt) Logical	Form	M	1.0

Syntax	Base Class	M/P	Ver
mouseDouble(const *x* LongInt, const *y* LongInt, const *state* SmallInt) Logical	UIObject	M	1.0
mouseDown(const *x* LongInt, const *y* LongInt, const *state* SmallInt) Logical	Form	M	1.0
mouseDown(const *x* LongInt, const *y* LongInt, const *state* SmallInt) Logical	UIObject	M	1.0
mouseEnter(const *x* LongInt, const *y* LongInt, const *state* SmallInt) Logical	Form	M	1.0
mouseEnter(const *x* LongInt, const *y* LongInt, const *state* SmallInt) Logical	UIObject	M	1.0
mouseExit(const *x* LongInt, const *y* LongInt, const *state* SmallInt) Logical	Form	M	1.0
mouseExit(const *x* LongInt, const *y* LongInt, const *state* SmallInt) Logical	UIObject	M	1.0
mouseMove(const *x* LongInt, const *y* LongInt, const *state* SmallInt) Logical	Form	M	1.0
mouseMove(const *x* LongInt, const *y* LongInt, const *state* SmallInt) Logical	UIObject	M	1.0
mouseRightDouble(const *x* LongInt, const *y* LongInt, const *state* SmallInt) Logical	Form	M	1.0
mouseRightDouble(const *x* LongInt, const *y* LongInt, const *state* SmallInt) Logical	UIObject	M	1.0
mouseRightDown(const *x* LongInt, const *y* LongInt, const *state* SmallInt) Logical	Form	M	1.0
mouseRightDown(const *x* LongInt, const *y* LongInt, const *state* SmallInt) Logical	UIObject	M	1.0
mouseRightUp(const *x* LongInt, const *y* LongInt, const *state* SmallInt) Logical	Form	M	1.0
mouseRightUp(const *x* LongInt, const *y* LongInt, const *state* SmallInt) Logical	UIObject	M	1.0
mouseUp(const *x* LongInt, const *y* LongInt, const *state* SmallInt) Logical	Form	M	1.0
mouseUp(const *x* LongInt, const *y* LongInt, const *state* SmallInt) Logical	UIObject	M	1.0
moveTo() Logical	Form	M	1.0
moveTo() Logical	UIObject	M	1.0
moveTo(const ***objectName*** String) Logical	Form	M	1.0
moveTo(const ***objectName*** String) Logical	UIObject	P	1.0

continues

TABLE D.1. CONTINUED

Syntax	Base Class	M/P	Ver
moveToPage(const *pageNumber* SmallInt) Logical	Form	M	1.0
moveToPage(const *pageNumber* SmallInt) Logical	Form	P	1.0
moveToPage(const *pageNumber* SmallInt) Logical	**Report**	M	1.0
moveToRecNo(const *recordNum* LongInt) Logical	TCursor	M	1.0
moveToRecNo(const *recordNum* LongInt) Logical	UIObject	M	1.0
moveToRecord(const *recordNum* LongInt) Logical	TCursor	M	1.0
moveToRecord(const *recordNum* LongInt) Logical	UIObject	M	1.0
moveToRecord(const *tc* TCursor) Logical	TableView	M	1.0
moveToRecord(const *tc* TCursor) Logical	UIObject	M	1.0
moy() String	**Date**	M	1.0
moy() String	**DateTime**	M	1.0
msgAbortRetryIgnore(const *caption* String, const *text* String) String	System	P	1.0
msgInfo(const *caption* String, const *text* String)	System	P	1.0
msgQuestion(const *caption* String, const *text* String) String	System	P	1.0
msgRetryCancel(const *caption* String, const *text* String) String	System	P	1.0
msgStop(const *caption* String, const *text* String)	System	P	1.0
msgyesNoCancel(const *caption* String, const *text* String) String	System	P	1.0
name() String	**FileSystem**	M	1.0
newValue() AnyType	**ValueEvent**	M	1.0
nextRecord() Logical	TCursor	M	1.0

Syntax	Base Class	M/P	Ver
nextRecord() Logical	UIObject	M	1.0
nFields() LongInt	Table	M	1.0
nFields() LongInt	TCursor	M	1.0
nFields() LongInt	UIObject	M	1.0
nFields(const *tableName* String) LongInt	Table	P	1.0
nKeyFields() LongInt	Table	M	1.0
nKeyFields() LongInt	TCursor	M	1.0
nKeyFields() LongInt	UIObject	M	1.0
nKeyFields(const *tableName* String) LongInt	Table	P	1.0
nRecords() LongInt	Table	M	1.0
nRecords() LongInt	TCursor	M	1.0
nRecords() LongInt	UIObject	M	1.0
nRecords(const *tableName* String) LongInt	Table	P	1.0
number(const *value* AnyType) Number	Number	P	1.0
Number(*numString* String, *formatSpec* String) Number	Number	P	5.0
numVal(const *value* AnyType) Number	Number	P	1.0
oemCode(const *char* String) SmallInt	String	P	1.0
open() Logical	Database	M	1.0
open(const *fileName* String, const *mode* String) Logical	TextStream	M	1.0
open(const *formName* String [, const *windowStyle* LongInt [, const *x* LongInt, const *y* LongInt, const *w* LongInt, const *h* LongInt]]) Logical	Form	M	4.5

continues

TABLE D.1. CONTINUED			
Syntax	*Base Class*	*M/P*	*Ver*
open(const *formName* String, [const *windowStyle* LongInt, [const *x* LongInt, const *y* LongInt, const *w* LongInt, const *h* LongInt]]) Logical	Form	M	1.0
open(const *libName* String) Logical	Library	M	1.0
open(const *libName* String, const *scopeType* SmallInt) Logical	Library	M	1.0
open(const openInfo FormOpenInfo) Logical	Form	M	1.0
open(const openInfo ReportOpenInfo) Logical	Report	M	1.0
open(const *reportName* String [, const *windowStyle* LongInt [, const *x* LongInt, const *y* LongInt, const *w* LongInt, const *h* LongInt]]) Logical	Report	M	4.5
open(const *reportName* String, [const *windowStyle* LongInt, [const *x* LongInt, const *y* LongInt, const *w* LongInt, const *h* LongInt]]) Logical	Report	M	1.0
open(const *server* String) Logical	DDE	M	1.0
open(const *server* String, const *topic* String) Logical	DDE	M	1.0
open(const *server* String, const *topic* String, const *item* String) Logical	DDE	M	1.0
open(const *tableName* String [, const *db* Database] [, const *indx* String]) Logical	TCursor	M	1.0
open(const *tableVar* Table) Logical	TCursor	M	1.0
open(const *tableViewName* String) Logical	TableView	M	1.0
open(const *tableViewName* String, const *windowStyle* LongInt) Logical	TableView	M	1.0
open(const *tableViewName* String, const *windowStyle* LongInt, const *x* LongInt, const *y* LongInt, const *w* LongInt, const *h* LongInt) Logical	TableView	M	1.0
open([const *aliasName* String,] [const *ses Session*,] [const *params* DynArray) Logical	Database	M	5.0
open([const *databaseName* String,] [const *ses Session*,] [const *params* DynArray) Logical	Database	M	4.5

Syntax	Base Class	M/P	Ver
open([const *databaseName* String,] [const *ses Session*]) Logical	Database	M	1.0
open([const *name* String]) Logical	Session	M	1.0
openAsDialog(const *formName* String [, const *windowStyle* LongInt [, const *x* LongInt, const *y* LongInt, const *w* LongInt, const *h* LongInt]]) Logical	Form	M	4.5
openAsDialog(const *formName* String, [const *windowStyle* LongInt, [const *x* LongInt, const *y* LongInt, const *w* LongInt, const *h* LongInt]]) Logical	Form	M	1.0
openAsDialog(const *openInfo* FormOpenInfo) Logical	Form	M	1.0
pixelsToTwips(const *pix* Point) Point	System	P	1.0
pixelsToTwips(const *pix* Point) Point	UIObject	M	1.0
play(const *scriptName* String) AnyType	System	P	1.0
pmt(const *interestRate* Number, const *periods* Number) Number	Number	M	1.0
point(const *newPoint* Point) Point	Point	P	1.0
point(const *x* LongInt, const *y* LongInt) Point	Point	P	1.0
position() LongInt	TextStream	M	1.0
postAction(const *actionId* SmallInt)	Form	M	1.0
postAction(const *actionId* SmallInt)	UIObject	M	1.0
postRecord() Logical	TCursor	M	1.0
postRecord() Logical	UIObject	M	1.0
pow(const *exponent* Number) Number	Number	M	1.0
pow10() Number	Number	M	1.0
print() Logical	Report	M	1.0
print(const *reportName* String [, const *refresh* SmallInt]) Logical	Report	M	1.0

continues

TABLE D.1. CONTINUED

Syntax	Base Class	M/P	Ver
print(const *ri ReportPrintInfo*) Logical	Report	M	1.0
printerGetInfo(var *printInfo PrinterInfo*) Logical	System	P	5.0
printerGetLayout(var *pageLayoutInfo* PageLayoutInfo) Logical	System	P	5.0
printerGetOptions(var *printSettings* PrinterOptionInfo) Logical	System	P	5.0
printerGetPaperSizes(var *paperSizes* Array[] String) Logical	System	P	5.0
printerGetType() SmallInt	System	P	5.0
printerSetCurrent(printerDesc String) Logical	System	P	5.0
printerSetOptions(printSettings PrinterOptionInfo) Logical	System	P	5.0
priorRecord() Logical	TCursor	M	1.0
priorRecord() Logical	UIObject	M	1.0
privDir() String	FileSystem	P	1.0
projectViewerClose() Logical	System	P	5.0
projectViewerIsOpen() Logical	System	P	5.0
projectViewerIsRestricted() Logical	System	P	5.0
projectViewerOpen() Logical	System	P	5.0
projectViewerRefresh() Logical	System	P	5.0
projectViewerRestrict() Logical	System	P	5.0
projectViewerUnRestrict() Logical	System	P	5.0
protect(const *tableName* String) Logical	Table	P	1.0
protect(const *tableName* String, const *password* String) Logical	Table	P	1.0
protect([const *password* String]) Logical	Table	M	1.0

Syntax	Base Class	M/P	Ver
pushButton() Logical	UIObject	M	1.0
pv(const *interestRate* Number, const *periods* Number) Number	Number	M	1.0
qLocate(const *exactMatch* String, …) Logical	TCursor	M	1.0
rand() Number	Number	P	1.0
readChars(var string String, const *nChars* SmallInt) Logical	TextStream	M	1.0
readEnvironmentString(const *key* String) String	System	P	1.0
readFromClipboard() Logical	Graphic	M	1.0
readFromClipboard() Logical	Ole	M	1.0
readFromClipboard(const *clipBoardFormat* String) Logical	Binary	M	5.0
readFromFile(const *fileName* String) Logical	Binary	M	1.0
readFromFile(const *fileName* String) Logical	Graphic	M	1.0
readFromFile(const *fileName* String) Logical	Memo	M	1.0
readFromFile(const *fileName* String) Logical	Query	M	5.0
readFromFile(const *fileName* String) Logical	SQL	M	5.0
readFromString(const *QueryString* String) Logical	Query	M	5.0
readFromString(const *QueryString* String) Logical	SQL	M	5.0
readLine(var stringArray Array[ ] String) Logical	TextStream	M	1.0
readLine(var *value* String) Logical	TextStream	M	1.0
readProfileString(const *fileName* String, const *section* String, const *key* String) String	System	P	1.0
reason() SmallInt	ActionEvent	M	1.0
reason() SmallInt	ErrorEvent	M	1.0

continues

Syntax	Base Class	M/P	Ver
reason() SmallInt	Event	M	1.0
reason() SmallInt	KeyEvent	M	1.0
reason() SmallInt	MenuEvent	M	1.0
reason() SmallInt	MouseEvent	M	1.0
reason() SmallInt	MoveEvent	M	1.0
reason() SmallInt	StatusEvent	M	1.0
reason() SmallInt	TimerEvent	M	1.0
reason() SmallInt	ValueEvent	M	1.0
recNo() LongInt	TCursor	M	1.0
recorderContinue( )	System	P	5.0
recorderFlush( )	System	P	5.0
recorderPause( )	System	P	5.0
recorderStart(const *fileName* String) Logical	System	P	5.0
recorderStop( ) Logical	System	P	5.0
recordStatus(const *statusType* String) Logical	TCursor	M	1.0
recordStatus(const *statusType* String) Logical	UIObject	M	1.0
reIndex(const *indexName* StringI, const *tagName* StringI) Logical	Table	M	1.0
reIndex(const *IndexName* StringI, const *TagName* StringI) Logical	TCursor	M	1.0
reIndexAll() Logical	Table	M	1.0
reIndexAll() Logical	TCursor	M	1.0
remove(const *index* LongInt)	Array	M	1.0

TABLE D.1. CONTINUED

Syntax	Base Class	M/P	Ver
remove(const *index* LongInt, const *numberOfElements* LongInt)	Array	M	1.0
remove(const *item* String)	Menu	M	1.0
remove(const *item* String)	PopUpMenu	M	1.0
removeAlias(const *alias* String) Logical	Session	M	1.0
removeAlias(const *alias* String) Logical	Session	P	1.0
removeAllItems(const *value* AnyType)	Array	M	1.0
removeAllPasswords()	Session	M	1.0
removeAllPasswords()	Session	P	1.0
removeItem(const *value* AnyType)	Array	M	1.0
removeItem(const *value* AnyType)	DynArray	M	1.0
removeMenu()	Menu	P	1.0
removePassword(const *password* String)	Session	M	1.0
removePassword(const *password* String)	Session	P	1.0
removeProjectAlias(const *alias* String) Logical	Session	M	5.0
removeProjectAlias(const *alias* String) Logical	Session	P	5.0
rename(const *destTableName* String) Logical	Table	M	1.0
rename(const *oldName* String, const *newName* String) Logical	FileSystem	M	1.0
rename(const *tableName* String, const *destTableName* String) Logical	Table	P	1.0
replaceItem(const *keyItem* AnyType, const *newItem* AnyType)	Array	M	1.0
resetCompileInformation()	System	P	5.0
resourceInfo(var *info* DynArray[ ] AnyType)	System	P	5.0

continues

TABLE D.1. CONTINUED

Syntax	Base Class	M/P	Ver
reSync(const *tc* TCursor) Logical	UIObject	M	1.0
retryPeriod() SmallInt	Session	M	1.0
retryPeriod() SmallInt	Session	P	1.0
rgb(const *red* SmallInt, const *green* SmallInt, const *blue* SmallInt) LongInt	UIObject	P	1.0
rollbackTransaction() Logical	Database	M	4.5
round(const *places* SmallInt) Number	Number	M	1.0
rTrim() String	String	M	1.0
run() AnyType	Script	M	5.0
run() Logical	Form	M	1.0
run() Logical	Report	M	1.0
save([const **newFormName** String]) Logical	Form	M	1.0
save([const **newLibName** String]) Logical	Library	M	5.0
save([const **newReportName** String]) Logical	Report	M	1.0
save([const **newScriptName** String]) Logical	Script	M	5.0
saveCFG([const **fileName** String]) Logical	Session	M	1.0
saveCFG([const **fileName** String]) Logical	Session	P	1.0
saveProjectAliases([const **fileName** String]) Logical	Session	M	5.0
saveProjectAliases([const **fileName** String]) Logical	Session	P	5.0
saveStyleSheet(filename String, **overwrite** Logical) Logical	Form	M	5.0
saveStyleSheet(filename String, **overwrite** Logical) Logical	Report	M	5.0

Syntax	Base Class	M/P	Ver
search(const *str* String) SmallInt	String	M	1.0
second() SmallInt	DateTime	M	1.0
second() SmallInt	Time	M	1.0
selectCurrentTool(**ObjType** SmallInt) Logical	Form	M	5.0
selectCurrentTool(**ObjType** SmallInt) Logical	Report	M	5.0
sendKeys(const *keys* String [, const *wait* Logical]) Logical	System	P	4.5
sendKeysActionId(const *actionId* SmallInt)	System	P	4.5
sendKeysFromFile(const *keysFileName* String, const *wait* Logical) Logical	System	P	5.0
sendKeysSpeed(const *speed* Number)	System	P	5.0
sendToBack()	UIObject	M	5.0
seqNo() LongInt	TCursor	M	1.0
setAliasPassword(const *aliasName* String, const *password* String) Logical	Session	M	4.5
setAliasPassword(const *aliasName* String, const *password* String) Logical	Session	P	4.5
setAliasPath(const *aliasName* String, const *aliasPath* String) Logical	Session	M	1.0
setAliasPath(const *aliasName* String, const *aliasPath* String) Logical	Session	P	1.0
setAliasProperty(const *aliasName* String, const *property* String, const *propertyValue* String) Logical	Session	M	4.5
setAliasProperty(const *aliasName* String, const *property* String, const *propertyValue* String) Logical	Session	P	4.5
setAltKeyDown(const *yesNo* Logical)	KeyEvent	M	1.0
setBatchOff() Logical	TCursor	M	4.5
setBatchOn() Logical	TCursor	M	4.5

continues

TABLE D.1. CONTINUED

Syntax	Base Class	M/P	Ver
setChar(const *char* String)	KeyEvent	M	1.0
setControlKeyDown(const *yesNo* Logical)	KeyEvent	M	1.0
setControlKeyDown(const *yesNo* Logical)	MouseEvent	M	1.0
setData(const *menuData* LongInt)	MenuEvent	M	1.0
setDefaultPrinterStyleSheet(const *fileName* String) Logical	System	P	5.0
setDefaultScreenStyleSheet(const *fileName* String) Logical	System	P	5.0
setDir(const *name* String) Logical	FileSystem	M	1.0
setDirLock(const *dirName* String) Logical	FileSystem	P	5.0
setDrive(const *name* String) Logical	FileSystem	M	1.0
setErrorCode(const *errorId* LongInt)	ActionEvent	M	1.0
setErrorCode(const *errorId* LongInt)	ErrorEvent	M	1.0
setErrorCode(const *errorId* LongInt)	Event	M	1.0
setErrorCode(const *errorId* LongInt)	KeyEvent	M	1.0
setErrorCode(const *errorId* LongInt)	MenuEvent	M	1.0
setErrorCode(const *errorId* LongInt)	MouseEvent	M	1.0
setErrorCode(const *errorId* LongInt)	MoveEvent	M	1.0
setErrorCode(const *errorId* LongInt)	StatusEvent	M	1.0
setErrorCode(const *errorId* LongInt)	TimerEvent	M	1.0
setErrorCode(const *errorId* LongInt)	ValueEvent	M	1.0
setErrorCode(const *errorId* SmallInt)	ActionEvent	M	5.0
setErrorCode(const *errorId* SmallInt)	ErrorEvent	M	5.0

Syntax	Base Class	M/P	Ver
setErrorCode(const *errorId* SmallInt)	Event	M	5.0
setErrorCode(const *errorId* SmallInt)	KeyEvent	M	5.0
setErrorCode(const *errorId* SmallInt)	MenuEvent	M	5.0
setErrorCode(const *errorId* SmallInt)	MouseEvent	M	5.0
setErrorCode(const *errorId* SmallInt)	MoveEvent	M	5.0
setErrorCode(const *errorId* SmallInt)	StatusEvent	M	5.0
setErrorCode(const *errorId* SmallInt)	TimerEvent	M	5.0
setErrorCode(const *errorId* SmallInt)	ValueEvent	M	5.0
setExclusive([const *yesNo* Logical])	Table	M	1.0
setFieldValue(const *fieldName* String, const *value* AnyType) Logical	TCursor	M	1.0
setFieldValue(const *fieldNum* SmallInt, const *value* AnyType) Logical	TCursor	M	1.0
setFileAccessRights(const *fileName* String, const *rights* String) Logical	FileSystem	P	1.0
setFilter([const *exactMatch* AnyType, ...] const *minVal* AnyType, const *maxVal* AnyType) Logical	UIObject	M	1.0
setFilter([const *exactMatch* AnyType, ...] const *minValue* AnyType, const *maxValue* AnyType) Logical	Table	M	1.0
setFilter([const *exactMatch* AnyType, ...] const *minValue* AnyType, const *maxValue* AnyType) Logical	TCursor	M	1.0
setFlyAwayControl([const *yesNo* Logical])	TCursor	M	1.0
setGenFilter(filters Array[] String) Logical	Table	M	5.0
setGenFilter(filters Array[] String) Logical	TCursor	M	5.0
setGenFilter(filters Array[] String) Logical	UIObject	M	5.0

continues

Table D.1. continued

Syntax	Base Class	M/P	Ver
setGenFilter(filters Array[ ] String, *names* Array[ ] AnyType) Logical	Table	M	5.0
setGenFilter(filters Array[ ] String, *names* Array[ ] AnyType) Logical	TCursor	M	5.0
setGenFilter(filters Array[ ] String, *names* Array[ ] AnyType) Logical	UIObject	M	5.0
setGenFilter(filters DynArray[ ] String) Logical	Table	M	5.0
setGenFilter(filters DynArray[ ] String) Logical	TCursor	M	5.0
setGenFilter(filters DynArray[ ] String) Logical	UIObject	M	5.0
setGenFilter(idxName String, *filters* Array[ ] String) Logical	TCursor	M	5.0
setGenFilter(idxName String, *filters* Array[ ] String) Logical	UIObject	M	5.0
setGenFilter(idxName String, *filters* Array[ ] String, *names* Array[ ] AnyType) Logical	TCursor	M	5.0
setGenFilter(idxName String, *filters* Array[ ] String, *names* Array[ ] AnyType) Logical	UIObject	M	5.0
setGenFilter(idxName String, *filters* DynArray[ ] String) Logical	TCursor	M	5.0
setGenFilter(idxName String, *filters* DynArray[ ] String) Logical	UIObject	M	5.0
setGenFilter(idxName String, *idxTag* String, *filters* Array[ ] String) Logical	TCursor	M	5.0
setGenFilter(idxName String, *idxTag* String, *filters* Array[ ] String) Logical	TCursor	M	5.0
setGenFilter(idxName String, *idxTag* String, *filters* Array[ ] String) Logical	UIObject	M	5.0
setGenFilter(idxName String, *idxTag* String, *filters* Array[ ] String, *names* Array[ ] AnyType) Logical	TCursor	M	5.0
setGenFilter(idxName String, *idxTag* String, *filters* Array[ ] String, *names* Array[ ] AnyType) Logical	UIObject	M	5.0
setGenFilter(idxName String, *idxTag* String, *filters* DynArray[ ] String) Logical	TCursor	M	5.0
setGenFilter(idxName String, *idxTag* String, *filters* DynArray[ ] String) Logical	UIObject	M	5.0
setId(const *actionId* SmallInt)	**ActionEvent**	M	1.0

Syntax	Base Class	M/P	Ver
setId(const *actionId* SmallInt)	MenuEvent	M	1.0
setIndex(const *indexName* String) Logical	Table	M	1.0
setIndex(const *indexName* String, const *indexTagName* String) Logical	Table	M	1.0
setInside(const *trueFalse* Logical)	MouseEvent	M	1.0
setItem(const *item* String)	DDE	M	1.0
setLanguageDriver(const *langDriver* String) Logical	Query	M	5.0
setLeftDown(const *yesNo* Logical)	MouseEvent	M	1.0
setMenu(Menu *menu*)	Form	M	5.0
setMenu(Menu *menu*)	Report	M	5.0
setMenuChoiceAttribute(const *menuChoice* String, const *menuAttribute* SmallInt)	Menu	P	1.0
setMenuChoiceAttributeById(const *menuId* SmallInt, const *menuAttribute* SmallInt)	Menu	P	1.0
setMiddleDown(const *yesNo* Logical)	MouseEvent	M	1.0
setMousePosition(const *p* Point)	MouseEvent	M	1.0
setMousePosition(const *xPosition* LongInt, const *yPosition* LongInt)	MouseEvent	M	1.0
setMouseScreenPosition(const *mousePosition* Point)	System	P	1.0
setMouseScreenPosition(const x LongInt, const y LongInt)	System	P	1.0
setMouseShape(const *mouseShapeId* LongInt) LongInt	System	P	1.0
setNewValue(const *newValue* AnyType)	ValueEvent	M	1.0
setPosition(const *offset* LongInt)	TextStream	M	1.0
setPosition(const x LongInt, const y LongInt, const w LongInt, const h LongInt)	Application	M	1.0
setPosition(const x LongInt, const y LongInt, const w LongInt, const h LongInt)	Form	M	1.0

continues

TABLE D.1. CONTINUED

Syntax	Base Class	M/P	Ver
setPosition(const *x* LongInt, const *y* LongInt, const *w* LongInt, const *h* LongInt)	Form	P	1.0
setPosition(const *x* LongInt, const *y* LongInt, const *w* LongInt, const *h* LongInt)	**Report**	M	1.0
setPosition(const *x* LongInt, const *y* LongInt, const *w* LongInt, const *h* LongInt)	TableView	M	1.0
setPosition(const *x* LongInt, const *y* LongInt, const *w* LongInt, const *h* LongInt)	UIObject	M	1.0
setPrivDir(const *path* String) Logical	**FileSystem**	P	5.0
setProperty(const *propertyName* String, const *propertyValue* AnyType)	UIObject	M	1.0
setProtoProperty(const *ObjType* SmallInt, *propertyName* String, *value* AnyType) Logical	Form	M	5.0
setProtoProperty(const *ObjType* SmallInt, *propertyName* String, *value* AnyType) Logical	Form	P	5.0
setProtoProperty(const *ObjType* SmallInt, *propertyName* String, *value* AnyType) Logical	**Report**	M	5.0
setQueryRestartOptions(const *qryRestartType* SmallInt) Logical	Database	M	1.0
setQueryRestartOptions(const *qryRestartType* SmallInt) Logical	Database	P	1.0
setQueryRestartOptions(const *qryRestartType* SmallInt) Logical	Query	M	5.0
setQueryRestartOptions(const *qryRestartType* SmallInt) Logical	**SQL**	M	5.0
setRange(const *arValues* Array[] AnyType) Logical	Table	M	5.0
setRange(const *arValues* Array[] AnyType) Logical	TCursor	M	5.0
setRange(const *arValues* Array[] AnyType) Logical	UIObject	M	5.0
setRange(const *arValues* Array[] AnyType) Logical	UIObject	P	5.0
setRange([const *exactMatch* AnyType, ...] [const *minVal* AnyType, const *maxVal* AnyType]) Logical	UIObject	M	5.0

Syntax	Base Class	M/P	Ver
setRange([const exactMatch AnyType, ...] [const minVal AnyType, const maxVal AnyType]) Logical	UIObject	P	5.0
setRange([const exactMatch AnyType, ...] [const minValue AnyType, const maxValue AnyType]) Logical	Table	M	5.0
setRange([const exactMatch AnyType, ...] [const minValue AnyType, const maxValue AnyType]) Logical	TCursor	M	5.0
setReadOnly([const yesNo Logical])	Table	M	1.0
setReason(const reasonId SmallInt)	ActionEvent	M	1.0
setReason(const reasonId SmallInt)	ErrorEvent	M	1.0
setReason(const reasonId SmallInt)	Event	M	1.0
setReason(const reasonId SmallInt)	KeyEvent	M	1.0
setReason(const reasonId SmallInt)	MenuEvent	M	1.0
setReason(const reasonId SmallInt)	MouseEvent	M	1.0
setReason(const reasonId SmallInt)	MoveEvent	M	1.0
setReason(const reasonId SmallInt)	StatusEvent	M	1.0
setReason(const reasonId SmallInt)	TimerEvent	M	1.0
setReason(const reasonId SmallInt)	ValueEvent	M	1.0
setRetryPeriod(const period SmallInt) Logical	Session	M	1.0
setRetryPeriod(const period SmallInt) Logical	Session	P	1.0
setRightDown(const yesNo Logical)	MouseEvent	M	1.0
setSelectedObjects(objects Array[] UIObject, const yesNo Logical)	Form	P	5.0
setShiftKeyDown(const yesNo Logical)	KeyEvent	M	1.0

continues

TABLE D.1. CONTINUED

Syntax	Base Class	M/P	Ver
setShiftKeyDown(const *yesNo* Logical)	MouseEvent	M	1.0
setSize(const *size* LongInt)	Array	M	1.0
setStatusValue(const *statusValue* AnyType)	StatusEvent	M	1.0
setStyleSheet(const *fileName* String)	Report	M	5.0
setStyleSheet(const *fileName* String) Logical	Form	M	5.0
setStyleSheet(const *fileName* String) Logical	Form	P	5.0
setTimer(const *milliSeconds* LongInt)	UIObject	M	1.0
setTimer(const *milliSeconds* LongInt, const *repeat* Logical)	UIObject	M	1.0
setTitle(const *text* String)	Application	M	1.0
setTitle(const *text* String)	Form	M	1.0
setTitle(const *text* String)	Form	P	1.0
setTitle(const *text* String)	Report	M	1.0
setTitle(const *text* String)	TableView	M	1.0
setUserLevel(const *level* String)	System	P	5.0
setVChar(const *char* String)	KeyEvent	M	1.0
setVCharCode(const *VKCode* SmallInt)	KeyEvent	M	1.0
setWorkingDir(const *path* String) Logical	FileSystem	P	5.0
setX(const *newXValue* LongInt)	Point	M	1.0
setX(const *xPosition* LongInt)	MouseEvent	M	1.0
setXY(const *newXValue* LongInt, const *newYValue* LongInt)	Point	M	1.0
setY(const *newYValue* LongInt)	Point	M	1.0

Syntax	Base Class	M/P	Ver
setY(const *yPosition* LongInt)	**MouseEvent**	M	1.0
show()	**Application**	M	1.0
show()	Form	M	1.0
show()	Form	P	1.0
show()	**Menu**	M	1.0
show()	**Report**	M	1.0
show()	TableView	M	1.0
show() String	PopUpMenu	M	1.0
show(const *xTwips* SmallInt, const *yTwips* SmallInt) String	PopUpMenu	M	1.0
showDeleted([const **yesNo** Logical]) Logical	Table	M	1.0
showDeleted([const **yesNo** Logical]) Logical	TCursor	M	1.0
showSpeedBar()	Form	P	1.0
showToolBar()	Form	P	5.0
sin() Number	Number	M	1.0
sinh() Number	Number	M	1.0
size() LongInt	Array	M	1.0
size() LongInt	**Binary**	M	1.0
size() LongInt	DynArray	M	1.0
size() LongInt	**FileSystem**	M	1.0
size() LongInt	**TextStream**	M	1.0
size() SmallInt	String	M	1.0

continues

TABLE D.1. CONTINUED

Syntax	Base Class	M/P	Ver
skip() Logical	TCursor	M	1.0
skip(const *nRecords* LongInt) Logical	TCursor	M	1.0
skip(const *nRecords* LongInt) Logical	UIObject	M	1.0
sleep()	System	P	1.0
sleep(const numberOfMilliSecs LongInt)	System	P	1.0
smallInt(const *value* AnyType) SmallInt	SmallInt	P	1.0
sortTo(const *destTable* Table, const *NumField* SmallInt, const *sortFields* Array[] String, const *sortOrder* Array[] SmallInt) Logical	TCursor	M	1.0
sortTo(const *tableName* String, const *NumField* SmallInt, const *sortFields* Array[] String, const *sortOrder* Array[] SmallInt) Logical	TCursor	M	1.0
sound(const *freqHertz* LongInt, const *durationMilliSecs* LongInt)	System	P	1.0
space(const numberOfSpaces SmallInt) String	String	P	1.0
splitFullFileName(const *fullFileName* String, var *driveName* String, var *pathName* String, var *fileName* String, var *extensionName* String)	FileSystem	P	1.0
splitFullFileName(const *fullFileName* String, var *fileNameParts* DynArray[] String)	FileSystem	P	1.0
SQLupdates(const *yesNo* Logical)	System	P	5.0
sqrt() Number	Number	M	1.0
startUpDir() String	FileSystem	P	1.0
statusValue() AnyType	StatusEvent	M	1.0
string(const *value* AnyType) String	String	P	1.0
string(const *value* AnyType, ...) String	String	P	1.0

Syntax	Base Class	M/P	Ver
strVal(const *value* AnyType) String	String	P	1.0
substr(const *startIndex* SmallInt) String	String	M	1.0
substr(const *startIndex* SmallInt, const *numberOfChars* SmallInt) String	String	M	1.0
subtract(const *destTable* Table) Logical	Table	M	1.0
subtract(const *destTable* Table) Logical	TCursor	M	1.0
subtract(const *destTableName* String) Logical	TCursor	M	1.0
subtract(const *destTableName* String) Logical	Table	M	1.0
subtract(const *destTCursor* TCursor) Logical	TCursor	M	1.0
subtract(const *tableName* String, const *destTableName* String) Logical	Table	P	1.0
switchIndex([const *indexName* String [, const *indexTagName* String]] [, const *stayOnRecord* Logical]) Logical	UIObject	M	1.0
switchIndex([const *indexName* String [,const *indexTagName* String]] [, const *stayOnRecord* Logical]) Logical	TCursor	M	1.0
sysInfo(var *info* DynArray[] AnyType)	**System**	P	1.0
tableName() String	TCursor	M	1.0
tableRights(const *rights* String) Logical	Table	M	1.0
tableRights(const *rights* String) Logical	TCursor	M	1.0
tableRights(const *tableName* String, const *rights* AnyType) Logical	Table	P	1.0
tableRights(const *tableName* String, const *rights* String) Logical	Table	P	5.0
tan() Number	Number	M	1.0
tanh() Number	Number	M	1.0
time() *DateTime*	**FileSystem**	M	1.0

continues

TABLE D.1. CONTINUED

Syntax	Base Class	M/P	Ver
time([const *value* AnyType]) *Time*	Time	P	1.0
toANSI() String	String	M	1.0
today() *Date*	Date	P	1.0
toHex(const *value* LongInt) String	AnyType	P	5.0
toOEM() String	String	M	1.0
totalDiskSpace(const *driveLetter* String) LongInt	FileSystem	M	1.0
trace(const *ar* Array[] AnyType)	AnyType	P	5.0
trace(const *dn* DynArray[] AnyType)	AnyType	P	5.0
trace(const *rec* Record)	AnyType	P	5.0
trace(const *value* AnyType)	AnyType	P	5.0
tracerClear()	System	P	1.0
tracerHide()	System	P	1.0
tracerOff()	System	P	1.0
tracerOn()	System	P	1.0
tracerSave(const *fileName* String)	System	P	1.0
tracerShow()	System	P	1.0
tracerToTop()	System	P	1.0
tracerWrite(const *message* String, …)	System	P	1.0
transactionActive() Logical	Database	M	4.5
truncate(const *places* SmallInt) Number	Number	M	1.0
twipsToPixels(const *twips* Point) Point	System	P	1.0

Syntax	Base Class	M/P	Ver
twipsToPixels(const *twips* Point) Point	UIObject	M	1.0
type() String	Table	M	1.0
type() String	TCursor	M	1.0
unAssign()	AnyType	M	4.5
unAssign() Logical	AnyType	M	1.0
unAttach() Logical	Table	M	1.0
unDeleteRecord() Logical	TCursor	M	1.0
unDeleteRecord() Logical	UIObject	M	1.0
unlock(const *lockType* String) Logical	Table	M	1.0
unlock(const *lockType* String) Logical	TCursor	M	1.0
unlock(const *tableName* {Table | TCursor}, const *lockType* String, …) Logical	Session	P	1.0
unlockRecord() Logical	TCursor	M	1.0
unlockRecord() Logical	UIObject	M	1.0
unProtect() Logical	Table	M	1.0
unProtect(const *password* String) Logical	Table	M	1.0
unProtect(const *tableName* String) Logical	Table	P	1.0
unProtect(const *tableName* String, const *password* String) Logical	Table	P	1.0
update(const *fieldName* String, const *fieldValue* AnyType, …) Logical	TCursor	M	4.5
update(const *fieldNum* Number, const *fieldValue* AnyType, …) Logical	TCursor	M	4.5
updateLinkNow() Logical	Ole	M	5.0
updateRecord() Logical	TCursor	M	1.0

continues

TABLE D.1. CONTINUED

Syntax	Base Class	M/P	Ver
updateRecord(const *moveTo* Logical) Logical	TCursor	M	1.0
upper() String	String	M	1.0
usesIndexes(const *indexName* String, ...) Logical	Table	M	1.0
vChar() String	**KeyEvent**	M	1.0
vCharCode() SmallInt	**KeyEvent**	M	1.0
version() String	**System**	P	1.0
view()	AnyType	M	1.0
view()	Array	M	1.0
view()	Currency	M	1.0
view()	**Date**	M	1.0
view()	**DateTime**	M	1.0
view()	DynArray	M	1.0
view()	Logical	M	1.0
view()	LongInt	M	1.0
view()	Number	M	1.0
view()	Point	M	1.0
view()	Record	M	1.0
view()	SmallInt	M	1.0
view()	String	M	1.0
view()	**Time**	M	1.0
view()	UIObject	M	1.0

Syntax	Base Class	M/P	Ver
view(const *title* String)	AnyType	M	1.0
view(const *title* String)	Array	M	1.0
view(const *title* String)	Currency	M	1.0
view(const *title* String)	**Date**	M	1.0
view(const *title* String)	**DateTime**	M	1.0
view(const *title* String)	DynArray	M	1.0
view(const *title* String)	Logical	M	1.0
view(const *title* String)	LongInt	M	1.0
view(const *title* String)	Number	M	1.0
view(const *title* String)	Point	M	1.0
view(const *title* String)	Record	M	1.0
view(const *title* String)	SmallInt	M	1.0
view(const *title* String)	String	M	1.0
view(const *title* String)	**Time**	M	1.0
view(const *title* String)	UIObject	M	1.0
vkCodeToKeyName(const *vkCode* SmallInt) String	String	P	1.0
wait()	TableView	M	1.0
wait() AnyType	Form	M	1.0
wait() AnyType	**Report**	M	5.0
wantInMemoryTCursor(const *yesNo* Logical])	Query	M	5.0
wantInMemoryTCursor(const *yesNo* Logical])	**SQL**	M	5.0
wasLastClicked() Logical	UIObject	M	1.0

continues

TABLE D.1. CONTINUED

Syntax	Base Class	M/P	Ver
wasLastRightClicked() Logical	UIObject	M	1.0
windowClientHandle() SmallInt	**Application**	M	1.0
windowClientHandle() SmallInt	Form	M	1.0
windowClientHandle() SmallInt	Form	P	1.0
windowClientHandle() SmallInt	**Report**	M	5.0
windowHandle() SmallInt	**Application**	M	1.0
windowHandle() SmallInt	Form	M	1.0
windowHandle() SmallInt	Form	P	1.0
windowHandle() SmallInt	**Report**	M	5.0
windowHandle() SmallInt	TableView	M	1.0
windowsDir() String	**FileSystem**	P	1.0
windowsSystemDir() String	**FileSystem**	P	1.0
winGetMessageId(const *msgName* SmallInt) SmallInt	System	P	1.0
winPostMessage(const *hWnd* SmallInt, const *msg* SmallInt, const *wParam* SmallInt, const *lParam* LongInt) Logical	System	P	1.0
winSendMessage(const *hWnd* SmallInt, const *msg* SmallInt, const *wParam* SmallInt, const *lParam* LongInt) LongInt	System	P	1.0
workingDir() String	**System**	P	1.0
writeEnvironmentString(const *key* String, const *value* String) Logical	**FileSystem**	P	1.0
writeLine(const *value* AnyType, ...) Logical	**System**	P	1.0
	TextStream	M	1.0

Syntax	Base Class	M/P	Ver
writeProfileString(const *fileName* String, const *section* String, const *key* String, const *value* String) Logical	System	P	1.0
writeQBE(const *fileName* String) Logical	Query	M	1.0
writeQBE(const *qbeVar* Query, const *fileName* String) Logical	Database	M	1.0
writeQBE(const *qbeVar* Query, const *fileName* String) Logical	Database	P	1.0
writeQBE(const *str* String, const *fileName* String) Logical	Database	M	1.0
writeQBE(const *str* String, const *fileName* String) Logical	Database	P	1.0
writeQBE(const *str* String, const *fileName* String) Logical	Query	P	4.5
writeSQL(const *fileName* String) Logical	SQL	M	4.5
writeSQL(const *str* String, const *fileName* String) Logical	SQL	P	4.5
writeString(const *value* AnyType, ...) Logical	TextStream	M	1.0
writeToClipboard() Logical	Graphic	M	1.0
writeToClipboard() Logical	Ole	M	1.0
writeToClipboard(const *clipBoardFormat* String) Logical	Binary	M	5.0
writeToFile(const *fileName* String) Logical	Binary	M	1.0
writeToFile(const *fileName* String) Logical	Graphic	M	1.0
writeToFile(const *fileName* String) Logical	Memo	M	1.0
x() LongInt	MouseEvent	M	1.0
x() LongInt	Point	M	1.0
y() LongInt	MouseEvent	M	1.0
y() LongInt	Point	M	1.0
year() SmallInt	Date	M	1.0
year() SmallInt	DateTime	M	1.0

PROPERTIES

Table E.1 lists the properties in ObjectPAL, grouped by object.

TABLE E.1. PROPERTIES GROUPED BY OBJECT.

Object	Property	Type	Sample Value	Ver
Band	Arrived	Logical	False	1.0
Band	BottomBorder	LongInt	0	5.0
Band	Breakable	Logical	True	1.0
Band	Class	String	Band	1.0
Band	ContainerName	String	#Report1	1.0
Band	Design.PinHorizontal	Logical	True	1.0
Band	Design.PinVertical	Logical	False	1.0
Band	Design.Selectable	Logical	True	4.5
Band	FieldName	String	ClassName	5.0
Band	First	String	#Band13.#Field15	1.0
Band	Focus	Logical	False	1.0
Band	FullName	String	#Band13	1.0
Band	FullSize	Point	(12225,195)	1.0
Band	Headings	Logical	PageAndGroup	1.0
Band	LeftBorder	LongInt	0	5.0
Band	Manager	String	#Report1	1.0
Band	Name	String	#Band13	1.0
Band	Next	String	#Page_Footer	1.0
Band	OtherBandName	String	#Band13	5.0

Object	Property	Type	Sample Value	Ver
Band	Owner	String	Blank	1.0
Band	Position	Point	(0,4787)	1.0
Band	PositionalOrder	SmallInt	3	5.0
Band	Prev	String	#Page_Header	1.0
Band	RightBorder	LongInt	15	5.0
Band	Select	Logical	False	4.5
Band	Shrinkable	Logical	True	1.0
Band	Size	Point	(12240,210)	1.0
Band	SortOrder	Logical	Ascending	1.0
Band	StartPageNumbers	Logical	False	5.0
Band	TopBorder	LongInt	15	5.0
Bitmap	Arrived	Logical	False	1.0
Bitmap	BottomBorder	LongInt	15	5.0
Bitmap	Class	String	Bitmap	1.0
Bitmap	ContainerName	String	#Page2	1.0
Bitmap	Design.ContainObjects	Logical	True	1.0
Bitmap	Design.PinHorizontal	Logical	False	1.0
Bitmap	Design.PinVertical	Logical	False	1.0
Bitmap	Design.Selectable	Logical	True	4.5

continues

TABLE E.1. CONTINUED

Object	Property	Type	Sample Value	Ver
Bitmap	Design.SizeToFit	Logical	True	1.0
Bitmap	First	String	Blank	1.0
Bitmap	Focus	Logical	False	1.0
Bitmap	Frame.Color	LongInt	Black	1.0
Bitmap	Frame.Style	SmallInt	SolidFrame	1.0
Bitmap	Frame.Thickness	SmallInt	15	1.0
Bitmap	FullName	String	#Page2.#Bitmap10	1.0
Bitmap	FullSize	Point	(1590,870)	1.0
Bitmap	HorizontalScrollBar	Logical	False	1.0
Bitmap	LeftBorder	LongInt	15	5.0
Bitmap	Magnification	SmallInt	Magnify100	1.0
Bitmap	Manager	String	#Form1	1.0
Bitmap	Name	String	#Bitmap10	1.0
Bitmap	Next	String	#Page2.#OLE11	1.0
Bitmap	Owner	String	Blank	1.0
Bitmap	PinHorizontal	Logical	False	1.0
Bitmap	PinVertical	Logical	False	1.0
Bitmap	Position	Point	(4590,2430)	1.0
Bitmap	Prev	String	#Page2.#Text9	1.0

Object	Property	Type	Sample Value	Ver
Bitmap	RasterOperation	LongInt	SourceCopy	1.0
Bitmap	RightBorder	LongInt	15	5.0
Bitmap	Scroll	Point	(0,0)	1.0
Bitmap	Select	Logical	False	4.5
Bitmap	Size	Point	(1620,900)	1.0
Bitmap	TopBorder	LongInt	15	5.0
Bitmap	Value	AnyType	Blank	1.0
Bitmap	VerticalScrollBar	Logical	False	1.0
Bitmap	Visible	Logical	True	1.0
Bitmap	WideScrollBar	Logical	False	5.0
Box	Arrived	Logical	False	1.0
Box	BottomBorder	LongInt	15	5.0
Box	Breakable	Logical	False	1.0
Box	Class	String	Box	1.0
Box	Color	LongInt	Transparent	1.0
Box	ContainerName	String	#Page2	1.0
Box	Design.ContainObjects	Logical	True	1.0
Box	Design.PinHorizontal	Logical	False	1.0
Box	Design.PinVertical	Logical	False	1.0

continues

Object	Property	Type	Sample Value	Ver
Box	Design.Selectable	Logical	True	4.5
Box	First	String	Blank	1.0
Box	FitHeight	Logical	True	1.0
Box	FitWidth	Logical	True	1.0
Box	Focus	Logical	False	1.0
Box	Frame.Color	LongInt	Black	1.0
Box	Frame.Style	SmallInt	SolidFrame	1.0
Box	Frame.Thickness	SmallInt	15	1.0
Box	FullName	String	#Page2.#Box6	1.0
Box	FullSize	Point	(1410,960)	1.0
Box	Invisible	Logical	False	1.0
Box	LeftBorder	LongInt	15	5.0
Box	Manager	String	#Form1	1.0
Box	Name	String	#Box6	1.0
Box	Next	String	#Page2.#Line7	1.0
Box	Owner	String	Blank	1.0
Box	Pattern.Color	LongInt	Black	1.0
Box	Pattern.Style	SmallInt	EmptyPattern	1.0
Box	PinHorizontal	Logical	False	1.0

Object	Property	Type	Sample Value	Ver
Box	PinVertical	Logical	False	1.0
Box	Position	Point	(7110,450)	1.0
Box	Prev	String	#Page2.#Field12	1.0
Box	RightBorder	LongInt	15	5.0
Box	Select	Logical	False	4.5
Box	Shrinkable	Logical	True	1.0
Box	Size	Point	(1440,990)	1.0
Box	TopBorder	LongInt	15	5.0
Box	Translucent	Logical	True	1.0
Box	Visible	Logical	True	1.0
Button	Arrived	Logical	False	1.0
Button	BottomBorder	LongInt	0	5.0
Button	ButtonType	SmallInt	PushButtonType	1.0
Button	CenterLabel	Logical	True	1.0
Button	CheckedValue	AnyType	Blank	5.0
Button	Class	String	Button	1.0
Button	ContainerName	String	#Page2	1.0
Button	Design.ContainObjects	Logical	True	1.0
Button	Design.PinHorizontal	Logical	False	1.0

continues

TABLE E.1. CONTINUED

Object	Property	Type	Sample Value	Ver
Button	Design.PinVertical	Logical	False	1.0
Button	Design.Selectable	Logical	True	4.5
Button	First	String	#Page2.#Button15.#Text16	1.0
Button	Focus	Logical	False	1.0
Button	FullName	String	#Page2.#Button15	1.0
Button	FullSize	Point	(1800,810)	1.0
Button	LabelText	String	LABEL	1.0
Button	LeftBorder	LongInt	0	5.0
Button	Manager	String	#Form1	1.0
Button	Name	String	#Button15	1.0
Button	Next	String	#Page2.#TableFrame17	1.0
Button	Owner	String	Blank	1.0
Button	Position	Point	(360,3510)	1.0
Button	Prev	String	#Page2.#OLE11	1.0
Button	RightBorder	LongInt	0	5.0
Button	Select	Logical	False	4.5
Button	Size	Point	(1800,810)	1.0
Button	Style	SmallInt	BorlandButton	1.0
Button	TabStop	Logical	False	1.0

Object	Property	Type	Sample Value	Ver
Button	TopBorder	LongInt	0	5.0
Button	UncheckedValue	AnyType	Blank	5.0
Button	Value	AnyType	False	1.0
Button	Visible	Logical	True	1.0
Cell	Arrived	Logical	False	1.0
Cell	BottomBorder	LongInt	0	5.0
Cell	Class	String	Cell	1.0
Cell	Color	LongInt	Transparent	1.0
Cell	ContainerName	String	#Page2.#Crosstab25	1.0
Cell	Design.ContainObjects	Logical	True	1.0
Cell	Design.PinHorizontal	Logical	True	1.0
Cell	Design.PinVertical	Logical	True	1.0
Cell	Design.SizeToFit	Logical	False	1.0
Cell	First	String	#Page2.#Crosstab25.#Cell26.#Field27	1.0
Cell	Focus	Logical	False	1.0
Cell	FullName	String	#Page2.#Crosstab25.#Cell26	1.0
Cell	FullSize	Point	(1590,390)	1.0
Cell	HorizontalScrollBar	Logical	False	1.0
Cell	LeftBorder	LongInt	0	5.0

continues

TABLE E.1. CONTINUED

Object	Property	Type	Sample Value	Ver
Cell	Manager	String	#Form1	1.0
Cell	Name	String	#Cell26	1.0
Cell	Next	String	#Page2.#Crosstab25.#Cell28	1.0
Cell	Owner	String	Blank	1.0
Cell	Position	Point	(1740,540)	1.0
Cell	Prev	String	#Page2.#Crosstab25.#Cell26	1.0
Cell	RightBorder	LongInt	0	5.0
Cell	Scroll	Point	(0,0)	1.0
Cell	Select	Logical	False	4.5
Cell	Size	Point	(1590,390)	1.0
Cell	TopBorder	LongInt	0	5.0
Cell	VerticalScrollBar	Logical	False	1.0
Crosstab	Arrived	Logical	False	1.0
Crosstab	BottomBorder	LongInt	90	5.0
Crosstab	Class	String	Crosstab	1.0
Crosstab	Color	LongInt	Transparent	1.0
Crosstab	ContainerName	String	#Page2	1.0
Crosstab	Design.PinHorizontal	Logical	False	1.0
Crosstab	Design.PinVertical	Logical	False	1.0

Object	Property	Type	Sample Value	Ver
Crosstab	Design.Selectable	Logical	True	4.5
Crosstab	First	String	#Page2.#Crosstab25.#Cell26	1.0
Crosstab	Focus	Logical	False	1.0
Crosstab	FullName	String	#Page2.#Crosstab25	1.0
Crosstab	FullSize	Point	(3330,930)	1.0
Crosstab	Grid.Color	LongInt	Black	1.0
Crosstab	Grid.GridStyle	SmallInt	tfDoubleLine	1.0
Crosstab	HorizontalScrollBar	Logical	False	1.0
Crosstab	LeftBorder	LongInt	105	5.0
Crosstab	Manager	String	#Form1	1.0
Crosstab	Name	String	#Crosstab25	1.0
Crosstab	Next	String	Blank	1.0
Crosstab	Owner	String	Blank	1.0
Crosstab	Position	Point	(7020,4680)	1.0
Crosstab	Prev	String	#Page2.#Graph24	1.0
Crosstab	RightBorder	LongInt	105	5.0
Crosstab	Scroll	Point	(0,0)	1.0
Crosstab	Select	Logical	False	4.5
Crosstab	Size	Point	(2160,720)	1.0

continues

TABLE E.1. CONTINUED

Object	Property	Type	Sample Value	Ver
Crosstab	TableName	String	Blank	1.0
Crosstab	TopBorder	LongInt	90	5.0
Crosstab	Touched	Logical	False	1.0
Crosstab	Translucent	Logical	True	1.0
Crosstab	VerticalScrollBar	Logical	False	1.0
Crosstab	Visible	Logical	True	1.0
Crosstab	WideScrollBar	Logical	False	5.0
EditRegion	Alignment	SmallInt	Left	1.0
EditRegion	Arrived	Logical	False	1.0
EditRegion	AvgCharSize	Point	(90,240)	5.0
EditRegion	BottomBorder	LongInt	15	5.0
EditRegion	Breakable	Logical	True	1.0
EditRegion	Class	String	EditRegion	1.0
EditRegion	Color	LongInt	Transparent	1.0
EditRegion	CompleteDisplay	Logical	False	1.0
EditRegion	ContainerName	String	#Page2.#Field12	1.0
EditRegion	Design.PinHorizontal	Logical	False	1.0
EditRegion	Design.PinVertical	Logical	False	1.0
EditRegion	Design.Selectable	Logical	True	4.5

Object	Property	Type	Sample Value	Ver
EditRegion	Design.SizeToFit	Logical	True	1.0
EditRegion	DisplayType	SmallInt	LabeledField	1.0
EditRegion	First	String	Blank	1.0
EditRegion	FitHeight	Logical	True	1.0
EditRegion	FitWidth	Logical	True	1.0
EditRegion	Focus	Logical	False	1.0
EditRegion	Font.Color	LongInt	Black	1.0
EditRegion	Font.Size	SmallInt	10	1.0
EditRegion	Font.Style	SmallInt	FontAttribNormal	1.0
EditRegion	Font.Typeface	String	Arial	1.0
EditRegion	Frame.Color	LongInt	Black	1.0
EditRegion	Frame.Style	SmallInt	NoFrame	1.0
EditRegion	Frame.Thickness	SmallInt	15	1.0
EditRegion	FullName	String	#Page2.#Field12.#EditRegion13	1.0
EditRegion	FullSize	Point	(3150,240)	1.0
EditRegion	LeftBorder	LongInt	15	5.0
EditRegion	Magnification	SmallInt	Magnify100	1.0
EditRegion	Manager	String	#Form1	1.0
EditRegion	Name	String	#EditRegion13	1.0

continues

TABLE E.1. CONTINUED

Object	Property	Type	Sample Value	Ver
EditRegion	Next	String	#Page2.#Field12.#Text14	1.0
EditRegion	NoEcho	Logical	False	1.0
EditRegion	Owner	String	Blank	1.0
EditRegion	PinHorizontal	Logical	False	1.0
EditRegion	PinVertical	Logical	False	1.0
EditRegion	Position	Point	(1515,80)	1.0
EditRegion	Prev	String	#Page2.#Field12.#Text14	1.0
EditRegion	Readonly	Logical	False	1.0
EditRegion	RightBorder	LongInt	15	5.0
EditRegion	Scroll	Point	(0,0)	1.0
EditRegion	Select	Logical	False	4.5
EditRegion	Size	Point	(3150,240)	1.0
EditRegion	TabStop	Logical	True	1.0
EditRegion	Text	String	RTL10.ClassName [A32]	4.5
EditRegion	TopBorder	LongInt	15	5.0
EditRegion	Translucent	Logical	True	1.0
EditRegion	Value	AnyType	RTL10.ClassName [A32]	4.5
EditRegion	Visible	Logical	True	1.0
EditRegion	WordWrap	Logical	False	1.0

Object	Property	Type	Sample Value	Ver
Ellipse	Arrived	Logical	False	1.0
Ellipse	BottomBorder	LongInt	15	5.0
Ellipse	Class	String	Ellipse	1.0
Ellipse	Color	LongInt	Transparent	1.0
Ellipse	ContainerName	String	#Page2	1.0
Ellipse	Design.ContainObjects	Logical	True	1.0
Ellipse	Design.PinHorizontal	Logical	False	1.0
Ellipse	Design.PinVertical	Logical	False	1.0
Ellipse	Design.Selectable	Logical	True	4.5
Ellipse	First	String	Blank	1.0
Ellipse	FitHeight	Logical	True	1.0
Ellipse	FitWidth	Logical	True	1.0
Ellipse	Focus	Logical	False	1.0
Ellipse	FullName	String	#Page2.#Ellipse8	1.0
Ellipse	FullSize	Point	(1680,870)	1.0
Ellipse	LeftBorder	LongInt	15	5.0
Ellipse	Line.Color	LongInt	Black	1.0
Ellipse	Line.LineStyle	SmallInt	SolidLine	1.0
Ellipse	Line.Thickness	SmallInt	15	1.0

continues

TABLE E.1. CONTINUED

Object	Property	Type	Sample Value	Ver
Ellipse	Manager	String	#Form1	1.0
Ellipse	Name	String	#Ellipse8	1.0
Ellipse	Next	String	#Page2.#Text9	1.0
Ellipse	Owner	String	Blank	1.0
Ellipse	Pattern.Color	LongInt	Black	1.0
Ellipse	Pattern.Style	SmallInt	EmptyPattern	1.0
Ellipse	PinHorizontal	Logical	False	1.0
Ellipse	PinVertical	Logical	False	1.0
Ellipse	Position	Point	(360,2340)	1.0
Ellipse	Prev	String	#Page2.#Line7	1.0
Ellipse	RightBorder	LongInt	15	5.0
Ellipse	Select	Logical	False	4.5
Ellipse	Shrinkable	Logical	False	1.0
Ellipse	Size	Point	(1710,900)	1.0
Ellipse	TopBorder	LongInt	15	5.0
Ellipse	Translucent	Logical	True	1.0
Ellipse	Visible	Logical	True	1.0
Field	Alignment	SmallInt	Left	1.0
Field	Arrived	Logical	False	1.0

Object	Property	Type	Sample Value	Ver
Field	AutoAppend	Logical	False	4.5
Field	AvgCharSize	Point	(90,240)	5.0
Field	BlankRecord	Logical	False	1.0
Field	BottomBorder	LongInt	15	5.0
Field	Breakable	Logical	True	1.0
Field	CalculatedField	Logical	False	5.0
Field	Class	String	Field	1.0
Field	Color	LongInt	Transparent	1.0
Field	CompleteDisplay	Logical	False	1.0
Field	ContainerName	String	#Page2	1.0
Field	Default	String	Blank	1.0
Field	DeleteWhenEmpty	Logical	False	5.0
Field	Deleted	Logical	False	1.0
Field	Design.PinHorizontal	Logical	False	1.0
Field	Design.PinVertical	Logical	False	1.0
Field	Design.Selectable	Logical	True	4.5
Field	Design.SizeToFit	Logical	True	1.0
Field	DisplayType	SmallInt	EditField	1.0
Field	Editing	Logical	False	1.0

continues

TABLE E.1. CONTINUED

Object	Property	Type	Sample Value	Ver
Field	FieldName	String	Blank	1.0
Field	FieldNo	SmallInt	1	1.0
Field	FieldRights	String	ReadWrite	1.0
Field	FieldSize	SmallInt	255	1.0
Field	FieldType	String	ALPHA	1.0
Field	FieldUnits2	SmallInt	0	1.0
Field	FieldValid	Logical	True	1.0
Field	First	String	#Page2.#Field12.#EditRegion13	1.0
Field	FitHeight	Logical	True	1.0
Field	FitWidth	Logical	True	1.0
Field	FlyAway	Logical	False	1.0
Field	Focus	Logical	False	1.0
Field	Font.Color	LongInt	Black	1.0
Field	Font.Size	SmallInt	10	1.0
Field	Font.Style	SmallInt	FontAttribNormal	1.0
Field	Font.Typeface	String	Arial	1.0
Field	Format.DateFormat	String	DWSMSDSYSOS	1.0
Field	Format.LogicalFormat	String	LT(True)	1.0
Field	Format.NumberFormat	String	W.W,ENWDWLW	1.0

Object	Property	Type	Sample Value	Ver
Field	Format.TimeFormat	String	THWMWSWNWOW	1.0
Field	Format.TimeStampFormat	String	DWSMSDSYSOS,THWMWSWNWOW	1.0
Field	Frame.Color	LongInt	Black	1.0
Field	Frame.Style	SmallInt	NoFrame	1.0
Field	Frame.Thickness	SmallInt	15	1.0
Field	FullName	String	#Page2.#Crosstab25.#Cell26.#Field27	1.0
Field	FullSize	Point	(1410,210)	1.0
Field	HorizontalScrollBar	Logical	False	1.0
Field	IndexField	Logical	False	1.0
Field	Inserting	Logical	False	1.0
Field	KeyField	Logical	False	1.0
Field	LabelText	String	ClassName :	1.0
Field	LeftBorder	LongInt	15	5.0
Field	Locked	Logical	False	1.0
Field	LookupTable	String	Blank	1.0
Field	LookupType	String	Blank	1.0
Field	Magnification	SmallInt	Magnify100	1.0
Field	Manager	String	#Form1	1.0
Field	Maximum	String	Blank	1.0

continues

Object	Property	Type	Sample Value	Ver
Field	Minimum	String	Blank	1.0
Field	NRecords	LongInt	1159	1.0
Field	Name	String	#Field12	1.0
Field	Next	String	#Page2.#Box6	1.0
Field	NextTabStop	String	Blank	5.0
Field	NoEcho	Logical	False	1.0
Field	Owner	String	Blank	1.0
Field	Pattern.Color	LongInt	Black	1.0
Field	Pattern.Style	SmallInt	EmptyPattern	1.0
Field	Picture	String	Blank	1.0
Field	PinHorizontal	Logical	True	1.0
Field	PinVertical	Logical	False	1.0
Field	Position	Point	(105,0)	1.0
Field	Prev	String	#Page2.#Crosstab25	1.0
Field	RasterOperation	LongInt	SourceCopy	1.0
Field	Readonly	Logical	False	1.0
Field	RecNo	LongInt	0	1.0
Field	Refresh	Logical	False	1.0
Field	Required	Logical	False	1.0

Object	Property	Type	Sample Value	Ver
Field	RightBorder	LongInt	15	5.0
Field	RowNo	SmallInt	0	1.0
Field	Scroll	Point	(0,0)	1.0
Field	Select	Logical	False	4.5
Field	SeqNo	LongInt	0	1.0
Field	Size	Point	(1440,240)	1.0
Field	SpecialField	SmallInt	DateField	5.0
Field	TabStop	Logical	True	1.0
Field	TableName	String	Blank	1.0
Field	Text	String	RTL10.ClassName [A32]	1.0
Field	TopBorder	LongInt	15	5.0
Field	Touched	Logical	False	1.0
Field	Translucent	Logical	True	1.0
Field	Value	String	RTL10.ClassName [A32]	1.0
Field	VerticalScrollBar	Logical	False	1.0
Field	Visible	Logical	True	1.0
Field	WideScrollBar	Logical	False	5.0
Field	WordWrap	Logical	False	1.0
Form	Arrived	Logical	False	1.0

continues

Table E.1. continued

Object	Property	Type	Sample Value	Ver
Form	AutoAppend	Logical	False	4.5
Form	BlankRecord	Logical	False	1.0
Form	Border	Logical	False	1.0
Form	Caption	Logical	False	1.0
Form	Class	String	Form	1.0
Form	ContainerName	String	Blank	1.0
Form	ControlMenu	Logical	False	1.0
Form	Deleted	Logical	False	1.0
Form	DesignModified	Logical	False	4.5
Form	DesktopForm	Logical	False	1.0
Form	DialogForm	Logical	False	1.0
Form	DialogFrame	Logical	False	1.0
Form	Editing	Logical	False	1.0
Form	FieldView	Logical	False	1.0
Form	First	String	#Page2	1.0
Form	FlyAway	Logical	False	1.0
Form	Focus	Logical	False	1.0
Form	FrameObjects	Logical	True	5.0
Form	FullName	String	#Form1	1.0

Object	Property	Type	Sample Value	Ver
Form	FullSize	Point	(9601,6631)	1.0
Form	GridValue	Point	(1440,1440)	5.0
Form	HorizontalScrollBar	Logical	True	1.0
Form	Inserting	Logical	False	1.0
Form	Locked	Logical	False	1.0
Form	Manager	String	#Form1	1.0
Form	MaximizeButton	Logical	False	1.0
Form	MemoView	Logical	False	1.0
Form	MinimizeButton	Logical	False	1.0
Form	Modal	Logical	False	1.0
Form	MouseActivate	Logical	True	1.0
Form	NRecords	LongInt	0	1.0
Form	Name	String	#Form1	1.0
Form	Next	String	Blank	1.0
Form	PersistView	Logical	False	1.0
Form	Position	Point	(0,0)	1.0
Form	Prev	String	Blank	1.0
Form	PrinterDocument	Logical	False	5.0
Form	RecNo	LongInt	0	1.0

continues

TABLE E.1. CONTINUED

Object	Property	Type	Sample Value	Ver
Form	Refresh	Logical	False	1.0
Form	Scroll	Point	(0,0)	1.0
Form	SeeMouseMove	Logical	False	5.0
Form	SeqNo	LongInt	0	1.0
Form	ShowGrid	Logical	False	5.0
Form	Size	Point	(7845,3825)	1.0
Form	SizeToFit	Logical	False	1.0
Form	SnapToGrid	Logical	True	5.0
Form	StandardMenu	Logical	True	1.0
Form	TableName	String	RTL10.DB	1.0
Form	ThickFrame	Logical	False	1.0
Form	Title	String	Form Design : RTLP10	1.0
Form	Touched	Logical	False	1.0
Form	VerticalScrollBar	Logical	True	1.0
Graph	Arrived	Logical	False	1.0
Graph	BackWall.Color	LongInt	13112735	1.0
Graph	BackWall.Pattern.Color	LongInt	Black	1.0
Graph	BackWall.Pattern.Style	SmallInt	EmptyPattern	1.0
Graph	Background.Color	LongInt	Transparent	1.0

Object	Property	Type	Sample Value	Ver
Graph	Background.Pattern.Color	LongInt	Black	1.0
Graph	Background.Pattern.Style	SmallInt	EmptyPattern	1.0
Graph	BaseFloor.Color	LongInt	13172735	1.0
Graph	BaseFloor.Pattern.Color	LongInt	Black	1.0
Graph	BaseFloor.Pattern.Style	SmallInt	EmptyPattern	1.0
Graph	BindType	SmallInt	GraphTabular	1.0
Graph	BottomBorder	LongInt	15	5.0
Graph	Class	String	Graph	1.0
Graph	Color	LongInt	Transparent	1.0
Graph	ContainerName	String	#Page2	1.0
Graph	CurrentSeries	SmallInt	1	1.0
Graph	CurrentSlice	SmallInt	1	1.0
Graph	Design.ContainObjects	Logical	True	1.0
Graph	Design.PinHorizontal	Logical	False	1.0
Graph	Design.PinVertical	Logical	False	1.0
Graph	Design.Selectable	Logical	True	4.5
Graph	First	String	Blank	1.0
Graph	Focus	Logical	False	1.0
Graph	Frame.Color	LongInt	Black	1.0

continues

	TABLE E.1. CONTINUED			
Object	Property	Type	Sample Value	Ver
Graph	Frame.Style	SmallInt	SolidFrame	1.0
Graph	Frame.Thickness	SmallInt	15	1.0
Graph	FullName	String	#Page2.#Graph24	1.0
Graph	FullSize	Point	(1770,780)	1.0
Graph	GraphType	SmallInt	Graph2DBar	1.0
Graph	Label.Font.Color	LongInt	Black	1.0
Graph	Label.Font.Size	SmallInt	10	1.0
Graph	Label.Font.Style	SmallInt	FontAttribNormal	1.0
Graph	Label.Font.Typeface	String	Arial	1.0
Graph	Label.LabelFormat	SmallInt	GraphPercent	1.0
Graph	Label.LabelLocation	SmallInt	Above	1.0
Graph	Label.NumberFormat	String	W.2,ET	1.0
Graph	LeftBorder	LongInt	15	5.0
Graph	LeftWall.Color	LongInt	13172735	1.0
Graph	LeftWall.Pattern.Color	LongInt	Black	1.0
Graph	LeftWall.Pattern.Style	SmallInt	EmptyPattern	1.0
Graph	LegendBox.Color	LongInt	Transparent	1.0
Graph	LegendBox.Font.Color	LongInt	Black	1.0
Graph	LegendBox.Font.Size	SmallInt	10	1.0

Object	Property	Type	Sample Value	Ver
Graph	LegendBox.Font.Style	SmallInt	FontAttribNormal	1.0
Graph	LegendBox.Font.Typeface	String	Arial	1.0
Graph	LegendBox.LegendPos	SmallInt	Bottom	1.0
Graph	LegendBox.Pattern.Color	LongInt	Black	1.0
Graph	LegendBox.Pattern.Style	SmallInt	EmptyPattern	1.0
Graph	Manager	String	#Form1	1.0
Graph	MaxGroups	SmallInt	8	1.0
Graph	MaxXValues	SmallInt	8	1.0
Graph	MinXValues	SmallInt	8	1.0
Graph	Name	String	#Graph24	1.0
Graph	Next	String	#Page2.#Crosstab25	1.0
Graph	NextTabStop	String	Blank	5.0
Graph	Options.Elevation	SmallInt	60	1.0
Graph	Options.Rotation	SmallInt	30	1.0
Graph	Options.ShowAxes	Logical	True	1.0
Graph	Options.ShowGrid	Logical	True	1.0
Graph	Options.ShowLabels	Logical	False	1.0
Graph	Options.ShowLegend	Logical	False	1.0
Graph	Options.ShowTitle	Logical	True	1.0

continues

TABLE E.1. CONTINUED

Object	Property	Type	Sample Value	Ver
Graph	Owner	String	Blank	1.0
Graph	Pattern.Color	LongInt	Black	1.0
Graph	Pattern.Style	SmallInt	EmptyPattern	1.0
Graph	PinHorizontal	Logical	False	1.0
Graph	PinVertical	Logical	False	1.0
Graph	Position	Point	(7290,3600)	1.0
Graph	Prev	String	#Page2.#Multirecord22	1.0
Graph	RightBorder	LongInt	15	5.0
Graph	Scroll	Point	(0,0)	1.0
Graph	Select	Logical	False	4.5
Graph	Series.Color	LongInt	Blue	1.0
Graph	Series.Graph_Title.Text	String	Blank	1.0
Graph	Series.Graph_Title.UseDefault	Logical	True	1.0
Graph	Series.Line.Color	LongInt	Black	1.0
Graph	Series.Line.LineStyle	SmallInt	SolidLine	1.0
Graph	Series.Line.Thickness	SmallInt	15	1.0
Graph	Series.Marker	SmallInt	MarkerFilledBox	1.0
Graph	Series.Marker.Size	SmallInt	MarkerSize18	5.0
Graph	Series.Marker.Style	SmallInt	MarkerFilledBox	5.0

Object	Property	Type	Sample Value	Ver
Graph	Series.Pattern.Color	LongInt	Black	1.0
Graph	Series.Pattern.Style	SmallInt	EmptyPattern	1.0
Graph	Series.TypeOverride	SmallInt	None	1.0
Graph	SeriesName	String	[Undefined Field]	5.0
Graph	Size	Point	(1800,810)	1.0
Graph	Slice.Color	LongInt	Blue	1.0
Graph	Slice.Explode	Logical	False	1.0
Graph	Slice.Pattern.Color	LongInt	Black	1.0
Graph	Slice.Pattern.Style	SmallInt	EmptyPattern	1.0
Graph	TabStop	Logical	True	1.0
Graph	TableName	String	Blank	1.0
Graph	TitleBox.Color	LongInt	Transparent	1.0
Graph	TitleBox.Graph_Title.Font.Color	LongInt	Black	1.0
Graph	TitleBox.Graph_Title.Font.Size	SmallInt	12	1.0
Graph	TitleBox.Graph_Title.Font.Style	SmallInt	FontAttribNormal	1.0
Graph	TitleBox.Graph_Title.Font.Typeface	String	Arial	1.0
Graph	TitleBox.Graph_Title.Text	String	Blank	1.0
Graph	TitleBox.Graph_Title.UseDefault	Logical	True	1.0
Graph	TitleBox.Pattern.Color	LongInt	Black	1.0

continues

TABLE E.1. CONTINUED

Object	Property	Type	Sample Value	Ver
Graph	TitleBox.Pattern.Style	SmallInt	EmptyPattern	1.0
Graph	TitleBox.Subtitle.Font.Color	LongInt	Black	1.0
Graph	TitleBox.Subtitle.Font.Size	SmallInt	10	1.0
Graph	TitleBox.Subtitle.Font.Style	SmallInt	FontAttribNormal	1.0
Graph	TitleBox.Subtitle.Font.Typeface	String	Arial	1.0
Graph	TitleBox.Subtitle.Text	String	Blank	1.0
Graph	TitleBox.Subtitle.UseDefault	Logical	True	1.0
Graph	TitleBoxName	String	[Undefined Field]	5.0
Graph	TopBorder	LongInt	15	5.0
Graph	Touched	Logical	False	1.0
Graph	Translucent	Logical	True	1.0
Graph	Visible	Logical	True	1.0
Graph	XAxis.Graph_Title.Font.Color	LongInt	Black	1.0
Graph	XAxis.Graph_Title.Font.Size	SmallInt	10	1.0
Graph	XAxis.Graph_Title.Font.Style	SmallInt	FontAttribNormal	1.0
Graph	XAxis.Graph_Title.Font.Typeface	String	Arial	1.0
Graph	XAxis.Graph_Title.Text	String	Blank	1.0
Graph	XAxis.Graph_Title.UseDefault	Logical	True	1.0
Graph	XAxis.Scale.AutoScale	Logical	True	1.0

Object	Property	Type	Sample Value	Ver
Graph	XAxis.Scale.HighValue	Number	100.00	1.0
Graph	XAxis.Scale.Increment	Number	0.00	1.0
Graph	XAxis.Scale.Logarithmic	Logical	False	1.0
Graph	XAxis.Scale.LowValue	Number	0.00	1.0
Graph	XAxis.Ticks.Alternate	Logical	False	1.0
Graph	XAxis.Ticks.DateFormat	String	W.2,ET	1.0
Graph	XAxis.Ticks.Font.Color	LongInt	Black	1.0
Graph	XAxis.Ticks.Font.Size	SmallInt	10	1.0
Graph	XAxis.Ticks.Font.Style	SmallInt	FontAttribNormal	1.0
Graph	XAxis.Ticks.Font.Typeface	String	Arial	1.0
Graph	XAxis.Ticks.NumberFormat	String	W.2,ET	1.0
Graph	XAxis.Ticks.TimeFormat	String	W.2,ET	4.5
Graph	XAxis.Ticks.TimeStampFormat	String	W.2,ET	4.5
Graph	XAxisName	String	[Undefined Field]	5.0
Graph	YAxis.Graph_Title.Font.Color	LongInt	Black	1.0
Graph	YAxis.Graph_Title.Font.Size	SmallInt	10	1.0
Graph	YAxis.Graph_Title.Font.Style	SmallInt	FontAttribNormal	1.0
Graph	YAxis.Graph_Title.Font.Typeface	String	Arial	1.0
Graph	YAxis.Graph_Title.Text	String	Blank	1.0

continues

TABLE E.1. CONTINUED

Object	Property	Type	Sample Value	Ver
Graph	YAxis.Graph_Title.UseDefault	Logical	True	1.0
Graph	YAxis.Scale.AutoScale	Logical	True	1.0
Graph	YAxis.Scale.HighValue	Number	50.00	1.0
Graph	YAxis.Scale.Increment	Number	50.00	1.0
Graph	YAxis.Scale.Logarithmic	Logical	False	1.0
Graph	YAxis.Scale.LowValue	Number	0.00	1.0
Graph	YAxis.Ticks.Alternate	Logical	False	1.0
Graph	YAxis.Ticks.DateFormat	String	W.2,ET	1.0
Graph	YAxis.Ticks.Font.Color	LongInt	Black	1.0
Graph	YAxis.Ticks.Font.Size	SmallInt	10	1.0
Graph	YAxis.Ticks.Font.Style	SmallInt	FontAttribNormal	1.0
Graph	YAxis.Ticks.Font.Typeface	String	Arial	1.0
Graph	YAxis.Ticks.NumberFormat	String	W.2,ET	1.0
Graph	YAxis.Ticks.TimeFormat	String	W.2,ET	4.5
Graph	YAxis.Ticks.TimeStampFormat	String	W.2,ET	4.5
Graph	YAxisName	String	[Undefined Field]	5.0
Graph	ZAxis.Graph_Title.Text	String	Blank	1.0
Graph	ZAxis.Graph_Title.UseDefault	Logical	True	1.0
Graph	ZAxis.Ticks.Font.Color	LongInt	Black	1.0

Object	Property	Type	Sample Value	Ver
Graph	ZAxis.Ticks.Font.Size	SmallInt	10	1.0
Graph	ZAxis.Ticks.Font.Style	SmallInt	FontAttribNormal	1.0
Graph	ZAxis.Ticks.Font.Typeface	String	Arial	1.0
Graph	ZAxisName	String	Blank	5.0
Header	Arrived	Logical	False	1.0
Header	BottomBorder	LongInt	0	5.0
Header	Class	String	Header	1.0
Header	Color	LongInt	Transparent	1.0
Header	ContainerName	String	#Page2.#TableFrame17	1.0
Header	Design.ContainObjects	Logical	True	1.0
Header	Design.PinHorizontal	Logical	True	1.0
Header	Design.PinVertical	Logical	True	1.0
Header	Design.Selectable	Logical	True	4.5
Header	First	String	#Page2.#TableFrame17.#Header18.#Text20	1.0
Header	Focus	Logical	False	1.0
Header	FullName	String	#Page2.#TableFrame17.#Header18	1.0
Header	FullSize	Point	(2340,391)	1.0
Header	LeftBorder	LongInt	0	5.0
Header	Manager	String	#Form1	1.0

continues

TABLE E.1. CONTINUED

Object	Property	Type	Sample Value	Ver
Header	Name	String	#Header18	1.0
Header	Next	String	#Page2.#TableFrame17.#Record19	1.0
Header	Owner	String	Blank	1.0
Header	PinHorizontal	Logical	False	1.0
Header	PinVertical	Logical	False	1.0
Header	Position	Point	(0,0)	1.0
Header	Prev	String	#Page2.#TableFrame17.#Record19	1.0
Header	RightBorder	LongInt	0	5.0
Header	Select	Logical	False	4.5
Header	Size	Point	(2340,391)	1.0
Header	TopBorder	LongInt	0	5.0
Header	Translucent	Logical	True	1.0
Header	Visible	Logical	True	1.0
Line	Arrived	Logical	False	1.0
Line	BottomBorder	LongInt	0	5.0
Line	Breakable	Logical	False	1.0
Line	Class	String	Line	1.0
Line	Color	LongInt	Black	1.0
Line	ContainerName	String	#Page2	1.0

Object	Property	Type	Sample Value	Ver
Line	Design.PinHorizontal	Logical	False	1.0
Line	Design.PinVertical	Logical	False	1.0
Line	Design.Selectable	Logical	True	4.5
Line	End	Point	(8550,2160)	1.0
Line	First	String	Blank	1.0
Line	Focus	Logical	False	1.0
Line	FullName	String	#Page2.#Line7	1.0
Line	FullSize	Point	(1800,450)	1.0
Line	Invisible	Logical	False	1.0
Line	LeftBorder	LongInt	0	5.0
Line	LineEnds	SmallInt	NoArrowEnd	1.0
Line	LineStyle	SmallInt	SolidLine	1.0
Line	LineType	SmallInt	StraightLine	1.0
Line	Manager	String	#Form1	1.0
Line	Name	String	#Line7	1.0
Line	Next	String	#Page2.#Ellipse8	1.0
Line	Owner	String	Blank	1.0
Line	PinHorizontal	Logical	False	1.0
Line	PinVertical	Logical	False	1.0

continues

TABLE E.1. CONTINUED

Object	Property	Type	Sample Value	Ver
Line	Position	Point	(6750,1710)	1.0
Line	Prev	String	#Page2.#Box6	1.0
Line	RightBorder	LongInt	0	5.0
Line	Select	Logical	False	4.5
Line	Size	Point	(1800,450)	1.0
Line	Start	Point	(6750,1710)	1.0
Line	Thickness	SmallInt	15	1.0
Line	TopBorder	LongInt	0	5.0
Line	Visible	Logical	True	1.0
Multirecord	Arrived	Logical	False	1.0
Multirecord	AutoAppend	Logical	False	4.5
Multirecord	BlankRecord	Logical	False	1.0
Multirecord	BottomBorder	LongInt	15	5.0
Multirecord	Breakable	Logical	True	1.0
Multirecord	ByRows	Logical	True	5.0
Multirecord	Class	String	Multirecord	1.0
Multirecord	Color	LongInt	Transparent	1.0
Multirecord	ContainerName	String	#Page2	1.0
Multirecord	Deleted	Logical	False	1.0

Object	Property	Type	Sample Value	Ver
Multirecord	Design.PinHorizontal	Logical	False	1.0
Multirecord	Design.PinVertical	Logical	False	1.0
Multirecord	Design.Selectable	Logical	True	4.5
Multirecord	Editing	Logical	False	4.5
Multirecord	First	String	#Page2.#Multirecord22.#Record23	1.0
Multirecord	FirstRow	String	#Record23	5.0
Multirecord	FitHeight	Logical	True	1.0
Multirecord	FitWidth	Logical	True	1.0
Multirecord	FlyAway	Logical	False	1.0
Multirecord	Focus	Logical	False	1.0
Multirecord	Frame.Color	LongInt	Black	1.0
Multirecord	Frame.Style	SmallInt	SolidFrame	1.0
Multirecord	Frame.Thickness	SmallInt	15	1.0
Multirecord	FullName	String	#Page2.#Multirecord22	1.0
Multirecord	FullSize	Point	(1830,1470)	1.0
Multirecord	Inserting	Logical	False	1.0
Multirecord	LeftBorder	LongInt	15	5.0
Multirecord	Locked	Logical	False	1.0
Multirecord	Manager	String	#Form1	1.0

continues

TABLE E.1. CONTINUED

Object	Property	Type	Sample Value	Ver
Multirecord	NCols	SmallInt	2	1.0
Multirecord	NRecords	LongInt	0	1.0
Multirecord	NRows	SmallInt	2	1.0
Multirecord	Name	String	#Multirecord22	1.0
Multirecord	Next	String	#Page2.#Graph24	1.0
Multirecord	Owner	String	Blank	1.0
Multirecord	Pattern.Color	LongInt	Black	1.0
Multirecord	Pattern.Style	SmallInt	EmptyPattern	1.0
Multirecord	PinHorizontal	Logical	False	1.0
Multirecord	PinVertical	Logical	False	1.0
Multirecord	Position	Point	(4950,3780)	1.0
Multirecord	Prev	String	#Page2.#TableFrame17	1.0
Multirecord	Readonly	Logical	False	1.0
Multirecord	RecNo	LongInt	0	1.0
Multirecord	Refresh	Logical	False	1.0
Multirecord	RightBorder	LongInt	15	5.0
Multirecord	RowNo	SmallInt	1	1.0
Multirecord	Scroll	Point	(0,0)	1.0
Multirecord	Select	Logical	False	4.5

Object	Property	Type	Sample Value	Ver
Multirecord	SeqNo	LongInt	0	1.0
Multirecord	Size	Point	(1890,1530)	1.0
Multirecord	TableName	String	Blank	1.0
Multirecord	TopBorder	LongInt	15	5.0
Multirecord	Touched	Logical	False	1.0
Multirecord	Translucent	Logical	True	1.0
Multirecord	VerticalScrollBar	Logical	False	1.0
Multirecord	Visible	Logical	True	1.0
Multirecord	WideScrollBar	Logical	False	5.0
Multirecord	Xseparation	SmallInt	144	5.0
Multirecord	Yseparation	SmallInt	144	5.0
OLE	Arrived	Logical	False	1.0
OLE	BottomBorder	LongInt	15	5.0
OLE	Class	String	OLE	1.0
OLE	ContainerName	String	#Page2	1.0
OLE	Design.ContainObjects	Logical	True	1.0
OLE	Design.PinHorizontal	Logical	False	1.0
OLE	Design.PinVertical	Logical	False	1.0
OLE	Design.Selectable	Logical	True	4.5

continues

TABLE E.1. CONTINUED

Object	Property	Type	Sample Value	Ver
OLE	Design.SizeToFit	Logical	True	1.0
OLE	First	String	Blank	1.0
OLE	Focus	Logical	False	1.0
OLE	Frame.Color	LongInt	Black	1.0
OLE	Frame.Style	SmallInt	SolidFrame	1.0
OLE	Frame.Thickness	SmallInt	15	1.0
OLE	FullName	String	#Page2.#OLE11	1.0
OLE	FullSize	Point	(1590,780)	1.0
OLE	HorizontalScrollBar	Logical	False	1.0
OLE	LeftBorder	LongInt	15	5.0
OLE	Magnification	SmallInt	Magnify100	1.0
OLE	Manager	String	#Form1	1.0
OLE	Name	String	#OLE11	1.0
OLE	Next	String	#Page2.#Button15	1.0
OLE	Owner	String	Blank	1.0
OLE	PinHorizontal	Logical	False	1.0
OLE	PinVertical	Logical	False	1.0
OLE	Position	Point	(6570,2610)	1.0
OLE	Prev	String	#Page2.#Bitmap10	1.0

Object	Property	Type	Sample Value	Ver
OLE	RightBorder	LongInt	15	5.0
OLE	Scroll	Point	(0,0)	1.0
OLE	Select	Logical	False	4.5
OLE	Size	Point	(1620,810)	1.0
OLE	TopBorder	LongInt	15	5.0
OLE	Value	AnyType	Blank	1.0
OLE	VerticalScrollBar	Logical	False	1.0
OLE	Visible	Logical	True	1.0
OLE	WideScrollBar	Logical	False	5.0
Page	Arrived	Logical	False	1.0
Page	BottomBorder	LongInt	15	5.0
Page	Class	String	Page	1.0
Page	Color	LongInt	Transparent	1.0
Page	ContainerName	String	#Form1	1.0
Page	First	String	#Page2.#Field3	1.0
Page	Focus	Logical	False	1.0
Page	FullName	String	#Page2	1.0
Page	FullSize	Point	(9598,6628)	1.0
Page	LeftBorder	LongInt	15	5.0

continues

TABLE E.1. CONTINUED

Object	Property	Type	Sample Value	Ver
Page	Manager	String	#Form1	1.0
Page	Name	String	#Page2	1.0
Page	Next	String	Blank	1.0
Page	Owner	String	Blank	1.0
Page	Pattern.Color	LongInt	Black	1.0
Page	Pattern.Style	SmallInt	EmptyPattern	1.0
Page	Position	Point	(0,0)	1.0
Page	PositionalOrder	SmallInt	1	5.0
Page	Prev	String	#Page2	1.0
Page	RightBorder	LongInt	15	5.0
Page	Select	Logical	False	4.5
Page	Size	Point	(9600,6630)	1.0
Page	TopBorder	LongInt	15	5.0
Page	Translucent	Logical	True	1.0
Page	Visible	Logical	True	5.0
Page_Footer	Arrived	Logical	False	1.0
Page_Footer	BottomBorder	LongInt	0	5.0
Page_Footer	Class	String	Band	1.0
Page_Footer	ContainerName	String	#Report1	1.0

Object	Property	Type	Sample Value	Ver
Page_Footer	Design.PinHorizontal	Logical	True	1.0
Page_Footer	Design.PinVertical	Logical	True	1.0
Page_Footer	Design.Selectable	Logical	True	4.5
Page_Footer	First	String	Blank	1.0
Page_Footer	Focus	Logical	False	1.0
Page_Footer	FullName	String	#Page_Footer	1.0
Page_Footer	FullSize	Point	(12224,195)	1.0
Page_Footer	LeftBorder	LongInt	0	5.0
Page_Footer	Manager	String	#Report1	1.0
Page_Footer	Name	String	#Page_Footer	1.0
Page_Footer	Next	String	#Report_Footer	1.0
Page_Footer	OtherBandName	String	#Page_Header	5.0
Page_Footer	Owner	String	Blank	1.0
Page_Footer	Position	Point	(0,4997)	1.0
Page_Footer	PositionalOrder	SmallInt	6	5.0
Page_Footer	Prev	String	#Band14	1.0
Page_Footer	PrintOn1stPage	Logical	True	1.0
Page_Footer	RightBorder	LongInt	15	5.0
Page_Footer	Select	Logical	False	4.5

continues

TABLE E.1. CONTINUED

Object	Property	Type	Sample Value	Ver
Page_Footer	Size	Point	(12239,210)	1.0
Page_Footer	TopBorder	LongInt	15	5.0
Page_Header	Arrived	Logical	False	1.0
Page_Header	BottomBorder	LongInt	0	5.0
Page_Header	Class	String	Band	1.0
Page_Header	ContainerName	String	#Report1	1.0
Page_Header	Design.PinHorizontal	Logical	True	1.0
Page_Header	Design.PinVertical	Logical	True	1.0
Page_Header	Design.Selectable	Logical	True	4.5
Page_Header	First	String	#Page_Header.#Field6	1.0
Page_Header	Focus	Logical	False	1.0
Page_Header	FullName	String	#Page_Header	1.0
Page_Header	FullSize	Point	(12224,445)	1.0
Page_Header	LeftBorder	LongInt	0	5.0
Page_Header	Manager	String	#Report1	1.0
Page_Header	Name	String	#Page_Header	1.0
Page_Header	Next	String	#Band13	1.0
Page_Header	OtherBandName	String	#Page_Footer	5.0
Page_Header	Owner	String	Blank	1.0

Object	Property	Type	Sample Value	Ver
Page_Header	Position	Point	(0,210)	1.0
Page_Header	PositionalOrder	SmallInt	2	5.0
Page_Header	Prev	String	#Report_Header	1.0
Page_Header	PrintOn1stPage	Logical	True	1.0
Page_Header	RightBorder	LongInt	15	5.0
Page_Header	Select	Logical	False	4.5
Page_Header	Size	Point	(12239,460)	1.0
Page_Header	TopBorder	LongInt	15	5.0
Record	Arrived	Logical	False	1.0
Record	AutoAppend	Logical	False	4.5
Record	BlankRecord	Logical	False	1.0
Record	BottomBorder	LongInt	0	5.0
Record	Breakable	Logical	False	4.5
Record	Class	String	Record	1.0
Record	Color	LongInt	Transparent	1.0
Record	ContainerName	String	#Page2.#Multirecord22	1.0
Record	DeleteWhenEmpty	Logical	True	1.0
Record	Deleted	Logical	False	1.0
Record	Design.PinHorizontal	Logical	False	1.0

continues

TABLE E.1. CONTINUED

Object	Property	Type	Sample Value	Ver
Record	Design.PinVertical	Logical	False	1.0
Record	Design.Selectable	Logical	True	4.5
Record	Editing	Logical	False	4.5
Record	First	String	#Page2.#TableFrame17.#Record19.#Field21	1.0
Record	FitHeight	Logical	True	1.0
Record	FitWidth	Logical	True	1.0
Record	FlyAway	Logical	False	1.0
Record	Focus	Logical	False	1.0
Record	Frame.Color	LongInt	Black	1.0
Record	Frame.Style	SmallInt	SolidFrame	1.0
Record	Frame.Thickness	SmallInt	15	1.0
Record	FullName	String	#Page2.#Multirecord22.#Record23	1.0
Record	FullSize	Point	(2340,290)	1.0
Record	Inserting	Logical	False	1.0
Record	LeftBorder	LongInt	0	5.0
Record	Locked	Logical	False	1.0
Record	Manager	String	#Form1	1.0
Record	NRecords	LongInt	0	1.0
Record	Name	String	#Record19	1.0

Object	Property	Type	Sample Value	Ver
Record	Next	String	Blank	1.0
Record	Owner	String	Blank	1.0
Record	Pattern.Color	LongInt	Black	1.0
Record	Pattern.Style	SmallInt	EmptyPattern	1.0
Record	Position	Point	(0,391)	1.0
Record	Prev	String	#Page2.#Multirecord22.#Record23	1.0
Record	Readonly	Logical	False	1.0
Record	RecNo	LongInt	0	1.0
Record	Refresh	Logical	False	1.0
Record	RightBorder	LongInt	0	5.0
Record	RowNo	SmallInt	1	1.0
Record	Scroll	Point	(0,0)	1.0
Record	Select	Logical	False	4.5
Record	SeqNo	LongInt	0	1.0
Record	Shrinkable	Logical	True	1.0
Record	Size	Point	(2340,290)	1.0
Record	TableName	String	Blank	1.0
Record	TopBorder	LongInt	0	5.0
Record	Touched	Logical	False	1.0

continues

TABLE E.1. CONTINUED

Object	Property	Type	Sample Value	Ver
Record	Translucent	Logical	True	1.0
Record	Visible	Logical	True	1.0
Record_Band	Arrived	Logical	False	1.0
Record_Band	BottomBorder	LongInt	0	5.0
Record_Band	Breakable	Logical	True	1.0
Record_Band	Class	String	Band	1.0
Record_Band	ContainerName	String	#Report1	1.0
Record_Band	Design.PinHorizontal	Logical	True	1.0
Record_Band	Design.PinVertical	Logical	True	1.0
Record_Band	Design.Selectable	Logical	True	4.5
Record_Band	First	String	#Record_Band.#Field17	1.0
Record_Band	Focus	Logical	False	1.0
Record_Band	FullName	String	#Record_Band	1.0
Record_Band	FullSize	Point	(12224,3172)	1.0
Record_Band	LeftBorder	LongInt	0	5.0
Record_Band	Manager	String	#Report1	1.0
Record_Band	Name	String	#Record_Band	1.0
Record_Band	Next	String	#Band14	1.0
Record_Band	OtherBandName	String	#Record_Band	5.0

Object	Property	Type	Sample Value	Ver
Record_Band	Owner	String	Blank	1.0
Record_Band	Position	Point	(0,1600)	1.0
Record_Band	PositionalOrder	SmallInt	4	5.0
Record_Band	Prev	String	#Band13	1.0
Record_Band	RightBorder	LongInt	15	5.0
Record_Band	Select	Logical	False	4.5
Record_Band	Shrinkable	Logical	True	1.0
Record_Band	Size	Point	(12239,3187)	1.0
Record_Band	StartPageNumbers	Logical	False	5.0
Record_Band	TopBorder	LongInt	15	5.0
Report	Arrived	Logical	False	1.0
Report	AutoAppend	Logical	False	4.5
Report	Class	String	Report	1.0
Report	ContainerName	String	Blank	1.0
Report	DesignModified	Logical	False	4.5
Report	DesktopForm	Logical	False	1.0
Report	First	String	#Report_Header	1.0
Report	Focus	Logical	False	1.0
Report	FrameObjects	Logical	True	5.0

continues

Table E.1. continued

Object	Property	Type	Sample Value	Ver
Report	FullName	String	#Report1	1.0
Report	FullSize	Point	(12241,5418)	1.0
Report	GridValue	Point	(1440,1440)	5.0
Report	HorizontalScrollBar	Logical	True	1.0
Report	Manager	String	#Report1	1.0
Report	Margins.Bottom	LongInt	720	5.0
Report	Margins.Left	LongInt	720	5.0
Report	Margins.Right	LongInt	720	5.0
Report	Margins.Top	LongInt	720	5.0
Report	Name	String	#Report1	1.0
Report	Next	String	Blank	1.0
Report	PageSize	Point	(12240,15840)	5.0
Report	Position	Point	(0,0)	1.0
Report	Prev	String	Blank	1.0
Report	PrinterDocument	Logical	True	5.0
Report	RefreshOption	SmallInt	0	5.0
Report	RemoveGroupRepeats	Logical	False	5.0
Report	Scroll	Point	(0,0)	1.0
Report	ShowGrid	Logical	False	5.0

Object	Property	Type	Sample Value	Ver
Report	Size	Point	(7455,3435)	1.0
Report	SizeToFit	Logical	False	1.0
Report	SnapToGrid	Logical	False	5.0
Report	StandardMenu	Logical	True	1.0
Report	TableName	String	NRTL50.DB	1.0
Report	Title	String	Report Design : RTLP10	1.0
Report	VerticalScrollBar	Logical	True	1.0
Report_Footer	Arrived	Logical	False	1.0
Report_Footer	BottomBorder	LongInt	15	5.0
Report_Footer	Breakable	Logical	True	1.0
Report_Footer	Class	String	Band	1.0
Report_Footer	ContainerName	String	#Report1	1.0
Report_Footer	Design.PinHorizontal	Logical	True	1.0
Report_Footer	Design.PinVertical	Logical	True	1.0
Report_Footer	Design.Selectable	Logical	True	4.5
Report_Footer	First	String	Blank	1.0
Report_Footer	Focus	Logical	False	1.0
Report_Footer	FullName	String	#Report_Footer	1.0
Report_Footer	FullSize	Point	(12224,180)	1.0

continues

TABLE E.1. CONTINUED

Object	Property	Type	Sample Value	Ver
Report_Footer	LeftBorder	LongInt	0	5.0
Report_Footer	Manager	String	#Report1	1.0
Report_Footer	Name	String	#Report_Footer	1.0
Report_Footer	Next	String	Blank	1.0
Report_Footer	OtherBandName	String	#Report_Header	5.0
Report_Footer	Owner	String	Blank	1.0
Report_Footer	Position	Point	(0,5207)	1.0
Report_Footer	PositionalOrder	SmallInt	7	5.0
Report_Footer	Prev	String	#Page_Footer	1.0
Report_Footer	RightBorder	LongInt	15	5.0
Report_Footer	Select	Logical	False	4.5
Report_Footer	Shrinkable	Logical	True	1.0
Report_Footer	Size	Point	(12239,210)	1.0
Report_Footer	TopBorder	LongInt	15	5.0
Report_Header	Arrived	Logical	False	1.0
Report_Header	BottomBorder	LongInt	0	5.0
Report_Header	Breakable	Logical	True	1.0
Report_Header	Class	String	Band	1.0
Report_Header	ContainerName	String	#Report1	1.0

Object	Property	Type	Sample Value	Ver
Report_Header	Design.PinHorizontal	Logical	True	1.0
Report_Header	Design.PinVertical	Logical	True	1.0
Report_Header	Design.Selectable	Logical	True	4.5
Report_Header	First	String	Blank	1.0
Report_Header	Focus	Logical	False	1.0
Report_Header	FullName	String	#Report_Header	1.0
Report_Header	FullSize	Point	(12224,195)	1.0
Report_Header	LeftBorder	LongInt	0	5.0
Report_Header	Manager	String	#Report1	1.0
Report_Header	Name	String	#Report_Header	1.0
Report_Header	Next	String	#Page_Header	1.0
Report_Header	OtherBandName	String	#Report_Footer	5.0
Report_Header	Owner	String	Blank	1.0
Report_Header	Position	Point	(0,0)	1.0
Report_Header	PositionalOrder	SmallInt	1	5.0
Report_Header	PrecedePageHeader	Logical	True	1.0
Report_Header	Prev	String	#Report_Footer	1.0
Report_Header	RightBorder	LongInt	15	5.0
Report_Header	Select	Logical	False	4.5

continues

TABLE E.1. CONTINUED

Object	Property	Type	Sample Value	Ver
Report_Header	Shrinkable	Logical	True	1.0
Report_Header	Size	Point	(12239,210)	1.0
Report_Header	TopBorder	LongInt	15	5.0
TableFrame	Arrived	Logical	False	1.0
TableFrame	AttachedHeader	Logical	True	5.0
TableFrame	AutoAppend	Logical	False	4.5
TableFrame	BlankRecord	Logical	False	1.0
TableFrame	BottomBorder	LongInt	0	5.0
TableFrame	Breakable	Logical	True	1.0
TableFrame	Class	String	TableFrame	1.0
TableFrame	Color	LongInt	Transparent	1.0
TableFrame	ColumnPosition	SmallInt	0	5.0
TableFrame	ContainerName	String	#Page2	1.0
TableFrame	CurrentColumn	SmallInt	0	5.0
TableFrame	DeleteWhenEmpty	Logical	False	1.0
TableFrame	Deleted	Logical	False	1.0
TableFrame	Design.PinHorizontal	Logical	False	1.0
TableFrame	Design.PinVertical	Logical	False	1.0
TableFrame	Design.Selectable	Logical	True	4.5

Object	Property	Type	Sample Value	Ver
TableFrame	Design.SizeToFit	Logical	True	1.0
TableFrame	Editing	Logical	False	4.5
TableFrame	First	String	#Page2.#TableFrame17.#Header18	1.0
TableFrame	FirstRow	String	#Record19	5.0
TableFrame	FitHeight	Logical	True	1.0
TableFrame	FitWidth	Logical	False	1.0
TableFrame	FlyAway	Logical	False	1.0
TableFrame	Focus	Logical	False	1.0
TableFrame	FullName	String	#Page2.#TableFrame17	1.0
TableFrame	FullSize	Point	(2340,1440)	1.0
TableFrame	Grid.Color	LongInt	Black	1.0
TableFrame	Grid.GridStyle	SmallInt	tfDoubleLine	1.0
TableFrame	Grid.RecordDivider	Logical	False	1.0
TableFrame	Header	String	#Header18	5.0
TableFrame	HorizontalScrollBar	Logical	False	1.0
TableFrame	Inserting	Logical	False	1.0
TableFrame	LeftBorder	LongInt	0	5.0
TableFrame	Locked	Logical	False	1.0
TableFrame	Manager	String	#Form1	1.0

continues

TABLE E.1. CONTINUED

Object	Property	Type	Sample Value	Ver
TableFrame	NCols	SmallInt	1	1.0
TableFrame	NRecords	LongInt	0	1.0
TableFrame	NRows	SmallInt	3	1.0
TableFrame	Name	String	#TableFrame17	1.0
TableFrame	Next	String	#Page2.#Multirecord22	1.0
TableFrame	Owner	String	Blank	1.0
TableFrame	Pattern.Color	LongInt	Black	1.0
TableFrame	Pattern.Style	SmallInt	EmptyPattern	1.0
TableFrame	PinHorizontal	Logical	False	1.0
TableFrame	PinVertical	Logical	False	1.0
TableFrame	Position	Point	(2520,3780)	1.0
TableFrame	Prev	String	#Page2.#Button15	1.0
TableFrame	Readonly	Logical	False	1.0
TableFrame	RecNo	LongInt	0	1.0
TableFrame	Refresh	Logical	False	1.0
TableFrame	RepeatHeader	Logical	True	5.0
TableFrame	RightBorder	LongInt	0	5.0
TableFrame	RowNo	SmallInt	1	1.0
TableFrame	Scroll	Point	(0,0)	1.0

Object	Property	Type	Sample Value	Ver
TableFrame	Select	Logical	False	4.5
TableFrame	SeqNo	LongInt	0	1.0
TableFrame	Size	Point	(2340,1440)	1.0
TableFrame	TableName	String	Blank	1.0
TableFrame	TopBorder	LongInt	0	5.0
TableFrame	Touched	Logical	False	1.0
TableFrame	Translucent	Logical	True	1.0
TableFrame	VerticalScrollBar	Logical	False	1.0
TableFrame	Visible	Logical	True	1.0
TableFrame	WideScrollBar	Logical	False	5.0
Text	Alignment	SmallInt	Center	1.0
Text	Arrived	Logical	False	1.0
Text	AvgCharSize	Point	(90,240)	5.0
Text	BottomBorder	LongInt	0	5.0
Text	Breakable	Logical	True	1.0
Text	Class	String	Text	1.0
Text	Color	LongInt	Transparent	1.0
Text	ContainerName	String	#Page2	1.0
Text	CursorColumn	LongInt	0	1.0

continues

Object	Property	Type	Sample Value	Ver
Text	CursorLine	LongInt	1	1.0
Text	CursorPos	LongInt	0	1.0
Text	Design.ContainObjects	Logical	False	1.0
Text	Design.PinHorizontal	Logical	False	1.0
Text	Design.PinVertical	Logical	False	1.0
Text	Design.Selectable	Logical	True	4.5
Text	DesignSizing	SmallInt	TextFixedSize	1.0
Text	First	String	Blank	1.0
Text	FitHeight	Logical	False	1.0
Text	FitWidth	Logical	False	1.0
Text	Focus	Logical	False	1.0
Text	Font.Color	LongInt	Black	1.0
Text	Font.Size	SmallInt	10	1.0
Text	Font.Style	SmallInt	FontAttribNormal	1.0
Text	Font.Typeface	String	Arial	1.0
Text	Frame.Color	LongInt	Black	1.0
Text	Frame.Style	SmallInt	NoFrame	1.0
Text	Frame.Thickness	SmallInt	15	1.0
Text	FullName	String	#Page2.#Button15.#Text16	1.0

Object	Property	Type	Sample Value	Ver
Text	FullSize	Point	(1185,240)	1.0
Text	HorizontalScrollBar	Logical	False	1.0
Text	Invisible	Logical	False	1.0
Text	LeftBorder	LongInt	0	5.0
Text	LineSpacing	SmallInt	TextSingleSpacing	1.0
Text	Manager	String	#Form1	1.0
Text	MarkerPos	LongInt	0	1.0
Text	Name	String	#Text14	1.0
Text	Next	String	#Page2.#Bitmap10	1.0
Text	OverStrike	Logical	False	1.0
Text	Owner	String	#Page2.#Button15	1.0
Text	Pattern.Color	LongInt	Black	1.0
Text	Pattern.Style	SmallInt	EmptyPattern	1.0
Text	PinHorizontal	Logical	True	1.0
Text	PinVertical	Logical	False	1.0
Text	Position	Point	(105,75)	1.0
Text	Prev	String	#Page2.#Button15.#Text16	1.0
Text	RightBorder	LongInt	0	5.0
Text	Scroll	Point	(0,0)	1.0

continues

TABLE E.1. CONTINUED

Object	Property	Type	Sample Value	Ver
Text	Select	Logical	False	4.5
Text	SelectedText	String	Blank	1.0
Text	Size	Point	(1185,240)	1.0
Text	Text	String	Blank	1.0
Text	TopBorder	LongInt	0	5.0
Text	TopLine	LongInt	1	1.0
Text	Translucent	Logical	True	1.0
Text	Value	AnyType	Blank	1.0
Text	VerticalScrollBar	Logical	False	1.0
Text	Visible	Logical	True	1.0
Text	WideScrollBar	Logical	False	5.0
Text	WordWrap	Logical	False	1.0

CONSTANTS

The tables in this appendix list the constants, grouped by class. The three columns show the constant name, the constant value, and the version of Paradox in which the constant was introduced. The second column, constant value, is listed here for reference only with version 5.0. Don't use these constant numbers in your code, because they might change in a future version. For version 5.0, however, the error numbers can be useful.

TABLE F.1. ActionClasses (SmallInt).

Constant	Value	Ver
DataAction	12	1.0
EditAction	10	1.0
FieldAction	11	1.0
MoveAction	8	1.0
SelectAction	9	1.0

TABLE F.2. ActionDataCommands (SmallInt).

Constant	Value	Ver
DataArriveRecord	3111	1.0
DataBegin	3076	1.0
DataBeginEdit	3078	1.0
DataBeginFirstField	3105	1.0
DataCancelRecord	3082	1.0
DataDeleteRecord	3085	1.0
DataDesign	3102	1.0
DataDitto	3098	1.0
DataEnd	3077	1.0
DataEndEdit	3079	1.0
DataEndLastField	3106	1.0
DataFastBackward	3101	1.0
DataFastForward	3100	1.0
DataFilter	3093	5.0
DataHideDeleted	3096	1.0
DataInsertRecord	3084	1.0
DataLockRecord	3080	1.0
DataLookup	3086	1.0
DataLookupMove	3099	1.0

Constant	Value	Ver
DataLostLock	3113	4.5
DataNextRecord	3072	1.0
DataNextSet	3074	1.0
DataPostRecord	3094	1.0
DataPrint	3103	1.0
DataPriorRecord	3073	1.0
DataPriorSet	3075	1.0
DataRecalc	3110	1.0
DataRefresh	3104	1.0
DataRefreshOutside	3112	1.0
DataSaveCrosstab	3107	1.0
DataSearch	3089	1.0
DataSearchNext	3090	1.0
DataSearchRecord	3092	4.5
DataSearchReplace	3091	1.0
DataShowDeleted	3095	1.0
DataTableView	3087	1.0
DataToggleDeleteRecord	3109	1.0
DataToggleDeleted	3097	1.0
DataToggleEdit	3088	1.0
DataToggleLockRecord	3083	1.0
DataUnDeleteRecord	3108	1.0
DataUnlockRecord	3081	1.0

TABLE F.3. ACTIONEDITCOMMANDS (SMALLINT).		
Constant	Value	Ver
EditCommitField	2574	1.0
EditCopySelection	2570	1.0
EditCopyToFile	2579	1.0
EditCutSelection	2569	1.0
EditDeleteBeginLine	2564	1.0
EditDeleteEndLine	2565	1.0
EditDeleteLeft	2560	1.0
EditDeleteLeftWord	2562	1.0
EditDeleteLine	2567	1.0
EditDeleteRight	2561	1.0
EditDeleteRightWord	2563	1.0
EditDeleteSelection	2568	1.0
EditDeleteWord	2566	1.0
EditDropDownList	2585	1.0
EditEnterFieldView	2583	1.0
EditEnterMemoView	2588	1.0
EditEnterPersistFieldView	2591	1.0
EditExitFieldView	2584	1.0
EditExitMemoView	2589	1.0
EditExitPersistFieldView	2592	1.0
EditHelp	2581	1.0
EditInsertBlank	2571	1.0
EditInsertLine	2572	1.0
EditInsertObject	2596	5.0
EditLaunchServer	2586	1.0
EditPaste	2573	1.0
EditPasteFromFile	2580	1.0
EditPasteLink	2595	5.0
EditProperties	2577	1.0

Constant	Value	Ver
EditReplace	2576	1.0
EditSaveCrossTab	2594	5.0
EditTextSearch	2593	1.0
EditToggleFieldView	2582	1.0
EditToggleMemoView	2587	4.5
EditTogglePersistFieldView	2590	4.5
EditUndoField	2575	1.0
EditUpdateNow	2597	5.0

TABLE F.4. ActionFieldCommands (SmallInt).

Constant	Value	Ver
FieldBackward	2817	1.0
FieldDown	2824	1.0
FieldEnter	2820	1.0
FieldFirst	2821	1.0
FieldForward	2816	1.0
FieldGroupBackward	2819	1.0
FieldGroupForward	2818	1.0
FieldLast	2822	1.0
FieldLeft	2825	1.0
FieldNextPage	2827	1.0
FieldPriorPage	2828	1.0
FieldRight	2826	1.0
FieldRotate	2829	1.0
FieldUp	2823	1.0

TABLE F.5. ActionMoveCommands (SmallInt).		
Constant	Value	Ver
MoveBegin	2058	1.0
MoveBeginLine	2054	1.0
MoveBottom	2057	1.0
MoveBottomLeft	2061	1.0
MoveBottomRight	2063	1.0
MoveDown	2051	1.0
MoveEnd	2059	1.0
MoveEndLine	2055	1.0
MoveLeft	2048	1.0
MoveLeftWord	2052	1.0
MoveRight	2049	1.0
MoveRightWord	2053	1.0
MoveScrollDown	2067	1.0
MoveScrollLeft	2064	1.0
MoveScrollPageDown	2075	1.0
MoveScrollPageLeft	2072	1.0
MoveScrollPageRight	2073	1.0
MoveScrollPageUp	2074	1.0
MoveScrollRight	2065	1.0
MoveScrollScreenDown	2071	1.0
MoveScrollScreenLeft	2068	1.0
MoveScrollScreenRight	2069	1.0
MoveScrollScreenUp	2070	1.0
MoveScrollUp	2066	1.0
MoveTop	2056	1.0
MoveTopLeft	2060	1.0
MoveTopRight	2062	1.0
MoveUp	2050	1.0

TABLE F.6. ACTIONSELECTCOMMANDS (SMALLINT).

Constant	Value	Ver
SelectBegin	2314	1.0
SelectBeginLine	2310	1.0
SelectBottom	2313	1.0
SelectBottomLeft	2317	1.0
SelectBottomRight	2319	1.0
SelectDown	2307	1.0
SelectEnd	2315	1.0
SelectEndLine	2311	1.0
SelectLeft	2304	1.0
SelectLeftWord	2308	1.0
SelectRight	2305	1.0
SelectRightWord	2309	1.0
SelectScrollDown	2323	1.0
SelectScrollLeft	2320	1.0
SelectScrollPageDown	2331	1.0
SelectScrollPageLeft	2328	1.0
SelectScrollPageRight	2329	1.0
SelectScrollPageUp	2330	1.0
SelectScrollRight	2321	1.0
SelectScrollScreenDown	2327	1.0
SelectScrollScreenLeft	2324	1.0
SelectScrollScreenRight	2325	1.0
SelectScrollScreenUp	2326	1.0
SelectScrollUp	2322	1.0
SelectSelectAll	2332	4.5
SelectSelectall	2332	1.0
SelectTop	2312	1.0
SelectTopLeft	2316	1.0
SelectTopRight	2318	1.0
SelectUp	2306	1.0

TABLE F.7. AGGMODIFIERS (SMALLINT).

Constant	Value	Ver
CumUniqueAgg	192	5.0
CumulativeAgg	128	5.0
RegularAgg	0	5.0
UniqueAgg	64	5.0

TABLE F.8. BUTTONSTYLES (SMALLINT).

Constant	Value	Ver
BorlandButton	0	1.0
Windows3dButton	2	5.0
WindowsButton	1	1.0

TABLE F.9. BUTTONTYPES (SMALLINT).

Constant	Value	Ver
CheckboxType	2	1.0
PushButtonType	0	1.0
RadioButtonType	1	1.0

TABLE F.10. COLORS (LONGINT).

Constant	Value	Ver
Black	0	1.0
Blue	16711680	1.0
Brown	32896	1.0
DarkBlue	8388608	1.0
DarkCyan	8421376	1.0
DarkGray	8421504	1.0
DarkGreen	32768	1.0
DarkMagenta	8388736	1.0
DarkRed	128	1.0
Gray	12632256	1.0
Green	65280	1.0
LightBlue	16776960	1.0
Magenta	16711935	1.0
Red	255	1.0
Translucent	−16777216	1.0
Transparent	−1	1.0
White	16777215	1.0
Yellow	65535	1.0

TABLE F.11. COMPLETEDISPLAY (SMALLINT).

Constant	Value	Ver
DisplayAll	1	1.0
DisplayCurrent	0	1.0

TABLE F.12. DATERANGETYPES (SMALLINT).

Constant	Value	Ver
ByDay	0	5.0
ByMonth	2	5.0
ByQuarter	3	5.0
ByWeek	1	5.0
ByYear	4	5.0

TABLE F.13. DEVICETYPE (SMALLINT).

Constant	Value	Ver
Display	1	5.0
Printer	2	5.0

TABLE F.14. ERRORREASONS (SMALLINT).

Constant	Value	Ver
ErrorCritical	1	1.0
ErrorWarning	2	1.0

TABLE F.15. ERRORS (SMALLINT).

Constant	Value	Ver
ValCheckMayNotBeEnforced	12810	4.5
peARYFixedSizeArray	−30589	1.0
peARYIndexOutOfBounds	−30588	1.0
peARYNoMemory	−30591	1.0

Constant	Value	Ver
peARYRangeTooLarge	−30590	1.0
peARYTooLarge	−30592	1.0
peAccessDisabled	9222	4.5
peAccessError	−31721	1.0
peActionNotSupported	−31652	4.5
peActiveIndex	10035	1.0
peActiveTrans	−30347	5.0
peActiveTransaction	10256	4.5
peAliasInUse	−30391	1.0
peAliasIsServer	−28153	4.5
peAliasMismatch	−30349	5.0
peAliasNotDefined	−30393	1.0
peAliasNotOpen	10044	4.5
peAliasPathNonExistant	−30358	4.5
peAliasProjectConflict	−30342	5.0
peAliasPublicConflict	−30341	5.0
peAlias_X_Db	−30411	1.0
peAllFieldsReadOnly	−31184	1.0
peAlreadyLocked	10247	1.0
peArgumentNumber	−30400	1.0
peArgumentTypeInvalid	−30350	5.0
peBOF	8705	1.0
peBad1Sep	−31980	1.0
peBad1TSep	−31970	1.0
peBad2Sep	−31979	1.0
peBad2TSep	−31969	1.0
peBad3Sep	−31978	1.0
peBad3TSep	−31968	1.0
peBad4Sep	−31977	1.0
peBad4TSep	−31967	1.0

continues

Constant	Value	Ver
peBad5Sep	−31976	1.0
peBad5TSep	−31966	1.0
peBad6TSep	−31965	1.0
peBadAMPM	−31971	1.0
peBadAlias	−31731	1.0
peBadArgument	−30397	1.0
peBadArrayResize	−30379	1.0
peBadBlobHeader	−31662	1.0
peBadCharsInAlias	−28147	4.5
peBadConstantGroup	−30585	5.0
peBadDate	−31986	1.0
peBadDay	−31983	1.0
peBadDriverType	−28156	4.5
peBadField	−31699	1.0
peBadFieldType	−30423	4.5
peBadFileFormat	−31722	1.0
peBadHandle	−32482	1.0
peBadHour	−31974	1.0
peBadLinkIndex	−31637	5.0
peBadLogical	−31975	1.0
peBadMinutes	−31973	1.0
peBadMonth	−31984	1.0
peBadObject	−30525	5.0
peBadRecordTag	−32496	1.0
peBadSeconds	−31972	1.0
peBadTable	−31700	1.0
peBadTime	−31985	1.0
peBadTypeArray	−30390	1.0
peBadVersion	−31697	1.0

TABLE F.15. CONTINUED

Constant	Value	Ver
peBadWeekday	−31982	1.0
peBadXtabAction	−31664	1.0
peBadYear	−31981	1.0
peBad_FieldType	−30423	1.0
peBigXtab	−31728	1.0
peBlankField	−31220	1.0
peBlankTableName	−30418	1.0
peBlankValue	−30703	1.0
peBlobFileMissing	8714	1.0
peBlobModified	13058	1.0
peBlobNotOpened	10755	1.0
peBlobOpened	10754	1.0
peBlobReaderror	−31707	1.0
peBlobVersion	12037	1.0
peBracketMismatch	−31995	1.0
peBreak	−30672	1.0
peBufferSizeError	−32488	1.0
peBufferTooSmall	−31998	1.0
peCFunction	−30383	1.0
peCancel	−31705	1.0
peCancelDatabaseOpen	−28158	4.5
peCancelPassword	−28148	4.5
peCannotArrive	−31646	1.0
peCannotClose	10034	1.0
peCannotCloseAlias	−28145	5.0
peCannotCopy	−31724	1.0
peCannotCopyTo	−31172	1.0
peCannotCut	−31725	1.0
peCannotCutTo	−31173	1.0
peCannotDelete	−31174	1.0

continues

TABLE F.15. CONTINUED		
Constant	Value	Ver
peCannotDeleteLine	−31179	1.0
peCannotDepart	−31647	1.0
peCannotDitto	−31694	1.0
peCannotEdit	−31739	1.0
peCannotEditField	−31203	1.0
peCannotEditRefresh	−31675	1.0
peCannotExitField	−31227	1.0
peCannotExitRecord	−31226	1.0
peCannotFindFile	−31629	4.5
peCannotInsert	−31730	1.0
peCannotInsertText	−31169	1.0
peCannotLoadDriver	15877	1.0
peCannotLoadLanguageDriver	15878	4.5
peCannotLock	−31740	1.0
peCannotLockServerDependent	−31656	4.5
peCannotLookupFill	−31209	1.0
peCannotLookupFillCorr	−31208	1.0
peCannotLookupMove	−31207	1.0
peCannotMakeQuery	−31666	1.0
peCannotMove	−31658	4.5
peCannotOpenClip	−31716	1.0
peCannotOpenTable	−31206	1.0
peCannotOrderRange	−31167	1.0
peCannotPaste	−31723	1.0
peCannotPasteFrom	−31171	1.0
peCannotPasteLink	−31175	1.0
peCannotPerformAction	−31170	1.0
peCannotPutField	−31743	1.0
peCannotPutRecord	−31742	1.0

Constant	Value	Ver
peCannotRotate	−31695	1.0
peCannotUndelete	−31669	1.0
peCantDropPrimary	−30345	5.0
peCantOpenTable	−30435	4.5
peCantSearchField	−31192	1.0
peCantSetFilter	−30367	1.0
peCantShowDeleted	−30381	1.0
peCantToggleToTable	−31153	5.0
peCatalogCountError	−32484	1.0
peCatalogSizeError	−32483	1.0
peCfgCannotWrite	8453	1.0
peCfgMultiFile	8454	1.0
peClientsLimit	9486	1.0
peCompatERR	−30454	1.0
peCompatErr	−30454	4.5
peConstantNotFound	−30584	5.0
peConversion	−30701	1.0
peCopyLinkedTables	12807	4.5
peCopyOverSelf	−30468	5.0
peCorruptLockFile	8966	1.0
peCreateERR	−30455	1.0
peCreateErr	−30455	4.5
peCreateWarningRange	−30364	1.0
peCursorLimit	9478	1.0
peDBLimit	9489	1.0
peDDEAllocate	−30557	1.0
peDDEExecute	−30553	1.0
peDDEInitiate	−30558	1.0
peDDENoLock	−30556	1.0
peDDENotOpened	−30559	1.0

continues

TABLE F.15. CONTINUED		
Constant	*Value*	*Ver*
peDDEPoke	−30555	1.0
peDDERequest	−30554	1.0
peDDETimeOut	−30552	1.0
peDDEUnassigned	−30560	1.0
peDataLoss	−31734	1.0
peDataTooLong	−28149	4.5
peDatabaseERR	−30461	1.0
peDatabaseErr	−30461	4.5
peDeadlock	10255	4.5
peDeliveredDocument	−31665	1.0
peDependentMustBeEmpty	9747	4.5
peDestMustBeIndexed	10047	4.5
peDetailRecExistsEmpty	9744	4.5
peDetailRecordsExist	9734	1.0
peDetailTableExists	9743	4.5
peDetailTableOpen	9746	4.5
peDiffSortOrder	13313	1.0
peDifferentPath	10061	4.5
peDifferentTables	10020	1.0
peDirBusy	10244	1.0
peDirLocked	10246	1.0
peDirNoAccess	9219	1.0
peDirNotPrivate	11269	1.0
peDiskError	−30465	5.0
peDivideByZero	−30687	4.5
peDriveNotFound	−30471	5.0
peDriverLimit	9491	1.0
peDriverNotLoaded	10762	1.0
peDriverUnknown	−30368	1.0

Constant	Value	Ver
peDuplicateAlias	−28157	4.5
peDuplicateMoniker	−31643	5.0
peDynamicBind	−30695	4.5
peEOF	8706	1.0
peEditObjRequired	−31686	1.0
peEmbedDataProblem	−31654	4.5
peEmbedNotAllowed	−31653	4.5
peEmbedWontFit	−31655	4.5
peEmptyClipboard	−31668	1.0
peEmptyTable	−31223	1.0
peEndOfBlob	8711	1.0
peEngineQueryMismatch	12038	4.5
peEnumERR	−30453	1.0
peEnumErr	−30453	4.5
peExpressionIllegal	−31650	4.5
peExtInvalid	−30348	5.0
peFAILEDMETHOD	−30403	1.0
peFS_CREATEERR	−32479	4.5
peFS_WRITEOPENERR	−32478	4.5
peFailNoError	−30715	4.5
peFailedDatabaseOpen	−28159	4.5
peFailedMethod	−30403	4.5
peFailedStdDB	−30429	1.0
peFamFileInvalid	8967	1.0
peFieldIsBlank	9740	1.0
peFieldLimit	9492	1.0
peFieldMultiLinked	9750	4.5
peFieldNotCurrent	−31204	1.0
peFieldNotInEdit	−31687	1.0
peFieldNotInLookupTable	9736	4.5

continues

TABLE F.15. CONTINUED		
Constant	Value	Ver
peFieldValueERR	−30378	1.0
peFieldValueErr	−30378	4.5
peFileBusy	10243	1.0
peFileCorrupt	8962	1.0
peFileCreate	−30660	5.0
peFileDeleteFail	9220	1.0
peFileExists	13057	1.0
peFileIsDirectory	−28152	4.5
peFileLocked	10245	1.0
peFileNoAccess	9221	1.0
peFileNotFound	−30473	5.0
peFileOpenError	−32490	1.0
peFileReadError	−32494	1.0
peFileWriteError	−32492	1.0
peFilterErrAt	−30351	5.0
peFixedType	−30697	1.0
peFmlMemberNotFound	8713	1.0
peForeignKeyErr	9733	1.0
peFormClosed	−30541	1.0
peFormCompileError	−31685	1.0
peFormCompileErrors	−30534	4.5
peFormInvalidName	−30539	1.0
peFormInvalidOptions	−30540	1.0
peFormNotAttached	−30542	1.0
peFormOpenFailed	−30533	1.0
peFormQueryOpen	−31640	5.0
peFormQueryViewMismatch	−31639	5.0
peFormReadError	−31720	1.0
peFormTableOpen	−31718	1.0

Constant	Value	Ver
peFormTableReadonly	−31735	1.0
peFormWriteError	−31719	1.0
peFormatError	−32493	1.0
peGENERICERR	−30404	1.0
peGeneralErr	−30404	4.5
peGeneralSQL	13059	4.5
peGroupLocked	10250	1.0
peHasOpenCursors	10765	1.0
peHeaderCorrupt	8961	1.0
peIXPBlockRange	−28926	4.5
peIXPConversion	−28925	4.5
peIXPDataTooSparse	−28875	4.5
peIXPDbClose	−28909	4.5
peIXPDbOpen	−28910	4.5
peIXPExcelFileType	−28888	4.5
peIXPExcelIndexRecord	−28889	4.5
peIXPExportTable	−28878	4.5
peIXPFieldCount	−28924	4.5
peIXPFieldDesc	−28904	4.5
peIXPFileClose	−28919	4.5
peIXPFileCreate	−28921	4.5
peIXPFileName	−28880	4.5
peIXPFileOpen	−28920	4.5
peIXPFileRead	−28912	4.5
peIXPFileWrite	−28911	4.5
peIXPGetField	−28896	4.5
peIXPGetProp	−28903	4.5
peIXPHome	−28892	4.5
peIXPImportTable	−28879	4.5
peIXPInputFile	−28923	4.5

continues

TABLE F.15. CONTINUED		
Constant	*Value*	*Ver*
peIXPInsertRecord	−28893	4.5
peIXPNextRecord	−28894	4.5
peIXPPageName	−28876	4.5
peIXPPassword	−28922	4.5
peIXPPutField	−28895	4.5
peIXPRange	−28927	4.5
peIXPRecordCount	−28891	4.5
peIXPRecordInit	−28890	4.5
peIXPRecordLength	−28877	4.5
peIXPRecordSize	−28873	4.5
peIXPSkip	−28874	4.5
peIXPTableName	−28887	4.5
peIXPTblClose	−28906	4.5
peIXPTblCreate	−28908	4.5
peIXPTblLock	−28905	4.5
peIXPTblOpen	−28907	4.5
peIllFormedCalcField	−31706	1.0
peIllegalAliasProperty	−30363	4.5
peIllegalCharacter	−31147	5.0
peIllegalConversion	−30699	1.0
peIllegalIndexName	−30376	1.0
peIllegalIndexName1	−30343	5.0
peIllegalOpForInMem	−30344	5.0
peIllegalOperator	−30717	1.0
peIllegalTableName	−30357	4.5
peIllegalXtabSpec	−31689	1.0
peImcompatibleRecStructs	10045	4.5
peInUse	−31684	1.0
peInappropriateFieldType	−31214	1.0

Constant	Value	Ver
peInappropriateSubType	−31213	1.0
peIncompatibleDataType	−30366	1.0
peIncompatibleDataTypes	−30428	1.0
peIncompatibleRecStructs	10045	5.0
peIncompleteExponent	−31990	1.0
peIncompletePictureMatch	−31667	1.0
peIncompleteSymbol	−31992	1.0
peIncompleteXtab	−31729	1.0
peIncorrectParmFormat	−30466	5.0
peIndexCorrupt	8965	1.0
peIndexDoesntExist	−31634	5.0
peIndexERR	−30457	1.0
peIndexErr	−30457	4.5
peIndexExists	10027	1.0
peIndexFailed	−30421	1.0
peIndexLimit	9487	1.0
peIndexNameRequired	10010	1.0
peIndexOpen	10028	1.0
peIndexOutOfdate	12034	1.0
peIndexReadOnly	10767	4.5
peIndexStartFailed	−30419	1.0
peInfiniteInsert	−31663	1.0
peInterfaceVer	12033	1.0
peInternal	−30718	1.0
peInternalError	−32510	1.0
peInternalLimit	9482	1.0
peInvalidAttribute	−30469	5.0
peInvalidBlobHandle	10030	1.0
peInvalidBlobLen	10029	1.0
peInvalidBlobOffset	9998	1.0

continues

TABLE F.15. CONTINUED		
Constant	*Value*	*Ver*
peInvalidBookmark	10021	1.0
peInvalidCallbackBuflen	10017	1.0
peInvalidCfgParam	12550	1.0
peInvalidChar	−31994	1.0
peInvalidColumn	−31231	1.0
peInvalidDBSpec	12545	1.0
peInvalidDataBase	−30438	1.0
peInvalidDataTypeCompare	−30427	1.0
peInvalidDate	10059	4.5
peInvalidDesc	10004	1.0
peInvalidDescNum	9999	1.0
peInvalidDir	10018	1.0
peInvalidDrive	−28155	4.5
peInvalidExpression	−31648	5.0
peInvalidExpressionInFld	−31635	5.0
peInvalidExpressionWStr	−31644	5.0
peInvalidFieldDesc	10001	1.0
peInvalidFieldName	10038	1.0
peInvalidFieldType	10000	1.0
peInvalidFieldXform	10002	4.5
peInvalidFileAttributes	−30469	5.0
peInvalidFileExt	10042	1.0
peInvalidFileExtension	−30524	5.0
peInvalidFileName	9987	1.0
peInvalidFilter	10051	4.5
peInvalidFormat	−31999	1.0
peInvalidHandle	9990	1.0
peInvalidIndexCreate	10054	4.5
peInvalidIndexDelete	10055	4.5

Constant	Value	Ver
peInvalidIndexDesc	10023	1.0
peInvalidIndexName	10022	1.0
peInvalidIndexStruct	10005	1.0
peInvalidIndexType	10048	4.5
peInvalidIsolationLevel	−30356	4.5
peInvalidKey	10026	1.0
peInvalidLanguageDriver	10043	4.5
peInvalidLinkExpr	10040	1.0
peInvalidMasterTableLevel	9735	4.5
peInvalidMode	10033	1.0
peInvalidModifyRequest	9996	1.0
peInvalidOperationForTableType	−30365	1.0
peInvalidOptParam	11522	1.0
peInvalidOption	9989	1.0
peInvalidParam	9986	1.0
peInvalidParameter	−30696	4.5
peInvalidPassword	10015	1.0
peInvalidPath	−28154	4.5
peInvalidPrefferedFile	−31224	1.0
peInvalidProperty	−31212	1.0
peInvalidQuery	−30439	1.0
peInvalidRecNum	−1	5.0
peInvalidRecStruct	10003	1.0
peInvalidRecordNumber	−31673	1.0
peInvalidRefIntgDesc	9994	4.5
peInvalidRefIntgStruct	10007	4.5
peInvalidRestrTableOrder	10008	1.0
peInvalidRestructureOperation	10012	4.5
peInvalidRow	−31225	1.0
peInvalidSQL	−30361	4.5

continues

TABLE F.15. CONTINUED		
Constant	Value	Ver
peInvalidSession	−30408	1.0
peInvalidSessionHandle	10011	4.5
peInvalidSysData	12547	1.0
peInvalidTCursor	−30441	1.0
peInvalidTable	−28151	4.5
peInvalidTableCreate	10052	4.5
peInvalidTableDelete	10053	4.5
peInvalidTableLock	−30338	5.0
peInvalidTableName	10039	1.0
peInvalidTableVar	−30436	1.0
peInvalidTime	10058	4.5
peInvalidTimeStamp	10060	4.5
peInvalidTranslation	10019	1.0
peInvalidUserPassword	10036	1.0
peInvalidValChkStruct	10006	1.0
peKeyFieldTypeMismatch	9995	1.0
peKeyOrRecDeleted	8708	1.0
peKeyViol	9729	1.0
peLDNotFound	8715	1.0
peLOCATEFAILED	−30402	1.0
peLanguageDriveMisMatch	10049	4.5
peLinkWontFit	−31148	5.0
peLinkedTableProtected	9749	4.5
peListTooBig	−31671	1.0
peLiveQueryDead	−31636	5.0
peLocateERR	−30458	1.0
peLocateErr	−30458	4.5
peLocateFailed	−30402	4.5
peLockFileLimit	9495	4.5

Constant	Value	Ver
peLockInvalid	−30388	1.0
peLockTimeout	10249	1.0
peLocked	10241	1.0
peLookupTableErr	9736	1.0
peLostExclusiveAccess	10252	1.0
peLostTableLock	10251	1.0
peMasterExists	9741	1.0
peMasterReferenceErr	9745	4.5
peMasterTableOpen	9742	1.0
peMatchNotFound	−31714	1.0
peMathError	−30688	1.0
peMaxValErr	9731	1.0
peMemoCorrupt	8963	1.0
peMethodNotFound	−30713	4.5
peMethodNotValid	−30712	4.5
peMinValErr	9730	1.0
peMisMatchedOperands	−30698	1.0
peModifiedSinceOpen	−31647	5.0
peMultiLevelCascade	10037	1.0
peMultiResults	10057	4.5
peMultipleInit	10759	1.0
peMultiplePoints	−31993	1.0
peMultipleSigns	−31996	1.0
peNA	10756	1.0
peNameNotUnique	10009	1.0
peNameReserved	10041	1.0
peNan	−31989	1.0
peNeedExclusiveAccess	10253	4.5
peNeedRestructure	10032	1.0
peNetFileLocked	11268	1.0

continues

TABLE F.15. CONTINUED		
Constant	*Value*	*Ver*
peNetFileVersion	11267	1.0
peNetInitErr	11265	1.0
peNetMultiple	11270	1.0
peNetUnknown	11271	1.0
peNetUserLimit	11266	1.0
peNo1Sep	−31948	1.0
peNo1TSep	−31938	1.0
peNo2Sep	−31947	1.0
peNo2TSep	−31937	1.0
peNo3Sep	−31946	1.0
peNo3TSep	−31936	1.0
peNo4Sep	−31945	1.0
peNo4TSep	−31935	1.0
peNo5Sep	−31944	1.0
peNo5TSep	−31934	1.0
peNo6TSep	−31933	1.0
peNoAMPM	−31939	1.0
peNoActiveTransaction	−30354	4.5
peNoArguments	−30401	1.0
peNoAssocIndex	10764	1.0
peNoCallback	10016	1.0
peNoConfigFile	8452	1.0
peNoCurrRec	8709	1.0
peNoDMChangeInRun	−31457	5.0
peNoDay	−31951	1.0
peNoDayOrMonthSpec	−31987	1.0
peNoDestRecord	−30424	1.0
peNoDetailRoom	−31727	1.0
peNoDiskSpace	9475	1.0

Constant	Value	Ver
peNoFamilyRights	10499	1.0
peNoFieldRights	10497	1.0
peNoFieldRoom	−31726	1.0
peNoFile	−32487	1.0
peNoFileHandles	9474	1.0
peNoHour	−31942	1.0
peNoHourSpec	−31988	1.0
peNoKeyField	−31691	1.0
peNoLock	−30339	5.0
peNoLockedRecord	−31649	4.5
peNoLogical	−31943	1.0
peNoLookup	−31733	1.0
peNoLookupMove	−31182	1.0
peNoMemoView	−31732	1.0
peNoMemory	9473	1.0
peNoMinutes	−31941	1.0
peNoMonth	−31952	1.0
peNoNumber	−31991	1.0
peNoPage	−31702	1.0
peNoPictureMatch	−31738	1.0
peNoProperty	−31679	1.0
peNoRecordNos	−31191	1.0
peNoRecords	−31704	1.0
peNoSearchField	−31715	1.0
peNoSeconds	−31940	1.0
peNoSelect	−31701	1.0
peNoSelection	−31717	1.0
peNoSeqnums	−31703	1.0
peNoServerAnsTable	−30360	4.5
peNoSession	−31708	1.0

continues

TABLE F.15. CONTINUED		
Constant	*Value*	*Ver*
peNoSoftDeletes	−31185	1.0
peNoSortField	−30417	1.0
peNoSrcRecord	−30425	1.0
peNoSuchFile	9988	1.0
peNoSuchFilter	10050	4.5
peNoSuchIndex	9997	1.0
peNoSuchTable	10024	1.0
peNoTableName	−30430	1.0
peNoTableRights	10498	1.0
peNoTableSupport	10766	4.5
peNoTempFile	−31711	1.0
peNoTempTableSpace	9476	1.0
peNoTextTable	−28143	5.0
peNoTransaction	10257	4.5
peNoWeekday	−31950	1.0
peNoWorkPrivAlias	−30387	1.0
peNoYear	−31949	1.0
peNonExistantAlias	−28160	4.5
peNotABlob	10753	1.0
peNotAValidField	−30380	1.0
peNotAllowedFieldType	−30389	1.0
peNotAllowedInPlace	−31155	5.0
peNotCoEdit	−30444	1.0
peNotEnoughRights	−30394	4.5
peNotEnoughtRights	−30394	1.0
peNotField	−30446	1.0
peNotFieldNum	−30445	1.0
peNotImplemented	12290	1.0
peNotInEditMode	−31736	1.0

Constant	Value	Ver
peNotInRunMode	−31659	1.0
peNotIndexed	10757	1.0
peNotInitialized	10758	1.0
peNotLiveView	−31154	5.0
peNotLocked	10248	1.0
peNotNumericField	−30448	1.0
peNotOleField	−31696	1.0
peNotOnThatNet	12549	1.0
peNotOpenIndex	−30396	1.0
peNotSameSession	10760	1.0
peNotSupported	12289	1.0
peNotSupportedFiltered	−31638	5.0
peNotValidSearchField	−30375	1.0
peNullFieldName	−31709	1.0
peOSAccessDenied	11013	1.0
peOSArgListTooLong	11028	1.0
peOSBadFileNo	11014	1.0
peOSCrossDevLink	11030	1.0
peOSExecFmt	11029	1.0
peOSFileExist	11043	1.0
peOSInvalidAccCode	11020	1.0
peOSInvalidArg	11027	1.0
peOSInvalidData	11021	1.0
peOSInvalidEnviron	11018	1.0
peOSInvalidFormat	11019	1.0
peOSInvalidFunc	11009	1.0
peOSInvalidMemAddr	11017	1.0
peOSLockViol	11059	1.0
peOSMathArg	11041	1.0
peOSMemBlocksDestroyed	11015	1.0

continues

TABLE F.15. CONTINUED		
Constant	Value	Ver
peOSNetErr	11109	1.0
peOSNoDevice	11023	1.0
peOSNoFATEntry	11010	1.0
peOSNoMemory	11016	1.0
peOSNoMoreFiles	11026	1.0
peOSNoPath	11011	1.0
peOSNotSameDev	11025	1.0
peOSOutOfRange	11042	1.0
peOSRemoveCurDir	11024	1.0
peOSShareViol	11058	1.0
peOSTooManyOpenFiles	11012	1.0
peOSUnknown	11047	1.0
peObjImplicitlyDropped	12801	1.0
peObjImplicitlyModified	12803	1.0
peObjMayBeTruncated	12802	1.0
peObjNotFound	8712	4.5
peObjectImplicityTruncated	12809	4.5
peObjectNotFound	−30646	1.0
peObjectTreeTooBig	−31670	1.0
peOk	0	1.0
peOldVersion	12035	1.0
peOleActivateFailed	−32485	1.0
peOpenBlobLimit	9494	1.0
peOpenDetailFailed	9738	4.5
peOpenErr	−31646	5.0
peOpenLookupFailed	9737	4.5
peOpenMasterFailed	9739	4.5
peOpenTableLimit	9483	1.0
peOpenedByPal	−31150	5.0

Constant	Value	Ver
peOperatorNotAllowed	−30700	1.0
peOptRecLockFailed	10259	4.5
peOptRecLockRecDel	10260	4.5
peOtherServerLoaded	12808	4.5
peOutOfHandles	−32491	1.0
peOutOfMemory	−32511	1.0
peOutOfRange	9985	1.0
peOverFlow	−30702	1.0
pePart1Sep	−31916	1.0
pePart1TSep	−31906	1.0
pePart2Sep	−31915	1.0
pePart2TSep	−31905	1.0
pePart3Sep	−31914	1.0
pePart3TSep	−31904	1.0
pePart4Sep	−31913	1.0
pePart4TSep	−31903	1.0
pePart5Sep	−31912	1.0
pePart5TSep	−31902	1.0
pePart6TSep	−31901	1.0
pePartAMPM	−31907	1.0
pePartDay	−31919	1.0
pePartHour	−31910	1.0
pePartLogical	−31911	1.0
pePartMinutes	−31909	1.0
pePartMonth	−31920	1.0
pePartSeconds	−31908	1.0
pePartWeekday	−31918	1.0
pePartYear	−31917	1.0
pePasswordLimit	9490	1.0
pePasswordRequired	−28142	5.0

continues

Constant	Value	Ver
Table F.15. CONTINUED		
pePasteNeedPage	−31692	1.0
pePastePage	−31693	1.0
pePathNonExistant	−30392	1.0
pePathNotFound	−30472	5.0
pePdx10Table	13061	1.0
pePdxDriverNotActive	10761	1.0
pePictureErr	−31200	1.0
pePrecisionExceeded	−31997	1.0
pePrimaryKeyRedefine	9993	1.0
pePropertyAccess	−31677	1.0
pePropertyBadValue	−31678	1.0
pePropertyGet	−30652	1.0
pePropertyNotFound	−30650	1.0
pePropertySet	−30653	1.0
pePublicAliasExists	−28144	5.0
peQBETerminated	−30353	4.5
peQBEbadFileName	−30416	1.0
peQryAmbOutPr	11780	1.0
peQryAmbSymAs	11781	1.0
peQryAmbigJoAsy	11777	1.0
peQryAmbigJoSym	11778	1.0
peQryAmbigOutEx	11779	1.0
peQryAseToPer	11782	1.0
peQryAveNumDa	11783	1.0
peQryBadExpr1	11784	1.0
peQryBadFieldOr	11785	1.0
peQryBadFormat	11885	1.0
peQryBadVName	11786	1.0
peQryBitmapErr	11787	1.0

Constant	Value	Ver
peQryBlobErr	11896	1.0
peQryBlobTerm	11895	1.0
peQryBuffTooSmall	11888	1.0
peQryCalcBadR	11788	1.0
peQryCalcType	11789	1.0
peQryCancExcept	11880	1.0
peQryChNamBig	11797	1.0
peQryChgTo1ti	11790	1.0
peQryChgToChg	11791	1.0
peQryChgToExp	11792	1.0
peQryChgToIns	11793	1.0
peQryChgToNew	11794	1.0
peQryChgToVal	11795	1.0
peQryChkmrkFi	11796	1.0
peQryChunkErr	11798	1.0
peQryColum255	11799	1.0
peQryConAftAs	11800	1.0
peQryDBExcept	11881	1.0
peQryDel1time	11801	1.0
peQryDelAmbig	11802	1.0
peQryDelFrDel	11803	1.0
peQryEgFieldTyp	11804	1.0
peQryEmpty	11886	1.0
peQryExaminOr	11805	1.0
peQryExprTyps	11806	1.0
peQryExtraCom	11807	1.0
peQryExtraOro	11808	1.0
peQryExtraQro	11809	1.0
peQryFatalExcept	11883	1.0
peQryFind1Att	11810	1.0

continues

TABLE F.15. CONTINUED		
Constant	*Value*	*Ver*
peQryFindAnsT	11811	1.0
peQryGrpNoSet	11812	1.0
peQryGrpStRow	11813	1.0
peQryIdfPerli	11815	1.0
peQryIdfinlco	11814	1.0
peQryInAnExpr	11816	1.0
peQryIns1Time	11817	1.0
peQryInsAmbig	11818	1.0
peQryInsDelCh	11819	1.0
peQryInsExprR	11820	1.0
peQryInsToIns	11821	1.0
peQryIsArray	11822	1.0
peQryLabelErr	11823	1.0
peQryLinkCalc	11824	1.0
peQryLngvName	11825	1.0
peQryLongExpr	11878	1.0
peQryLongQury	11826	1.0
peQryMemExcept	11882	1.0
peQryMemVProc	11827	1.0
peQryMisSrtQu	11830	1.0
peQryMisngCom	11828	1.0
peQryMisngRpa	11829	1.0
peQryNIY	11884	1.0
peQryNamTwice	11831	1.0
peQryNoAnswer	11856	1.0
peQryNoChkmar	11832	1.0
peQryNoDefOcc	11833	1.0
peQryNoGroups	11834	1.0
peQryNoPatter	11836	1.0

Constant	Value	Ver
peQryNoQryToPrep	11887	1.0
peQryNoSuchDa	11837	1.0
peQryNoValue	11838	1.0
peQryNonsense	11835	1.0
peQryNotHandle	11890	1.0
peQryNotParse	11889	1.0
peQryNotPrep	11857	1.0
peQryOnlyCons	11839	1.0
peQryOnlySetR	11840	1.0
peQryOutSens1	11841	1.0
peQryOutTwic1	11842	1.0
peQryPaRowCnt	11843	1.0
peQryPersePar	11844	1.0
peQryProcPlsw	11845	1.0
peQryPwInsrts	11846	1.0
peQryPwModrts	11847	1.0
peQryQbeFieldFound	11848	1.0
peQryQbeNoFence	11849	1.0
peQryQbeNoFenceT	11850	1.0
peQryQbeNoHeaderT	11851	1.0
peQryQbeNoTab	11852	1.0
peQryQbeNumCols	11853	1.0
peQryQbeOpentab	11854	1.0
peQryQbeTwice	11855	1.0
peQryQuaInDel	11858	1.0
peQryQuaInIns	11859	1.0
peQryQxFieldCount	11892	1.0
peQryQxFieldSymNotFound	11893	1.0
peQryQxTableSymNotFound	11894	1.0
peQryRagInIns	11860	1.0

continues

TABLE F.15. CONTINUED		
Constant	Value	Ver
peQryRagInSet	11861	1.0
peQryRefresh	11879	1.0
peQryRegister	11877	1.0
peQryRestartQry	11897	1.0
peQryRowUsErr	11862	1.0
peQrySQLg_Alpho	11902	1.0
peQrySQLg_Avera	11915	1.0
peQrySQLg_BadPt	11917	1.0
peQrySQLg_Chini	11907	1.0
peQrySQLg_Cntln	11906	1.0
peQrySQLg_Count	11914	1.0
peQrySQLg_DateA	11916	1.0
peQrySQLg_Dateo	11903	1.0
peQrySQLg_FndSu	11920	1.0
peQrySQLg_IDcco	11922	1.0
peQrySQLg_IfDcs	11921	1.0
peQrySQLg_Liken	11901	1.0
peQrySQLg_MDist	11899	1.0
peQrySQLg_NoAri	11900	1.0
peQrySQLg_NoQuery	11925	1.0
peQrySQLg_OTJvr	11910	1.0
peQrySQLg_Onlyc	11905	1.0
peQrySQLg_Onlyi	11923	1.0
peQrySQLg_Patrn	11919	1.0
peQrySQLg_Quant	11912	1.0
peQrySQLg_RegSo	11913	1.0
peQrySQLg_RelPa	11918	1.0
peQrySQLg_Relop	11904	1.0
peQrySQLg_SQLDialect	11924	1.0

Constant	Value	Ver
peQrySQLg_SlfIn	11909	1.0
peQrySQLg_StRow	11911	1.0
peQrySQLg_Union	11908	1.0
peQrySetExpec	11863	1.0
peQrySetVAmb1	11864	1.0
peQrySetVBad1	11865	1.0
peQrySetVDef1	11866	1.0
peQrySumNumbe	11867	1.0
peQrySyntErr	11891	1.0
peQryTableIsWP3	11868	1.0
peQryTokenNot	11869	1.0
peQryTwoOutr1	11870	1.0
peQryTypeMIsM	11871	1.0
peQryUnknownAnsType	11898	1.0
peQryUnrelQ1	11872	1.0
peQryUnusedSt	11873	1.0
peQryUseInsDe	11874	1.0
peQryUseOfChg	11875	1.0
peQryVarMustF	11876	1.0
peQueryERR	−30459	1.0
peQueryErr	−30459	4.5
peQueryView	−31151	5.0
peREGExpressionTooLarge	−30622	1.0
peREGInvalidBracketRange	−30616	1.0
peREGNestedSQP	−30617	1.0
peREGOperandEmpty	−30618	1.0
peREGSPQFollowsNothing	−30613	1.0
peREGTooManyParens	−30621	1.0
peREGTrailingBackSlash	−30612	1.0
peREGUnmatchedBrackets	−30615	1.0

continues

Constant	Value	Ver
	TABLE F.15. CONTINUED	
peREGUnmatchedParens	−30620	1.0
peReadAccessError	−32495	1.0
peReadErr	9217	1.0
peReadOnlyDB	10501	1.0
peReadOnlyDir	10500	1.0
peReadOnlyField	10502	4.5
peReadOnlyProperty	−31681	1.0
peRecAlreadyLocked	−30407	1.0
peRecDeleted	8708	1.0
peRecLockFailed	10258	4.5
peRecLockLimit	9485	1.0
peRecMoved	8707	1.0
peRecNotFound	8710	1.0
peRecTooBig	9477	1.0
peRecordAlreadyLocked	−31737	1.0
peRecordGroupConflict	10254	4.5
peRecordIsDeleted	−31165	1.0
peRecordIsNotDeleted	−31164	1.0
peRecordNotLocked	−30377	1.0
peRefIntgReqIndex	9748	4.5
peReqOptParamMissing	11521	1.0
peReqSameTableTypes	−30386	1.0
peReq_WLock_TC	−30413	1.0
peReq_XLock_TC	−30340	5.0
peReqdErr	9732	1.0
peRequiredField	−31741	1.0
peRequiresPDOXtable	−30399	1.0
peReservedOsName	10046	4.5
peSKCantInstallHook	−30632	4.5

Constant	Value	Ver
peSKInvalidCount	−30634	4.5
peSKInvalidKey	−30636	4.5
peSKMissingCloseBrace	−30637	4.5
peSKMissingCloseParen	−30635	4.5
peSKStringTooLong	−30633	4.5
peSameTable	−30346	5.0
peSerNumLimit	9481	1.0
peServerPathIllegal	−30362	4.5
peSessionERR	−30460	1.0
peSessionErr	−30460	4.5
peSessionsLimit	9488	1.0
peShareNotLoaded	11273	1.0
peSharedFileAccess	11272	1.0
peSortERR	−30456	1.0
peSortErr	−30456	4.5
peSortFailed	−30422	1.0
peSortStartFailed	−30420	1.0
peSrvAccessDenied	−32476	4.5
peSrvCannotGetLock	−32480	4.5
peSrvCapacityLimit	−32483	4.5
peSrvCopyFailed	−32472	4.5
peSrvDeleteFailed	−32473	4.5
peSrvDiskError	−32471	4.5
peSrvFileDoesNotExist	−32487	4.5
peSrvFormat	−32493	4.5
peSrvGraphicPasteFailed	−32465	5.0
peSrvInvalidCount	−32496	4.5
peSrvInvalidExtension	−32481	4.5
peSrvInvalidHandle	−32482	4.5
peSrvInvalidName	−32469	4.5

continues

TABLE F.15. CONTINUED		
Constant	Value	Ver
peSrvMemoryAllocation	−32511	4.5
peSrvNameTooLong	−32470	4.5
peSrvNoReadRights	−32495	4.5
peSrvNoWriteRights	−32489	4.5
peSrvNotSameDevice	−32475	4.5
peSrvOleActivateFailed	−32485	4.5
peSrvOleCantUpdateNow	−32463	5.0
peSrvOleInsertObjectFailed	−32466	5.0
peSrvOlePasteFailed	−32468	4.5
peSrvOlePasteLinkFailed	−32467	5.0
peSrvOpen	−32490	4.5
peSrvPathNotFound	−32477	4.5
peSrvRead	−32494	4.5
peSrvRenameFailed	−32474	4.5
peSrvTextPasteFailed	−32464	5.0
peSrvUnknowError	−32510	4.5
peSrvUseCountLimit	−32484	4.5
peSrvWrite	−32492	4.5
peStackOverflow	−30716	4.5
peStringTooLong	−30470	5.0
peSysCorrupt	8451	1.0
peSysFileIO	8450	1.0
peSysFileOpen	8449	1.0
peSysReEntered	8455	4.5
peTCursorAttach	−30382	1.0
peTCursorERR	−30463	1.0
peTCursorErr	−30463	4.5
peTableClose	−30508	1.0
peTableCopy	−30510	1.0

Constant	Value	Ver
peTableCreate	−30512	1.0
peTableCursorLimit	9484	1.0
peTableERR	−30462	1.0
peTableEncrypted	10503	4.5
peTableErr	−30462	4.5
peTableExists	13060	1.0
peTableFull	9479	1.0
peTableInUse	−31672	1.0
peTableLevelChanged	12806	4.5
peTableMismatch	−31690	1.0
peTableOpen	10031	1.0
peTableProtected	−30395	1.0
peTableReadOnly	10763	1.0
peTableRename	−30511	1.0
peTableRights	−30509	1.0
peTableSQL	12291	1.0
peTableViewTableReadOnly	−31187	1.0
peTableLockLimit	9493	1.0
peTblNotImplemented	−30359	4.5
peTblUtilInUse	−28146	5.0
peTextWontFit	−31149	5.0
peTooFewSeries	−31674	1.0
peTooManyTables	−31710	1.0
peToolsRead	−31683	1.0
peToolsWrite	−31682	1.0
peTransactionImbalance	−31651	4.5
peTransactionNA	−30355	4.5
peUIObjectErr	−30352	5.0
peUnassigned	−30704	1.0
peUnboundXtab	−31712	1.0

continues

Constant	Value	Ver
peUnknownDB	10014	1.0
peUnknownDBType	12546	1.0
peUnknownDataBase	−30433	1.0
peUnknownDriver	10013	1.0
peUnknownExtension	−31698	1.0
peUnknownFieldName	−31215	1.0
peUnknownFieldNum	−31216	1.0
peUnknownFile	9992	1.0
peUnknownIndex	−30384	1.0
peUnknownNetType	12548	1.0
peUnknownSQL	13059	1.0
peUnknownTableType	9991	1.0
peUnknownVersion	−31657	4.5
peUnlockFailed	10242	1.0
peUnsupportedOption	−30641	5.0
peUntranslatableCharacters	−28150	4.5
peUpdateNOIndex	−30405	1.0
peUpdateNoIndex	−30405	4.5
peUseCount	10025	1.0
peValFieldModified	12805	1.0
peValFileCorrupt	8968	1.0
peValFileInvalid	12036	1.0
peValidateData	12804	1.0
peVendInitFail	15879	4.5
peWorkStationSessionLimit	9480	4.5
peWriteAccessError	−32489	1.0
peWriteErr	9218	1.0
peWriteOnlyProperty	−31680	1.0
peWrongDriverName	15873	1.0

TABLE F.15. CONTINUED

Constant	Value	Ver
peWrongDriverType	15876	1.0
peWrongDriverVer	15875	1.0
peWrongObjectVersion	−32486	1.0
peWrongSysVer	15874	1.0
peWrongTable	−31713	1.0
peXtabAnswerError	−31688	1.0
peXtabNotRunning	−31645	5.0
pecantOpenTable	−30435	1.0

TABLE F.16. EVENTERRORCODES (SMALLINT).		
Constant	Value	Ver
CanNotArrive	−31646	1.0
CanNotDepart	−31647	1.0
Can_Arrive	0	1.0
Can_Depart	0	1.0

TABLE F.17. EXECUTEOPTIONS (SMALLINT).		
Constant	Value	Ver
ExeHidden	0	1.0
ExeMinimized	6	1.0
ExeShowMaximized	3	1.0
ExeShowMinimized	2	1.0
ExeShowMinimizedNoActivate	7	1.0
ExeShowNoActivate	4	1.0
ExeShowNormal	1	1.0

TABLE F.18. FIELDDISPLAYTYPES (SMALLINT).

Constant	Value	Ver
CheckBoxField	4	1.0
ComboField	1	1.0
EditField	0	1.0
LabeledField	5	1.0
ListField	2	1.0
RadioButtonField	3	1.0

TABLE F.19. FILEBROWSERFILETYPES (LONGINT).

Constant	Value	Ver
fbASCII	8192	1.0
fbAllTables	512	1.0
fbBitmap	8388608	1.0
fbDBase	4096	1.0
fbDM	33554432	5.0
fbExcel	1048576	1.0
fbFiles	1	1.0
fbForm	8	1.0
fbGraphic	128	1.0
fbIni	2097152	1.0
fbLibrary	4194304	1.0
fbLotus1	524288	1.0
fbLotus2	262144	1.0
fbMailmerge	32	1.0
fbParadox	2048	1.0
fbPrinterStyle	134217728	5.0
fbQuattro	131072	1.0
fbQuattroPro	65536	1.0

Constant	Value	Ver
fbQuattroProWindows	32768	1.0
fbQuery	4	1.0
fbReport	16	1.0
fbSQL	16777216	5.0
fbScreenStyle	67108864	5.0
fbScript	64	1.0
fbTable	2	1.0
fbTableView	1024	1.0
fbText	256	1.0

TABLE F.20. FONTATTRIBUTES (SMALLINT).

Constant	Value	Ver
FontAttribBold	2	1.0
FontAttribItalic	4	1.0
FontAttribNormal	1	1.0
FontAttribStrikeOut	8	1.0
FontAttribUnderline	16	1.0

TABLE F.21. FRAMESTYLES (SMALLINT).

Constant	Value	Ver
DashDotDotFrame	4	1.0
DashDotFrame	3	1.0
DashedFrame	1	1.0
DottedFrame	2	1.0
DoubleFrame	6	1.0
Inside3DFrame	10	1.0

continues

TABLE F.21. CONTINUED		
Constant	Value	Ver
NoFrame	5	1.0
Outside3DFrame	11	1.0
ShadowFrame	9	1.0
SolidFrame	0	1.0
WideInsideDoubleFrame	8	1.0
WideOutsideDoubleFrame	7	1.0
Windows3DFrame	12	5.0
Windows3DGroup	13	5.0

TABLE F.22. GENERAL (LOGICAL—EXCEPT FOR PI, WHICH IS A NUMBER).		
Constant	Value	Ver
No	False	1.0
Off	False	1.0
On	True	1.0
PI	3.141593	1.0
Yes	True	1.0

TABLE F.23. GRAPHBINDTYPES (SMALLINT).		
Constant	Value	Ver
Graph1DSummary	2	1.0
Graph2DSummary	3	1.0
GraphTabular	1	1.0

TABLE F.24. GRAPHLABELFORMATS (SMALLINT).

Constant	Value	Ver
GraphHideY	0	1.0
GraphPercent	2	1.0
GraphShowY	4	1.0

TABLE F.25. GRAPHLABELLOCATION (SMALLINT).

Constant	Value	Ver
LabelAbove	2	1.0
LabelBelow	4	1.0
LabelBottom	7	1.0
LabelCenter	0	1.0
LabelLeft	1	1.0
LabelMiddle	6	1.0
LabelRight	3	1.0
LabelTop	5	1.0

TABLE F.26. GRAPHLEGENDPOSITION (SMALLINT).

Constant	Value	Ver
LegendBottom	0	1.0
LegendRight	1	1.0

TABLE F.27. GRAPHMARKERS (SMALLINT).

Constant	Value	Ver
MarkerBoxedCross	11	1.0
MarkerBoxed_Plus	9	1.0
MarkerCross	10	1.0
MarkerFilledBox	0	1.0
MarkerFilledCircle	4	1.0
MarkerFilledDownTriangle	2	1.0
MarkerFilledTriangle	6	1.0
MarkerFilledTriangles	12	1.0
MarkerHollowBox	1	1.0
MarkerHollowCircle	5	1.0
MarkerHollowDownTriangle	3	1.0
MarkerHollowTriangle	7	1.0
MarkerHollowTriangles	13	1.0
MarkerHorizontalLine	14	1.0
MarkerPlus	8	1.0
MarkerVerticalLine	15	1.0

TABLE F.28. GRAPHTYPEOVERRIDE (SMALLINT).

Constant	Value	Ver
GraphArea	3	1.0
GraphBar	1	1.0
GraphDefault	0	1.0
GraphLine	2	1.0

TABLE F.29. GRAPHTYPES (SMALLINT).

Constant	Value	Ver
Graph2DArea	3	1.0
Graph2DBar	1	1.0
Graph2DColumns	21	1.0
Graph2DLine	5	1.0
Graph2DPie	20	1.0
Graph2DRotatedBar	9	1.0
Graph2DStackedBar	6	1.0
Graph3DArea	14	1.0
Graph3DBar	11	1.0
Graph3DColumns	23	1.0
Graph3DPie	22	1.0
Graph3DRibbon	12	1.0
Graph3DRotatedBar	26	1.0
Graph3DStackedBar	24	1.0
Graph3DStep	13	1.0
Graph3DSurface	17	1.0
GraphXY	19	1.0

TABLE F.30. GRAPHICMAGNIFICATION (SMALLINT).

Constant	Value	Ver
Magnify100	100	1.0
Magnify200	200	1.0
Magnify25	25	1.0
Magnify400	400	1.0
Magnify50	50	1.0
MagnifyBestFit	−1	1.0

TABLE F.31. IdRanges (SmallInt).

Constant	Value	Ver
UserAction	0	1.0
UserActionMax	2047	1.0
UserError	0	1.0
UserErrorMax	2047	1.0
UserMenu	8000	1.0
UserMenuMax	10000	1.0

TABLE F.32. KeyBoardStates (SmallInt).

Constant	Value	Ver
Alt	128	1.0
Control	8	1.0
LeftButton	1	1.0
RightButton	2	1.0
Shift	4	1.0

TABLE F.33. Keyboard (SmallInt).

Constant	Value	Ver
VK_ADD	107	1.0
VK_BACK	8	1.0
VK_CANCEL	3	1.0
VK_CAPITAL	20	1.0
VK_CLEAR	12	1.0
VK_CONTROL	17	1.0
VK_DECIMAL	110	1.0

Constant	Value	Ver
VK_DELETE	46	1.0
VK_DIVIDE	111	1.0
VK_DOWN	40	1.0
VK_END	35	1.0
VK_ESCAPE	27	1.0
VK_EXECUTE	43	1.0
VK_F1	112	1.0
VK_F10	121	1.0
VK_F11	122	1.0
VK_F12	123	1.0
VK_F13	124	1.0
VK_F14	125	1.0
VK_F15	126	1.0
VK_F16	127	1.0
VK_F2	113	1.0
VK_F3	114	1.0
VK_F4	115	1.0
VK_F5	116	1.0
VK_F6	117	1.0
VK_F7	118	1.0
VK_F8	119	1.0
VK_F9	120	1.0
VK_HELP	47	1.0
VK_HOME	36	1.0
VK_INSERT	45	1.0
VK_LBUTTON	1	1.0
VK_LEFT	37	1.0
VK_MBUTTON	4	1.0
VK_MENU	18	1.0
VK_MULTIPLY	106	1.0

continues

Constant	Value	Ver
VK_NEXT	34	1.0
VK_NUMLOCK	144	1.0
VK_NUMPAD0	96	1.0
VK_NUMPAD1	97	1.0
VK_NUMPAD2	98	1.0
VK_NUMPAD3	99	1.0
VK_NUMPAD4	100	1.0
VK_NUMPAD5	101	1.0
VK_NUMPAD6	102	1.0
VK_NUMPAD7	103	1.0
VK_NUMPAD8	104	1.0
VK_NUMPAD9	105	1.0
VK_PAUSE	19	1.0
VK_PRINT	42	1.0
VK_PRIOR	33	1.0
VK_RBUTTON	2	1.0
VK_RETURN	13	1.0
VK_RIGHT	39	1.0
VK_SELECT	41	1.0
VK_SEPARATOR	108	1.0
VK_SHIFT	16	1.0
VK_SNAPSHOT	44	1.0
VK_SPACE	32	1.0
VK_SUBTRACT	109	1.0
VK_TAB	9	1.0
VK_UP	38	1.0

Table caption: TABLE F.33. CONTINUED

TABLE F.34. LibraryScope (SmallInt).

Constant	Value	Ver
GlobalToDesktop	2	1.0
PrivateToForm	1	1.0

TABLE F.35. LineEnds (SmallInt).

Constant	Value	Ver
ArrowBothEnds	2	1.0
ArrowOneEnd	1	1.0
NoArrowEnd	0	1.0

TABLE F.36. LineStyles (SmallInt).

Constant	Value	Ver
DashDotDotLine	4	1.0
DashDotLine	3	1.0
DashedLine	1	1.0
DottedLine	2	1.0
NoLine	5	1.0
SolidLine	0	1.0

TABLE F.37. LineThickness (SmallInt).

Constant	Value	Ver
LWidth10Points	200	1.0
LWidth1Point	20	1.0

continues

TABLE F.37. CONTINUED

Constant	Value	Ver
LWidth2Points	40	1.0
LWidth3Points	60	1.0
LWidth6Points	120	1.0
LWidthHairline	5	1.0
LWidthHalfPoint	10	1.0

TABLE F.38. LINETYPES (SMALLINT).

Constant	Value	Ver
CurvedLine	2	1.0
StraightLine	0	1.0

TABLE F.39. MENUCHOICEATTRIBUTES (SMALLINT).

Constant	Value	Ver
MenuChecked	1	1.0
MenuDisabled	64	1.0
MenuEnabled	128	1.0
MenuGrayed	32	1.0
MenuHilited	512	1.0
MenuNotChecked	2	1.0
MenuNotGrayed	16	1.0
MenuNotHilited	1024	1.0

TABLE F.40. MENUCOMMANDS (SMALLINT).

Constant	Value	Ver
MenuAddPage	7404	5.0
MenuAlignBottom	7209	5.0
MenuAlignCenter	7207	5.0
MenuAlignLeft	7205	5.0
MenuAlignMiddle	7210	5.0
MenuAlignRight	7206	5.0
MenuAlignTop	7208	5.0
MenuBuild	7464	4.5
MenuCanClose	7102	1.0
MenuChangedPriv	7469	5.0
MenuChangedWork	7467	5.0
MenuChangingPriv	7468	5.0
MenuChangingWork	7466	5.0
MenuCompileWithDebug	5176	5.0
MenuControlClose	−4000	1.0
MenuControlKeyMenu	−3840	1.0
MenuControlMaximize	−4048	1.0
MenuControlMinimize	−4064	1.0
MenuControlMouseMenu	−3952	1.0
MenuControlMove	−4080	1.0
MenuControlNextWindow	−4032	1.0
MenuControlPrevWindow	−4016	1.0
MenuControlRestore	−3808	1.0
MenuControlSize	−4096	1.0
MenuCopyToolBar	7213	5.0
MenuDataModel	7402	5.0
MenuDataModelDesigner	186	5.0
MenuDeliver	7418	5.0

continues

TABLE F.40. CONTINUED		
Constant	Value	Ver
MenuDesignBringFront	7203	5.0
MenuDesignDuplicate	7202	5.0
MenuDesignGroup	7201	5.0
MenuDesignLayout	7214	5.0
MenuDesignSendBack	7204	5.0
MenuEditCopy	132	1.0
MenuEditCopyTo	140	1.0
MenuEditCut	131	1.0
MenuEditDelete	134	1.0
MenuEditLinks	164	5.0
MenuEditPaste	133	1.0
MenuEditUndo	130	1.0
MenuFileAliases	124	1.0
MenuFileAutoRefresh	1501	1.0
MenuFileExit	108	1.0
MenuFileExport	1006	1.0
MenuFileImport	1005	1.0
MenuFileMultiBlankZero	15009	1.0
MenuFileMultiUserDrivers	15007	1.0
MenuFileMultiUserInfo	15006	1.0
MenuFileMultiUserLock	15004	1.0
MenuFileMultiUserLockInfo	15001	1.0
MenuFileMultiUserRetry	15005	1.0
MenuFileMultiUserUserName	15002	1.0
MenuFileMultiUserWho	15003	1.0
MenuFilePrint	7401	1.0
MenuFilePrinterSetup	120	1.0
MenuFilePrivateDir	112	1.0
MenuFileTableAdd	1104	1.0

Constant	Value	Ver
MenuFileTableCopy	1102	1.0
MenuFileTableDelete	1105	1.0
MenuFileTableEmpty	1106	1.0
MenuFileTableInfoStructure	4001	1.0
MenuFileTablePasswords	1108	1.0
MenuFileTableRename	1103	1.0
MenuFileTableRestructure	1001	1.0
MenuFileTableSort	1101	1.0
MenuFileTableSubtract	1107	1.0
MenuFileWorkingDir	111	1.0
MenuFolderOpen	1305	1.0
MenuFormDesign	7520	1.0
MenuFormEditData	7409	1.0
MenuFormFieldView	7704	1.0
MenuFormFilter	7465	5.0
MenuFormMemoView	7393	5.0
MenuFormNew	7871	1.0
MenuFormOpen	7851	1.0
MenuFormOrderRange	7446	1.0
MenuFormPageFirst	7451	1.0
MenuFormPageGoto	7455	1.0
MenuFormPageLast	7452	1.0
MenuFormPageNext	7453	1.0
MenuFormPagePrevious	7454	1.0
MenuFormPersistView	7392	5.0
MenuFormShowDeleted	7447	1.0
MenuFormTableView	7426	1.0
MenuFormView	7520	5.0
MenuFormViewData	7410	5.0
MenuHelpAbout	176	1.0

continues

TABLE F.40. CONTINUED		
Constant	Value	Ver
MenuHelpCoach	197	5.0
MenuHelpContents	170	1.0
MenuHelpExpert	198	5.0
MenuHelpKeyboard	173	1.0
MenuHelpObjectPAL	191	5.0
MenuHelpSearch	199	5.0
MenuHelpSpeedBar	172	1.0
MenuHelpSupport	175	1.0
MenuHelpUsingHelp	174	1.0
MenuInit	7462	1.0
MenuInsertObject	163	5.0
MenuLibraryNew	7875	1.0
MenuLibraryOpen	7855	1.0
MenuObjectTree	7414	5.0
MenuOpenProjectView	1307	5.0
MenuPageLayout	7408	5.0
MenuPasteFrom	142	1.0
MenuPasteLink	136	1.0
MenuPropertiesBandLabels	7313	5.0
MenuPropertiesCurrent	7212	1.0
MenuPropertiesDesigner	7329	1.0
MenuPropertiesDesktop	123	1.0
MenuPropertiesExpandedRuler	7319	1.0
MenuPropertiesFormRestoreDefaults	7327	1.0
MenuPropertiesFormSaveDefaults	7322	1.0
MenuPropertiesGridSettings	7318	5.0
MenuPropertiesGroupRepeats	7407	5.0
MenuPropertiesHorizontalRuler	7309	1.0
MenuPropertiesMethods	7341	5.0

Constant	Value	Ver
MenuPropertiesShowGrid	7317	5.0
MenuPropertiesSizeToFit	7391	5.0
MenuPropertiesSizeandPos	7311	5.0
MenuPropertiesSnapToGrid	7300	5.0
MenuPropertiesStandardMenu	7390	5.0
MenuPropertiesStyleSheet	7312	5.0
MenuPropertiesVerticalRuler	7310	1.0
MenuPropertiesWindow	7328	5.0
MenuPropertiesZoom100	7303	1.0
MenuPropertiesZoom200	7304	1.0
MenuPropertiesZoom25	7301	1.0
MenuPropertiesZoom400	7305	1.0
MenuPropertiesZoom50	7302	1.0
MenuPropertiesZoomBestFit	7308	1.0
MenuPropertiesZoomFitHeight	7307	1.0
MenuPropertiesZoomFitWidth	7306	1.0
MenuQueryNew	1303	1.0
MenuQueryOpen	1304	1.0
MenuRecordCancel	7449	1.0
MenuRecordDelete	7432	1.0
MenuRecordFastBackward	7421	1.0
MenuRecordFastForward	7424	1.0
MenuRecordFirst	7420	1.0
MenuRecordInsert	7431	1.0
MenuRecordLast	7425	1.0
MenuRecordLocateNext	7444	1.0
MenuRecordLocateRecordNumber	7445	1.0
MenuRecordLocateSearchAndReplace	7434	1.0
MenuRecordLocateValue	7433	1.0
MenuRecordLock	7430	1.0

continues

Constant	Value	Ver
MenuRecordLookup	7460	1.0
MenuRecordMove	7461	1.0
MenuRecordNext	7423	1.0
MenuRecordPost	7448	1.0
MenuRecordPrevious	7422	1.0
MenuReportAddBand	7406	5.0
MenuReportNew	7872	1.0
MenuReportOpen	7852	1.0
MenuReportPageFirst	7451	5.0
MenuReportPageGoto	7455	5.0
MenuReportPageLast	7452	5.0
MenuReportPageNext	7453	5.0
MenuReportPagePrevious	7454	5.0
MenuReportPrintDesign	7215	5.0
MenuReportRestartOpts	7415	5.0
MenuRotatePage	7405	5.0
MenuSQLFileNew	7876	4.5
MenuSQLFileOpen	7856	4.5
MenuSQLToolsOpen	5001	4.5
MenuSave	106	1.0
MenuSaveAs	107	1.0
MenuSaveCrossTab	7104	5.0
MenuScriptNew	7874	1.0
MenuScriptOpen	7854	1.0
MenuSearchText	141	1.0
MenuSelectAll	138	1.0
MenuSizeMaxHeight	7221	5.0
MenuSizeMaxWidth	7220	5.0
MenuSizeMinHeight	7218	5.0

TABLE F.40. CONTINUED

Constant	Value	Ver
MenuSizeMinWidth	7217	5.0
MenuSpaceHorz	7223	5.0
MenuSpaceVert	7224	5.0
MenuStackPages	7456	5.0
MenuTableNew	3001	1.0
MenuTableOpen	3002	1.0
MenuTileHorizontal	7457	5.0
MenuTileVertical	7458	5.0
MenuWindowArrangeIcons	152	1.0
MenuWindowCascade	151	1.0
MenuWindowCloseAll	153	1.0
MenuWindowTile	150	1.0
MenuWorkGroupOpen	5000	4.5

TABLE F.41. MENUREASONS (SMALLINT).

Constant	Value	Ver
MenuControl	2	1.0
MenuDesktop	1	1.0
MenuNormal	0	1.0

TABLE F.42. MOUSESHAPES (LONGINT).

Constant	Value	Ver
MouseArrow	32512	1.0
MouseCross	32515	1.0
MouseIBeam	32513	1.0
MouseUpArrow	32516	1.0
MouseWait	32514	1.0

TABLE F.43. MoveReasons (SmallInt).

Constant	Value	Ver
PalMove	2	1.0
RefreshMove	5	1.0
ShutDownMove	4	1.0
StartupMove	3	1.0
UserMove	1	1.0

TABLE F.44. PageTilingOptions (SmallInt).

Constant	Value	Ver
StackPages	8192	5.0
TileHorizontal	16384	5.0
TileVertical	0	5.0

TABLE F.45. PatternStyles (SmallInt).

Constant	Value	Ver
BricksPattern	50	1.0
CrosshatchPattern	17	1.0
DiagonalCrosshatchPattern	21	1.0
DottedLinePattern	66	1.0
EmptyPattern	0	1.0
FuzzyStripesDownPattern	22	1.0
HeavyDotPattern	78	1.0
HorizontalLinesPattern	1	1.0
LatticePattern	54	1.0
LeftDiagonalLinesPattern	9	1.0
LightDotPattern	70	1.0

Constant	Value	Ver
MaximumDotPattern	86	1.0
MediumDotPattern	74	1.0
RightDiagonalLinesPattern	13	1.0
ScalesPattern	34	1.0
StaggeredDashesPattern	58	1.0
ThickHorizontalLinesPattern	6	1.0
ThickStripesDownPattern	18	1.0
ThickStripesUpPattern	14	1.0
ThickVerticalLinesPattern	10	1.0
VerticalLinesPattern	5	1.0
VeryHeavyDotPattern	82	1.0
WeavePattern	46	1.0
ZigZagPattern	2	1.0

TABLE F.46. PRINTCOLOR (LONGINT).

Constant	Value	Ver
prnColor	2	5.0
prnMonochrome	1	5.0

TABLE F.47. PRINTDUPLEX (LONGINT).

Constant	Value	Ver
prnHorizontal	3	5.0
prnSimplex	1	5.0
prnVertical	2	5.0

TABLE F.48. PRINTQUALITY (LONGINT).

Constant	Value	Ver
prnDraft	−1	5.0
prnHigh	−4	5.0
prnLow	−2	5.0
prnMedium	−3	5.0

TABLE F.49. PRINTSOURCES (LONGINT).

Constant	Value	Ver
prnAuto	7	5.0
prnCassette	14	5.0
prnEnvManual	6	5.0
prnEnvelope	5	5.0
prnLargeCapacity	11	5.0
prnLargeFmt	10	5.0
prnLower	2	5.0
prnManual	4	5.0
prnMiddle	3	5.0
prnOnlyOne	1	5.0
prnSmallFmt	9	5.0
prnTractor	8	5.0
prnUpper	1	5.0

TABLE F.50. PRINTERORIENTATION (LONGINT).

Constant	Value	Ver
prnLandscape	2	5.0
prnPortrait	1	5.0

TABLE F.51. PRINTERSIZES (LONGINT).		
Constant	Value	Ver
prn10x14	16	5.0
prn11x17	17	5.0
prnA3	8	5.0
prnA4	9	5.0
prnA4Small	10	5.0
prnA5	11	5.0
prnB4	12	5.0
prnB5	13	5.0
prnCSheet	24	5.0
prnDSheet	25	5.0
prnESheet	26	5.0
prnEnv10	20	5.0
prnEnv11	21	5.0
prnEnv12	22	5.0
prnEnv14	23	5.0
prnEnv9	19	5.0
prnEnvB4	33	5.0
prnEnvB5	34	5.0
prnEnvB6	35	5.0
prnEnvC3	29	5.0
prnEnvC4	30	5.0
prnEnvC5	28	5.0
prnEnvC6	31	5.0
prnEnvC65	32	5.0
prnEnvDL	27	5.0
prnEnvItaly	36	5.0
prnEnvMonarch	37	5.0
prnEnvPersonal	38	5.0

continues

TABLE F.51. CONTINUED		
Constant	Value	Ver
prnExecutive	7	5.0
prnFanfoldLegalGerman	41	5.0
prnFanfoldStandardGerman	40	5.0
prnFanfoldUS	39	5.0
prnFolio	14	5.0
prnLedger	4	5.0
prnLegal	5	5.0
prnLetter	1	5.0
prnLetterSmall	2	5.0
prnNote	18	5.0
prnQuarto	15	5.0
prnStatement	6	5.0
prnTabloid	3	5.0

TABLE F.52. PRINTERTYPE (SMALLINT).		
Constant	Value	Ver
prnHPPCL	1	5.0
prnPostscript	2	5.0
prnTTY	4	5.0
prnUnknown	0	5.0

TABLE F.53. QUERYRESTARTOPTIONS (SMALLINT).		
Constant	Value	Ver
QueryDefault	0	1.0
QueryLock	2	1.0

Constant	Value	Ver
QueryNoLock	1	1.0
QueryRestart	3	1.0

TABLE F.54. RASTEROPERATIONS (LONGINT).

Constant	Value	Ver
MergePaint	12255782	1.0
NotSourceCopy	3342344	1.0
NotSourceErase	1114278	1.0
SourceAnd	8913094	1.0
SourceCopy	13369376	1.0
SourceErase	4457256	1.0
SourceInvert	6684742	1.0
SourcePaint	15597702	1.0

TABLE F.55. REPORTORIENTATION (SMALLINT).

Constant	Value	Ver
PrintDefaultOrientation	0	1.0
PrintLandscape	2	1.0
PrintPortrait	1	1.0

TABLE F.56. REPORTPRINTPANEL (SMALLINT).

Constant	Value	Ver
PrintHorizontalPanel	3	1.0
PrintClipToWidth	0	1.0

continues

TABLE F.56. CONTINUED		
Constant	Value	Ver
PrintHorizontalPanel	1	4.5
PrintOverflowPages	1	1.0
PrintVerticalPanel	2	1.0

TABLE F.57. REPORTPRINTRESTART (SMALLINT).		
Constant	Value	Ver
PrintFromCopy	1	1.0
PrintLock	0	1.0
PrintNoLock	2	1.0
PrintRestart	3	1.0
PrintReturn	4	1.0

TABLE F.58. SPECIALFIELDTYPES (SMALLINT).		
Constant	Value	Ver
DateField	0	5.0
NofFieldsField	5	5.0
NofPagesField	7	5.0
NofRecsField	4	5.0
PageNumField	6	5.0
RecordNoField	3	5.0
TableNameField	2	5.0
TimeField	1	5.0
TimeStampField	8	5.0

TABLE F.59. STATUSREASONS (SMALLINT).

Constant	Value	Ver
ModeWindow1	1	1.0
ModeWindow2	2	1.0
ModeWindow3	3	1.0
StatusWindow	0	1.0

TABLE F.60. TABLEFRAMESTYLES (SMALLINT).

Constant	Value	Ver
tf3D	3	1.0
tfDoubleLine	1	1.0
tfNoGrid	4	1.0
tfSingleLine	0	1.0
tfTripleLine	2	1.0

TABLE F.61. TEXTALIGNMENT (SMALLINT).

Constant	Value	Ver
TextAlignBottom	6	1.0
TextAlignCenter	1	1.0
TextAlignJustify	3	1.0
TextAlignLeft	0	1.0
TextAlignRight	2	1.0
TextAlignTop	4	1.0
TextAlignVCenter	5	1.0

TABLE F.62. TextDesignSizing (SmallInt).

Constant	Value	Ver
TextFixedSize	0	1.0
TextGrowOnly	2	1.0
TextSizeToFit	1	1.0

TABLE F.63. TextSpacing (SmallInt).

Constant	Value	Ver
TextDoubleSpacing	2	1.0
TextDoubleSpacing2	3	1.0
TextSingleSpacing	0	1.0
TextSingleSpacing2	1	1.0
TextTripleSpacing	4	1.0

TABLE F.64. UIObjectTypes (SmallInt).

Constant	Value	Ver
BandTool	19	5.0
BoxTool	1	1.0
ButtonTool	7	1.0
ChartTool	11	1.0
EllipseTool	3	1.0
FieldTool	8	1.0
GraphicTool	5	1.0
LineTool	2	1.0
OleTool	6	1.0
PageBrkTool	18	5.0

Constant	Value	Ver
PageTool	14	5.0
RecordTool	10	1.0
SelectionTool	0	5.0
TableFrameTool	9	1.0
TextTool	4	1.0
XtabTool	12	1.0

TABLE F.65. UPDATELINK (SMALLINT).

Constant	Value	Ver
OLEUpdateAutomatic	1	5.0
OLEUpdateManual	3	5.0

TABLE F.66. VALUEREASONS (SMALLINT).

Constant	Value	Ver
EditValue	1	1.0
FieldValue	0	1.0
StartupValue	3	1.0

TABLE F.67. WINDOWSTYLES (LONGINT, *SMALLINT).

Constant	Value	Ver
WinDefaultCoordinate*	−32768	1.0
WinStyleBorder	8388608	1.0
WinStyleControlMenu	524288	1.0
WinStyleDefault	8192	1.0

continues

	Table F.67. continued	
Constant	Value	Ver
WinStyleDialog	–2147483648	1.0
WinStyleDialogFrame	4194304	1.0
WinStyleHScroll	1048576	1.0
WinStyleHidden	16384	1.0
WinStyleMaximize	16777216	1.0
WinStyleMaximizeButton	65536	1.0
WinStyleMinimize	536870912	1.0
WinStyleMinimizeButton	131072	1.0
WinStyleModal	2	1.0
WinStyleThickFrame	262144	1.0
WinStyleTitleBar	12582912	1.0
WinStyleVScroll	2097152	1.0

APPENDIX

ERRORS

Table G.1 lists all the error constants and messages. The second column lists the corresponding value for each constant. Do not use this value in your code; use only the error constant. The third column lists the corresponding error message. Many of the error contants do not have a corresponding error message. The last column shows the version of Paradox in which the error constant was introduced.

NOTE Some of the following errors are unmapped; they do not have a corresponding error message. These unmapped errors are underlying errors that should never surface in ObjectPAL; however, they are included here for completeness.

TABLE G.1. ERROR CONSTANTS AND MESSAGES.

Error Constant	Value	Error Message	Ver
peAccessDisabled	9222	Access to table disabled because of previous error.	4.5
peAccessError	−31721	Invalid file access.	1.0
peActionNotSupported	−31652	Action not supported for this object	4.5
peActiveIndex	10035	Index is being used to order table.	1.0
peActiveTrans	−30347	A Transaction is currently active.	5.0
peActiveTransaction	10256	A user transaction is already in progress.	4.5
peAliasInUse	−30391	The alias '%0ds' is in use.	1.0
peAliasIsServer	−28153	Alias is a server.	4.5
peAliasMismatch	−30349	The destination table of the rename has a conflicting alias.	5.0
peAliasNotDefined	−30393	The alias '%0ds' has not been defined.	1.0
peAliasNotOpen	10044	Alias is not currently opened.	4.5
peAliasPathNonExistant	−30358	The path for the alias '%0ds' does not exist.	4.5
peAliasProjectConflict	−30342	The Public Alias being added '%0ds' is already a Project Alias.	5.0
peAliasPublicConflict	−30341	The Project Alias being added '%0ds' is already a Public Alias.	5.0
peAlias_X_Db	−30411	The alias '%0ds' and the Database '%1ds' do not match.	1.0
peAllFieldsReadOnly	−31184	All fields are read only.	1.0
peAlreadyLocked	10247	Record already locked by this session.	1.0
peArgumentNumber	−30400	'%0ds' failed because it has the wrong number of arguments supplied.	1.0
peArgumentTypeInvalid	−30350	A method which takes an indeterminate number of arguments has an argument which is not a valid type.	5.0
peARYFixedSizeArray	−30589	The '%0ds' operation is not allowed on fixed-size arrays.	1.0
peARYIndexOutOfBounds	−30588	The specified array index is out of bounds. The index is %0dl, and the array limit is %1dl.	1.0
peARYNoMemory	−30591	Not enough memory to allocate or grow the array.	1.0
peARYRangeTooLarge	−30590	The starting and ending indexes are not valid for this array. The starting index is %0dl, ending index is %1dl, and the array size is %2dl.	1.0
peARYTooLarge	−30592	You cannot allocate an array with a size larger than 64k.	1.0
peBad1Sep	−31980	Bad Date Separator.	1.0
peBad1TSep	−31970	Bad Time Separator.	1.0

Error Constant	Value	Error Message	Ver
peBad2Sep	−31979	Bad Date Separator.	1.0
peBad2TSep	−31969	Bad Time Separator.	1.0
peBad3Sep	−31978	Bad Date Separator.	1.0
peBad3TSep	−31968	Bad Time Separator.	1.0
peBad4Sep	−31977	Bad Date Separator.	1.0
peBad4TSep	−31967	Bad Time Separator.	1.0
peBad5Sep	−31976	Bad Date Separator.	1.0
peBad5TSep	−31966	Bad Time Separator.	1.0
peBad6TSep	−31965	Bad Time Separator.	1.0
peBadAlias	−31731	Unknown alias.	1.0
peBadAMPM	−31971	Bad AM-PM Specification.	1.0
peBadArgument	−30397	'%0ds' failed because argument %1di was not legal.	1.0
peBadArrayResize	−30379	Could not resize a dynamic array.	1.0
peBadBlobHeader	−31662	Blob has invalid header.	1.0
peBadCharsInAlias	−28147	Illegal characters in alias	4.5
peBadConstantGroup	−30585	The constant group '%0ds' was not found.	5.0
peBadDate	−31986	Bad Date Specification.	1.0
peBadDay	−31983	Bad Day Specification.	1.0
peBadDriverType	−28156	Invalid driver name.	4.5
peBadField	−31699	Invalid field.	1.0
peBadFieldType	−30423	Field '%0ds' has a badly formed type '%1ds'.	4.5
peBadFileFormat	−31722	Cannot interpret file. It could be corrupt.	1.0
peBadHandle	−32482		1.0
peBadHour	−31974	Bad Hour Specification.	1.0
peBadLinkIndex	−31637	Index used to join tables is no longer valid.	5.0
peBadLogical	−31975	Bad Logical Specification.	1.0
peBadMinutes	−31973	Bad Minute Specification.	1.0
peBadMonth	−31984	Bad Month Specification.	1.0
peBadObject	−30525	The method, '%0ds', is not allowed on a '%1ds' object.	5.0
peBadRecordTag	−32496		1.0
peBadSeconds	−31972	Bad Seconds Specification.	1.0
peBadTable	−31700	Invalid table.	1.0
peBadTime	−31985	Bad Time Specification.	1.0
peBadTypeArray	−30390	Trying to do a copyToArray or copyFromArray with an array type that does not correspond.	1.0
peBadVersion	−31697	The ObjectPAL version used in this form is incompatible with this version of Paradox. You must recompile from source.	1.0
peBadWeekday	−31982	Bad Day of Week Specification.	1.0
peBadXtabAction	−31664	Action is not supported in a crosstab	1.0
peBadYear	−31981	Bad Year Specification.	1.0
peBad_FieldType	−30423		1.0

continues

TABLE G.1. CONTINUED

Error Constant	Value	Error Message	Ver
peBigXtab	−31728	Crosstab contains too many fields.	1.0
peBlankField	−31220	The field is blank.	1.0
peBlankTableName	−30418	A blank table name was provided.	1.0
peBlankValue	−30703	Value is illegal or blank.	1.0
peBlobFileMissing	8714	BLOB file is missing.	1.0
peBlobModified	13058	BLOB has been modified.	1.0
peBlobNotOpened	10755	BLOB not opened.	1.0
peBlobOpened	10754	BLOB already opened.	1.0
peBlobReaderror	−31707	Problem reading data from .MB file on disk.	1.0
peBlobVersion	12037	BLOB file version is too old.	1.0
peBOF	8705	At beginning of table.	1.0
peBracketMismatch	−31995	Mismatched brackets.	1.0
peBreak	−30672	Stopped program at your request.	1.0
peBufferSizeError	−32488	Buffer size error.	1.0
peBufferTooSmall	−31998	Buffer is too small.	1.0
peCancel	−31705	User selected Cancel.	1.0
peCancelDatabaseOpen	−28158	Canceled open database operation.	4.5
peCancelPassword	−28148	Cancelled password entry.	4.5
peCannotArrive	−31646		1.0
peCannotClose	10034	Cannot close index.	1.0
peCannotCloseAlias	−28145	Alias currently in use.	5.0
peCannotCopy	−31724	Cannot copy selection to Clipboard.	1.0
peCannotCopyTo	−31172	Unable to copy to file.	1.0
peCannotCut	−31725	Cannot cut selection to Clipboard.	1.0
peCannotCutTo	−31173	Unable to cut to file.	1.0
peCannotDelete	−31174	Unable to delete.	1.0
peCannotDeleteLine	−31179	Unable to delete line.	1.0
peCannotDepart	−31647		1.0
peCannotDitto	−31694	Cannot duplicate field.	1.0
peCannotEdit	−31739	You cannot modify this field.	1.0
peCannotEditField	−31203	This field cannot be edited.	1.0
peCannotEditRefresh	−31675	Cannot modify data during refresh.	1.0
peCannotExitField	−31227	Unable to exit field.	1.0
peCannotExitRecord	−31226	Unable to exit record.	1.0
peCannotFindFile	−31629		4.5
peCannotInsert	−31730	Cannot insert record here.	1.0
peCannotInsertText	−31169	Unable to insert text.	1.0
peCannotLoadDriver	15877	Cannot load driver.	1.0

Error Constant	Value	Error Message	Ver
peCannotLoadLanguageDriver	15878	Cannot load language driver.	4.5
peCannotLock	−31740	Cannot lock record.	1.0
peCannotLockServerDependent	−31656	Cannot lock record dependent on server.	4.5
peCannotLookupFill	−31209	Unable to fill field from lookup table.	1.0
peCannotLookupFillCorr	−31208	Unable to fill corresponding fields from lookup table.	1.0
peCannotLookupMove	−31207	Unable to fill field from master table.	1.0
peCannotMakeQuery	−31666	Cannot create query from the selected file.	1.0
peCannotMove	−31658	Cannot move in that direction.	4.5
peCannotOpenClip	−31716	Could not open Clipboard.	1.0
peCannotOpenTable	−31206	Unable to open table.	1.0
peCannotOrderRange	−31167	Unable to set Order/Range.	1.0
peCannotPaste	−31723	Cannot paste from Clipboard into the selected object.	1.0
peCannotPasteFrom	−31171	Unable to paste from file.	1.0
peCannotPasteLink	−31175	Unable to paste link.	1.0
peCannotPerformAction	−31170	Unable to perform action.	1.0
peCannotPutField	−31743	The value is not legal in this field.	1.0
peCannotPutRecord	−31742	Record contains illegal field values.	1.0
peCannotRotate	−31695	Cannot rotate columns.	1.0
peCannotUndelete	−31669	Cannot undelete record.	1.0
peCantDropPrimary	−30345	The Primary Index cannot be dropped because another index is maintained on the table.	5.0
pecantOpenTable	−30435		1.0
peCantOpenTable	−30435	Could not open table '%0ds'. Engine error %1dx.	4.5
peCantSearchField	−31192	Unable to search in this field.	1.0
peCantSetFilter	−30367	A %0ds cannot be done on %1ds %2ds because it is an expression index.	1.0
peCantShowDeleted	−30381	Table does not show deleted records.	1.0
peCantToggleToTable	−31153	Cannot toggle to table view.	5.0
peCatalogCountError	−32484		1.0
peCatalogSizeError	−32483		1.0
peCfgCannotWrite	8453	Cannot write to Engine configuration file.	1.0
peCfgMultiFile	8454	Cannot initialize with different configuration file.	1.0
peCFunction	−30383	Found problem in a CFunction operation.	1.0
peClientsLimit	9486	Too many clients.	
peCompatErr	−30454	An error was triggered in the '%0ds' procedure.	4.5
peCompatERR	−30454		1.0
peConstantNotFound	−30584	The constant name was not found.	5.0
peConversion	−30701	Could not convert data of type '%0cc' to type '%1cc'. The types are mismatched or the values are incompatible.	1.0
peCopyLinkedTables	12807	Copy linked tables?	4.5
peCopyOverSelf	−30468	Cannot copy a file over itself. Use rename instead.	5.0

continues

TABLE G.1. CONTINUED

Error Constant	Value	Error Message	Ver
peCorruptLockFile	8966	Corrupt lock file.	1.0
peCreateErr	–30455	An error was triggered in a Create operation.	4.5
peCreateERR	–30455		1.0
peCreateWarningRange	–30364	The %0ds of field %1ds is outside range %2di–%3di. Setting it to %4di.	1.0
peCursorLimit	9478	Too many open cursors.	1.0
peDatabaseErr	–30461	An error was triggered in the '%0ds' method on an object of Database type.	4.5
peDatabaseERR	–30461		1.0
peDataLoss	–31734	Character(s) not supported by Table Language.	1.0
peDataTooLong	–28149	Data is too long for field.	4.5
peDBLimit	9489	Too many open databases.	1.0
peDDEAllocate	–30557	DDE: Buffer allocation failed.	1.0
peDDEExecute	–30553	DDE: Execute server command failed.	1.0
peDDEInitiate	–30558	DDE: Specified DDE server is not responding.	1.0
peDDENoLock	–30556	DDE: Could not lock memory.	1.0
peDDENotOpened	–30559	DDE: Session not opened. Use Open.	1.0
peDDEPoke	–30555	DDE: Send data (poke) request failed.	1.0
peDDERequest	–30554	DDE: Could not receive data.	1.0
peDDETimeOut	–30552	DDE: Time out while waiting for data.	1.0
peDDEUnassigned	–30560	DDE: Server and Topic were not assigned. Use Open.	1.0
peDeadlock	10255	A deadlock was detected.	4.5
peDeliveredDocument	–31665	Cannot modify this document.	1.0
peDependentMustBeEmpty	9747	Cannot make this master a detail of another table if its details are not empty.	4.5
peDestMustBeIndexed	10047	Destination must be indexed.	4.5
peDetailRecExistsEmpty	9744	Master has detail records. Cannot empty it.	4.5
peDetailRecordsExist	9734	Master has detail records. Cannot delete or modify.	1.0
peDetailTableExists	9743	Detail table(s) exist.	4.5
peDetailTableOpen	9746	Detail table is open.	4.5
peDifferentPath	10061	Tables in different directories.	
peDriverUnknown	–30368	The driver type '%0ds' is unknown.	1.0
peDuplicateAlias	–28157	Duplicate alias name.	4.5
peDuplicateMoniker	–31643	Table monicker already in use.	5.0
peDynamicBind	–30695	The data type %00cc does not support dynamic binding.	4.5
peEditObjRequired	–31686	Method requires an edit object.	1.0
peEmbedDataProblem	–31654	Object to be embedded violates data constraints when placed in container.	4.5
peEmbedNotAllowed	–31653	Chosen container cannot embed or disembed other objects.	4.5

Error Constant	Value	Error Message	Ver
peEmbedWontFit	−31655	Object to be embedded falls outside edges of container.	4.5
peEmptyClipboard	−31668	Cannot paste—Clipboard is empty.	1.0
peEmptyTable	−31223	The table is empty.	1.0
peEndOfBlob	8711	End of BLOB.	1.0
peEngineQueryMismatch	12038	Query and Engine DLLs are mismatched.	4.5
peEnumErr	−30453	An error was triggered in an Enum.	4.5
peEnumERR	−30453		1.0
peEOF	8706	At end of table.	1.0
peExpressionIllegal	−31650	Cannot use an expression for linking in this data model.	4.5
peExtInvalid	−30348	The destination table of the rename has an extension mismatch.	5.0
peFailedDatabaseOpen	−28159	Could not open database.	4.5
peFailedMethod	−30403	The method '%0ds' failed.	4.5
peFAILEDMETHOD	−30403		1.0
peFailedStdDB	−30429	Could not open standard database. Engine error %0dx.	1.0
peFailNoError	−30715	You have called `fail()` without any error code or error message.	4.5
peFamFileInvalid	8967	Corrupt family file.	1.0
peFieldIsBlank	9740	Field is blank.	1.0
peFieldLimit	9492	Too many fields in Table Create.	1.0
peFieldMultiLinked	9750	Field(s) linked to more than one master.	4.5
peFieldNotCurrent	−31204	The specified field is not the current field.	1.0
peFieldNotInEdit	−31687	Must be in Field View to search.	1.0
peFieldNotInLookupTable	9736	Field value out of lookup table range.	4.5
peFieldValueErr	−30378	Could not get a field's value.	4.5
peFieldValueERR	−30378		1.0
peFileBusy	10243	Table is busy.	1.0
peFileCorrupt	8962	Corrupt file—other than header.	1.0
peFileCreate	−30660		5.0
peFileDeleteFail	9220	File Delete operation failed.	
peFmlMemberNotFound	8713	Could not find family member.	1.0
peForeignKeyErr	9733	Master record missing.	1.0
peFormatError	−32493		1.0
peFormClosed	−30541	You have tried to access a design object that is not open.	1.0
peFormCompileError	−31685	Form has PAL syntax errors. Reopening in design window.	1.0
peFormCompileErrors	−30534	The design object has compile errors and will not run.	4.5
peFormInvalidName	−30539	%01ds is not a valid name for a %0ds.	1.0
peFormInvalidOptions	−30540	Invalid WinStyle combination for opening the design object.	1.0
peFormNotAttached	−30542	You have tried to access a design object that is not open.	1.0
peFormOpenFailed	−30533	The design object could not be opened.	1.0
peFormQueryOpen	−31640	Could not open query.	5.0

continues

Error Constant	Value	Error Message	Ver
peFormQueryViewMismatch	−31639	Query needs to be saved and/or re–executed.	5.0
peFormReadError	−31720	Error occurred reading file.	1.0
peFormTableOpen	−31718	Could not open tables.	1.0
peFormTableReadonly	−31735	Cannot modify this table.	1.0
peFormWriteError	−31719	Could not write to file.	1.0
peFS_CREATEERR	−32479	Could not create file. Protection or access error.	4.5
peFS_WRITEOPENERR	−32478	Could not open output file. Protection or access error.	4.5
peGeneralErr	−30404	Unknown error.	4.5
peGeneralSQL	13059	General SQL error.	4.5
peGENERICERR	−30404		1.0
peGroupLocked	10250	Key group is locked.	1.0
peHasOpenCursors	10765	Table(s) open. Cannot perform this operation.	1.0
peHeaderCorrupt	8961	Corrupt table/index header.	1.0
peIllegalAliasProperty	−30363	The property '%0ds' is not associated with the alias '%1ds'.	4.5
peIllegalCharacter	−31147	Illegal character.	5.0
peIllegalConversion	−30699	Cannot convert data of type '%0cn' to %1cc.	1.0
peIllegalIndexName	−30376	Trying to create index named '%0ds' when index name must be '%1ds'.	1.0
peIllegalIndexName1	−30343	Trying to create a Paradox index '%0ds' which can't be named the same as a field.	5.0
peIllegalOperator	−30717	An illegal PAL operator was found.	1.0
peIllegalOpForInMem	−30344	Can't perform an '%0ds' on an InMemory TCursor.	5.0
peIllegalTableName	−30357	'%0ds' is not a valid table name.	4.5
peIllegalXtabSpec	−31689	Crosstab specification is not allowed.	1.0
peIllFormedCalcField	−31706	Incorrect expression syntax.	1.0
peImcompatibleRecStructs	10045	Incompatible record structures.	4.5
peInappropriateFieldType	−31214	The specified field type is invalid.	1.0
peInappropriateSubType	−31213	The specified field subtype is invalid.	1.0
peIncompatibleDataType	−30366	Trying to store incompatible data type.	1.0
peIndexCorrupt	8965	Corrupt index.	1.0
peIndexDoesntExist	−31634	Index does not exist.	5.0
peIndexErr	−30457	An error was triggered in an Index operation.	4.5
peIndexERR	−30457		1.0
peIndexExists	10027	Index already exists.	1.0
peIndexFailed	−30421	Index could not be created.	1.0
peIndexLimit	9487	Too many indexes on table.	1.0
peIndexNameRequired	10010	Index name required.	1.0
peIndexOpen	10028	Index is open.	1.0
peIndexOutOfdate	12034	Index is out of date.	1.0

Error Constant	Value	Error Message	Ver
peIndexReadOnly	10767	Index is read only.	4.5
peIndexStartFailed	−30419	Could not start Index.	1.0
peInfiniteInsert	−31663	Infinite record insertion attempted.	1.0
peInterfaceVer	12033	Interface mismatch. Engine version different.	1.0
peInternal	−30718	An unexpected error occurred.	1.0
peInternalError	−32510		1.0
peInternalLimit	9482	Some internal limit (see context).	1.0
peInUse	−31684	Cannot delete object(s) that are in use.	1.0
peInvalidAttribute	−30469	Invalid File Attributes: %0ds.	5.0
peInvalidBlobHandle	10030	Invalid BLOB handle in record buffer.	1.0
peInvalidBlobLen	10029	Invalid BLOB length.	1.0
peInvalidBlobOffset	9998	Invalid offset into the BLOB.	1.0
peInvalidBookmark	10021	Bookmarks do not match table.	1.0
peInvalidCallbackBuflen	10017	Invalid callback buffer length.	1.0
peInvalidCfgParam	12550	Invalid configuration parameter.	1.0
peInvalidChar	−31994	Invalid character.	1.0
peInvalidColumn	−31231	The specified column number is invalid.	1.0
peInvalidDataBase	−30438	Database not opened.	1.0
peInvalidDataTypeCompare	−30427	Cannot compare data types—Memo, Bitmap, OLE.	1.0
peInvalidDate	10059	Invalid Date.	
peInvalidFileName	9987	Invalid file name.	1.0
peInvalidFilter	10051	Invalid Filter.	4.5
peInvalidFormat	−31999	Invalid format.	1.0
peInvalidHandle	9990	Invalid handle to the function.	1.0
peInvalidIndexCreate	10054	Invalid index create request.	4.5
peInvalidIndexDelete	10055	Invalid index delete request.	4.5
peInvalidIndexDesc	10023	Invalid index descriptor.	1.0
peInvalidIndexName	10022	Invalid index/tag name.	1.0
peInvalidIndexStruct	10005	Invalid array of index descriptors.	1.0
peInvalidIndexType	10048	Invalid index type.	4.5
peInvalidIsolationLevel	−30356	'%0ds' is not a valid isolation level.	4.5
peInvalidKey	10026	Key does not pass filter condition.	1.0
peInvalidLanguageDriver	10043	Invalid language Driver.	4.5
peInvalidLinkExpr	10040	Invalid linked cursor expression.	1.0
peInvalidMasterTableLevel	9735	Master table level is incorrect.	4.5
peInvalidMode	10033	Invalid mode.	1.0
peInvalidModifyRequest	9996	Invalid modify request.	1.0
peInvalidOperationForTableType	−30365	Can't perform %0ds for table of type %1ds.	1.0
peInvalidOption	9989	Invalid option.	1.0
peInvalidOptParam	11522	Invalid optional parameter.	1.0

continues

TABLE G.1. CONTINUED

Error Constant	Value	Error Message	Ver
peInvalidParam	9986	Invalid parameter.	1.0
peInvalidParameter	−30696	%00ds:%01ds:%02ds: The value of the parameter, '%3ds', is not legal. %4rs.	4.5
peInvalidPassword	10015	Invalid password given.	1.0
peInvalidPath	−28154	Invalid path.	4.5
peInvalidPrefferedFile	−31224	The specified file name is invalid.	1.0
peInvalidTCursor	−30441	TCursor not opened.	1.0
peInvalidTime	10058	Invalid Time.	4.5
peInvalidTimeStamp	10060	Invalid Datetime	4.5
peInvalidTranslation	10019	Translate Error. Value out of bounds.	1.0
peInvalidUserPassword	10036	Unknown user name or password.	1.0
peInvalidValChkStruct	10006	Invalid array of validity check descriptors.	1.0
peIXPBlockRange	−28926	Selected range of cells is too wide to import.	4.5
peIXPConversion	−28925	String conversion error on line %ld.	4.5
peIXPDataTooSparse	−28875	Data in the selected block is too sparse to import.	4.5
peIXPDbClose	−28909	Unable to close database.	4.5
peIXPDbOpen	−28910	Unable to open database.	4.5
peIXPExcelFileType	−28888	Not an Excel file.	4.5
peIXPExcelIndexRecord	−28889	Excel Index record not found.	4.5
peIXPExportTable	−28878	Table selected to load is not a valid Export Specification table.	4.5
peIXPFieldCount	−28924	An error occured while parsing the specification table.	4.5
peIXPFieldDesc	−28904	Unable to get table field descriptions.	4.5
peIXPFileClose	−28919	Could not close the file.	4.5
peIXPFileCreate	−28921	Could not create the file.	4.5
peIXPFileName	−28880	Not a valid file name.	4.5
peIXPFileOpen	−28920	Could not open the file.	4.5
peIXPFileRead	−28912	Could not read from file.	4.5
peIXPFileWrite	−28911	Could not write to file.	4.5
peIXPGetField	−28896	Unable to get table field.	4.5
peIXPGetProp	−28903	Unable to get table properties.	4.5
peIXPHome	−28892	Unable to set table cursor to top.	4.5
peIXPImportTable	−28879	Table selected to load is not a valid Import Specification table.	4.5
peIXPInputFile	−28923	Input file is incorrect.	4.5
peIXPInsertRecord	−28893	Unable to insert table record.	4.5
peIXPNextRecord	−28894	Unable to get next table record.	4.5
peIXPPageName	−28876	Invalid page name.	4.5
peIXPPassword	−28922	The input file is password protected.	4.5

Error Constant	Value	Error Message	Ver
peIXPPutField	−28895	Unable to put table field.	4.5
peIXPRange	−28927	Invalid cell range.	4.5
peIXPRecordCount	−28891	Unable to get table record count.	4.5
peIXPRecordInit	−28890	Unable to initialize table record.	4.5
peIXPRecordLength	−28877	Invalid record length.	4.5
peIXPRecordSize	−28873	Record size is limited to 32000 characters.	4.5
peIXPSkip	−28874	Errors encountered during import, records were skipped.	4.5
peIXPTableName	−28887	Not a valid table name.	4.5
peIXPTblClose	−28906	Unable to close database table.	4.5
peKeyViol	9729	Key violation.	1.0
peLanguageDriveMisMatch	10049	Language Drivers of Table and Index do not match.	4.5
peLDNotFound	8715	Could not find language driver.	1.0
peLinkedTableProtected	9749	A table linked by referential integrity requires password to open.	4.5
peLinkWontFit	−31148	Link information will not fit in field.	5.0
peListTooBig	−31671	Maximum number of items in a list is 2500.	1.0
peLiveQueryDead	−31636	Live answer set forced to disk for this operation.	5.0
peLocateErr	−30458	An error was triggered in a Locate operation.	4.5
peLocateERR	−30458		1.0
peLocateFailed	−30402	Could not perform locate operation.	4.5
peLOCATEFAILED	−30402		1.0
peLocked	10241	Record locked by another user.	1.0
peLockFileLimit	9495	Lock file has grown too large.	4.5
peLockInvalid	−30388	Trying to '%0ds' (un)lock table '%1ds' by name which can't be done in PAL.	1.0
peLockTimeout	10249	Lock time out.	1.0
peLookupTableErr	9736		1.0
peLostExclusiveAccess	10252	Exclusive access was lost.	1.0
peLostTableLock	10251	Table lock was lost.	1.0
peMasterExists	9741	Link to master table already defined.	1.0
peMasterReferenceErr	9745	Self referencing referential integrity must be entered one at a time with no other changes to the table.	4.5
peMasterTableOpen	9742	Master table is open.	1.0
peMatchNotFound	−31714	"%s" was not found.	1.0
peMathError	−30688	An arithmetic error occurred during '%0ds' execution. Reason: '%1ds'.	1.0
peMaxValErr	9731	Maximum validity check failed.	1.0
peMemoCorrupt	8963	Corrupt Memo/BLOB file.	1.0
peMethodNotFound	−30713	The method, '%0ds' is not visible from the object, '%01un'.	4.5
peMethodNotValid	−30712	The method is not valid for the object.	4.5
peMinValErr	9730	Minimum validity check failed.	1.0

continues

Table G.1. continued

Error Constant	Value	Error Message	Ver
peMisMatchedOperands	–30698	Cannot perform '%0ds' between %1cc and %2cc.	1.0
peModifiedSinceOpen	–31647	The disk file has been modified since it was loaded.	5.0
peNetUnknown	11271	Unknown network error.	1.0
peNetUserLimit	11266	Network user limit exceeded.	1.0
peNo1Sep	–31948	Date Separator missing.	1.0
peNo1TSep	–31938	Time Separator missing.	1.0
peNo2Sep	–31947	Date Separator missing.	1.0
peNo2TSep	–31937	Time Separator missing.	1.0
peNo3Sep	–31946	Date Separator missing.	1.0
peNo3TSep	–31936	Time Separator missing.	1.0
peNo4Sep	–31945	Date Separator missing.	1.0
peNo4TSep	–31935	Time Separator missing.	1.0
peNo5Sep	–31944	Date Separator missing.	1.0
peNo5TSep	–31934	Time Separator missing.	1.0
peNo6TSep	–31933	Time Separator missing.	1.0
peNoActiveTransaction	–30354	No active transaction to commit or rollback.	4.5
peNoAMPM	–31939	AM-PM Specification missing.	1.0
peNoArguments	–30401	'%0ds' failed because it has no arguments supplied.	1.0
peNoAssocIndex	10764	No associated index.	1.0
peNoCallback	10016	No callback function.	1.0
peNoConfigFile	8452	Cannot find Engine configuration file.	1.0
peNoCurrRec	8709	No current record.	1.0
peNoDay	–31951	Day Specification missing.	1.0
peNoDayOrMonthSpec	–31987	Format is display only. Need day or month.	1.0
peNoDestRecord	–30424	Trying to store into a nonexistent record.	1.0
peNoDetailRoom	–31727	Insufficient room for detail records of %s.	1.0
peNoDiskSpace	9475	Insufficient disk space.	1.0
peNoDMChangeInRun	–31457	Cannot modify the Data Model in Run Mode.	5.0
peNoFamilyRights	10499	Insufficient family rights for operation.	1.0
peNoFieldRights	10497	Insufficient field rights for operation.	1.0
peNoFieldRoom	–31726	Could not fit field %s in layout.	1.0
peNoFile	–32487		1.0
peNoFileHandles	9474	Not enough file handles.	1.0
peNoHour	–31942	Hour Specification missing.	1.0
peNoHourSpec	–31988	Format is display only. Need hour.	1.0
peNoKeyField	–31691	No key field in this table.	1.0
peNoLock	–30339	The table(tcursor) is not '%0ds' locked.	5.0
peNoPage	–31702	Invalid page.	1.0

Error Constant	Value	Error Message	Ver
peNoPictureMatch	–31738	Invalid character(s) in this field.	1.0
peNoProperty	–31679	The property is not valid for the given object.	1.0
peNoRecordNos	–31191	The table does not support record numbers.	1.0
peNoRecords	–31704	Table is empty.	1.0
peNoSearchField	–31715	Active object is not a field or has a value that cannot be searched.	1.0
peNoSeconds	–31940	Seconds Specification missing.	1.0
peNoSelect	–31701	Must be in Field View (F2) to select.	1.0
peNoSelection	–31717	There is no object selected to cut or copy.	1.0
peNoSeqnums	–31703	Table does not support sequence numbers.	1.0
peNoServerAnsTable	–30360	The answer table cannot be on a server.	4.5
peNoSession	–31708	Database information is missing from Desktop.	1.0
peNoSoftDeletes	–31185	The table does not support soft deletes.	1.0
peNoSortField	–30417	No field identified on Sort from table '%0ds'.	1.0
peNoSrcRecord	–30425	Trying to read from a nonexistent record.	1.0
peNoSuchFile	9988	File does not exist.	1.0
peNoSuchFilter	10050	Filter handle is invalid.	4.5
peNoSuchIndex	9997	Index does not exist.	1.0
peNoSuchTable	10024	Table does not exist.	1.0
peNoTableName	–30430	Specify the table to be associated for TCursor.	1.0
peNoTableRights	10498	Insufficient table rights for operation.	1.0
peNoTableSupport	10766	Table does not support this operation.	4.5
peNotABlob	10753	Field is not a BLOB.	1.0
peNotAllowedFieldType	–30389	Field '%0ds' of type '%1ds' is not a valid type for a sort or index operation.	1.0
peNotAllowedInPlace	–31155	This operation is not allowed while in place.	5.0
peNotAValidField	–30380	The field number or name is not in the table.	1.0
peNotCoEdit	–30444	Table needs to be in Edit mode to perform operation.	1.0
peNoTempFile	–31711	Could not create temporary table.	1.0
peNoTempTableSpace	9476	Temporary table resource limit.	1.0
peNotEnoughRights	–30394	Cannot perform operation '%0ds' on '%1ds' because of insufficient rights.	4.5
peNotEnoughtRights	–30394		1.0
peNoTextTable	–28143	Unrecognized table type.	5.0
peNotField	–30446	Field '%0ds' is not a field in table '%1ds'.	1.0
peNotFieldNum	–30445	Field '%0di' is not a field in table '%1ds'.	1.0
peNotImplemented	12290	Not implemented yet.	1.0
peNotIndexed	10757	Table is not indexed.	
peNoTransaction	10257	No user transaction is currently in progress.	4.5
peNotSameSession	10760	Attempt to mix objects from different sessions.	1.0
peNotSupported	12289	Capability not supported.	1.0

continues

TABLE G.1. CONTINUED

Error Constant	Value	Error Message	Ver
peNotSupportedFiltered	−31638	Operation not supported on filtered record set	5.0
peNotValidSearchField	−30375	Illegal field type for '%0ds' in '%1ds' for locate.	1.0
peNoWeekday	−31950	Day of Week Specification missing.	1.0
peNoWorkPrivAlias	−30387	Cannot change the path of the default working or private directories.	1.0
peNoYear	−31949	Year Specification missing.	1.0
peNullFieldName	−31709	Field has no name.	1.0
peObjectImplicityTruncated	12809	Object implicitly truncated.	4.5
peObjectNotFound	−30646	You have tried to reference the object named '%0ds' from the object named '%1un'. The referenced object could not be found. The name is either incorrect or the object is not visible from '%2ds'.	1.0
peObjectTreeTooBig	−31670	Too many objects for object tree.	1.0
peObjImplicitlyDropped	12801	Object implicitly dropped.	1.0
peObjImplicitlyModified	12803	Object implicitly modified.	1.0
peObjMayBeTruncated	12802	Object may be truncated.	1.0
peObjNotFound	8712	Could not find object.	4.5
peOk	0		1.0
peOldVersion	12035	Older version (see context).	1.0
peOleActivateFailed	−32485		1.0
peOpenBlobLimit	9494	Too many open BLOBs.	1.0
peOpenDetailFailed	9738	Detail Table Open operation failed.	4.5
peOpenedByPal	−31150	This table view was opened by ObjectPal.	5.0
peOpenErr	−31646	Cannot open file.	5.0
peOpenLookupFailed	9737	Lookup Table Open operation failed.	4.5
peOpenMasterFailed	9739	Master Table Open operation failed.	4.5
peOpenTableLimit	9483	Too many open tables.	1.0
peOperatorNotAllowed	−30700	Operation '%0ds' is not allowed on the data type %1cc.	1.0
peOptRecLockFailed	10259	Couldn't perform the edit because another user changed the record.	4.5
peOptRecLockRecDel	10260	Couldn't perform the edit because another user deleted or moved the record.	4.5
peOSNetErr	11109	Operating system network error.	1.0
peOSNoDevice	11023	Device does not exist.	1.0
peOSNoFATEntry	11010	File or directory does not exist.	1.0
peOSNoMemory	11016	Not enough memory.	1.0
peOSNoMoreFiles	11026	No more files.	1.0
peOSNoPath	11011	Path not found.	1.0
peOSNotSameDev	11025	Not same device.	1.0
peOSOutOfRange	11042	Result is too large.	1.0

Error Constant	Value	Error Message	Ver
peOSRemoveCurDir	11024	Attempt to remove current directory.	1.0
peOSShareViol	11058	Share violation.	1.0
peOSTooManyOpenFiles	11012	Too many open files. You may need to increase MAXFILEHANDLE limit in ODAPI configuration.	1.0
peOSUnknown	11047	Unknown internal operating system error.	1.0
peOtherServerLoaded	12808		4.5
peOutOfHandles	–32491	Out of internal file handles ??	1.0
peOutOfMemory	–32511		1.0
peOutOfRange	9985	Number is out of range.	1.0
peOverFlow	–30702	Overflow. The source data is numerically too large (positive or negative) to store in the destination.	1.0
pePart1Sep	–31916	Incomplete Date Separator.	1.0
pePart1TSep	–31906	Incomplete Time Separator.	1.0
pePart2Sep	–31915	Incomplete Date Separator.	1.0
pePart2TSep	–31905	Incomplete Time Separator.	1.0
pePart3Sep	–31914	Incomplete Date Separator.	1.0
pePart3TSep	–31904	Incomplete Time Separator.	1.0
pePart4Sep	–31913	Incomplete Date Separator.	1.0
pePart4TSep	–31903	Incomplete Time Separator.	1.0
pePart5Sep	–31912	Incomplete Date Separator.	1.0
pePart5TSep	–31902	Incomplete Time Separator.	1.0
pePart6TSep	–31901	Incomplete Time Separator.	1.0
pePartAMPM	–31907	Incomplete AM-PM Specification.	1.0
pePartDay	–31919	Incomplete Day Specification.	1.0
pePartHour	–31910	Incomplete Hour Specification.	1.0
pePartLogical	–31911	Incomplete Logical Specification.	1.0
pePictureErr	–31200	The field value fails picture validity check.	1.0
pePrecisionExceeded	–31997	Number is out of range for the given type.	1.0
pePrimaryKeyRedefine	9993	Cannot redefine primary key.	1.0
pePropertyAccess	–31677	Cannot access the property in the current mode of the object.	1.0
pePropertyBadValue	–31678	Attempted to assign an illegal value to the property.	1.0
pePropertyGet	–30652	An error occurred when trying to get the property named '%0ds' of the object named '%1un' of type '%2uc'.	1.0
pePropertyNotFound	–30650	You have tried to access the property named '%0up' which does not belong to the object named '%1un' of type '%2uc'.	1.0
pePropertySet	–30653	An error occurred when setting the property named '%0ds' of the object named '%1un' of type '%2uc'.	1.0
pePublicAliasExists	–28144	Alias(es) already defined—discarding new ones.	5.0
peQBEbadFileName	–30416	File '%0ds' does not exist for executeQBEfile.	1.0
peQBETerminated	–30353	QBE terminated by user.	4.5
peQryAmbigJoAsy	11777	Ambiguous use of ! (inclusion operator).	1.0

continues

TABLE G.1. CONTINUED

Error Constant	Value	Error Message	Ver
peQryAmbigJoSym	11778	Ambiguous use of ! (inclusion operator).	1.0
peQryAmbigOutEx	11779	Ambiguous use of ! (inclusion operator).	1.0
peQryAmbOutPr	11780	Ambiguous use of ! (inclusion operator).	1.0
peQryAmbSymAs	11781	Ambiguous use of ! (inclusion operator).	1.0
peQryAseToPer	11782	A SET operation cannot be included in its own grouping.	1.0
peQryAveNumDa	11783	Only numeric and date fields can be averaged.	1.0
peQryBadExpr1	11784	Invalid expression.	1.0
peQryBadFieldOr	11785	Invalid OR expression.	1.0
peQryBadFormat	11885	Query format is not supported.	1.0
peQryBadVName	11786	Invalid variable name.	1.0
peQryBitmapErr	11787	Bitmap.	1.0
peQryBlobErr	11896	General BLOB error.	1.0
peQryBlobTerm	11895	Operation is not supported on BLOB fields.	1.0
peQryBuffTooSmall	11888	Buffer too small to contain query string.	1.0
peQryCalcBadR	11788	CALC expression cannot be used in INSERT, DELETE, CHANGETO, and SET rows.	1.0
peQryCalcType	11789	Type error in CALC expression.	
peQryEmpty	11886	Query string is empty.	1.0
peQryExaminOr	11805	Cannot use example elements in an OR expression.	1.0
peQryExprTyps	11806	Expression in this field has the wrong type.	1.0
peQryExtraCom	11807	Extra comma found.	1.0
peQryExtraOro	11808	Extra OR found.	1.0
peQryExtraQro	11809	One or more query rows do not contribute to the ANSWER.	1.0
peQryFatalExcept	11883	Unexpected exception.	1.0
peQryFind1Att	11810	FIND can be used in only one query form at a time.	1.0
peQryFindAnsT	11811	FIND cannot be used with the ANSWER table.	1.0
peQryGrpNoSet	11812	A row with GROUPBY must contain SET operations.	1.0
peQryGrpStRow	11813	GROUPBY can be used only in SET rows.	1.0
peQryIdfinIco	11814	Use only INSERT, DELETE, SET, or FIND in leftmost column.	1.0
peQryIdfPerli	11815	Use only one INSERT, DELETE, SET, or FIND per line.	1.0
peQryInAnExpr	11816	Syntax error in expression.	1.0
peQryIns1Time	11817	INSERT can be used in only one query form at a time.	1.0
peQryInsAmbig	11818	Cannot perform operation on INSERTED table together with an INSERT query.	1.0
peQryInsDelCh	11819	INSERT, DELETE, CHANGETO and SET rows may not be checked.	1.0
peQryInsExprR	11820	Field must contain an expression to insert (or be blank).	1.0
peQryInsToIns	11821	Cannot insert into the INSERTED table.	1.0

Error Constant	Value	Error Message	Ver
peQryIsArray	11822	Variable is an array and cannot be accessed.	1.0
peQryLabelErr	11823	Label.	1.0
peQryLinkCalc	11824	Rows of example elements in CALC expression must be linked.	1.0
peQryLngvName	11825	Variable name is too long.	
peQryOnlySetR	11840	Incomplete query statement. Query only contains a SET definition.	1.0
peQryOutSens1	11841	Example element with ! makes no sense in expression.	1.0
peQryOutTwic1	11842	Example element cannot be used more than twice with a ! query.	1.0
peQryPaRowCnt	11843	Row cannot contain expression.	1.0
peQryPersePar	11844	Period cannot be used as a decimal separator.	1.0
peQryProcPlsw	11845	Processing Deletes, Changes, or Inserts. Please wait.	1.0
peQryPwInsrts	11846	Insufficient password rights to insert or delete records.	1.0
peQryPwModrts	11847	Insufficient password rights to modify field.	1.0
peQryQbeFieldFound	11848	Field not found in table.	1.0
peQryQbeNoFence	11849	Expecting a column separator in table header.	1.0
peQryQbeNoFenceT	11850	Expecting a column separator in table.	1.0
peQryQbeNoHeaderT	11851	Expecting column name in table.	1.0
peQryQbeNoTab	11852	Expecting table name.	1.0
peQryQbeNumCols	11853	Expecting consistent number of columns in all rows of table.	1.0
peQryQbeOpentab	11854	Cannot open table.	1.0
peQryQbeTwice	11855	Field appears more then once in table.	1.0
peQryQuaInDel	11858	DELETE rows cannot contain quantifier expression.	1.0
peQryQuaInIns	11859	Invalid expression in INSERT row.	1.0
peQryQxFieldCount	11892	Query extended syntax field count error.	1.0
peQryQxFieldSymNotFound	11893	Field name not found in sort or field clause of query script.	1.0
peQryQxTableSymNotFound	11894	Table name not found in sort or field clause of query script.	1.0
peQryRagInIns	11860	Invalid expression in INSERT row.	1.0
peQryRagInSet	11861	Invalid expression in SET definition.	
peQrySQLg_NoQuery	11925		1.0
peQrySQLg_Onlyc	11905		1.0
peQrySQLg_Onlyi	11923		1.0
peQrySQLg_OTJvr	11910		1.0
peQrySQLg_Patrn	11919		1.0
peQrySQLg_Quant	11912		1.0
peQrySQLg_RegSo	11913		1.0
peQrySQLg_Relop	11904		1.0
peQrySQLg_RelPa	11918		1.0
peQrySQLg_SlfIn	11909		1.0
peQrySQLg_SQLDialect	11924		1.0

continues

Table G.1. CONTINUED

Error Constant	Value	Error Message	Ver
peQrySQLg_StRow	11911		1.0
peQrySQLg_Union	11908		1.0
peQrySumNumbe	11867	Only numeric fields can be summed.	1.0
peQrySyntErr	11891	QBE syntax error.	1.0
peQryTableIsWP3	11868	Table is write protected.	1.0
peQryTokenNot	11869	Token not found.	1.0
peQryTwoOutr1	11870	Cannot use example element with ! more than once in a single row.	1.0
peQryTypeMIsM	11871	Type mismatch in expression.	1.0
peQryUnknownAnsType	11898	Unknown answer table type.	1.0
peQryUnrelQ1	11872	Query appears to ask two unrelated questions.	1.0
peQryUnusedSt	11873	Unused SET row.	1.0
peQryUseInsDe	11874	INSERT, DELETE, FIND, and SET can be used only in the leftmost column.	1.0
peQryUseOfChg	11875	CHANGETO cannot be used with INSERT, DELETE, SET, or FIND.	1.0
peQryVarMustF	11876	Expression must be followed by an example element defined in a SET.	1.0
peQueryErr	−30459	An error was triggered in the '%0ds' method on an object of Query type.	4.5
peQueryERR	−30459		1.0
peQueryView	−31151	This table view is a query view.	5.0
peReadAccessError	−32495		1.0
peReadErr	9217	Read failure.	1.0
peReadOnlyDB	10501	Database is read only.	1.0
peRecTooBig	9477	Record size is too big for temporary table.	1.0
peRefIntgReqIndex	9748	Referential integrity fields must be indexed.	4.5
peREGExpressionTooLarge	−30622	Matching error: Expression is too big.	1.0
peREGInvalidBracketRange	−30616	Matching error: Invalid bracket range.	1.0
peREGNestedSQP	−30617	Matching error: Nested operand.	1.0
peREGOperandEmpty	−30618	Matching error: Operand is empty.	1.0
peREGSPQFollowsNothing	−30613	Matching error: *, +, ? must follow an expression.	1.0
peREGTooManyParens	−30621	Matching error: Too many parentheses.	1.0
peREGTrailingBackSlash	−30612	Matching error: Trailing back slash.	1.0
peREGUnmatchedBrackets	−30615	Matching error: Unmatched brackets.	1.0
peREGUnmatchedParens	−30620	Matching error: Unmatched parentheses.	1.0
peReqdErr	9732	Field value required.	1.0
peReqOptParamMissing	11521	Optional parameter is required.	1.0
peReqSameTableTypes	−30386	Operation requires the same table types.	1.0
peRequiredField	−31741	This field cannot be blank.	1.0

Error Constant	Value	Error Message	Ver
peRequiresPDOXtable	−30399	The table created must be a Paradox table type.	1.0
peReq_WLock_TC	−30413	The operation you are trying to perform requires write-lock access to the table which could not be achieved.	1.0
peReq_XLock_TC	−30340	The operation you are trying to perform requires exclusive-lock access to the table which could not be achieved.	5.0
peReservedOsName	10046	Name is reserved by DOS.	4.5
peSameTable	−30346	Table Names the same.	5.0
peSerNumLimit	9481	Serial number limit (Paradox).	1.0
peServerPathIllegal	−30362	A server alias does not have a path.	4.5
peSessionErr	−30460	An error was triggered in the '%0ds' method on an object of Session type.	4.5
peSessionERR	−30460		1.0
peSessionsLimit	9488	Too many sessions.	1.0
peSharedFileAccess	11272	Not initialized for accessing network files.	1.0
peShareNotLoaded	11273	SHARE not loaded. It is required to share local files.	1.0
peSKCantInstallHook	−30632	Cannot do sendKeys( ) while another sendKeys( ) is already playing.	4.5
peSKInvalidCount	−30634	The repeat count is not correct.	4.5
peSKInvalidKey	−30636	The key name is not correct.	4.5
peSKMissingCloseBrace	−30637	Missing closing brace.	4.5
peSKMissingCloseParen	−30635	Missing closing parenthesis.	4.5
peSKStringTooLong	−30633	The keys string is too long.	4.5
peSortErr	−30456	An error was triggered in a Sort operation.	4.5
peSortERR	−30456		1.0
peSortFailed	−30422	Sort from '%0ds' to '%1ds' could not be performed.	1.0
peSrvGraphicPasteFailed	−32465	Unable to paste graphic.	5.0
peSrvInvalidCount	−32496	File is corrupt. Record tag error.	4.5
peSrvInvalidExtension	−32481	Invalid file extension for this file type.	4.5
peSrvInvalidHandle	−32482	Internal invalid handle.	4.5
peSrvInvalidName	−32469	File name is invalid.	4.5
peSrvMemoryAllocation	−32511	Out of memory.	4.5
peSrvNameTooLong	−32470	File name is too long.	4.5
peSrvNoReadRights	−32495	No read access to file.	4.5
peSrvNotSameDevice	−32475	Rename not allowed to a different device.	4.5
peSrvNoWriteRights	−32489	File does not exist or is write protected.	4.5
peSrvOleActivateFailed	−32485	Cannot activate OLE server.	4.5
peSrvOleCantUpdateNow	−32463	Unable to update OLE object.	5.0
peSrvOleInsertObjectFailed	−32466	Unable to insert OLE object.	5.0
peSrvOlePasteFailed	−32468	Unable to paste OLE object.	4.5
peSrvOlePasteLinkFailed	−32467	Unable to paste link OLE object.	5.0

continues

Table G.1. continued

Error Constant	Value	Error Message	Ver
peSrvOpen	−32490	File does not exist or is read protected.	4.5
peSrvPathNotFound	−32477	Could not find requested path.	4.5
peSrvRead	−32494	Disk error occurred while reading file.	4.5
peSrvRenameFailed	−32474	Could not rename the specified file.	4.5
peSrvTextPasteFailed	−32464	Unable to paste text.	5.0
peSrvUnknowError	−32510	Internal error.	4.5
peSrvUseCountLimit	−32484	Internal catalog usecount error.	4.5
peSrvWrite	−32492	Error occurred while writing to file. Check disk space.	4.5
peStackOverflow	−30716	Stack overflow. Your method or procedures are nested too deeply.	4.5
peStringTooLong	−30470	String too long. Cannot exceed %0di characters.	5.0
peSysCorrupt	8451	Data structure corruption.	1.0
peSysFileIO	8450	I/O error on a system file.	1.0
peSysFileOpen	8449	Cannot open a system file.	1.0
peSysReEntered	8455	System has been illegally re-entered.	4.5
peTableClose	−30508		1.0
peTableCopy	−30510		1.0
peTableCreate	−30512		1.0
peTableCursorLimit	9484	Too many cursors per table.	1.0
peTableEncrypted	10503	Encrypted dBASE tables not supported.	4.5
peTableErr	−30462	An error was triggered in the '%0ds' method of an object of Table type.	4.5
peTableERR	−30462		1.0
peTableExists	13060	Table already exists.	1.0
peTableFull	9479	Table is full.	
peTableRename	−30511		1.0
peTableRights	−30509		1.0
peTableSQL	12291	SQL replicas not supported.	1.0
peTableViewTableReadOnly	−31187	Table is read only.	1.0
peTblNotImplemented	−30359	'%0ds' has not been implemented.	4.5
peTblUtilInUse	−28146	Cannot perform utility while table is in use.	5.0
peTCursorAttach	−30382	Could not attach TCursor to another object.	1.0
peTCursorErr	−30463	An error was triggered in the '%0ds' method on an object of TCursor type.	4.5
peTCursorERR	−30463		1.0
peTextWontFit	−31149	Text will not fit in field.	5.0
peTooFewSeries	−31674	Surface graph needs two or more series.	1.0
peToolsRead	−31683	Could not read the default speed bar properties.	1.0
peToolsWrite	−31682	Could not save the default speed bar properties.	1.0

Error Constant	Value	Error Message	Ver
peTooManyTables	–31710	Crosstab uses too many tables.	1.0
peTransactionImbalance	–31651	Transaction mismatch—cannot commit changes	4.5
peTransactionNA	–30355	Transactions are not supported by this database.	4.5
peUIObjectErr	–30352	An error was triggered in the '%0ds' method on an object of UIObject type.	5.0
peUnassigned	–30704	You have tried to use an unassigned variable. A variable must be assigned a value before you can use it.	1.0
peUnboundXtab	–31712	Crosstab has no defining table.	1.0
peUnknownDataBase	–30433	The database or alias supplied for opening a TCursor was not known.	1.0
peUnknownDB	10014	Unknown database.	1.0
peUnknownDBType	12546	Unknown database type.	1.0
peUnknownDriver	10013	Driver not known to system.	1.0
peUnknownExtension	–31698	Cannot recognize file extension.	1.0
peUnknownFieldName	–31215	The specified field name is invalid.	1.0
peUnknownFieldNum	–31216	The specified field number is invalid.	1.0
peUnknownFile	9992	Cannot open file.	1.0
peUnknownIndex	–30384	%0ds %1ds is an unknown index.	1.0
peUnknownNetType	12548	Network type unknown.	1.0
peUnknownSQL	13059		1.0
peUnknownTableType	9991	Unknown table type.	1.0
peUnknownVersion	–31657	Cannot read file—version is too high.	4.5
peUnlockFailed	10242	Unlock failed.	1.0
peUnsupportedOption	–30641	This printer does not support the setting: %0ds.	5.0
peUntranslatableCharacters	–28150	Character(s) not supported by Table Language.	4.5
peUpdateNoIndex	–30405	The Add or Sub routines require an indexed destination table in order to do updates.	4.5
peUpdateNOIndex	–30405		1.0
peWriteErr	9218	Write failure.	1.0
peWriteOnlyProperty	–31680	You do not have write access to this property. It is read only. It cannot be modified.	1.0
peWrongDriverName	15873	Wrong driver name.	1.0
peWrongDriverType	15876	Wrong driver type.	1.0
peWrongDriverVer	15875	Wrong driver version.	1.0
peWrongObjectVersion	–32486	Object could not be read. Continuing read.	1.0
peWrongSysVer	15874	Wrong system version.	1.0
peWrongTable	–31713	Cannot rebind to chosen table.	1.0
peXtabAnswerError	–31688	Error in crosstab ANSWER table.	1.0
peXtabNotRunning	–31645	Cannot save the table while the crosstab is not running.	5.0
Unmapped Error	–27125	&Design.	5.0
Unmapped Error	–27132	Unknown error. One of your files may be corrupted. Try reinstalling Coaches.	5.0

continues

TABLE G.1. CONTINUED

Error Constant	Value	Error Message	Ver
Unmapped Error	−27133	Coaches from another Borland product are already running. Cancel the other Coaches.	5.0
Unmapped Error	−27134	One or more files are missing. Reinstall Coaches.	5.0
Unmapped Error	−27135	Not enough memory is available to run Coaches. Close other applications that are running.	5.0
Unmapped Error	−27136	You are running a version of Windows that is incompatible with Coaches. Install Windows 3.1 or greater.	5.0
Unmapped Error	−27391	Private directory was not changed. Could not close all open windows.	1.0
Unmapped Error	−27474	Reached limit on count of ValChecks per table.	1.0
Unmapped Error	−27475	A lookup table has not been defined.	1.0
Unmapped Error	−27476	You have changed field %s which has validity checks. Continue?	1.0
Unmapped Error	−27477	No destination file was specified.	1.0
Unmapped Error	−27478	This table is a referential integrity master: the existing records will not be affected by the new or changed validity check on field %s.	1.0
Unmapped Error	−27479	You may not change the primary key of a referential integrity master (dependent table is named %s).	1.0
Unmapped Error	−27480	Do you wish to Cancel without saving your changes?	1.0
Unmapped Error	−27481	A referential integrity rule (named %s) already exists for this combination.	1.0
Unmapped Error	−27482	Two indexes named %s have been specified, please erase any index(es) of this name then try again.	1.0
Unmapped Error	−27483	A composite index or primary key is needed to match referential integrity rule %s.	1.0
Unmapped Error	−27484	Since no dBASE IV features were used, the table is also dBASE III+ compatible.	1.0
Unmapped Error	−27485	The table required dBASE IV features and has been upgraded.	1.0
Unmapped Error	−27486	The table required Paradox for Windows features and has been upgraded.	1.0
Unmapped Error	−27487	Value is valid so far, but may not be complete.	1.0
Unmapped Error	−27488	Illegal characters in filename.	1.0
Unmapped Error	−27489	Extension was specified but not filename.	1.0
Unmapped Error	−27490	No source file was specified.	1.0
Unmapped Error	−27492	Cannot perform this operation with table open.	1.0
Unmapped Error	−27493	Rename cannot overwrite an existing file.	1.0
Unmapped Error	−27494	The destination file does not exist.	1.0
Unmapped Error	−27495	Rename cannot move a file to a new directory.	1.0
Unmapped Error	−27496	The source file does not exist.	1.0
Unmapped Error	−27497	The source and destination files are the same.	1.0
Unmapped Error	−27503	The char '%s' cannot be used in the language for this table.	1.0

Error Constant	Value	Error Message	Ver
Unmapped Error	−27504	Field no. %u in %s %s not found so %s will be erased.. Continue?	1.0
Unmapped Error	−27505	Validity checks and lookup tables can be specified only for sortable field types.	1.0
Unmapped Error	−27506	The specified table name is too long.	1.0
Unmapped Error	−27507	Path name is too long.	1.0
Unmapped Error	−27508	Self referential integrity requires that at least one child field is not keyed.	1.0
Unmapped Error	−27509	New sorted table must be different from the source table.	1.0
Unmapped Error	−27510	Do you really want to delete the password %s?	1.0
Unmapped Error	−27511	Do you really want to delete the referential integrity rule %s?	1.0
Unmapped Error	−27512	Do you really want to delete the index %s?	1.0
Unmapped Error	−27513	An existing password must be selected for change.	1.0
Unmapped Error	−27514	Cannot use a table for its own lookup.	1.0
Unmapped Error	−27515	Table object will be deleted or modified. Continue?	1.0
Unmapped Error	−27516	Invalid database alias.	1.0
Unmapped Error	−27517	Should the new and modified validity check(s) be enforced on existing data?	1.0
Unmapped Error	−27518	An index of this type already exists.	1.0
Unmapped Error	−27519	Current language driver is not valid for the selected table type.	1.0
Unmapped Error	−27520	Not enough memory to complete operation.	1.0
Unmapped Error	−27521	Picture does not accept value.	1.0
Unmapped Error	−27522	Value is valid.	1.0
Unmapped Error	−27523	One or more syntax errors were found in the picture.	1.0
Unmapped Error	−27524	The picture is correct.	1.0
Unmapped Error	−27525	Data loss occurred in the %s validity check during OEM to ANSI translation.	1.0
Unmapped Error	−27526	Data loss occurred in the %s validity check during ANSI to OEM translation.	1.0
Unmapped Error	−27527	Converting an ANSI string to an OEM string may cause data loss. Continue?	1.0
Unmapped Error	−27528	Converting an OEM string to an ANSI string may cause data loss. Continue?	1.0
Unmapped Error	−27529	The selected database or directory is read-only.	1.0
Unmapped Error	−27530	Change canceled. Reverting to the original password.	1.0
Unmapped Error	−27531	Invalid password.	1.0
Unmapped Error	−27532	You do not have rights to perform this operation.	1.0
Unmapped Error	−27533	Choose New to define a password, or choose a password from the list.	1.0
Unmapped Error	−27534	Modify the current password or its access rights.	1.0
Unmapped Error	−27535	Define a new password and specify its access rights.	1.0
Unmapped Error	−27536	Delete master password and all auxiliary passwords.	1.0

continues

TABLE G.1. CONTINUED

Error Constant	Value	Error Message	Ver
Unmapped Error	−27537	Enter new master and confirmation passwords.	1.0
Unmapped Error	−27538	Password already exists.	1.0
Unmapped Error	−27539	No field is selected.	1.0
Unmapped Error	−27540	No password has been specified.	1.0
Unmapped Error	−27541	Confirmation and master passwords do not match.	1.0
Unmapped Error	−27542	Invalid password.	1.0
Unmapped Error	−27543	The only valid table extensions are .DB and .DBF.	1.0
Unmapped Error	−27544	The specified source table was not found.	1.0
Unmapped Error	−27546	The new table's name cannot match the source table's name.	1.0
Unmapped Error	−27547	Specify the table's extension.	1.0
Unmapped Error	−27548	At least one table has not been specified.	1.0
Unmapped Error	−27549	Table already has that name.	1.0
Unmapped Error	−27550	Invalid character(s) in table name.	1.0
Unmapped Error	−27551	Cannot perform the selected operation on a SQL table.	1.0
Unmapped Error	−27552	Could not sort the view.	1.0
Unmapped Error	−27553	Select only one index.	1.0
Unmapped Error	−27554	Select a field for sorting.	1.0
Unmapped Error	−27555	Could not sort the table.	1.0
Unmapped Error	−27556	Could not remove an associated file.	1.0
Unmapped Error	−27557	Could not include an associated file in the operation.	1.0
Unmapped Error	−27558	Could not add the table to the folder.	1.0
Unmapped Error	−27559	The limit of 47 indexes has been reached.	1.0
Unmapped Error	−27560	The limit of 15 composite secondary indexes has been reached.	1.0
Unmapped Error	−27561	A tag name is required for an index with a subset condition (filter).	1.0
Unmapped Error	−27562	The primary key can include only the first 16 fields.	1.0
Unmapped Error	−27563	A primary index is required when maintained indexes or referential integrity are used.	1.0
Unmapped Error	−27564	The maximum number of fields per index (16) has been reached.	1.0
Unmapped Error	−27565	Index cannot contain more than 16 fields.	1.0
Unmapped Error	−27566	The index was not named.	1.0
Unmapped Error	−27567	An index was not specified.	1.0
Unmapped Error	−27568	Index contains no fields.	1.0
Unmapped Error	−27569	Field names are reserved for automatically named single-field indexes.	1.0
Unmapped Error	−27570	An index named %s already exists. Overwrite?	1.0
Unmapped Error	−27571	Invalid source field type.	1.0
Unmapped Error	−27572	Field types do not match.	1.0

Error Constant	Value	Error Message	Ver
Unmapped Error	–27573	Could not find the specified lookup table.	1.0
Unmapped Error	–27574	Could not get dBASE lock information record length.	1.0
Unmapped Error	–27575	Could not get language driver information.	1.0
Unmapped Error	–27576	Internal error: Could not get field value.	1.0
Unmapped Error	–27577	Could not place value in field.	1.0
Unmapped Error	–27578	Could not get field value.	1.0
Unmapped Error	–27579	Internal error: Wrong table operation.	1.0
Unmapped Error	–27583	A table named %s already exists. Overwrite it?	1.0
Unmapped Error	–27584	Changing the strict referential integrity rule affects all referential integrity definitions.	1.0
Unmapped Error	–27585	This table lookup enforces referential integrity. It must be located in the same directory as the lookup table.	1.0
Unmapped Error	–27586	Could not find the referential integrity target table.	1.0
Unmapped Error	–27587	A name is required for the referential integrity relationship.	1.0
Unmapped Error	–27588	Table lookup for field %s does not completely match the lookup table.	1.0
Unmapped Error	–27589	A table lookup matching this referential integrity relationship already exists.	1.0
Unmapped Error	–27590	Lookup is not listed.	1.0
Unmapped Error	–27591	There are no more fields to specify. To make a change, use the Remove button.	1.0
Unmapped Error	–27592	A referential integrity relationship named %s	
Unmapped Error	–27597	Cannot specify a number of digits for this field type.	1.0
Unmapped Error	–27598	This operation requires at least one field having a sortable type.	1.0
Unmapped Error	–27599	Could not get the selected table type.	1.0
Unmapped Error	–27600	Default value must be between the minimum and maximum.	1.0
Unmapped Error	–27601	Validity checks are not allowed on this field type.	1.0
Unmapped Error	–27602	Validity checks for all the fields of this table will be erased. Continue?	1.0
Unmapped Error	–27603	The number of key fields is limited to 16.	1.0
Unmapped Error	–27604	Keys are not allowed on memo, formatted memo, binary, graphic, or OLE field types.	1.0
Unmapped Error	–27605	Key fields must be consecutive, starting with the first field in the Field Roster.	1.0
Unmapped Error	–27606	One or more validity check data types are different than the field types.	1.0
Unmapped Error	–27607	Invalid entry in validity check field.	1.0
Unmapped Error	–27608	Invalid entry in key field.	1.0
Unmapped Error	–27609	Invalid field type.	1.0
Unmapped Error	–27610	Field No. %i:	1.0
Unmapped Error	–27611	You cannot specify a size for a field of this type.	1.0

continues

TABLE G.1. CONTINUED

Error Constant	Value	Error Message	Ver
Unmapped Error	−27612	Invalid field size.	1.0
Unmapped Error	−27613	Field name already exists. Rename one of the fields.	1.0
Unmapped Error	−27614	The maximum number of fields for this table has been reached, no more may be added.	1.0
Unmapped Error	−27615	The field name, type, and size are missing.	1.0
Unmapped Error	−27616	The field type and size are missing.	1.0
Unmapped Error	−27617	The field name and size are missing.	1.0
Unmapped Error	−27618	The field name and type are missing.	1.0
Unmapped Error	−27619	The field size is missing.	1.0
Unmapped Error	−27620	The field type is missing.	1.0
Unmapped Error	−27621	Field name is missing.	1.0
Unmapped Error	−27622	Blank field is not allowed.	1.0
Unmapped Error	−27623	No field has been specified.	1.0
Unmapped Error	−27624	A table cannot borrow a structure from itself.	1.0
Unmapped Error	−27625	Invalid path name.	1.0
Unmapped Error	−27626	Invalid table name.	1.0
Unmapped Error	−27627	Invalid table-name extension.	1.0
Unmapped Error	−27628	Invalid table name extension. %s is the valid extension.	1.0
Unmapped Error	−27629	%s is not allowed as a table name.	1.0
Unmapped Error	−27630	Paradox requires a new table name.	1.0
Unmapped Error	−27631	You do not have rights to restructure %s.	1.0
Unmapped Error	−27632	Could not close database.	1.0
Unmapped Error	−27633	Could not open database.	1.0
Unmapped Error	−27634	Could not write STRUCT.DB file.	1.0
Unmapped Error	−27635	Cannot create STRUCT.DB file.	1.0
Unmapped Error	−27636	Could not open the table.	1.0
Unmapped Error	−27637	Could not find any database drivers.	1.0
Unmapped Error	−27638	Could not get a list of databases.	1.0
Unmapped Error	−27639	The table type will change from dBASE III+ to dBASE IV. Continue?	1.0
Unmapped Error	−27640	The table type will change from Paradox 3.5 to Paradox for Windows. Any 3.5 "Family" objects for this table will be orphaned! Continue?	1.0
Unmapped Error	−27641	Cannot restructure in a read-only database.	1.0
Unmapped Error	−27642	Cannot restructure in a read-only directory.	1.0
Unmapped Error	−27643	You do not have rights to perform the restructure operation.	1.0
Unmapped Error	−27644	You do not have table rights to perform the restructure operation.	1.0
Unmapped Error	−27645	Field %s: existing field type cannot be converted to requested type.	1.0

Error Constant	Value	Error Message	Ver
Unmapped Error	−27646	Do you really want to delete the field %s?	1.0
Unmapped Error	−27647	Possible data loss in the field %s. Do you want to trim it?	1.0
Unmapped Error	−27887	DDE link cannot be started.	1.0
Unmapped Error	−27888	Could not find DDE expression.	1.0
Unmapped Error	−27889	DDE link is not allowed in a BLOB field.	1.0
Unmapped Error	−27890	Only one DDE link is allowed.	1.0
Unmapped Error	−27891	Cannot run query while waiting for DDE.	1.0
Unmapped Error	−27892	This query does not produce an ANSWER table.	1.0
Unmapped Error	−27893	SQL is not available for this query.	1.0
Unmapped Error	−27894	Could not create SQL viewer.	1.0
Unmapped Error	−27895	The query is empty.	1.0
Unmapped Error	−27896	Could not write query file.	1.0
Unmapped Error	−27897	Syntax error in query.	1.0
Unmapped Error	−27898	This query has the maximum number of tables.	1.0
Unmapped Error	−27899	Could not create temporary tables.	1.0
Unmapped Error	−27900	Insufficient memory.	1.0
Unmapped Error	−27901	Query is too long.	1.0
Unmapped Error	−27902	Could not open query file.	1.0
Unmapped Error	−27903	Could not read query file.	1.0
Unmapped Error	−28668	Cannot delete object in text.	1.0
Unmapped Error	−28669	Only ANSI RTF files are supported.	1.0
Unmapped Error	−28670	This is not an RTF file.	1.0
Unmapped Error	−28671	Character limit in field exeeded.	1.0
Unmapped Error	−28672	No such group in search string.	1.0
Unmapped Error	−28863	No fields can be exported to Paradox DOS.	5.0
Unmapped Error	−28864	Cannot export a table to itself.	5.0
Unmapped Error	−28871	Cannot export a table with more than 256 fields.	1.0
Unmapped Error	−28872	Operation canceled by user.	1.0
Unmapped Error	−29171	Error occurred while using bitmap.	1.0
Unmapped Error	−29172	The GIF file is formatted incorrectly.	1.0
Unmapped Error	−29173	The EPS file is formatted incorrectly.	1.0
Unmapped Error	−29174	The TIF file is formatted incorrectly.	1.0
Unmapped Error	−29175	The PCX file is formatted incorrectly.	1.0
Unmapped Error	−29176	The graphic file contains an invalid palette.	1.0
Unmapped Error	−29177	The graphic file contains an invalid header.	1.0
Unmapped Error	−29178	Error occurred while writing graphic file.	1.0
Unmapped Error	−29179	Error occurred while reading graphic file.	1.0
Unmapped Error	−29180	The graphic file could not be opened.	1.0
Unmapped Error	−29181	The graphic is not defined.	1.0
Unmapped Error	−29182	The graphic is not defined.	1.0

continues

TABLE G.1. CONTINUED

Error Constant	Value	Error Message	Ver
Unmapped Error	–29183	The graphic is not defined.	1.0
Unmapped Error	–29676	Printer/font manager combination invalid. Printing disabled.	1.0
Unmapped Error	–29679	Invalid function parameter.	5.0
Unmapped Error	–29680	Invalid or null HDC.	5.0
Unmapped Error	–29683	User selected Cancel.	1.0
Unmapped Error	–29685	No printer installed or no printer active. Using screen settings.	5.0
Unmapped Error	–29688	Insufficient memory.	5.0
Unmapped Error	–29689	Invalid printer driver.	5.0
Unmapped Error	–29690	Cannot find printer driver.	5.0
Unmapped Error	–29691	No printer installed or Windows cannot print.	1.0
Unmapped Error	–29692	Null or invalid window handle.	5.0
Unmapped Error	–29948	Invalid font specification.	1.0
Unmapped Error	–29949	Invalid font handle.	1.0
Unmapped Error	–29951	Font System error.	1.0
Unmapped Error	–30337	The information about the QBE executing locally is only available after it has executed.	5.0
Unmapped Error	–30452	An error was triggered in the '%0ds' method on an object of SQL type.	1.0
Unmapped Error	–30474	Function not available in the runtime version.	5.0
Unmapped Error	–30479	Cannot format data of type, '%0cc'.	1.0
Unmapped Error	–30480	There is an ObjectPAL syntax error in another method or calculated field.	1.0
Unmapped Error	–30481	Duplicate object name.	1.0
Unmapped Error	–30482	Unknown method name.	1.0
Unmapped Error	–30483	Parameter mismatch.	1.0
Unmapped Error	–30484	Constant object or parameter cannot be modified.	1.0
Unmapped Error	–30485	Cannot find file name in module database.	1.0
Unmapped Error	–30486	Cannot lock the module database.	1.0
Unmapped Error	–30487	Cannot create the temporary DLL file.	1.0
Unmapped Error	–30488	Cannot open the DLL file.	1.0
Unmapped Error	–30489	Cannot generate a unique name for the temporary DLL file.	1.0
Unmapped Error	–30490	Windows could not load the library.	1.0
Unmapped Error	–30491	No name was given to load.	1.0
Unmapped Error	–30492	This form was created with a pre-alpha version of Paradox for Windows. It can no longer be loaded.	1.0
Unmapped Error	–30493	This delivered form was compiled with an earlier version of Paradox for Windows. You must recompile the source form with the current version.	1.0
Unmapped Error	–30494	Cannot find reference '%0ds' in DLL library '%1ds'.	1.0

Error Constant	Value	Error Message	Ver
Unmapped Error	−30495	Could not find DLL, %0ds, referenced in the USES statement. You cannot call methods from this DLL.	1.0
Unmapped Error	−30496	This form references external procedures or DLLs which could not be found.	1.0
Unmapped Error	−30521	No more file handles. Cannot open file.	1.0
Unmapped Error	−30522	Cannot create a unique file name.	1.0
Unmapped Error	−30526	The number of linked fields in the master table must be the same as the detail table.	1.0
Unmapped Error	−30527	Could not get the value from [%0ds.%1ds].	1.0
Unmapped Error	−30528	Could not put the value to [%0ds.%1ds].	1.0
Unmapped Error	−30529	You cannot create an object in a running report.	1.0
Unmapped Error	−30530	You cannot call the wait() method for a form which is being viewed as a dialog and which has also been compiled with trace or debug options.	1.0
Unmapped Error	−30531	Cannot save a design object (form/report) which is in View mode.	1.0
Unmapped Error	−30532	Cannot load DLL library. Probable file name conflict with existing DLL.	1.0
Unmapped Error	−30535	You cannot deliver an unnamed form. You must save it first.	1.0
Unmapped Error	−30536	You have tried to close a form which is waiting on a message box or another form.	1.0
Unmapped Error	−30537	You have tried to use a tableframe '%0ds' before it was open.	1.0
Unmapped Error	−30538	The method, '%0ds', is not allowed on a form which is in View mode.	1.0
Unmapped Error	−30543	An unexpected error occurred. You were referencing a form.	1.0
Unmapped Error	−30550	DDE: No command specified. You must specify a command in the EXECUTE method.	1.0
Unmapped Error	−30551	DDE: No item specified. You must use SETITEM to specify an item.	1.0
Unmapped Error	−30575	A record/array operation was performed between two Record/Array objects which do not have the same structure or which contain elements other than AnyType.	1.0
Unmapped Error	−30576	An error occurred trying to access a record structure. An unexpected field number was encountered. => %0di.	1.0
Unmapped Error	−30587	Array sizes are not equal.	1.0
Unmapped Error	−30611	Matching error: Corrupted pattern program.	1.0
Unmapped Error	−30614	Matching error: Invalid pattern.	1.0
Unmapped Error	−30619	Matching error: Code unreadable.	1.0
Unmapped Error	−30623	Matching error: Null expressions.	1.0
Unmapped Error	−30624	Matching error: Illegal argument.	1.0
Unmapped Error	−30638	String exceeds 32K.	1.0
Unmapped Error	−30640	Tried to assign NULL to a string.	1.0
Unmapped Error	−30642	This function is not available in the Runtime Version.	1.0
Unmapped Error	−30643	'%0ds' is not a valid property name.	1.0

continues

TABLE G.1. CONTINUED

Error Constant	Value	Error Message	Ver
Unmapped Error	−30644	:%00ds:Format: There is an error in the format specification,'%01ds'. %02ds.	1.0
Unmapped Error	−30645	Cannot move to '%0ds' from '%1un'.	1.0
Unmapped Error	−30647	The method, '%0ds', is not allowed on an object which is in use.	1.0
Unmapped Error	−30648	Tried to assign NULL to a property.	1.0
Unmapped Error	−30649	The data type '%0cc' does not support the property named '%1up'.	1.0
Unmapped Error	−30651	Illegal property conversion.	1.0
Unmapped Error	−30654	%00ds:%02ds=>Could not find the directory path, '%3ds'. %4rs.	1.0
Unmapped Error	−30655	%00ds:%02ds=>The file, '%3ds', could not be found. %4rs.	1.0
Unmapped Error	−30656	%00ds:%02ds=>Could not perform the seek operation on the file, '%3ds'. %4rs.	1.0
Unmapped Error	−30657	%00ds:%02ds=>Could not perform the read operation on the file, '%3ds'. %4rs.	1.0
Unmapped Error	−30658	%00ds:%02ds=>Could not perform the write operation on the file, '%3ds'. %4rs.	1.0
Unmapped Error	−30659	%00ds:%02ds=>The file, '%3ds', could not be opened. %4rs.	1.0
Unmapped Error	−30660	%00ds:%02ds=>The file, '%3ds', could not be created. %4rs.	1.0
Unmapped Error	−30661	%00ds:%02ds=>You have tried to perform a TextStream operation without first opening or creating it.	1.0
Unmapped Error	−30662	Error occurred trying to execute the specified program %0ds.	1.0
Unmapped Error	−30663	EXECPROC could not find the method named '%0ds' in UIObject '%1un'.	1.0
Unmapped Error	−30664	The play procedure could not find the script named '%0ds'.	1.0
Unmapped Error	−30711	Error: %0rs.	1.0
Unmapped Error	−30714	Could not allocate memory.	1.0
Unmapped Error	−31144	Record cannot be posted. Reactivate the table to finish editing.	5.0
Unmapped Error	−31161	Low value is invalid.	1.0
Unmapped Error	−31162	Unable to initiate DDE.	1.0
Unmapped Error	−31163	Unable to scroll until OLE value is posted.	1.0
Unmapped Error	−31166	Unable to select fields when record is locked.	1.0
Unmapped Error	−31168	Invalid field type for search.	1.0
Unmapped Error	−31176	Unable to paste.	1.0
Unmapped Error	−31177	Unable to copy.	1.0
Unmapped Error	−31178	Unable to cut.	1.0

Error Constant	Value	Error Message	Ver
Unmapped Error	−31180	Mismatched table name is in property file.	1.0
Unmapped Error	−31181	Invalid heading in property file.	1.0
Unmapped Error	−31183	No lookup available for this field.	1.0
Unmapped Error	−31186	Translation errors found in text.	1.0
Unmapped Error	−31188	Unable to initialize objects.	1.0
Unmapped Error	−31189	DDE is not allowed here.	1.0
Unmapped Error	−31190	User selected Cancel.	1.0
Unmapped Error	−31193	Unable to open properties.	1.0
Unmapped Error	−31194	Unable to save properties.	1.0
Unmapped Error	−31195	Unable to launch server.	1.0
Unmapped Error	−31196	Unable to initiate DDE with server.	1.0
Unmapped Error	−31197	Unable to scan for DDE link information.	1.0
Unmapped Error	−31199	Cannot duplicate field.	1.0
Unmapped Error	−31201	Unable to find lookup value.	1.0
Unmapped Error	−31202	Unable to open lookup table.	1.0
Unmapped Error	−31205	The record is already locked.	1.0
Unmapped Error	−31210	Cannot use the lookup table.	1.0
Unmapped Error	−31211	The first field of the lookup table is not of the appropriate type.	1.0
Unmapped Error	−31217	Unable to delete file.	1.0
Unmapped Error	−31218	Unable to copy to default.	1.0
Unmapped Error	−31219	Unable to set field value.	1.0
Unmapped Error	−31222	The value was not found.	1.0
Unmapped Error	−31228	Not in Edit mode.	1.0
Unmapped Error	−31229	The specified indicator is invalid.	1.0
Unmapped Error	−31230	The specified line style is invalid.	1.0
Unmapped Error	−31456	Please wait, cannot prepare report while cancel button is up.	5.0
Unmapped Error	−31458	Unique summary not allowed on a field of this type.	1.0
Unmapped Error	−31459	Query only allowed on the master table in reports.	1.0
Unmapped Error	−31460	Illegal report design.	1.0
Unmapped Error	−31461	A report group with a many to one link to a dBase table is not allowed.	1.0
Unmapped Error	−31462	Unknown restart option.	1.0
Unmapped Error	−31463	Requested printing range is beyond end of report.	1.0
Unmapped Error	−31464	Cannot add a group band without a master table.	1.0
Unmapped Error	−31465	Preferred report is not for this table. Generating a default report.	1.0
Unmapped Error	−31466	Could not use new sort order.	1.0
Unmapped Error	−31467	Selected band cannot be moved in the indicated direction.	1.0
Unmapped Error	−31468	Cannot sort. There is no table associated with this mail merge.	1.0

continues

TABLE G.1. CONTINUED			
Error Constant	*Value*	*Error Message*	*Ver*
Unmapped Error	−31469	The indicated design is not a mail merge.	1.0
Unmapped Error	−31470	Cannot convert this design to a report.	1.0
Unmapped Error	−31471	A page break cannot cross an object.	1.0
Unmapped Error	−31472	Cannot put a page break in the page band.	1.0
Unmapped Error	−31473	Page break must be within a band.	1.0
Unmapped Error	−31474	Page header and footer are too tall for the logical page size.	1.0
Unmapped Error	−31475	Could not open tables.	1.0
Unmapped Error	−31476	Compilation error.	1.0
Unmapped Error	−31477	Could not initialize report.	1.0
Unmapped Error	−31478	Printer problem. Canceling report.	1.0
Unmapped Error	−31479	Could not initialize printer.	1.0
Unmapped Error	−31480	Memory error. Canceling report.	1.0
Unmapped Error	−31481	File is not a report.	1.0
Unmapped Error	−31482	Requested page is past the end of the report.	1.0
Unmapped Error	−31483	Data has changed. Interrupted report.	1.0
Unmapped Error	−31484	Report contains undefined tables or multi-record objects.	1.0
Unmapped Error	−31485	Report design is corrupted.	1.0
Unmapped Error	−31486	User canceled report.	1.0
Unmapped Error	−31487	Report contains object too large to fit on page.	1.0
Unmapped Error	−31660	Limit on number of open indexes exceeded.	1.0
Unmapped Error	−31661	A query is not allowed in the data model.	1.0
Unmapped Error	−31676	Invalid field type for search.	1.0
Unmapped Error	−31744	Error.	1.0
Unmapped Error	−31889	Cannot delete default format.	5.0
Unmapped Error	−31890	Cannot delete default format.	1.0
Unmapped Error	−31891	True and false values must be different.	1.0
Unmapped Error	−31892	True and false value missing.	1.0
Unmapped Error	−31893	At least one active symbol required.	1.0
Unmapped Error	−31894	Invalid active symbol in order string.	1.0
Unmapped Error	−31895	Only one of each symbol is allowed in order string.	1.0
Unmapped Error	−31896	Add %N to time order.	1.0
Unmapped Error	−31897	Remove %N from time order.	1.0
Unmapped Error	−31898	Thousand separator cannot be equal to decimal point.	1.0
Unmapped Error	−31899	Invalid thousand separator.	1.0
Unmapped Error	−31900	Invalid decimal point.	1.0
Unmapped Error	−31921	Missing.	1.0
Unmapped Error	−31922	Missing.	1.0
Unmapped Error	−31923	Missing.	1.0
Unmapped Error	−31924	Missing.	1.0

Error Constant	Value	Error Message	Ver
Unmapped Error	–31925	Missing.	1.0
Unmapped Error	–31926	Missing.	1.0
Unmapped Error	–31927	Missing.	1.0
Unmapped Error	–31928	Missing.	1.0
Unmapped Error	–31929	Missing.	1.0
Unmapped Error	–31930	Missing.	1.0
Unmapped Error	–31931	Missing.	1.0
Unmapped Error	–31932	Missing.	1.0
Unmapped Error	–31953	Bad.	1.0
Unmapped Error	–31954	Bad.	1.0
Unmapped Error	–31955	Bad.	1.0
Unmapped Error	–31956	Bad.	1.0
Unmapped Error	–31957	Bad.	1.0
Unmapped Error	–31958	Bad.	1.0
Unmapped Error	–31959	Bad.	1.0
Unmapped Error	–31960	Bad.	1.0
Unmapped Error	–31961	Bad.	1.0
Unmapped Error	–31962	Bad.	1.0
Unmapped Error	–31963	Bad.	1.0
Unmapped Error	–31964	Bad.	1.0
Unmapped Error	–32216	Design.	1.0
Unmapped Error	–32235	&Design.	5.0
Unmapped Error	–32242	Unknown error. One of your files may be corrupted. Try reinstalling Coaches.	5.0
Unmapped Error	–32243	Coaches from another Borland product are already running. Cancel the other Coaches.	5.0
Unmapped Error	–32244	One or more files are missing. Reinstall Coaches.	5.0
Unmapped Error	–32245	Not enough memory is available to run Coaches. Close other applications that are running.	5.0
Unmapped Error	–32246	You are running a version of Windows that is incompatible with Coaches. Install Windows 3.1 or greater.	5.0
Unmapped Error	–32253	Out of GDI font handles.	1.0
Unmapped Error	–32254	Out of user memory. Close some applications and try again.	1.0
Unmapped Error	–32255	Out of GDI memory. Close some windows and try again.	1.0
Unmapped Error	–32257	Unknown error %x.	1.0
Unmapped Error	–32258	Unknown error %x.	1.0
Unmapped Error	–32259	Unknown error %x.	1.0
Unmapped Error	–32423	Design.	1.0
Unmapped Error	–32424	&Design.	5.0
Unmapped Error	–32431	Unknown error. One of your files may be corrupted. Try reinstalling Coaches.	5.0

continues

TABLE G.1. CONTINUED

Error Constant	Value	Error Message	Ver
Unmapped Error	−32432	Coaches from another Borland product are already running. Cancel the other Coaches.	5.0
Unmapped Error	−32433	One or more files are missing. Reinstall Coaches.	5.0
Unmapped Error	−32434	Not enough memory is available to run Coaches. Close other applications that are running.	5.0
Unmapped Error	−32435	You are running a version of Windows that is incompatible with Coaches. Install Windows 3.1 or greater.	5.0
Unmapped Error	−32442	Out of GDI font handles.	5.0
Unmapped Error	−32443	Out of user memory. Close some applications and try again.	5.0
Unmapped Error	−32444	Out of GDI memory. Close some windows and try again.	5.0
Unmapped Error	−32460	Out of GDI font handles.	1.0
Unmapped Error	−32461	Out of user memory. Close some applications and try again.	1.0
Unmapped Error	−32462	Out of GDI memory. Close some windows and try again.	1.0
Unmapped Error	10056	Invalid table specified.	1.0
Unmapped Error	10062	Mismatch in the number of arguments.	5.0
Unmapped Error	10063	Function not found in service library.	
Unmapped Error	10768	Table does not support this operation because it is not uniquely indexed.	1.0
Unmapped Error	10769	Operation must be performed on the current session.	5.0
Unmapped Error	10770	Invalid use of keyword.	5.0
Unmapped Error	11060	Critical DOS Error.	1.0
Unmapped Error	11061	Drive not ready.	1.0
Unmapped Error	11108	Not exact read/write.	1.0
Unmapped Error	11110	Error from NOVELL file server.	1.0
Unmapped Error	11111	NOVELL server out of memory.	1.0
Unmapped Error	11112	Record already locked by this workstation.	1.0
Unmapped Error	11113	Record not locked.	1.0
Unmapped Error	11274	Not on a network. Not logged in or wrong network driver.	1.0
Unmapped Error	11275	Lost communication with SQL server.	1.0
Unmapped Error	11926	Blob cannot be used as grouping field.	1.0
Unmapped Error	11927	Query properties have not been fetched.	1.0
Unmapped Error	11928	Answer table type is not yet supported in query.	1.0
Unmapped Error	11929	Answer table is not yet supported under server alias.	1.0
Unmapped Error	11930	Non-null blob field required. Can't insert records.	1.0
Unmapped Error	11931	Unique index required to perform CHANGETO.	1.0
Unmapped Error	11932	Unique index required to delete records.	1.0
Unmapped Error	11933	Update of table on the server failed.	1.0
Unmapped Error	11934	Can't process this query remotely.	1.0
Unmapped Error	11935	Unexpected end of command.	5.0

Error Constant	Value	Error Message	Ver
Unmapped Error	11936	Parameter not set in SQL statement.	
Unmapped Error	16148	Alias.	1.0
Unmapped Error	16149	Drive.	1.0
Unmapped Error	16150	Server error.	1.0
Unmapped Error	16151	Server message.	1.0
Unmapped Error	16152	Line Number.	5.0
Unmapped Error	16153	Capability.	5.0
Unmapped Error	16239	WORK.	1.0

H

APPENDIX

ASCII AND ANSI CHARACTER SETS

Dec	Hex	OEM (DOS)	ANSI (Windows)	Dec	Hex	OEM (DOS)	ANSI (Windows)
000	00			024	18	↑	□
001	01	☺	□	025	19	↓	□
002	02	☻	□	026	1A	→	□
003	03	♥	□	027	1B	←	□
004	04	♦	□	028	1C	∟	□
005	05	♣	□	029	1D	↔	□
006	06	♠	□	030	1E	▲	
007	07	•	□	031	1F	▼	□
008	08	◘	□	032	20		
009	09	○	□	033	21	!	!
010	0A	◙	□	034	22	"	"
011	0B	♂	□	035	23	#	#
012	0C	♀	□	036	24	$	$
013	0D	♪	□	037	25	%	%
014	0E	♫	□	038	26	&	&
015	0F	¤	□	039	27	'	'
016	10	►	□	040	28	(	(
017	11	◄	□	041	29	)	)
018	12	↕	□	042	2A	*	*
019	13	‼	□	043	2B	+	+
020	14	¶	□	044	2C	,	,
021	15	§	□	045	2D	–	'
022	16	▬	□	046	2E	.	.
023	17	↨	□	047	2F	/	/

Dec	Hex	OEM (DOS)	ANSI (Windows)	Dec	Hex	OEM (DOS)	ANSI (Windows)
048	30	0	0	072	48	H	H
049	31	1	1	073	49	I	I
050	32	2	2	074	4A	J	J
051	33	3	3	075	4B	K	K
052	34	4	4	076	4C	L	L
053	35	5	5	077	4D	M	M
054	36	6	6	078	4E	N	N
055	37	7	7	079	4F	O	O
056	38	8	8	080	50	P	P
057	39	9	9	081	51	Q	Q
058	3A	:	:	082	52	R	R
059	3B	;	;	083	53	S	S
060	3C	<	<	084	54	T	T
061	3D	=	=	085	55	U	U
062	3E	>	>	086	56	V	V
063	3F	?	?	087	57	W	W
064	40	@	@	088	58	X	X
065	41	A	A	089	59	Y	Y
066	42	B	B	090	5A	Z	Z
067	43	C	C	091	5B	[	[
068	44	D	D	092	5C	\	\
069	45	E	E	093	5D	]	]
070	46	F	F	094	5E	^	^
071	47	G	G	095	5F	_	_

Dec	Hex	OEM (DOS)	ANSI (Windows)	Dec	Hex	OEM (DOS)	ANSI (Windows)
096	60	`	`	120	78	x	x
097	61	a	a	121	79	y	y
098	62	b	b	122	7A	z	z
099	63	c	c	123	7B	{	{
100	64	d	d	124	7C				
101	65	e	e	125	7D	}	}
102	66	f	f	126	7E	~	~
103	67	g	g	127	7F	⌂	□
104	68	h	h	128	80	Ç	□
105	69	i	i	129	81	ü	□
106	6A	j	j	130	82	é	,
107	6B	k	k	131	83	â	ƒ
108	6C	l	l	132	84	ä	"
109	6D	m	m	133	85	à	…
110	6E	n	n	134	86	å	†
111	6F	o	o	135	87	ç	‡
112	70	p	p	136	88	ê	^
113	71	q	q	137	89	ë	‰
114	72	r	r	138	8A	è	Š
115	73	s	s	139	8B	ï	‹
116	74	t	t	140	8C	î	Œ
117	75	u	u	141	8D	ì	□
118	76	v	v	142	8E	Ä	□
119	77	w	w	143	8F	Å	□

Dec	Hex	OEM (DOS)	ANSI (Windows)	Dec	Hex	OEM (DOS)	ANSI (Windows)
144	90	É	□	168	A8	¿	¨
145	91	æ	'	169	A9	⌐	©
146	92	Æ	'	170	AA	¬	a
147	93	ô	"	171	AB	½	«
148	94	ö	"	172	AC	¼	¬
149	95	ò	•	173	AD	¡	—
150	96	û	–	174	AE	«	®
151	97	ù	—	175	AF	»	—
152	98	ÿ	˜	176	B0	▓	°
153	99	Ö	™	177	B1	▓	±
154	9A	Ü	š	178	B2	▓	2
155	9B	¢	>	179	B3	│	3
156	9C	£	œ	180	B4	┤	'
157	9D	¥	□	181	B5	╡	µ
158	9E	û	□	182	B6	╢	¶
159	9F	ƒ	Ÿ	183	B7	╖	•
160	A0	á	□	184	B8	╕	,
161	A1	í	¡	185	B9	╣	1
162	A2	ó	¢	186	BA	║	°
163	A3	ú	£	187	BB	╗	»
164	A4	ñ	¤	188	BC	╝	¼
165	A5	Ñ	¥	189	BD	╜	½
166	A6	ª	¦	190	BE	╛	¾
167	A7	º	§	191	BF	┐	¿

Dec	Hex	OEM (DOS)	ANSI (Windows)	Dec	Hex	OEM (DOS)	ANSI (Windows)
192	C0	└	À	216	D8	╪	ø
193	C1	┴	Á	217	D9	┘	Ù
194	C2	┬	Â	218	DA	┌	Ú
195	C3	├	Ã	219	DB	█	Û
196	C4	─	Ä	220	DC	▄	Ü
197	C5	┼	Å	221	DD	▌	Ý
198	C6	╞	Æ	222	DE	▐	Þ
199	C7	╟	Ç	223	DF	▀	ß
200	C8	╚	È	224	E0	α	à
201	C9	╔	É	225	E1	β	á
202	CA	╩	Ê	226	E2	Γ	â
203	CB	╦	Ë	227	E3	π	ã
204	CC	╠	Ì	228	E4	Σ	ä
205	CD	=	Í	229	E5	σ	å
206	CE	╬	Î	230	E6	μ	æ
207	CF	╧	Ï	231	E7	γ	ç
208	D0	╨	Đ	232	E8	Φ	è
209	D1	╤	Ñ	233	E9	Θ	é
210	D2	╥	Ò	234	EA	Ω	ê
211	D3	╙	Ó	235	EB	δ	ë
212	D4	╘	Ô	236	EC	∞	ì
213	D5	╒	Õ	237	ED	ø	í
214	D6	╓	Ö	238	EE	ε	î
215	D7	╫	×	239	EF	η	ï

Dec	Hex	OEM (DOS)	ANSI (Windows)	Dec	Hex	OEM (DOS)	ANSI (Windows)
240	F0	≡	δ	248	F8	°	ø
241	F1	±	ñ	249	F9	•	ù
242	F2	≥	ò	250	FA	·	ú
243	F3	≤	ó	251	FB	√	û
244	F4	⌠	ô	252	FC	ⁿ	ü
245	F5	⌡	õ	253	FD	²	ý
246	F6	÷	ö	254	FE	∎	p
247	F7	≈	÷	255	FF		ÿ

GLOSSARY

alpha test—The preliminary testing of a new product in which research and development are still in progress.

Alpha field type—A general-purpose field type that can contain letters and numbers.

ANSI—An acronym for American National Standards Institute. The ANSI set consists of 8-bit codes that represent 256 standard characters—letters, numbers, and symbols. The ANSI set is used by Windows applications.

answer set—When you execute a specific SQL query—either through a QBE query or an SQL file—you refer to the data returned by the server as an answer set.

answer table—A temporary table used to store the results of a query. Its default name is ANSWER.DB. An answer table is saved to your private directory.

API—An acronym for *application programming interface*. The Windows API is the set of DLLs that makes up Windows. It comprises all the functions, messages, data structures, data types, statements, and files that a programmer needs for developing Windows applications.

application—A group of forms, tables, reports, and other things in a directory. *Application* refers to the Paradox desktop. Specifically, an application is an ObjectPAL data type that provides a handle to the desktop.

arithmetic operators—The +, -, *, /, and ( ) operators used to construct arithmetic expressions in queries and calculated fields.

array—A data type that is a collection of variables (much like a table is a collection of fields). There are two types: fixed and resizeable. A fixed array has a predetermined—by the programmer—number of elements. A resizeable does not; therefore you need to set its size before using it. *See also DynArray.*

ascending order sort—The sort order of a table depends on the language driver. Usually, ascending order is A to Z, and it is case sensitive for alpha fields and low to high for numeric fields. *Warning:* Numbers in an alphanumeric field type sort alphanumerically —for example, 1, 101, 11, 2, 20, 210, 22, 23, 4, 404, 408.

ASCII—An acronym for *American Standard Code for Information Interchange*. The ASCII set consists of 7-bit codes that represent 128 standard characters, including letters, numbers, and symbols. The first 128 characters in the ASCII set, the extended ASCII set, and the ANSI set are the same.

asymmetrical outer join—A type of query in which an inclusive link is specified for only one of the tables involved.

autoincrement—To supply a unique value by automatically adding a value to any new records created; it increments the maximum value by 1 in database terms. This is unique for each new record.

axis—The horizontal or vertical line that defines the range of values plotted on a graph. The x-axis is the horizontal line, and the y-axis is the vertical line.

back-end—In a client server model, the SQL server is referred to as the back-end. *See also front-end.*

band—The repeating horizontal section of a report design. The Report Design window shows the report, page, and record bands by default. Group bands are optional.

batch file—A text file that contains one or more DOS commands. A batch file always has an extension of .BAT. The commands in a batch file are executed sequentially.

BDE—An acronym for Borland Database Engine (also referred to as IDAPI and previously referred to as ODAPI).

beep—An audible sound produced by a computer speaker. `beep()` is a command in some computer languages, including ObjectPAL.

beta test—A stage in product testing in which testing is done with actual users in the users' environment.

binary field—A field used by programmers to store custom data that Paradox cannot interpret. A binary field typically is used for sound and animation.

bind—To associate a UIObject (user-interactive object) with a table or a table's field. The data model brings data from a table to be displayed on a form in a UIObject.

binding—When the compiler compiles your source code, it casts all the variables in your code. This process is called *binding*.

BLOB—An acronym for *binary large object*. A BLOB is not a field type, but rather a data type. Field types that can contain BLOBs include binary, memo (both Paradox and dBASE), formatted memo, graphic, and OLE.

braces—The symbols { and }, which designate blocks of comments and are useful for disabling blocks of code.

branch—Normally, a programming language executes line after line in sequential order. This is true whether the language is a line-oriented language, such as BASIC, or a statement-oriented language, such as C. A branch transfers program control to an instruction other than the next sequential instruction.

breakpoint—A flag you can set in your code that stops a form during runtime and enters the Debugger. A breakpoint enables you to inspect variables, step through your code, and much more.

bubbling—A process in which external events are passed from the target object up through the containership hierarchy until the event is meaningful to an object's method or it reaches the form.

bug—An error or mistake in a program.

built-in method—The triggers that start your code, such as **pushButton**, **open**, and **changeValue**. Built-in methods are part of the event handler.

cascade—In referential integrity, cascade enables you to update child tables when a value changes in the parent table.

cascading menu—The object that pops up when a pull-down menu or a pop-up menu displays another pop-up menu.

check box—A box you can check or uncheck to set an option. You can check more than one check box in a set of check boxes.

checkmark—The symbol used in a Query statement to indicate that a field will be displayed in the answer table.

client (network)—A device that receives data from the server in a local area network.

client (OOP)—In object-oriented programming (OOP), an object that uses the resources of another object by operating on it or referencing it.

column—The vertical section of a table frame or a table view. Each cell of a column represents a single field in a record.

commit—Part of a concept for entering data. The idea is to enter data into a temporary table and commit—that is, copy—the data to a main table.

comparison operators—The operators used to compare two values in a query, in a calculated field, or in an ObjectPAL expression. The comparison operators are <, >, <=, >=, and =.

compiler—Generates code for maximum performance and distribution security.

Complete Display—A mode of a memo, formatted memo, graphic, and OLE fields that enables you to see all the record values displayed all the time. Turn off Complete Display to see only the value of the current field. You can move through the records of the table more quickly if you turn off Complete Display.

composite key or index—A key or index composed of two or more fields of a table. Together, the combination of the fields in the key sorts the table.

concatenate—To combine two or more alphanumeric values with the + operator.

constant—A specific, unchanging value used in calculations and defined in the Const window of an object.

container object—An object that completely surrounds and controls the behavior of all the objects within it. When you move a container, its contained objects also move. When you delete a container, its contained objects are also deleted.

control structure—In programming languages, control structures are keywords used to branch or loop. With control structures, you can alter the sequence of execution and add logic to your code.

crosstab—An object that enables you to summarize data in one field by expressing it in terms of two other fields. These spreadsheet-like structures are easy for the user to understand. Unfortunately, crosstabs aren't used enough by developers.

cursor—A cursor is a pointer to a row in an SQL answer set. Cursors are implemented in ObjectPAL as a TCursor object. *See also TCursor.*

custom method—A method that you create. It consists of methods and procedures from the runtime library and from other custom methods and procedures. Custom methods are subroutines that objects can access.

custom procedure—Similar to a custom method, except that the scope for a custom procedure is much more limited. Scope determines the availability of a custom procedure to other objects.

data integrity—A guarantee that the values in a table are protected from corruption. Data integrity for autoincrementing means that no two records have the same key values.

data model—A diagram of the table relationships for a form. Each form has only one data model. With the Data Model dialog box, you can bind tables to documents and specify how they are linked to one another.

database—An organized collection of information. For Paradox users, this meaning is stretched to mean a set of related tables in a directory.

database application—A cohesive set of files: your database with all its tables, forms, queries, reports, and anything else you include within the scope of the files, including utilities and accessories.

datatype—The type of data a variable or element of an array can contain.

DDE—Dynamic data exchange. A way for two or more applications to share data.

DDE client—The application that receives data from the server application. The client application is responsible for starting the DDE or OLE conversation.

DDE item—Represents the piece of data sent between applications.

DDE server—The application that responds to the calling application—that is, the client—in a DDE or OLE conversation, usually by sending data.

DDE topic—The subject of a DDE conversation. Usually, it is the name of a data file of the application.

Debugger—Part of the ObjectPAL Integrated Development Environment (IDE). The Debugger aids you in finding problem areas in your code.

define—To attach a design object to data from a table. For example, you define a field object in a form as a field in a table.

deliver—The final step in the development cycle in which the application is prepared. In ObjectPAL, it's the process of compiling an object for a special Paradox-only dynamic link library.

descending order—The sort order of a table depends on the language driver. For alpha fields, descending order is Z to A and is case sensitive. To illustrate another example, data fields are ordered from the latest date to the earliest date—for example, 5/1/93, 4/1/93, 1/15/89, 10/10/72.

design document—A form or a report.

design objects—The objects from the speedbar tools that you can place in forms and reports.

desk accessory—A term usually used in the Macintosh world to refer to a small application that adds functionality to an application. You can create or use small Windows or Paradox applications with your application.

Desktop—The main window in Paradox. The Desktop is the highest level of interaction with all Paradox objects. The Desktop is also known as your application workspace. In ObjectPAL, there is an application variable type for manipulating it. The application variable is discussed in Chapter 13, "The Display Managers."

detail table—In multitable relationships, the table whose records are subordinate to those of the master table. A detail table is also called a *slave table* or a *many table*.

dialog box—A box that requests or provides information. Many dialog boxes present options from which you must choose before you can perform an action. Other dialog boxes display warnings or error messages.

display manager—A group of ObjectPAL data types, including the application, the form, the report, and TableView. These object types are used to display data.

distributed processing—In a client/server model, the database processes are shared between the client and the server. This is called distributed processing. *See also transaction.*

DLL—An acronym for *dynamic link library*. A DLL is a type of application used by other applications. It usually contains a library of functions.

drop-down edit list—A type of field with a single-line text box that opens to display more choices when you click the down arrow button.

DynArray—A dynamic array (DynArray) is analogous to a two-field table, where the first field represents the DynArray index and the second field represents the value.

embedded SQL—When you place SQL commands within another programming language such as ObjectPAL, this is referred to as embedded SQL.

encapsulation—In OOP, the bundling of methods and variables within an object so that access to the variables is permitted only through the object's own methods.

enum procedure—A procedure that enumerates information and puts it in a table.

event—An action that triggers an ObjectPAL method. For example, pushing a button, clicking the mouse, and opening a form are events.

event handler—A type of developing environment that sets up triggers that are trapped for when the user interacts with the application.

event model—A map of the order in which events are triggered in an event handler.

event packet—The packet of information that is sent from one built-in method to another. This packet of information contains such items as error codes and information about the target.

example element—A character or group of characters that represents a value in a field of a query. An example element is similar to a variable.

export—To convert data from a native format—either Paradox or dBASE—to a foreign format, such as ASCII.

extended ASCII—A character set designed by IBM. IBM extended the standard ASCII set from 7-bit codes to 8-bit codes and added more characters. The extended ASCII set contains 256 characters.

field—A single value in a record—for example, *City*. A column of a table.

field types—Paradox field types are Alpha, Number, Money, Date, Time, TimeStamp, Logical, Short, Long Integer, BCD, Autoincrement, Memo, Formatted Memo, Binary, Byte, Graphic, and OLE. dBASE field types are Character, Float, Number, Date, Logical, Memo, and OLE.

Field view—A mode that enables you to edit a field at the character level. Use this mode to view field values that are too large to display within the width of the current field or to edit a memo field value. Don't confuse Field view with Complete Display.

flag—A variable used in a routine to indicate whether a condition has occurred.

fly away—The default behavior that occurs in a table view and table frame when you add a new record or change the key of a record. The new or altered record moves to its ordered location in the table and appears to fly away.

footer—Information that appears at the bottom of every section of a report. Footers are created in the page, report, and group bands of Paradox reports.

foreign key—The fields in one table that are linked to the key of another table.

front-end—A client application, such as Paradox, is referred to as the front-end. *See also back-end.*

GPF—An acronym for *general protection fault*. A GPF is a special type of error that Windows catches. Windows displays the name of the application that caused the error in an error box.

grid—Horizontal and vertical lines that help you place objects. You can show or hide the grid; you also can resize it. Use Snap To Grid when you first design a form. Doing so cuts down the time needed to design the form.

group band—The section of a report that defines the group. It repeats for every group of records.

group by operator—In a query, the operator that groups records by field without displaying the field's values in the Answer table.

header—Information that appears at the top of every section of a report. Headers are created in the section, report, and group bands of Paradox reports.

high-level language—A programming language that enables programmers to code in familar notation rather than obscure machine code.

Hungarian notation—A variable naming scheme. All variables of a given type should start with a lowercase prefix. The API consists of Hungarian notation for variable names.

IDAPI—An acronym for Independent Database Application Programming Interface. IDAPI is the database engine that Paradox 5 for Windows and dBASE V for Windows use.

IDE—An acronym for Borland's Integrated Development Environment built into Paradox. The IDE includes the Editor and the Debugger.

import—To convert data from a foreign format, such as ASCII, to a native format—either Paradox or dBASE.

inclusion operator—The ! symbol. It is used in a query with example elements to include a complete set of records in the answer table, regardless of whether those records match records in another table.

index—A file that determines the order in which a table displays records. It also enables a TCursor or Table window to move to any record faster. Paradox tables have a primary key and secondary indexes, whereas a dBASE table has only indexes—that is, files with .MDX or .NDX extensions. You can refer to any file that sorts a table as an index.

inheritance—In OOP, a mechanism for automatically sharing methods and data types among objects.

keycode—A code that represents a keyboard character in ObjectPAL scripts. A keycode can be an ASCII number, an IBM extended keycode number, or a string that represents a keyname known to Paradox.

keyword—A word reserved for use with certain commands in ObjectPAL.

library—A Paradox object that stores custom ObjectPAL code. Libraries are useful for storing and maintaining frequently used routines and for sharing custom methods and variables among forms, scripts, and other libraries.

link—To establish a relationship between tables by linking corresponding fields.

list—A type of field. A list is similar to a drop-down edit list, except that it's always down.

lock—A feature of the database engine that prevents other users from viewing, changing, or locking a table or a record while one user has a lock on it.

logic error—An error in thinking. Often, you try to code something that doesn't make sense because it's a logic error. Logic errors are among the most difficult types of errors to diagnose. If you knew that your thinking was wrong, you wouldn't try to implement the code in the first place!

logical operators—Three operators used in queries, in calculated fields, and in ObjectPAL methods. The three logical operators are AND, OR, and NOT.

logical value—A true or false value that is assigned to an expression when it is evaluated.

lookup table—Establishes a one-to-one relationship between two tables that ensures that a value entered in one table matches an existing value in another table.

loop—A set of instructions that is repeated a predetermined number of times or until a specified condition is met.

low-level language—A machine-dependent programming language, such as assembly language, C, or Pascal, that is translated by an assembler into instructions for a particular machine.

master table—In a multitable relationship, the primary table of your data model. If there is only one table in your data model, it is the master table.

MDI—An acronym for Multiple Document Interface. Among other things, this standard suggests how child windows should behave within an application.

Memo field type—A special type of BLOB field used for storing text. The file is divided into blocks of 512 characters. Each block is referenced by a sequential number, beginning at zero. Block 0 begins with a four-byte number in hexadecimal format in which the least significant byte comes first. This number specifies the number of the next available block. It is, in effect, a pointer to the end of the memo file. The remainder of Block 0 isn't used.

menu—A set of options. Typically, a menu is a list that appears horizontally across the menu bar of an application. Menus in ObjectPAL also can take the form of buttons on a form, pull-down menus, or pop-up menus.

method (built-in)—ObjectPAL code attached to an object that defines the object's response to an event.

method (RTL)—A function or command in ObjectPAL that acts on an object. A method uses dot notation to work on an object set by the programmer, as in *object.method*.

MIDI—An acronym for *musical instrument digital interface*. MIDI is a standard protocol that computers and musical instruments use to communicate with and control one other.

modal dialog box—A dialog box that the user can't leave to interact with Paradox until he or she responds to it.

multirecord—An object that displays several records at once in a box. Used with forms and reports.

network—A system of interconnected computer systems and terminals that share software and data.

network control file—A file that controls items such as table access. A network control file is often called a *net file*.

normalized data structure—Normalized tables arrange data to minimize disk space. Each record includes the smallest number of fields necessary to establish a category. Instead of dumping all possible fields into a large table, normalized tables distribute information over many tables. This saves disk space each time a user doesn't need a particular table. In addition, normalized tables provide more flexibility in terms of analysis. Normalized data should be your goal at all times.

null—A field or value that is either blank or zero. Whenever you store an empty field, Paradox and dBASE actually store a null. This condition for a field is called `blank` in Paradox.

Number field—A field that can contain numbers. A Number field can contain some valid nonnumerical characters, such as a decimal point or a minus sign.

object—An item—such as a button, field, or box—that the user interacts with to create events.

ObjectPAL—Paradox's event-driven application language. Although Paradox is powerful, it still can't do some things interactively. An example of a task that requires ObjectPAL is adding a menu to control a form.

ODAPI—An acronym for Object Database Application Programming Interface. ODAPI is the database engine that Paradox for Windows versions 1 and 4.5 and Quattro Pro for Windows versions 1 through 5 use.

OLE—Object linking and embedding. You use OLE to insert files from OLE servers into Paradox tables or OLE objects.

OLE client—An application that uses the documents provided by an OLE server. Paradox is both an OLE server and client.

OLE object—An OLE document. This document is similar to the document that an OLE server can save. An OLE object is stored in the OLE client much as a document is stored on a disk.

OLE server—An application that can provide access to its documents by means of OLE. Paradox is both an OLE server and client.

OLE variable—A handle to an OLE object in ObjectPAL used to manipulate that object.

operator—A symbol that represents an operation to be performed on a value or values. For example, the + operator represents addition, and the * operator represents multiplication.

orphaning records—In a referential integrity link, when you change the blank primary key to a nonblank value, the child records that were linked to it will remain blank. This is known as orphaning records.

outer join—A query that uses the inclusion operator to retrieve all the records in a table, regardless of whether those records match records in another table.

Paradox engine—The Paradox engine prior to ODAPI and IDAPI. The DOS versions of Paradox along with ObjectVision and many other third party applications use this engine to gain Paradox table support. Version 2 is compatible with Paradox 3.5, and version 3 is compatible with Paradox 4.

picture—A pattern of characters that defines what a user can type into a field during editing or data entry. A picture aids data entry and promotes—but does not ensure—consistent data.

polymorphism—In OOP, the capability of the same command to be interpreted differently when used with or received by different objects.

pop-up menu—A vertical list of options.

procedure—A function or command in ObjectPAL that has no object on which to work. The programmer doesn't specify an object.

prototyping—A process of application development in which small parts or the general structure of an application are designed and tested. These models are used as the basis for building the finished system.

pull-down menu—A list of items that appears when you choose a menu item from the horizontal menu list. A pull-down menu displays further options for you to choose.

query—A method or tool that asks a database questions. A query is a means of extracting sets of information from a database or table.

query by example (QBE)—The technique of asking questions about data by providing an example of the answer you expect.

Query operators—The reserved words that Paradox uses in queries.

Query statement—One or more filled-out query images in the Query window. A query image is one line in a multiline query.

record—The horizontal row in a Paradox table that represents a set of data for that item—for example, a person's address information.

record number—For Paradox tables, the position of the record, based on the active index. For dBASE tables, record numbers represent the physical location in the table, and they don't change when you change the active index.

referential integrity—A way of ensuring that the ties between similar data in separate tables can't be broken. Referential integrity is defined at the table level in Paradox.

reserved words—The names of commands, keywords, functions, system variables, and operators. These words may not be used as ObjectPAL variable names.

restricted view—In a multitable form, the first table in the data model is the master and controlling table. All other linked tables are detail tables. The second table shows only those records that match the current master record.

restructure—To change the structure of an existing table. You can change the field names, field types, field order, keys, indexes, validity checks, referential integrity, password protection, table language, and table lookup easily.

rollback—Part of a concept for entering data. The idea is to enter data into a temporary table with the opportunity to empty the temporary table and to leave the main table untouched.

row—The horizontal section of a table frame or a table view. Each row represents a single record.

Run mode—An alternative name for View Data mode.

runtime error—An error that occurs while a form is being run, even though the routine has passed a syntax check.

runtime library (RTL)—A predefined set of methods and procedures used for operating on objects, including UIObjects, data types, and TCursors.

script—A Paradox object that consists of ObjectPAL code that can be run independently of a form or called from ObjectPAL. Unlike a form or a report, a script has no objects. Unlike a library, a script can be run without ObjectPAL.

SDF—An acronym for *standard delimited format*. An SDF is a text file formatted in a particular style. Each field is enclosed in quotation marks and separated by a comma. Each line ends with a carriage return and a linefeed.

secondary index—An index used for linking, querying, and sorting tables.

self—self has different meanings depending on when it's used. When it's used in a library, self refers to the calling object. When it's used in a form, self refers to the object to which the code is attached.

server—The central, or controlling, computer in a local area network. Although it could be used as a regular computer, a server usually is dedicated to sending data to and receiving data from devices that are connected to a network.

set—A group of specific records in a query about which you ask questions.

set comparison operators—The reserved words used to compare a defined set of records to other records. The set comparison operators are ONLY, NO, EVERY, and EXACTLY.

Short field type—A Paradox field type that can contain integers from –32,767 through 32,767—no decimal. A short number field type uses less disk space than the number field type. It's perfect for storing ages, years of employment, invoice numbers, item numbers, and so on.

special field—A field, placed in a design document, that contains information about a table or design.

string—An alphanumeric value or an expression consisting of alphanumeric characters. You can convert a number to a string with string(x).

structure—The arrangement of fields in a table: their data types, indexes, validity checks, and so on.

subroutine—A sequence of instructions that performs a specific task, usually more than once in a program. The sequence may be invoked many times by the current program or by multiple applications. Although ObjectPAL doesn't have *actual* subroutines, you can think of custom methods and custom procedures as subroutines.

summary operators—The operators that answer questions about groups of records in a query. The summary operators are AVERAGE, COUNT, MAX, MIN, and SUM.

syntax error—An error that occurs because of an incorrectly expressed statement. Syntax errors usually occur when you mistype a command or when you attempt to use a command that doesn't exist.

table—An object that consists of rows of records and columns of fields. In ObjectPAL, a Table variable is a handle to a table.

table alias—With version 5, Borland introduced the concept of a *table alias* to the data model. In a data model, a table alias is an alternate name for a table.

table frame—A design object for forms and reports that represents a table and consists of columns and rows. Don't confuse a table frame with a table view.

TCursor—A tool used to manipulate a table behind the scenes. A TCursor (*table cursor*) is a pointer to a record in a table.

Type Definition—In C++, typedef is a keyword that assigns a symbol name (identifier) to the data type definition (type definition).

UIObjects—Objects you can draw using the speedbar, including circles, lines, fields, and buttons. You can attach a method to any of these objects.

utility—An application that helps the developer run, create, or analyze other applications.

variable—A place in memory used to store data temporarily.

WAD—An acronym for *works as designed*. WAD describes program behavior that you don't like, even though the program's designers planned it.

.WAV file—A sound file format that is the standard on the Windows platform.

wildcard operators—Special characters that Paradox uses to match patterns in queries or to locate values.

INDEX

W-X-Y-Z

What's on the Disks

The two disks included with this book contain more than 7 megabytes of sample applications, bonus forms, tutorial answers, and more. All the support files, sample applications, and utilities were developed exclusively for this book. Here's what you'll find on the disks:

- Source code, forms, and other files used in the book's tutorials.
- More than a dozen complete Paradox for Windows applications, including:

    Info Center
    Invoice Generator
    EduCalc
    Wedding Planner
    Personnel Management
    Rolodex
    Reference Tables

- Utilities and tools for the Paradox developer, including:

    SourceView
    Paradox Desktop
    Property

- Plus, more than 30 example Paradox Forms, including menuing, looping, DDE, sound, and graphics examples.

Installing the Software

Insert disk one in your floppy disk drive and follow these steps. To install all the software, you'll at least 8 megabytes of free space on your hard drive. You can also choose to install only a porti the software.

1. From Windows File Manager or Program Manager, choose **F**ile + **R**un from the menu.
2. Type `B:\INSTALL` and press Enter. If the disk is in your A drive, type `A:\INSTALL` instead.
3. Choose **F**ull Install to install all the software; choose **C**ustom Install to install only some the software.
4. Follow the on-screen instructions in the installation program. Insert disk two when the program prompts you.

The files will be installed to a directory named C:\SECRETS2, unless you changed this name du the install program.

When the installation is complete, the file SECRETS2.TXT will be displayed for you to read. Thi contains important information on the files and programs that were installed. A Program Man group name *Secrets2* will be created by the installation program.